Requirements Analysis and System Design

Visit the *Requirements Analysis and Systems Design, third edition* Companion Website at **www.pearsoned.co.uk/maciaszek** to find valuable **student** learning material including:

- Printable lecture slides.
- Model files for solutions to the case studies, the tutorial, and all other modeling examples in the textbook.

PEARSON
Education

We work with leading authors to develop the
strongest educational materials in computing,
bringing cutting-edge thinking and best
learning practice to a global market.

Under a range of well-known imprints, including
Addison Wesley, we craft high-quality print and
electronic publications that help readers to understand
and apply their content, whether studying or at work.

To find out more about the complete range of our
publishing, please visit us on the World Wide Web at:
www.pearsoned.co.uk

REQUIREMENTS ANALYSIS AND SYSTEM DESIGN

third edition

LESZEK A. MACIASZEK

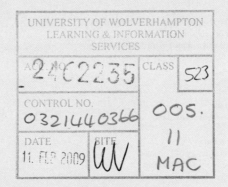

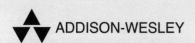
ADDISON-WESLEY

An imprint of **Pearson Education**
Harlow, England • London • New York • Boston • San Francisco • Toronto • Sydney • Singapore • Hong Kong
Tokyo • Seoul • Taipei • New Delhi • Cape Town • Madrid • Mexico City • Amsterdam • Munich • Paris • Milan

Pearson Education Limited
Edinburgh Gate
Harlow
Essex CM20 2JE
England

and Associated Companies throughout the world

Visit us on the World Wide Web at:
www.pearsoned.co.uk

First published 2001
Second edition published 2005
Third edition published 2007

ISBN 978-0-321-44036-5

British Library Cataloguing-in-Publication Data
A catalogue record for this book is available from the British Library

Library of Congress Cataloging-in-Publication Data
A catalog record for this book is available from the Library of Congress

10 9 8 7 6 5 4 3 2
10 09 08

Typeset in 10/12 pt TimesNewRoman by 30
Printed and bound in Malaysia (CTP-PJB)

The publisher's policy is to use paper manufactured from sustainable forests.

Brief contents

Contents

Contents for case studies

- AE – advertising expenditure
- CC – currency converter
- CM – contact management
- TL – time logging
- TM – telemarketing
- UE – university enrolment
- VS – video store

TL

VS

Supporting resources

Visit **www.pearsoned.co.uk/maciaszek** to find valuable online resources

Companion Website for students

- Printable lecture slides.
- Model files for solutions to the case studies, the tutorial, and all other modeling examples in the textbook.

For instructors

- Lecture slides in PowerPoint that can be downloaded and used for presentations.
- Solutions Manual with annotated answers to all review and exercise questions from the end of each chapter of the textbook.
- Ready-to-use assignments and projects for students, with model answers.
- Examination testbank – ready-to-use examples of examination questions with answers.

For more information please contact your local Pearson Education sales representative or visit **www.pearsoned.co.uk/maciaszek**

Preface

Outline of the book

The development of an *information system (IS)* – from its inception to the deployment to stakeholders – comprises three iterative and incremental phases: analysis, design and implementation. This book describes the methods and techniques used in the *analysis* and *design* phases. The implementation issues, including code examples, are addressed only to the extent to which they need to be considered in the design phase. Quality and change management are addressed separately in Chapter 9.

The text concentrates on *object-oriented software development*. The *Unified Modeling Language (UML)* is used to capture modeling artifacts. Emphasis is placed on the development by elaboration where the same modeling language (UML) is used throughout the development lifecycle. Analysts, designers and programmers "speak" the same language, although they perhaps use the dialects (profiles) of the language fitting their individual needs.

The early applications of object technology targeted graphical user interfaces (GUIs) and focused on the speed of developing new systems and the speed of program execution. In this book, I emphasize the application of object technology in *enterprise information systems (EIS)* development. The challenges are the large volume of data, complex data structures, shared access to information by many concurrent users, transaction processing, changing requirements and so on. The main advantage of object technology for EIS development is in facilitating *system adaptiveness* (understandability, maintenance and scalability).

Developing enterprise information systems is synonymous with doing *analysis and design "in the large"*. No EIS project can succeed without following strict *development processes* and without understanding the underlying *software architectures*. The EIS development is large-scale, object-oriented, iterative and incremental.

The book proposes a detailed approach to the analysis and design of enterprise information systems with UML. It identifies ways to:

- analyze and model business processes
- harness the complexity of large system models
- improve software architectures
- facilitate system adaptiveness
- handle detailed design issues

- understand graphical user interfaces
- appreciate the significance of databases
- manage quality, change, and so on.

Distinguishing features

This book has a number of features that, when combined, create a unique offering. The *"teach by example" approach* is the cornerstone of the text. The main discussion is based on seven case studies and a tutorial-style review and reinforcement chapter. The *case studies* are drawn from seven application domains, each with its own unique features and educational benefits. The domains are *university enrolment*, *video store*, *contact management*, *telemarketing*, *advertising expenditure*, *time logging* and *currency converter*. The *tutorial* relates to an *online shopping* application for purchasing a computer on the Internet.

To facilitate self-education, the case studies and the tutorial are formulated using *question-and-answer* and *exercise-and-solution* principles. The practical material is further extended and diversified through questions and exercises formulated at the ends of chapters. Selected questions/exercises are provided with answers/solutions. Each chapter contains *review quizzes* with answers and *multiple-choice tests* with answers. Moreover, definitions of *key terms* are given for each chapter.

The book discusses principles, methods and techniques of good analysis and design. Special attention is paid to the design phase. Design is not treated as a straightforward transformation from analysis. The book acknowledges the difficulties and intricacies of large-scale system development. In many ways, it takes a fresh look at *"design in the large,"* iterative and incremental development of large systems and the capabilities and limitations of tools and methods in large software production.

A unique character of the book comes from a balanced blend of practical explanation and theoretical insight. A major premise is to avoid unnecessary overcomplication, but without the loss of rigor. The book speaks from experience. Topics that are not relevant to industry or only of specialized research interest have been excluded.

The book is on the cutting edge of information technology. It uses the standard in visual system modeling – UML. It addresses the developments in web and database technologies. In this context, the Internet-driven shift from "thick clients" (that is, large desktop computers) back to server-based computing is acknowledged. The analysis and design principles discussed in the text apply equally well to conventional client/server solutions and modern component-based distributed applications.

Software development is not amenable to "black–white", "true–false", "zero–one" solutions. Good software solutions come from good business analysts and system designers, not blindly applied algorithms. A policy of the book is to warn the reader about potential difficulties that the advocated approach cannot entirely resolve. In consequence, it is hoped that readers will apply their acquired knowledge with care and not assume unrealistic expectations of the ease with which the approach can be applied (and thereby, possibly, fail more dramatically).

In summary, the distinguishing features of the book are as follows.

- The book relates the theories to reality – in the form of practical problems and limitations, that will have to be addressed when applying the approach "in the field".

- The book gives special attention to the design phase. Design is *not* treated as simply a straightforward transformation from analysis, and the difficulties and intricacies of large-scale enterprise system development are acknowledged.

- There is a wealth of non-trivial examples and questions, exercises, quizzes and multiple-choice tests. The majority of the answers and solutions are included in the book. The remainder are included in the supplementary materials available to instructors from the book's website. The instructor's manual is not an afterthought – it has been written concurrently with the text and is meticulous.

Intended readership

In tune with the growing demand for university courses to be more relevant to industry practice, this textbook is aimed at students and practitioners alike. This has been a difficult task but, it is hoped, it has been achieved. To ensure a lasting educational benefit, the implementation aspects of software development are discussed in non-vendor-specific terms (although commercial CASE tools have been used in illustrations and solutions).

The book is aimed at computer science and information systems curricula. As it contains both high-level system modeling topics and low-level user interface and database design issues, the book should be attractive to courses in systems analysis, systems design, software engineering, databases and object technology, as well as software project courses that require students to develop a system following the development lifecycle: from requirements determination to the user interface and database implementation. The book is designed for a one-semester course, but it can potentially be used over two one-semester courses – one on requirements analysis and the other on system design.

For the practitioner's audience, the presented theories are related to realities. Many problem domains, examples and exercises are drawn from the consulting practice of the author. We have adopted a policy of warning the reader of potential difficulties or limitations with advocated approaches. The following categories of practitioner are likely to benefit most from the book: business and system analysts, designers, programmers, system architects, project leaders and managers, reviewers, testers, technical writers and industry trainers.

Organization of the book

The book provides comprehensive coverage of object-oriented analysis and design of enterprise information systems. The material is presented in an order consistent with modern development processes. The book consists of ten chapters and an appendix on the fundamentals of object technology. The coverage is more or less equally balanced between analysis and design topics.

Readers with varying amounts of background knowledge should be able to accommodate the text. The last chapter of the book is dedicated to review and reinforcement of the entire material. Having such a chapter at the end of the book should meet the expectations of many university courses. After all, the review and reinforcement principle is the cornerstone of any lasting education.

Summary of changes in the second edition

Although the first edition of *Requirements Analysis and System Design* had a very good reception and resulted in translations of the book into several languages, there is always scope for improvement, particularly in technology-influenced areas such as systems development. The main changes (hopefully improvements) in the second edition were the following.

- Elimination of the subtitle "Developing information systems with UML". Contemporary systems development implies modeling in UML. There is no need any more to assert to the reader that the book uses UML.

- Answers to odd-numbered questions and solutions to selected exercises have been added at the ends of chapters. This makes the book more useful for self-education. The remaining answers and solutions are available to instructors on the book's website, together with a wealth of other teaching material.

- "Guided Tutorial", previously in Chapters 2 and 6, has been extracted into a separate chapter. Moreover, the tutorial has been relocated to Chapter 10 and extensively revamped and extended to serve as a review and reinforcement chapter entitled "Tutorial-style Review and Reinforcement".

- Chapters 2 and 3 have been swapped. This is because the requirements analysis (now in Chapter 2) does not need a prior knowledge of objects and object modeling (now in Chapter 3).

- The title of Chapter 3 has been changed to "Objects and Object Modeling" to reflect the change from the explanation of objects in general and by a guided tutorial to the explanation of objects via UML and by examples.

- Chapter 4 ("Requirements Specification") has been enriched by an explanation of the overriding importance of the system's architectural framework to the supportability of the developed system. Accordingly, the chapter has introduced an architectural framework subsequently enforced in the discussion in the following chapters.

- The content of Chapter 6 has been changed, mostly as a result of the relocation of the material from/to other chapters. The tutorial has been moved to Chapter 10. Some program design topics have been obtained from Chapter 9. The discussion on system architecture has been significantly extended. Consequently, the new title of the chapter is "System Architecture and Program Design".

- Chapter 7 ("User Interface Design") has been modified and enriched in several ways. The benefits of the Java Swing library have been used to explain some UI design principles. The window navigation models based previously on the UML activity diagrams have been replaced by a new UML profile – the user experience (UX) storyboards.

■ Chapter 8, now entitled "Persistence and Database Design", has been extended with discussion about designing persistent objects, including the patterns for managing persistency within the adopted architectural framework. Previous detailed discussion about object and object-relational databases has been dropped (because of the continuing dominance of the relational databases in enterprise information systems and the difficulty of the material). The saved space has been filled with database topics moved from the previous Chapter 9, such as transaction management.

■ After the material from the previous Chapter 9 had been moved to the earlier chapters, the previous Chapter 10 became the new Chapter 9. This chapter, too, has been extended. In particular, a section on test-driven development has been added.

Summary of changes in the third edition

The third edition is approximately 25 per cent longer than the second edition. Review quizzes (with answers), multiple-choice tests (also with answers) and definitions of key terms have been introduced in each chapter. Changes and additions have been made to the content of all chapters (with the exception of the database chapter (Chapter 8)). The internal organization of some chapters has been improved. The main changes in this third edition are as follows:

■ Chapter 1 has been extended throughout – new sections have been added on solution management frameworks (ITIL and COBIT), aspect-oriented development and system integration (to emphasize the claim that today's enterprise systems are rarely developed as standalone applications and most development projects are also, if not predominantly, integration projects).

■ Chapter 2 has also been extended – a new section has been added at the beginning on process hierarchy modeling, business process modeling and solution envisioning.

■ Chapter 3 has been changed – what was Section 3.1 in the second edition has been moved to the Appendix and Section 3.2 made into Chapter 3, after being modified and extended to fully conform to the latest improvements in the UML standard.

■ Chapter 4 has been extended and modified to make use of UML changes and to better explain architectural prerogatives and frameworks.

■ Chapter 5 has been modified and extended with a section at the end on advanced interaction modeling.

■ Chapter 6 has been extended and modified. There is a new discussion in the logical architecture section (Section 6.2) on architectural complexity and patterns and the collaboration modeling section (Section 6.5) has been modified to reflect relevant changes in the UML standard.

■ Chapter 7 has been extended to include a new discussion on Web GUI design.

■ Chapter 9 has been reorganized and modified regarding some details.

■ Chapter 10 has been modified to reflect relevant changes in the UML standard.

■ As mentioned earlier, there is now an Appendix on "Fundamentals of object technology".

Supplementary materials

A comprehensive package of supplementary material is provided on the companion website. Most of the documents there are freely available to readers, but some material is password-protected for the benefit of instructors who have adopted the textbook in their teaching. The home page for the book is simultaneously maintained at:

http://www.booksites.net/maciaszek
http://www.comp.mq.edu.au/books/rasd3ed

The web package includes:

1 Instructor's resources with:

- lecture slides in Microsoft PowerPoint
- answers and solutions manual containing annotated answers and solutions to all review and exercise questions from the ends of the chapters
- assignments and projects – ready-to-use assignments and projects for students, complete with model answers and solutions
- examination testbank – ready-to-use examples of examination questions with answers and solutions.

2 Students' resources with:

- printable lecture slides in Acrobat Read format
- model files for solutions to the case studies, tutorial and all other modeling examples in the textbook (in the formats of Rational Rose, Magic Draw, Enterprise Architect, PowerDesigner and Visio Professional).

3 Errata and Addendum document dedicated to corrections of errors and omissions in the book.

For further information

Your comments, corrections, suggestions for improvements, contributions and so on are very much appreciated. Please direct any correspondence to:

Leszek A. Maciaszek
Department of Computing
Macquarie University
Sydney, NSW 2109
Australia
e-mail: leszek@ics.mq.edu.au
website: www.comp.mq.edu.au/~leszek
phone: +61 2 98509519
facsimile: +61 2 98509551
courier: North Ryde, Herring Road, Bld. E6A, Room 319

Acknowledgements

The writing of this book would be impossible without interactions with friends, colleagues, students, industry gurus and all the other people who, consciously or not, have shaped my knowledge in the subject area. I am truly indebted to all of them. An attempt to list all their names would be injudicious and impractical – please accept a blanket "thank you".

I wish to express my appreciation to lecturers and students at universities and practitioners around the world who cared to provide feedback and point out deficiencies in the first and second editions of this book. Their feedback is gratefully acknowledged in this third edition.

I would like to thank my editors at Pearson Education in London. Special thanks go to Keith Mansfield who was the initial Acquisition Editor for the first edition of the *RASD* book as well as my other book *PSE – Practical Software Engineering*. Keith was also responsible for the second edition of *RASD*. After Keith left Pearson, a great continuity was provided by Simon Plumtree. His careful analysis of *RASD*'s competitive position resulted in Pearson's decision to publish new editions of *RASD* every couple of years.

During the production of *PSE* and *RASD* (2nd edition), and throughout the whole process of preparing the third edition of *RASD* for publication, my primary point of contact at Pearson was Owen Knight. His responsiveness and openess were for me a constant source of encouragement and support. Thank you, Owen, from the depth of my heart.

Book editing and production is a surprisingly complex process in which many people are involved and many remain anonymous to the author. Many thanks to you all. A special responsibility is with a Desk Editor and I would like to thank Georgina Clark-Mazo for the excellent job in bringing this edition of *RASD* to production.

Guided tour

Chapter objectives present the key areas that each chapter will cover.

Review quizzes within the chapters help reinforce learning.

Extensive use of **UML diagrams**.

Summaries at the end of each chapter help clarify the key points of that section.

Key terms are listed and defined at the end of each chapter.

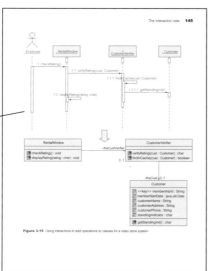

Numerous **annotated screen shots** draw out key points.

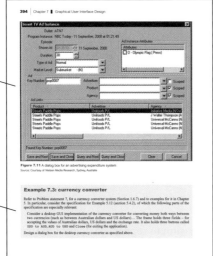

The book is based upon seven **case studies** to illustrate the concepts in real-life applications.

Multiple-choice tests at the end of each chapter help reinforce learning.

General **end of chapter questions**.

End of chapter exercises specific to each case study.

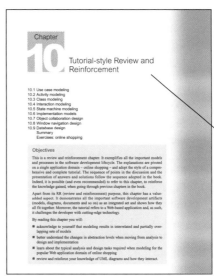

A **tutorial-style Review and Reinforcement chapter** to further consolidate learning.

Publisher's acknowledgements

We are grateful to the following for permission to reproduce copyright material:

Figure 1.5 IBM Rational Unified Process, Rational Suite Tutorial 2002, from Rational Suite Tutorial 2002, IBM Corporation; from Nielsen Media Research, Sydney: Figure 5.31 Category-Product window (advertising expenditure); Figure 6.35 Update Product window (advertising expenditure); Figure 6.39 Ad Link Row Browser and Modify Ad Links windows; Figure 7.1 Analysis phase window prototype (contact management); Figure 7.2 Design-phase window prototype (contact management); Figure 7.3 Implemented window (contact management); Figure 7.5 The main components of a primary window (advertising expenditure); Figure 7.6 A primary window showing list of products (advertising expenditure); Figure 7.7 A row browser (advertising expenditure); Figure 7.8 A multi-pane row browser window (advertising expenditure); Figure 7.9 A window with a tree browser and row browser panes (advertising expenditure); Figure 7.10 A simple secondary window-a logon window (advertising expenditure); Figure 7.11 A dialog box (advertising expenditure); Figure 7.13 A tab folder (contact management); Figure 7.14 A drop-down list (advertising expenditure); Figure 7.15 A message box (advertising expenditure); Figure 7.34 Organization status (contact management); Figure 7.35 A window to insert new organization status (contact management); Figure 7.40 A primary window (contact management); Figure 7.41 A dialog box (contact management); Figure 7.42 A tab folder (contact management); Figure 7.43 A sequence diagram for UX behavioural collaboration (contact management); Figure 7.44 A class diagram for UX structural collaboration (contact management); Figure 9.11 Traceability from features to use cases and use case requirements; Figure 9.12 Traceability from test plan to test case and test case requirements; Figure 9.13 Hyperlinking document to use case graphical icon; Figure 9.14 Hyperlinking document to use case graphical icon; Figure 9.15 Traceability for use case requirement and test requirement; Figure 9.16 Traceability from test requirement to defect; and Figure 9.17 Enhancements; from © Pearson Education Ltd: Figure 7.16 Menus; Figure 7.17 Toolbars; Figure 7.18 Buttons and other controls; Figure 9.1 JUnit as the composite pattern; Figure 9.2 Testing activities versus development phases; Figure 9.5 Test environment; Figure 9.6 Change and quality management interplay; Figure 9.7 Change management with IBM Rational Clearquest; and Figure 9.9 Defect management with IBM Rational Clearquest in *Practical Software Engineering: A*

Case-Study Approach Fisher, Maciaszek and Liong (2005); Figure 7.19 Addison-Wesley web page from Addison-Wesley; Figure 7.22 from National Australia Bankweb site © Image copyright National Australia Bank Limited 2006, reproduced with permission; Figure 10.12 Example custom configuration web page (on-line shopping) and Figure 10.13 Example custom configuration summary web page (on-line shopping), Courtesy of Sony Electronics Inc.

In some instances we have been unable to trace the owners of copyright material, and we would appreciate any information that would enable us to do so.

Chapter

1

The Software Process

Objectives

Objectives

The intention of this chapter is to describe – at an overview level – a number of strategic issues in the software development process. The educational value of this chapter is in introducing the reader to processes and approaches that underlie modern software development. By reading this chapter you will:

- understand the nature of software development, the social underpinnings of it and why development of business systems cannot be solely based on strict engineering and science principles

- learn about software process standards (CMM, ISO 9000, ITIL) and compliance frameworks (COBIT)

- gain knowledge of strategic system planning and approaches (SWOT, VCM, BPR, ISA) to ensuring that business objectives determine information systems projects

- realize that information systems differ widely depending on which management level they serve and what competitive advantage they present

- understand the difference between structured and object-oriented approaches to software development

- learn about the phases of the software development lifecycle and activities that span that lifecycle
- find out about contemporary and emerging software development models/methods (the spiral model, IBM Rational Unified Process, model-driven architecture, agile software development, aspect-oriented software development)
- be introduced to seven case studies used for examples and exercises throughout the book.

1.1 The nature of software development

The literature on information systems (IS) management is full of examples of failed projects, exceeded deadlines and budgets, faulty solutions, unmaintainable systems and so on. Even if the much cited Standish Chaos report (claiming that 70 per cent of software projects fail) is an exaggeration (Glass 2005), there is no doubt that many "successful" systems (that is, paid for and delivered to the customers) are plagued by reliability, performance, security, maintainability and other problems.

To understand the reasons for these problems, we first need to understand the nature of software development. In a now classic paper, Brooks (1987) identified the essence and accidents of software engineering. The *essence* of software engineering is embodied in the difficulties inherent in the software itself. These difficulties can only be acknowledged – they are not amenable to breakthroughs or "silver bullets". According to Brooks, the essence of software engineering is a consequence of the inherent complexity, conformity, changeability and invisibility of the software.

The "essential difficulties" of software define software development invariants. The invariants state that software is a product of a creative act of development – a craft or an art in the sense of an activity performed by an artisan rather than a fine artist. In a typical state of affairs, software is not a result of a repetitive act of manufacturing.

Once the invariants of software development are understood, one should address the *accidents* of software engineering – the difficulties due to software production practices, which are amenable to human intervention. We group various "accidental difficulties" into three categories:

- stakeholders
- process
- modeling.

1.1.1 The software development invariants

There are some essential properties of software that are not susceptible to human intervention. These properties remain invariant in all software projects. They need to be acknowledged in the projects. The task of software development is to ensure that the invariants do not get out of control and do not exert any undue negative impact on the project.

Software is inherently *complex*. In contemporary systems, the complexity is the function of the mere size of the software (such as expressed in lines of written code) and the function of interdependencies between the components of which the software product is composed.

The complexity of software varies with the nature of application domains to which the software is applied. It turns out that application domains that are computationally intensive typically lead to less complex systems than domains that are data-intensive. Data-intensive applications include e-business systems, which are the subject of this book. Such systems process huge volumes of data and business rules, which are frequently inconsistent or ambiguous. Building software that is able to accommodate all business data, rules and special cases is inherently (invariantly) difficult.

The difficulty is increased by three other essential properties reported by Brooks: *conformity*, *changeability* and *invisibility*. Application software must conform to a particular hardware/software platform on which it is built and must conform and integrate with existing information systems. Because business processes and requirements are in a constant state of flux, application software must be built to accommodate change. Although application software produces visible output, the code responsible for the output is frequently buried deeply in "invisible" programming statements, binary library code and surrounding system software.

Software is *developed* rather than *manufactured* (Pressman 2005). Of course, one cannot deny that advances in software engineering introduce more certainty into development practices, but the success of a software project cannot be guaranteed. This can be contrasted with traditional branches of engineering, such as civil or mechanical engineering. In traditional engineering, the products (artifacts) are designed with mathematical precision and then manufactured (frequently in multiple quantities) using machinery and production lines.

The software product, once developed, can be duplicated (manufactured) at minimal cost, but, in the case of enterprise information systems, the duplication is never needed. Each system is unique and is developed for a specific enterprise. The difficulty is in the development, not in the manufacturing. Accordingly, the entire cost of software production is in its development.

To ease the development effort and cost, the software industry offers partial solutions in the form of reusable software components, which can be taken advantage of in the development process. The challenge is in putting together little pieces of the solution into a coherent enterprise system that meets the needs of complex business processes.

Software practices encourage the development of systems from customizable software frameworks or packages – *commercial off-the-shelf* (**COTS**) solutions or *enterprise resource planning* (**ERP**) systems. However, a software framework can only deliver a routine accounting, manufacturing or human resources system. These routine solutions must be adapted to particular business processes that an enterprise wants and needs to conduct. These business processes must be defined and a model for the system must then be developed. The emphasis is changed from "developing from scratch" to "developing by customizing the software framework", but the very nature of the development process is still the same in both cases.

Conceptual constructs (models) for a final solution – to ensure so that they satisfy the specific needs of an organization – have to be created for any system. Once created, the software framework's functionality is customized to correspond to the conceptual constructs. Programming tasks may be different, but requirements analysis and system design activities are similar to those involved in development from scratch. After all, a conceptual construct (model) is the same under many possible representations (implementations).

Equally importantly, it is unlikely that an organization can find a software framework to automate its *core business activites*. A core business activity of a telephone company is telephony, not human resources or accounting. Accordingly, the software in support of core business activities has less opportunity to rely on software components or frameworks. Moreover, the software in support of other business activities (such as accounting) must include targeted and unique solutions to deliver a competitive advantage to an organization. As noticed by Szyperski (1988: 5), "Standard packages create a level playing field and the competition has to come from other areas."

In every case, the development process should take advantage of component technology (Allen and Frost 1998; Szyperski 1998). A **component** is an executable unit of software with well-defined functionality (services) and communication protocols (interfaces) to other components. Components can be configured to satisfy application requirements. Most influential and directly competing component technology standards are J2EE/EJB from Sun and .NET from Microsoft. A related technology of **SOA** (Service-Oriented Architecture) advocates constructing systems from **services** – that is, running software instances (as opposed to components, which need to be loaded, installed, composed, deployed and initialized before they can be run).

Packages, components, services and similar techniques do not change the essence of software production. In particular, the principles and tasks of requirements analysis and system design remain invariant. A final software product can be assembled from standard and custom-made components, but the "assembly" process is still an art. As Pressman (2005) observes, we do not even have software "spare parts" to replace broken components in systems "on the road".

1.1.2 The software development "accidents"

The software development invariants define the essence of, and create the greatest challenges in, software production. It is critically important that the "accidents" of software development do not add to the complexity and potential lack of supportability of the software product. **Supportability** (*adaptiveness*) is defined by a set of three system features: software understandability, maintainability and scalability (extensibility).

The accidents of software development can be attributed mostly to the fact that an information system is a social system. Its success or failure depends on people, their acceptance and support for the system, the processes used in the development, management practices, the use of software modeling techniques and so on.

1.1.2.1 Stakeholders

Stakeholders are people who have a stake in a software project. Any person affected by the system or who has influence on system development is a stakeholder. There are two main groups of stakeholders:

- customers (users and system owners)
- developers (analysts, designers, programmers and so on).

In ordinary communication, the term "user" is routinely used to mean "customer". Not withstanding this fact, the term "customer" better reflects the desired meaning. First, the customer is the person who pays for the development and is responsible for making decisions. Second, even if the customer is not always right, the customer's requirements cannot be arbitrarily changed or rejected by developers – any conflicting, unfeasible or illegal requirements must be renegotiated with customers.

Information systems are *social systems*. They are developed *by* people (developers) *for* people (customers). The success of a software project is determined by social factors – technology is secondary. There are many examples of technically inferior systems that work and benefit customers. The inverse is not true. A system with no benefit (perceived or real) to the customer will be abandoned no matter how technically brilliant it is.

In a typical situation, the main causes of software failure can be traced to the stakeholder factor. At the *customer* end, projects fail because (see, for example, Pfleeger, 1998):

- customers' needs are misunderstood or not fully captured
- customers' requirements change too frequently
- customers are not prepared to commit sufficient resources to the project
- customers do not want to cooperate with developers
- customers have unrealistic expectations
- the system is no longer of benefit to customers.

Projects also fail because the *developers* may not be up to the task. With the escalation in software complexity, there is a growing recognition that the skills and knowledge of developers are critical. Good developers can deliver an acceptable solution. Great developers can deliver a superior solution quicker and more cheaply. As Fred Brooks (1987: 13) famously says, "Great designs come from great designers."

The excellence and commitment of developers is the factor that contributes most to software quality and productivity. To ensure that a software product is successfully delivered to a customer, and, more importantly, to reap productivity benefits from it, a software organization must employ proper management practices with regard to developers (Brooks 1987; Yourdon 1994) namely:

- hire the best developers
- provide ongoing training and education to existing developers
- encourage exchange of information and interaction between developers so that they stimulate each other
- motivate developers by removing obstacles and channeling their efforts into productive work
- offer an exciting working environment (this tends to be much more important to people than an occasional salary increase)
- align personal goals with organizational strategies and objectives
- emphasize teamwork.

1.1.2.2 Process

A software **process** defines the activities and organizational procedures used in software production and maintenance. The process aims to manage and improve collaboration in the development and maintenance team so that a quality product is delivered to the customers and it is properly supported afterwards. A process model:

- states an order for carrying out activities
- specifies what development artifacts are to be delivered and when
- assigns activities and artifacts to developers
- offers criteria for monitoring a project's progress, measuring the outcomes and planning future projects.

Unlike modeling and programming languages, software processes are not susceptible to standardization. Each organization has to develop its own process model or customize it from a generic process template, such as the template known as the *Rational Unified Process*® (**RUP**®) (Kruchten 2003). A *software* process is an important part of the organization's overall *business* process and determines the organization's unique character and competitive position in the marketplace.

The process adopted by an organization must be aligned with its development culture, social dynamics, developers' knowledge and skills, managerial practices, customers' expectations, project sizes and even kinds of application domain. Because all these factors are subject to change, an organization may need to diversify its process model and create variants of it for each software project. For example, depending on the developers' familiarity with the modeling methods and tools, special training courses may need to be included in the process.

Project size has probably the greatest influence on the process. In a small project (of ten or so developers), a formal process may not be needed at all. Such a small team is likely to communicate and respond to changes well informally. In larger projects, however, an informal communication network will not suffice and so a well-defined process for controlled development is necessary.

1.1.2.2.1 *Iterative and incremental process*

Modern software development processes are invariably *iterative* and *incremental*. System models are refined and transformed through analysis, design and implementation phases. Details are added in successive **iterations**, changes and improvements are introduced as needed and **incremental** *releases* of software modules maintain user satisfaction and provide important feedback to modules still under development.

The **builds** of executable code are delivered to the customer in chunks, each next build being an increment adding to the previous build. An increment does not extend the project's *scope* as determined by the set of functional user requirements that the system must satisfy. *Iterations* are short – in weeks rather than months. The customer feedback is frequent, the planning is continual, the change management is a vital aspect of the **lifecycle**, and regular collection of metrics and risk analysis set up the agenda for successive iterations.

There are various variants of this iterative and incremental process. The variants of special significance include (Maciaszek and Liong 2005):

- the spiral model
- the Rational Unified Process (RUP)
- Model-Driven Architecture (**MDA**)
- the agile development process
- aspect-oriented software development.

The *spiral model*, defined by Boehm (1988), serves as a reference point for the more recent models, including the three models listed above. *RUP* is a relatively flexible process that offers a support environment (called the RUP platform) to guide developers with various document templates, explanations of concepts, development ideas and so on. *MDA* is based on the idea of executable specifications – generating the software from models and components. *Agile* development proposes a framework in which people and team collaboration are considered more important than planning, documentation and other formalities. *Aspect-oriented* development introduces an orthogonal idea of crosscutting concerns (aspects) and advocating the production of separate software modules for these concerns. Each aspect (such as software security, performance or concurrency) is treated as an independent development concern, but also the one that has to be carefully integrated (weaved) with the rest of the system.

The success of an iterative and incremental process is predicated on early identification of the *system's architectural modules*. The modules should be of similar size, highly cohesive and have minimal overlaps (coupling). The order in which the modules are to be implemented is also important. Some modules may not be able to be *released* if they depend for information or computation on other modules yet to be developed. Unless iterative and incremental development is planned and controlled, the process can degenerate into "ad hoc hacking" with no control over the project's real progress.

Capability maturity model   1.1.2.2.2

A major challenge for every organization engaged in software production is to improve its development process. Naturally enough, to introduce process improvements, the organization has to know what the problems are with its current process. The *capability maturity model* (**CMM**) is a popular method for process assessment and improvement (CMM 1995).

CMM has been specified by the Software Engineering Institute (SEI) at Carnegie Mellon University in Pittsburgh, USA. Originally used by the US Department of Defence to assess the IT capabilities of organizations bidding for defence contracts, it is now widely used by the IT industry in America and elsewhere.

CMM is essentially a *questionnaire* that an IT organization fills in. The questionnaire is followed by a verification and attestation process that assigns the organization to one of the five CMM levels. The higher the level, the better the process maturity in the organization. Figure 1.1 defines the levels, gives a short description of the main features of each level and indicates the main areas of process improvement necessary for the organization to achieve a higher level.

Figure 1.1
Process maturity
levels in CMM

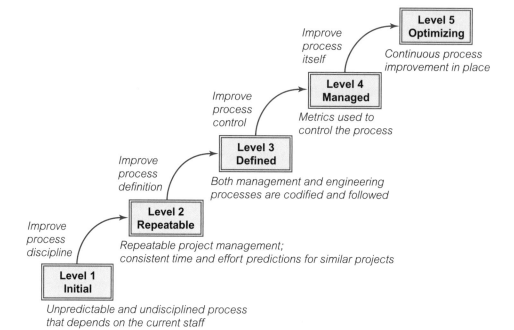

Arthur (1992) calls the levels of maturity "the stairway to software excellence." The five steps on the stairway are chaos, project management, methods and tools, measurement and continuous quality improvement. Experience has shown that it takes several years to progress one level up the maturity scale. Most organizations are at level 1, some at level 2; very few are known to be at level 5. The following few questions show the difficulty of the task. An organization that wants to be at CMM level 2 must provide positive answers to all these questions – and more (Pfleeger 1998).

- Does the software quality assurance function have a management reporting channel separate from the software development project management?
- Is there a software configuration control function for each project that involves software development?
- Is a formal process used in the management review of each software development prior to making contractual commitments?
- Is a formal procedure used to produce software development schedules?
- Are formal procedures applied to estimating software development costs?
- Are statistics on software code and test errors gathered?
- Does senior management have a mechanism for the regular review of the status of software development projects?
- Is a mechanism used for controlling changes to the software requirements?

The ISO 9000 family of quality standards *1.1.2.2.3*

There are other process improvement models besides CMM. Of particular interest are the **ISO** 9000 family of quality standards, developed by the International Organization for Standardization. The ISO standards apply to the *quality* management and the *process* to produce a quality product. The standards are generic – they apply to any industry and all types of business, including software development.

The main premise of the ISO 9000 family of standards is that if the process is right, then the process outcome (product or service) will also be right. "The objective of quality management is to produce quality products by building quality into the products rather than testing quality into the products" (Schmauch, 1994:1).

As per our earlier discussion about the process, the ISO standards do not enforce or specify processes. The standards provide models of *what* must be accomplished, not *how* activities must be performed. An organization requesting an ISO certification (also called registration) must say what it does, do what it says and demonstrate what it has done (Schmauch 1994).

A litmus test for an ISO-certified organization is that it should be able to make a quality product or provide a quality service even if its entire workforce were to be replaced. To this aim, the organization has to *document and record* all its formal activities. Written procedures must be defined for each activity, including what to do when things go wrong or customers complain.

As with CMM, ISO certification can only be granted after an *on-site audit* by an ISO registrar. These audits are then repeated at regular intervals. Organizations are impelled into the scheme through competitive forces stipulated by customers demanding that the suppliers of products and services be certified. Many countries have adopted ISO 9000 as their national standards. Such adoption is particularly strong in Europe.

The ITIL framework *1.1.2.2.4*

From a business perspective, software (or information technology – IT – in general) is an infrastructure service that is fast becoming a commodity. IT is still a leading source of competitive advantage for early adopters but the time span of that advantage is much shorter lived than it used to be. The reasons are many and include the existence of open source software, free-of-charge educational licences for commercial software, short cycles of iterative and incremental software development and so on.

Increasingly, software becomes merely a service-enabling business solution. The strength of influences between business and software is such that we need to talk about *solution (service) delivery*, not merely software or system delivery. A delivered solution needs to be further managed. *Solution management* refers to all aspects of the management of the IT solution provision. This fact has been recognized in the IT Infrastructure Library (**ITIL**®) – the most widely used and accepted framework of best practices for IT service management (ITIL 2004).

"The challenges for IT managers are to coordinate and work in partnership with the business to deliver high-quality IT services. This has to be achieved while reducing the overall TCO (total cost of ownership) and often increasing the frequency, complexity and the volume of change. ... IT management is all about the efficient and effective use of the

4 Ps, people, processes, products (tools and technology) and partners (suppliers, vendors and outsourcing organizations)." (ITIL 2004: 5).

Figure 1.2 presents the ITIL approach to implementing solution management as a continuous service improvement programme (CSIP). The CSIP programme starts with the determination of high-level business objectives, continues to checking if the milestones (deliverables) have been reached and maintains the momentum by consolidating the improvements reached and continuing with the cycle of tasks.

High level *business objectives* are determined in a strategic planning and business modeling exercise. Objectives are analyzed in the context of the current organizational status to assess the gaps that need to be bridged. Such assessment of *IT organizational maturity* should include internal reviews, external benchmarking and process verification against industry standards (such as ITIL, CMM or ISO 9000).

Once a gap assessment report has been completed, a business case for the CSIP needs to be made. The business case should identify 'quick wins' (if any), but, first of all, it should determine *measurable targets* as specific short-term goals in support of the business objectives. Equipped with all this preliminary information, a *process improvement plan* is produced. The plan determines the scope, approach and process to be followed, as well as the terms of reference for the CSIP project.

Figure 1.2
ITIL approach to
solution (service)
management

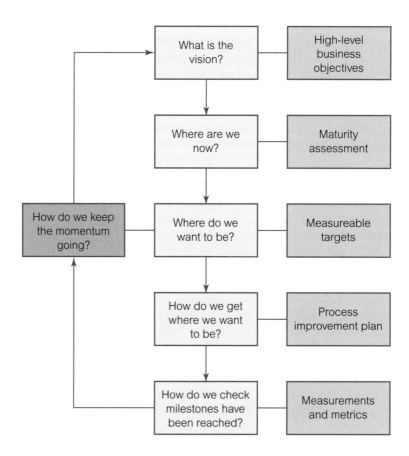

The progress and performance of the CSIP is assessed against a set of measurable milestones, deliverables, critical success factors (CSFs) and key performance indicators (KPIs). While it is important to include *measurements and metrics* that directly relate to business benefits, it must be remembered that quality business improvements are conditional on software quality factors.

The COBIT framework

1.1.2.2.5

ITIL addresses the operational side of the solution delivery and management. **COBIT**® (Control OBjectives for Information and related Technology) is a compliance framework and addresses the control side of the solution management (COBIT 2000).

ITIL, CMM and ISO 9000 are *process standards*. They state requirements for how the organization must manage processes to be able to provide a quality product or service. By contrast, COBIT is a *product standard*. It focuses on *what* an organization needs to do rather than *how* it needs to do it.

The target audience for COBIT is not software developers. COBIT targets senior IT managers, senior business managers and auditors. "Due to its high level and broad coverage and because it is based on many existing practices, COBIT is often referred to as the 'integrator', bringing disparate practices under one umbrella and, just as important, helping to link these various IT practices to business requirements." (COBIT 2005: 10).

The COBIT framework is quite prescriptive. It groups IT-related efforts into four *domains*:

- plan and organize
- acquire and implement
- deliver and support
- monitor.

The domains are assigned *control objectives*. There are 34 high-level control objectives. Associated with these objectives is an *audit guideline* for evaluating IT processes against COBIT's 318 recommended detailed control objectives. The objectives serve the purpose of assurance management and improvement advice.

The first domain – *planning and organization* – is a system planning activity (Section 1.3). It looks at IT as part of the organization's strategic and tactical plan. It is concerned with the identification of how IT can best contribute to the realization of the business's vision and objectives. It also looks at the short-term planning for the IT function. It assesses existing systems, conducts feasibility studies, allocates resources, builds an information **architecture** model, looks at technological directions, systems architecture, migration strategies, organizational placement of the IT function, data and system ownership, people management, IT operating budgets, cost and benefit justification, risk assessment, quality management and so on.

The second domain – *Acquisition and implementation* – is concerned with the realization of the IT strategy. It identifies automated solutions that would satisfy the business's goals and user requirements. It determines if an IT solution has to be developed or can be acquired. It then proposes a software development or acquisition process. It does not just concentrate on the application software but also on the technology infrastructure. It prescribes development, testing, installation and maintenance procedures, service requirements and training materials. It also introduces change management practices.

The third domain – *delivery and support* – encompasses the delivery of IT services, actual processing of **data** by application systems (known as application controls) and the necessary IT support processes. It defines service level agreements, manages third-party services, addresses performance and workloads, takes responsibility for a continuous service, ensures systems security, links with a cost accounting system, educates and trains users, assists and advises customers, manages system configuration, handles problems and incidents, manages data, facilities and operations.

The fourth domain – *Monitoring* – assesses IT processes over time for their quality and compliance with control requirements. It monitors the processes, assesses performance targets and customer satisfaction, looks at the adequacy of the internal control mechanisms, obtains independent assurance with regard to security, service effectiveness, compliance with laws, professional ethics and so on.

1.1.2.3 Modeling

Stakeholders and processes are two elements in the triangle for success. The third element is *software modeling* – that is, the very activity of software development looked at as the modeling of software artifacts. A **model** is an abstraction from reality, an abstract representation of reality. An implemented and working system is also a model of reality.

Modeling artifacts have to be communicated (language) and documented (tools). Developers need a *language* with which to build visual and other models and discuss them with customers and fellow developers. The language should allow the construction of models at varying levels of abstraction to present proposed solutions at different levels of detail. The language should have a strong *visual* component, as per the popular saying that "a picture is worth a thousand words." It should also have strong *declarative semantics* – that is, it should allow for the capturing of "procedural" meaning in "declarative" sentences. We should be able to communicate by saying "what" needs to be done rather than "how" to go about doing it.

Developers also need a *tool* or, rather, a sophisticated computer-based *environment* for the software development process. Such tools and environments are known as Computer-Assisted Software Engineering (**CASE**). A CASE enables the storage and retrieval of models in a central repository and graphical and textual manipulation of models on a computer screen. Ideally, a repository should provide for shareable multi-user (multi-developer) access to models. Typical functions of a *CASE repository* are to:

- coordinate access to models
- facilitate collaboration between developers
- store multiple versions of models
- identify differences between versions
- allow sharing of the same concepts in different models
- check the consistency and integrity of models
- generate project reports and documents
- generate data structures and programming code (forward engineering)
- generate models from existing implementation (reverse engineering).

Note that a CASE-generated program is just a code skeleton – computational algorithms need to be coded by programmers in the usual way.

Unified modeling language

"The Unified Modeling Language (**UML**) is a general-purpose visual modeling language that is used to specify, visualize, construct, and document the artifacts of a software system. It captures decisions and understanding about systems that must be constructed. It is used to understand, design, browse, configure, maintain, and control information about such systems. It is intended for use with all development methods, **lifecycle** stages, application domains, and media." (Rumbaugh et al., 2005: 3).

The Rational Software Corporation, currently part of IBM, developed UML, which unifies the best features of earlier methods and notations. In 1997, the Object Management Group (**OMG**) approved UML as a standard modeling language. Since its inception, UML has been embraced by the IT industry, widely accepted and further developed. UML version 2.0 was adopted by OMG in 2005.

UML is independent of any software development process, although Rational has proposed a matching process called the *Rational Unified Process* (*RUP*: Kruchten 2003). A process that adopts UML must support an *object-oriented approach* to software production. UML is not appropriate for old-style structured approaches that result in systems implemented with procedural programming languages, such as COBOL.

UML is also independent of implementation technologies (as long as they are object-oriented). This makes UML somewhat deficient in supporting the detailed design phase of the development lifecycle. By the same token, however, it does make UML resilient to specificities and frequent changes in implementation platforms.

The UML language constructs allow modeling of the static structure and dynamic behavior of a system. A system is modeled as a set of collaborating **objects** (software modules) that react to external events to perform tasks of benefit to customers (users). Particular models emphasize some aspects of the system and ignore others that are stressed in other models. Together, a set of integrated models provides a complete description for the system.

UML models can be categorized into three groups:

- *state models* – which describe the static data structures
- *behavior models* – which describe object collaborations
- *state change models* – which describe the allowed states for the system over time.

UML also contains a limited number of *architectural constructs* that allow the system to be modularized for iterative and incremental development. However, UML does not advocate any particular *architectural framework* that the systems can or should conform to. Such a framework would define a layered structure of system components and specify how they need to communicate and would, therefore, contradict the UML's objective of being a general-purpose language.

CASE and process improvement

Process improvement is much more than the introduction of new methods and techniques. In fact, the introduction of new methods and techniques to an organization at a low level of process maturity can bring with it more harm than good.

An example in point is the CASE technology when applied as an integrated *environment* allowing multiple developers to collaborate and share design information in order to produce new design artifacts. Such a CASE environment imposes certain processes that the development team has to obey to take advantage of this technology. However, if the development team has not been previously able to improve its processes, it is extremely unlikely that it will assimilate the process dictated by the CASE tool. As a result, the potential productivity and quality gains offered by the new technology will not materialize.

This observation is not to say that the CASE technology is a risky business. It is only risky when used to drive the entire development process and the development team is not ready to embrace that process. However, the same CASE methods and techniques would always bring personal productivity and quality improvements to individual developers who use the technology within a *tool* on their own local workstations. Modeling software artifacts with pencil and paper may make sense in a classroom situation, but never for real projects.

1.1.3   Development or integration?

The development of new software systems that automate exclusively manual processes is almost non-existent today. Most development projects replace or extend existing software solutions or integrate them into larger solutions that provide new levels of automation. Accordingly, *integration development* (as opposed to standalone, "from scratch" *application development*) is conducted using the same iterative lifecycle approaches and is producing the same software product models. The differences are in emphasis related to the integration level and in the enabling technology.

We divide integration approaches into three general categories (Hohpe and Woolf 2003; Linthicum 2004):

- information- and/or portal-oriented
- interface-oriented
- process-oriented.

Information-oriented integration relies on exchanges of **information** between source and target applications. This is an integration on the level of databases or application programming interfaces (APIs) that externalize information for consumption by other applications.

Portal-oriented integration can be seen as a special kind of information-oriented integration in which information is externalized from multiple software systems into a common user interface, typically in a Web browser's portal. The difference is that information-oriented integration focuses on the real-time exchange of information whereas portals require human intervention to act on information externalized from back-end systems.

Interface-oriented integration links application interfaces (that is, *services* defined via an interface abstraction). Interfaces expose services performed by one application that can benefit another. Interface-oriented integration does not require detailed business processes of participating applications to be visible. The supply of services can be *informational* (when data is supplied) or *transactional* (when a piece of functionality is supplied). The former is really a variation on information-based integration, but the latter requires changes to the source and target applications or may result in a new application (composite application).

Process-oriented integration links applications by defining a new layer of processes on top of an existing set of processes and data in existing applications. Arguably, this is an ultimate integration solution in which new process logic is separated from the application logic of participating applications and is likely to create a new solution that automates tasks once performed manually. Process-oriented integration starts with building a new process model and assumes the complete visibility of the internal processes of applications being integrated. It has a strategic dimension, aimed at leveraging existing business processes and delivering competitive advantage.

Review quiz 1.1

RQ1 Do "accidents" of software development define the software development invariants?

RQ2 What are the two main groups of stakeholders in software projects?

RQ3 Does each incremental release within an iteration add a new functionality to the software product under development?

RQ4 Is COBIT a product or a process standard?

RQ5 Is portal-oriented integration a special kind of interface-oriented integration?

System planning

1.2

Information system projects have to be planned for. They have to be identified, classified, ranked and selected for initial development, improvement or, perhaps, elimination. The question is, which IS technologies and applications will return the most value to the business? Ideally, the decision should be based on a clearly defined *business strategy* and careful and methodical planning (Bennett et al., 2002; Hoffer et al., 2002; Maciaszek, 1990).

Business strategy can be determined by various processes known as *strategic planning, business modeling, business process re-engineering, strategic alignment, information resource management* or similar. All these approaches undertake to study fundamental business processes in an organization in order to determine a long-term vision for the business and then prioritize business issues that can be resolved by the use of information technology.

This said, there are many organizations – in particular, many small organizations – with no clear business strategy. Such organizations are likely to decide on information systems development by simply identifying the current most pressing business problems that need to be addressed. When external environment or internal business conditions change, the existing information systems will have to be modified or even replaced. Such a modus operandi allows small organizations to refocus quickly on their current situation, take advantage of new opportunities and rebuff new threats.

Large organizations cannot afford to make constant changes to their business direction. In reality, they frequently dictate directions for other organizations in the same line of business. To some degree, they can mould the environment to their *current* needs. However, large organizations also have to look carefully into the *future*. They have to use a planning-based approach to identify development projects. These are typically large projects that take a long time to complete. They are too cumbersome to be changed or replaced easily. They need to accommodate, or even target, future opportunities and threats.

System planning can be carried out in a number of different ways. A traditional approach is nicknamed **SWOT** – *strengths, weaknesses, opportunities, threats*. Another popular strategy is based on **VCM** – *value chain model*. More modern variations used for developing a business strategy are known as **BPR** – *business process re-engineering*. The information needs of an organization can also be assessed by using blueprints for **ISA** – *information system architecture*. Such blueprints can be obtained by taking analogies from descriptive frameworks that have proved successful in disciplines other than IT – for example, in the construction industry.

All system planning approaches have an important common denominator: they are concerned with *effectiveness* (doing the right thing) rather than *efficiency* (doing things right). 'More efficiently' means doing the same job quicker with the existing resources or cheaper with fewer resources. More effectively means employing alternative resources and ideas to do a better job. 'More effectively' can also mean achieving competitive *edge* by doing innovative new things.

1.2.1 The SWOT approach

The SWOT (strengths, weaknesses, opportunities, threats) approach allows for the identification, classification, ranking and selection of IS development projects in a manner that is aligned with an organization's strengths, weaknesses, opportunities and threats. This is a top-down approach that starts with the determination of an organization's mission.

The *mission statement* captures the unique character of an organization and specifies its vision of where it wants to be in the future. In a good mission statement, emphasis is placed on customers' needs rather than on the products or services that an organization delivers.

The mission statement, and a business strategy developed from it, take into consideration the company's *internal strengths and weaknesses* in the areas of management, production, human resources, finance, marketing, research and development and so on. These strengths and weaknesses must be recognized, agreed and prioritized. A successful organization has a good understanding of its current set of strengths and weaknesses that guide the development of its business strategy.

Examples of *strengths* include:

- ownership of brand names and patents
- a good reputation among customers and suppliers
- exclusive access to resources or technology
- cost advantage due to production volume, proprietary know-how, exclusive rights or partnerships.

Frequently, a *weakness* is the absence of a potential strength. Examples of weaknesses include:

- unreliable cash flow
- inferior skills base of the staff and reliance on some key staff members
- poor location of the business.

The identification of internal company strengths and weaknesses is a necessary, but not sufficient, condition for successful business planning. An organization does not function in a vacuum – it depends on external economic, social, political and technological factors. An organization has to know of *external opportunities* to be taken advantage of and *external threats* to be avoided. These are factors that an organization cannot control, but knowledge of them is essential in determining the organization's objectives and goals.

Examples of *opportunities* include:

- new, less restrictive regulations, removal of trade barriers
- a strategic alliance, a joint venture or a merger
- the Internet as a new market
- the collapse of a competitor and the resulting opening of the market.

Any changes to the environment with a potential negative impact are threats. Examples of *threats* include:

- potential for a price war with competitors
- technology changes extending beyond the capability of assimilating them
- new tax barriers on the product or service.

Organizations pursue one or very few *objectives* at any given time. Objectives are normally long-term (three to five years) or even "timeless". Typical examples of objectives are to improve customer satisfaction, introduce new services, address competitive threats or increase control over suppliers. Each strategic objective must be associated with specific *goals*, usually expressed as annual targets. For example, the objective "to improve customer satisfaction" can be supported by the goal of fulfilling customer orders more quickly – within two weeks, say.

Objectives and goals require management *strategies* and specific *policies* for the implementation of these strategies. Such managerial instruments would adjust organizational structures, allocate resources and determine development projects, including information systems.

Figure 1.3 shows the relationships and derivation rules between concepts involved in SWOT analysis. The SWOT matrix defines the position of an organization in the marketplace and matches the organization's capabilities to the competitive environment in which it operates.

The VCM approach   1.2.2

The VCM (value chain model) assesses competitive advantage by analyzing the full chain of activities in an organization – from raw materials to final products sold and shipped to customers. In the value chain approach, the product or service is the medium that transfers *value* to customers. The chain metaphor reinforces the point that a single weak link will cause the whole chain to break. The model serves the purpose of understanding which value chain configurations will yield the greatest competitive advantage. The IS development projects can then target those segments, operations, distribution channels, marketing approaches and so on that give the most competitive advantage.

Figure 1.3
SWOT framework

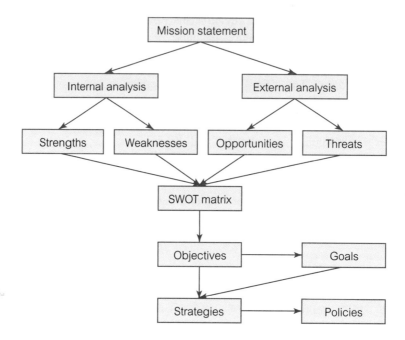

In the original VCM approach (Porter 1985), organizational functions are categorized into *primary activities* and *support activities*. The primary activities create or add value to a final product. They are divided into five successive stages:

1 *inbound logistics* – receiving inputs to the product or service

2 *operations* – using inputs to create the product or service

3 *outbound logistics* – distributing the product or service to buyers

4 *sales and marketing* – inducing buyers to purchase the product or service

5 *services* – to maintain or enhance the value of the product or service.

These five stages utilize pertinent information technologies and are assisted by relevant categories of information systems, such as:

1 warehousing systems for inbound logistics

2 computer manufacturing systems for operations

3 shipment and scheduling systems for outbound logistics

4 ordering and invoicing systems for sales and marketing

5 equipment maintenance systems for services.

The support activities do not add value, at least not directly. They are still essential, but they do not enrich the product. The support activities include administration and infrastructure, human resource management, research and development and, quite understandably, IS development.

While VCM is a useful tool for strategic planning and determination of IS development projects, the reverse is also true. The omnipresent computerization facilitates business changes and this in turn creates efficiencies, cost reductions and competitive advantages. In other words, *IT can transform an organization's value chains*. A self-reinforcing loop between IT and VCM can be established.

Porter and Millar (1985) identified five steps that an organization can take to exploit IT opportunities:

1   assess the information intensity of products and processes

2   assess the role of IT in industry structure

3   identify and rank ways in which IT could create a competitive advantage

4   consider how IT could create new businesses

5   develop a plan to take advantage of IT.

The BPR approach   1.2.3

The BPR (business process re-engineering) approach to system planning is based on the premise that today's organizations must reinvent themselves and abandon the functional decomposition, hierarchical structures and operational principles that they are now using.

The concept was introduced by Hammer (1990) and Davenport and Short (1990). It immediately generated interest as well as controversy. An extended description of BPR can be found in the books by the originators (Davenport 1993; Hammer and Champy 1993a).

Most contemporary organizations are structured into *vertical units* that focus on functions, products or regions. These structures and work styles can be traced back to the eighteenth century and Adam Smith's principle of the division of labor and the consequent fragmentation of work. No one employee or department is responsible for a *business process*, which is defined as "a collection of activities that takes one or more kinds of input and creates an output that is of value to the customer" (Hammer and Champy 1993a).

BPR challenges Smith's industrial principles of the division of labor, hierarchical control and economies of scale. In today's world, organizations must be able to adapt quickly to market changes, new technologies, competitive factors, customers' demands and so on.

Rigid organizational structures in which business processes have to cut across many departments are obsolete. Organizations must focus on business processes rather than individual tasks, jobs, people or departmental functions. These processes cut *horizontally* across the business and end at points of contact with customers. "The most visible difference between a process enterprise and a traditional organization is the existence of process owners" (Hammer and Stanton 1999).

The main objective of BPR is to radically redesign business processes in an organization (hence, BPR is sometimes known as a *process redesign*). Business processes have to be identified, streamlined and improved. The processes are documented in *work flow diagrams* and subjected to a *workflow analysis*. Workflows capture the flow of events, documents and information in a business process and can be used to calculate the time, resources and costs needed for these activities.

Davenport and Short (1990) recommend a five-step approach to BPR:

1 determine the business vision and process objectives (the business vision derives from the mission statement; the objectives concentrate on cost and time reductions, quality improvements, staff empowerment, knowledge acquisition and so on)

2 determine the processes to be re-engineered

3 understand and measure the existing processes (in order to avoid past mistakes and establish the baseline for process redesign and improvement)

4 identify information technology (IT) levers and how they can influence the process redesign and improvement

5 design and build a *prototype* of the new process (the prototype is a workflow system that is the subject of iterative and incremental development).

The major hurdle in implementing BPR in organizations lies in the need to embed a horizontal process in a traditional vertical management structure. A serious BPR initiative requires changing the organization so that it centres on the development teams as the primary organizational units. These teams are responsible for one or more end-to-end business processes.

Sometimes a radical change is unacceptable. The traditional structures cannot be changed overnight. A radical push can be met with defiance and then the potential benefits of BPR can be compromised. Under such circumstances, an organization can still benefit from modeling its business processes and attempting to improve them only, rather than re-engineer them. The term *business process improvement* (BPI) is used to characterize an improvement initiative (Allen and Frost 1998).

Once business processes have been defined, the process owners require IT support to improve the efficiency of these processes further. The resulting IS development projects concentrate on implementing the identified workflows. The combination of the *effectiveness* of BPR and the *efficiency* of IT can give dramatic improvements in all contemporary measures of an organization's performance, such as quality, service, speed, cost, price, competitive advantage and flexibility.

1.2.4 The ISA approach

Unlike the approaches already described, ISA (information systems architecture) is a bottom-up approach that offers a *neutral architectural framework* for IS solutions that can suit a variety of business strategies. As such, the ISA approach does not include a system planning methodology – it simply offers a framework that leverages most business strategies.

The ISA approach was introduced in a paper by Zachman (1987) and later extended by Sowa and Zachman (1992). An insignificantly modified version of the original paper has been published (Zachman 1999).

The ISA framework is represented as a table of 30 cells organized into 5 rows (labeled 1 through 5) and six columns (labeled A through F). The rows represent the different *perspectives* used in the construction of a complex engineering product, such as an information system. These perspectives are those of five major "players in the game" – the five IS participants:

1 planner – determines the scope of the system
2 owner – defines an enterprise conceptual model
3 designer – specifies a system physical model
4 builder – provides detailed technological solutions
5 subcontractor – delivers system components.

The six columns represent the six different *descriptions* or *architectural models* that each of the participants engages with. Like perspectives, the descriptions are quite different from each other, but, at the same time, they are intrinsically related to one another. The descriptions provide answers to six questions that are key to each of the participant.

A *What* is the thing made of? (That is, data, in the case of IS.)
B *How* does the thing function? (That is, the business processes.)
C *Where* is the thing located? (That is, the location of the processing components.)
D *Who* works with the thing? (That is, the users.)
E *When* does the thing occur? (That is, the scheduling of events and states.)
F *Why* is the thing taking place? (That is, the motivation of the enterprise.)

The combination of perspectives and descriptions in the 30 cells provides a powerful taxonomy that establishes a complete architecture for an IS development. The vertical perspectives may differ in detail, but, more importantly, they differ in essence and employ different modeling representations. Different models emphasize the different viewpoints of the participants. Likewise, the horizontal descriptions are prepared for different reasons – they each answer one of the six questions.

   The most attractive feature of the ISA approach comes from providing a framework that is likely to be flexible enough to accommodate future changes in business conditions and resources. This is because an ISA solution is not derived from any particular business strategy. It is just a framework for a complete description of an IS system. The framework draws from the experiences of more established disciplines – some with a thousand or so years of history (such as classical architecture).

Review quiz 1.2

RQ1 What is the main target of system planning – effectiveness or efficiency?
RQ2 In a SWOT analysis, are objectives derived from goals or vice versa?
RQ3 In the VCM approach, is 'sales and marketing' a primary or support activity?
RQ4 According to the BPR approach, what is the most visible difference between a process enterprise and a traditional organization?
RQ5 What are the five 'perspectives' of the ISA framework?

1.3 Systems for three management levels

Associated with system planning is the recognition that an organization has three management levels:

1 strategic

2 tactical

3 operational.

The three levels are characterized by a unique focus of decision making, by a distinct set of required IS applications, and by the specific support required from IT. It is the task of system planning to define a blend of IS applications and IT solutions that is most effective for an organization at a particular point in time. Table 1.1 defines the issues involved in matching decision making levels to IS applications and IT solutions (see Benson and Standing, 2002; Jordan and Machesky 1990; Robson 1994).

The IS applications and IT solutions that offer the greatest returns to an organization are those at the *strategic level*. However, these are also solutions that are the most difficult to implement – they use "bleeding-edge" technology and demand very skillful and specialized design. After all, these are the systems that can give an organization a competitive edge in the marketplace.

At the other end of the spectrum, systems in support of the *operational management level* are quite routine, use conventional database technology and are frequently customized from prepackaged solutions. These systems are unlikely to provide a competitive edge, but, without them, the organization is not able to function properly.

Every modern organization has a full suite of operational-level systems, but only the best-managed organizations have an integrated set of strategic-level IS applications. The main technology for storing and retrieving data for high-level strategic and tactical decision making is known as a *data warehouse* (Kimball 1996).

Table 1.1 IS and IT support for different levels of decision making

Level of decisionmaking	Focus of decisionmaking	Typical IS applications	Typical IT solutions	Pivotal concept
Strategic (executive and senior management levels)	Strategies in support of organization's long-term objectives	Market and sales analysis, product planning, performance evaluation	Datamining, knowledge management	*Knowledge*
Tactical (line management level)	Policies in support of short-term goals and resource allocation	Budget analysis, salary forecasting, inventory scheduling, customer service	Data warehouse, analytical processing, spreadsheets	*Information*
Operational (operative management level)	Day-to-day staff activities and production support	Payroll, invoicing, purchasing, accounting	Database, transactional processing, application generators	*Data*

The last column in Table 1.1 associates three pivotal IS concepts – knowledge, information and data – with systems at the three levels of decision making. The definitions of the pivotal concepts are:

- *data* – raw facts representing values, quantities, concepts and events pertaining to business activities.
- *information* – value-added facts; data that have been processed and summarized to produce value-added facts, revealing new features and trends.
- *knowledge* – understanding of information, obtained by experience or study and resulting in the ability to do things effectively and efficiently, which can be in a person's mind (*tacit knowledge*) or documented in some structured form.

As an example, a telephone number is a piece of *data*. Grouping telephone numbers by geographical areas or by customer rating of their owners results in *information*. Understanding how to use this information in telemarketing to entice people to buy products is *knowledge*. As jokingly noted by Benson and Standing (2002), deciding not to phone someone in the middle of the night is *wisdom*. More seriously, wisdom is sometimes considered to be the ultimate pivotal IS concept. It is then defined as the ability to use the knowledge to make good judgments and decisions.

Transactional processing systems   1.3.1

The main class of systems at the operational level of decision making are OnLine Transaction Processing (**OLTP**) systems. A **transaction** is defined as a logical unit of work that accomplishes a particular business task and guarantees the integrity of the database after the task completes (Maciaszek and Liong 2005). From the transactional perspective, *integrity* means that the data is left consistent and correct after the transaction completes its execution.

Transactional processing systems are inherently associated with the technology of databases. A *database* is a central repository of enterprise data and the key strategic resource of any enterprise. A *database system* has the key responsibility of enabling concurrent multi-user access to data by any number of users and application programs. This access to data is demarcated (bracketed) by the notion of business transactions that dictate which data can or cannot be accessed concurrently and under what conditions the data can be modified.

The size of a database is measured in gigabytes (Gb – 10^9 bytes) or even terabytes (Tb – 10^{12} bytes). Accordingly, the database resides on a non-volatile (*persistent*) secondary storage, such as magnetic or optical disks. The data is said to be persistent because it stays on the disks permanently, whether or not the disk drives are powered and in use.

Apart from the *concurrency* control, the notion of a transaction is fundamental to ensuring that the database can always recover from software and hardware failures. Any *recovery* from failures must ensure that the data is returned (rolled back) to a correct state that existed before the transaction started. Alternatively, a failed transaction can be automatically restarted (rolled forward) so that a new correct state, as determined by the transaction processing logic, is achieved.

Although the state of the database is by and large determined by the processing logic of various transactions executing on the data, that logic is subjected to a careful control of enterprise-wide business rules. This introduces the distinction between the *application logic* governed by transactions and the *business logic* governed by other database programming mechanisms, namely referential integrity constraints and triggers. For example, if a business rule states that to enroll on a course a student must have passed a prerequisite exam, no application transaction will be permitted to overpass that business rule so that ineligible students are enrolled.

As stated, a database is a key strategic resource of any enterprise. As a consequence, database technology provides mechanisms to guarantee the *security* of the data by ensuring that only authenticated and authorized users and application programs can access the data and execute internal database programs (stored procedures).

1.3.2 Analytical processing systems

The main class of systems at the tactical level of decision making are OnLine Analytical Processing (**OLAP**) systems. As opposed to transactional processing that typically results in changes to data, analytical processing is concerned with the *analysis* of pre-existing historical data to facilitate decision making. Hence, instead of asking for detailed sales data, the analytical processing systems try to answer queries such as "How much profit did we get from the promotional sales of some products to female customers last month as opposed to normal sales in the same month last year?" The more historical data is available for any such analysis, the more reliable the decision making can be.

Analytical processing systems are associated with the technology of data warehouses. A **data warehouse** is normally created by taking incremental copies of the data in one or more transactional databases. The new data is always added. The historical data is never removed. Consequently, data warehouses become quickly many times larger than the databases from which the data is drawn. Large data warehouses require terabytes (Tb – 10^{12} bytes) or even petabytes (Pb – 10^{15} bytes) of storage. The size of the data warehouse is the issue, but fortunately the data is static – that is, it is not subject to changes (except any changes due to the discovery of incorrect, inconsistent or missing data in the original database).

As required and expected by tactical-level managers, analytical systems are designed to support data-intensive ad hoc querying. This places particular demands on the data warehouse technology. On the front end of the technology, programmingless access tools to query the data need to be provided to managers. On the back end of the technology, a single data warehouse needs to be created and organized to enable easy querying of historical, detailed and appropriately partitioned, presummarized and prepackaged data.

Summarizing and packaging the data constitute a unique feature of data warehouses aimed at adding value to the data extracted from the source systems. *Summarizing* (aggregation) selects, joins and groups data in order to provide precalculated measures and trends for direct access by the end users. *Packaging* transforms the operational and summarized data into more useful formats, such as graphs, charts, spreadsheets, animations. *Partitioning* uses technical means and user profiling to reduce the amount of data that the system needs to scan as it searches for the answers to queries.

As the creation of a large, monolithic data warehouse for all enterprise data proves to be a real challenge, other related technologies have emerged. A popular practical solution is to build **data marts**. Like a data warehouse, a data mart is a special-purpose database dedicated to analytical processing. Unlike a data warehouse, a data mart holds only a subset of enterprise data relevant to a particular department or business function. Also, a data mart tends to hold mostly summarized historical data and leaves detailed operational data on original storage sources.

A new emerging trend is towards **data webhouses**. A data webhouse is defined as "a distributed data warehouse that is implemented over the Web with no central data repository" (Connolly and Begg 2005: 1152). A data webhouse provides a natural answer to the difficulty associated with the extraction, cleansing and loading of large volumes of potentially inconsistent data from multiple data sources into single data storage. A data webhouse offers an alternative technology for analytical processing on enterprise intranets. Its potential use on the Internet is naturally restricted by the confines of the privacy and security of data as the most guarded strategic asset of any enterprise. Outside of these confines, data webhouses can offer very useful analytical analysis of data associated with the behavior of Internet users (so-called *clickstreams* of data).

Knowledge processing systems 1.3.3

The main class of systems at the strategic level of decision making are knowledge processing systems. **Knowledge** is usually defined as know-how – intellectual capital accumulated as a result of experience. As noted by Rus and Lindvall (2002: 26), "The major problem with intellectual capital is that it has legs and walks home every day. At the same rate experience walks out the door, inexperience walks in the door. Whether or not many software organizations admit it, they face the challenge of sustaining the level of competence needed to win contracts and fulfil undertakings."

To sustain intellectual capital present in an enterprise information system (EIS), the know-how has to be managed. Effectively, *knowledge management* has to be engaged to help organizations discover, organize, distribute and apply the knowledge encoded in information systems. **Datamining** is an area of knowledge management concerned with exploratory data analysis to discover relationships and patterns (perhaps previously unknown or forgotten) that can (re-)discover knowledge and support decision making.

The main objectives of datamining are (Kifer et al. 2006; Oz 2004):

■ *association (path analysis)* – finding patterns in data where one event leads to another related event, such as predicting which people who rent a property are likely to move out of the rental market and buy a property in the near future

■ *classification* – finding if certain facts fall into predefined interesting categories, such as predicting which customers are likely to be the least loyal and may change to another mobile phone provider

■ *clustering* – similar to classification, but the categories are not previously known and are discovered by a clustering algorithm rather than being specified by the human analyst, such as predicting the response to a telemarketing initiative.

As with OLAP systems, the main source of data for datamining is a data warehouse rather than operational databases. Datamining extends OLAP's capabilities to reach the demands of strategic management. It offers *predictive* rather than *retrospective* models. It uses artificial intelligence (AI) techniques to discover trends, correlations and patterns in data. It attempts to find hidden and unexpected knowledge rather than the knowledge that is anticipated as it is the hidden and unexpected knowledge that has more strategic value for decision making.

Review quiz 1.3

RQ1 Which level of decisionmaking is primarily supported by data warehouse technology?

RQ2 What are the two main functions of transaction management in OLTP systems?

RQ3 What kind of OLAP technology aims to support individual departments or business functions, and stores only summarized historical data?

RQ4 What is the main technology underpinning knowledge processing systems?

1.4   The software development lifecycle

Software development follows a lifecycle. This lifecycle is an orderly set of activities conducted and managed for each development project. The processes and methods are the machinery for a lifecycle implementation. The lifecycle consists of:

- the applied modeling approach
- the exact phases, during the sequence of which the software product is transformed – from initial inception to phasing it out
- the method (methodology) and associated development process.

A typical lifecycle begins with a business *analysis* of the current situation and proposed solution. The analysis models are subjected to more detailed *design*. The design is followed by programming (*implementation*). The implemented parts of the system are *integrated* and *deployed* to customers. At this point, the system becomes *operational* (it supports daily business operations). For successful operation, the system undergoes *maintenance* tasks.

This book concentrates on analysis and design, touching on implementation. Risking some simplification, business analysis is about what to do whereas system design is about how to do it using the available technology, and implementation is about doing it (in the sense that a tangible software product is delivered to the customer).

The development approach 1.4.1

The "software revolution" has introduced some significant changes to the ways in which software products work. In particular, software has become much more *interactive*. The tasks and behavior of programs dynamically adapt to users' requests.

Looking back, the *procedural* logic of a COBOL-like program of the past was inflexible and not very responsive to unexpected events. Once started, the program executed to completion in a more or less deterministic fashion. Occasionally, the program would request input information from the user and would then follow a different execution path. In general, however, interaction with the user was limited and the number of different execution paths was predetermined. The program was in control, not the user.

With the advent of modern graphical user interfaces (GUIs), the approach to computing has changed dramatically. GUI programs are *event-driven* and execute in a random and unpredictable fashion dictated by user-generated events, from a keyboard, mouse or other input device.

In a GUI environment, the user is (largely) in control of the program's execution, not vice versa. Behind every event, there is a software *object* that knows how to service that event in the current state of the program's execution. Once the service has been accomplished, control returns to the user.

This contemporary style of program–user interaction necessitates a different approach to software development. Conventional software has been well served by the so-called *structured approach*. Modern GUI systems require object programming, so the *object approach* is the best way to design such systems.

The structured approach 1.4.1.1

The *structured approach* to systems development is also called functional, procedural and imperative. This approach was popularized (and de facto standardized) in the 1980s. From a system modeling perspective, the structured approach is based on two techniques:

- data flow diagrams (**DFD**) for process modeling
- entity relationship diagrams (**ERD**) for data modeling.

The structured approach is *processcentric* and uses DFDs as a driving development force. In this approach, the system is broken down into manageable units in the activity called *functional decomposition*. The system is hierarchically divided into business processes linked by data flows.

Over the years, the structured approach has evolved slightly from being process-centered to becoming more data-centered. This has been the direct result of the popularity of the relational database model. The importance of DFDs in structured development has faded a bit in favour of the ERD datacentric technique.

The combination of DFDs and ERDs delivers relatively complete analysis models that capture all of a system's functions and data at a desirable level of abstraction, which does not depend on the software/hardware considerations. The analysis model is transformed later into a design model, expressed typically in relational database terms. The implementation phase can then follow.

The structured approach to analysis and design is characterized by a number of features, some of which do not align well with modern software engineering. For example, the approach:

- tends to be *sequential and transformational* rather than iterative and incremental – that is, does not facilitate a seamless development process via iterative refinement and incremental software delivery
- tends to deliver inflexible solutions that satisfy the set of identified business functions but can be hard to scale up and extend in the future
- assumes development from scratch and does not support the reuse of pre-existing components.

The transformational nature of the approach introduces a considerable risk of misinterpreting original users' requirements down the development track. This risk is exacerbated by the progressive need to trade off the relatively declarative semantics of analysis models for procedural solutions in design models and implementation code (this is because the analysis models are semantically richer than the underlying design and implementation models).

1.4.1.2   The object-oriented approach

The *object-oriented approach* to systems development breaks a system down into components of various granularity, with classes of objects at the bottom of this decomposition. Classes are linked by various relationships and communicate by sending messages that invoke operations on objects.

Although object-oriented programming languages (Simula) existed as early as the beginning of the 1970s, the object-oriented approach to system development was popularized only in the 1990s. Later on, the Object Management Group approved a series of UML (Unified Modeling Language) standards in support of the approach.

Compared with the structured approach, the object-oriented approach is more *datacentric* – it evolves around class models. In the analysis phase, classes do not need to have their operations defined, only their attributes. However, the growing significance of *use cases* in UML shifts the emphasis slightly from data to processes.

There is a perception that developers use object approaches because of the technical advantages of the object paradigm, such as abstraction, encapsulation, reuse, inheritance, message passing and polymorphism. Indeed, these technical properties can lead to greater reusability of code and data, shorter development times, increased programmer productivity, improved software quality and greater understandability. While attractive, these advantages of object technology do not always materialize in practice, however. Nevertheless, we do use objects today and will be using them tomorrow. The reasons for this have to do with the need for the *event-driven* programming demanded by modern interactive GUI-based applications.

Other reasons for the popularity of the object approach have to do with addressing the needs of *newly emerging applications* and the preferred ways to fight *application backlogs* (the quantity of software products the planned or agreed date of which has expired and are still to be delivered, typically in the process of expanding and integrating with the existing legacy systems). Two of the most important new categories of application that demand object technology are *workgroup computing* and *multimedia systems*. The idea of stopping the application backlog from growing by means of the concept known as *object wrapping* has proved to be both attractive and workable.

The object approach to systems development follows the *iterative and incremental* process. A single model (and a single design document) is "elaborated" in the analysis, design and implementation phases. Details are added in successive iterations, changes and refinements are introduced as needed and incremental releases of selected modules maintain user satisfaction and provide additional feedback for other modules.

Development by elaboration is possible because all development models (analysis, design and implementation) are semantically rich and based on the same "language" – the underlying vocabulary is essentially the same (classes, attributes, methods, inheritance, polymorphism, and so on). However, note that whenever the implementation is based on a relational database, there is still a need for a complex transformation because the underlying semantics of the relational model is quite poor by comparison and is orthogonal to object technology.

The object approach alleviates the most important shortcomings of the structured approach, but it does introduce a few new problems.

- The analysis phase is conducted at an even higher level of abstraction and – if the implementation server solution assumes a relational database – the *semantic gap* between the object-oriented modeling artifacts and the implementation of the datacentric artifacts with relational database technology can be significant. Although the analysis and design can be conducted in an iterative and incremental fashion, eventually the development reaches the implementation stage, which requires transformation into a relational database. If the implementation platform is an object or object-relational database, then the transformation from design is much easier.

- *Project management* is more difficult. Managers measure development progress by clearly defined work breakdown structures, deliverables and milestones. In object-oriented development that occurs by means of "elaboration" there are no clear boundaries between phases and so project documentation evolves continuously. An attractive solution to this difficulty lies in dividing the project into small modules and managing the progress by frequent executable releases of these modules (some of these releases can be internal, others delivered).

- Object solutions are significantly more complex than old-style structured systems. The *complexity* results mostly from the need for extensive inter-object and inter-component communication. The situation can be aggravated by bad architectural design, such as that which permits unrestricted networks of intercommunication objects. Systems built in this way are difficult to maintain and evolve.

The difficulties with the object approach do not change the fact that "the future isn't what it used to be", in Arthur C. Clarke's words. There is no going back to the procedural style of programming reminiscent of batch COBOL applications. All stakeholders in IS development projects are aware of the Internet, e-business, computer games and other interactive applications.

New software applications are thus much more complex to build and the structured approach is inadequate for the task. The object-oriented approach – and the technologies built on the object paradigm, such as components and Web services – is currently the dominant and practical method to harness the development of new highly interactive event-driven software.

1.4.2 Lifecycle phases

There are some well-defined chronological sequences of action in software production. At a coarse level of granularity, the lifecycle includes five phases:

1 business analysis
2 system design
3 implementation
4 integration and deployment
5 operation and maintenance.

The *business analysis* phase concentrates on system requirements. Requirements are determined and specified (modeled). Function and data models for the system are developed and integrated. Non-functional requirements and other system constraints are also captured.

The *system design* phase divides into two major subphases – namely, architectural and detailed design. The program design that involves user interface at the client end and database objects at the server end is explained in terms of its structure (architecture) and technical solutions (detailed design). Various design issues that influence a system's understandability, maintainability and scalability are raised and documented.

The *implementation* phase consists of the activity of coding client application programs and server databases. Incremental and iterative implementation processes are emphasized. *Round-trip engineering* between design models and the implementation of client applications and server databases is essential to successful product delivery.

It is impracticable and unrealistic today for software to be developed in one big chunk in a single iteration of analysis, design and implementation. The software is developed in smaller modules (components) and these need to be assembled as well as integrated with modules already operational prior to deployment to customers for production use. This is called the *integration and deployment* phase.

The *operation and maintenance* phase begins at the point when the pre-existing business solution or system is phased out and the new system takes over day-to-day operations. Perhaps paradoxically, the operation phase also signifies the beginning of system maintenance, which includes any corrections and extensions to software. To a large degree, maintenance is not a reflection on the quality of delivered software. It is, rather, a sign of the times and the fact that the business environment is in a constant state of flux, demanding regular changes to software.

1.4.2.1 Business analysis

Business analysis (or *requirements analysis*) is the activity of determining and specifying customers' requirements. The requirements determination and specification are related but separate activities and sometimes conducted by different people. Accordingly, a distinction is sometimes made between a business analyst and a system analyst. The former determines requirements, the latter specifies (or models) them.

Business analysis, even when conducted in the context of a small application domain, takes a careful look at the enterprise's business processes. In this sense, business analysis is linked to *business process re-engineering* (BPR, Section 1.2.3). The aim of BPR is to propose new ways of conducting business and gaining competitive advantage. These "new ways" are supposed to be freed from the luggage of existing solutions, including existing information systems.

As a result of BPR initiatives and the normal activity of adding engineering rigor to system development, business analysis increasingly becomes an act of *requirements engineering*. Indeed, requirements engineering is a software development discipline of growing importance – one that links smoothly to the whole field of software engineering (Maciaszek and Liong 2005).

Requirements determination 1.4.2.1.1

Kotonya and Sommerville (1998) define a **requirement** as "a statement of a system service or constraint." A *service statement* describes how the system should behave with regard to an individual user or the whole user community. In the latter case, a service statement really defines a *business rule* that must be obeyed at all times (such as "fortnightly salaries are paid on Wednesdays"). A service statement may also be some computation that the system must carry out ("calculate salesperson commission based on sales in the last fortnight using a particular formula", for example).

A *constraint statement* expresses a restriction on the system's behavior or its development. An example of the former may be the security constraint: "only direct managers can see the salary information of their staff." An example of the latter may be, "we must use Sybase development tools." Notice that sometimes the distinction between a constraint statement on the system's behavior and a business rule service statement is blurred. This is not a problem as long as all requirements are identified and duplications eliminated.

The task of the requirements determination phase is to determine, analyze and negotiate requirements with customers. The phase involves various techniques for gathering information from customers. It is a concept exploration, carried out by means of structured and unstructured interviews with users, questionnaires, the study of documents and forms, video recordings and so on. An ultimate technique of the requirements phase is *rapid prototyping* of the solution so that difficult requirements can be clarified and misunderstandings avoided.

Requirements analysis includes negotiations between developers and customers. This step is necessary to eliminate contradicting and overlapping requirements and conform to the project budget and deadline.

The product of the requirements phase is a *requirements document*. This is mostly a narrative text document with some informal diagrams and tables. No formal models are included, except perhaps a few easy and popular notations that can be easily grasped by customers and facilitate developer–customer communication.

Requirements specification 1.4.2.1.2

The requirements specification phase begins when the developers start modeling the requirements using a particular method (such as UML). A CASE tool is used to enter, analyze and document the models. As a result, the requirements document is enriched with graphical models and CASE-generated reports. In essence, a *specifications document* (the *specs* in the jargon) replaces the requirements document.

The two most important specification techniques in object-oriented analysis are *class diagrams* and *use case diagrams*. These are techniques for data and function specifications. A typical specification document will also describe other requirements, such as performance, "look and feel", usability, maintainability, security and political and legal requirements.

Specification models can and will overlap. Overlapping allows for the proposed solution to be viewed from many different angles so that specific aspects of the solution are emphasized and analyzed. Consistency and completeness of requirements are also carefully checked.

Ideally, the specification models should be independent of the hardware/software platform on which the system is to be deployed. *Hardware/software considerations* impose heavy restrictions on the vocabulary (and therefore expressiveness) of the modeling language. Moreover, the vocabulary may be difficult for customers to understand, thus inhibiting developer–customer communication.

This said, some of the constraint statements would, in fact, impose hardware/software considerations on developers. Moreover, the customers themselves express their requirements in relation to a particular hardware/software technology or even demand a particular technology. In general, however, the task of the business analysis should not be to consider or relate to a hardware/software platform on which the system will be deployed.

1.4.2.2   System design

The definition of *system design* is broader than the definition of *software design*, although undoubtedly software design takes center stage. System design includes the description of a structure of the system and the detailed design of internals of system components. Accordingly, system design is sometimes separated into architectural design and detailed design.

Design continues from analysis. While this observation is certainly true, architectural design can be seen as a relatively self-governing activity aimed at using good and proven design practices to achieve architectural excellence. By contrast, detailed design flows directly from analysis models.

The specification document from the analysis phase is like a *contract* between developers and customers for delivery of the software product. It lists all the requirements that the software product must satisfy. Specifications are handed over to system/software architects, designers and engineers to develop lower-level models of a system's architecture and its internal workings. Design is done in terms of the software/hardware platform on which the system is to be implemented.

1.4.2.2.1   *Architectural design*

The description of the system in terms of its modules (components) is called its *architectural design*. The architectural design includes decisions about the solution strategies for the client and server aspects of the system. The architectural design is also concerned with the selection of a solution strategy and the modularization of the system. The *solution strategy* needs to resolve client (user interface) and server (database) issues as well as any *middleware* needed to "glue" client and server processes together. The decision about the basic building blocks (components) to use is relatively independent of a solution strategy, but the detailed design of components must conform to a selected client/server solution.

Client/server models are frequently extended to provide *three-tier architecture*, where application logic constitutes a separate layer. The middle tier is a logical tier and, as such, may or may not be supported by separate hardware. Application logic is a process that can run on either the client or the server – that is, it can be compiled into the client or server process and implemented as a dynamic link library (DLL), application programming interface (API), remote procedure calls (RPC) and so on.

The quality of the architectural design is tremendously important to the long-lasting success of the system. A good architectural design produces **adaptive (supportable)** *systems* – that is, systems that are understandable, maintainable and scalable (extensible). Without these qualities, the inherent complexity of a software solution escapes control. It is, therefore, crucial that architectural design delivers an adaptive system structure and this structure is adhered to during programming and carefully maintained after system delivery.

Detailed design   *1.4.2.2.2*

The description of the internal workings of each software component is called its *detailed design*. It develops detailed algorithms and data structures for each component. The components are eventually deployed on the client, server or middleware processes of the underlying implementation platform. Accordingly, the algorithms and data structures are tailored to constraints (both reinforcing and obstructive) of the underlying implementation platform.

The detailed design of the *client* (user interface) needs to conform to the GUI design supportable by Internet browsers, for Web-based applications, or the guidelines provided by the creator of a particular GUI interface (Windows, Motif, Macintosh), for conventional applications. Such guidelines are normally provided online as part of the electronic GUI documentation (for example, Windows 2000).

A major principle for an object-oriented GUI design is that the *user is in control*, not the program. The program reacts to randomly generated user events and provides the necessary software services. Other GUI design principles are a consequence of this fact. Of course, the "the user is in control" principle should not be taken literally – the program would still validate the user's privileges and might disallow certain actions.

The detailed design of the *server* defines objects on a database server – most likely a relational (or possibly object-relational) server. Some of these objects are data containers (tables, views and so on). Other objects are procedural (such as stored procedures and triggers).

The detailed design for the *middleware* layer is concerned with the application logic and business rules. This layer provides a separation and mapping between the user interface and database aspects of the solution. This separation is crucial if there is to be an acceptable level of ease regarding the independent evolution of the application software handling the user interface and the database software handling access to data sources.

Implementation   1.4.2.3

·The *implementation* of an information system involves the *installation* of the purchased software and *coding* of the custom-written software. It also involves other important activities, such as the loading of test and production databases, testing, user training and hardware issues.

Typically an implementation team is organized into two groups of programmers – those responsible for client programming and those in charge of server database programming. Client programs implement windows and application logic (even if the application logic is deployed on a separate application server, there are always aspects of it that have to reside on the client). Client programs also initiate business transactions, which result in the activation of server database programs (stored procedures). The responsibility for database consistency and transactional correctness lies with server programs.

In a true spirit of iterative and incremental development, the detailed design of *user interfaces* is prone to implementation changes. Application programmers may opt for a different appearance of implemented windows to conform to the vendor's GUI principles, facilitate programming or improve the user's productivity.

Similarly, server *database* implementation may force changes to design documents. Unforeseen database problems, difficulties with the programming of stored procedures and triggers, concurrency issues, integration with client processes and performance tuning are just a few reasons for modifying a design.

1.4.2.4 Integration and deployment

Incremental development implies *incremental integration and deployment* of software modules (subsystems). This task is not trivial. For large systems, module integration can take more time and effort than any one of the earlier lifecycle phases, including implementation. As Aristotle observed, "The whole is more than the sum of the parts."

Module integration must be carefully planned from the very beginning of the software lifecycle. Software units that are to be implemented individually must be identified in the early stages of system analysis. They need to be readdressed in detail during the architectural design process. The sequence of implementation must allow for the smoothest possible incremental integration.

The main difficulty with incremental integration lies in intertwined circular dependencies between the modules. In a well-designed system, circular *coupling* of modules is minimized or even eliminated altogether. On the other hand, linear coupling between modules is a way of achieving the system's desired functionality.

What can we do if we need to deliver one module before the other is ready? The answer lies in writing special code to temporarily "fill the gaps" so that all modules can be integrated. Programming routines to simulate the activity of the missing module are called *stubs*.

Object-oriented systems must be designed for integration and deployment. Each module should be as independent as possible. Dependencies between modules should be identified and minimized in the analysis and design phases. Ideally, each module should constitute a single thread of processing that executes as a response to a particular customer need. The use of stubs as replacement operations should be minimized when possible. If not properly designed, the integration phase will result in chaos and put at risk the entire development project.

1.4.2.5 Operation and maintenance

Operation and maintenance follow a successful handover to a customer of each incremental software module and, eventually, of the entire software product. Maintenance is not only an inherent part of the software lifecycle but accounts for most of it as far as IT personnel time and effort is concerned. Schach (2005) estimates that 75 percent of lifecycle time is spent on software postdelivery maintenance.

Operation signifies the *changeover* from the existing business solution, whether in software or not, to the new one. A changeover is usually a gradual process. If it is possible, the old and new systems should run in parallel for a while to allow a fallback if the new system does not stand up to the task.

Maintenance consists of three distinct stages (Ghezzi *et al.* 2003; Maciaszek 1990):

1 housekeeping
2 adaptive maintenance
3 perfective maintenance.

Housekeeping involves carrying out the routine maintenance tasks necessary to keep the system accessible to users and operational. *Adaptive maintenance* involves monitoring and auditing the system's operations, adjusting its functionality to satisfy the changing environment and adapting it to meet performance and throughput demands. *Perfective maintenance* is the redesigning and modifying of the system to accommodate new or substantially changed requirements.

Eventually, the continuing maintenance of a software system becomes unsustainable and the system has to be phased out. *Phasing out* would normally happen due to reasons that have little to do with the *usefulness* of the software. The software is probably still useful, but it has become unmaintainable. Schach (2005) lists four reasons for phasing out (retiring) software:

- proposed changes go beyond the immediate capability of perfective maintenance
- the system is out of the maintainers' control and the effects of changes cannot be predicted
- there is a lack of documentation to base future software extensions on
- the implementation hardware/software platform has to be replaced and no migration path is available.

Activities spanning the lifecycle 1.4.3

Some experts and authors also include project *planning* and *testing* as two distinct lifecycle phases. However, these two important activities are not really *separate* lifecycle phases because they span the *whole* lifecycle.

A software project management plan is drawn up early on in the process, significantly enriched after the specification phase and evolves through the rest of the lifecycle. Similarly, testing is most intensive after implementation, but also applies to software artifacts produced in every other phase.

A project's progress is tracked to the project plan. Tracking of a project's progress links to another activity that also spans the lifecycle – the activity of collecting project **metrics** – that is, measuring the development processes and their outcomes.

1.4.3.1   Project planning

A familiar maxim is that if you can't plan it, you can't do it. Planning spans the software project lifecycle. It begins once the *system planning* activities determine the business strategy for the organization and the software projects are identified. **Project planning** is the activity of estimating the project's deliverables, costs, time, risks, milestones and resource requirements. It also includes the selection of development methods, processes, tools, standards and team organization.

Project planning is a moving target. It is not something you do once and never change. Within the framework of a few *fixed constraints*, project plans evolve with the lifecycle.

Typical constraints are *time* and *money* – each project has a clear deadline and a tight budget. One of the first tasks in project planning is to assess whether or not the project is feasible in terms of these time, budget and other constraints. If it is feasible, then the constraints are documented and can only be changed in the course of a formal approval process.

Project feasibility is assessed bearing several factors in mind (Hoffer et al., 2002; Whitten and Bentley 1998):

- *operational feasibility* readdresses the issues originally undertaken in *system planning* when the project was identified – it is the study of how the proposed system will affect organizational structures, procedures and people
- *economic feasibility* assesses the costs and benefits of the project (also known as cost–benefit analysis)
- *technical feasibility* assesses the practicality of the proposed technical solution and the availability of technical skills, expertise and resources
- *schedule feasibility* assesses the reasonability of the project timetable.

Not all constraints are known or could be evaluated at the time of a project's initiation. Additional constraints will be discovered during the requirements phase and will also need to be evaluated in terms of their feasibility. These will include legal, contractual, political and security constraints.

Subject to feasibility assessment, a *project plan* will be constructed and this will constitute the guidance for project and process management. The issues addressed in the project plan include (Whitten and Bentley 1998):

- **project scope**
- project tasks
- directing and controlling the project
- quality management
- metrics and measurement
- project scheduling
- allocation of resources (people, material, tools)
- people management.

Metrics 1.4.3.2

Measuring development time and effort and taking other *metrics* of project artifacts is an important part of *project and process management*. Although an important part, it is frequently neglected in organizations at low levels of process maturity. The price is high. Without measuring the past, the organization is not able to plan accurately for the future.

Metrics are usually discussed in the context of *software quality* and *complexity* – they apply to the quality and complexity of the *software product* (Fenton and Pfleeger 1997; Henderson-Sellers 1996; Pressman 2005). Metrics are used to measure such quality factors as correctness, reliability, efficiency, integrity, usability, maintainability, flexibility and testability. For example, software reliability can be evaluated by measuring the frequency and severity of failures, mean time between failures, accuracy of output results, ability to recover from failure and so on.

An equally important application of metrics is that of measuring the development models (*development products*) at different phases of the lifecycle. Metrics are then used to assess the effectiveness of the *process* and improve the quality of work at various lifecycle phases.

Typical metrics that apply to the *software process* and can be taken at various lifecycle phases are (Schach 2005):

- requirements volatility – the percentage of requirements that changed by the time the requirements phase had finished, which may reflect on the difficulty of obtaining requirements from the customers
- requirements volatility after the requirements phase – this may point to a poor-quality requirements document
- prediction of hot spots and bottlenecks in the system – the frequency of users attempting to execute different functions in the prototype of the software product
- the size of the specification document generated by the CASE tool and other more detailed metrics from the CASE repository, such as the number of classes in a class model (if used on a few past projects where the costs and times to complete them are known, these metrics provide an ideal planning "database" to use to predict the time and effort that will be required for similar future projects)
- record of fault statistics – when they were introduced into the product and when they were discovered and rectified, which may reflect on the thoroughness of the quality assurance, review processes and testing activities
- average number of tests before a test unit is considered acceptable for integration and release to customers – this may reflect on the programmers' debugging procedures.

Testing 1.4.3.3

Like project planning and metrics, *testing* is an activity that spans the whole software lifecycle. It is not just a separate phase that happens after the implementation. Indeed, it is much too late to start testing after the software product has been implemented. The escalating costs of fixing faults introduced in earlier lifecycle phases is likely to be exorbitant (Schach 2005).

Thus, testing activities should be carefully planned from the beginning. At the start, *test cases* have to be identified. Test cases (or test plans) define the test steps to be undertaken in an attempt to "break" the software. Test cases should be defined for each functional module (*use case*) described in the requirements document. Relating test cases to use cases establishes a *traceability* path between tests and users' requirements. To be testable, a software artifact must be traceable.

Naturally enough, all developers test products of their work. However, original developers are blindfolded by the work that they have done to produce the software artifact in the first place. To be most effective, a third party should conduct testing, methodically. The task can be assigned to the software quality assurance (SQA) group in the organization. This group should include some of the best developers in the organization. Their job is to test, not develop. The SQA group (not the original developers) is then charged with responsibility for the products' quality.

The more testing is done in the early development phases, the better the payoff. Requirements, specifications and any documents (including program source code) can be tested in *formal reviews* (so-called *walkthroughs* and *inspections*). Formal reviews are carefully prepared meetings that target a particular part of the documentation or system. An appointed reviewer studies a document beforehand and raises various questions. The meeting decides if a question is in fact a fault, but no attempt should be made to offer an immediate solution to the problem at this point. The original developer will address the fault later. Provided that the meetings are friendly and finger pointing is avoided, the "team synergy" will lead to the early detection and correction of many faults.

Once software prototypes and the first versions of the software product are made available, *execution-based testing* can be undertaken. There are two kinds of execution-based testing:

- testing to specs – black box testing
- testing to code – white box or glass box testing.

Testing to specs treats the program itself as a black box – that is, as something about which nothing is known except that it takes some input and produces some output. The program is given some input and the resulting output is analyzed for the presence of errors. Testing to specs is particularly useful for discovering incorrect or missing requirements.

Testing to code "looks through" the program logic to derive the input needed to *exercise* various execution paths in the program. Testing to code complements testing to specs as the two tests tend to discover different categories of error.

Incremental development involves not only incremental integration of software modules but also *incremental* or *regression testing*. Regression testing is the re-execution of the previous test cases on the same *baseline data set* after a previously released software module has been incrementally extended. The assumption is that the old functionality should remain the same and should not have been broken by an extension.

Regression testing can be well supported by *capture–playback tools* that allow the user's interactions with the program to be captured and played back without further user intervention. The main difficulty with regression testing is enforcement of the baseline data set. Incremental development does not just extend the procedural program logic but also extends (and modifies) underlying data structures. An extended software product may force changes to the baseline data set, thus ruling out the sensible comparison of results.

Review quiz 1.4

RQ1 Which software development approach, structured or object-oriented, takes advantage of the activity of functional decomposition?

RQ2 What is another name for business analysis?

RQ3 Which development phase is largely responsible for producing/delivering an adaptive system?

RQ4 The notion of a stub is associated with what development phase?

RQ5 Which activities span the development lifecycle and are not, therefore, distinct lifecycle phases?

Development models and methods   1.5

Development models and methods is about the "how" of software production. Similar to the notion of *lifecycle models and processes* (Section 1.1.2.2), development models and methods constitute a concept rather than a process standard used for organizational accreditation (such as CMM, ISO 9000 or ITIL) or a compliance framework (such as COBIT).

This implies that an organization can develop its own lifecycle process by mixing elements of various models and methods. After all, the development process is something that should reflect the unique character of each organization. The process is the consequence of social, cultural, organizational, environmental and other similar aspects of development. The process will also differ from project to project according to its size, application domain, required software tools and so on.

Modern development processes are *iterative and incremental* (Section 1.1.2.2.1). A system development project consists of many iterations. Each iteration delivers an incremental (improved) version of the product. Iterations and increments apply to the same scope of the system. This means that a new increment does not normally add any new large chunk of functionality (such as a new subsystem) to the previous increment. An increment improves existing functionality, usability, performance and other qualities of the system while not changing the system's scope. Adding a new functionality to an existing system is the responsibility of software *integration* (Section 1.1.3), which in itself is iterative and incremental.

Various representative models and methods exist for iterative and incremental development. Models and methods of significant popularity – discussed next – include (Maciaszek and Liong 2005):

- the spiral model
- the IBM Rational Unified Process (RUP)
- model-driven architecture
- agile software development
- aspect-oriented development.

1.5.1 The spiral model

The *spiral model* (Boehm 1988) is a de facto reference model for all iterative and incremental development processes. The model was proposed at a time when the structured development approach (Section 1.4.1.1) still dominated, but, being really a meta-model, it can be applied equally well to the object-oriented approach (Section 1.4.1.2). The model places the software engineering activities within the wider context of system planning, risk analysis and customer evaluation. These four activities are visualized graphically as quadrants, which together create spiral loops in a Cartesian diagram (Figure 1.4).

According to the spiral model, system development begins with the *planning* activities. Planning involves the project feasibility studies and initial requirements gathering. It also builds project schedules and defines budgetary components.

Next, the project enters the *risk analysis* quadrant, in which the impacts of risks on the project are assessed. *Risks* are any potential adverse circumstances and uncertainties facing the development. Risk analysis assesses expected project outcomes and the acceptable level of tolerance of risk against the probabilities of achieving these outcomes. Risk analysis is responsible for a "go, no-go" decision to move on to the next, engineering quadrant. The decision is purely risk-driven and is looking into the future (it must not be motivated by the project costs committed so far).

The *engineering* quadrant addresses down-to-earth development efforts. The project's progress is measured in this quadrant. "Engineering" includes all sorts of system modeling, programming, integration and deployment activities.

Before the project enters the next iteration, it is subjected to *customer evaluation*. This is a formal process by means of which customers' feedback is obtained. The evaluation is conducted against known requirements that the system should satisfy, but any other feedback from customers is also addressed on entry to the next planning quadrant.

Figure 1.4
The spiral model

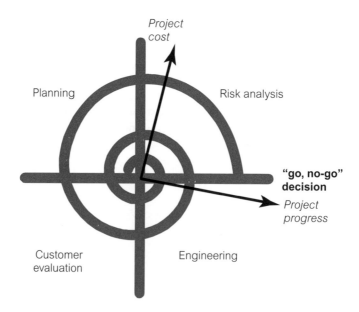

IBM Rational Unified Process 1.5.2

The IBM Rational Unified Process (RUP) is defined as a software development process platform (RUP, 2003). The platform provides a development support environment consisting of guiding and learning documents, good practice templates, Web-based facilitation techniques and so on. RUP organizes projects in two-dimensional terms. The horizontal dimension represents the successive *phases* of each project iteration. RUP proposes four phases – inception, elaboration, construction and transition. The vertical dimension represents software development *disciplines* – namely business modeling, requirements, analysis and design, implementation, testing, deployment and the supporting activities of configuration and change management, project management and environment. The disciplines represent the project's focus areas or work flows.

The division into phases and disciplines has its merits, but it is fair to say that it causes as many problems as it solves. Its aim is to show the imposition of the horizontal dynamic dimension on the vertical static dimension. Dynamic dimensions represent a project's progress in terms of iterations and milestones. The progress is measured with regard to the static dimension's focus areas and issues such as activities and artifacts.

In practice, the distinction between the horizontal and vertical dimensions is not always clear. Questions such as "What is the difference between construction and implementation or between transition and deployment?" are frequently asked. In order not to add to the confusion, Figure 1.5 shows the vertical RUP disciplines organized in a cycle of activities. The horizontal phases are not shown, but they apply (albeit with varying strength) to each discipline. For example, the inception phase dominates in business modeling, but it does not exist at all in deployment. On the other hand, the transition phase is very involved during deployment, but not in business modeling.

Figure 1.5
IBM Rational
Unified Process
Source: Reprinted by
permssion from
Rational Suite Tutorial
2002, copyright 2002
International Business
Machines Corporation

Like the spiral model, RUP emphasizes iterative development and the importance of early and continuous risk analysis. Frequent executable releases underpin the nature of RUP. RUP assumes that the process configuration is customized to the project. The customization means that RUP process components can be selected specifically for the organization, the task, the whole team and even individual team members. RUP has a universal applicability, but it provides specific guidance for teams that use IBM Rational software development tools.

1.5.3 Model-driven architecture

Model-driven architecture (MDA) (Kleppe et al. 2003; MDA 2006) is an old idea and its time has (possibly) come. It dates back to the programming concept of formal specifications and transformation models (Ghezzi et al. 2003). MDA is a framework for executable modeling and the generation of programs from specifications.

MDA uses various Object Management Group (OMG) standards to completely specify platform-independent and platform-specific models for a system. The standards that enable such specifications include:

- Unified Modeling Language (UML) for modeling tasks
- Meta-Object Facility (MOF) for using a standard meta-model repository so that derived specifications can work together
- XML Meta-Data Interchange (XMI) for mapping UML to XML for interchange purposes
- Common Warehouse Meta-model (CWM) for mapping of MDA to database schemas and permitting flexible datamining.

MDA aims at deriving platform-independent models, which include complete specifications of the system's state and behavior. This allows for the separation of business applications from the technology changes. In the next step, MDA provides tools and techniques to produce platform-specific models for realization in environments such as J2EE, .NET or Web Services.

Figure 1.6 shows how MDA concepts link to the three main development phases of analysis, design and implementation. PSM and code bridges are interoperability facilities to permit the system under development to span multiple platforms.

As a natural consequence of executable modeling, MDA also reaches in the direction of component technology. Components are defined in platform-independent models and then implemented in platform-specific ways. OMG uses MDA to create transformable models and reusable components to offer standard solutions for vertical operations, such as telecommunications or hospitals.

1.5.4 Agile software development

Agile software development is a more recent contribution to iterative and incremental development models. The concept has been popularized by the Agile Alliance, a non-profit organization committed to agility in software production (Agile 2006). Agile

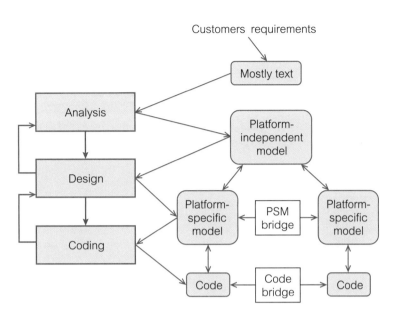

Figure 1.6
Model-driven
architecture

development embraces change as an inherent aspect of software production, proposes "lightweight" methods to accommodate changing requirements and gives programming center stage in system development.

In the "Manifesto for agile software development", the Agile Alliance formulated the key points of agility in software production:

- individuals and interactions over and above processes and tools
- working software over comprehensive documentation
- customer collaboration over contract negotiation
- responding to changeover following a plan.

Agile development is an iterative and incremental process with a zest to replace formalities with the frequent delivery of executable programs to customers. This zest is made clear in its terminology. Thus the names of the typical lifecycle phases of analysis, design, implementation and deployment give way to new terms of user stories, acceptance tests, refactoring, test-driven development and continuous integration (Figure 1.7). A closer look reveals that the change in terminology does not change the fact that agile development blends nicely with more established iterative and incremental processes.

User stories in agile development terms correspond to requirements analysis in other models. The stories list and describe the users' views on the features that the system under development should support. The stories are used to plan the development iterations in terms of time and money.

Agile development replaces design-level modeling and implementation with a cycle of acceptance tests, refactoring and test-driven development. *Acceptance tests* are specifications of programs that an application program under development must pass to satisfy users' requirements. As a consequence, implementation is test-driven. Programs are written to pass acceptance tests. This process is known as *test-driven development* and leads

Figure 1.7
Agile software
development

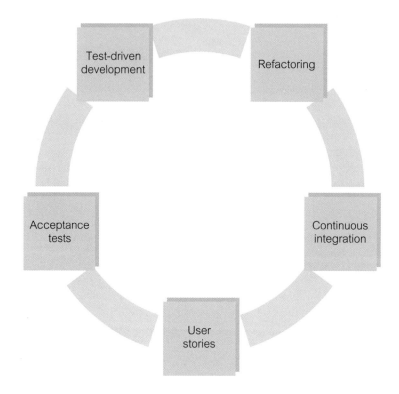

to so-called *intentional programming* – the ability and opportunity to specify the intent of the program in the acceptance test before starting to code the program.

Test-driven development is conducted by pairs of programmers. All programming is done by two programmers using a single workstation to allow discussion, the exchange of ideas and immediate verification of concepts with another person. *Pair programming*, as it is called, also introduces the benefits of *collective ownership* – no one person owns the code and there is always a second person who understands the code that has already been written.

Agile development is strong on *refactoring*, which is the activity of improving the code by restructuring (re-architecting) it without changing its behavior. Refactoring assumes that the initial architecture is sound and flexible. It also assumes that programming is carried out according to good practices and established design and implementation patterns.

Each iteration in agile development is planned to be completed in a *short cycle* of about two weeks duration. Short cycles imply *continuous integration* of the new code with the code that already exists. The code integrated at the end of two weeks is a *minor delivery* for customer evaluation. A major delivery for production use is normally planned after three short cycles – that is, after six weeks.

Agile development contributes some important practices to iterative and incremental development. There are various specific variants and practices that either fall into the category of agile development or can be combined with agile development. The best-known representatives include:

- extreme programming (XP) (Beck 1999; Extreme 2006)
- feature-driven development (Feature 2006)
- lean development (Poppendieck and Poppendieck 2003).

There have been doubts about the scalability of agile development to large and very large projects. Agile development seems more suited to smaller teams, of 50 or fewer developers, highly integrated, committed to outcomes and low-key on plans, formalities, accountability to project managers and even the delivery to a contract. This kind of approach is at odds with developing large-scale mission-critical enterprise information systems. Such developments are normally done according to the formal and documented practices of process standards and compliance frameworks (Section 1.1.2.2).

Aspect-oriented sotware development 1.5.5

Aspect-oriented Programming (AOP) (Kiczales et al. 1997) is not a revolutionary idea – few truly useful ideas are. Most concepts underpinning AOP have been known about and used before, although frequently under different names and using different technologies. The main objective of AOP is to produce more modular systems by identifying so-called *crosscutting concerns* and producing separate software modules for these concerns. The modules are called *aspects*. The aspects are integrated using the process called *aspect weaving*.

A starting point for AOP is the realization that a software system consists of many vertical modules. The pivotal module contains software components that implement the functional requirements of the system. However, each system must also obey non-functional requirements that determine such software qualities as correctness, reliability, security, performance, concurrency and so on. These qualities need to be addressed from various (or even most) software components responsible for the system's functions. In "conventional" object-oriented programming, the code implementing these qualities would be duplicated (scattered) in many components. These non-functional qualities are known in AOP as *concerns* – goals that the application must meet. Because the object-oriented implementation of these concerns would cut across many components, they are known as *crosscutting concerns*.

To avoid code scattering due to crosscutting concerns, AOP advocates the gathering together of such code into separate modules, called *aspects*. Although aspects tend to be units implementing non-functional requirements, in general they could also be units of the system's functional decomposition. In particular, they could implement various enterprise-wide business rules that need to be enforced by classes responsible for an application's program logic.

Thus, AOP decomposes systems into aspects built around the core functional components, known as the *base code*. The aspects constitute the separate *aspect code*. For such a system to work, software components have to be composed with aspects or, to put it the other way around, aspects have to weaved into the program logic flow. Such a process of software composition is called *aspect weaving*. Some aspects can be weaved into a system at compile time (*static weaving*), while others can only be weaved at runtime (*dynamic weaving*).

Aspect weaving applies to *join points* in a program's execution. Join points are predefined points of software composition, such as a call to a method, an access to an attribute, an instantiation of an object, throwing an exception and so on. A particular action that needs to be taken for a join point is called an *advice* (checking security permissions of the user or starting a new business transaction, for example). An advice can run before the join point it operates over (*before advice*) after a join point completes (*after advice*) or it can replace the join point it operates over (*around advice*).

In general, the same advice may apply to many join points in the program. A set of join points related to a single advice is called a *pointcut*. Pointcuts are often defined programmatically with wildcards and regular expressions. Compositions of pointcuts may also be possible (and desirable).

Like agile development, aspect-oriented software development concentrates on the programming tasks and introduces a fair share of new terminology (see Figure 1.8). As with agile development, a closer look at this terminology reveals that aspect-oriented development is just another way of applying iterative and incremental processes to produce adaptive software.

With all its good intentions to improve software modularization (and therefore adaptiveness), AOP can be a potential source of emergent or even incorrect behavior (see, for example, Murphy and Schwanninger 2006). This is because aspects modify behavior at join points in a way that may not be obvious to the developer responsible for the application's functional logic. Moreover, aspects themselves are not necessarily independent and multiple aspects can affect each other in subtle ways, resulting in emergent behavior.

Figure 1.8
Aspect-oriented
software
development

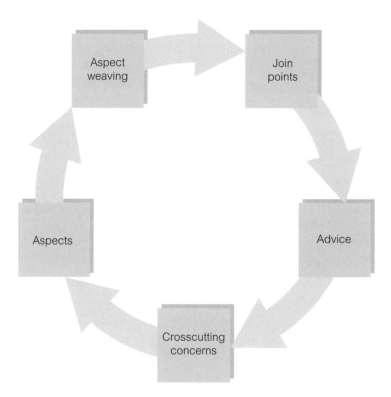

There is a clear need for AOP development practices to ensure that the aspect code and the base code evolve gracefully together and the crosscutting concerns are well-documented and known to application developers at all times. A resolution to this dilemma is particularly difficult in the presence of dynamic weaving (see, for example, Hirschfeld and Hanenberg 2005). A necessary condition for being able to tackle these issues is the developer's awareness of the mutual impact of changes in the base and aspect code.

Review quiz 1.5

RQ1 Is adding a new functionality to a software project the responsibility of a software iteration or integration?

RQ2 Which of the development models and methods is most explicit about risk analysis?

RQ3 Which development model and method is directly linked to the traditional concept of formal specifications?

RQ4 Which development model and method is directly linked to the concept of intentional programming?

RQ5 Which development model and method is directly linked to the concept of crosscutting concerns?

Problem statements for case studies

1.6

Apart from a tutorial-style case study (online shopping (OS)) placed in a separate chapter at the end of the book, this edition of the book uses seven case studies to exemplify software development concepts and modeling activities. At first glance, you will only get a vague idea from the problem statements that follow what is involved, but return to these statements when studying consecutive chapters and encountering references, questions or answers to these case studies.

The presentation style of the end-of-the-book tutorial and the case studies is similar – that is, the questions are defined and then the solutions are given. This allows the reader to attempt a solution and then compare it with the solution offered. The case studies are:

- university enrolment (UE)
- video store (VS)
- contact management (CM)
- telemarketing (TM)
- advertising expenditure (AE)
- time logging (TL)
- currency converter (CC).

1.6.1 University enrolment

University enrolment is a classic textbook example (see Quatrani 2000; Stevens and Pooley 2000). It is a surprisingly complex application domain with a rich set of business rules that change relatively frequently, yet historical information has to be carefully maintained in relation to the business rules that are in force at different times.

No two universities are the same. Each has its own interesting peculiarities that can be used in case studies to emphasize particular facets of system analysis and design. The emphasis in our case study is on the intricacies of state modeling with regard to handling the time dimension (temporal information) and capturing business rules in data structures.

Problem statement 1: university enrolment

A medium-sized university offers a number of undergraduate and postgraduate degrees to full-time and part-time students. The educational structure of the university consists of divisions. Divisions contain several departments. While a single division administers each degree, the degree may include courses from other divisions. In fact, the university prides itself on the freedom of choice given to students in selecting courses towards their degrees.

The flexibility of this course selection process puts strains on the university enrolment system. Individually tailored programs of study must not contradict the rules governing the degree, such as the structure of prerequisite courses so that the student can qualify for the degree's compulsory courses. A student's choice of courses may be restricted by timetable clashes, maximum class sizes and so on.

The flexibility of education offered by the university has been the main reason behind the steady growth in student numbers. However, to maintain its traditional strength, the current enrolment system – still partly manual – has to be replaced by a new software solution. The preliminary search for an off-the-shelf software package has not been successful. The university enrolment system is sufficiently unique to warrant in-house development.

The system is required to assist in pre-enrolment activities and handle the enrolment procedures themselves. The pre-enrolment activities must include mail-outs of last semester's examination grades to students, together with any enrolment instructions. During enrolment sessions, the system must accept the students' proposed programs of study and validate them for prerequisites, timetable clashes, class sizes, special approvals and so on. Resolution of some of the problems may require consultation with academic advisers or academics in charge of course offerings.

1.6.2 Video store

The second case study is a routine business application that is typical of those needed for small businesses. It is the application to support the operation of a small video store. The video store keeps in stock a wide-ranging disk and tape library of entertainment material. The main operation of the store is rental services.

A typical computer system to support a small video store would be customized from off-the-shelf software or some other proprietary solution. The system would be based on one of the popular database management systems available for small business computers.

Although, with the database software underneath, the system may be deployed initially on a single machine, GUI development is likely to be done with a simple fourth-generation language (4GL) with screen painting, code generation capability and a connection to a simple database.

A distinguishing aspect of the video store as a case study is the extensive chain of activities – from ordering of entertainment material through stock management to the accounting associated with rentals and sales to customers. In a way, it is a small-scale *value chain model* operation (Section 1.2.2).

Problem statement 2: video store

A new video store intends to offer rentals (and sales) of entertainment material to the wider public. The store management is determined to launch its operations with the support of a computer system. The management has sourced a number of small business software packages that might be suitable for customization and further development. To assist with the package selection, the store has hired a business analyst whose job it is to determine and specify the requirements.

The video store will keep a stock of videotapes, CDs (games and music) and DVDs. The inventory has already been ordered from one supplier, but more suppliers will be approached for future orders. All videotapes and disks will be barcoded so that a scanning machine integrated with the system can support the rentals and returns. Customer membership cards will also be barcoded.

Existing customers will be able to place reservations on entertainment material to be collected at a specific date. The system must have a flexible search engine to answer customers' enquiries, including enquiries about material that the video store does not stock but may order on request.

Contact management   1.6.3

Contact management is a "hot" application domain. Frequently known by the abbreviation CRM (contact or customer relationship management), contact management is an important component of enterprise resource planning (ERP) systems. ERP systems automate *back office* transaction processing applications. Three typical components of an ERP system are accounting, manufacturing and human resources. CRM belongs to the human resources component.

ERP systems are very large customizable solutions. Some people refer to them as megapackages. Naturally enough, a CRM component of an ERP solution can be very complex. The case study addresses only a small portion of the problems associated with CRM.

Contact management applications are characterized by interesting GUI solutions by means of which the employees of customer relations, or a similarly named department, can schedule their activities with regard to customers. In essence, the contact management system's GUI acts as a diary to record customer-related tasks and events and keep track of their progress.

The diary has to be database-driven to allow dynamic scheduling and monitoring of tasks and events across many employees. Like most human resource systems, contact management applications require a sophisticated authorization scheme to control access to sensitive information.

Problem statement 3: contact management

A market research company has an established customer base of organizations that buy its market analysis reports. Some larger customers have also purchased specialized reporting software from the company. These customers are then provided with raw and preaggregated information for their own report generation.

The company is constantly on the search for new customers, even if the new customers may be interested only in one-off, narrowly targeted market reports. As prospective customers are not quite customers yet, the company prefers to call them contacts – hence, *contact* management system (contacts are prospective, actual and past customers).

A new contact management system is to be developed internally and made available to all employees in the company, but with varying levels of access. Employees of the Customer Services Department will take ownership of the system. The system will permit flexible scheduling and rescheduling of contact-related activities so that employees can collaborate successfully to win new customers and foster existing relationships.

1.6.4   Telemarketing

Many organizations market their products and services by telemarketing – that is, by directly contacting customers over the telephone. A telemarketing system needs to support an elaborated process of scheduling the phone calls to automatically connect telemarketers to customers, facilitating the conversation and recording conversation outcomes.

Special aspects of a telemarketing system are heavy reliance on the database capability to actively schedule and dynamically reschedule phone calls while supporting concurrent conversations. Another interesting aspect is the ability to dial the scheduled phone numbers automatically.

Problem statement 4: telemarketing

A charitable society sells lottery tickets to raise funds. The fundraising is carried out in the form of *campaigns* to support currently important charitable causes. The society keeps a list of past contributors (*supporters*). For each new campaign, a subset of these supporters is preselected for telemarketing and/or direct mail contact.

The society uses some innovative schemes to gain new supporters. These schemes include special *bonus campaigns* to reward supporters for bulk buying, attracting new contributors and so on. The society does not randomly target potential supporters by using telephone directories or similar means.

To support its work, the society has decided to contract out the development of a new telemarketing application. The new system is required to support a significant number of telemarketers working simultaneously. The system must be able to schedule the phone calls according to prespecified priorities and other known constraints.

The system is required to dial the numbers for the scheduled phone calls. Unsuccessful connections must be rescheduled and tried again later. Telephone callbacks to supporters must also be arranged. The conversation outcomes, including ticket orders and any changes to supporter records, ought to be maintained.

Advertising expenditure 1.6.5

In the age of globalization and geographical separation of buyers and sellers, selling a product or service is not possible without spending large sums of money on advertising. Not surprisingly, companies are profoundly interested in knowing how their advertising budgets have been used and how their advertising expenditure (and targets) compare with the expenditure (and targets) of their competitors. Such information can be bought from market research companies, which collect and analyze advertising data.

A special feature of the advertising expenditure domain is a necessary close processing alignment between collecting and storing advertising data in a transactional database and adding the latest data collections to a data warehouse. The data warehouse is then used for the analysis of collected information to produce and sell requested advertising expenditure reports.

Problem statement 5: advertising expenditure

A market research organization collects data on advertising from various media outlets, such as television and radio stations, newspapers and magazines, as well as cinema, outdoor and Internet advertisers. The collected data can be analyzed in various ways to measure the advertising expenditure of companies advertising their products. The organization needs to develop an advertising expenditure (AE) application.

The AE system will provide two areas of reporting to the clients of the market research organization. A client may request a report that the advertisements they paid for appeared as they were supposed to (this is called campaign monitoring). A client can also request a report outlining their competitive advertising position in their specific industry (this is called expenditure reporting). The expenditure reports capture the expenditure achieved by an advertiser or an advertised product by various criteria (time, geographical regions, media and so on).

The expenditure reporting is the core business of the organization. In fact, any AE client (not just an advertising client) can purchase expenditure reports, either in the form of custom-designed reporting software or as hard copies. The AE's customer base comprises individual advertisers, advertising agencies, media companies and media-buying consultancies, as well as sales and marketing executives, media planners and buyers.

The AE has contractual arrangements with many media outlets to receive from them regularly electronic log files with information pertaining to the advertising content of these outlets. The log information is transferred to the AE database and is then subjected to careful verification – partly automatic and partly manual. The task of verification is to confirm that all captured advertisement details are valid and logical in the context of the surrounding information. The manual entry (monitoring) of advertisements for which there are no electronic logs remains a major part of the AE operation.

Once entered and verified, the advertisements undergo valorization – the process of assigning an expenditure estimate to an advertisement.

Time logging 1.6.6

There is a difference between *application* software and *system* software. The difference has to do with the fact that system software is a tool marketed and sold in large quantities to the public at large. Examples are wordprocessors, spreadsheets and database management systems. Increasingly, many such tools provide a generic solution to a well-defined application domain. Time logging is such a tool. Companies can buy a time logging tool to serve as a time and billing application that keeps track of time spent by employees on various projects and tasks.

A special feature of the time logging domain is that it produces a software tool. As such, the tool has to be attractive to buyers, very reliable in use and designed for the future production of new versions. This imposes special requirements with regard to the GUI aspect of the product, the necessary rigorous testing and a scalable architecture of the software.

Problem statement 6: time logging

A software production company is given the task of developing a time logging (TL) tool for public sale to organizations in need of time control software for their employees. The company hopes that the TL tool will be in a position to compete with the market leader – the tool called Time Logger from Responsive Software (Responsive 2003).

The scope of the TL project is delineated by the functionality offered by the exisiting Time Logger tool. Responsive Software's website contains a detailed description of Time Logger's functions. Similar functions need to be present in the TL tool. The following points list the main functions.

The TL tool will allow employees to enter time records – that is, time spent working on various projects and tasks and time without any work done (pauses, lunches, holidays and so on). The time can be entered by directly (manually) recording the start and end times or using the stopwatch facility. The stopwatch facility links to the computer clock and allows the employee to use start/stop command buttons to say when an activity started and ended.

The TL tool will allow clients for whom the work is performed to be identified. Related functions are to bill the clients, produce invoices and keep track of payments. Work expenses can be calculated using hourly rates and/or a fixed expense component. Some activities recorded in the TL tool will not be billable to clients.

The TL tool will allow the production of customized time reports with various reporting details suppressed or added, as required by the employee.

The TL tool will allow easy changes to be made to time records already entered. It will also provide various sorting, searching and filtering capabilities.

1.6.7 Currency converter

Banks, other financial institutions and even general-purpose Web portals provide currency converter facilities to Internet users. Currency converters are Web applications that act as online calculators for converting money and other currencies (such as traveler checks) from one foreign currency to another. The calculators use the current exchange rates, but some facilities may allow calculations using past rates from previous dates.

A currency converter is a small utility but still offering a range of interesting implementation possibilities and functional variations. Being a small utility, it gives us a possibility to explain detailed design issues and even present some code excerpts. Being a Web-based application, it allows us to explain architectural design issues for solutions that use a browser client and access a database server for data destined for the browser's form fields (supported currencies and the exchange rates).

Problem statement 7: currency converter

A bank needs to offer in its Web portal a special-purpose calculator to enable its customers and the public at large to find out what amount of money would be obtained by converting an entered amount in one currency into another foreign currency. Routinely, the currency converter would apply the most current exchange rates, but the application can be extended to permit the user to select the date in the past for which the calculations should be made.

The application may be implemented by means of one or two web pages. In the case of two web pages, the first page would enable the user to enter the amount of money to be converted, select from combo boxes the "from" and "to" currencies, then to press "Calculate" or a similar button. The second page would then show the results of the calculation and provide an option (such as a "Start over" button) to return to the first page and do another calculation, if desired.

In the case of a one-page solution, the form would contain a calculation result field, not editable by the user or perhaps not even visible at first. This result field would display the conversion outcome value on the user's pressing the "Calculate" button.

Summary

This chapter has looked at strategic issues relating to the software development process. For some readers, the content of this chapter may have amounted to little more than "motherhood" statements. For readers with some experience in software development, the chapter could have delivered additional cerebral ammunition. For all readers, the intent of the chapter is to serve (not necessarily gently) as an introduction to the much more comprehensive discussions to come.

The *nature* of software development is that of a *craft* or even an *art*. An outcome of a software project cannot be ascertained completely at its start. The main *accidental difficulty* in software development relates to *stakeholders* – a software product must give a tangible benefit to stakeholders; it will fail otherwise. The triangle for success includes, in addition to the stakeholders' factor, a sound *process* and the support of a *modeling language and tools*. Process improvement models and frameworks include the Capability Maturity Model, the ISO 9000 standards, the ITIL and COBIT frameworks. The UML is the standard modeling language.

Software development is concerned with delivering *efficient* software products. *System planning* precedes software development and determines which products can be most *effective* to the organization. There are various ways in which system planning can be conducted. Four popular approaches were discussed: SWOT, VCM, BPR and ISA.

Information systems are constructed for three *levels of management*: operational, tactical and strategic. The corresponding software systems are classified as transaction processing, analytical processing and knowledge processing systems. Systems that support the strategic level of decision making offer the greatest effectiveness. These are also systems that create the greatest challenges to software developers.

In the past, software products were *procedural* – a programmed procedure executed its task more or less sequentially and predictably and then terminated. The *structured development approach* has been successfully used to produce such systems.

Modern software products are *object-oriented* – that is, a program consists of programming objects that execute randomly and unpredictably and the program does not terminate unless closed by the user. The objects "hang around", waiting for user-generated events to start a computation. They may request the services of other objects to complete the task and then become idle again but remain alert, just in case a user generates another event. Modern GUI-based distributed IS applications are object-oriented and the *object-oriented development approach* is best equipped to produce such applications. The rest of the book concentrates on the object-oriented approach.

Software development follows a *lifecycle*. The main lifecycle phases are analysis, design, implementation, integration and deployment, then operation and maintenance. Some important activities span all lifecycle phases. They include project planning, metrics and testing.

This book concentrates on two phases of the lifecycle: *analysis* and *design*. Other phases include implementation, integration and maintenance. Software development comprises a range of other important activities, such as project planning, collection of metrics, testing and change management. We do not consider any of those to be a separate phase because they occur repeatedly throughout the lifecycle.

Modern development processes are *iterative and incremental*. The predecessor and reference model for all iterative and incremental processes is the spiral model. This observation also includes the CMM and ISO 9000 standards used for organization accreditation purposes. Other important and popular models include IBM Rational Unified Process® (RUP®), model-driven architecture (MDA), agile software development and aspect-oriented software development.

Finally, this chapter defined the problem statements for seven case studies used in successive chapters (alongside the guided tutorial placed in the Appendix) to exemplify and explain any non-trivial modeling concepts and techniques. The case studies relate to distinct domains – university enrolment, a video store, contact management, telemarketing, advertising expenditure, a time logging application and an online currency converter.

Key terms

Adaptiveness (supportability) a software quality defined by a set of three system features: software understandability, maintainability and scalability (extensibility).

Architecture the description of the system in terms of its modules (*components*). It defines how a system is designed and how the components are connected with each other.

BPR Business Process Re-engineering.

Build executable code delivered to a customer as an *increment* of a system development or integration project.

CASE Computer-Aided Software Engineering.

CMM Capability Maturity Model.

COBIT Control OBjectives for Information and related Technology.

Component an executable unit of software with well-defined functionality (services) and communication protocols (interfaces) to other components.

COTS Commercial Off-The Shelf software package.

Data raw facts representing values, quantities, concepts and events pertaining to business activities.

Data mart a smaller variant of *data warehouse* that holds only a subset of enterprise data relevant to a particular department or business function.

Datamining an area of knowledge management concerned with exploratory data analysis to discover relationships and patterns (perhaps previously unknown or forgotten) that can (re-)discover *knowledge* and support decision making.

Data webhouse a distributed *data warehouse* that is implemented over the Web with no central data repository.

Data warehouse a database containing historical information and geared towards OLAP-style business intelligence and decision making.

DFD Data Flow Diagram.

ERD Entity Relationship Diagram.

ERP Enterprise Resource Planning system.

Increment the next improved version of a software product obtained as a result of one *iteration* of a system development or integration project; an increment does not extend the *project scope*.

Information value-added facts; *data* that have been processed and summarized to produce value-added facts revealing new features and trends.

ISA Information Systems Architecture.

ISO International Organization for Standardization.

Iteration one cycle in a system development or integration project resulting in a *build*.

ITIL IT Infrastructure Library.

Knowledge understanding of *information*, obtained by experience or study, and resulting in the ability to do things effectively and efficiently.

Lifecycle the *process* used to build and support (over their useful "life") the deliverables (products and services) produced by the software project.

MDA Model-Driven Architecture.

Metrics measurements of software attributes, such as correctness, reliability, efficiency, integrity, usability, maintainability, flexibility and testability.

Model an abstraction from reality; a representation of some aspect of external reality in software.

Object a software module that can react to external events/messages to perform tasks required by a software system. It consists of data and the operations associated with that data.

OLAP OnLine Analytical Processing.

OLTP OnLine Transaction Processing.

OMG Object Management Group.

Process the activities and organizational procedures used in software production and maintenance.

Project planning the activity of estimating the project's deliverables, costs, time, risks, milestones and resource requirements.

Project scope the set of functional user requirements that the system must satisfy and agreed in the project contract.

Requirement a statement of a system service or constraint.

RUP Rational Unified Process.

Service a running software instance, able to be located and used by other software systems using XML based messages conveyed by Internet protocols.

SOA Service-Oriented Architecture.

Stakeholder any person affected by the system or who has influence on system development.

Supportability see *adaptiveness*.

SWOT Strengths, Weaknesses, Opportunities, Threats.

System planning a planning initiative that defines strategic directions for an organization.

Transaction a logical unit of work that accomplishes a particular business task and guarantees the integrity of the database after the task completes.

UML Unified Modeling Language.

VCM Value Chain Model.

Multiple-choice test

MC1 According to Brooks, which of the following is *not* an essential difficulty of software development?

   a conformity

   b invisibility

   c correctness

   d changeability.

MC2 The software quality of supportability (adaptiveness) includes:

   a reliability

   b usability

   c maintainability

   e all of the above.

MC3 The "repeatable" level of CMM (Level 2) means that:

   a both management and engineering processes are codified and followed

   b metrics are used to control the process

   c continuous process improvement is in place

   d none of the above.

MC4 The Continuous Service Improvement Programme (CSIP) is part of:

   a CMM

   b ISO 9000

   c ITIL

   d COBIT.

MC5 UML models include:

   a state models

   b state change models

   c behavior models

   d all of the above.

MC6 Process-oriented integration is an integration:

   a on the level of databases or application programming interfaces (APIs) that externalize information for consumption by other applications

b in which information is externalized from multiple software systems into a common user interface

c that links application interfaces (that is, *services* defined through an interface abstraction)

d none of the above.

MC7 Which of the following is *not* an approach to carry out system planning:

    a ERP

    b SWOT

    c ISA

    d all of the above.

MC8 Which of the following is a primary activity of the VCM approach:

    a human resource management

    b services

    c administration and infrastructure

    d none of the above.

MC9 Which of the following is *not* considered a participant (perspective) in the ISA approach:

    a subcontractor

    b owner

    c manager

    d all of the above.

MC10 Which of the following is an OLAP technology:

    a data webhouse

    b data warehouse

    c data mart

    d all of the above.

MC11 Which of the following is *not* an objective/task of datamining:

    a classification

    b clustering

    c packaging

    d none of the above.

MC12 Which of the following is *not* a modeling technique of the structured approach to systems development:

    a UML

    b ERD

    c DFD

    d all of the above.

MC13 Which of the following is *not* considered to be an iterative and incremental development model/method:

    a the spiral model

    b functional decomposition

    c model-driven architecture

    d none of the above.

MC14 Which of the following development models/methods directly embraces intentional programming:

    a aspect-oriented development

    b agile software development

    c genetic programming

    d none of the above.

Questions

Q1 Based on your experiences with software products, how would you interpret Fred Brooks' observation that the *essence of software engineering* is determined by inherent software complexity, conformity, changeability and invisibility? How would you explain these four factors? How is software engineering different from traditional engineering, such as civil or mechanical engineering?

Q2 The notion of *component* is defined as an executable unit of software with well-defined functionality (services) and communication protocols (interfaces) to other components. Search in the latest UML specification document (UML 2005 – refer to the Bibliography for access information) and provide the definitions for *package*, *subsystem* and *module*. What are the similarities and differences between the notion of *component* and the concepts of *package*, *subsystem*, and *module*?

Q3 This chapter argues that *software production is an art or craft*. This observation can be supplemented with the quotation that "Art is a collaboration between God and the artist, and the less the artist does, the better" (André Gide). What lesson, if any, is this quotation providing to software developers? Do you agree with it?

Q4 Recall the definition of a *stakeholder*. Is a software vendor or a technical support person a stakeholder? Explain.

Q5 Which *CMM level of maturity* is needed for an organization to be able to respond successfully to a crisis situation? Explain.

Q6 Read the "ITIL Overview" paper (ITIL 2004 – refer to the Bibliography for access information). How does ITIL ensure that IT processes are aligned to business processes and IT delivers solutions that are most timely and relevant to the business? What are the seven core modules of ITIL? What "best practice" guidelines within these modules contribute directly to the desired alignment of business and IT processes?

Q7 Read the "Aligning COBIT, ITIL" paper (COBIT 2005 – refer to the Bibliography for access information). How does COBIT check for the compliance that IT processes are aligned to business processes and that IT delivers solutions that are most timely and relevant to the business? List the COBIT control objectives that check on the desired alignment of business and IT processes.

Q8 When explaining the SWOT approach to system planning, the book states that in a good mission statement emphasis is placed on customers' needs rather than on the products or services that an organization delivers. Explain and exemplify how targeting the products or services in the *mission statement* can defeat the *effectiveness* objective of system planning.

Q9 Search the Internet for papers describing the ISA Zachman framework. If you do not know it, find out (perhaps using the Internet) the meaning of the old Roman dictum, "divida et impera" (divide and conquer or divide and rule). Explain the observation that the ISA approach is a convenient framework for the "divide and conquer" method in the realization of large and complex systems.

Q10 Explain how a BPR *business process* relates to the notion of *work flow*.

Q11 What are the three *management levels*? Consider a banking application that monitors the usage patterns of a credit card by its holder in order to block the card automatically when the bank suspects misuse (theft, fraud and so on). Which management level is addressed by such an application? Give reasons.

Q12 What are the main modeling techniques in the structured development approach?

Q13 What are the main reasons for the shift from the structured to object-oriented development approach?

Q14 An object-oriented system should be *designed for integration*. What does this mean?

Q15 System planning and software metrics are inherently correlated. Explain why this is so.

Q16 Explain the relationship between traceability and testing.

Q17 Read the papers about RUP and the spiral model (available from the *References* link on the book's website – see Bibliography). How does RUP relate to the spiral model?

Q18 Explain how MDA uses and integrates the four OMG standards – UML, MOF, XMI, and CWM. Search the Internet for the latest information on these standards. Good places to start are: www.omg.org/mda/ and www.omg.org/technology/documents/_modeling_spec_catalog.htm

Q19 Briefly explain the following three agile development models and methods – extreme programming (XP), aspect-oriented software development, and feature-driven development. Compare the second and the third model and method with XP from the generic viewpoint of emphasis placed on the phases of the analysis–design–implementation cycle. Search the Internet for information on these models and methods.

Q20 List the similarities and differences between RUP® and XP. To assist you in this task, read the paper "RUP vs XP" (Smith 2003 – refer to the Bibliography for access information).

Review quiz answers

Review quiz 1.1
RQ1 No, they don't. The "essential difficulties" define the invariants.
RQ2 Customers and developers.
RQ3 No, it does not. An *increment* improves non-functional software qualities, such as software correctness, reliability, robustness, performance, usability and so on.
RQ4 COBIT is a *product standard*. ITIL, CMM and ISO 9000 are *process standards*.
RQ5 No, it is not. *Portal-oriented integration* can be seen as a special kind of information-oriented integration. Interface-oriented integration refers to the programming notion of interface (that is, a declaration of services/operations), not to the user interface (that is, not to the GUI rendered in a browser).

Review quiz 1.2
RQ1 Effectiveness.
RQ2 Vice versa – goals are derived from objectives.
RQ3 A primary activity.
RQ4 The existence of process owners.
RQ5 Planner, owner, designer, builder and subcontractor.

Review quiz 1.3
RQ1 The tactical level of decisionmaking.
RQ2 Concurrency control and recovery from failures.
RQ3 Data marts.
RQ4 Datamining.

Review quiz 1.4
RQ1 The structured approach.
RQ2 Requirements analysis.
RQ3 Architectural design.
RQ4 With the integration and deployment phase.
RQ5 Planning, testing and metrics.

Review quiz 1.5
RQ1 Integration.
RQ2 The spiral model.
RQ3 Model-driven architecture.
RQ4 Agile software development.
RQ5 Aspect-oriented software development.

Multiple-choice test answers

MC1 c
MC2 c
MC3 d
MC4 c

MC5 d
MC6 d
MC7 a
MC8 b
MC9 c
MC10 d
MC11 c
MC12 a
MC13 b
MC14 b

Answers to odd-numbered questions

Q1

The Brooks paper (Brooks 1987) is really concerned with the identification of *reasons for failures of software projects*. Some reasons for failures are a consequence of "essential difficulties" and are therefore invariant. Other reasons – "accidental difficulties" – can be controlled, managed and perhaps restrained.

The four essential difficulties are (1) complexity, (2) conformity, (3) changeability and (4) invisibility. The first difficulty – *complexity* – is the most intractable. Many software problems derive from it and from its exponential growth with software size (where "size" can be determined by the number of possible states of the program and the number of communication paths between software objects). Any scaling-up of software always faces a combinatorial explosion in software complexity. "Development in the large" is very different to "development in the small". The difficulty is inherent. It can be constrained only by applying good design practices based on "divide and conquer" approaches and hierarchical layering of software modules (Maciaszek and Liong 2005).

As opposed to natural systems (such as are studied in biology or physics), the complexity of software is aggravated by three other essential difficulties: conformity, changeability and invisibility. Software systems have to *conform* to a human-made, messy and random environment. Being part of this human environment, a new software system must conform to already established "interfaces", no matter how unreasonable they may be.

Software is a model of reality set in a human-made environment. As the environment changes, (so far) successful software is subject to pressures for *change*. The change demands frequently go beyond what is feasible or practical.

Finally, software is an intangible object. It cannot be pinpointed in space. If software is *invisible*, then it cannot be readily *visualizable*. The problem is not in a lack of graphical modeling representations for the software (this book is mostly about such representations!) The point is that no *single* graphical model can fully represent the structure and behavior of software. Developers have to work with a large number of graphical abstractions, superimposed one upon another, to represent a software system – a truly difficult task, in particular if the models are incapable of dividing the solution space into hierarchical layers.

The difference between software and traditional engineering can be established from Brooks' observation that the above four *difficulties* are an essential property of software, but only accidental properties in traditional engineering.

Any attempt to describe software to abstract away its complexity, conformity, changeability or invisibility frequently also abstracts away the software essence. A software engineer is in the unenviable position of often not being able to ignore (abstract away) some aspects of the problem because all of them constitute an intertwined essence of the solution. Sooner rather than later, all ignored properties must be reinstated in successive models and the models have to be conveniently linked for complete interpretation. The lesson is clear – *a great software developer is first and foremost a great abstractionist.*

Q3

This question is related to question 1 above. If we acknowledge essential difficulties in software engineering, then we have no choice but to try to harness these difficulties by delivering *simple solutions*.

"Simple" does not mean "simplistic". Simple, in this context, means "just right" for the users and "easy enough" for developers – not too creative, not too ambitious, without unnecessary bells and whistles. The analysis of completed software projects consistently shows that users are only distracted by unnecessary and complex features. Indeed, some projects fail precisely as a result of such unnecessary complications.

Perhaps the most important advice that a novice developer can get is contained in the *KISS* (*keep it simple, stupid*) acronym. There is also an equally unflattering version of Murphy's law: *"Build a system that even a fool can use and only a fool will use it"*.

Q5

An organization would need to be at least at *level 3* of CMM maturity to respond successfully to a crisis situation. An organization at *level 1* relies on key individuals for process management. The process itself is not documented. Even if the development is guided by some established procedures, there is no understanding of how these procedures should change to react to a crisis.

An organization at *level 2* has an intuitive process derived from past experiences. A crisis situation introduces an unfamiliar aspect to the process and is likely to cause the process to break down. If the organization is able to learn from the crisis, then the improvements to its process can make it more resilient in the face of future adversities.

An organization at *level 3* of process maturity has the processes codified and followed for all projects. When faced with a crisis, the organization will not panic and will continue to use the defined process. This "steady as it goes" principle can restore orderliness and calm to the project management, which may be sufficient to overcome the crisis. However, if the crisis is of large proportions, then *level 3* may also be insufficient ("steady as it goes" may turn out to be "steady as it sinks").

Q7

COBIT is a compliance framework aimed at controlling organizational processes to support good IT governance. It divides the IT management issues into four groups: (1) plan and organize, (2) acquire and implement, (3) deliver and support, and (4) monitor.

The compliance of business and IT processes is mainly addressed by the first group – plan and organize (PO). The relevant PO control objectives are:

- PO1.1 – IT as part of the organization's long- and short-range plans
- PO1.2 – IT long-range plan
- PO1.3 – IT long-range planning – approach and structure
- PO1.4 – IT long-range plan changes
- PO1.8 – assessment of existing systems
- PO3.3 – technological infrastructure contingency
- PO3.4 – hardware and software acquisition plans

- PO4.3 – review of organizational achievements
- PO4.5 – responsibility for quality assurance
- PO6.1 – positive information control environment
- PO9.1 – business risk assessment.

Q9

The old Roman dictum, "divida et impera" (divide and conquer or divide and rule) recommends that a position of power can be achieved by isolating the adversaries and working towards causing disagreements between them. In problem solving, this dictum is frequently used with a slightly different meaning. It requires that a large problem be divided into smaller problems so that once the solution to the smaller problem is found, a larger problem can be addressed.

The "divida et impera" principle leads to hierarchical modularization of the problem space. In system development, it results in the division of the system into subsystems and packages. The division has to be carefully planned to reduce dependencies in the hierarchy of subsystems and packages.

ISA provides a framework within which manageable system development units can be addressed with various *perspectives* and *descriptions*. With ISA, the development resources can be allocated to the individual *cells* (intersections of perspectives and descriptions), thus facilitating development process and control.

The related benefits of ISA include:

- improved communication between stakeholders
- identification of tools that best support various development cells
- identification of areas of development strengths and weaknesses
- integration and placement of development methods and tools with relation to one another
- providing the basis for risk assessment.

Q11

The three levels of management are (1) strategic, (2) tactical and (3) operational. An IS application at the lowest level of decisionmaking (that is, the operational level) processes business data into *information*. An IS application at the highest level processes business data into *knowledge*. The upward movement through the levels of decisionmaking coincides with the desire to turn information into knowledge. Having knowledge gives an organization a competitive advantage.

The banking application for credit card monitoring belongs to at least the tactical management level. It involves *analytical* rather than *transactional* processing. It analyzes credit card transactions against such issues as:

- typical card usage patterns by the card owner
- probability of fraud based on the location (such as the country) where the card has been used
- if the card has been used to withdraw money (for which a PIN has to be entered)
- if the owner has been checking the account over the Internet or by phone (for which a user ID and password have to be entered)
- any past problems with the card
- if the owner can be reached by phone (before the card is blocked by the bank, an attempt to contact the owner by phone must be made).

Q13

The object-oriented technology is not "a new kid on the block". In fact, it dates back to the language called Simula developed in the late 1960s. The center-stage position that object technology occupies today is due to a number of factors. The most important factor relates to the advances in hardware, in particular GUIs (graphical user interfaces), which have *enabled* the widespread application of object solutions. Modern GUIs demand *event-driven programming*, which is best served by object technology.

The shift to object-oriented development is also driven by the needs of *new applications* that can be implemented on modern hardware/software platforms. Two main categories of such applications are *workgroup computing* and *multimedia systems*.

Object-oriented technology is also essential for addressing the ever-growing *application backlog* of large systems that are difficult to maintain and even more difficult to re-engineer into modern solutions. *Object wrapping* is a promising approach to fight the application backlog.

Q15

Gathering the *metrics* of software process and software product is relatively meaningless the first time it is done in an IT organization. The metrics start being useful when they are linked on project completion to such issues as project duration and expended budget. Once such correlation between software metrics and *planning targets* is known for one project, the next project can be planned better.

Metrics from a current project can be compared with what happened on the previous project. If the metrics are comparable with those obtained before, then the system planning can assume that the planning constraints (time, money and so on) will be comparable as well. This is particularly true if the development team is unchanged, the processes are similar, the application is in the same domain area (that of accounting applications, for example) and the customer base is analogous.

If the metrics are taken consistently on many projects, then the benefits to system planning are even greater. More metrics means more planning precision and the possibility of finding useful past metrics for planning of untypical projects and modifying plans due to changed circumstances.

Q17

RUP® is a commercial development framework, while the spiral model is a rather theoretical concept. Risking some discord, RUP® can be seen as an implementation of the spiral model. Because RUP® is a customizable framework, it can be tailored to define a process in which each iteration follows the spiral of planning–risk analysis–engineering–customer evaluation.

As a customized process framework, RUP® specifies activities and methods that unify developers and customers. RUP® also offers patterns, work flows, templates of documents, project dashboards and development guidance. The spiral model does not address project management issues, nor does it propose any specific development practices.

To adhere to the spiral model, a particular RUP® process must consider the main concerns of the spiral model in each iteration. These concerns include cyclical changes to schedules and budget, adjustments based on users' objectives and constraints, risk identification and resolution, a readiness to kill the project purely on the basis of risk analysis and engineering activities resulting in prototypes and artifacts that can be immediately evaluated by customers.

Q19

Extreme programming (XP) is the original, most popular and most comprehensive of the agile development methods. Although it has "programming" in its name, it is really an approach to a software development lifecycle.

XP embraces object technology and embodies some of the best practices of object-oriented development. The practices include development to user stories by on-site customers, test-driven development to, pair programming, streamlining of code and improving the design by means of refactoring, and time-boxed small releases of code to customers. These practices are integrated into a well-defined process.

Aspect-oriented software development is an architecture centric framework. It emphasizes modularization of software according to so-called crosscutting concerns. The concerns can be of various granularities and can be functional or non-functional. Examples of concerns are system security, required concurrency level and object caching strategy. The argument is that development by concerns (or aspects) delivers scalable solutions with stable architecture resistant to refactoring.

The concerns are programmed separately and factored out of the application code. Because existing programming languages lack the facilities for factoring out the aspect code and rejoining it to the main application code, aspect programming demands special tools (such as AspectJ) to separate application logic and crosscutting concerns. In AspectJ, a rejoining point is any well-defined instant in the execution of the program. This can be an entry or return from a method or an object construction.

Compared with XP, aspect development is merely a programming technique, albeit with an influence on architectural design. As such, aspect programming can be used as an alternative to the frequent refactoring advocated in XP.

Feature-driven development consists of five processes: (1) development of an overall business object model, (2) construction of a features list, (3) planning by feature, (4) designing by feature and (5) building by feature. Process 1 is done by domain experts and produces a high-level class diagram. Process 2 delivers functional decomposition reminiscent of data flow diagrams. The decomposition is done by subject areas, business activities and business activity step. Features at the bottom of functional decomposition should not demand more than two weeks of work. Such features are broken down into discrete milestones. The remaining three processes create a plan–design–build cycle. Features are prioritized, designed one feature at a time and built using extensive unit testing.

Compared to XP, feature-driven development covers similar parts of the lifecycle – that is, analysis–design–implementation. However, XP iterations lean more on implementation, whereas feature-driven development follows a more classic lifecycle that depends on analysis/design prior to any programming.

Chapter

2

Requirements Determination

Objectives

Objectives

Requirements determination is about social, communication and managerial skills. This is the least technical phase of system development but, if not done thoroughly, the consequences are more serious than for other phases. The downstream costs of not capturing, omitting or misinterpreting customers' requirements may prove unsustainable later in the process.

This chapter introduces a broad spectrum of issues in requirements determination. By reading this chapter you will:

- understand the necessity of aligning business and IT processes when converging on the solution
- learn about process hierarchy modeling and business process modeling
- understand the relationship between implementation strategies and requirements analysis and system design tasks

- distinguish between functional and non-functional requirements
- gain knowledge of the methods of requirements elicitation, negotiation and validation, as well as the principles of requirements management
- be able to construct requirements business models, including business use case models and business class models
- learn about the desired structure of a typical requirements document.

From business processes to solution envisioning

The contemporary business landscape of an adaptive enterprise requires that business capabilities are explored and the solutions to meet changing demands are identified. Business processes define the need for IT projects and systems. In many cases, IT solutions merely address business problems. In other cases, IT solutions are true enablers of business innovation and generate new business ideas. In all cases, an IT solution is an infrastructure service that may initially offer an important competitive advantage but eventually becomes a *commodity* that competitors will also have.

Businesses need to take the initiative. However, because of the dynamic development of new technologies, including ready-to-customize prepackaged solutions, IT specialists are increasingly seen as *providers of business solutions* rather than just system developers. The alignment of business strategy and IT is the objective of system planning initiatives and is recognized in IS development processes, standards and compliance frameworks. As noticed by Polikoff et al. (2006: 47): "Nearly all best practices now reflect the need to perform fundamental *business strategy*, *modeling*, and *envisioning work* as indispensable inputs to software requirements and development. However, no proven, repeatable means are provided or evidenced for executing these essential activities."

The main difficulty in linking a business idea to a corresponding IT solution can be attributed to the lack of proper communication channels between business people and IT experts. These channels have important social and organizational dimensions, but the initial difficulty (and the necessary condition for communication) must be linked to the existence (or lack) of a common modeling language that would provide a graphical notation for drawing business processes.

While many languages and notations have been proposed to bridge the gap between business process design and process implementation, the main language of choice is the *Business Process Modeling Notation* (**BPMN**) (White, 2004; BPMN 2006). Originally developed by a consortium called Business Process Management Initiative, it is now managed by the OMG within the task force called Business Modeling & Integration Domain Task Force (BMI DTF).

2.1.1 Process hierarchy modeling

BPMN is specifically dedicated to modeling **business processes** defined as activities that produce something of value to the organization or to its external stakeholders. The concept of process is hierarchical – a process may contain other processes (*subprocesses*). An atomic activity within a process is called a **task**.

A **business process model** can be defined for processes of various sizes – from an enterprise-wide process to a process performed by a single person. Formally, BPMN does not provide support for modeling structures of processes, but, in practice, a functional breakdown of processes comes in handy. In the past, data flow **diagrams** served as a (quite sophisticated) technique of functional decomposition. In contemporary practice, simpler process hierarchy diagrams tend to be used.

A **process hierarchy diagram** defines the static structure of the business process model. It shows a process hierarchy structure as the decomposition of a top-level business process into its subprocesses. It is normally not customary or necessary to decompose subprocesses down to the atomic tasks.

2.1.1.1 Processes and process decompositions

A business process can be an activity performed manually or an automated service. A process has at least one input flow and one output flow. When the process gains the control, it performs its activity, typically by transforming the input flow into the output flow.

A process can be atomic or composite. An atomic process (task) does not contain any subprocesses. A composite process uses subprocesses to describe its actions. Process decomposition links are used to define composite processes. Figure 2.1 shows the relevant notation.

2.1.1.2 Process hierarchy diagram

A *diagram* is a graphical representation of a model. Frequently, a diagram provides a particular viewpoint on the model and the complete representation of the model may consist of many diagrams. Moreover, the same diagram can be presented with varying levels of details – the symbols of the same graphical objects can be displayed with different kinds of information to emphasize some aspects of the model and facilitate understanding.

Figure 2.1
Process hierarchy
diagram – notation

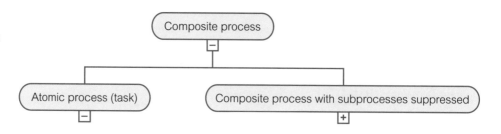

Example 2.1: advertising expenditure

Consider Problem statement 5 for an advertising expenditure system (Section 1.6.5) and construct a process hierarchy diagram for it. There is no need to attempt a complete decomposition of high-level processes. It is sufficient (for illustration purposes) to decompose a single selected high-level process.

Consider the following additional observations.

■ The problem statement describes the main workflow of processes involved in gathering details about the advertisements and measuring advertising expenditures. However, the supporting management processes are not explicitly listed. At least two of these processes constitute an important part of the process hierarchy model. These are concerned with the contracts, and with the management of contacts and accounts receivable.

■ Contact management involves activities such as the acquiring of new customers, the ongoing management of existing customers, tracking contact management activities and the management of suppliers of advertising information.

■ Contracts and accounts receivable consist of such tasks as the negotiation of contracts, invoice creation, monitoring of contracts, invoice processing and payments, and sales analysis.

Figure 2.2 represents a process hierarchy diagram for Example 2.1. It shows six high-level composite processes within the scope of the overall business process called `Advertising expenditure measurements`. For illustration purposes, the decomposition of the process `Measurement collection` into three tasks is also shown.

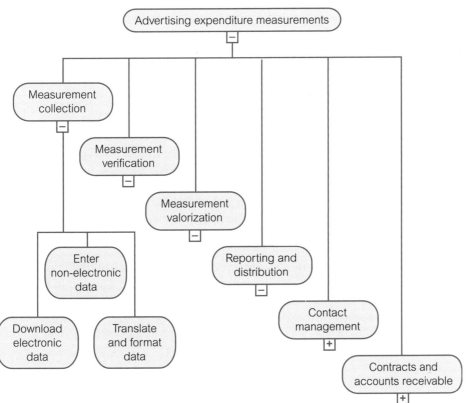

Figure 2.2
Process hierarchy model for an advertising expenditure system

2.1.2 Business process modeling

BPMN allows for the creation of many types of diagrams for modeling end-to-end business processes in a workflow within a single organization and for the modeling of interactions between business processes governed by different business entities. The former models are known as *internal* business processes, the latter *collaborative* business-to-business (B2B) processes.

BPMN is not a notation for any specific process modeling methodology. Rather, its aim is to provide a common communication language for business and IT people. There are other competing notations and methodologies, one of which is the UML activity diagrams, which are explained later in the book. There is an expectation that because both BPMN and UML are being developed by OMG, some kind of consolidation of business process diagrams and activity diagrams will result. A related goal is to map these notations to an executable language, in particular to the Business Process Execution Language (**BPEL**) – a standard for process execution in systems based on the Service-Oriented Architecture (SOA) (White 2005).

2.1.2.1 Flow objects, connecting objects, swimlanes and artifacts

BPMN offers four basic categories of modeling elements (White 2004):

- **flow objects**
- **connecting objects**
- **pools** (swimlanes)
- **artifacts**

Flow objects are the core BPMN elements. There are three categories of flow objects – events, activities and gateways (see Figure 2.3).

An *event* is something that "happens". It usually has a cause (trigger) or an impact (result). The start event indicates where a particular process will start. The end (stop) event indicates where the process will end. Intermediate events occur between a start event and an end event. There are various types of events, such as timer, error or cancel.

An *activity* is some work that must be done. This could be a task or a subprocess. A subprocess can have a plus sign in the bottom line of the rounded rectangle to indicate that it is a compound activity. A compound activity can be broken down into a set of subactivities and visualized as an expanded subactivity. Additional graphical annotations at the bottom of rounded rectangle symbols determine additional properties, such as looping or multiple-instance executions.

A *gateway* is used to control the divergence and convergence of multiple sequence flows. There are six types of gateway, ranging from a simple decision to determine branching to parallel forking and joining of paths.

The *connecting objects* (or *connectors* for short) are used to connect flow objects in order to define the structure of a business process. There are three categories of connecting objects – sequence flows, message flows and associations (see Figure 2.4).

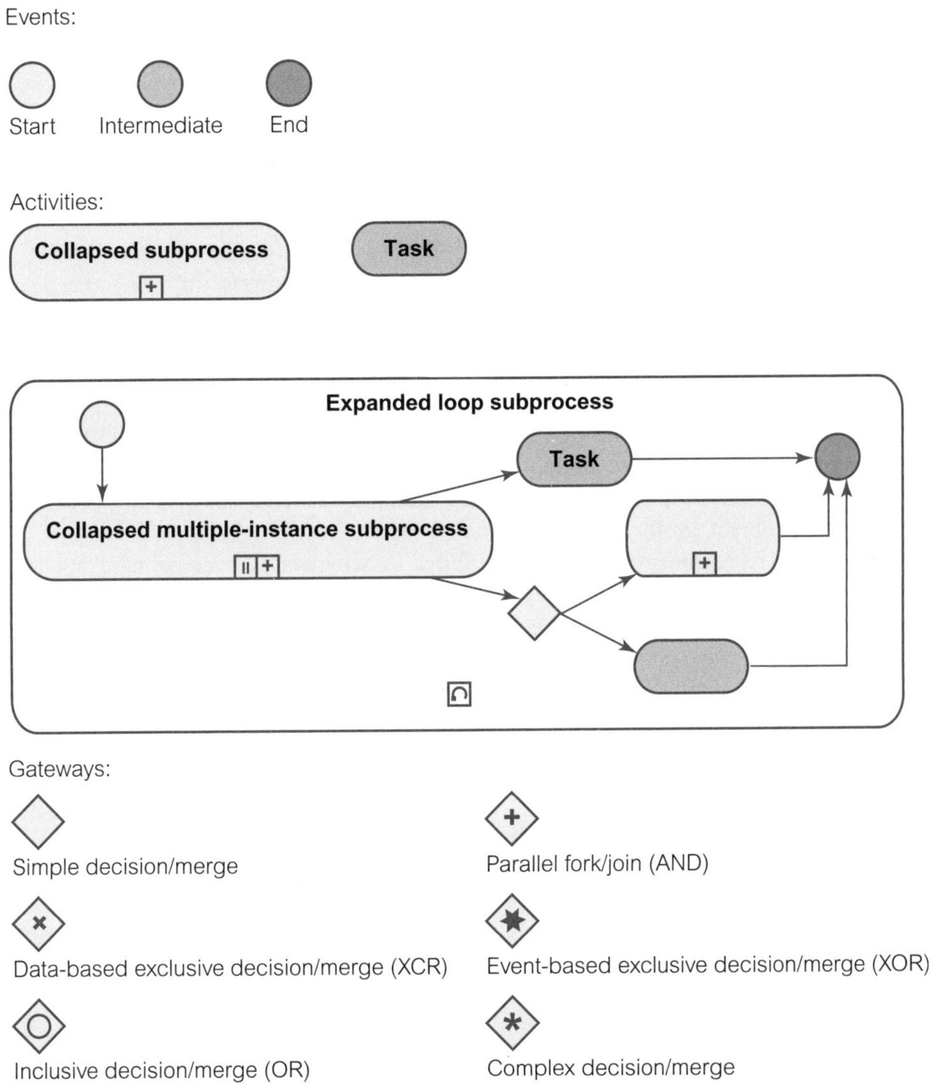

Figure 2.3
BPMN – flow
objects

Events:

Start   Intermediate   End

Activities:

Collapsed subprocess   Task

Expanded loop subprocess

Task

Collapsed multiple-instance subprocess

Gateways:

Simple decision/merge

Parallel fork/join (AND)

Data-based exclusive decision/merge (XCR)

Event-based exclusive decision/merge (XOR)

Inclusive decision/merge (OR)

Complex decision/merge

A *sequence flow* is used to show the order in which the activities will be performed in a process. A *message flow* is used to show the flow of messages (data) between two business entities (two process participants) that are prepared to send and receive them. An *association* is used to associate flow objects or an artifact with a flow object.

A *pool* represents a business entity (participant) in a process. It acts as a "swimlane" mechanism to organize activities into separate visual categories in order to illustrate different functional capabilities or responsibilities. Pools represent sets of self-contained processes. Accordingly, the sequence flow may not cross the boundary of a pool. Participants in various pools can communicate via message flows or associations to artifacts.

Figure 2.4
BPMN –
connecting
objects

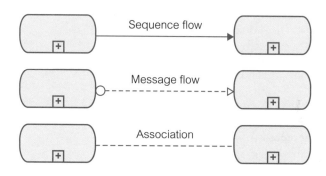

There are two kinds of pool – horizontal and vertical (see Figure 2.5). The choice between the two is determined by the graphical convenience.

Artifacts provide additional modeling flexibility by allowing us to extend the basic notation to respond to specific modeling situations, such as for so-called vertical markets (telecommunication, hospitals or banking, for example). Three types of artifacts are pre-defined – data object, group and annotation (see Figure 2.6)

Data objects represent data required or produced by activities. They do not have any direct effect on the sequence or message flow of the process, but they do provide additional information about activities. A *group* is a grouping of activities that does not affect the sequence flow of the process. The grouping can be used for documentation or analysis purposes (such as to identify the activities of a distributed transaction across pools). *Annotations* provide additional text information for the reader of a business process diagram.

2.1.2.2 Business process diagram

Using the notational elements just explained, business process models can be visualized with the chosen level of precision. Many business process diagrams and multiple-level diagrams can be created.

Figure 2.5
BPMN – pools
(swimlanes)

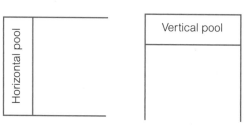

Figure 2.6
BPMN – artifacts

Example 2.2: advertising expenditure

Consider Problem statement 5, for an advertising expenditure system (Section 1.6.5) and the process hierarchy diagram in Example 2.1 (Section 2.1.1.2). Construct a business process diagram for the process "Measurement collection".

Consider the following additional observations about measurement collection.

■ The major data collection method used is electronic transfer from the data suppliers. This process occurs on a daily basis and, in the majority of cases, is performed automatically in the middle of the night. The data is collected from television stations, radio stations, press publishers and cinema outdoor advertisers. A specialized communications package is used for the data transfer from the data logs located at the suppliers. The supplier is responsible for placing the contents of the previous day's advertising log on to a dedicated file server prior to the data downloading process, which typically begins at 2am every night.

■ Data not collected electronically has to be entered from the source documents. This type of collection applies mostly to press sources – advertisements in newspapers and magazines – but also advertising catalogues delivered to households.

■ Each of the suppliers of information has its own unique format that it uses to provide its data. Thus, the first process performed on this data is to convert it into a standard format so that uniform processing can be performed on it. In the case of television, some networks provide a single file and this first needs to be split into the individual station components.

Figure 2.7 is a business process diagram for Example 2.2. It shows both an external `Supplier` process and the two processes managed by internal business entities (shown as the pools called `IT department` and `Data entry`). The diagram takes advantage of intermediate event timers in the `IT department` and the `Data entry` pools. It also indicates that `Transfer advertising data` and `Download electronic data` are multiple-instance subprocesses. Three data objects engaged in the process are also modeled.

Solution envisioning   2.1.3

Solution envisioning (Polikoff et al. 2006) is a business value-driven approach to delivering an IT service (that is, it is not merely a software system) to solve an as-is business problem or foster a to-be business innovation. Solution envisioning makes a close connection between business and IT stakeholders and integrates business strategy methods and software development capabilities.

Solution envisioning can be seen as an "Internet-age" extension and a combined application of system planning approaches discussed in Section 1.2 and the three levels of systems discussed in Section 1.3. The three Es – efficiency, effectiveness and edge (Section 1.2) – underpin the solution envisioning exercise and determine the resulting degree of change in the business. The uniqueness and novelty of solution envisioning is largely in the recognition of the fact that modern software development projects are rarely standalone, from-scratch custom developments, but they are packaged and component-based (Section 1.1.1) and integration projects (Section 1.1.3).

Figure 2.7
Business process model for an advertising expenditure system

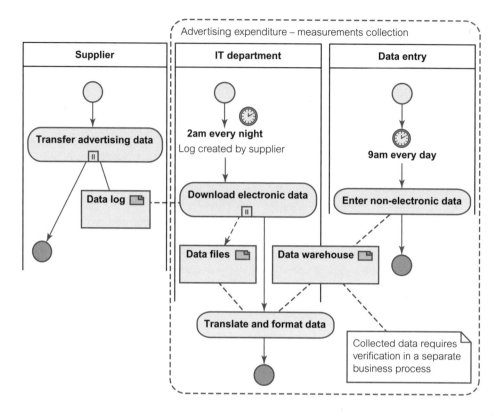

2.1.3.1 Solution envisioning process

The solution envisioning process is preoccupied with establishing an effective linkage between business and IT processes. Polikoff et al. (2006) divide the process into three phases, each of which consists of activity groups and activities within those groups. Figure 2.8 uses a business process diagram to show the elements of the solution envisioning process. The three phases are visualized as vertical pools, activity groups are shown as expanded subprocesses and activities are structured as tasks.

The first phase of the solution envisioning process – **business capability exploration** – determines **business capabilities**, which are understood as the capacities relating to how a business IT solution can deliver specific results. This phase describes **capability cases** – solution ideas, making the business case for each capability. From the IT perspective, each capability case can be seen as a reusable software component for achieving a business objective.

"The (first) phase is completed when an understanding is reached on the nature of the business problems and on the specific results a solution will need to bring about. This understanding is documented in a preliminary vision of the proposed solution that can be communicated to a broader set of stakeholders for evaluation and further decision making within an envisioning workshop" (Polikoff et al. 2006: 156).

The second phase – **solution capability envisioning** – aims at developing the capability case into a **solution concept** and ensuring that the solution is agreed on by the

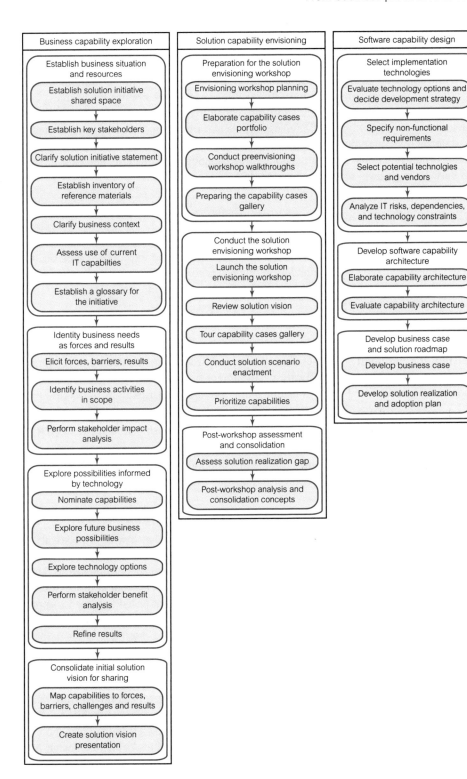

Figure 2.8
Solution envisioning process

stakeholders. The solution concept takes the business context as an input and produces future scenarios for new ways to work as output. The solution concept converges on the ultimate solution architecture and is developed in solution envisioning workshops.

The third phase – **software capability design** – decides on system implementation technologies, develops software **capability architecture** and elaborates the business case with project plans and risk analysis. Software capability design is an activity in software modeling – it develops high-level models and plans for building the solution. The modeling undertakings include functional capabilities (functional requirements), quality attributes (non-functional requirements) and the capability architecture, showing interactions between high-level software components.

2.1.3.2 Implementation strategies and capability architecture

In the first phase of the solution envisioning process, capability cases function as multiple *solution sketches* to allow many solution possibilities to be explored. Later on, the selected capability cases become technical *blueprints* for the solution. The feedback loop between the business case and the IT solution necessitates quite early determination of the implementation strategy.

As pointed out earlier, there are three prevalent *implementation strategies* (Polikoff et al. 2006):

- **custom development** – hand-crafted, standalone, from-scratch software development covering all phases of the software development process (lifecycle), performed in-house and/or contracted out to consulting and development firms
- **package-based development** – derives the solution by customizing pre-existing software packages, such as COTS, ERP or Customer Relationship Management (**CRM**) systems
- **component-based development** – builds the solution by integrating software components sourced from multiple vendors and business partners and likely to be based on SOA and/or MDA.

Despite the obvious differences between implementation strategies, which strategy is chosen has only a limited impact on the modeling activities that it will be necessary to undertake for the requirements analysis and system design. To begin with (and as explained and evidenced later in the book) *requirements analysis* is supposed to be (at least in principle) implementation-independent. It should model business processes, not IT processes. The proviso is that package-based and component-based approaches supply predeveloped IT solutions for selected business processes (but this does not free the developer from modeling the business processes for the specific enterprise!).

System design, however, is affected by which implementation strategy is chosen. The impact is not with regard to typical design activities per se (they apply equally well to all implementation strategies) but, rather, in terms of the need for explicit visualization in the design models as to which elements are custom built and which customized from packages or serviced by components. Clearly, the custom built elements are "white box" (to use a software testing term). This means that the design of these elements must show all their internal details. For package-based and component-based elements, the design may be "black box". This means, that the external functionality of these elements must be incorporated and integrated into the design models, but their internal workings may remain unexplained.

One of the controversies brought about by modern solution envisioning approaches relates to the role and place of the *system architecture* (and, therefore, the role and place of *architectural design*) in the overall software development process. As explained in the previous section, software capability design develops software capability architecture – that is, a model that identifies high-level system functional components and the interactions between them. Within the solution envisioning approach, the capability architecture is developed early in the process and in parallel with business analysis and identification of capability cases and users' requirements. Moreover, the capability architecture assumes the implementation strategy and provides strong guidance for the realization of the solution.

The shift of architectural design activities to the very early stages of the system development process is both motivated and explained by the differences in implementation strategies. The author of this book shares the experience of Polikoff et al. (2006: 252) that "the absence of such an architectural model, or a poorly developed one, has often served as a warning sign of a project heading for trouble." The reader is asked to remember this point when undertaking any development project and excuse us that more complete discussion of architectural design, which is placed (purely for educational reasons) in later chapters (in particular, Chapters 4 and 6).

Review quiz 2.1

RQ1 What is the name of the most popular language for visual modeling of business processes that aims at bridging the gap between business and IT people?

RQ2 What are the four categories of modeling elements in BPMN?

RQ3 Can a sequence flow connect two pools?

RQ4 What is the name of a business value-driven approach to delivering an IT service to solve an as-is business problem or foster a to-be business innovation?

RQ5 What is the main modeling outcome of software capability design?

RQ6 What are the three distinct implementation strategies to be considered in the solution envisioning process?

Requirements elicitation

2.2

A business analyst discovers the system requirements as a result of consultation, which involves customers and experts in the problem domain. In some cases, the business analyst has sufficient domain experience, so the help of a domain expert may not be required. A business analyst is then a kind of domain expert, modeled using a generalization relationship (a line with a white arrowhead), as shown in Figure 2.9. (The figure uses the notation of the UML use case model, which is explained in detail in Chapter 3. Here, the use case notation is used only for its convenience.)

Figure 2.9
Influences during
requirements
determination

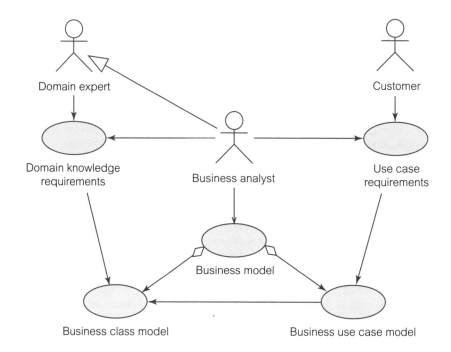

Requirements elicited from domain experts constitute the domain knowledge. They capture widely acknowledged time-independent business rules and processes applicable to typical organizations and systems. Requirements elicited from customers are expressed in use case scenarios. They go beyond the basic domain knowledge and capture the unique character of the organization – the way the business is done here and now or how it should be done.

The task of a business analyst is to combine the two sets of requirements into a business model. As shown in Figure 2.9 by means of aggregation relationships (signified by a diamond on the lines), the business model contains a **business class model** and **business use case model**.

The *business class model* is a high-level class diagram. A **class** is an abstraction that describes a set of objects with common attributes, operations, relationships and semantic constraints. A class model identifies and relates together **business objects** – the fundamental classes in the business domain.

The *business use case model* is a high-level use case diagram that identifies major functional building blocks in the system. The model represents **business use cases**, relationships between them and how **business actors** interact with them. A business use case may represent a similar functional block to that of a capability case (Section 2.1.3.1). The difference is in the emphasis and the role and place of these two concepts in the development lifecycle. The focus of a *capability case* is the business value of a piece of the functionality. The *business use case* assumes the business value and describes an interaction between a user (actor) and the system to realize that business value.

In general, domain classes (business objects) do not have to be derived or result from use cases (Rumbaugh 1994). In practice, however, a business class model should be validated against the business use case model. The validation is likely to lead to some adjustments or extensions to the business class model.

Following Hoffer et al. (2002), this book distinguishes between traditional and modern methods of fact finding and information gathering (Sections 2.2.2 and 2.2.3).

System requirements   2.2.1

System planning (Section 1.2) defines strategic directions for an organization. *Business process modeling* flows from system planning and documents both routine business processes and new process ideas that can give an organization a competitive edge. Together, system planning and business process modeling determine what information systems need to be developed.

Requirements determination is the first phase in the system development and implementation lifecycle. The purpose of requirements determination is to provide a narrative definition of functional and other requirements that the stakeholders expect to be satisfied in the implemented and deployed system. The boundary of the system is expected to be derived from a business process model. Accordingly, the business process model can serve as the main reference point for the identification of high-level system requirements. It is also desirable to classify these initial requirements into those that can be implemented by software and those that require manual processing or other forms of human intervention.

As noted in Section 1.4.2.1.1, requirements define the expected services of the system – (**service statements**) and constraints that the system must obey (**constraint statements**). The service statements constitute the system's **functional requirements**. Functional requirements can be grouped into those that describe the scope of the system, necessary business functions and required data structures.

The constraint statements can be classified according to different categories of restriction imposed on the system, such as the required system's "look and feel", performance and security. The constraint statements constitute the system's **non-functional requirements**. Non-functional requirements are also known as *supplementary requirements*.

Functional requirements   2.2.1.1

Using the notational elements just explained, business process models can be visualized with the chosen level of precision. Many business process diagrams and multiple-level hierarchical diagrams can be created.

Functional requirements need to be obtained from customers (users and system owners). This is a *requirements elicitation* activity conducted by a business (or system) analyst. There are many techniques that can be employed – often traditional interviews with customers culminating (if necessary) in building a software prototype with which to discover more requirements.

The collected functional requirements must be subjected to careful analysis to eliminate duplications and contradictions. This invariably leads to *requirements reviews and renegotiations* with customers. The agreed-on set of functional requirements is modeled using graphical notations and further defined in text.

2.2.1.2 Non-functional requirements

Non-functional requirements are not behavioral in nature. Rather, they are constraints on the development and implementation of the system. The level of adherence to these constraints determines the software's quality. Non-functional requirements can be divided into those that relate to (Ghezzi et al. 2003; Lethbridge and Laganière 2001; Maciaszek and Liong 2005):

- **usability**
- **reusability**
- **reliability**
- **performance**
- efficiency
- adaptiveness (supportability)
- other constraints.

Usability defines the ease of use of the system. A system is more usable when it is easier to use. Usability is determined by such issues as documentation and help facilities, the training necessary for efficient and effective use, aesthetics and consistency of the user interface, error handling and so on. Usability is a bit in the eye of the beholder. What is usable for an expert user may be unusable for a novice, and vice versa.

Reusability defines the ease of reuse of previously implemented software components in new system developments. "Software component" is understood here loosely, to mean any part of implemented software or even an idea (pattern) that can be reused. Reuse applies to interfaces, classes, packages, frameworks and so on. Reusability is a reflection on the maturity of software development teams and software engineering as an industrial field.

Reliability relates to the frequency and seriousness of system failures and how gracefully the system can recover from failures. Reliability is determined by the demanded availability of the system during its operational hours, acceptable mean time between failures, accuracy of produced results and so on. A reliable system is a dependable system – that is, the user can depend on it.

Performance is defined by expectations regarding the response time of the system, transactions throughput, resource consumption, possible number of concurrent users and so on. Performance demands may differ for different business functions, pick workloads (pick times) and users.

Efficiency relates to the cost and time of achieving the software's outcomes and objectives, including the expected level of performance. This includes the cost of the hardware, software people and other resources. A more efficient system uses fewer resources to perform tasks.

Adaptiveness (supportability) is a set of three constraints – understandability, maintainability and scalability. Adaptiveness defines the ease with which the system can be understood, corrected, perfected and extended. Adaptiveness is determined by the clarity and simplicity of the architectural design and faithfulness of the implementation to the design.

The notion of *other constraints* covers all other non-functional requirements for a system. Issues that belong in this category include policy decisions about the project's infrastructure, legal issues that may affect the project, demanded level of software portability, system interoperability requirements and timeliness for product delivery.

Once acceptable to customers, the requirements are defined, classified, numbered and prioritized in the *requirements document*. This document is structured according to a *template* chosen by the organization for documenting requirements.

Although the requirements document is largely a narrative document, a high-level diagrammatic *business model* is likely to be included. The business model will normally consist of a **system scope model**, a *business use case model* and a *business class model*.

Customers' requirements are a moving target. To handle volatile requirements, we need to be able to manage change. *Requirements management* includes activities such as estimating the impacts of change on other requirements and the rest of the system.

Traditional methods of requirements elicitation

2.2.2

Traditional methods of eliciting requirements include interviews, questionnaires, observation and studying business documents. These are simple and cost-effective methods. The effectiveness of traditional methods is inversely proportional to the degree of **risk** of the project. High risk implies that the system is difficult to implement – even the high-level business requirements are not quite clear. In such projects, traditional methods are unlikely to suffice.

Interviewing customers and domain experts

2.2.2.1

Interviews are a primary technique of fact finding and information gathering. Most interviews are conducted with customers. Interviews with customers elicit mostly use case requirements (see Figure 2.9). Domain experts can also be interviewed if the business analyst does not have sufficient domain knowledge. Interviews with domain experts are frequently a simple knowledge transfer process – a learning exercise for the business analyst.

Interviews with customers are more complex (Kotonya and Sommerville 1998; Sommerville and Sawyer 1997). Customers may have only a vague picture of their requirements. They may be unwilling to cooperate or unable to express their requirements in understandable terms. They may also demand requirements that exceed the project's budget or are not implementable. Finally, it is likely that the requirements of different customers may be in conflict.

There are two basic kinds of interview: structured (formal) and unstructured (informal). A *structured interview* is prepared in advance and has a clear agenda, many of the questions being predetermined. Some questions may be *open-ended* (for which possible responses cannot be anticipated); others may be *close-ended* (with the answer to be picked from a range of provided answers or a simple "yes" or "no").

Structured interviews need to be supplemented with *unstructured interviews*. Unstructured interviews are more like informal meetings, with no predetermined questions nor anticipated objectives. The purpose of an unstructured interview is to encourage the customer to speak his or her mind and, in the process, elicit requirements that the business analyst would not have expected and would not, therefore, have asked questions about.

Both structured and unstructured interviews must be provided with some starting point and context for discussion. This may be a short written document or e-mail sent to the interviewee prior to the meeting, explaining the interviewer's objective or posing some questions.

Three kinds of questions should, in general, be avoided (Whitten and Bentley 1998):

- *opinionated questions* – the interviewer expresses (directly or indirectly) his or her opinion on the issue, such as "Do we have to do things the way we do them?"

- *biased questions* – similar to opinionated ones, except that the interviewer's opinion is clearly biased, such as "You are not going to do this, are you?"

- *imposing questions* – the answer is assumed in the question, such as "You do things this way, don't you?"

Lethbridge and Laganière (2001) recommend that the following categories of questions be asked during an interview. Questions about:

- *specific details* for any issue raised during interview – ask about the five w's: what, who, when, where and why

- *vision for the future* – as interviewees are likely to be blissfully unaware of various system constraints and may be coming up with very innovative, yet unimplementable, ideas

- *alternative ideas* – these can be questions to an interviewee and suggestions from the interviewer, asking for opinions

- the *minimum acceptable as a solution* to the problem – good, usable systems are simple systems, so finding out what is the minimum required is therefore essential to determine the workable scope of the system

- *other sources of information* – to discover important documents and other knowledge sources hitherto unknown to the interviewer

- *soliciting diagrams* – simple graphical models drawn by an interviewee to explain business processes may prove invaluable to understanding the requirements.

There are many factors to a successful interview, but perhaps the most important are the interviewer's *communication and interpersonal* skills. While the interviewer asks questions and maintains control, it is equally important that he or she listens carefully and is patient so that the interviewee is at ease. To ascertain correct understanding, the interviewer should seek confirmation by paraphrasing the interviewee's statements back to him or her.

To maintain good interpersonal rapport and obtain additional feedback, a memorandum summarizing the interview should be sent to the interviewee within a day or two, along with a request for comments.

Interviews have a unique set of advantages and disadvantages (Bennett et al. 2002). The *advantages* are:

- flexibility and timeliness of information gathering because of the ability to react dynamically to the interviewee's observations
- possibility of obtaining deeper understanding of the requirements by progressively asking more inquisitive questions and gathering relevant documents
- possibility of conducting interviews even with geographically dispersed stakeholders by means of video conferencing.

On the negative side, the *disadvantages* of interviews are that they are:

- time-consuming and costly as they are conducted in meetings and require a number of follow-up activities, such as listening to interview recordings, reporting back to the interviewees and resolving any misunderstandings
- subject to misinterpretations and bias (but this disadvantage is shared with many other requirements determination techniques)
- subject to obtaining conflicting information from different interviewees on the same subject matter (this can be alleviated by means of group interviews and modern requirements elicitation methods, such as **brainstorming** and other workshop methods).

Questionnaires   2.2.2.2

Questionnaires are an efficient way to gather information from many customers. Questionnaires are normally used in addition to interviews, not in lieu of them. An exception may be a low-risk project with well-understood objectives. In such a project, the passive nature and lesser depth of a questionnaire may not prove disadvantageous.

In general, questionnaires are less productive than interviews because no clarification can be sought regarding the questions or possible responses. Questionnaires are passive, which is both an advantage and a disadvantage. It is an advantage because the respondent has time to consider the responses and can remain anonymous. It is a disadvantage because the respondent cannot easily clarify the questions.

A questionnaire should be designed so that it is as easy as possible to answer the questions. In particular, open-ended questions should be avoided – most questions should be closed. *Closed questions* can take three forms (Whitten and Bentley 1998):

- *multiple-choice questions* – the respondent must pick one or more answers from the set of answers provided (additional comments from the respondent may also be allowed)
- *rating questions* – the respondent has to express his or her opinion about a statement, commonly circling numbers or, for example, "strongly agree, agree neutral, disagree, strongly disagree or don't know".
- *ranking questions* – the answers provided are ranked by means of sequential numbers, percentage values or similar ordering means.

A well-designed, easy-to-answer questionnaire will encourage respondents to return the completed documents promptly. However, when evaluating the results, the business analyst should consider possible distortions due to the fact that people who did not respond would have been likely to provide different responses (Hoffer et al. 2002).

Questionnaires are particularly useful and economical when the views of a large number of people are sought and they are geographically dispersed. However, careful planning is required to prepare a good questionnaire and the statistical analysis of the answers demands appropriate skills.

2.2.2.3   Observation

There are situations where the business analyst finds it difficult to obtain complete information from interviews and questionnaires. The customer may be unable to convey the information effectively or have only fragmentary knowledge of the complete business process. In such cases, *observation* may be an effective fact-finding technique. After all, the best way to learn how to tie a tie is by observing the process.

Observation can take three forms:

- *passive observation* – the business analyst observes business activities without interruption or direct involvement and even, in some cases, video cameras may be used for less intrusive observation
- *active observation* – the business analyst participates in the activities and effectively becomes part of the team
- *explanatory observation* – the user explains his or her activities to the observer while doing the job.

To be representative, observations should be carried out for a prolonged period of time, at different time intervals and cover different workloads (pick times).

The main difficulty with observation is that people tend to behave differently when they are being watched. In particular, they tend to work according to formal rules and procedures. This distorts the reality by hiding any work shortcuts – positive or negative. We ought to remember that "work to rule" is an effective form of industrial action. There are also ethical, privacy or even legal problems because the nature of some jobs requires dealing with sensitive personal information and organizational secrets.

On the positive side, observation is an indispensable technique for capturing the time needed to perform certain tasks. Also, it is a great validator of the information obtained via other requirements elicitation methods. Finally, because of its visual character, observation can uncover some work practices so deeply entrenched in the work performed that they are not picked up by other elicitation techniques.

2.2.2.4   Study of documents and software systems

The *study of documents and software systems* is an invaluable technique for finding both use case and domain knowledge requirements. The technique is always used, although it may target only the selective aspects of the system.

Use case requirements are discovered by studying existing enterprise documents and system forms/reports (if a computerized solution for the current system exists, as is typically the case in large organizations). One of the most valuable insights into use case requirements is the record (if one exists) of defects and change requests for an existing system.

Organization documents to study include business forms (completed, if possible), work procedures, job descriptions, policy manuals, business plans, organizational charts, inter-office correspondence, minutes of meetings, accounting records, external correspondence and customers' complaints.

System forms and reports to study include computer screens and reports, together with the associated documentation – system operating manuals, user documentation, technical documentation and system analysis and design models.

Domain knowledge requirements are discovered by researching business domain jour-nals and reference books. The studies of proprietary software packages, such as COTS, ERP and CRM systems, can also provide a wealth of domain knowledge. Hence, visits to libraries and software vendors are a part of the requirements elicitation process (although the Internet allows many such "visits" to be accomplished without leaving the office).

Modern methods of requirements elicitation 2.2.3

Modern methods of requirements elicitation include the use of software **prototypes**, brainstorming, joint application development (**JAD**), and rapid application development (**RAD**). They offer better insights into the requirements than the other methods discussed, but come at a higher cost and require more effort. However, the long-term payoff may be very rewarding.

Modern methods are typically employed when the *risks* for the project are high. The factors for high-risk projects are many. They include unclear objectives, undocumented procedures, unstable requirements, eroded user expertise, inexperienced developers and insufficient user commitment.

Prototyping 2.2.3.1

Prototyping is the most frequently used modern requirements elicitation method. Software prototypes are constructed to visualize either the whole system or just part of it to customers in order to obtain their feedback. A *prototype* is a demonstration system – a "quick and dirty" working model of the solution that presents a graphical user interface (GUI) and simulates the system behavior for various user events. The information content of GUI screens is hard-coded in the prototype program rather than obtained dynamically from the database.

The complexity (and growing expectations of customers) of modern GUIs makes pro-totyping an indispensable element in software development. The feasibility and usefulness of the system can be estimated by means of prototypes well before real imple-mentation is undertaken.

In general, a system prototype is a very effective way of eliciting requirements difficult to obtain from customers by other means. This is frequently the case with systems that are to deliver new business functionality. It is also the case where there are conflicting requirements or communication problems exist between customers and developers.

There are two kinds of prototype (Kotonya and Sommerville 1998):

- The *"throw-away" prototype*, which is to be discarded when the requirements elicitation is completed. The throw-away prototype targets the requirements determination phase of the lifecycle. It typically concentrates on the least understood requirements.

- The *evolutionary prototype*, which is retained after the requirements elicitation process and used to produce the final product. The evolutionary prototype targets the speed of product delivery. It typically concentrates on well-understood requirements so that the first version of the product can be delivered quickly (although with incomplete functionality).

An additional argument in favor of the throw-away prototype is that it avoids the risk of retaining "quick and dirty" or otherwise inefficient solutions in the final product. However, the power and flexibility of contemporary software production tools have weakened that argument. There is no reason, in a well-managed project, for inefficient prototype solutions not to be eradicated.

2.2.3.2 Brainstorming

Brainstorming is a conference technique to form new ideas or find a solution to a specific problem by putting aside judgment, social inhibitions and rules (Brainstorming 2003). In general, brainstorming is not for problem analysis or decision making but generating new ideas and possible solutions. The analysis and decision making is done afterwards and does not involve brainstorming techniques.

Brainstorming is useful in requirements elicitation because of the difficulty of reaching consensus among stakeholders on what the concrete requirements are. Moreover, stakeholders tend to have a narrow view of their requirements – one that corresponds to what they are most familiar with – and brainstorming can help them to be a bit more creative.

Brainstorming requires a person to lead and moderate the session – the facilitator. Prior to the meeting, the facilitator should define the problem/opportunity area for which ideas will be generated. This is known as a *probortunity statement* (Brainstorming 2003). The term "**probortunity**" was made by merging of the words "problem" and "opportunity" (which also removes the negative connotations of the word "problem").

The probortunity statement defines the scope for a particular brainstorming session and takes forms such as question, challenge, concern, difficulty, mystery or puzzle. In the case of requirements elicitation, the probortunity statement is likely to consist of *trigger questions*.

Lethbridge and Laganière (2001) give the following examples of trigger questions for a brainstorming session targeting requirements elicitation:

- What features should be supported by the system?
- What are the input data and what are the outputs of the system?
- What classes are needed in the business or domain object model?
- What questions should be raised in interviews or questionnaires?
- What issues still need to be considered?
- What are the main risks in the project?
- What trigger questions should be asked during this or future brainstorming sessions?

The brainstorming session should be restricted to between 12 and 20 people sitting in a circle. A large round table is best for this purpose. The idea is that the facilitator is just "one of the crowd" and all participants feel equal. The session inventory should include notepads, pens, large flipcharts behind each two to three participants and a projector to present the probortunity statement and trigger questions.

During the session, participants think of answers to trigger questions and either shout them for writing down or write them down on sheets of paper, one idea per sheet. The latter approach is normally preferred because it does not intimidate people. The answers may then be passed in a circular way to the next person on the left. This serves the purpose of stimulating people to generate even more ideas.

This process lasts until no new ideas are forthcoming or after a fixed period of time (say, 15 minutes) passes (Lethbridge and Laganière 2001). At this point, participants are asked to read the ideas on the sheets in front of them, which are likely to be from the other participants (this ensures anonymity). The ideas are written down on a flipchart. A brief discussion may follow.

In the last stage of the meeting, the group votes to prioritize the ideas. This can be done by assigning a certain number of votes to each participant. A good technique is to distribute a fixed number of small sticky notes to each participant and let them stick the notes next to the ideas on the flipchart. The counting of how many notes are next to each idea is the final vote.

Joint application development 2.2.3.3

Joint application development (JAD) is a brainstorming-like technique. It is what the name implies – a joint application development in one or more workshops that bring together all stakeholders – customers and developers (Wood and Silver 1995). JAD is included here in modern methods of requirements elicitation even though the technique has a long history. It was introduced (by IBM) in the late 1970s.

There are many JAD brands and there are many consulting firms that offer the service of organizing and running a JAD session. A JAD meeting can take a few hours, a few days or even a couple of weeks. The number of participants should not exceed 25 to 30. The meeting's participants are (Hoffer et al. 2002; Whitten and Bentley 1998) as follows.

- *Leader* – the person who conducts and moderates the meeting. This person has excellent communication skills, is not a stakeholder in the project (apart from being a JAD leader) and has a good knowledge of the business domain (but not necessarily good software development knowledge).

- *Scribe* – the person who records the JAD session on a computer. This person should have touch-typing skills and possess strong knowledge of software development. The scribe can use CASE tools to document the session and develop initial solution models.

- *Customers (users and managers)* – these are the main participants and communicate and discuss the requirements, make decisions, approve the project's objectives and so on.

- *Developers* – business analysts and other members of the development team. They listen rather than speak as they are at the meeting to elicit facts and gather information, not to dominate the process.

JAD capitalizes on the benefits of group dynamics. "Group synergy" is likely to produce better solutions to problems as groups increase productivity, learn faster, make more educated judgments, eliminate more errors, take riskier decisions (this may be a negative though!), focus participants' attention on the most important issues, integrate people and so on.

When conducted according to the rules, JAD sessions tend to deliver surprisingly good outcomes. Be warned, though, as the "Ford Motor Co. in the 1950s experienced a marketing disaster with the Edsel – a car designed by a committee" (Wood and Silver 1995: 176)!

2.2.3.4   Rapid application development

Rapid application development (RAD) is more than a requirements elicitation method – it is an approach to software development as a process (Hoffer et al. 2002). As the name suggests, RAD aims at delivering system solutions fast. Technical excellence is secondary to the speed of delivery.

According to Wood and Silver (1995), RAD combines five techniques:

- evolutionary prototyping (Section 2.2.3.1)
- CASE tools with code generation and round-trip engineering between the design models and the code
- specialists with advanced tools (SWAT) – the RAD development team, which includes the best analysts, designers and programmers the organization can get, works to a strict time regime and is co-located with the users
- interactive JAD – a JAD session (Section 2.2.3.3), during which the scribe is replaced by the SWAT team with CASE tools
- timeboxing – a project management method that imposes a fixed time period (timebox) on the SWAT team to complete the project. The method forbids "scope creep" (if the project is running late, the scope of the solution is trimmed down to allow the project to complete on time).

The RAD approach may be an attractive proposition for many projects – in particular smaller ones that are not in the organization's core business area and do not, therefore, set the agenda for other development projects. Fast solutions are unlikely to be optimal or sustainable for core business areas.

Problems associated with RAD include:

- inconsistent GUI designs
- specialized rather than generic solutions, so as to facilitate software reuse
- deficient documentation
- software that is difficult to maintain and scale up.

Review quiz 2.2

RQ1 What is the name of the profession charged with the responsibility of eliciting and documenting domain knowledge requirements and use case requirements?

RQ2 What are the two main kinds of requirements?

RQ3 What are the three forms of closed questions in questionnaires?

RQ4 Who are the participants in a JAD session?

RQ5 What is the RAD development team called?

Requirements negotiation and validation
2.3

Requirements elicited from customers may overlap or conflict. Some requirements may be ambiguous or unrealistic. Others may remain undiscovered. For these reasons, requirements need to be negotiated and validated before they find their way into the requirements document.

In reality, *requirements negotiation and validation* are done in parallel with *requirements elicitation*. As requirements are elicited, they are subjected to a certain degree of scrutiny. This is naturally so with all modern techniques of requirements elicitation that involve so-called *group dynamics*. Nevertheless, once the elicited requirements have been compiled into a list, they still need to undergo careful negotiation and validation.

Requirements negotiation and validation cannot be dissociated from the process of writing up a requirements document. *Requirements negotiation* is typically based on a draft of the document. The requirements listed in the draft document are negotiated and modified, if necessary. Spurious requirements are removed. Newly discovered requirements are added.

Requirements validation requires a more complete version of the requirements document, with all the requirements clearly identified and classified. Stakeholders read the document and conduct formal review meetings. *Reviews* are frequently structured into so-called *walkthroughs* or *inspections*. They are a form of *testing*.

Out-of-scope requirements
2.3.1

The choice of IT projects and, therefore, the systems to be implemented (and, in broad terms, their scope) are determined during the system planning and business modeling activities (Sections 1.2 and 2.1). However, the detailed interdependencies of the systems can only be uncovered during the *requirements analysis* phase. It is the task of requirements analysis to determine the *system boundary* (*system scope*) so that scope creep can be addressed early on in the process.

To be able to decide if any particular requirement is within or outside the system scope, a reference model is needed against which such a decision can be made. Historically, such a reference model has been provided in the form of a **context diagram**

– a top-level diagram of the popular structured modeling technique called data flow diagrams (DFD). Although DFDs have been superseded in UML by use case diagrams, a context diagram is still a superior method of establishing the system's boundary.

However, there may be other reasons for classifying a requirement as being outside the system scope (Sommerville and Sawyer 1997). For example, a requirement may be too difficult to implement in the computerized system and should be left to a human process or it may be of low priority and excluded from the first version of the system. A requirement may also be implemented in the hardware or other external device and so be beyond the control of the software system.

2.3.2   Requirements dependency matrix

Assuming that all requirements are clearly identified and numbered (Section 2.4.1), a *requirements dependency matrix* (or *interaction matrix*) can be constructed (Kotonya and Sommerville 1998; Sommerville and Sawyer 1997). The matrix lists requirement identifiers in sorted order in the row and column headings, as shown in Table 2.1.

The upper right part of the matrix (above and including the diagonal – that is, the blue area) is not used. The remaining cells indicate whether or not any two requirements overlap, are in conflict or are independent (empty cells).

Conflicting requirements should be discussed with customers and reformulated where possible to alleviate conflicts (a record of the conflict, visible to subsequent development, should be kept). *Overlapping requirements* should also be restated to eliminate overlaps.

The requirements dependency matrix is a simple but effective technique for finding conflicts and overlaps when the number of requirements is relatively small. When this is not the case, then the technique may still be used if requirements are grouped into categories and then compared separately within each category.

2.3.3   Requirements – risks and priorities

Once conflicts and overlaps in requirements have been resolved and a revised set of requirements has been produced, they need to undergo risk analysis and prioritization. *Risk analysis* identifies requirements that are likely to cause difficulties during development. *Prioritization* is needed to allow easy re-scoping of the project when faced with delays.

Table 2.1 Requirements dependency matrix

Requirement	R1	R2	R3	R4
R1				
R2	Conflict			
R3				
R4		Overlap	Overlap	

The *feasibility* of the project is contingent on the amount of risk that the project carries. *Risk* is a threat to the project plan (in terms of the budget, time, resource allocation and so on). By identifying risks, the project manager can attempt to control them. Requirements may be "risky" due to a variety of factors. Typical risk categories are (Sommerville and Sawyer 1997):

- *technical risk* – a requirement is technically difficult to implement
- *performance risk* – a requirement, when implemented, can adversely affect the response time of the system
- *security risk* – a requirement, when implemented, can expose the system to security breaches
- *database integrity risk* – a requirement cannot easily be validated and can cause data inconsistency
- *development process risk* – a requirement calls for the use of unconventional development methods unfamiliar to developers, such as formal specification methods
- *political risk* – a requirement may prove difficult to fulfil for internal political reasons
- *legal risk* – a requirement may fall foul of current laws or anticipated changes to the law
- *volatility risk* – a requirement is likely to keep changing or evolving during the development process.

Ideally, requirements *priorities* are obtained from individual customers in the requirements elicitation process. They are then negotiated in meetings and modified again when the risk factors have been attached to them.

To eliminate ambiguity and facilitate prioritization, the number of priority classifications should be small. Three to five different priorities are sufficient. They can be named "high", "medium", "low", and "not sure". An alternative list might be "essential", "useful", "hardly matters", and "to be decided".

Review quiz 2.3

RQ1 What is (arguably) the best visual modeling method for capturing the system boundary?

RQ2 What kinds of dependencies between requirements are made explicit in a requirement dependency matrix?

RQ3 What is the name of a risk category associated with a scenario in which a requirement is likely to keep changing or evolving during the development process?

Requirements management   2.4

Requirements have to be managed. *Requirements management* is really a part of overall project management. It is concerned with three main issues:

- identifying, classifying, organizing and documenting the requirements

- changes to requirements – that is, processes need to be in place that set out how inevitable changes to requirements are proposed, negotiated, validated and documented
- requirements traceability – that is, processes need to be set up that maintain dependency relationships between requirements and other system artifacts as well as between the requirements themselves.

2.4.1 Requirements – identification and classification

Requirements are described in *natural language statements*, such as:

- "The system shall schedule the next phone call to a customer on the telemarketer's request."
- "The system shall automatically dial the scheduled phone number and simultaneously display on the telemarketer's screen the customer's information, including phone number, customer number, and name."
- "On successful connection, the system shall display an introductory text that the telemarketer should communicate to the customer to establish conversation."

A typical system would consist of hundreds or thousands of requirements statements like the above. To manage such large numbers of requirements properly, they have to be numbered following some *identification scheme*. The scheme may include a *classification* of requirements into more manageable groups.

There are several techniques for identifying and classifying requirements (Kotonya and Sommerville 1998):

- *unique identifier* – usually a sequential number assigned manually or generated by a CASE tool's database – that is, the database (or *repository*) where the CASE tool stores the analysis and design artifacts
- *sequential number within document hierarchy* – a number is assigned with consideration to the requirement's position in the requirements document, so, for example, the seventh requirement in the third section of the second chapter would be numbered 2.3.7
- *sequential number within requirements category* – a number is assigned in addition to a mnemonic name that identifies the category of the requirement, which can be a function, data, performance, security or other requirement.

Each identification method has its pros and cons. The most flexible and least error-prone is the *database-generated unique identifier*. Databases have a built-in capability to generate unique identifiers for every new record of data in a situation of concurrent multi-user access to data.

Some databases can, additionally, support the maintenance of multiple versions of the same record by extending the unique identifier value with the version number. Finally, databases can maintain *referential integrity* links between the modeling artifacts, including requirements, and can therefore provide necessary support for requirements change management and traceability.

Requirements hierarchies

Requirements can be hierarchically structured in *parent–child relationships*. A parent requirement is composed of child requirements. A child requirement is, effectively, a subrequirement of the parent requirement.

Hierarchical relationships introduce an additional level of requirements classification. This may or may not be reflected directly in their identification numbers (by using dot notation). If it were to be, the requirement numbered 4.9, for example, would be the ninth child of the parent identified by the number four.

The following is an example of a set of hierarchical requirements:

1　The system shall schedule the next phone call to a customer on the telemarketer's request.

　1.1　The system shall activate Next Call push button upon entry to the Telemarketing Control form or when the previous call has terminated.

　1.2　The system shall remove the call from the top of the queue of scheduled calls and make it the current call.

　1.3　… and so on.

Hierarchies of requirements allow them to be defined at different *levels of abstraction*. This is consistent with the overall modeling principle of systematically adding details to models when moving to the lower levels of abstraction. As a result, high-level models can be constructed for parent requirements and lower-level models can be linked to child requirements.

Change management

Requirements change. A requirement may change, be removed or a new requirement may be added, at any phase of the development lifecycle. In itself, change is not a kick in the teeth, but unmanaged change is.

The more advanced the development, the more costly the change is. In fact, the *downstream cost* of putting the project back on track after change will always grow and, frequently, grow exponentially. Changing a requirement just created and not linked to other requirements is a straightforward editing exercise. Changing the same requirement after it has been implemented in software, however, may be prohibitively costly.

A change may be linked to a human error, but is more frequently caused by internal policy changes or external factors, such as competitive forces, global markets or technological advances. Whatever the reason, strong management policies are needed to document *change requests*, assess a *change impact* and effect the changes.

Because changes to requirements are costly, a formal *business case* must be made for each change request. A valid change, not dealt with previously, is assessed for technical feasibility, the impact on the rest of the project and cost. Once approved, the change is incorporated into relevant models and implemented in the software.

Change management involves tracking large amounts of interlinked information over long periods of time. Without tool support, change management is doomed. Ideally, the requirements changes should be stored and tracked by a *software configuration management tool* used by developers to handle versions of models and programs across the development lifecycle. A good CASE tool should either have its own configuration management capability or be linked to a standalone configuration management tool.

2.4.4 Requirements traceability

Requirements traceability is just a part – albeit a critically important part – of *change management*. Requirements traceability is about maintaining traceability relationships to track changes from/to a requirement throughout the development lifecycle.

Consider the following requirement: "The system shall schedule the next phone call to a customer on the telemarketer's request." This requirement could then be modeled using a sequence diagram, activated from the GUI by an action button labeled "Next call" and programmed in a database trigger. If a traceability relationship exists between all these elements, a change to any element will make the relationship open again to discussion – the trace becomes *suspect* (to use one tool's parlance).

A traceability relationship can cut across many models in successive lifecycle phases. Only adjacent traceability links can be directly modified. For example, if an element *A* is traced to an element *B* and *B* traced to *C*, then change at either endpoint of the relationship will need to be effected in two steps – modifying link *A–B*, then *B–C*. (Chapter 9 explains traceability and change management in detail.)

Review quiz 2.4

RQ1   What are the techniques for identifying requirements?

RQ2   What is the name of a tool dedicated to change management?

RQ3   What is a suspect trace?

2.5 Requirements business model

The *requirements determination* phase captures requirements and defines them (predominantly) in natural language statements. A formal modeling of requirements using UML is conducted afterwards in the *requirements specification* phase. Nevertheless, a high-level visual representation of gathered requirements – called *requirements business modeling* – is routinely undertaken during requirements determination.

As a minimum, high-level visual models are needed to determine the system scope, identify principal use cases and establish the most essential business classes. Figure 2.10 shows the dependencies between these three models of the requirements determination phase and the models of the remaining lifecycle phases.

Figure 2.10
Models in the
lifecycle

The leading role of use case diagrams in the lifecycle is indicated in Figure 2.10 by recognizing that the test cases, user documentation and project plans are all derived from the use case model. Apart from that, use case diagrams and class models are used concurrently and drive each other in successive development iterations. The design and implementation are also intertwined and can feed back to the requirements specification models.

System scope model

Perhaps the main concern in system development is *scope creep* due to ever-changing requirements. While some changes to requirements are unavoidable, we have to ensure that the requested changes do not go beyond the accepted scope of the project.

The question is, "How do we define the scope of the system?" Answering that question is not straightforward because any system is only a part of a larger environment – a part of a set of systems that together constitute that environment. The systems collaborate by exchanging information and invoking the services of each other. Hence, the above question could be interpreted as, "Should we implement the requirements or is the requested functionality a responsibility of another system?"

To be able to answer the scope questions, we need to know the *context* in which our system operates. We need to know the *external entities* – other systems, organizations, people, machines and so on that expect some services from us or provide services to us. In business systems, those services translate into information – *data flows*.

The system scope, therefore, can be determined by identifying external entities and input/output data flows between the external entities and our system. Our system obtains the input information and does the necessary *processing* to produce the output information.

Any requirement that cannot be supported by the system's internal processing is outside the project's scope.

UML does not provide a good visual model to define the scope of the system. Therefore, the old-fashioned *context diagram* of DFDs is frequently used for the task. Figure 2.11 shows the notation for a context diagram.

Figure 2.11
Context diagram –
notation

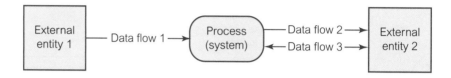

Example 2.3: telemarketing

Consider Problem statement 4, for a telemarketing system (Section 1.6.4) and construct a context diagram for it. Additionally, consider the following observations.

■ Campaigns are planned on recommendations from the society's trustees, who decide on worthy and timely charitable causes. The campaigns have to be approved by local government. The design and planning of campaigns is supported by a separate campaign database application system.

■ There is also a separate supporter database that stores and maintains information about all supporters, past and present. This database is used to select supporters to be contacted for a particular campaign. The selected *segment* of supporters is made available to telemarketing activities for the campaign.

■ Orders from supporters for lottery tickets are recorded during telemarketing for perusal by the order processing system. An order processing system maintains the status of orders in the supporter database.

A possible context diagram for this example is shown in Figure 2.12. The rounded rectangle in the center of the diagram represents the system. The squares around it designate external entities. The arrows depict data flows. The detailed information content of data flows is not visible on the diagram – that is defined separately and stored in the CASE tool's repository.

The `Telemarketing` system obtains information about the current campaign from the external entity `Campaign database`. This information includes the number and prices of tickets, lottery prizes and the campaign's duration.

Similarly, `Telemarketing` obtains supporter details from the `Supporter database`. During a telemarketing call, new information about a supporter may emerge (for instance, that the supporter intends to change his or her phone number). The `Supporter database` needs to be updated accordingly, hence, the data flow `Supporter details` is bidirectional.

The main activity is between `Telemarketing` and the `Supporter` entity. The data flow `Conversation` contains information that is exchanged on the telephone. A supporter's reply to the telemarketer's offer to buy lottery tickets is transferred along the data flow `Outcome`. A separate data flow called `Ticket placement` is used to record details of tickets ordered by a `Supporter`.

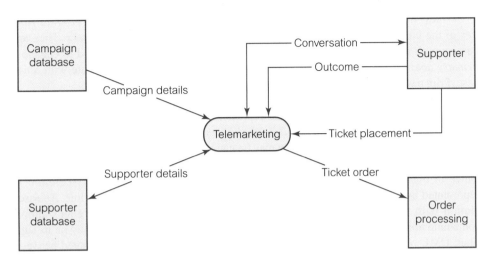

Figure 2.12
Context diagram
for a telemarketing
system

Further processing of ticket orders is outside the scope of the system. The data flow
`Ticket order` is forwarded to the external entity `Order processing`. It can be
assumed that, after orders are entered, other external entities can handle payments from
supporters, ticket mail-outs, prize draws and so on. These are not of concern as long as
the current status of orders, payments and so on is available to the system from the external entities `Campaign database` and `Supporter database`.

Business use case model

2.5.2

A *business use case model* (Kruchten 2003) is a use case model at a high level of abstraction. It identifies high-level business processes – *business use cases*. Such a use case can
define a process in a way that is abstracted completely from its realization. A *business
process* is then dissociated from an *information system process* and the whole model represents the business point of view, emphasizing organizational activities and work tasks
(these are not necessarily supported by computerized system solutions).

In practice, however, business use case models are constructed in order for business
processes to be supported by the information system under development. In such cases, a
business process is conceived as a kind of information system process. A business use
case then corresponds to what is sometimes called a *system feature*. (System features are
identified in a *vision document*. If the vision document is present, then it may be used as a
replacement for the business use case model.)

The focus of a business use case diagram is the *architecture* of business processes. The
diagram provides a bird's-eye view of desired business and system behavior. The narrative
description for each business use case is brief, business-oriented and focused on the main
flow of activities. A business use case model is not adequate for communicating to developers exactly what the system should do.

Business use cases are turned into *use cases* in the requirements specification phase. It
is in that phase that the detailed use cases are identified, narrative descriptions are
extended to include subprocesses and alternative processes, some GUI screens are
mocked up and the relationships between use cases are established.

Business actors in a business use case diagram can sometimes represent *external entities* of the context diagram. Such actors are also known as *secondary actors*. They are passive with regard to use cases. To communicate with a use case they need to engage a *primary actor* – one central to the system and able to actively communicate with a use case. Primary business actors instigate use cases by sending *events* to them.

Use cases are event-driven. The communication lines between actors and use cases are not data flows. The communication lines represent the flow of *events* from actors and the flow of *responses* from use cases. In UML, the *communication relationships* between actors and use cases are expressed as lines and may be named (stereotyped) as «communicate».

Business use cases can be linked by various relationships. The relationship of significance in business use case models is an *association relationship*. An *association* is represented by a line with or without arrowheads on one or both ends of the line. An association with an arrowhead is a *client–supplier* association – that is, a client knows something about its supplier. This also means that a client depends in some way on its supplier. UML relationships, other than associations, are not normally encouraged between business use cases. Figure 2.13 illustrates the notation for business use case diagrams.

There is an interesting dichotomy with regard to actors. Many actors must be seen as both external *and* internal to the system. They are *external* because they interact with the system from the outside, but they are also *internal* because the system may maintain information about the actors so that it can knowingly interact with the "external" actors. The system specification must describe, as a model, the system and its environment. The environment contains actors. The system may itself keep information about the actors. Hence, the specification holds two models related to actors – a model of the actor and a model of what the system records about the actor.

Figure 2.13
Business use
case diagram –
notation

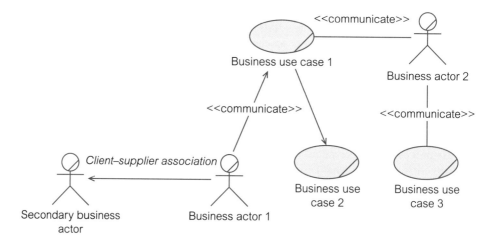

Example 2.4: telemarketing

Consider Problem statement 3 and the context diagram for a telemarketing system (Sections 1.6.4 and 2.5.1) and construct a business use case diagram.

A possible business use case diagram is presented in Figure 2.14. There are two business actors: Telemarketer and Supporter. Telemarketer is a primary actor, Supporter a secondary actor.

Telemarketer asks the system for the phone call to a supporter to be scheduled and dialed up. On successful connection, Supporter is involved as a secondary actor. The business use case Schedule phone conversation (which includes here the establishment of the connection) becomes a piece of functionality of value to both actors.

During the telephone conversation, Telemarketer may need to access and modify campaign and supporter details. This functionality is captured in the business use case CRUD campaign and supporter details (CRUD is a popular acronym that stands for the four main operations concerning data – create, read, update, delete).

There is a client–server association relationship between Schedule phone conversation and CRUD campaign and supporter details. Another way of looking at this relationship is that Phone conversation depends on CRUD campaign and supporter details.

The business use case Enter conversation outcome serves the purpose of entering the successful or unsuccessful results of the telemarketing action. This use case delivers an identifiable value to both actors.

The omission of other relationships between use cases is arbitrary. In general, all relationships between use cases can be suppressed to avoid cluttering and overcrowding the diagram. Use cases tend to have some sort of communication with most other use cases and the inclusion of *all* these relationships could defeat the abstraction principle of modeling.

Business glossary   2.5.3

One of the inconspicuous but important aspects of software development is the clarity of business and system terminology. Without such clarity, communication between project stakeholders lacks precision and can result in solving the wrong problem. To improve

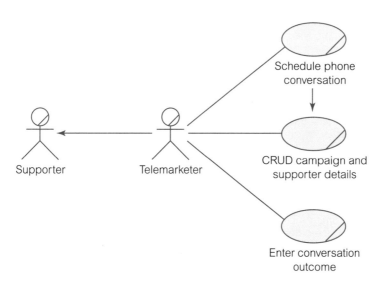

Figure 2.14
Business use case diagram for a telemarketing system

communication and avoid misunderstandings, a *glossary* of terms and definitions must be created and shared with the stakeholders.

In practice, at least a partial glossary of terms is likely to exist in the enterprise, possibly from the development of related systems. If it does not exist, building the glossary should start in the requirements determination phase. If a glossary exists, it needs to be reviewed and extended.

The glossary can be written in table format. It should provide the terms and definitions, sorted alphabetically by the terms and possibly with links to closely related terms.

Example 2.5: telemarketing

Consider Problem statement 3 and the context diagram for a telemarketing system (Sections 1.6.4 and 2.5.1) and construct a business glossary.

Table 2.2 presents an initial glossary of business terms for telemarketing. Words written in italics in the Definition column are references to terms defined elsewhere in the glossary.

Table 2.2 Business glossary (telemarketing)

Term	Definition
bonus campaign	A special series of activities, conducted within a *campaign*, to additionally entice *supporters* to buy the campaign *tickets*. Typical examples are giving free tickets for bulk or early buying or attracting new supporters. A particular kind of bonus campaign can be used in many campaigns.
campaign	A government-approved and carefully planned series of activities that are intended to achieve a *lottery* objective.
draw	An act of randomly choosing a particular *lottery ticket* as a winning ticket.
lottery	A fund-raising game of chance, organized by the charity in order to make money, in which people (*supporters*) buy numbered *tickets* to have a chance of winning a *prize* if their number is chosen in a *draw*.
placement	Acquisition of one or more *lottery tickets* by a *supporter* during *telemarketing*. The placement is paid for by a supporter with a credit card.
prize	A reward to a *supporter* who bought a *lottery ticket* that wins in the *draw*.
segment	A group of *supporters*, from the supporters database, who become targets of a particular *campaign* in its *telemarketing* activities.
supporter	A person or organization that exists in the charity database as a previous or potential buyer of *lottery tickets*.
ticket	A *lottery ticket* with a determined money value, identifying a *campaign* and uniquely numbered within all campaign tickets.
ticket order	A confirmed *placement* for tickets, with an allocated order number, and treated as a customer order by the order processing department.
telemarketer	An employee conducting *telemarketing*.
telemarketing	The activity of advertising and possibly selling *lottery tickets* by telephone.

Business class model 2.5.4

A *business class model* is a UML *class model*. Just as with the business use case model, the business class model is a higher level of abstraction than more concrete class models. A business class model identifies the main categories of business objects in the system.

Business objects have a persistent presence in an enterprise's database. They have to be contrasted with instances of other software classes, such as those handling the user interface or responsible for the application program logic.

Business classes are normally presented as business data structures with operations (services) on data suppressed. Even more, a business class model is frequently not explicit about the attribute structure of classes – class names and a brief description are sometimes sufficient.

Business classes can be linked in the model by three UML relationships: association, generalization and aggregation. Association and aggregation express semantic relationships between instances of classes (that is, objects). Generalization is a relationship between classes (that is, types of objects).

Association represents the knowledge that objects of one class have with regard to objects of another class (or with regard to different objects of the same class). The knowledge is about semantic links from an object to one or more other objects. The existence of the links enables navigation between objects (a program can navigate to linked objects).

Associations have the important properties of multiplicity and participation. *Multiplicity* defines the number of possible instances of a class that can be linked to a single instance of another class. Multiplicity is defined at both ends of an association line between classes and can be 0, 1 or n (where "n" means that many objects can be linked).

To show a possibility that some objects in an association may have zero linked objects, the multiplicity may be represented by a pair of values, namely 0..1 or 0..n. The value 0 in the pair indicates that the *participation* of an object in an association to other objects is optional (the object may or may not have association links).

Aggregation is a semantically stronger kind of association, so for example, an instance of one class "has" instances of another class. It is said that a superset class "has" a subset class or that a subset class "is a part of" the superset class. For example, Book "has" Chapter.

Generalization is a relationship of classes, such that a class "can be" another class. It is said that a superclass "can be" a subclass or that a subclass "is a kind of" the superclass. For example, Employee "can be" Manager.

Interestingly enough, it is frequently the case that the *business actors* of a business use case model are represented as *business classes* in the business class model. This is consistent with the observation that actors are frequently both external and internal to the system (Section 2.5.2). Figure 2.15 shows the notation used for business class modeling.

A first-cut business class model is shown in Figure 2.16. The diagram contains six classes, two of which (`Supporter` and `Telemarketer`) are derived from the actors in the business use case model. The call scheduling algorithm obtains a phone number and other information from the class `Supporter` and schedules the call to one of the currently available `Telemarketers`. The algorithm will ultimately be implemented in the system's database in the form of a *stored procedure*.

Figure 2.15
Business class
diagram – notation

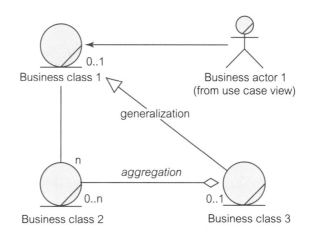

Example 2.6 telemarketing

Consider Problem statement 3, the context diagram, business use case diagram and business glossary for a Telemarketing system, (Sections 1.6.4, 2.5.1, 2.5.2 and 2.5.3) and construct a business class diagram. The following hints may be of assistance.

- ▪ The emphasis in the system is on call scheduling. The call scheduling itself is a procedural computation – that is, the solution to it is algorithmic and computational. Nevertheless, the scheduled call queues and the outcomes of calls must be stored in some data structure.

- ▪ As discussed above, information about actors may need to be stored in classes.

Figure 2.16
Business class
diagram for a
telemarketing
system

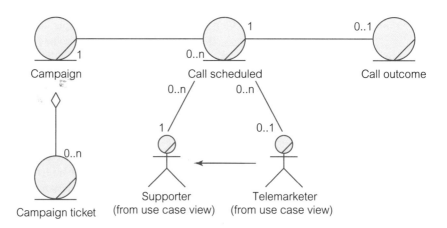

The class `Call scheduled` contains the current queue of calls, including those that are currently active. Call outcomes, such as ticket placement, are recorded in `Call outcome` as well as propagated to other affected classes, such as `Campaign ticket` or `supporter`.

The class `Campaign` contains `Campaign tickets` and can have many `Call scheduled events`. Similarly, `Supporter` and `Telemarketer` may also have many `Call scheduled`. The association between `Call scheduled` and `Call outcome` is one to one.

Review quiz 2.5

RQ1 What is another name for a business use case?

RQ2 What is the name of a relationship representing the flow of events between actors and use cases?

RQ3 What are the three main categories of relationships between business classes?

RQ4 How is the optional participation between business classes visualized in UML?

Requirements document   2.6

The *requirements document* is a tangible outcome of the requirements determination phase. Most organizations produce a requirements document according to a predefined template. The *template* defines the structure (table of contents) and the style of the document.

The main body of a requirements document consists of requirements statements. As discussed in Section 2.2.1, the requirements need to be grouped into *functional requirements* (service statements) and *non-functional requirements* (constraint statements). Although this can be confusing, functional requirements can be further classified into *function requirements* and *data requirements*. (In the literature, the term "functional requirements" is used interchangeably in its broad or narrow sense. When used in the narrow sense, the term corresponds to function requirements.)

Apart from the requirements per se, the requirements document has to address *project issues*. Normally, the project issues are discussed at the beginning of the document and again at the end. In the introductory part of the document, the project's business context is discussed, including the project's purpose, stakeholders and main constraints. Towards the end of the document, all other project issues are raised, including schedule, budget, risks and documentation.

Document templates   2.6.1

Templates for requirements documents are available from textbooks, standards organizations (IEEE, ANSI and others), web pages of consulting firms, vendors of software engineering tools and so on. Over time, each organization develops its own standard that fits its organizational practices, culture, expected readership, types of system and so on.

A requirements document template defines the structure of the document and gives detailed guidelines about what to write in each section. The guidelines may include content matters, motivation, examples and additional considerations (Robertson and Robertson 2003).

Figure 2.17 shows a typical table of contents for a requirements document. Explanations of the contents are given in the following sections.

2.6.2 Project preliminaries

The project preliminaries part of the document targets managers and decisionmakers, who are unlikely to study the whole document in detail. The *purpose and scope* of the project needs to be explained clearly at the beginning of the document, followed by the business context.

The requirements document has to make a *business case* for the system. In particular, any system planning and business modeling efforts (Sections 1.2 and 2.1), which established the need for the system, have to be referred to. The requirements document should explain how the proposed system will contribute to the organization's business objectives and goals.

Stakeholders (Section 1.1.2.1) of the system have to be identified. It is important that the *customer* is not just an impersonal department or office – people's names should be

Figure 2.17
The requirements document – table of contents

> **Requirements Document**
> *Table of contents*
>
> **1 Project preliminaries**
>   1.1 Purpose and scope of the project
>   1.2 Business context
>   1.3 Stakeholders
>   1.4 Ideas for solutions
>   1.5 Document overview
> **2 System services**
>   2.1 The scope of the system
>   2.2 Functional requirements
>   2.3 Data requirements
> **3 System constraints**
>   3.1 Interface requirements
>   3.2 Performance requirements
>   3.3 Security requirements
>   3.4 Operational requirements
>   3.5 Political and legal requirements
>   3.6 Other constraints
> **4 Project matters**
>   4.1 Open issues
>   4.2 Preliminary schedule
>   4.3 Preliminary budget
> **Appendices**
>   Glossary
>   Business documents and forms
>   References

listed. In the end, it is a person who will decide whether or not the delivered software product is acceptable.

Although a requirements document should be as far away from the technical solutions as possible, it is important to brainstorm ideas for the solution early in the development lifecycle. Indeed, the *solution envisioning* process is largely a predevelopment undertaking (Section 2.1). Any off-the-shelf solutions are of special interest. It always makes good business sense to buy a product rather than develop it from scratch where possible.

The requirements document should provide a list of existing software packages and components that ought to be investigated further as potential solutions. Note that taking up an off-the-shelf solution varies the development processes but does not dispense with the requirements analysis and system design!

Finally, it is a good idea to include an *overview* of the *rest* of the document in the project preliminaries section. This may entice a busy reader to study other parts of the document and will facilitate understanding of the document content. The overview should also explain the analysis and design methodology embraced by the developers.

System services   2.6.3

The main part of the requirements document is dedicated to the definition of the *system's services* (Section 2.2.1). This part is likely to account for more than half of the entire document. This is also just about the only part of the document that may contain high-level models for the solution – *requirements business models* (Section 2.5). Note, however, that the glossary is moved to the Appendices section.

The *scope of the system* can be modeled with a *context diagram* (Section 2.5.1). In explaining the context diagram, the boundaries for the proposed project must be clearly defined. Without this definition, the project will not be able to stand up to the demands of scope creep.

Functional requirements can be modeled using a *business use case diagram* (Section 2.5.2). However, the diagram will provide only a high-level embrace of the detailed listing of functional requirements. As discussed in Section 2.4, each requirement has to be identified, classified and defined.

Data requirements can be modeled using a *business class diagram* (Section 2.5.4). As with functional requirements, the business class diagram is not a complete definition of business data structures. Each business class needs to be explained further. The attribute content of classes ought to be described. Identifying attributes of classes must be determined. Otherwise, it is not possible to explain associations properly.

System constraints   2.6.4

System services define *what* the system must accomplish. *System constraints* (Section 2.2.1) describe *how* the system is constrained when accomplishing its services. System constraints may be set with regard to:

- interface requirements
- performance requirements

- security requirements
- operational requirements
- political and legal requirements, as well as others.

Interface requirements define how the product interfaces with users. In the requirements document, we only define the "look and feel" of the GUI. The initial design (screen painting) of the GUI will be conducted during *requirements specification* and later during *system design*.

Depending on the application domain, *performance requirements* can become quite central to the success of the project. In a narrow sense, they specify the speed (the system's *response times*) at which various tasks have to be accomplished. In a broader sense, performance requirements include other constraints – related to the system's reliability, availability, throughput and so on.

Security requirements describe users' access privileges to the information under the system's control. Users can be given restricted access to data and/or restricted rights to execute certain operations on data.

Operational requirements determine the hardware/software environment, if known, in which the system will operate. These requirements may have an impact on other aspects of the project, such as user training and system maintenance.

Political and legal requirements are frequently assumed rather than explicitly stated in the requirements document. This can be a very costly mistake. Unless these requirements are brought out into the open, the product may be difficult or impossible to deploy for political or legal reasons.

Other constraints are also possible. For example, some systems may place extra stress on ease of use (*usability requirements*) or ease with which the system can be maintained (*maintainability requirements*).

The importance of watertight definitions for system constraints cannot be overstated. There are numerous examples of failed projects due to omitted or misinterpreted system constraints. The issue is as sensitive for customers as it is for developers. Unscrupulous or desperate developers can play the system constraints card to their advantage in an effort to evade their responsibilities.

2.6.5 Project matters

The final main part of the requirements document addresses other project matters. An important section in this part is *open issues*. In here, we specify any issues that can affect the success of the project but have not been discussed under other headings in the document. These may include the expected growth in importance of some requirements that are currently out of scope and any potential problems or malpractices that deployment of the system can trigger.

A *preliminary schedule* for major tasks on the project needs to be developed. This should include the preliminary allocation of human and other resources. A project management software tool can be used to produce standard planning charts, such as PERT or Gantt charts (Maciaszek and Liong 2005).

As a direct upshot of the schedule, the *preliminary budget* can be provided. The cost of the project can be expressed as a range rather than a single, precise figure. If the requirements are well documented, one of the estimating methods for assessing the cost (such as *function point analysis*) can be used.

Appendices 2.6.6

Finally, the *appendices* contain other useful information for understanding requirements. The main inclusion here is a business glossary (Section 2.5.3). The glossary defines terms, acronyms and abbreviations used in the requirements document. The importance of a good glossary cannot be overestimated. Terminology misinterpretations can be very damaging.

One of the frequently overlooked aspects of the requirements document is that the business domain it defines can be quite well understood by studying the *documents and forms* used in workflow processes. Whenever possible, completed business forms should be included – empty forms do not convey the same level of insight.

References provide citations to documents referred to in the document or used in its preparation. These may include books and other published sources of information, but, even more importantly, the minutes of meetings, memoranda and other internal documents should also be cited.

Review quiz 2.6

RQ1 How can functional requirements be classified?

RQ2 How can any out-of-scope, but relevant, requirements be addressed in a requirements document?

Summary

This chapter took a comprehensive look at requirements determination. The determination of requirements precedes their specification. The determination process is about discovering requirements and documenting them in a mostly narrative requirements document. The requirements specification (discussed in Chapter 4) provides more formal models of requirements.

The analysis of *business processes* drives the development of information systems. On the other hand, *IT processes* can be true enablers of business innovation and create new business ideas. It is, therefore, critically important to consider *implementation strategies* when constructing *business process models*. In particular, the choice of implementation strategy determines the *capability architecture* of the system. Accordingly, architectural design should be a consideration alongside business process modeling.

Requirements elicitation follows two lines of discovery – from the domain knowledge and use cases. These complement each other and lead to the determination of a business model for the system to be developed.

There are various *methods of requirements elicitation*, including interviewing customers and domain experts, questionnaires, observation, study of documents and software systems, prototyping, brainstorming, JAD and RAD.

Requirements elicited from customers may overlap and conflict. It is a business analyst's job to resolve these overlaps and conflicts via *requirements negotiation and validation*. To do this job properly, the business analyst ought to construct a *requirements dependency matrix* and assign *risks* and *priorities* to the requirements.

Large projects *manage* large volumes of requirements. It is essential in such projects that the requirement statements be *identified and classified. Requirements hierarchies* can then be defined. These steps ensure proper *requirements traceability* in the next project stages, as well as proper handling of *change requests*.

Even though the requirements determination does not include formal system modeling, a basic *requirements business model* may be constructed. The business model can result in three generic diagrams – the context diagram, business use case diagram and business class diagram. It also initiates definitions of terms in the glossary.

A document that results from the requirements determination – the *requirements document* – begins with a high-level description of the *project preliminaries* (mostly for the benefit of the managerial readership). The main parts of the document describe *system services* (functional requirements) and *system constraints* (non-functional requirements). The final part handles other project matters, including the *schedule* and *budget* details.

Key terms

Artifact a BPMN element that provides additional modeling flexibility by allowing you to extend the basic notation; three types of artifacts are predefined: data object, group and annotation.

BPEL Business Process Execution Language.

BPMN Business Process Modeling Notation.

Brainstorming conference technique to find new ideas or a solution to a specific problem by putting aside judgment, social inhibitions and rules.

Business actor a human, organizational unit, computer system, device or other kind of active object that can interact with the system and expects a business value from that interaction.

Business capability any capacity relating to how a business IT solution can deliver specific results.

Business capability exploration the first phase of the solution envisioning process that determines business capabilities.

Business class model a high-level business model showing business objects and relationships between them.

Business object a fundamental class in the business domain; a business entity.

Business process activity that produces something of value to the organization or to its external stakeholders.

Business process model the diagram that shows the dynamic structure of the business process.

Business use case a high-level business function; a functional system feature.

Business use case model a high-level use case diagram that identifies major functional building blocks in the system.

Capability architecture an architectural design for the system that identifies high-level components of the system and interactions between them.

Capability case a solution idea making the business case for a business capability.

Class an abstraction that describes a set of objects with common attributes, operations, relationships and semantic constraints.

Component-based development the development process that builds the solution by integrating software components sourced from multiple vendors and business partners and likely to be based on SOA and/or MDA.

Connecting object a BPMN element used to connect flow objects in order to define the structure of a business process; there are three categories of connecting objects – sequence flows, message flows and associations.

Constraint statement a constraint that the system must obey.

Context diagram the top-level diagram of a DFD.

CRM Customer Relationship Management.

Custom development hand-crafted, standalone, from-scratch software development, covering all phases of the software development process (lifecycle), performed in-house and/or contracted out to consulting and development firms.

Diagram a graphical representation of a model.

Flow object the core BPMN element; there are three categories of flow objects – events, activities and gateways.

Functional requirement see *service statement*.

JAD Joint Application Development.

Non-functional requirement see *constraint statement*.

Package-based development the development process that derives the solution by customizing pre-existing software packages, such as COTS, ERP or CRM systems.

Performance a non-functional requirement that is defined by expectations regarding the response time of the system, transactions throughput, resource consumption, possible number of concurrent users and so on.

Pool a BPMN element that represents a business entity (participant) in a process; also called swimlane.

Probortunity the merging of the words "problem" and "opportunity"; used in *brainstorming*.

Process see *business process*.

Process hierarchy diagram diagram that shows the static structure of the business process.

Prototype a "quick and dirty" working model of the solution that presents a graphical user interface (GUI) and simulates the system behavior for various user events.

RAD Rapid Application Development.

Reliability a non-functional requirement that relates to the frequency and seriousness of system failures and how gracefully the system can recover from failures.

Reusability a non-functional requirement that defines the ease of reuse of previously implemented software components in new system developments.

Risk a threat to the project plan (budget, time, resource allocation and so on).

Service statement a requirement that defines a service expected of the system.

Software capability design the third phase of the solution envisioning process that decides on system implementation technologies, develops software capability architecture – and elaborates the business case with project plans and risk analysis.

Solution capability envisioning the second phase of the solution envisioning process that aims to develop the capability case into a solution concept and ensure that the solution is agreed on by the stakeholders.

Solution concept an artifact of solution capability envisioning that takes the business context as an input and produces future scenarios for new ways to work as an output.

Solution envisioning a business value-driven approach to delivering an IT service to solve an as-is business problem or to foster a to-be business innovation.

System scope model a high-level business model determining the boundaries and main responsibilities of the system.

Task an atomic activity within a process.

Usability a non-functional requirement that defines the ease of use of the system.

Multiple-choice test

MC1 In BPMN, an atomic process is also called an:

   a activity

   b task

   c event

   d job.

MC2 In BPMN, a message flow is the following modeling element:

   a flow object

   b swimlane

   c artifact

   d connector.

MC3 In solution envisioning, the modeling element that determines the business value of a piece of the functionality is a:

   a business use case

   b solution case

   c capability case

   d business case.

MC4 Which requirements elicitation method works with the notion of a probortunity statement:

   a questionnaire

   b brainstorming

   c JAD

   d none of the above.

MC5 Which requirements elicitation method works with the notion of trigger question:

   a questionnaire

   b RAD

   c JAD

   d none of the above.

MC6 A relationship stating that a class "can be" another class is called:

   a generalization

   b aggregation

   c association

   d none of the above.

MC7 An interface requirement is a:

   a functional requirement

   b system service

   c system constraint

   d none of the above.

Questions

Q1 Section 2.1.2 mentions that an important aim of business process modeling is to be able to map BPMN to Business Process Execution Language (BPEL). Use the Internet's Wikipedia (http://en.wikipedia.org/wiki/Main_Page) to find out about BPEL. Access and read Michelson (2005) (refer to the Bibliography for access information). Consider the following definition of BPEL: "BPEL is … an XML-based language, built on top of Web services specifications, which is used to define and manage long-lived service orchestrations or processes" (Michelson 2005: 4). "Decipher" this definition by explaining the constituent concepts.

Q2 A pivotal idea in solution envisioning is the solution envisioning workshop. Each workshop is conducted over one to two days and guided by a series of focal points that address key questions. The focal points are: (1) exploring the present, (2) exploring change – analyzing forces and trends, (3) capability-based design – interplay of technology and business design, (4) making commitments, and (5) future roadmap. For each of the focal points, think about possible key questions. What key questions would you be interested in asking during the workshop?

Q3 Search the Internet and/or other sources of information to decipher Hewlett-Packard's FURPS acronym. Briefly describe the meaning of the acronym's letters. Discuss how the FURPS model can be related to functional and non-functional requirements.

Q4 Search the Internet and/or other sources of information to learn about McCall's software quality model. Briefly describe the model and show how can it be helpful in requirements determination.

Q5 Requirements elicitation aims at reconciling domain knowledge requirements and use case requirements. Explain the difference between these two kinds of requirement. Should one of them take precedence over the other in the requirements determination process? Give reasons for your answer.

Q6 During interviews, it is recommended that opinionated, biased or imposing questions be avoided. Can you think about the situations where such questions may be necessary for the benefit of the project?

Q7 What is the difference between a survey and a questionnaire in requirements determination and similar tasks?

Q8 What steps would you take to prepare and conduct observation as a requirements determination technique? What practical guidelines would you apply?

Q9 What is prototyping? How is it useful for requirements determination?

Q10 What are the advantages of brainstorming and JAD in comparison with other requirements determination methods?

Q11 What is scope creep? How can it be addressed during requirements determination?

Q12 What are the typical characteristics and capabilities of requirements management tools? Search the Internet for the answer.

Q13 Why should requirements be numbered?

Q14 How are actors in a business use case diagram different from external entities in a context diagram?

Exercises: advertising expenditure

E1 Consider Problem statement 5, for the advertising expenditure example (Section 1.6.5) and the process hierarchy diagram in Example 2.1 (Section 2.1.1.2). Consider the following additional details about the way in which the AE organization manages contracts and accounts receivable:

- The majority of contacts (customers) are on annual contracts. Contracts are renegotiated once a year based on the event log for each customer. The event log makes it possible to assess how much the customer has been using our services and if the client has experienced any problems during the year. Having the complete information from the log enables our staff to conclude their negotiations quickly, possibly in a single meeting.
- For each customer on a contract, we generate an invoice on a monthly basis. The contents of the invoice are compiled from the details stored when the contract was negotiated, plus any additional services beyond the contract.
- If a contract has expired or outstanding invoices to a customer exceed a predefined limit, data delivery and other services should be suspended until the contract is renegotiated.
- Invoices are generated and sent at the end of each month. The payments are tracked. The details of invoices and payments are recorded for reporting purposes.

Construct a business process diagram for the process "Contracts and accounts receivable".

E2 Refer to Problem statement 5 in Section 1.6.5. Refer solely to the business processes as described in the problem statement. In particular, ignore "Contact management" and "Contracts and accounts receivable" (Figure 2.2 in Section 2.1.1.2 and elsewhere in Chapter 2).

Draw a context diagram for the AE system. Explain the model.

E3 Refer to Problem statement 5 in Section 1.6.5. Refer solely to the business processes as described in the problem statement. In particular, ignore "Contact management" and "Contracts and accounts receivable" (Figure 2.2 in Section 2.1.1.2 and elsewhere in Chapter 2).

Draw a business use case diagram for the AE system. Explain the model.

E4 Refer to Problem statement 5 in Section 1.6.5.

Develop an initial business glossary. Identify only entries most essential for the core AE business – advertisement measurement.

E5 Refer to Problem statement 5 in Section 1.6.5.

Draw a business class diagram for the AE system. Refer to the business glossary entries you compiled above for Exercise E4 and model only business classes most essential for the core AE business – advertisement measurement. Explain the model.

Exercises: time logging

F1 Refer to Problem statement 6 in Section 1.6.6.

Draw a high-level use case diagram for the TL software tool. Explain the model.

F2 Refer to Problem statement 6 in Section 1.6.6.

Develop a glossary of terms for the TL project.

F3 Refer to Problem statement 6 in Section 1.6.6.

Draw a high-level class diagram for the TL software tool. Explain the model.

Review quiz answers

Review quiz 2.1
RQ1   Business Process Modeling Notation (BPMN).
RQ2   Flow objects, connecting objects, pools and artifacts.
RQ3   No, it can't. Pools can communicate via message flows or via associations to common artifacts.
RQ4   Solution envisioning.
RQ5   Capability architecture.
RQ6   Custom development, package-based development and component-based development.

Review quiz 2.2

RQ1 Business analyst.

RQ2 Functional requirements (service statements) and non-functional requirements (constraint statements, supplementary requirements).

RQ3 Multiple-choice questions, rating questions and ranking questions.

RQ4 Leader, scribe, customers and developers.

RQ5 Specialists With Advanced Tools (SWAT).

Review quiz 2.3

RQ1 Context diagram.

RQ2 Conflicting requirements and overlapping requirements.

RQ3 Volatility risk.

Review quiz 2.4

RQ1 Unique identifier, sequential number within document hierarchy and sequential number within requirements category.

RQ2 Software configuration management tool.

RQ3 A suspect trace is an indication in a traceability matrix that a relationship between two linked requirements could have been invalidated as a result of changes to any of these two linked requirements or other related requirement.

Review quiz 2.5

RQ1 System feature.

RQ2 Communication relationship.

RQ3 Association, generalization and aggregation.

RQ4 It is visualized in the multiplicity definition by putting a 0 (zero) value on the relevant end of the association.

Review quiz 2.6

RQ1 Functional requirements can be classified into function requirements and data requirements.

RQ2 They can be listed in the "open issues" section.

Multiple-choice test answers

MC1 b

MC2 d

MC3 c

MC4 b

MC5 d (brainstorming works with this notion)

MC6 a

MC7 c

Answers to odd-numbered questions

Q1

BPEL is a language for the formal specification of business processes and interaction models between processes. It is an XML-based language. XML (Extensible Markup Language) is a language that describes the structure of data in Web documents so as to allow for the exchange of structured documents and data over the Internet.

BPEL extends the Web services interaction model. A Web service is a software component that uses an XML messaging system and is available over the Internet. In order to be available over Internet, a Web service explains its functionality via a public interface and provides assistance so interested parties can locate it. A Web service is one type of service that can be part of a SOA.

BPEL targets programming-in-the-large and provides support for the specification of large business transactions between collaborating services. "Orchestration is a type of collaboration in which the primary service directly invokes other services. The primary service knows the sequence of actions and the interfaces, responses, and return states of the called services." (Michelson 2005: 3)

Q3

Hewlett-Packard's FURPS is a model for assessing software quality (Grady 1992). The acronym identifies a set of five quality factors – functionality, usability, reliability, performance and supportability:

- *Functionality* defines the feature set and capabilities of the software system. The definition includes a list of delivered functions and the security aspects of the system.

- *Usability* considers human perception of the ease of use of the system. It includes such issues as system esthetics, consistency, documentation, help facilities and the training required for effective and efficient use of the system.

- *Reliability* measures the frequency and severity of system failures, accuracy of produced output, mean time to failure, ability to recover from failure and overall predictability of the system.

- *Performance* evaluates the response time of the system (on average and at pick times), transaction throughput, resource consumption, efficiency under varying workloads and so on.

- *Supportability* defines how easy it is to support the system. It combines a number of related properties, such as software understandability, maintainability (adaptability to change, serviceability), scalability (extendibility), testability, configurability, ease of installation and ease of localizing problems.

The FURPS model normally applies to assessing quality in a delivered software product. However, the five quality factors can serve as a handy classification for user requirements to be delivered in the system under development. In such a classification, the FURPS functionality component relates to *functional requirements*, while the remaining four factors define *non-functional requirements*.

The one-to-four proportion between functional and non-functional requirements is by no means a reflection on the relative importance of these two categories of requirements. In system development, the effort and cost expended on functional requirements (system services) frequently outweighs the effort and cost of ensuring non-functional requirements (system constraints).

Q5

The *domain knowledge requirements* are obtained from the generic understanding of the application domain. This includes the domain expert's (or the analyst's) experience in the domain, published work about the domain, any widely disseminated practices and regulations and solutions employed in off-the-shelf systems.

The *use case requirements* are obtained from studying the specific business practices and processes. They capture the ways in which business is done in a particular organization. While some use case requirements will align with the domain knowledge requirements, others will not (because they reflect the specific ways that the things are done in that organization).

Normally, both kinds of requirements are collected more or less in parallel. It is possible that the initial investigations will focus on the domain knowledge requirements, but eventually all these requirements must be validated with customers. In other words, the domain knowledge requirements are either incorporated into a use case (and become use case requirements) or they are discarded.

The process of validating *domain knowledge requirements* is frequently centered on revisions to the business class model (and – in later stages – to the class model). This is shown in Figure 2.9 by means of a dependency relationship between the business use case model and the business class model.

Although not shown in Figure 2.9, feedback from the business class model (and therefore domain knowledge requirements) to the business use case model (and therefore use case requirements) is also possible. If such feedback happens, it may signify that "the customer is not always right" – that is, the customer is prepared to reassess a use case requirement to make it correspond to a generic domain knowledge requirement.

Later in the analysis and design process, the use case requirements take center stage. All development models and artifacts are driven by and validated against the use case requirements.

Q7

Both a survey and a questionnaire for requirements determination are questionnaires. The main difference is that a *survey* seeks public verification of some facts, whereas a *questionnaire* (in requirements determination and similar tasks) is a fact-finding device.

Surveys and questionnaires bring about different kinds of inaccuracies and respondent bias. Survey results can be distorted because of the inability of the respondents to answer a question or their deliberate "coloring" of the facts. Questionnaire results can suffer from similar deficiencies, but the distortions can be aggravated by questions asking for an opinion or subjective assessment. Adding to the trouble are questions asking for answers using scaling values.

Q9

Prototyping is a quick modeling and implementation of a proposed system. A *prototype* is an inefficient, low-quality solution with many implementation compromises. The main purpose of a prototype is to give users an idea of the "look and feel" of the actual system.

The prototype is evaluated by the users and used to validate and refine requirements for the system to be developed. The prototype provides dynamic visual displays and simulates interaction with human users. This facilitates the users' understanding of requirements supported by the software and allows appraisal of software behavior.

Provided that proper customer resources are committed to the evaluation of the prototype and the required changes to the requirements are made in a timely fashion, the prototype is one of the most powerful techniques for requirements determination.

Q11

Scope creep is the growth of customers' expectations as the project progresses and the associated demand for new requirements to be implemented in the system. The new requirements are normally not accounted for in the schedule and budget.

A good technique to counteract scope creep is to document all *requests for change* and address them in the context of the system scope model in the requirements document. A high-level scope model is frequently modeled in the context diagram for the system. More detailed requirements are captured in use case diagrams.

Any demands for new requirements should be modeled in the context diagram and/or use case diagrams and the dynamics of changing project parameters should be explained to customers. The parameters should include the impact on the project's schedule and cost.

Scope creep is due not only to changing business conditions but also shortcomings in the work done during the requirements determination phase. Employing modern methods of requirements elicitation, such as prototyping, can diminish the risk of scope creep.

Finally, developing the system in short iterations with frequent deliveries reduces the need for requirements changes within iterations. Changes between iterations are less troublesome.

Q13

The system is constructed to satisfy customers' requirements. In all but trivial systems, the requirements are defined on several levels, with a higher-level requirement consisting of a number of more specific lower-level requirements. The total number of requirements can easily reach thousands.

To ensure that all customers' requirements will be implemented in the system, they need to be *structured and numbered* to start with. Only then can the implementation of requirements be systematically checked and managed.

The project and change management are dependent on the precise *identification* of all requirements. Requirements are allocated to developers and other resources, the project plans are structured in relation to groupings of requirements, defects are traced back to the numbered requirements and so on.

Solutions to exercises: AE

Note that Maciaszek and Liong (2005) offer additional discussion and solutions for the AE domain.

E1

The *business process diagram* is shown in Figure 2.18. The processes and tasks are distributed across two pools – Customer relationship department and Accounts receivable. Event timers and event rules are used to add precision to sequence flows.

E2

The *context diagram*, as shown in Figure 2.19, is a high-level model that identifies the scope of the AE system. There are two external entities: `Media outlet` and `AE client`. Media outlets supply advertising data to `AE`. AE clients receive campaign monitoring reports and expenditure reports from `AE`.

The transformation of advertising data into reports is the internal function of `AE`. The verification of advertisements, manual entry and other individual `AE` functions will acquire and supply data, but these are considered internal data flows within the `AE` "bubble". For example, the supply of newspapers, magazines, video reels and so on for manual entry is treated as internal to the system (at least for the time being).

Figure 2.18
Business process
diagram for an
advertising
expenditure
system

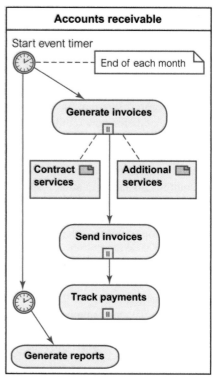
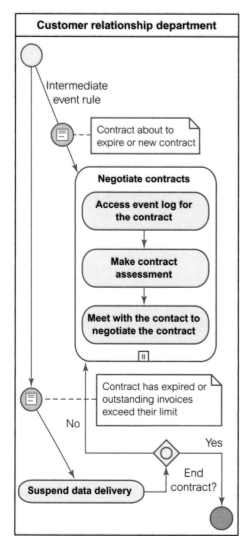

Figure 2.19
Context diagram
for an advertising
expenditure
system

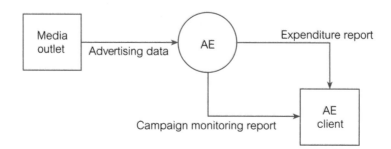

E3

The business use cases in Figure 2.20 have been organized from top to bottom to signify the sequence of performing the business functions. They constitute the main functional modules of the AE system.

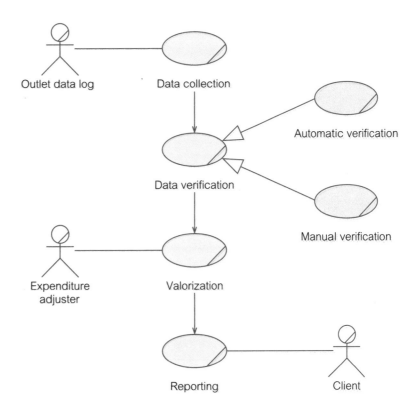

Figure 2.20
Business use case diagram for an advertising expenditure system

The business use case model divides the AE system into four business uses cases connected by unidirectional associations. The sequence of associations signifies the main AE business work flow – from data collection to verification, valorization and reporting.

Data collection communicates with Outlet data log to obtain advertising log information (this is normally done by electronic transfer). The process of data collection includes matching received advertisement details with the advertisements previously recorded in the AE database. The matching process is not distinguished in the model as a separate use case.

Data verification confirms that the advertisement details obtained are valid and logical in the context of surrounding information (other advertisements, programs and so on). Once entered and verified, the advertisements undergo Valorization. This is the process of assigning expenditure estimates to advertisements.

Reporting produces customized reports to clients who buy or subscribe to the reports. Reports can be distributed in various forms, such as e-mail, CDs or on paper.

E4

The glossary is presented in Table 2.3.

Table 2.3 Business glossary for advertising expenditure

Term	Definition
ad instance	A particular occurrence of an *ad* – that is, each incidence of an ad's broadcast, screening or publication.
adlink	An association between an *ad*, the *product* it advertises, the *advertiser* who pays for the exposure of the ad and the *agency* responsible for the booking of that exposure.
advertisement (ad)	A unique piece of creative work that may be broadcast, screened, published or otherwise exposed any number of times. Each ad exposure by a media outlet is known in the AE system as an *ad instance*.
advertiser	A company that uses an *outlet* to expose an *advertisement* in order to promote a *product*.
agency	An organization that handles the advertising planning and media buying for an *advertiser*. The goal of an *agency* is to optimize advertising expenditure.
category	A name in a hierarchical classification of products. There are an unlimited number of levels in the hierarchy (that is, category, subcategories, down to products). *Products* may only be categorized at the lowest level of the category hierarchy.
organization	A business entity that AE deals with. There are different types of organization, including *advertisers*, *agencies* and *outlets*. An organization may be one, many or none of these types.
outlet	An organization that exposes an *advertisement*. This could be a television or radio station, publication or company advertising in cinemas and outdoors.
product	Merchandise or service that may be advertised. Products may be categorized (that is, a product can belong to a *category* of products).

E5

Six business classes are recognized (see Figure 2.21). `AdvertisementInstance` embodies individual occurrences of an advertisement. `Advertisement` is a unique piece of creativity that may be broadcast, screened or published any number of times. `AdvertisementProduct` captures the product that is the aim of the advertisement.

There are also three organizational classes. `Outlet` stores information about media companies. `Advertiser` is an organization that uses the media to advertise a product. `Agency` is an organization that handles advertising planning and media buying on behalf of an advertiser.

The diagram also shows the principal relationships between business classes. The relationship between `Agency` and `Advertiser` is an aggregation. Other relationships are associations.

Figure 2.21
Business class
diagram for an
advertising
expenditure
system

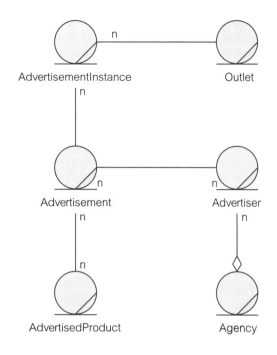

Chapter

3

Fundamentals of Visual Modeling

Objectives

This chapter presents the fundamentals of visual object modeling demonstrating various UML diagrams and explaining how they fit together. Each UML diagram emphasizes a particular *view* on the system under development. To understand the system in its entirety, multiple UML diagrams, representing different views, have to be developed and integrated. To illustrate the integrative principle behind various UML views, the presented diagrams are drawn from the same application domain – the video store (VS) case study (Section 1.6.2).

This chapter teaches UML modeling, but it assumes that the reader has some prior understanding of object-oriented technology. If this is not the case, the reader is invited to study beforehand the material in the Appendix: Fundamentals of object technology. For readers familiar with object technology, the Appendix may serve as a refresher.

By reading this chapter you will:

- learn how UML models provide various intersecting views on the system under development
- understand that the real value of some models is not in the graphical representation but in textual descriptions and other forms of specification, the use case view being a case in point
- recognize that behavior modeling with use cases and activities sets the agenda for structural models, including class diagrams
- understand that class diagrams are the most complete definition of the system under development and the resulting implementation is a realization of classes and other objects defined in the class model
- appreciate the importance of interaction modeling for defining and analyzing the run-time behavior of the system
- learn about the necessity of constructing state machine models for these classes and other elements of the system that exhibit dynamic state changes and need to conform to strict business rules
- gain knowledge of the component and deployment models that allow you to capture the implementation view of the system.

The use case view

3.1

The *use case model* is the main UML representative and the focal point of behavior modeling. *behavior modeling* presents the dynamic view of the system – it models function requirements. A behavior model represents business transactions, operations and algorithms on data. There are several visualization techniques for behavior modeling – the use case diagram, sequence diagram, communication diagram and activity diagram.

In practice, the importance of **use cases** goes even further. Use cases drive the entire software development lifecycle, from requirements analysis to testing and maintenance. They are the focal point and reference for most development activities (see Figure 2.10 in Section 2.5).

System behavior is what a system does when it is responding to external events. In UML, the outwardly visible and testable system behavior is captured in use cases. Consistently with a model being able to be applied at various levels of abstraction, a use case model may capture the behavior of a system as a whole or the behavior of any part of the system – a subsystem, component or class, for example.

A *use case* performs a business function that is *outwardly visible* to an actor and can be separately *tested* later in the development process. An *actor* is whoever or whatever (person, machine) interacts with a use case. The actor interacts with the use case in expectation of receiving a useful result.

A *use case diagram* is a visual representation of actors and use cases, together with any additional definitions and specifications. A use case diagram is not just a diagram but also a fully documented partial model of the system's intended behavior. The same understanding applies to other UML diagrams. The model is said to be "partial" because normally a *UML model* consists of many diagrams (and related documentation) representing various viewpoints on the model.

It is worthwhile emphasizing again the point made in Section 2.5.2, that a use case model can be viewed as a generic technique for describing all business processes, not just information system processes. When used in such a capacity, a use case model would include all manual business processes and then identify which of these processes should be automated (and become information system processes). However, despite the attractiveness of this proposition, this is not typical practice in system modeling. Normally only automated processes are captured.

3.1.1 Actors

Actors and use cases are determined from the analysis of the function requirements. Function requirements are materialized in use cases. Use cases satisfy function requirements by providing a result of value to an actor. It is immaterial whether the business analyst chooses to identify actors first and then use cases or the other way around.

An actor is a **role** that somebody or something *external* to the subject plays with regard to a use case. An actor is not a particular instance of somebody or something, so somebody named "Joe" is not an actor. "Joe" can play the role of customer and be represented in the use case model by the actor Customer. In general, Customer does not even have to be a person. It could be an organization or a machine.

A *subject* is any group of use cases for which a use case model is drawn (such as a subsystem, component, class). An actor *communicates* with the subject by, for example, exchanging signals and data.

A typical graphical image for an actor is a "stick person" (see Figure 3.1). In general, an actor can be shown as a **class** rectangular symbol. Like a normal class, an actor can have attributes and operations (events that it sends or receives). Figure 3.1 demonstrates three graphical representations of actors.

3.1.2 Use cases

A *use case* represents a unit of functionality of value to an actor. However, not all use cases need to be directly associated with an actor. Such use cases bring value to an actor by being associated with one or more other use cases that, in turn, are associated with an actor.

Use cases can be grouped together to represent a subject. "Each use case specifies some behavior, possibly including variants, that the subject can perform in collaboration with one or more actors. Use cases define the offered behavior of the subject without reference to its internal structure" (UML 2005: 578).

Use cases can be derived from the identification of tasks of the actor. The question to ask is, "What are the actor's responsibilities towards the subject and expectations from the subject?" Use cases can also be determined from direct analysis of functional requirements. In many instances, a *functional requirement* maps directly to a *use case*.

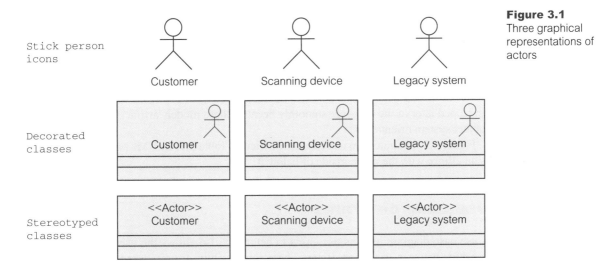

Figure 3.1
Three graphical
representations of
actors

Table 3.1 shows how selected function requirements for the video store system can be used to identify actors and use cases. Two actors are involved in all four requirements, but clearly the level of the actors' involvement varies from requirement to requirement. The `Scanning device` is not selected as an actor – it is considered to be internal to the system.

Table 3.1 Assignment of requirements to actors and use cases for a video store

Requirement no.	Requirement	Actors	Use case(s)
1	Before a video can be rented out, the system confirms the customer's identity and standing by swiping over scanner his/her video store membership card	`Customer, Employee`	`Scan membership card`
2	A videotape or disk can be swiped over a scanner to obtain its description and price (fee) as part of the customer's enquiry or rental request	`Customer, Employee`	`Scan video medium`
3	Customer pays the nominal fee before the video can be rented out. Payment may be in cash or by debit/credit card	`Customer, Employee`	`Accept payment Charge payment to card`
4	The system verifies all conditions for renting out the video, acknowledges that the transaction can go ahead, and prints the receipt for the customer	`Employee, Customer`	`Print receipt`

The use cases can be named using the subject's or actors' viewpoint. Table 3.1 leans towards the employee's viewpoint, evidenced by the wording, for example, `Accept payment` rather than `Make payment`.

Naming use cases from the actor's perspective is not always a recommended practice. It is easy to argue that they should be named from the external actor's perspective. However, the latter approach makes it difficult to connect use cases and models/artifacts developed later in the lifecycle smoothly because these models/artifacts will take a strong subject/system orientation.

Figure 3.2 illustrates the use cases identified in Table 3.1. In UML, a use case is drawn as an ellipse with the name inside or below it.

3.1.3 Use case diagrams

A use case diagram assigns use cases to actors. It also allows the user to establish relationships between use cases, if any. These relationships are discussed in Chapter 4. The use case diagram is the principal visualization technique for a behavioral model of the system. The diagram elements (use cases and actors) need to be described further to provide a document with complete *use case specifications* (see next section).

Figure 3.3 incorporates the use cases of Figure 3.2 into a diagram with the actors. Figure 3.4 represents the same model with use cases assigned to a subject. Although the relative placement of the actors and use cases in the diagram is arbitrary, modeling with subjects makes it necessary to place the actors around the subject box. Note that the same actor can be shown multiple times on the drawing.

The models in Figures 3.3 and 3.4 show that the `Employee` actor engages directly with all use cases. The `Customer` actor depends on the `Employee` actor to achieve most of his or her goals, so there is a *dependency* relationship between `Customer` and `Employee`. The direct communication between `Customer` and `Charge payment to card` signifies the need for the `Customer` to enter his or her PIN and confirm the payment on the card-scanning device.

Figure 3.2
Use cases for a video store system

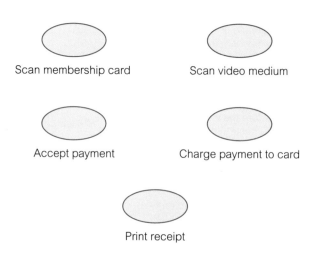

Scan membership card

Scan video medium

Accept payment

Charge payment to card

Print receipt

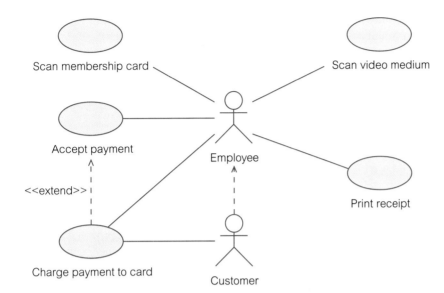

Figure 3.3
A use case
diagram for a
video store
system

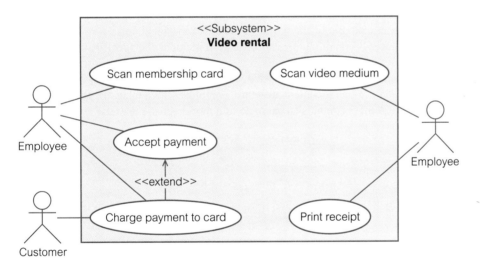

Figure 3.4
A use case
diagram featuring
a subject for a
video store
system

In general, use case diagrams allow a few kinds of relationships between modeling elements. These relationships are discussed in Chapter 4. The «extend» relationship in Figures 3.3 and 3.4 signifies that the functionality of Accept payment may sometimes be extended (supported) by the use case Charge payment to card.

Documenting use cases   3.1.4

The dynamics of each use case should be specified separately using other UML models (such as interactions, activities or state machines) and/or described in a *flow of events* document. The latter is a textual document that defines what the system has to do when

USE CASE Description !!!

the actor activates a use case. The structure of a *use case document* can vary, but a typical description would contain the following information (Quatrani 2000):

■ a brief description

■ the actors involved

■ the preconditions necessary for the use case to start

■ a detailed description of the flow of events, including:

    – the main flow of events, which can be broken down to show subflows of events (subflows can be further divided into smaller subflows to improve the document's readability)

    – alternative flows to define exceptional situations

■ postconditions, which define the state of the system after the use case ends.

The use case document evolves as the development of the project progresses. In the early stage of requirements determination, only a brief description is written. Other parts of the document are written gradually and iteratively. A complete document emerges at the end of the requirements specification phase. At that stage, the prototypes of GUI screens can be added to the document. Later on, the use case document is used to produce the user documentation for the implemented system.

Table 3.2 is an example of the narrative specification for the use case `Accept payment` from Figures 3.3 and 3.4. The specification includes the specification for `Charge payment to card`, which extends `Accept payment`. The tabular form is not the usual way of documenting use cases. Use case documents can consist of many pages (ten or so on average) and a normal document structure, complete with a table of contents, would be the norm. Section 6.5.3 contains an example of a more realistic use case document.

Review quiz 3.1

RQ1 What are the most important behavior modeling techniques?

RQ2 Is the use case diagram the same as the use case specification?

3.2 The activity view

The *activity model* represents a behavior as being composed of individual elements. The behavior may be a specification of a use case. It may also be a piece of functionality that can be reused in many places. Activity models fill a gap between a high-level representation of system behavior in *use case models* and much lower-level representation of behavior in *interaction models* (sequence and communication diagrams).

The activity diagram shows the steps of a computation. The execution steps for an **activity** are called **actions**. Actions cannnot be broken down further within an activity. The diagram depicts which steps are executed in sequence and which can be executed

Table 3.2 Narrative specification for use case for the video store

Use case	Accept payment
Brief description	This use case allows an Employee to accept payment from a `Customer` for a video rental. The payment may be made in cash or by debit/credit card.
Actors	`Employee, Customer`
Preconditions	`Customer` expresses readiness to rent the video, he/she possesses a valid membership card and the video is available for rental.
Main flow	The use case begins when the `Customer` decides to pay for the video rental and offers cash or debit/credit card payment.
	The `Employee` requests the system to display the rental charge together with basic customer and video details.
	If the `Customer` offers cash payment, the `Employee` handles the cash, confirms to the system that the payment has been received and asks the system to record the payment as made.
	If the `Customer` offers debit/credit card payment, the `Employee` swipes the card, requests the `Customer` to type the card's PIN, select debit or credit account and transmit the payment. Once the payment has been confirmed electronically by the card provider, the system records the payment as made.
	The use case ends
Alternative flows	The `Customer` does not have sufficient cash and does not offer card payment. The `Employee` asks the system to verify the `Customer's` rating (derived from the customer's history of payments). The `Employee` decides whether to rent out the video with no or with partial payment. Depending on the decision, the `Employee` cancels the transaction (and the use case terminates) or proceeds with partial payment (and the use case continues)
	The `Customer`'s card does not swipe properly through the scanner. After three unsuccessful attempts, the `Employee` enters the card number manually. The use case continues
Postconditions	If the use case was successful, the payment is recorded in the system's database. Otherwise, the system's state is unchanged

concurrently. The flow of control from one action to the next is called a **control flow**. "By flow, we mean that the execution of one node affects, and is affected by, the execution of other nodes, and such dependencies are represented by *edges* in the activity diagram" (UML 2005: 324).

If a use case document has been completed, then activities and actions can be discovered from the description of the *main and alternative flows*. However, activity models can have other uses in system development apart from providing detailed specifications for use cases (Fowler 2004). They can be used to understand a business process at a high level of abstraction before any use cases are produced. Alternatively, they can be used at a much lower level of abstraction to design complex sequential algorithms or design concurrency in multithreaded applications.

3.2.1 Actions

If the activity modeling is used to visualize the sequencing of actions in a use case, then actions can be established from the use case document. Table 3.3 lists the statements in the main and alternative flows of the use case document and identifies the actions relating to them.

An action is represented in UML by a round-cornered rectangle. The actions identified in Table 3.3 are drawn in Figure 3.5.

3.2.2 Activity diagrams

An *activity diagram* shows flows connecting actions and other **nodes**, such as decisions, forks, joins, merges and object nodes. Typically, there is one-to-one correspondence between an activity and the activity diagram – that is, activities are shown as activity diagrams. However, nesting of activities in a single diagram is also permitted.

Table 3.3 Finding actions in main and alternative flow for the video store

No.	Use case statement	Action
1	The `Employee` requests the system to display the rental charge together with basic customer and video details	`Display transaction details`
2	If the `Customer` offers cash payment, the `Employee` handles the cash, confirms to the system that the payment has been received and asks the system to record the payment as made	`Key in cash amount` `Confirm transaction`
3	If the `Customer` offers debit/credit card payment, the `Employee` swipes the card and then requests the `Customer` to type the card's PIN, select debit or credit account and transmit the payment. Once the payment has been confirmed electronically by the card provider, the system records the payment as made	`Swipe the card` `Accept card number` `Select card account` `Confirm transaction`
4	The `Customer` does not have sufficient cash and does not offer card payment. The `Employee` asks the system to verify the `Customer`'s rating (which accounts for the customer's history of payments). The `Employee` decides whether or not to rent out the video with no or partial payment. Depending on the decision, the `Employee` cancels the transaction (and the use case terminates) or proceeds with partial payment (and the use case continues)	`Verify customer rating` `Refuse transaction` `Allow rent with no payment` `Allow rent with partial payment`
5	The `Customer`'s card does not swipe properly through the scanner. After three unsuccessful attempts, the `Employee` enters the card number manually	`Enter card number manually`

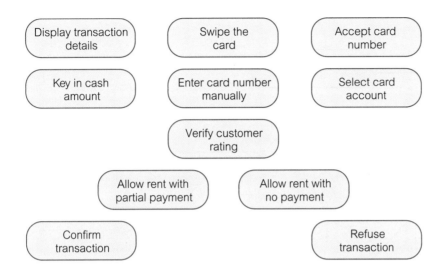

Figure 3.5
The actions for a use case for a video store system

Unless an activity diagram represents a continuous loop, the diagram may have an initial action that starts the activity and one or more final actions. A solid filled circle represents the start of an activity. The end of an activity is shown using a bull's eye symbol.

Flows can *branch* and *merge*. These create *alternative* computation *threads*. A diamond box shows a branch condition. The exit from a branch condition is controlled by an event (such as Yes, No) or by a guard condition (such as [green light], [good rating]).

Flows can also *fork* and *rejoin*. This creates *concurrent* (parallel) computation *threads*. The fork or join of flows is represented by a bar line. An activity diagram without concurrent processes resembles a conventional *flowchart* (there is no example of concurrent behavior in this section).

To draw the diagram for the video store example, the actions identified in Figure 3.5 have to be connected by flows, as demonstrated in Figure 3.6. `Display transaction details` is the initial action. The *recursive flow* for this action recognizes the fact that the display is continuously refreshed until the computation moves to the next node.

During `Display transaction details`, the customer can offer cash or card payment, which leads to the execution of one of two possible computation threads. Several actions to manage a card payment are combined in Figure 3.6 in an activity node called `Handle card payment`. This kind of nesting of actions is convenient when a flow is possible from any of the nested actions. If this is the case, the flow can be drawn from the activity node, as shown for the flow to the branch condition called `Payment problems?`

The need to test the condition `Payment problems?` may arise from problems with the card payment as well as the possibility of it being due to the customer having insufficient cash. If there are no payment issues, then the rental transaction is confirmed and the processing terminates on the final action. Otherwise, the customer rating is verified. Depending on the rating, the rent transaction is declined (if `[Bad]` rating), allowed with partial payment (if `[Good]` rating) or allowed with no payment (if `[Excellent]` rating).

Figure 3.6
An activity diagram for a use case for a video store system

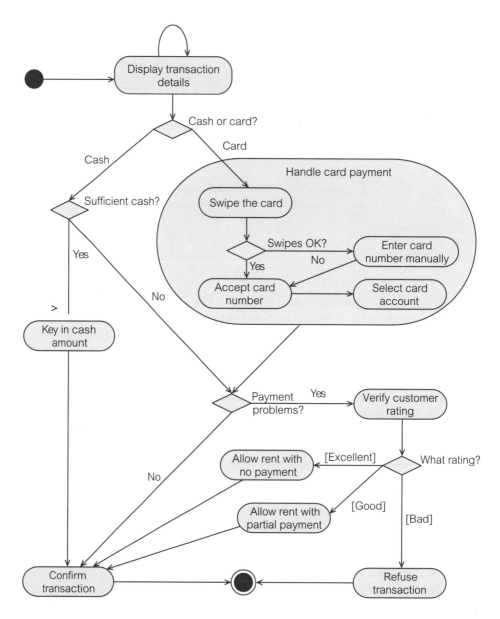

Review quiz 3.2

RQ1 Can an activity model be used as a specification of a use case?

RQ2 Flows in an activity diagram connect actions and other diagram nodes. What are these other nodes?

The structure view

The *structure view* represents the *static view* of the system – it represents data structures and their relationships and identifies operations that act on these data. The main visualization technique for static modeling is the *class diagram* – that is, the main kind of *structure diagram* (other structure diagrams are component and deployment diagrams).

Class modeling integrates and embodies all other modeling activities. Class models define the structures that capture the internal state of the system. They identify classes and their attributes, including relationships. They also define the operations necessary to fulfill the dynamic behavioral requirements of the system specified in use cases. When implemented in a programming language, classes represent both the static structure and the dynamic behavior of the application.

Accordingly, class models are constructed by referring to most, if not all, fundamental object technology concepts (see Appendix). Understanding these concepts is a necessary but not sufficient condition for working with class models. It is a necessary condition for reading (understanding) class models, but it is not a sufficient condition for writing (developing) them. Developing class models demands additional skills that have to do with the proper use of abstraction and the ability to (iteratively) integrate a variety of inputs into a single coherent solution.

The outcome of class modeling is a class diagram and related textual documentation. In this chapter, class modeling is discussed after use case modeling, but, in practice, these two activities are typically conducted in parallel. The two models feed off each other by providing auxiliary but complementary information. Use cases facilitate class discovery and, conversely, class models can lead to the discovery of overlooked use cases.

Classes

In the discussion so far, we have used classes to define *business objects*. Our class examples have all been long-lived (persistent) business entities, such as order, shipment, customer, student and so on. These are the classes that define the *database model* for an application domain. For that reason, such classes are frequently called *entity classes* (model classes). They represent persistent database objects.

Entity classes define the essence of any information system. Indeed, requirements analysis is interested predominantly in entity classes. However, for the system to function, other classes are needed as well. The system needs classes that define GUI objects (such as screen forms) – called the *presentation* (*boundary, view*) *classes*. The system also needs classes that control the program's logic and process user events – the *control classes*. Other categories of classes are needed as well, such as the classes responsible for communication with external data sources – sometimes called *resource classes*. The responsibility for managing entity objects in the memory cache in order to satisfy business transactions is given to yet another category of classes – *mediator classes*.

Depending on the particular modeling approach used, classes other than entity classes may or may not be addressed in any detail in a requirements analysis. The same thinking may apply to the definition of operations in early class models. Initial modeling of non-entity classes and the definition of operations may be postponed to the interaction view (Section 3.4) and more detailed modeling may be postponed to the system design phase.

Following the approach taken for finding actors and use cases (see Table 3.1), we can construct a table that assists in finding classes from the analysis of functional requirements. Table 3.4 assigns the functional requirements to the entity classes.

Finding classes is an iterative task as the initial list of candidate classes is likely to change. Answering a few questions may help to determine whether a concept in a requirement statement is a candidate class or not. The questions are the following:

- Is the concept a container for data?
- Does it have separate attributes that will take on different values?
- Would it have many instance objects?
- Is it in the scope of the application domain?

The list of classes in Table 3.4 still raises many questions.

- What's the difference between `Video` and `Videotape`/`VideoDisk`? Is `Video` just a generic term for `Videotape`/`VideoDisk`? If so, don't we need a class to describe the video `Movie` or other content of the video medium? Perhaps a class called `Movie` is required?
- Is the meaning of `Rental` in requirements 2, 3 and 4 the same? Is it all about a rental transaction?
- Perhaps `MembershipCard` is part of `Customer`?
- Is there a need to distinguish separate classes for `CashPayment` and `CardPayment`?

Table 3.4 Assignment of requirements to entity classes for a video store

Requirement no.	Requirement	Entity class
1	Before a video can be rented out, the system confirms the customer's identity and standing by swiping his/her video store membership card over a scanner	`Video, Customer` `MembershipCard`
2	A videotape or disk can be swiped over the scanner to obtain its description and price (fee) as part of a customer's enquiry or rental request	`Videotape,` `VideoDisk` `Customer, Rental`
3	The customer must pay the nominal fee before the video can be rented out. The payment may be in cash or by debit/credit card	`Customer, Video,` `Rental, Payment`
4	The system verifies all conditions for renting out the video, acknowledges that the transaction can go ahead and prints the receipt for the customer	`Rental, Receipt`

- Although a video store employee, as an actor, is not explicitly mentioned in the requirements in Table 3.4, it is clear that the system must have knowledge of which employees have been involved in rental transactions. Clearly, there is a need for the class `Employee`.

Answering these and similar questions is not easy and requires an in-depth knowledge of application requirements. Figure 3.7 includes all the classes identified in Table 3.4 as well as those raised in the above discussion. Note that the classes `Customer` and `Employee` have already appeared as *actors* in the use case diagram, hence the annotation "from use case view." This duality of actors as external entities interacting with the system and as internal entities about which the system must have some knowledge is quite common in system modeling.

Attributes   3.3.2

The structure of a class is defined by its **attributes** (see Appendix, Section A.3.1). The analyst must have some appreciation of the attribute structure when initially declaring a class. In practice, the main attributes are usually allocated to a class immediately after the class has been added to the model.

Attributes are discovered from user requirements and domain knowledge. Initially, the modeler concentrates on defining *identifying attributes* for each class – that is, the one or more attributes in a class that have unique values across all instances of the class. Such attributes are frequently referred to as *keys*. Ideally, a key should consist of one attribute. In some cases, a set of attributes constitutes a key.

Once the identifying attributes are known, the modeler should define the main *descriptive attributes* for each class. These are attributes that describe the main informational content of the class. There is no need, as yet, to start defining *non-primitive types* for attributes (see Appendix, Section A.3.1). Most attributes that look like they require non-primitive types can be typed as strings of characters. The strings can be converted to non-primitive types in later modeling stages.

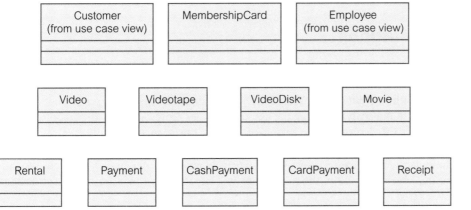

Figure 3.7
Classes for a video store system

Figure 3.8
Primitive attributes
in classes for a
video store
system

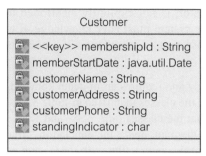
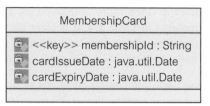

Figure 3.8 shows two video store classes with primitive attributes. Both classes have identical keys (`membershipId`). This confirms the question, raised in Section 3.3.1, that `MembershipCard` has some interesting relationships to `Customer`. This issue will definitely resurface in later modeling stages.

Some attributes in Figure 3.8 are typed as `java.util.Date`. This is a `Date` data type provided by a Java library and, although it is a non-primitive data type, it is not *user-defined* (and, therefore, not contradicting the assumption that only primitive types are used).

In fact, from the Java viewpoint, the `String` data type is also a non-primitive type. Some attributes, such as `customerAddress`, are likely to be given a user-defined non-primitive type later on (that is, some kind of `Address` class will need to be created). For now, such attributes are typed as `String`.

The attribute `standingIndicator` is typed as `char`. This attribute captures the standing (rating) assigned to each customer based on his or her past history of payments, timely return of videos and so on. The rating can range from, say, A to E, where A can mean an excellent rating and E the worst rating given to the customer – that is, a customer who is about to be excluded from membership.

Admittedly and understandably, there is a significant number of arbitrary decisions in defining attributes in Figure 3.8. For example, the presence of `memberStartDate` in `Customer` instead of `Membership card`, can be questioned. Similarly, the omission of `customerName` and `customerAddress` in `MembershipCard` would raise a few eyebrows.

3.3.3 Associations

Associations between classes establish pathways for easy object collaboration (see Appendix, Section A.3.1). In the implemented system, the associations will be represented with attribute types that designate associated classes (see Appendix, Section A.3.1.1). In the analysis model, the association lines represent these associations.

Figure 3.9 demonstrates two associations between three video store classes – `Customer`, `Rental` and `Payment`. Both associations are of the same one-to-many multiplicity (see Appendix , Section A.5.2). The role names for the associations are shown. In the implemented system, the role names will be converted into attributes that designate classes (see Appendix, Section A.3.1.1).

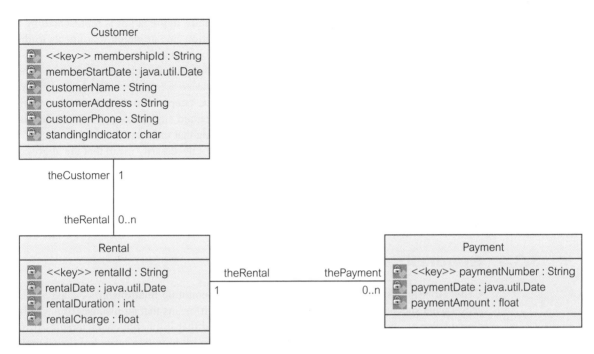

Figure 3.9 Associations for a video store system

`Customer` can be associated with many video `Rental` transactions. Each `Rental` applies to a single `Customer`. There is no indication in the model if more than one video can be rented in a single transaction. Even if this is allowed, all videos have to be rented for the same period of time (as only one value of `rentalDuration` is possible).

It is possible to pay for a `Rental` in more than one `Payment`. This implies that the `paymentAmount` does not have to be paid in full and can be smaller than `rentalCharge`. It is also possible to rent a video without immediate payment (a `Rental` object may be associated with zero `Payment` objects). This is allowed by an alternative flow in the use case specification (see Table 3.2).

The model in Figure 3.9 does not include an explicit association between `Payment` and `Customer`. From the semantic point of view, such an association is not necessary. The customer for a payment can be identified by "navigating" through the rental transaction. This is possible because each `Payment` object is associated with a single `Rental` object and each `Rental` object is associated with a single `Customer`. However, it is likely that an association between `Payment` and `Customer` will be added to the model during the design stage (this may be motivated by considerations related to processing efficiency).

Aggregation   3.3.4

Aggregation *and* **composition** are stronger forms of association with ownership semantics (see Appendix, Section A.6). In a typical commercial programming environment, aggregations and compositions are likely to be implemented like associations – with attribute types that designate associated classes. Visually, aggregation is represented by a white diamond adornment on the end of the association line at which it connects to the aggregate (superset) class. A black diamond is used for compositions.

Figure 3.10 illustrates an aggregation relationship for the classes `Customer` and `MembershipCard`. `Customer` contains zero or one `MembershipCard`. The system allows information to be stored about potential customers, i.e. people who do not yet have membership cards. Such a potential `Customer` does not contain any `MembershipCard` details, so its `memberStartDate` is set to a null value (meaning that the value does not exist).

The white diamond on the aggregation line does not necessarily mean that the aggregation is by reference (see Appendix, Section A.6). It can also mean that the modeler has not yet decided on the implementation of the aggregation. If the presented diagram is an analysis model, then the implementation of the aggregation is undecided. If it is a design model, then the white diamond indeed means aggregation by reference.

3.3.5 Generalization

Generalization (see Appendix, Section A.7) is a taxonomic relationship of classes that shows what subclasses *specialize* from a superclass. It means that an instance of any subclass is also an indirect instance of its superclass and that it inherits characteristics from the superclass. Generalization is visualized by a solid line with a large hollow triangle attached to the superclass.

Generalization is a powerful software reuse technique that also greatly simplifies the semantics and graphical presentation of models. The simplification is achieved in two diverse manners, depending on modeling circumstances.

By the fact that a subclass type is also the superclass type, it is possible to draw an association from any class in the model to the superclass and assume that, in reality, any object in the generalization hierarchy can be linked in that association. On the other hand, it is possible to draw an association to a more specific class lower in the generalization hierarchy to capture the fact that only objects of that specific subclass can be linked in the association.

Figure 3.11 is an example of a generalization hierarchy rooted at the *Payment* class. Because only two kinds of payment are allowed in the video store (cash or card payment), the *Payment* class has become an abstract class hence its name is in italics – (see Appendix, Section A.8). `Receipt` is associated with `Payment`. In reality, objects of concrete subclasses of *Payment* will be linked to `Receipt` objects.

Figure 3.10
Aggregation for a video store system

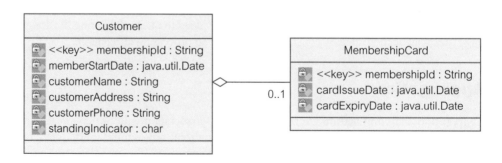

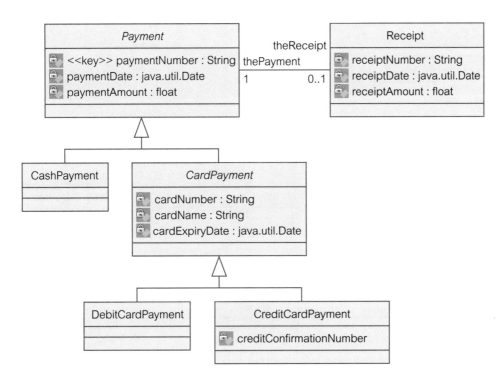

Figure 3.11
Generalization for
a video store
system

The diagram in Figure 3.11 has introduced two new classes to the video store model. The new classes are DebitCardPayment and CreditCardPayment, which are subclasses of CardPayment. As a result, CardPayment has become an abstract class.

Class diagrams   3.3.6

The class diagram is the heart and soul of an object-oriented design. The video store examples so far have demonstrated the *static modeling* ability of the class model. The classes have contained some attributes, but no **operations**. The operations belong more to the design than analysis realm. When operations are eventually included in classes, the class model implicitly defines system *behavior*.

Figure 3.12 illustrates the class diagram for a video store. The model demonstrates only classes identified in the previous examples. Other potential classes, such as Sale, CD or TVProgram, are not shown. Apart from Payment and CardPayment, Video turns out to be an abstract class. All other classes are concrete.

A careful analysis of the multiplicities of associations in Figure 3.12 reveals that the Rental class refers to *current* rentals only. Each rented video is associated with one, and only one, rental transaction. *Past* rentals of the same video are not remembered in the Rental class.

A Video (that is, a videotape or disk) contains one or more Movie. A movie can be available on zero, one or more videotapes or disks.

Figure 3.12
A class diagram
for a video store
system

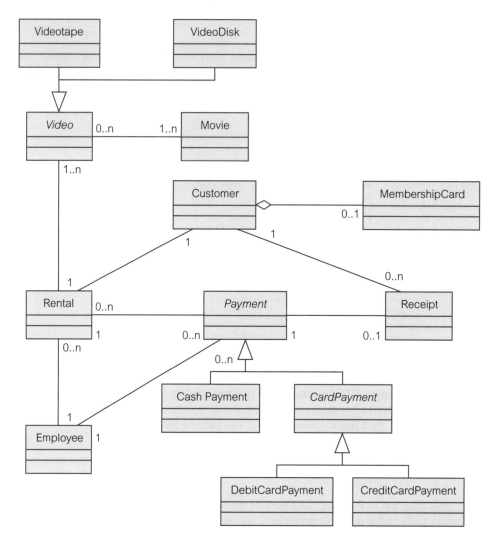

Each rental transaction is associated with an `Employee` responsible for it. Similarly, each payment is linked to an employee. The `Customer` information for payment can be obtained by navigating from `payment` to `customer` via a `rental` transaction or via `receipt`.

Review quiz 3.3

RQ1 Are the notions of an entity class and a business object synonymous?

RQ2 Does the concept of multiplicity apply to aggregation?

The interaction view

Interaction modeling captures the **interactions** between objects that need to communicate to execute a use case or part of it. Interaction models are used in the more advanced stages of requirements analysis, when a basic class model is known so that the references to objects are backed up by the class model.

The above observation underpins the main distinction between activity modeling (Section 3.2) and interaction modeling. *Activity modeling* is frequently done at a higher level of abstraction – it shows the sequencing of events without assigning the events to objects. *Interaction modeling*, however, shows the sequencing of **events (messages)** between collaborating objects.

Both activity and interaction modeling represent the realization of use cases. Activity diagrams, being more abstract, frequently capture the behavior of an entire use case. Interaction diagrams, being more detailed, tend to model portions of a use case. Sometimes an interaction diagram models a single activity in the activity diagram.

There are two kinds of interaction diagrams – *sequence diagrams* and *communication diagrams* (called *collaboration diagrams* prior to UML 2.0). They can be used interchangeably and, indeed, many CASE tools provide automatic conversion from one model to the other. The difference is in emphasis. Sequence models concentrate on time sequences, while communication models emphasize object relationships (Rumbaugh et al. 2005).

Sequence diagrams

An *interaction* is a set of *messages* in some behavior that are exchanged between *roles* across *links* (persistent or transient links (see Appendix, Section A.2.3). The sequence diagram is a two-dimensional graph. *Roles* (objects) are shown along the horizontal dimension. Sequencing of messages is shown top to bottom on the vertical dimension. Each vertical line is called the object's **lifeline**. A method activated on a lifeline is called the **activation** (or *execution specification*) and it is shown on a sequence diagram as a vertical tall rectangle.

Figure 3.13 shows a simple sequence diagram representing the sequence of messages necessary to fulfil the activity "Verify customer rating" in the activity diagram shown in Figure 3.6. The diagram engages the *objects* of four classes: `Employee`, `RentalWindow`, `CustomerVerifier`, and `Customer`. `Employee` is an actor, `RentalWindow` is a presentation class, `CustomerVerifier` is a control class and `Customer` is an entity class. Object *lifelines* are shown as vertical dotted lines. *Activations* are shown as narrow rectangles on the lifelines.

Processing begins when an `Employee` requests `RentalWindow` to `checkRating()`. When the message is received, `RentalWindow` displays information about the rental transaction being conducted for that particular customer. This means that the `RentalWindow` object holds (has a reference to) the relevant `Customer` object. Accordingly, `RentalWindow` passes to `CustomerVerifier` the `Customer` object in the argument of the `verifyRating()` message.

Figure 3.13
A sequence diagram for the activity "Verify customer" for a video store system

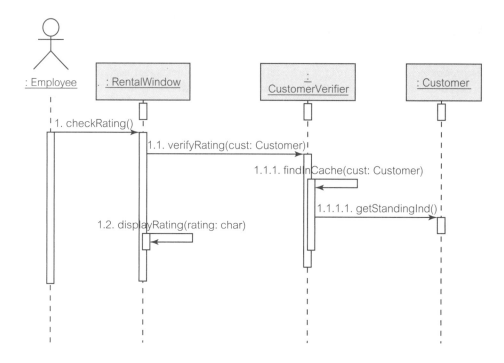

CustomerVerifier is a control object responsible for the program's logic and managing the memory cache of entity objects. Because the current rental transaction relates to a particular Customer object processed by RentalWindow, it can be assumed that the Customer object resides in the memory cache (that is, it does not have to be retrieved from the database). Consequently, CustomerVerifier sends a *self-message* (a message to its own method) to find the OID of Customer. This is done by the findInCache() method.

Once the handle (the OID) on the Customer object is known to CustomerVerifier, it requests Customer – in the getStandingInd() message – to reveal his or her rating. Objects returned to the original caller by the invoked methods are not explicitly shown in sequence diagrams. A *return* from a message call is implicit at the end of the object activation (that is, when the flow of control is returned to the caller). Therefore, the value of the Customer's standingInd attribute is (implicitly) returned to RentalWindow. At this point, RentalWindow sends a self-message to displayRating() for the employee's consideration.

Figure 3.13 uses hierarchical numbering of messages to show activation dependencies between messages and the corresponding methods. Note that a message to self within an activation results in a new activation. There are other important modeling facilities in sequence diagrams, which are discussed later in the book. Below is a quick recap of the main features of sequence diagrams.

An arrow represents a *message* from a calling object (*sender*) to an operation (method) in the called object (*target*). As a minimum, the message is named. *Actual arguments* of the message and other control information can also be included. The actual arguments correspond to the *formal arguments* in the method of the target object.

The actual argument can be an *input argument* (from the sender to the target) or an *output argument* (from the target back to the sender). The input argument may be identified by the keyword `in` (if there is no keyword then the input argument is assumed). The output argument is identified by the keyword `out`. Arguments that are `inout` are also possible, but they are rare in object-oriented solutions.

As mentioned, showing the *return* of control from the target to the sender object is not necessary. The "synchronous" message arrow to the target object implies the automatic return of control to the sender. The target knows the OID of the sender.

A message can be sent to a *collection* of objects (a collection could be a set, list or array of objects, for example). This frequently happens when a calling object is linked to multiple receiver objects (because the multiplicity of the association is one to many or many to many). An *iteration marker* – an asterisk in front of the message label – would indicate iterating over a collection.

Communication diagrams 3.4.2

A communication diagram is an alternative representation of a sequence diagram. There is a difference in emphasis, though. There are no lifelines or activations in communication diagrams. Both are implicit in the messages shown as arrows. As in sequence diagrams, the hierarchical numbering of messages may help in understanding the model, but the numbering does not necessarily document the sequence of method invocations. Indeed, some models are more truthful if no numbering is used.

Figure 3.14 is a communication diagram corresponding to the sequence diagram in Figure 3.13. Many CASE tools are able to convert any sequence diagram into a communication diagram automatically (and vice versa).

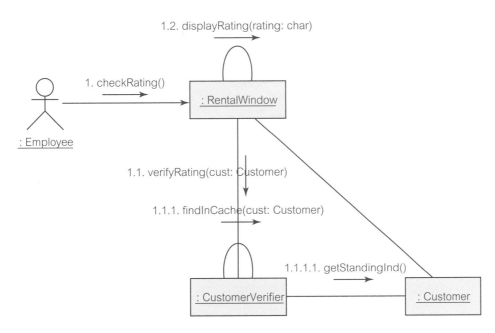

Figure 3.14
A communication diagram for the activity "Verify customer" for a video store system

In general, communication diagrams tend to be more useful graphically than sequence diagrams when representing models involving many objects. Also, and unlike sequence diagrams, the solid lines between objects may (and should) indicate the need for associations between classes of these objects. Building such associations legitimates the fact that the objects of these classes communicate.

3.4.3 Class methods

Examining the interactions can lead to the discovery of **methods** (operations) in classes. The dependencies between interactions and operations are straightforward. Each message invokes a method on the called object. The operation has the same name as the message.

The one-to-one mapping between *messages* in interaction models and *methods* in implemented classes has its limits and depends on whether or not the interaction model constitutes a detailed technical design – something neither possible nor desirable in the analysis phase. Thus, additional methods are defined during the detailed design and implementation phrases.

As an aside, note that similar one-to-one mapping exists between *messages* and *associations*, in particular for messages sent between *persistent* (*entity*) objects. Such messages should be supported by persistent links (see Appendix, Section A.2.3.1). Similar thinking should also apply to transient in-memory objects, which includes entity objects loaded in the memory (see Appendix, Section A.2.3.2). Therefore, the presence of a message in a sequence diagram stipulates the need for an association in the class diagram.

Figure 3.15 illustrates how interactions can be used to add operations to classes. The messages received by objects in the sequence diagram translate to methods (operations) in the classes representing these objects. The class diagram also reveals the return types and visibility of methods. These two characteristics of methods are not apparent in sequence diagrams.

`RentalWindow` receives the request to `checkRating()` and delegates this request to `CustomerVerifier`'s `verifyRating()`. Because `RentalWindow` holds the handle on the `Customer` object that it is currently processing (displays), it passes this object in the argument of `verifyRating()`. The delegation itself uses the association link to `CustomerVerifier`. The association is conducted via the role `theCustVerifier`, which will be implemented as a private attribute in `RentalWindow` (the private visibility is indicated by the minus sign in front of the role name).

The `verifyRating()` method utilizes the private method `findInCache()` to ascertain that the `Customer` object is in the memory and set the `theCust` attribute to reference this `Customer` object (if the attribute has not been previously set). Consequently, `CustomerVerifier` asks `Customer` to `getStandingInd()` by reading its attribute `standingIndicator`. The `char` value of this attribute is returned all the way to `RentalWindow`'s `checkRating()`.

To display the customer's rating in the GUI window under the control of `RentalWindow`, `checkRating()` sends a message to `displayRating()`, passing the rating value along. The `displayRating()` method has private visibility because it is called within `RentalWindow` by a self-message.

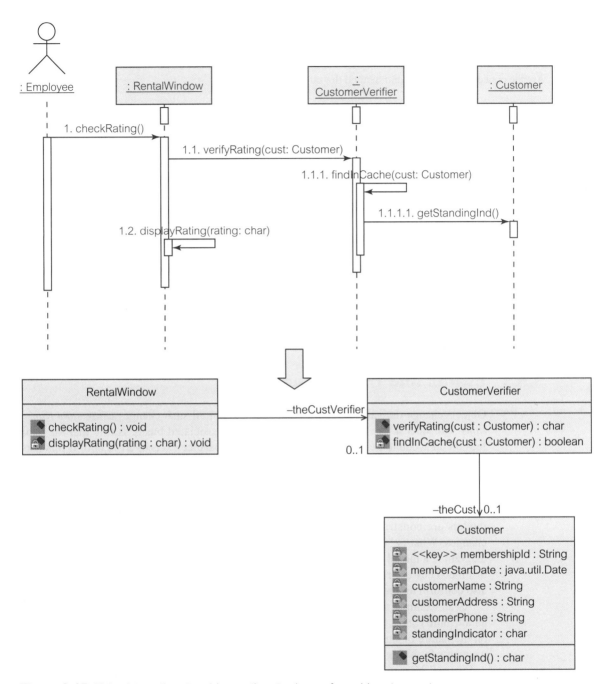

Figure 3.15 Using interactions to add operations to classes for a video store system

3.5   The state machine view

An *interaction model* provides a detailed specification for a use case, part of it or one or more activities. A *state machine model* specifies dynamic changes in a class. It describes various **states** in which objects of the class can be. These dynamic changes describe the behavior of an object across all use cases that involve the class from which the object is instantiated.

A *state* of an object is designated by the current values of the object's attributes (both primitive and those that designate other classes). A state machine model captures the life history of the class. An object is one and the same during its lifetime – its identity never changes (Appendix, Section A.2.3). However, the state of an object changes. A state machine diagram is a bipartite graph of *states* and **transitions** caused by *events*.

3.5.1   States and transitions

Objects change the values of their attributes, but not all such changes cause *state transitions*. Consider a Bank account object and an associated business rule that the bank fees on an account are waived when the account's balance exceeds $100,000. If this happens, we can say that Bank account has entered a privileged state. It is in a normal state otherwise. The account's balance changes after each withdrawal/deposit transaction, but its *state* changes only when the balance goes above or below $100,000.

The above example captures the essence of state machine modeling. State machine models are constructed for classes that have *interesting* state changes, not *any* state changes. What is "interesting," or not, is a business modeling decision. A state machine diagram is a model of business rules. The *business rules* are invariable over some periods of time. They are relatively independent of particular use cases. In fact, use cases must also conform to business rules.

As an example, consider the class Rental in the video store case study. Rental has an attribute (thePayment) that associates it with Payment (see Figure 3.9). Depending on the nature of this association, a Rental object can be in different states as far as the payments for hiring a video are concerned.

Figure 3.16 is a state machine model for the class Rental. The states are depicted as rounded rectangles. Events are shown as arrows. The initial state (pointed to by the arrow with the solid blue circle) of Rental is Unpaid. There are two possible transitions out of the Unpaid state. On the "Partial payment" event, the Rental object goes into the Partly Paid state. Only one partial payment is allowed according to the model. The

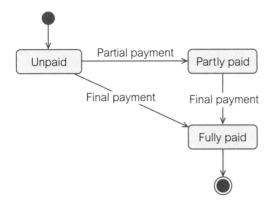

Figure 3.16
States and events
for the class
`Rental` for a video
store system

"Final payment" event, when in an `Unpaid` or `Partly paid` state, fires a transition to the `Fully paid` state. This is the final state (indicated by a solid blue circle with another circle around it).

State machine diagrams   3.5.2

A state machine diagram is normally attached to a class, but, in general, it can be attached to other modeling concepts, such as a use case. When attached to a class, the diagram determines how objects of that class react to events. More precisely, it determines – for each object state – what *action* the object will perform when it receives an event. The same object may perform a different action for the same event, depending on the object's state. The action's execution will typically cause a state change.

The complete description of a *transition* consists of three parts:

```
event(parameters) [guard] / action
```

Each part is optional. It is possible to omit all of them if the transition line by itself is self-explanatory. The *event* is a quick occurrence that affects the object. It can have parameters, such as `mouse button clicked (right_button)`. The event can be guarded by a *condition*, for example `mouse button clicked (right_button)` `[inside the window]`. Only when the condition evaluates to "true" does the event fire and affect the object.

The distinction between an event and a **guard** is not always obvious. The distinction is that an *event* "happens" and may even be saved before the object is ready to handle it. At the point of handling the event, the *guard* condition is evaluated to determine if a transition should fire.

An *action* is a short atomic computation that executes when the transition fires. An action can also be associated with a state. In general, an action is an object's response to a detected event. The states can, additionally, contain longer computations, called *activities*.

States can be composed of other states – *nested states*. The *composite state* is abstract – it is simply a generic label for all nested states. A transition taken out of a composite state's boundary means that it can fire from any of the nested states. This can improve the clarity and expressiveness of the diagram. A transition out of a composite state's boundary can also be fired from a nested state.

Consider again the class `Rental` in the video store case study and think about all the states in which `Rental` can be (not just with regard to payments, as in Figure 3.16, but to all attributes in `Rental`). Figure 3.17 illustrates a state machine diagram for the class `Rental`. The diagram has been purposely drawn to take advantage of a variety of state modeling features.

The state machine model in Figure 3.17 enters the state `Transaction started` once the *guard condition* [Customer validated and video scanned] is true. The transition to the next state (`Rental charge determined`) requires the firing of the *action* `/Calculate fees`. On the *event* `Customer wants to proceed`, the `Rental` object enters the `Unpaid` state.

The `Unpaid` state is one of two nested states within the composite state `Not fully paid`. The other nested state is `Partly paid`. The `Partly paid` state accepts the *transition to self* with the event `Partial payment`. This allows multiple partial payments before the transaction is paid in full.

Figure 3.17
State machine diagram for the class `Rental` for a video store system

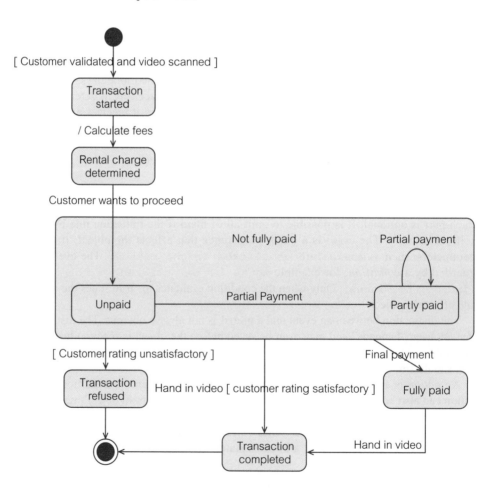

In the `Unpaid` state, when the guard condition [`Customer rating unsatisfactory`] is evaluated as true, a transition is fired into the state `Transaction refused`. This is one of two possible final states.

The second final state is `Transaction completed`. This state is achievable in two ways. First, and preferably, the event `Final payment` from the state `Not fully paid` results in the state `Fully paid`. When in this state, the event `hand in video` places the `Rental` object in the state `Transaction completed`. The second possibility for achieving the state `Transaction completed` is by the transition from the state `Not fully paid`, which is fired by the event `Hand in video` under the condition [`Customer rating satisfactory`].

Review quiz 3.5

RQ1   Can the state of an object depend on that object's association links?

RQ2   How is a guard different from an event?

The implementation view   3.6

UML provides tools for the architectural/structural modeling of the physical implementation of a system. The two main tools are the *component diagram* and *deployment diagram* (Alhir 2003; Maciaszek and Liong 2005). Both these diagrams belong to the broader category of *structure diagrams*, of which the main representative is a *class diagram* (Section 3.3.6).

Implementation models are in the physical modeling realm, but they must be defined with due consideration to the logical structure of the system. The main logical building block is the *class* and the main logical structural model is the *class diagram*. Other logical structuring concepts are the notions of *subsystem* and **package**

Subsystems and packages   3.6.1

The old Latin dictum *divida et impera* (divide and conquer or divide and rule) recommends that a position of power can be achieved by isolating adversaries and working towards causing disagreements between them. In problemsolving, this dictum is frequently used with a slightly different meaning. It requires that a large problem be divided into smaller problems so that, once the solution to the smaller problem has been found, a larger problem can be addressed.

The *divida et impera* principle leads to hierarchical modularization of the problem space. In system development, it results in the division of the system into subsystems and packages. The division has to be planned carefully to reduce dependencies in the hierarchy of subsystems and packages.

The notion of a *subsystem* specializes (inherits from) the concept of **component** (Ferm 2003) and is modeled as a stereotype of it. A subsystem encapsulates some part of intended system behavior. The services that a subsystem provides are the result of the services provided by its internal parts – its classes. This also means that a subsystem is not instantiable (Selic 2003).

The services of the *subsystem* can and should be defined using **interfaces** (see Appendix, Section A.9). The benefits of encapsulating behavior and providing services via interfaces are many and include insulation from change, replaceable implementation of services, extendibility, and reusability.

Subsystems can be structured in architectural layers, such that dependencies between layers are acyclic and minimized. Within each layer, subsystems can be nested. This means that a subsystem can contain other subsystems.

A *package* is a grouping of modeling elements under an assigned name. Like a subsystem, the services that a package provides are the result of the services provided by its internal parts – that is, classes. Unlike a subsystem, the package does not reveal its behavior by exposing interfaces. As noted by Ferm (2003: 2), "The difference between a subsystem and a package is that, for a package, a client asks for *some element inside the package* to fulfil a behavior; for a subsystem, a client asks *the subsystem itself* to fulfill the behavior."

Like a subsystem, a package may contain other packages. Unlike a subsystem, though, a package can be directly mapped to a programming language construct, such as a Java package or a .NET namespace. Like a subsystem, a package owns its members. A member (class, interface) can belong to only one direct subsystem or package.

All in all, a subsystem is a richer concept that embodies both the structural aspects of packages and the behavioral aspects of classes. The behavior is provided via one or more interfaces. The client requests the subsystem's services via these interfaces.

Figure 3.18 illustrates the UML graphical difference between a subsystem and a package. A subsystem is a component stereotyped as «subsystem». The fact that a subsystem encapsulates its behavior is represented by *provided interfaces* (see the next section). The interface `FinanceInterface` is implemented by the subsystem `Financial transaction` and is used by the class `RentalWindow` in the package GUI.

In general, to minimize system dependencies, interfaces should be placed outside the subsystems that implement them (Maciaszek and Liong 2005). Although not shown in Figure 3.18, placing all or most interfaces in a package that exclusively holds interfaces is allowed. Alternatively, if the GUI classes in Figure 3.18 were the only classes using `FinanceInterface`, then that interface could be located in the GUI package.

3.6.2 Components and component diagrams

"A *component* represents a modular part of a system that encapsulates its contents and whose manifestation is replaceable within its environment. A component defines its behavior in terms of provided and required interfaces" (UML 2005: 158).

A *provided interface* is one realized by a component (or other **classifier**, such as a class). It represents services that instances of that component offer to their clients. A *required interface* is one that can be used by a component (or other classifier, such as a

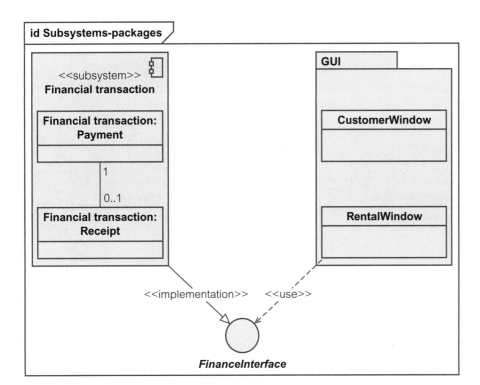

Figure 3.18
Subsystem and
package

class). It specifies services that a component needs in order to perform its function and fulfil its own services to its clients.

The *component diagram* is concerned with modeling the structure and dependencies of components in the implemented systems. Although a subsystem can be viewed as a special-ization of the concept of a component, UML uses a separate graphical element to visualize components. This visualization is different from the stereotyped package (see Figure 3.18). A component is shown as a rectangle with the keyword «component» and, optionally, a component icon in the top right-hand corner of the rectangle (see Figure 3.19).

The component concept addresses the area of component-based development (Section 2.1.3.2). The notation for components emphasizes their composition by visually assem-bling provided and required interfaces. A *provided* interface is shown as a small circle attached to a component. A *required* interface is shown as a small semicircle attached to a component.

Figure 3.19 shows three components – `ReceiptGenerator`, `CardVerifier` and `Payment`. `Payment` has three provided and three required interfaces. One of its required interfaces (`ICardVerifier`) is provided by `CardVerifier`. One of its provided inter-faces (`IPayTracking`) is required by `ReceiptGenerator`. The diagram shows two different visual ways in which provided and required interfaces can be assembled. The dashed dependency line linking `IPayTracking` interfaces is only necessary because the two interfaces have different names.

Separately, the specification of the interface `ICardVerifier` is also shown in Figure 3.19. The interface defines three operations to verify the card used for payment. The first

Figure 3.19
Component
diagram for a
video store
system

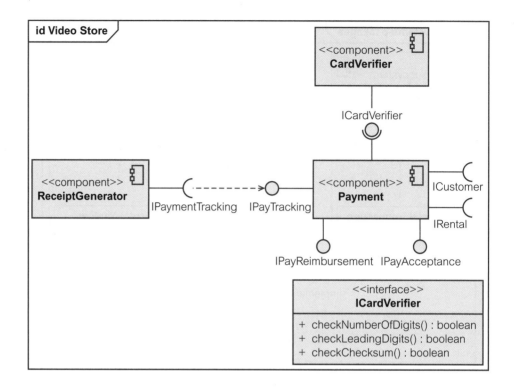

listed, `checkNumberOfDigits()`, ensures that the card consists of the right number of digits for that card type (credit cards can have either 13, 15 or 16 digits, for example), while the next, `checkLeadingDigits()`, ensures the correctness of the initial digits for that card type. Finally, `checkChecksum()` calculates the checksum for the card number and compares the checksum and the number to ensure that the card number has a valid number structure.

3.6.3 Nodes and deployment diagrams

"A *node* is a computational resource upon which artifacts may be deployed for execution. Nodes can be interconnected through communication paths to define network structures." (UML, 2005: 205). "An **artifact** is the specification of a physical piece of information that is used or produced by a software development process, or by deployment and operation of a system. Examples of artifacts include model files, source files, scripts, and binary executable files, a table in a database system, a development deliverable, or a word-processing document, a mail message" (UML 2005: 192).

The *deployment diagram* is concerned with modeling the structure and dependencies of nodes that define the implementation environment of the system. Nodes are connected by associations to show communication paths. The multiplicity values on association ends indicate the numbers of node instances involved in the association.

A *deployment diagram* also defines the deployment of components and other run-time processing elements on computer nodes (Alhir 2003). The node can be any server (such as a printer, e-mail, application, Web or database server) or any other computing or even human resource available to components and other processing elements.

Nodes are denoted as cubes. A «deploy» dependency from an artifact to a node signifies the deployment. Alternatively, artifact symbols can be placed within node symbols to indicate where they are deployed.

Figure 3.20 shows an example of a deployment diagram with three nodes – Client machine, Application server and Database server. There could be many client machines communicating with the Application server. There is only one application server connected to a single database server. The Application server houses the three components shown in Figure 3.19. The VideoStore.exe artifact is deployed on the Client machine and the schema.xml artifact is deployed on the Database server.

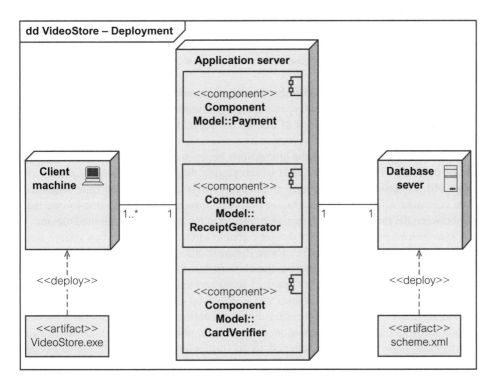

Figure 3.20
Deployment diagram for a video store system

Review quiz 3.6

RQ1 Is a subsystem modeled as a stereotype of a package or a stereotype of a component?

RQ2 Give some examples of artifacts that can be deployed on a node.

Summary

This chapter has covered quite a lot of ground. It has explained the fundamental terminology and concepts of object technology. It has also introduced all major UML models and diagrams and illustrated them using a single case study – a video store. For a novice to the topic, the task must have been daunting. The rewards will come in the following chapters.

The UML standard defines a large number of models and diagrams to enable in-depth and multi-focal software modeling. The models and diagrams can be classified according to various *views* they offer on a system – on its behavior and structure.

The *use case model* is the main UML representative and the focal point of behavior modeling. The model defines use cases, actors and the relationships between these modeling elements. Each use case is specified in a text document.

The *activity model* can graphically represent the flow of events in a use case. Activity models fill a gap between a high-level representation of system behavior in *use case models* and much lower-level representations of behavior in *interaction models* (sequence and communication diagrams).

Class modeling integrates and embodies all other modeling activities. Class models identify classes and their attributes, including relationships. Classes belong to various architectural layers. Typical groups of classes are presentation, control, entity, mediator and foundation classes.

Interaction modeling captures the interactions between objects needed to execute a use case or part of it. There are two kinds of interaction diagram, which are *sequence diagrams* and *communication diagrams*. Sequence models concentrate on time sequences, while communication models emphasize object relationships. There is one-to-one mapping between the messages in interaction models and methods in implemented classes.

A *state machine model* specifies dynamic changes in a class. It describes various states in which objects of the class can be. These dynamic changes describe the behavior of an object across all use cases that involve the class from which the object is instantiated. A state machine diagram is a bipartite graph of states and transitions caused by events.

UML provides *component diagrams* and *deployment diagrams* as two tools for architectural/structural modeling of physical implementation of the system. The dominant notions in these diagrams are component, interface, node and artifact. Other relevant architectural design concepts referred to in implementation models are *subsystem* and *package*.

Key terms

Action "the fundamental unit of behavior specification. An action takes a set of inputs and converts them into a set of outputs, though either or both sets may be empty" (UML 2005: 229).

Activation called also execution specification it "models the execution of a behavior or operation, including the period during which an operation calls other subordinate operations" (Rumbaugh et al. 2005: 344).

Activity "the specification of parameterized behavior as the coordinated sequencing of subordinate units whose individual elements are actions" (UML 2005: 322).

"a form of association that specifies a whole–part relationship between an
⟨ ⟩hole) and a constituent part" (Rumbaugh et al. 2005: 164).

⟨ ⟩ification of a physical piece of information that is used or produced by
⟨ ⟩opment process, or by deployment and operation of a system" (UML
⟨ ⟩ 192).

⟨A⟩ssociation "the semantic relationship between two or more classifiers that involves connections among their instances" (Rumbaugh et al. 2005: 174).

Attribute "the description of a named element of a specified type in a class; each object of the class separately holds a value of the type" (Rumbaugh et al. 2005: 186).

Class "a kind of classifier whose features are attributes and operation" (UML 2005: 61).

Classifier "a classification of instances, it describes a set of instances that have features in common. … Classifier is an abstract model element, and so properly speaking has no notation" (UML 2005: 64).

Component "represents a modular part of a system that encapsulates its contents and whose manifestation is replaceable within its environment" (UML 2005: 158). See also Component, Key terms, Chapter 1.

Composition a composite aggregation; "a strong form of aggregation that requires a part instance be included in at most one composite at a time" (UML 2005: 54).

Control flow "an edge that starts an activity node after the previous one is finished" (UML 2005: 344).

Event "the specification of some occurrence that may potentially trigger effects by an object" (UML 2005: 428).

Generalization "a taxonomic relationship between a more general classifier and a more specific classifier. Each instance of the specific classifier is also an indirect instance of the general classifier. Thus, the specific classifier inherits the features of the more general classifier" (UML 2005: 83).

Guard "a constraint that provides a fine-grained control over the firing of the transition. The guard is evaluated when an event occurrence is dispatched by the state machine. If the guard is true at that time, the transition may be enabled, otherwise, it is disabled" (UML 2005: 569).

Interaction "a specification of how messages are exchanged over time between roles within a context to perform a task. An interaction specifies a pattern of behavior. The context is supplied by a classifier or collaboration" (Rumbaugh et al. 2005: 406).

Interface "a kind of classifier that represents a declaration of a set of coherent public features and obligations. An interface specifies a contract; any instance of a classifier that realizes the interface must fulfill that contract" (UML 2005: 98).

Lifeline "represents an individual participant in the interaction" (UML 2005: 491).

Message "defines one specific kind of communication in an interaction. A communication can be, for example, raising a signal, invoking an operation, creating or destroying an instance." (UML 2005: 493).

Method "the implementation of an operation. It specifies the algorithm or procedure that produces the results of an operation" (Rumbaugh et al. 2005: 459).

Node "computational resource upon which artifacts may be deployed for execution" (UML 2005: 221).

Operation "a behavioral feature of a classifier that specifies the name, type, parameters, and constraints for invoking an associated behavior" (UML 2005: 115).

Package "used to group elements, and provides a namespace for the grouped elements" (UML 2005: 119).

Role "a constituent element of a structured classifier that represents the appearance of an instance (or, possibly, set of instances) within the context defined by the structured classifier" (Rumbaugh et al. 2005: 575).

State "models a situation during which some (usually implicit) invariant condition holds. The invariant may represent a static situation such as an object waiting for some external event to occur. However, it can also model dynamic conditions such as the process of performing some behavior" (UML 2005: 547).

Transition "a relationship within a state machine between two states indicating that an object in the first state, when a specified event occurs and specified guard conditions are satisfied, will perform specified effects (action or activity) and enter the second state. On such a change of state, the transition is said to fire" (Rumbaugh et al. 2005: 657).

Use case "the specification of a set of actions performed by a system, which yields an observable result that is, typically, of value for one or more actors or other stakeholders of the system" (UML 2005: 594).

Multiple-choice test

MC1 An actor is:

   a a role

   b external to the subject

   c communicates with a use case

   d all of the above.

MC2 An execution step for an activity is called a:

   a case

   b action

   c job

   d flow.

MC3 A concurrent computation threat in activity diagrams is defined by means of a:

   a branch and rejoin

   b fork and merge

   c guard and merge

   d none of the above.

MC4 Classes responsible for communication with external data sources are called:

   a external classes

   b communication classes

   c resource classes

   d none of the above.

MC5 The black diamond on the aggregation line means that:

    a the aggregation is by value

    b the aggregation is a composition

    c a subset object can be part of only one superset object

    d all of the above.

MC6 A formal argument may be supplied as part of the definition of a:

    a method

    b message

    c call

    d all of the above.

MC7 A state machine diagram is a bipartite graph of states and transitions caused by:

    a activities

    b triggers

    c events

    d all of the above.

MC8 A computational resource on which artifacts may be deployed for execution is called a:

    a component

    b node

    c package

    d none of the above.

Questions

Q1 Explain the main characteristics and complementary properties of a static model, behavioral model and state machine model.

Q2 Can an actor have attributes and operations? Explain your answer.

Q3 Explain the role and place of activity diagrams in system modeling.

Q4 What are entity classes? What other categories of class need to be distinguished in class modeling? Explain your answer.

Q5 What is an actual argument and what is a formal argument?

Q6 What is the difference between an action and an activity in state machine diagrams? Give examples in your answer.

Q7 Explain why subsystems implement interfaces and packages do not. What would be the consequences for implementation models if the subsystems they refer to did not implement interfaces?

Q8 How does an artifact relate to a node? How is that relationship modeled visually?

Exercises

E1 Refer to Figure A.2 in the Appendix (Section A.2.2). Consider the following changes to the logic of object collaboration for shipping products and replenishing stock.

Shipment and replenishment are separate processing threads. When `Order` creates a new `Shipment` object and requests its shipment, `Shipment` obtains `Product` objects as in Figure A.2. However, instead of `Stock` managing changes to product quantities, `Shipment` uses its handle on `Product` objects and requests `Product` to `getProdQuantity()` directly.

In this scenario, `Product` knows its quantity and when it has to be reordered. Consequently, when replenishment is needed, a new `Purchase` object is created to provide the `reorder()` service.

Modify the diagram in Figure A.2 to capture the above changes. There is no need to show messages that instantiate `Shipment` and `Purchase` objects, because the topic of object creation has not been sufficiently explained yet.

E2 Refer to Figure A.2 in the Appendix (Section A.2.2) and to Figure 3.23 (that is, the solution to Exercise E1). Define the return types for all messages in both diagrams. Explain how the return values are used in successive calls.

E3 Refer to Figure A.14 in the Appendix (Section A.5.2). Suppose that a course offering includes lectures and tutorials and it is possible that one teacher is in charge of the lecturing portion of the course offering and another teacher is in charge of the tutorials. Modify the diagram in Figure A.14 to capture the above fact.

E4 Refer to Figure A.16 in the Appendix (Section A.5.4). Provide an alternative model that does not use an association class, not a ternary association (which is not recommended in this book). Describe semantic differences, if any, between the model in Figure A.16 and your new model.

E5 Refer to Figure 3.21, in which `Book` contains `Chapter` objects and each `Chapter` contains `Paragraph` objects. The text of a book is stored in `Paragraph` objects. The `Finder` class is a control class. It depends on the `Book` class (this is indicated by the arrowed dotted line). Consider that `Finder` needs to display on screen all `chptNumber` and `paraNumber` that contain a particular search string within the text. Add operations to classes that are needed for such processing. Draw an object communication diagram and explain how the processing is done, including return types of operations.

E6 Refer to Figure 3.21 and the solution to Exercise E5 in Figure 3.25. Extend the class diagram by adding operations to classes that are needed for such processing. Provide pseudo-code or Java code for classes `Finder`, `Book` and `Chapter`.

E7 Refer to Figure A.22 in the Appendix (Section A.7.3). Extend the example by adding attributes to the classes `Teacher`, `Student`, `PostgraduateStudent` and `Tutor`.

E8 Refer to Figures A.24 (Section A.9.1) and A.25 (Section A.9.2), both in the Appendix. Extend Figures A.24 and A.25 (in the Solutions to odd-numbered exercises section, later in this chapter) to consider that `VideoMedium` is one kind of `EntertainmentMedium`, the other being `SoundMedium` (such as CDs). Of course, `VideoMedium` is also `SoundMedium`. A similar classification applies to equipment (housing media).

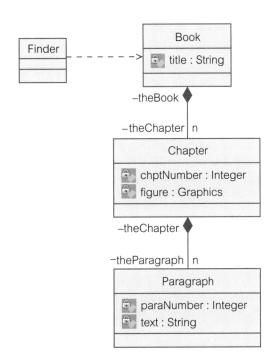

Figure 3.21
Aggregation for
the class Book

Exercises: video store

F1 The use case diagram in Figures 3.3 and 3.4 (Section 3.1.3) does not make it explicit that the model is about renting videos (it talks only about scanning cards and video devices, accepting payments and printing receipts). In practice, a use case will be required that a rental transaction is conducted and that it is eventually recorded on the video store's database. Moreover, the use case diagram does not check the age eligibility of customers (customers must be over 18 years old to be eligible to rent movies rated R or X).

Extend the use case diagram to include the above considerations. Also, take into account that the process of renting a video starts after scanning the customer's card and video or CD and that it is possible (1) to rent a video without making a payment (in some special cases), (2) age eligibility is checked if the customer is not 18 years old and movies are rated R or X and (3) customers can rent a video with or without receipt (depending on their request).

F2 Refer to the solution to Exercise F1 (Figure 3.27) and to the activity diagram in Figure 3.6 (Section 3.2.2). Develop a complementary activity diagram for the use case Rent video and the subordinate use cases that extend Rent video (there is no need to repeat the specifications for Accept payment, already developed in Figure 3.6).

F3 Refer to Figure 3.9 (Section 3.3.3). Assume that not every Payment is linked to Rental. Some videos are for sale, so Payment may be related to a Sale class. Also, assume that a single payment can pay for more than one rental. How do these changes impact on the model? Modify and extend the model accordingly.

F4 Refer to Figure 3.6 (Section 3.2.2). Draw a sequence diagram for the activity `Handle card payment`.

F5 Refer to the class diagram Figure 3.12 (Section 3.3.6) and consider the class `Video`. Apart from the information that can be obtained from the class model, consider that the video store sells videos that were previously available to rent once the movie activity threshold reaches certain level (such as when videos with that movie have not been rented out for a week). Also consider that videos are checked regularly to see if they are still operational and may be written off if damaged.

Develop a state machine diagram for the class `Video`. Develop also an alternative version of the diagram in which you use an abstract composite state called `In stock` to model that a video in stock can be available for rent or available for sale or damaged.

F6 Refer to the discussion on implementation models in Section 3.6. Consider the implementation model in Figure 3.22 with the relationships missing.

Assume that the components `Procurement` and `Video rental` are realized by classes within the `Inventory control` package. `Procurement` requires access to `Video rental`. `Stock server` is responsible for providing the functionality of `Procurement` and `Video shop server` for the functionality of `Video rental`. Complete the diagram in Figure 3.22 to show all the dependencies and other relationships.

Figure 3.22
An implementation model with the dependency and other relationships missing

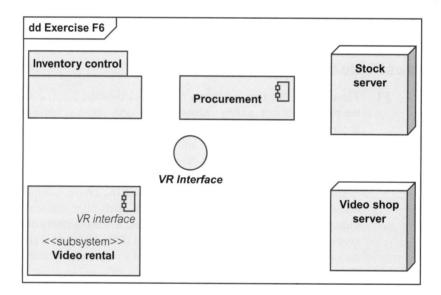

Review quiz answers

Review quiz 3.1
RQ1   Use case diagram, sequence diagram, communication diagram and activity diagram.
RQ2   No, the use case specification contains the diagram and a complete textual description of the use case intended behavior.

Review quiz 3.2
RQ1   Yes, it can. Activity modeling can be done at various abstraction levels, including for the internal specification of a use case's steps of computation.
RQ2   Decisions, forks, joins, merges and object nodes.

Review quiz 3.3
RQ1   Yes, they are synonymous.
RQ2   Yes, it does. Aggregation is merely a form of association.

Review quiz 3.4
RQ1   In sequence diagrams.
RQ2   No, they are not. Message is a call to a method.

Review quiz 3.5
RQ1   Yes, it can. Any attribute can influence the state of an object, including attributes that designate other classes (that is, associations).
RQ2   The guard condition is evaluated at the point of handling the event to determine if a transition will fire.

Review quiz 3.6
RQ1   In UML 2.0, a subsystem is modeled as a stereotype of a component. However, in earlier versions of UML it was modeled as a stereotype of a package.
RQ2   Model files, source files, scripts and binary executable files, a table in a database system, a development deliverable or a word-processing document, a mail message.

Multiple-choice test answers

MC1   d
MC2   b
MC3   d (it is defined by fork and rejoin)
MC4   c
MC5   d
MC6   a
MC7   c
MC8   b

Answers to odd-numbered questions

Q1

A *static model* describes the static structure of a system – classes, their internal structure and their relationships to each other. The main visualization technique for static modeling is the class diagram. A *behavior model* describes the actions of the objects in a system in support of business functions – interactions, operations and algorithms on data. Behavior modeling includes use case diagrams, sequence diagrams, communication diagrams, and activity diagrams. A *state machine model* describes the dynamic changes in object states over their lifetimes. The main visualization technique for state machine modeling is the state machine diagram.

The three models offer different but complementary viewpoints, frequently on the same modeling elements. The static view shows the kinds of elements that exist in a system. The behavioral view ensures that the elements are capable of executing the required system functionality. A good static model should be able to gracefully accommodate new or extended system functionality. The state machine view defines the framework for object evolution and the constraints on object states that both the behavioral and static model must conform to.

Q3

In older versions of UML, *activity diagrams* were considered a special case of a *state machine* and could even be used in lieu of state machine diagrams. To this aim, activity diagrams were extending the state machine notation and distinguished between *object states* (as in state machines) and *activity states* (not modeled directly in state machines). In the current UML, activity diagrams define only behavior by using the control and data flow model reminiscent of Petri nets (Ghezzi et al. 2003).

Unlike most other UML modeling techniques, the role and place of activity diagrams in the system development process is not clear-cut. The semantics of activity diagrams makes them usable at various levels of abstraction and in different phases of the lifecycle. They can be used in early analysis to depict the overall behavior of the system. They can be used to model the behavior of a use case or any part of it. They can also be used in design to give a flowchart-like specification of a specific method or even individual algorithms contained in a method.

All in all, activity diagrams can be seen as "gap fillers" in the system model. They are used as a complementary technique to provide a graphic visualization for a flow of events, data and processes within various other modeling elements.

Q5

Objects communicate by sending messages. Typically, a message from one object calls a method (operation) in another (or the same) object. A message signature includes a list of *actual arguments*. The method being invoked includes in its signature a corresponding list of *formal arguments*. In UML, the actual arguments of a message are called simply *arguments*, but the formal arguments of a method are called *parameters*.

Q7

A *package* is just a grouping of modeling elements and it is not concerned with how these modeling elements will be used by the clients. To address that concern, a stereotyped version of a component is provided in UML and is called a *subsystem* (in UML prior to version 2, a subsystem was a stereotyped version of a package).

Visually, a subsystem is a component stereotyped as «subsystem». Semantically, a subsystem hides its modeling elements and reveals only its public services to clients. The clients request the subsystem's services via its *provided interfaces*. In reality, a subsystem is merely a concept and so is not an instantiable – that is, it does not have a concrete implementation. A subsystem's services are realized (implemented) by classes that belong to the subsystem.

Modeling of access to a subsystem via provided interfaces implies that the implementation of all classes within that subsystem is hidden behind the interfaces. This has important benefits for implementation models. If interfaces were not specified for subsystems, other components would become dependent on the implementation of classes within subsystems. Such dependencies would impact negatively on the system's quality of adaptiveness (understandability, maintainability and scalability).

Solutions to odd-numbered exercises

E1
Figure 3.23 is a modified object collaboration. The two threads are numbered separately as 1 and 2. The shipment thread has two dependent messages, numbered hierarchically as 1.1 and 1.2.

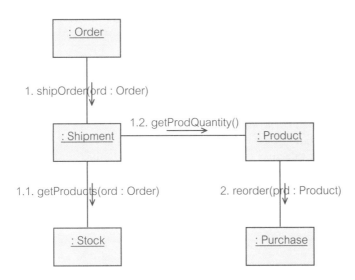

Figure 3.23
Object collaboration for shipment and replenishment

Apart from the lack of explanation of how the Shipment and Purchase objects are created, there are a few other details that remain unexplained. For example, the model does not explain how getProdQuantity() iterates over possibly many Product objects or what exactly makes Product send the reorder() messages.

E3
In the modified class diagram (Figure 3.24), two new classes are identified (Lecture and Tutorial) as subset classes of CourseOffering. The subset classes have their own associations to Teacher.

Because a Teacher can be in charge of both lectures and tutorials, the roles have different names – lect_in_charge_of and tut_in_charge_of. This is essential because two attributes will be needed in the implemented classes to capture these two roles (and the role names can then be used as attribute names).

E5
For explanatory reasons, the solution in Figure 3.25 shows return types, although they are not normally presented in communication diagrams. The messages iterateChapters and iterateParagraphs are just high-level descriptions of the requirement that Book has to iterate over many chapters and that Chapter needs

Figure 3.24
Modified class
diagram to
replace
association class

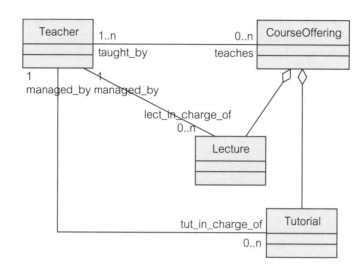

to iterate over many paragraphs. The details of such loop-based operations are not explained. Because `iterateChapters` and `iterateParagraphs` are just abstractions, rather than messages to methods, there are no parentheses after their names, which would signify a list of arguments.

Finder invokes the `search()` operation on `Book`. It eventually returns a `List` of chapter numbers and paragraph numbers containing the string value passed in the argument `what`. Before `Book` can return anything, it iterates over its `Chapter` objects to search for the string value.

Figure 3.25
An object
collaboration
diagram

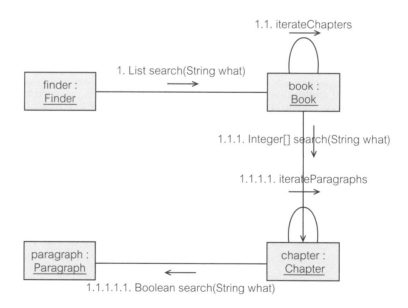

However, the text of a book is contained in `Paragraph` objects. Accordingly, `Chapter` iterates over its `Paragraph` objects and invokes the `search()` operation on each object. This operation in itself returns just true/false, but, for each true outcome, `Chapter` constructs an array of paragraph numbers. This array is returned to `Book`. `Book` can now build a list of chapter numbers and paragraph numbers and return it to `Finder`.

E7

Different (and arbitrary) solutions are possible. Figure 3.26 is an example. Note that the example is not Java-based, as Java does not support multiple inheritance.

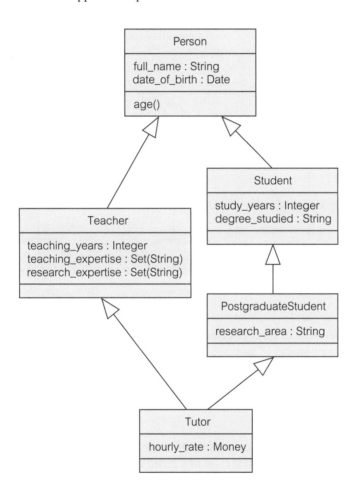

Figure 3.26
Multiple inheritance

The attributes `teaching_expertise` and `research_expertise` in `Teacher` are known as *parameterized types*. Both `Set` and `String` are classes. `String` is a parameter of `Set`. The values of these two attributes are sets of strings.

Solutions to odd-numbered exercises: video store

F1

Figure 3.27 presents an extended use case diagram. `Rent video` is extended by `Print receipt`, `Check age eligibility` and `Accept payment`. There are no direct relationships made to the two `Scan ...` use cases. The model assumes that `Rent video` has the information from scanning when the rental transaction is started.

Figure 3.27
An extended use
case diagram for
a video store
system

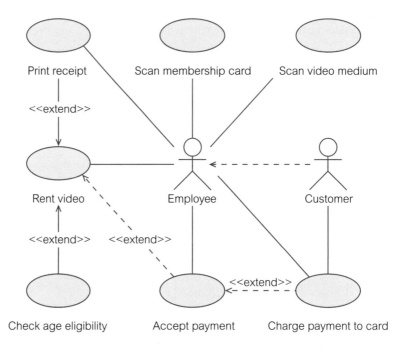

F3

Figure 3.28 illustrates that the introduction of the `Sale` class leads to new associations, but the "tricky" issue is elsewhere. There is a need in the new model to introduce an association between `Customer` and `Payment`. A payment can be made for more than one rental and it is possible (as this is not forbidden) that these rentals can be related to different customers. Consequently, without a `Payment–Customer` association, it may not be possible to identify a customer from a payment.

F5

Figure 3.29 is a state machine model for the class `Video`. Note the use of the event followed by a guard condition on the transition to the state `Damaged`. Note also the use of a guard followed by an action on the transition to state `For sale`. All other transitions are marked with events.

The model does not identify a start or end state. It has been decided that such identifications are not essential for modeling purposes.

Figure 3.30 is an alternative model. `Video` signifies a medium containing movie or other entertaining material. When a video is purchased and delivered to the `Video store` it becomes `Available for business`. On the event "Place in stock", the video is in the `In stock` state. This is an abstract state. In reality the video is in one of the three states `For rent`, `For sale` or `Damaged`. The internal transitions between these three states are not captured in the presented model (so that the picture is not cluttered).

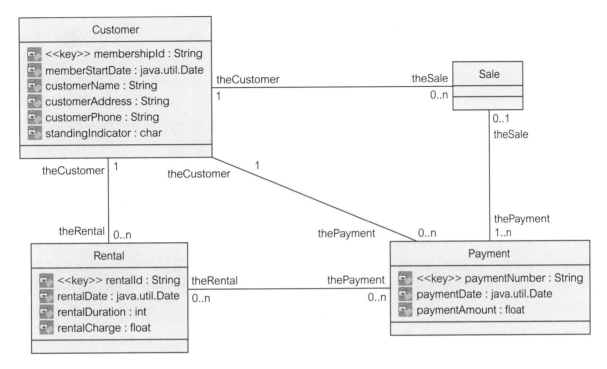

Figure 3.28 A modified and extended class model

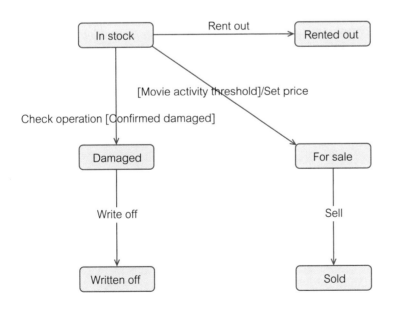

Figure 3.29
A state machine
diagram for the
class `Video`

Figure 3.30
Alternative state
machine diagram
for the class `Video`

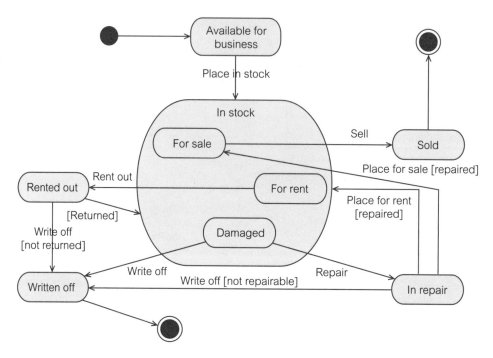

A video that is `Rented out` can be returned or not. When the `[Returned]` condition becomes true, the transition back to the `In stock` state follows. Otherwise the "Write off" event places the video in the `Written off` state. The `Written off` state can also be reached from the states `Damaged` and `In repair`.

There are three possible transitions from the `In repair` state. If the video is `[Repaired]`, it can be made available `For rent` or `For sale`. When in the latter state, the video can be `Sold`.

Requirements specification

Objectives

The requirements need to be specified in graphical and other formal models. Many models are necessary to specify the system completely. UML offers a plethora of integrated modeling techniques to assist a system analyst in this job. The process is iterative and incremental. The use of CASE tools is essential for successful modeling. The requirements specification produces three categories of model: state models, behavior models and state change models.

The requirements specification takes the narrative customer requirements as inputs and constructs specification models as outputs. The models (described in Chapter 3) provide a formal definition for various aspects (views) of the system. An outcome of the specification phase is an extended ("elaborated") *requirements document* (Section 2.6). The new document is frequently called a *specifications document* (or "spec" in the jargon). The structure of the original document is not changed, but the content is significantly extended. Eventually, the specifications document replaces the requirements document for the purposes of design and implementation (in practice, the extended document is likely to be still called a *requirements document*).

By reading this chapter you will:

- appreciate the importance of early architectural design as a prerogative for developing adaptive systems
- understand the most fundamental principles underpinning architectural frameworks (meta-models)
- be introduced to the PCBMER architectural framework advocated and used later in this book in case studies and examples
- gain practical knowledge about how to do modeling of classes, associations, other relationships and interfaces
- gain practical knowledge about how to do modeling of use cases, activities, interactions and operations
- learn how to model changes to object states.

4.1 Architectural prerogatives

Requirements specification is concerned with rigorous *modeling* of the customers' requirements that have been defined during the requirements determination phase. The emphasis is on the desired services that will be provided by the system (functional requirements). The system constraints (non-functional requirements) are frequently not developed further in the specification phase, but they serve to guide and validate modeling work. The guidance and validation takes the form of architectural prerogatives.

Software architecture defines the structure and organization of software components and **subsystems** that interact to form systems. "Software architecture captures and preserves designers' intentions about system structure and behavior, thereby providing a defense against design decay as a system ages. It's the key to achieving intellectual control over a sophisticated system's enormous complexity" (Kruchten et al. 2006: 23). Software architecture is the necessary and the most important condition to building into the software the quality of *adaptiveness* (supportability) – a triple of subqualities of understandability, maintainability and scalability (Section 2.2.1.2).

Consequently, before the work on any detailed system specifications can even begin, the software development team must adopt architectural patterns and principles to be obeyed by all developers (Maciaszek and Liong 2005). This is vitally important. Without a clear architectural vision for the system, the analysis phase will invariably deliver specifications for an unsupportable system (if it delivers anything at all!)

The underlying and overwhelming objective of all software modeling must be the minimization of component **dependencies**. To achieve this, the developers cannot allow for indiscriminate object communication, resulting in a messy and incomprehensible network of intercommunicating components. The complexity of such a (unsupportable) system would increase exponentially with the growth of the model and the addition of each new object. This cannot be tolerated and must be stopped before it starts to cause damage. A clear architectural model, with hierarchical layers of components and subsystems and restrictions in object intercommunication, must be adopted early in the lifecycle.

Model-View-Controller   4.1.1

Like anything in software design, there are many possible architectural designs for a system. Although it is possible to imagine a design that emerges in a bottom-up fashion from individual design decisions that occur during development, usually architects employ a top-down approach in which they derive a particular design from a predefined **architectural framework** (an **architectural meta-model**) (Maciaszek and Liong 2005).

Most modern architectural frameworks and related patterns are underpinned by a *Model-View-Controller* (**MVC**) framework, developed as part of the Smalltalk-80 programming environment (Krasner and Pope 1988). In Smalltalk-80, MVC forces programmers to divide application classes into three groups that specialize and inherit from three Smalltalk-provided abstract classes – Model, View and Controller.

Model objects represent data objects – the business entities and the business rules in the application domain. Changes to model objects are notified to view and controller objects via event processing. This uses the publisher/subscriber technique. Model is the publisher and it is therefore unaware of its views and controllers. View and controller objects subscribe to Model, but they can also initiate changes to model objects. To assist in this task, the model supplies necessary interfaces, which encapsulate the business data and behavior.

View objects represent user interface (UI) objects and present the state of the model in the format required by the user and rendered on the user's graphical interface. View objects are decoupled from model objects. View subscribes to Model so that it gets notified of changes to Model and can update its display. View objects can contain subviews, which display different parts of Model. Typically, each view object is paired with a controller object.

Controller objects represent mouse and keyboard events. Controller objects respond to the requests that originate from View and are the results of users' interactions with the system. Controller objects give meaning to keystrokes, mouse-clicks and so on and convert them into actions on the model objects. They mediate between view and model objects. By separating users' inputs from visual presentation, they allow changing system responses to users' actions without changing the UI presentation, and vice versa – changing UI without changing the system's behavior.

Figure 4.1 illustrates an actor's (user's) perspective on communication between MVC objects. The lines represent communication between objects. The user GUI events are intercepted by view objects and passed to controller objects for interpretation and further action. Mixing the behavior of View and Controller in a single object is considered bad practice in MVC.

Figure 4.1
The MVC
framework

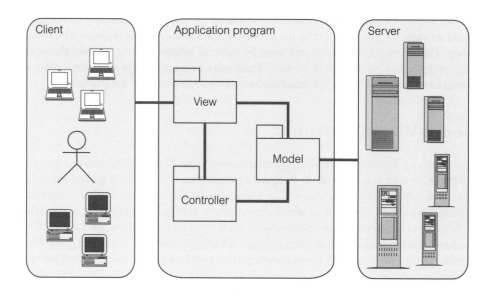

4.1.2 The Core J2EE architecture

MVC is the backbone of virtually all modern frameworks, which then extend the framework to enterprise and e-business systems. The Core J2EE architecture is one such framework (Alur et al. 2003; Roy-Faderman et al. 2004). As shown in Figure 4.2, the J2EE model consists of tiers – three embracing the application program components (presentation, business and integration) and two that are external to the application (client and EIS – Enterprise Information System).

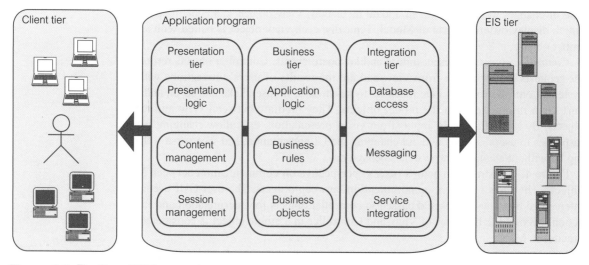

Figure 4.2 The Core J2EE framework

The user communicates with the system from the *client* tier. This tier can be a programmable client (such as a Java Swing-based client or applet), a HTML Web browser client, a WML mobile client or even an XML-based Web service client. The process that presents a user interface can execute on the client machine (a programmable client) or can execute from a Web or application server (such as a Java JSP/servlet application).

The *EIS* tier (also called the r   persistent information delivery system. This could be   nterprise system in an e-business solution   uted across many servers.

                                  ier (also known as the *Web* tier or
                                  , this tier contains the user inter-
f   on server. With reference to the
M   and controller components.
                                  gic not already implemented
as   sponsible for the validation
and   nsactions. It also manages
busi   e EIS tier to the application
mem
Th   g and maintaining connections   with databases via Java
Databa   cternal systems via Java
Messag

The   than regulatory. It introduces a   program's tiers. It also
dictates   ith integration components via   ample, enforce a strict
hierarchic   (invocation of methods) and th

There ar   t are quite regulatory
and address   gration of enterprise
and e-busine   rta Struts to allow
proper implei   services with technologies such   oss or Websphere
Application S   integration with
implementation

Presentat   Controller-Bean-Mediator-Entity-Resource   4.1.3

In the previous edition of this book and in Maciaszek and Liong (2005) we advocated the architectural model called *PCMEF*. This acronym stands for its five hierarchical layers of classes – presentation, control, mediator, entity and foundation. The layers could be modeled as subsystems or packages. More recently, the PCMEF framework has been extended to include six hierarchical layers and thus renamed **PCBMER**, which stands for presentation, controller, bean, mediator, entity and resource (Maciaszek 2006). The PCBMER architecture follows recognized trends in architectural design. For example, it aligns very well with the Core J2EE framework discussed in the previous section.

Figure 4.3 illustrates the *Core PCBMER* architectural framework. The framework borrows the names of the external tiers (the client tier and the EIS tier) from the Core J2EE framework. The tiers are represented as UML nodes. The dotted arrowed lines are *dependency relationships*. Hence, for example, presentation depends on controller and on **bean** and controller depends on bean. The PCBMER hierarchy is not strictly linear and a

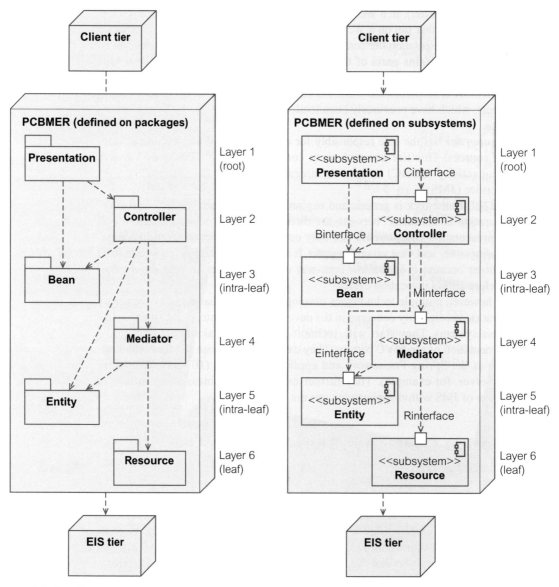

Figure 4.3 The Core PCBMER framework

higher layer can have more than one adjacent layer below (and that adjacent layer may be an *intra-leaf* – that is, it may have no layers below it).

A unidirectional dependency does not mean that objects cannot communicate in the other direction – they can. However, such communication must be done using dependency minimization techniques, such as using communication via interfaces or using publisher/subscriber protocols.

The PCBMER architecture, when adopted for a development project, forces developers to assign each class in the system to one of the six subsystems. This automatically improves the design because each class contributes to a predefined purpose of the subsystem. The class becomes more cohesive and dedicated to a single task.

Coupling between classes, to deliver complete services to clients, is allowed only along the dependency relationships. This may require the use of longer communication paths then would otherwise be needed, but it eliminates networks of intercommunicating objects. Together, the architecture provides for an optimal mix of object **cohesion** and coupling that satisfies all requirements of the system.

The PCBMER layers 4.1.3.1

Figure 4.3 shows two presentation variants of the *Core PCBMER* framework – one defined using UML packages and the other using UML subsystems (Section 3.6.1). Recall that a *package* is a grouping of modeling elements (classes and so on, including other packages) under an assigned name. The services that a package provides are the result of the services provided by its modeling elements. On the other hand, the notion of a *subsystem* is used to model large-scale components (that is, subsystem is a kind of component). A *component* (Section 3.6.2) is also a grouping of modeling elements (classes and so on, including other components) under an assigned name and such that its manifestation is replaceable within its environment. The services that a component provides are fully encapsulated and exposed as a set of **ports** that define the component's **provided** and **required interfaces**.

The *bean* layer represents the data classes and value objects that are destined for rendering on the user interface. Unless entered by the user, the bean data is built up from the entity objects (the entity layer). The Core PCBMER framework does not specify or endorse if access to bean objects is via message passing or event processing as long as the bean layer does not depend on other layers.

The *presentation* layer represents the screen and UI objects on which the beans can be rendered. It is responsible for maintaining consistency in its presentation when the beans change, so it depends on the bean layer. This dependency can be realized in one of two ways – by direct calls to methods (message passing) using the *pull model* or by event processing followed by message passing using the *push model* (or, rather, the *push-and-pull* model).

The *controller* layer represents the application logic. Controller objects respond to the UI requests that originate from Presentation and are results of users' interactions with the system. In a programmable GUI client, UI requests may be menu or button selections. In a Web browser client, UI requests appear as HTTP get or post requests.

The *entity* layer responds to Controller and Mediator. It contains classes representing "business objects". They store (in the program's memory) objects retrieved from the database or created in order to be stored on the database. Many entity classes are container classes.

The *mediator* layer establishes a channel of communication that mediates between entity and resource classes. This layer manages business transactions, enforces business rules, instantiates business objects in the entity layer and in general manages the memory cache of the application. Architecturally, Mediator serves two main purposes. First, it isolates the entity and resource layers so that changes in any one of them can be introduced independently. Second, it mediates between the controller and entity/resource layers when Controller requests data but it does not know if the data has been loaded to memory or it is only available on the database.

The *resource* layer is responsible for all communications with external persistent data sources (databases, Web services and so on). This is where the connections to the database and SOA servers are established, queries to persistent data are constructed and the database transactions are instigated.

4.1.3.2 The PCBMER principles

The Core PCBMER framework has a number of immediately visible advantages. One noticeable advantage is the *separation of concerns* between layers, allowing for modifications to be made within one layer without affecting the other (independent) layers or else having a predictable and manageable effect on the other (dependable) layers. For example, the presentation layer that provides a Java application UI could be switched to a mobile phone interface and still use the existing implementation of controller and bean layers. That is, the same pair of controller and bean layers can support more than one presentation UI at the same time.

The second important advantage is the *elimination of cycles* between dependency relationships and the resultant six-layer hierarchy with downward-only dependencies. Cycles would degenerate a hierarchy into a network structure. Cycles are disallowed both between PCBMER layers and within each PCBMER layer.

The third advantage is that the framework ensures a significant degree of *stability*. Higher layers depend on lower layers. Therefore, as long as the lower layers are stable (do not change significantly, in particular in interfaces), changes to the higher layers are relatively painless. Recall also that lower layers can be extended with new functionality (as opposed to changes to existing functionality) and such extensions should not impact on the existing functionality of the higher layers.

PCBMER enforces other properties and constraints that are not necessarily directly visible in Figure 4.3. Below is the list of the most important of PCBMER's *architectural principles* (Maciaszek 2006; Maciaszek and Liong 2005):

- *Downward Dependency Principle (DDP)*

  The **DDP** states that the main dependency structure is top-down. Objects in higher layers depend on objects in lower layers. Consequently, lower layers are more *stable* than higher layers. Interfaces, abstract classes, dominant classes and similar devices should encapsulate stable layers so that they can be extended when needed.

- *Upward Notification Principle (UNP)*

  The **UNP** promotes low coupling in a bottom-up communication between layers. This can be achieved by using *asynchronous communication* based on *event processing*. Objects in higher layers act as subscribers (*observers*) to state changes in lower layers.

When an object (*publisher*) in a lower layer changes its state, it sends notifications to its subscribers. In response, subscribers can communicate with the publisher (now in the downward direction) so that their states are synchronized with the state of the publisher.

- *Neighbor Communication Principle (NCP)*

  The **NCP** demands that a layer can only communicate directly with its neighbor layer as determined by direct dependencies between layers. This principle ensures that the system does not disintegrate to a network of intercommunicating objects. To enforce this principle, the message passing between non-neighboring objects uses *delegation* or *forwarding* (the former passes a reference to itself; the latter does not). In more complex scenarios, a special *acquaintance package* can be used to group interfaces to assist in collaboration that engages distant layers.

- *Explicit Association Principle (EAP)*

  The **EAP** visibly documents permitted message passing between classes. This principle recommends that *associations* are established on directly collaborating classes. Provided the design conforms to PCBMER, the downward dependencies between classes (as per DDP) are legitimized by corresponding associations. Associations resulting from DDP are uni-directional (otherwise they would create circular dependencies). It must be remembered, however, that not *all* associations between classes are due to message passing. For example, both-directional associations may be needed to implement referential integrity between classes in the entity layer.

- *Cycle Elimination Principle (CEP)*

  The **CEP** ensures that *circular dependencies* between layers and classes within layers are resolved (Maciaszek and Liong 2005). This is because such dependencies violate the separation of concerns guideline and are the main obstacle to reusability. Cycles can be resolved by placing offending classes in a new layer/package created specifically for that purpose or by forcing one of the communication paths in the cycle to communicate via an interface.

- *Class Naming Principle (CNP)*

  The **CNP** makes it possible to recognize in the *class name* the layer/package to which the class belongs. To this end, each class name is prefixed in PCBMER with the first letter of the layer name. So, for example, `EVideo` is a class in the entity layer. The same principle applies to interfaces. Each interface name is prefixed with two capital letters – the first is the letter "I" (signifying that this is an interface) and the second letter identifies the layer. Thus, `ICVideo` is an interface in the controller layer).

- *Acquaintance Package Principle (APP)*

  The **APP** is the consequence of the NCP. The acquaintance package consists of *interfaces* that an object passes, instead of concrete objects, in arguments to method calls. The interfaces can be implemented in any PCBMER layer. This effectively allows communication between non-neighboring layers while centralizing dependency management to a single acquaintance package.

Review quiz 4.1

RQ1 What is the necessary and most important condition for building the quality of adaptiveness (supportability) into the software?

RQ2 Which MVC objects represent mouse and keyboard events?

RQ3 Which Core J2EE tier is responsible for establishing and maintaining connections to data sources?

RQ4 Which PCBMER layer is responsible for establishing and maintaining connections to data sources?

4.2 State specifications

The *state* of an object is determined by the values of its attributes and associations. For example, the state of a `BankAccount` object may be "overdrawn" when the value of the attribute "balance" is negative. As object states are determined from the data structures, the models of data structures are called *state specifications*.

State specifications provide a *structure* (or *static*) *view* of the system (Section 3.3). The main task here is to define *classes* in an application domain, and their *attributes* and *relationships* with other classes. *Operations* of classes are normally omitted at first. They will be derived from the models of *behavior specifications*.

In a typical situation, *entity classes* (business objects) are identified first (Section 4.1.3). These are the classes that define the application domain and have *persistent* presence in the database for the system. Classes that service user events (*controller classes*), those that represent the GUI rendering (*presentation classes*) and those that manage data for GUI rendering (*bean classes*) are not established until the behavioral characteristics of the system are known. Similarly, other categories of classes, such as *resource* and *mediator classes*, are also defined later.

4.2.1 Modeling classes

The class model is the cornerstone of object-oriented system development. Classes set the foundation on which the state and behavior of the system are observable. Unfortunately, classes are chronically difficult to find and their properties are not always obvious. For the same non-trivial application domain, no two analysts will come up with an identical set of classes and their properties. Although the class models may be different, the eventual outcome and user satisfaction may be equally good (or equally bad).

Thus, class modeling is not a deterministic process – there is no recipe for how to find and define good classes; the process is highly *iterative* and *incremental*. Paramount to successful class design is the analyst's

- knowledge of class modeling
- understanding of the application domain
- experience with similar and successful designs

- ability to think forward and predict the consequences
- willingness to revise the model to eliminate imperfections.

The last point is related to the use of CASE tools. Large-scale application of CASE technology may hinder the system development in immature organizations (Section 1.1.2.3.2). However, the use of CASE tools for *personal productivity* is always warranted.

Discovering classes

As mentioned, no two analysts will come up with identical class models for the same application domain, nor will they use the same thinking processes to discover the classes. The literature is full of suggested approaches to *class discovery*. Analysts may follow one of these approaches initially, but the successive iterations will almost certainly involve unconventional and rather arbitrary mechanisms.

Bahrami (1999) goes over the main points for the four most popular approaches to identifying classes:

- noun phrase approach
- common class patterns approach
- use case-driven approach
- **CRC** (class–responsibility–collaborators) approach.

Bahrami (1999) attributes each approach to published work, but only the last approach has an indisputable origin. Next, the four approaches are summarized and examples given for the use of a *mixed approach*.

Noun phrase approach

The *noun phrase* approach advises that an analyst should read the statements in the requirements document, looking for noun phrases. Every noun is considered a *candidate class*. The list of candidate classes is then divided into three groups:

- relevant classes
- fuzzy classes
- irrelevant classes.

Irrelevant classes are those that are outside the problem domain. The analyst cannot formulate a statement of purpose for them. Experienced practitioners are unlikely to include irrelevant classes in their original list of candidate classes. In this way, the formal step of identifying and eliminating irrelevant classes is avoided.

Relevant classes are those that manifestly belong to the problem domain. The nouns representing the names of these classes appear frequently in the requirements document. Additionally, the analyst can confirm the significance and purpose of these classes from general knowledge of the application domain and the investigation of similar systems, textbooks, documents and proprietary software packages.

Fuzzy classes are those that the analyst cannot confidently and unanimously classify as relevant. They provide the greatest challenge. The analyst needs to analyze them further and either include them in the list of relevant classes or exclude them as irrelevant. The eventual classification of these classes into one or the other group will make a difference between a good class model and a bad one.

The noun phrase approach assumes that the requirements document is complete and correct. In reality, this is rarely true. Even if this were the case, a tedious search through large volumes of text might not necessarily lead to a comprehensive and accurate outcome.

4.2.1.1.2 *Common class pattern approach*

The *common class patterns* approach derives candidate classes from the generic classification theory of objects. *Classification theory* is a part of science concerned with partitioning the world of objects into useful groups so that it is possible to reason about them better.

Bahrami (1999) lists the following groups (patterns) for finding candidate classes:

- *concept class*: a *concept* is a notion that a large community of people share and agree on. Without concepts people are not able to communicate effectively or even to any satisfactory degree (for example, `Reservation` is a concept class in an airline reservation system)
- *events class*: an *event* is something that does not take time relative to our timescale (for example, `Arrival` is an event class in an airline reservation system)
- *organization class*: *organization* is any kind of purposeful grouping or collection of things (for example, `TravelAgency` is a class in an airline reservation system)
- *people class*: "people" is understood here as a role that a person plays in the system, rather than a physical person (for example, `Passenger` is a class in an airline reservation system)
- *places class*: *places* are physical locations relevant to the information system (`TravelOffice` is such a class in an airline reservation system).

Rumbaugh et al. (2005) propose a different classification scheme:

- *physical class* `Airplane`, for example
- *business class* `Reservation`, for example
- *logical class* `FlightTimetable`, for example
- *application class* `ReservationTransaction`, for example
- *computer class* `Index`, for example
- *behavioral class* `ReservationCancellation`, for example.

Thus, the common class patterns approach provides useful guidance, but does not offer a systematic process whereby a reliable and complete set of classes can be discovered. This approach may be used successfully to determine the initial set of classes or verify whether or not some classes (derived by other means) should be there or, perhaps, must not be there. However, the common class patterns approach is too loosely bound to specific users' requirements to offer a comprehensive solution.

A particular danger associated with the common class patterns approach relates to the possibilities for misinterpretation of class names. For example, what does an `Arrival` mean? Does it mean arrival on the runway (landing time), arrival at the terminal (disembarkation time), arrival at baggage reclaim (luggage clearance time)? Similarly, the word `Reservation` in the context of a Native American environment has an entirely separate meaning to the one understood here.

Use case-driven approach   *4.2.1.1.3*

The *use case-driven* approach is emphasized by IBM Rational Unified Process (Section 1.5.2). The graphical model of use cases is supplemented with narrative descriptions and activity and interaction models (Sections 3.2 and 3.4). These additional descriptions and models define the steps (and objects) needed for each use case to occur. From this information, we can generalize to discover candidate classes.

The use case-driven approach has a bottom-up flavor. Once the use cases are known and the *interaction models* of the system are at least partly defined, the objects used in these diagrams lead to the discovery of classes.

In reality, the use case-driven approach bears some similarity to the noun phrase approach. The common ground lies in the fact that the use cases specify the requirements. Both approaches study the statements in the requirements document to discover candidate classes. Whether these statements are narrative or graphical is secondary. In any case, at the analysis stage in the lifecycle, most use cases will only be described in text, with no interaction diagrams.

The use case-driven approach suffers from similar deficiencies to the noun phrase approach. Being a bottom-up approach, it relies for its accuracy on the completeness and correctness of the use case models. Partial use case models result in incomplete class models. Moreover, the class models correspond to specific functionality and so do not necessarily reflect *all* the important concepts of the addressed business domain. For all means and purposes, this leads to a *function-driven* approach (some proponents of object-oriented methods prefer to call it *problem-driven*).

CRC approach   *4.2.1.1.4*

The *CRC* (class–responsibility–collaborators) approach is more than a technique for class discovery – it is an attractive way of interpreting, understanding and teaching about objects (Wirfs-Brock and Wilkerson 1989; Wirfs-Brock et al. 1990). The CRC approach involves brainstorming sessions, made easy by the use of specially prepared cards. The cards have three compartments. The *class name* is written in the upper compartment, the class *responsibilities* are listed in the left compartment and the *collaborators* are listed in the right compartment. Responsibilities are the services (operations) that the class is prepared to perform on behalf of other classes. Many responsibilities to be fulfilled require the collaboration (services) of other classes. Such classes are listed as collaborators.

The CRC approach is an animated process during which the developers "play cards" – they fill cards with class names and assign responsibilities and collaborators while "executing" a processing scenario (such as a use case scenario). When services are needed and the existing classes do not contain them, a new class can be created. The new class is assigned appropriate responsibilities and collaborators. If a class becomes "too busy", it is divided into a number of smaller classes.

The CRC approach identifies classes from the analysis of messages passing between objects to fulfil the processing tasks. The emphasis is placed on the uniform distribution of intelligence in the system and some classes may be derived from the technical design need rather than discovered as "business objects" as such. In this sense, CRC may be more suitable for the verification of classes already discovered by other methods. CRC is also useful for the determination of class properties (as implied by the class responsibilities and collaborators).

4.2.1.1.5 Mixed approach

In practice, the process of class discovery is likely to be guided by different approaches at different times. Frequently, the elements of all four of the approaches explained above are involved. The analysts' overall knowledge, experience and intuition are also contributing factors. The process is neither top-down nor bottom-up, but middle-out. Such a process of class discovery can be called the *mixed approach*.

One possible scenario is as follows. The initial set of classes may be discovered from the generic knowledge and experience of analysts. The common class patterns approach can provide additional guidance. Other classes may be added from the analysis of high-level descriptions of the problem domain using the noun phrase approach. If use case diagrams are available, then the use case-driven approach can be used to add new and verify existing classes. Finally, the CRC approach will allow brainstorming on the list of classes discovered so far.

4.2.1.1.6 Guidelines for discovering classes

The following is an imperfect list of guidelines or rules of thumb that analysts should follow when selecting candidate classes. The guidelines apply to the discovery of *entity classes* (Section 4.1.3.1).

- Each class must have a clear *statement of purpose* in the system.
- Each class is a template description for a *set of objects*. *Singleton* classes – for which we can imagine only a single object – are very unlikely among "business objects". Such classes usually constitute a "common knowledge" aspect of the application and will be hard-coded in the application programs. As an example, if the system is designed for a single organization, the existence of the `Organization` class is not warranted.
- Each entity class must house a *set of attributes*. It is a good idea to determine identifying attribute(s) (*keys*) to assist in reasoning about the class cardinality – that is, an expected number of objects of that class in the database. However, remember that, in general, a class does not need to have a user-defined key. *Object identifiers* (OIDs) identify objects of classes (Appendix, Section A.2.3).
- Each class should be distinguished from an *attribute*. Whether a concept is a class or an attribute depends on the application domain. `Color` of a car is normally perceived as an attribute of the class `Car`. However, in a paint factory `Color` is definitely a class with its own attributes (brightness, saturation, transparency and so on).

- A class houses a *set of operations*. However, at this stage, the identification of operations can be ignored. The operations in the *interface* of the class (the services that the class provides in the system) are implied from the statement of purpose (see the first point above).

Examples of discovering classes   *4.2.1.1.7*

Example 4.1: university enrolment

Consider the following requirements for a university enrolment system and identify the candidate classes.

- Each university degree has a number of compulsory courses and a number of elective courses.
- Each course is at a given level and has a credit point value.
- A course can be a part of any number of degrees.
- Each degree specifies a minimum total credit points value required for degree completion. For exampe BIT (bachelor of information technology) requires 68 credit points, including compulsory courses.
- Students may combine course offerings into programs of study suited to their individual needs and leading to the degree in which a student is enrolled.

Let us analyze the requirements listed in Example 4.1 in order to discover the candidate classes. In the first point listed, the relevant classes are `Degree` and `Course`. These two classes conform to the five guidelines in Section 4.2.1.1.6. It is uncertain if the class `Course` should be specialized into classes `CompulsoryCourse` and `ElectiveCourse`. A course is compulsory or elective with respect to the degree. However, it is possible that the distinction between compulsory and elective courses can be captured by an association or even by an attribute of a class. Hence, `CompulsoryCourse` and `ElectiveCourse` are considered, at this stage, as fuzzy classes.

In the second point, only attributes of the class `Course` are identified – namely `courseLevel` and `creditPointValue`. The third point characterizes an association between the classes `Course` and `Degree`. The fourth introduces `minTotalCreditPoints` as an attribute of the class `Degree`.

The final point can lead to the discovery of three more classes – `Student`, `CourseOffering`, and `StudyProgram`. The first two are undoubtedly relevant classes, but `StudyProgram` may yet turn out to be an association between `Student` and `CourseOffering`. For that reason, `StudyProgram` is classified as a fuzzy class. This discussion is reflected in Table 4.1.

Table 4.1 Candidate classes for a university enrolment system

Relevant classes	Fuzzy classes
Course	CompulsoryCourse
Degree	ElectiveCourse
Student	StudyProgram
CourseOffering	

Example 4.2: video store

Consider the following requirements for a system for a video store and identify the candidate classes.

■ The video store keeps an extensive library of current and popular movie titles in stock. A particular movie may be held on videotapes or disks.

■ A movie can be rented for a particular rental duration (expressed in days), with a rental charge for that period.

■ The video store must be able to answer immediately any enquiries about a movie's stock availability. The current condition of each tape and disk must be known and recorded, together with generic information about the percentage of videotapes and disks in excellent renting condition.

The first requirement listed in Example 4.2 has a few nouns, but only some of them can be turned into candidate classes. The video store is not a class because the whole system is about it (there would be only one object of that class in the database). Similarly, the notions of stock and library are too generic to be considered classes, at least at this stage. The relevant classes seem to be MovieTitle, Videotape, and VideoDisk.

The second point is that each movie title has rental rates associated with it. However, it is not clear what is understood by "movie" – movie title or movie medium (tape or disk)? We will need to clarify this requirement with the customers. In the meantime, we may want to declare RentalRates to be a fuzzy class, rather than store information about rental period and rental charge in a movie title or a movie medium class.

The third requirment is that information about the current condition of each tape and disk needs to be stored. However, attributes such as videoCondition or percentExcellentCondition can be generically declared in a higher-level abstract class (let us call it VideoMedium) and inherited by the concrete subclasses (such as Videotape). This discussion is reflected in Table 4.2.

Table 4.2 Candidate classes for a system for a video store

Relevant classes	Fuzzy classes
MovieTitle	RentalRates
VideoMedium	
Videotape	
VideoDisk	

The first requirement given in Example 4.3 (overleaf) contains the notions of customer, contract and product. Our generic knowledge and experience tells us that these are typical classes. However, contract and product are not concepts within the scope of the contact management system and so should be refuted.

Example 4.3: contact management

Consider the following requirements for a contact management system and identify the candidate classes.

- The system supports the function of "keeping in touch" with all current and prospective customers so as to be responsive to their needs and win new contracts for products and services offered by the organization.
- The system stores the names, phone numbers, postal and courier addresses and so on of organizations and contact persons in these organizations.
- The system allows employees to schedule tasks and events that need to be carried out with regard to relevant contact persons. Employees schedule the tasks and events for other employees or themselves.
- A "task" is a group of events that take place to achieve a result. The result may be to convert a prospective customer into a customer, organize product delivery or solve a customer's problem. Typical types of events are phone calls, visits, sending faxes and arranging for training.

Customer is a relevant class, but we may prefer to call it Contact, on the understanding that not all contacts are current customers. The distinction between a current and a prospective customer may or may not warrant the introduction of classes CurrentCustomer and ProspectiveCustomer. As we are not sure, we will declare these two classes as fuzzy.

The second point in the list sheds new light on the discussion above. We need to distinguish between a contact *organization* and a contact *person*. Thus, Customer does not seem to be a good name for the class. After all, Customer implies only a current customer and the name can embody both an organization and a contact person. Our new proposal is to name the classes Organization, Contact (meaning a contact person), CurrentOrg (an organization that is our current customer) and ProspectiveOrg (an organization that is our prospective customer).

A few attributes of classes are mentioned in this second point, too. However, postal and courier addresses are composite attributes and they apply to the two classes Organization and Contact. As such, PostalAddress and CourierAddress are legitimate fuzzy classes.

The third point introduces three further relevant classes – Employee, Task and Event. The statement explains the scheduling activity. The last point listed further clarifies the meaning and relationships between the classes, but does not implicate any new classes. Table 4.3 shows the candidate classes for this example of contact management.

Table 4.3 Candidate classes for a contact management system

Relevant classes	Fuzzy classes
Organization	CurrentOrg
Contact	ProspectiveOrg
Employee	PostalAddress
Task	CourierAddress
Event	

4.2.1.2 Specifying classes

Once the list of candidate classes is known, they should be specified further by placing them on a class diagram and defining the classes' properties. Some properties can be entered and displayed inside graphical icons representing classes in class diagrams. Many other properties in the class specification have only textual representation. CASE tools provide easy editing capabilities to enter or modify such information via dialog windows with tabbed pages or similar techniques.

This section discusses class specification at a relatively high level of abstraction. The emphasis is placed on proper class naming and on the assignment of attributes to classes. Identification of class operations is not considered and more advanced modeling capabilities of UML are not used – they are discussed in Chapter 5 and later.

4.2.1.2.1 Naming classes

Each class has to be given a *name*. In some CASE tools, a *code* for the class – which is possibly different from the name – may also be assigned. The code would conform to the naming conventions demanded by a target programming language or database system. The code, not the name, is used for the generation of software code from the design models.

It is recommended practice to enforce a uniform convention for class names. The PCBMER convention (Section 4.1.3.2) is that a class name begins with a capital letter signifying the architectural layer (subsystem/package) to which the class belongs. The proper name of the class, following the letter identifying the layer, also begins with a capital letter. For compound names, the first letter of each word is capitalized (rather than separated by an underscore or hyphen). This is only a recommended convention, but it has a reasonable following among developers.

The name of the class should be a singular noun (such as Course) or an adjective and a singular noun (such as CompulsoryCourse) whenever possible. It is clear that a class is a template for many objects, so using plural nouns would not add any new information. At times, a singular noun does not capture the true intention of the class. In such situations, using plural nouns is acceptable (such as Videotape in Example 4.2).

A class name should be meaningful. It should capture the true nature of the class. It should be drawn from the users' vocabulary (not from the developers' jargon).

It is better to use a longer name than make it too cryptic. Names longer than 30 characters, though, are unwieldy (and some programming environments may not accept them, if the CASE tool is working with class names instead of class codes). Longer descriptions are also possible, in addition to class names and codes.

4.2.1.2.2 Discovering and specifying class attributes

The graphical icon representing a class consists of three compartments – class name, attributes and operations (Appendix, Section A.3). The specification of class attributes belongs to *state specifications* and is discussed here. The specification of class operations is discussed later in this chapter, under the heading Behavior specifications, Section 4.3.

Attributes are discovered in parallel with the discovery of classes. The identification of attributes is a side-effect of class determination. This does not mean that attribute discovery is a straightforward activity. On the contrary, it is a demanding and highly iterative process.

In the initial specification models, we define only the attributes that are essential to an understanding of the *states* (Section 3.5) in which objects of that class can be. Other attributes may be temporarily ignored (but the analyst must make sure that the existence of the ignored information is lost by failure to record it in the future). It is unlikely that *all* class attributes will be mentioned in the requirements document, but it is important to leave out attributes that are not implied by requirements. More attributes can be added in subsequent iterations.

Our recommended convention for *attribute names* is to use small letters but capitalize the first letters of successive words in a compound name (`streetName`, for example). An alternative approach is to separate words by inserting an underscore (such as `street_name`).

Examples of discovering and specifying class attributes   *4.2.1.2.3*

Example 4.4: university enrolment

Refer to Example 4.1 (section 4.2.1.1.7) and consider the following additional requirements from the requirements document.

■ A student's choice of courses may be restricted by timetable clashes and limitations on the number of students who can be enrolled on the current courses offered.

■ A student's proposed program of study is entered in the online enrolment system. The system checks the program's consistency and reports any problems. The problems need to be resolved with the help of an academic adviser. The final program of study is subject to academic approval by the delegate of the head of division and is then forwarded to the registrar.

The first point listed in Example 4.4 mentions timetable clashes, but we are not sure how to model this issue. It is possible that we are talking here about a use case that procedurally determines timetable clashes.

The second part of the first statement can be modeled by adding the `enrolmentQuota` attribute to the class `ECourseOffering`. It is also clear now that `ECourseOffering` should have the attributes of year and semester.

The second point in the list reinforces the need for the `EStudyProgram` class. We can see that `EStudyProgram` combines a number of course offerings currently on offer. Therefore, `EStudyProgram` should also have the attributes of year and semester.

On closer analysis of fuzzy classes `CompulsoryCourse` and `ElectiveCourse` (Table 4.1) we observe that a course is compulsory or elective *in relation to* a degree. The same course may be compulsory in relation to one degree, elective in relation to another degree and may even not be allowed for some other degrees. If so, `CompulsoryCourse` and `ElectiveCourse` are not classes in their own rights. (Note that we are not entering here into the realm of modeling with generalization – see Appendix, Section A.7.)

Figure 4.4 represents a class model conforming to the discussion so far. Additionally, we have used the *stereotypes* <<PK>> and <<CK>> to mean a primary key and a candidate

Figure 4.4
Class
specifications for
a university
enrolment system

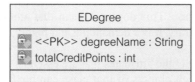

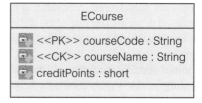

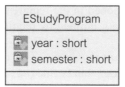

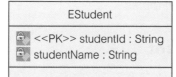

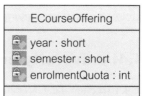

key, respectively. These are unique identifiers of objects in the classes concerned. Data types for attributes have been specified as well. Data types conform to Java.

The classes `EStudyProgram` and `ECourseOffering` do not have identifying attributes. They will be added to these classes when the *associations* (Appendix, Section A.5) between classes have been discovered.

Example 4.5: video store

Consider the combined requirements listed in Example 4.2 (Section 4.2.1.1.7) and the following additional requirements.

■ The rental charge for entertainment items (such as a movie) differs depending on the item category and the entertainment medium containing the item. In general, an "entertainment medium" can be a video medium or just a sound medium. A video medium can be a videotape, DVD or game CD. A music CD is a sound medium, but some music CDs are available in video formats, such as VCD or DVD-A.

■ The system stores information about employees and identifies the employee responsible for each rental transaction performed on behalf of a customer.

■ A separate transaction is generated for renting for different durations. Items in each rental transaction can relate to more than one medium (as long as all items are rented for the same duration). A medium can contain movies, TV programs, games or music.

■ The employees of the video store tend to remember the codes of the most popular movies. They frequently use a movie code, instead of its title, to identify the movie. This is a useful practice, because the same movie title may have more than one release by different directors.

The first statement in the list in Example 4.5 explains that rental charges vary depending on entertainment items and various categories of items – `EMovie`, `EGame`, and `EMusic`, for example They also vary depending on the entertainment medium housing the item, such as whether it is on an `EVideotape`, `EDVD` or `ECD`.

The second point establishes the need for the classes `EEmployee` and `ECustomer`. The associations between these classes and a class managing rental transactions (called `ERental`) will be defined later.

The main responsibilities of the `ERental` class are defined in the third point. Many rented items can be processed in a single transaction. This statement also explains that an entertainment medium can contain one of four categories of item – namely, movies, TV programs, games or music.

The final statement adds `movieCode` (as the key attribute) and `director` to the class `EMovie`. Other attributes are as discussed in Example 4.2 (Section 4.2.1.1.7).

Figure 4.5 shows the class model for the video store application as per the discussion in Examples 4.2 and 4.5 (above). `EMovie.isInStock` is a *derived* attribute. `EVideoMedium.percentExcellentCondition` is a *class scope* (*static*) attribute (Appendix, Section A.3.3). This attribute will contain the percentage of `EVideoMedium` objects, with the value of the attribute `videoCondition = "E"` (excellent). Although not shown in the diagram, a class-scope operation (named, for example, `computePercentageExcellentCondition`) would need to be associated with that attribute to compute its current value on demand.

Example 4.6: contact management

Refer to Example 4.3 (Section 4.2.1.1.7) and consider the following additional information.

- A customer is considered current if a contract with that customer exists for the delivery of our products or services. However, contract management is outside the scope of our system.
- The system allows the production of various reports on our contacts based on postal and courier addresses (find all customers by postcode, for example).
- The date and time of the task's creation is recorded. The "money value" expected from the completion of the task might also be stored.
- Events for the employee will be displayed on the employee's screen in calendar-like pages (one day per page). The priority of each event (low, medium or high) is distinguished visually on the screen.
- Not all events have a "due time" associated with them – some are "untimed" (they can be performed at any time during the day for which they were scheduled).
- The creation time of an event cannot be changed, but the due time can.
- On an event's completion, the completion date and time are recorded.
- The system also stores identifications for the employees who created the tasks and events, who are scheduled to do the event ("due employee") and who completed the event.

Analysis of the first extra piece of information in Example 4.6 tells us that the notion of the current customer is derived from the association between `EOrganization` (as a customer) and `Contract`. The association may be quite dynamic. Hence, the classes

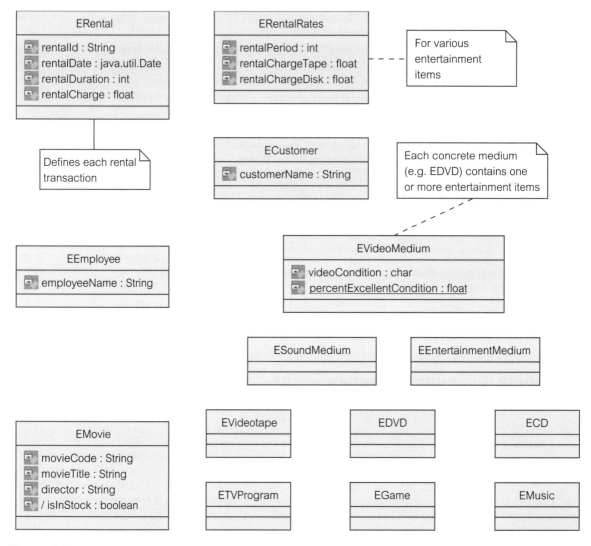

Figure 4.5 Class specifications for a video store system

`CurrentOrg` and `ProspectiveOrg` are not viable. Moreover, the system is not involved in contract management and is not responsible for the maintenance of the class `Contract`. The best we can do is to model the solution by a derived attribute, `EOrganization.isCurrent`, to be modified as necessary by the contract management subsystem.

The second point provides the reason for having two address classes – `EPostalAddress` and `ECourierAddress`.

The remaining statements provide additional information about the attribute contents of the classes. There are also some hints about association relationships and integrity constraints (to be discussed later).

The class specification for this contact management system is presented in Figure 4.6. No relationships have been modeled yet. Hence, for example, the final statement, which relates employees to tasks and events, is not reflected in the model.

From the first statement given in Example 4.7 (see overleaf), we can derive a few attributes in the class `ECampaign`. `ECampaign` contains `campaignCode` (primary key), `campaignTitle`, `dateStart` and `dateClosed`. The last sentence in this first statement refers to campaign prizes. A closer look should convince us that `EPrize` is a class on its own – it is drawn, it has a winner and it must have other properties not explicitly stated, such as description, value and ranking compared to the other prizes for that campaign.

We add `EPrize` to the class model, together with the attributes `prizeDescr`, `prizeValue` and `prizeRanking`. We observe that the date on which a draw is made is the same for all the prizes for a particular campaign. We add the attribute `dateDrawn` to the class `ECampaign`. A winner of the prize is a supporter. We can capture this fact later in an association between `EPrize` and `ESupporter`.

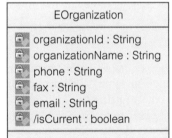

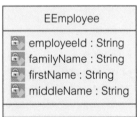

Figure 4.6
Class specifications for a contact management system

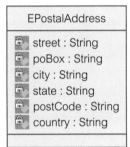

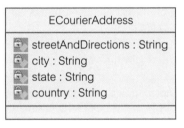

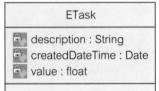

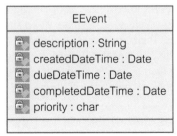

Example 4.7: telemarketing

Refer to Section 1.6.4 (problem statement 4) and Section 2.5, which presented the requirements business model and look at Example 2.3 concerning the telemarketing application. In particular, consider the business class diagram in Figure 2.16 (Section 2.5.4). Take into consideration the following additional information.

- A campaign has a title that is generally used to refer to it. It also has a unique code for internal reference. Each campaign runs over a fixed period of time. Soon after the campaign has closed, the draws for prizes are undertaken and the holders of winning tickets are advised.

- All tickets are numbered. The numbers are unique across all tickets in a campaign. The total number of tickets in a campaign, the number of tickets sold so far and the current status of each ticket are known (those available, ordered, paid for, prize winners and so on).

- To determine the performance of the society's telemarketers, the duration of calls and successful call outcomes (that is, those resulting in tickets being ordered) are recorded.

- Extensive information about supporters is maintained. Apart from normal contact details (address, phone number and so on), this information includes historical details, such as the first and most recent dates when a supporter had participated in a campaign, along with the number of campaigns in which they participated. Any details of known supporter's preferences and constraints (such as unwelcome times to call or the usual credit card used in ticket purchases) are also kept.

- The processing of telemarketing calls needs to be prioritized. Calls that are unanswered or where an answering machine was found need to be rescheduled to try again later. It is important to have alternative times when attempting repeat calls.

- We can try calling over and over again until a call attempt limit has been reached. The limit may be different for different call types. For example, a normal "solicitation" call may have a different limit to a call to remind a supporter of an outstanding payment.

- The possible outcomes of calls are categorized to facilitate data entry by telemarketers. Typical outcomes are success (tickets ordered), no success, call back later, no answer, engaged, answering machine, fax machine, wrong number and disconnected

The information in the second point is that each ticket has a number, but the number is not unique across all tickets ever (it is only unique within a campaign). We thus add the attribute `ticketNumber`, but we do not make it a primary key within `ECampaignTicket`. Two other attributes in `ECampaignTicket` are `ticketValue` and `ticketStatus`. The total number of tickets and the number of tickets sold are attributes of `ECampaign` (`numTickets` and `numTicketsSold`).

The third point uncovers a few challenging issues. What data structures do we need to compute telemarketers' performance? To start with, we need to come up with some measures to express their performance. One possibility is that we compute the average number of calls per hour for each telemarketer and the average number of successful calls per hour. We can then calculate a performance indicator by dividing the number of successful calls by the total number of calls. We add the attributes `averagePerHour` and `successPerHour` to the class `ETelemarketer`.

To calculate telemarketers' performance indicators, we need to store the duration of each call. The placeholder for this information is the class `ECallOutcome`. We add the attributes `startTime` and `endTime` to that class. We assume that each call outcome will be linked to a telemarketer by an association.

Analysis of the fourth point results in some attributes to be included in the class `ESupporter`. The attributes are `supporterId` (primary key), `supporterName`, `phoneNumber`, `mailingAddress`, `dateFirst`, `dateLast`, `campaignCount`, `preferredHours` and `creditCardNumber`. Some of these attributes (`mailingAddress`, `preferredHours`) are complex enough that we can expect that they will have to be converted into classes later in the development process, but we store them as attributes for now.

The fifth point refers to the class `ECallScheduled`. We add to it the attributes `phoneNumber`, `priority` and `attemptNumber`. We are not quite sure how to support the requirement that successive calls should be made at different times of day. This is obviously

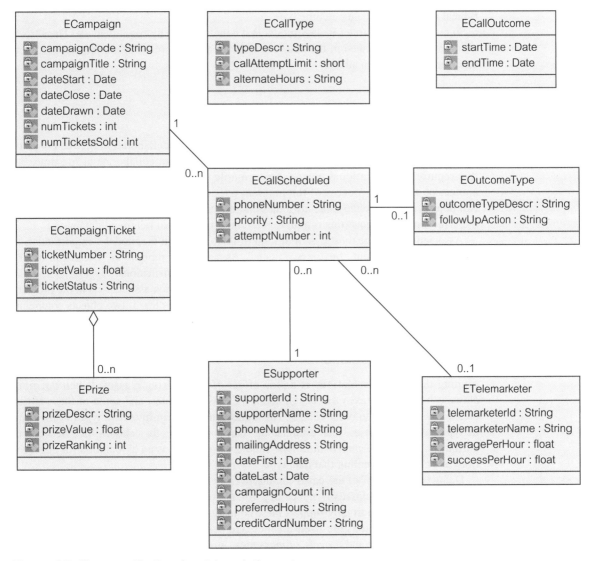

Figure 4.7 Class specifications for a telemarketing system

the responsibility of the scheduling algorithm, but a support in data structures will be necessary. Fortunately, some clarity on this issue is provided by the next statement.

The penultimate statement results in a new class – `ECallType`. The class contains the attributes `typeDescr`, `callAttemptLimit` and `alternativeHours`. The latter is a complex data structure, similar to `preferredHours` in `ESupporter`, and it will eventually result in a separate class.

The last point categorizes the calls' outcomes. This is a direct hint that a class `EOutcomeType` is needed. Possible outcome types can be stored in the attribute `outcomeTypeDescr`. It is not clear what other attributes can be included in `EOutcomeType`, but we are convinced that they will emerge with the study of detailed requirements. One such attribute could be `followUpAction`, to hold information about a typical next step for each outcome type.

Figure 4.7 demonstrates a class model that concludes the discussion above. The associations already established in the business class model (Figure 2.16) are retained. No new associations have been added.

4.2.2　Modeling associations

Associations connect objects in the system. They facilitate collaboration between objects. Without associations, the objects can still be related and can collaborate at run time, but this requires computational means. For example, an object can acquire an identity of another object in the process of the program passing objects in messages. Alternatively, two objects may share the same attributes and the program can search for the same attribute values in two objects (this is akin to referential integrity in relational databases).

Associations are the most essential kind of relationship in the model – in particular, in the model of persistent "business objects". Associations support the execution of use cases and, therefore, tie together the *state* and *behavior* specifications.

The PCBMER framework reasserts the importance of explicit associations in the program in the EAP principle (Section 4.1.3.2). The principle demands that if two objects communicate at run time, then a compile-time association between these objects should exist.

4.2.2.1　Discovering associations

Finding the main associations is a side-effect of discovering classes. When defining classes, the analyst makes a decision about the class attributes, and some of these attributes are associations to other classes. Attributes can have primitive data types or they can be typed as other classes, thus establishing relationships to other classes. In essence, any attribute with a *non-primitive data type* should be modeled as an association (or aggregation) to a class representing that data type.

Doing the "dry run" of use cases can discover the remaining associations. *Collaboration paths* between the classes – necessary for a use case execution – are determined. Associations should normally support these collaboration paths.

Although associations are used for message passing, there is a difference between a *cycle of associations* and a *cycle of messages*. Association cycles, such as the simplest possible cycle shown in Figure A.14 (Appendix, Section A.5.2), are frequent and perfectly acceptable. Message cycles, such as two or more objects exchanging messages back and forth in a circular manner, are troublesome because they introduce difficult-to-manage run-time dependencies. Accordingly, the PCBMER framework recommends that message cycles be eliminated (in the CEP principle, Section 4.1.3.2).

Occasionally, a *cycle of associations* does not have to *commute* (be closed) to fully express the underlying semantics (Maciaszek 1990). That is, at least one of the associations in the cycle can be *derived*. Figure 3.9 (Section 3.3.3) contains a relevant example. A *derived association* is redundant in the semantic sense and should be eliminated (a good semantic model should be non-redundant). It is possible and, indeed, likely that many derived associations will nevertheless be included in the design model (for efficiency reasons, for example).

Specifying associations   4.2.2.2

The specification of associations involves:

- naming them
- naming the association roles
- determining the association multiplicity (Appendix, Section A.5.2).

The rules for giving *names to associations* should loosely follow the convention for naming classes. However, the PCBMER's CNP principle for prefixing names with a letter identifying the architectural layer (Section 4.1.3.2) does not apply to *association* names. This is because association names do not have representations in the implemented system. They serve only a modeling purpose.

By contrast, association *roles* are represented in the implemented system by attributes in classes linked by the association (Appendix, Section A.3.1.1). Accordingly, the rules for giving *names for association roles* should follow the convention for attribute names – that is, starting with lower-case letters and capitalizing the first letter of any successive words, building up multiword names (Section 4.2.1.2.2). It is customary to begin role names with the word "the" – theOrderLine, for example.

If only one association connects two classes, the specification of association name and association roles between these classes is optional. A CASE tool would distinguish each association internally by means of system-provided identification names.

Role names can be used to explain more complicated associations – in particular, *self-associations* (*recursive associations* that relate objects of the same class). If provided, role names should be chosen with the understanding that, in the design models, they will become attributes in classes at the opposite end of an association.

The *multiplicities* should be specified for both ends (roles) of an association. If unclear, the lower and upper multiplicity bounds can be omitted at this stage.

Example of specifying associations   4.2.2.2.1

Example 4.8: contact management

Refer to Examples 4.3 (Section 4.2.1.1.7) and 4.6 (Section 4.2.1.2.3). Use the requirements given in these examples to discover and specify the associations on the classes in the contact management system.

The association model for the contact management system mentioned in Example 4.8 is presented in Figure 4.8. To demonstrate the flexibility of association modeling, the use of association names and role names is unsystematic. The figure also contains the code for the class `ETask`. The code has been generated automatically by the CASE tool used (IBM Rational Rose). Note that if role names are provided on the graphical model, then they are used by the code generator. Otherwise, the CASE tool generates the role names, as shown by the presence of the instance variable `theEEvent` in the generated code, even though the role name for the association to `EEvent` is not provided in the model.

The multiplicity of all associations between `EPostalAddress` and `ECourierAddress` on the one hand and `EOrganization` and `EContact` on the other is "one". However, exclusive `OR {Xor}` constraints are set on the two pairs of associations. In UML, "an *Xor-constraint* indicates a situation in which only one of several potential associations may be instantiated at one time for any single instance" (UML 2003). An Xor-constraint is shown as a dashed line named `{Xor}` connecting two or more associations (the curly brackets in UML signify a constraint condition imposed on the model). Let us explain using the association between `EOrganization` and `EPostalAddress`.

On the "one" end of the association, an `EOrganization` object is connected to a maximum of one `EPostalAddress` object, but only if the postal address of the organization is known. On the opposite end of the association, a particular `EPostalAddress` object relates to an `EOrganization` object *or* to an `EContact` object.

The multiplicity of the role –theContact, between `ETask` and `EContact`, is unspecified. The requirements have not explained if a task must be directly linked to a contact. If so, we are still not sure if it can be linked to more than one contact.

Finally, there are three associations between `EEvent` and `EEmployee`. These associations determine which employee created an event, which one is due to perform it and which one will eventually complete it. At the time of an event's creation, the employee who is going to complete that event is unknown (so the multiplicity on the employee end of association completed is "zero or one").

4.2.3 Modeling aggregation and composition relationships

Aggregation – and its stronger form, *composition* – carries the "whole–part" semantics between a composite (superset) class and a component (subset) class (Appendix, Section A.6). In UML, aggregation is treated as a constrained form of association. This is a gross underestimation of the modeling significance of aggregation. Suffice to say that aggregation, along with generalization, is the most important technique for reusing functionality in object-oriented systems.

The modeling power of UML would be greatly facilitated if the language supported the following four semantics for aggregation (Maciaszek et al. 1996b):

- *ExclusiveOwns* aggregation
- *Owns* aggregation
- *Has* aggregation
- *Member* aggregation.

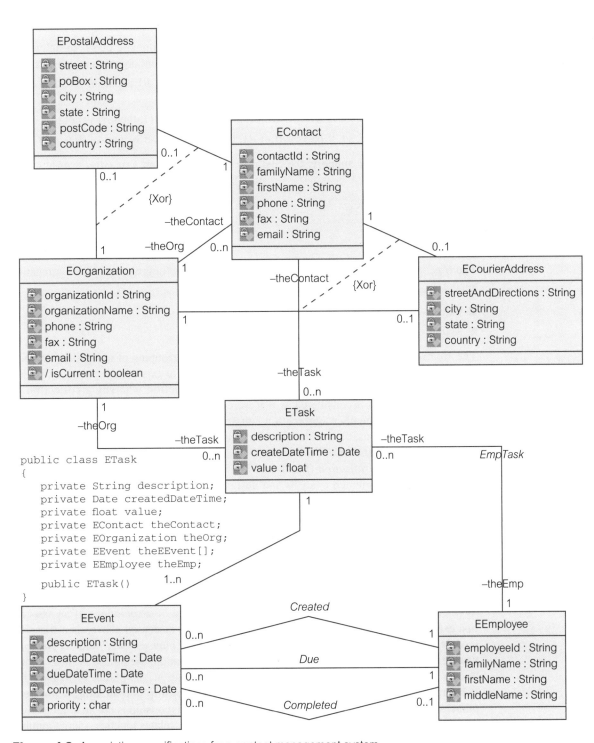

Figure 4.8 Association specifications for a contact management system

The *ExclusiveOwns* aggregation states that:

- component classes are *existence-dependent* on their composite class, so deleting a composite object propagates down and the related component objects are also deleted
- aggregation is *transitive*, so, if object *C*1 is part of *B*1, and *B*1 is part of *A*1, then *C*1 is part of *A*1
- aggregation is *asymmetric* (*irreflexive*), so, if *B*1 is part of *A*1, then *A*1 is not part of *B*1
- aggregation is *fixed*, so, if *B*1 is part of *A*1, then *B*1 can never be part of *Ai* ($i \neq 1$).

The *Owns* aggregation supports the first three properties of an *ExclusiveOwns* aggregation – that is:

- existence-dependency
- transitivity
- asymmetry.

The *Has* aggregation is semantically weaker than the *Owns* aggregation. This aggregation supports:

- transitivity
- asymmetry.

The *Member* aggregation has the property of purposeful grouping of independent objects – a grouping that does not make assumptions with regard to existence-dependency, transitivity, asymmetry or the fixed property. It is an abstraction whereby a collection of component members is considered as if it were a higher-level composite object. A component object in a member aggregation can at the same time belong to more than one composite object. Thus, the *multiplicity* of a member aggregation can be *many to many*.

Although *aggregation* has been recognized as a fundamental modeling concept for at least as long as *generalization* (Smith and Smith 1977), it has only been given marginal attention in object-oriented analysis and design (with the exception of "perfect match" application domains, such as multimedia systems). Fortunately, this trend may be reversed in the future because of the contributions and insights from the methodologists working on *design patterns*. This is evident, for example, in the treatment of aggregation (composition) in so-called "Gang of Four" (GoF) patterns (Gamma et al. 1995).

4.2.3.1 Discovering aggregations and composition

Aggregations are discovered in parallel with the discovery of *associations*. If an association exhibits one or more of the four semantic properties discussed above, then it can be modeled as an aggregation. The litmus test is to use the phrases "*has*" and "*is part of*" when explaining the relationship. In the top-down explanation, the phrase is "has" (Book "has" Chapter, for example). In the bottom-up interpretation, the phrase is "is part of" (Chapter "is part of" Book, for instance). If the relationship is read aloud with these phrases and the sentence does not make sense, then the relationship is *not* an aggregation.

From a structural point of view, aggregation frequently relates together a large number of classes whereas an association is quite meaningless beyond the binary degree

(Appendix, Section A.5.1). When we need to relate more than two classes together, a *member* aggregation may be an excellent modeling proposition. However, note that UML permits *n-ary associations* between three or more classes. Such associations are not recommended in this book.

Specifying aggregations and compositions 4.2.3.2

UML provides only limited support for aggregation. A strong form of aggregation in UML is called *composition*. In composition, the composite object may physically contain the part objects (the "by value" semantics). A part object can belong to only one composite object. The UML *composition* corresponds (more or less) to our *ExclusiveOwns* and *Owns* aggregations.

A weak form of aggregation in UML is simply called *aggregation*. It has the "by reference" semantics – the composite object does not physically contain the part objects. The same part object can have many aggregation or association links in the model. Loosely speaking, the UML *aggregation* corresponds to our *"has"* and *member* aggregations.

The *solid diamond* in UML represents a composition. The *hollow diamond* is used to define an aggregation. The rest of the aggregation specification is consistent with the association notation.

Example of aggregation and composition specifications 4.2.3.3

Example 4.9: university enrolment

Refer to Examples 4.1 (Section 4.2.1.1.7) and 4.4 (Section 4.2.1.2.3). Consider the following additional requirements.

■ The student's academic record should be available on demand. The record should include information about the grades obtained by the student in each course that the student enrolled on (and has not withdrawn from without penalty – that is within the first three weeks from the beginning of the semester).

■ Each course has one academic in charge of it, but additional academics may also teach it. There may be a different academic in charge of a course each semester, and there may be different academics for each course each semester.

Figure 4.9 demonstrates a class model constructed using the information in Example 4.9 and it emphasizes aggregation relationships. EStudent "has" EAcademicRecord is a UML composition ("by value" semantics). Each EAcademicRecord object is physically embedded in one EStudent object. Despite the existence of the association Takes, EAcademicRecord includes attribute courseCode. This is necessary because the association Takes will be implemented by the variable takesCrsoff in EStudent typed as a *collection* – Set[ECourseOffering], for example. The attribute takesCrsoff is independent of the information in the embedded EAcademicRecord object, although it ultimately links EStudent to ECourse.

Figure 4.9
Aggregation specifications for a university enrolment system

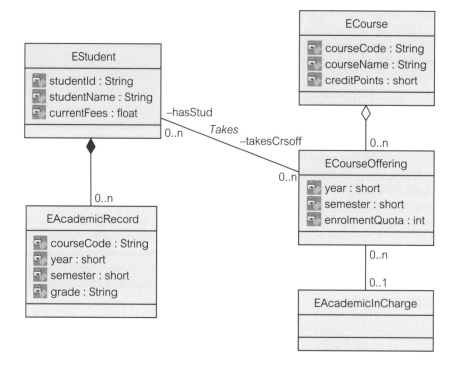

ECourse "has" ECourseOffering is a UML aggregation ("by reference" semantics). Each ECourseOffering object is logically contained in only one ECourse object. ECourseOffering can also participate in other aggregations and/or associations (such as with EStudent and EAcademicInCharge).

4.2.4 Modeling generalization relationships

Common *features* (attributes and operations) of one or more classes can be abstracted into a more generic class. This is known as *generalization* (Appendix, Section A.7). The generalization relationship connects a generic class (*superclass*) with more specific classes (*subclasses*). Generalization permits *inheritance* (*reuse*) of the superclass features by the subclasses. In a conventional object-oriented system, inheritance applies to classes, not objects (types are inherited, not values).

Apart from *inheritance*, generalization has two objectives (Rumbaugh et al. 2005):

▪ **substitutability**

▪ **polymorphism**.

Under the *substitutability* principle, a subclass object is a legal value for a superclass variable. For example, if a variable is declared to hold Fruit objects, then an Apple object is a legal value for that variable.

Under the *polymorphism* principle (Appendix, Section A.7.1), the same operation can have different implementations in different classes. A calling object can invoke an operation without knowing or caring which implementation of the operation will execute. The called object knows to what class it belongs and executes its own implementation.

Polymorphism works best when it is used hand in hand with inheritance. It is frequent that a polymorphic operation in the superclass is defined but no implementation is provided. That is, an operation is given a **signature** (the name and the list of formal arguments), but an implementation must be provided in each subclass. Such an *operation* is *abstract*.

Abstract operation should not be confused with **abstract class** (Appendix, Section A.8). The latter is a class that does not have any direct instance objects (but its subclasses may have instance objects). There may be no instances of `Vegetable`. The only direct instances are the objects of classes `Potato`, `Carrot` and so on.

In reality, a class with an abstract operation is abstract. A concrete class, such as `Apple`, cannot have abstract operations. While abstract operations are captured in *behavior specifications*, abstract classes are the domain of *state specifications*.

Discovering generalizations   4.2.4.1

An analyst observes many superclasses/subclasses when the initial list of classes is determined. Many other generalizations are detected when defining associations. Different associations (even from the same class) may need to be connected to a class at a different level of generalization/specialization. For example, the class `Course` may be associated with a `Student` (`Student` *takes* `Course`) and it may be connected to a `TeachingAssistant` (`TeachingAssistant` *teaches* `Course`). Further analysis can show that `TeachingAssistant` is a subclass of `Student`.

The litmus test for generalization is in using the phrases *"can be"* and *"is a kind of"* when explaining the relationship. In the top-down explanation, the phrase is "can be", so `Student` "can be" a `TeachingAssistant`, for example. In the bottom-up interpretation, the phrase is "is a kind of", so you would have `TeachingAssistant` "is a kind of" `Student`. Note that if a `TeachingAssistant` is also a kind of `Teacher`, then we have established *multiple inheritance* (Appendix, Section A.7.3).

Specifying generalization   4.2.4.2

A generalization relationship between classes shows that one class shares the structure and behavior defined in one or more other classes. Generalization is represented in UML by a solid line with an *arrowhead* pointing to the superclass.

A complete specification of generalization includes a number of powerful options. For example, one can further define a generalization relationship by specifying its *access*, identifying whether the class grants *rights* to another class or deciding what to do in a *multiple inheritance* situation. These issues are discussed in Section 5.2.

4.2.4.3 Examples of generalization specifications

Example 4.10: video store

Refer to Examples 4.2 (Section 4.2.1.1.7) and 4.5 (Section 4.2.1.2.3). The classes identified in Figure 4.5 (for Example 4.5) imply a generalization hierarchy rooted at the class EEntertainmentMedium. They also imply a parallel generalization hierarchy rooted at a class that can be named EEntertainmentItem or EEntertainmentItemCategory.

Our task is to extend the model in Figure 4.5 to include generalization relationships and establish the basic association relationship between the two generalization hierarchies. To capture some state differences between classes in the generalization hierarchy originating from the class EEntertainmentMedium, assume that the storage capacity of an EDVD allows multiple versions of the same movie to be held, each in a different language or with different endings. There is no need to decipher the peculiarities of game and music CDs in the model.

Figure 4.10 is a modified class model for a system for a video store described in Example 4.10 that emphasizes generalization. The generalization hierarchy states that EEntertainmentMedium "can be" EVideoMedium or ESoundMedium. EVideoMedium "has an" ESoundMedium. EVideoMedium "can be" EVideotape, EDVD or ECD. ECD is a "kind of" ESoundMedium, but in some cases ECD is also a "kind of" EVideoMedium. Further intricacies of ECD, such as classifications into game and music CDs or distinguishing between VCD and DVD-A formats, are not considered. The second generalization hierarchy states that an EEntertainmentItem "can be" EMovie, ETVProgram, EGame or EMusic. EEntertainmentMedium, EEntertainmentItem, EVideoMedium and ESoundMedium are *abstract classes* (shown by italicizing their names). Abstract classes do not instantiate objects (Appendix, Section A.8). EVideoMedium objects are instantiated by the *concrete classes* EVideotape, EDVD and ECD. The *abstract operation* computePercentExcellentCondition() must be declared (implemented) within these concrete classes.

The concrete classes inherit all attributes from their superclass. Hence, for example, all EVideotape objects have an instance variable videoCondition and a class variable percentExcellentCondition, and they are associated with an EEntertainmentItem object via instance variable theEEnterItem.

4.2.5 Modeling interfaces

Although they do not have implementation, *interfaces* provide some of the most powerful modeling capabilities (Appendix, Section A.9). Interfaces do not have attributes (except constants), associations or states. They only have *operations*, but all operations are implicitly public and abstract. Operations are *declared* (that is, turned into implemented methods) in classes that implement these interfaces.

Interfaces do not have associations to classes, but they may be targets of one-way associations from classes. This happens when an attribute that implements an association is typed with an interface rather than a class. The value of any such attribute will be a reference to some class that implements the interface.

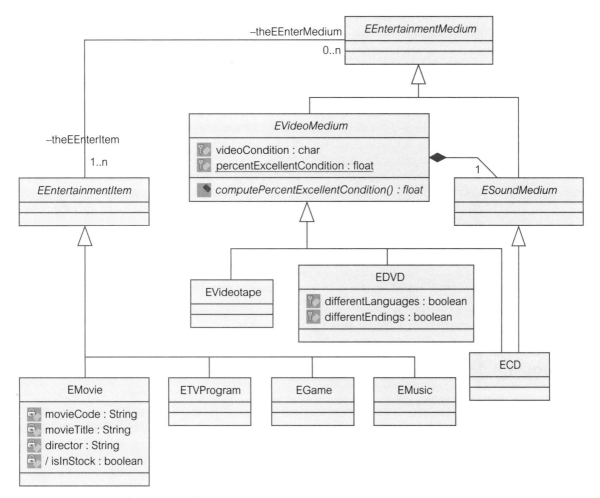

Figure 4.10 Generalization specifications for a video store system

An interface may have a generalization relationship to another interface. This means that an interface can extend another interface by inheriting its operations.

Discovering interfaces 4.2.5.1

Unlike other modeling elements discussed so far in this chapter, interfaces are not discovered from analysis of the application domain. Interfaces have more to do with using sound modeling principles that determine robust and supportable systems. By separating classes that *use* an interface from classes *implementing* that interface, interfaces result in systems that are easier to understand, maintain and evolve.

Interfaces are fundamental for enforcing architectural frameworks, such as the PCBMER framework (Section 4.1.3). They can be used to break cyclic dependencies in the system, implement publish/subscribe event schemes, hide the implementation from unauthorized clients and so on. In a typical situation, an interface reveals only a limited portion of the behavior of an actual class.

4.2.5.2   Specifying interfaces

Interfaces represent classes and, therefore, may be shown using a typical class rectangle stereotyped with the keyword <<interface>>. An alternative symbol that replaces the stereotype keyword with a small circle in the upper right-hand corner of the rectangle is also allowed. It is also possible to display an interface as a small circle with the name of the interface below the circle.

A class that *uses* (*requires*) the interface can be indicated by a dashed arrow pointing to the interface. For clarity, the arrow can be stereotyped with the keyword <<use>>. The class may use (require) only selected operations from the complete list of operations supplied by the interface.

A class that *implements* (*realizes*) the interface is indicated by a dashed line with a triangular end. This notation is similar to the generalization symbol, except that the line is dashed. For clarity, the line can be stereotyped with the keyword <<implement>>. The class must *implement* (*provide*) all operations supplied by the interface.

4.2.5.3   Examples of interface specifications

Example 4.11: contact management

Refer to Examples 4.3 (Section 4.2.1.1.7), 4.6 (Section 4.2.1.2.3), and 4.8 (Section 4.2.2.2.1). Consider in particular the classes EContact and EEmployee in Figure 4.8 for Example 4.8. These two classes have some attributes in common (firstName, familyName). The operations that provide access to these attributes can be extracted into a single interface.

Let us assume that there is a need to display information about overdue events on the screen. The relevant presentation layer class has the responsibility for displaying a list of overdue events together with names of contacts and employees, as well as the additional contact details (phone and e-mail) for contacts.

Our task is to propose a model such that the presentation class uses one or more interfaces implemented by EEmployee and EContact to support part of the "display overdue events" functionality.

Figure 4.11, for Example 4.11, contains two interfaces in two different graphical representations. The interface IAPerson is implemented by EEmployee. The interface IAContactInfo is implemented by EContact. Because IAContactInfo inherits from IAPerson, EContact also implements operations of IAPerson.

POverdueEvents is a presentation class. The model shows three operations in POverdueEvents. The operation displayEmployee() accepts IAPerson as an argument and is, therefore, able to perform getFirstName() and getFamilyName() methods on a given EEmployee object.

Similarly, the operation displayContact() obtains an IAContactInfo object. It can then call the methods, which are supplied by IAContactInfo and implemented in EContact. There are four such methods, which are getPhone(), getEmail(), getFirstName() and getFamilyName().

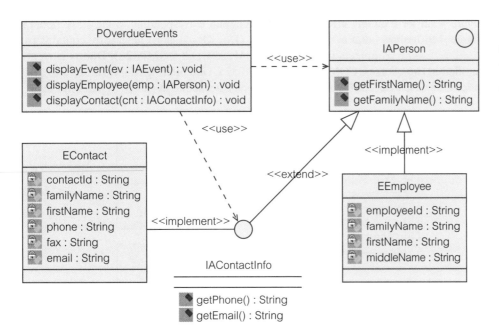

Figure 4.11
Interface
specifications for
a contact
management
system

Modeling objects 4.2.6

Modeling is concerned with definitions of *systems*. A model is not an executable system and, therefore, does not show instance objects. In any case, the number of objects in any non-trivial system is very large, so representing them graphically is impossible. Nevertheless, when modeling classes, we frequently imagine objects and discuss difficult scenarios using examples of objects.

Specifying objects 4.2.6.1

UML provides a graphical representation for an *object* (Appendix, Section A.2.1). We can draw object diagrams to illustrate data structures, including relationships between classes. Object diagrams can be useful as examples to illustrate more complex data structures and links between objects. Showing the links can clarify to people how objects can collaborate during an execution of the system.

Example of object specifications 4.2.6.2

Example 4.12: university enrolment

Our task in this example is to show a few objects representing the classes from the class model in Figure 4.9 (for Example 4.9, Section 4.2.3.3).

Figure 4.12, for Example 4.12, is an object diagram corresponding to the class model in Figure 4.9. It shows that a `Student` object (Don Donaldson) physically contains two `AcademicRecord` objects (for courses COMP224 and COMP326). Don is currently enrolled in two courses: COMP225 and COMP325. One offering of COMP325 was given in semester 2 in year 2007. Rick Richards was the academic in charge of that offering.

Figure 4.12
An object diagram for a university enrolment system

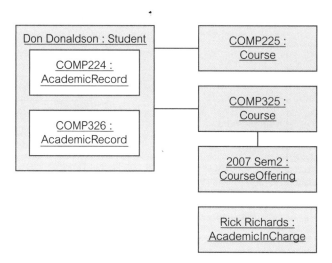

Review quiz 4.2

RQ1   What is the CRC approach used for?

RQ2   What are role names used for?

RQ3   What does transitivity mean in the context of aggregations?

RQ4   A subclass object may be a legal value for a superclass variable. Associated with that observation is the principle of what?

4.3   Behavior specifications

The behavior of the system, as it appears to an outside user, is depicted in *use cases* (Section 3.1). Use case models can be developed at different levels of abstraction. They can apply to the system as a whole in order to specify the main functional units in the application under development. They can also be used to capture the behavior of a UML *package*, a part of the package or even a *class* within the package.

During *analysis*, use cases capture the system requirements by focusing on *what* the system does or should do. During *design*, use case views can be used to specify the behavior of the system as it is to be implemented.

The behavior entailed by a use case requires that computations be performed and objects interact to execute a use case. *Computations* can be modeled with activity diagrams. *Interactions* of objects can be specified with sequence diagrams or communication diagrams.

Behavior specifications provide an *operational view* of the system. The main task here is to define *use cases* in the application domain and to determine which *classes* are involved in the execution of these use cases. We identify class *operations* and the *message passing* between objects. Although object interactions trigger changes to object states, in behavior specifications we define an *operational view on a frozen state* of the system. Changes in object states are explicitly depicted in *state change specifications*.

Use case models should be developed iteratively and concurrently with class models. The classes determined in state specifications will be elaborated further and the most important operations identified. However, note that state specifications mostly define *entity classes* ("business objects"). As behavior modeling proceeds, other layers of classes (Section 4.1.3.1) will be revealed.

Modeling use cases   4.3.1

Use case modeling is tightly integrated with requirements determination (Chapter 2). Textual requirements in the requirements document need to be traced down to use cases in the specifications document. If use cases drive the rest of the development process, then the process is *function-driven* (Section 4.2.1.1.3).

Like class modeling, use case modeling is inherently *iterative* and *incremental*. The initial use case diagram can be determined from the top-level requirements. This could be a *business use case model* (Section 2.5.2). Further refinements should be driven by more detailed requirements. If users' requirements change during the development lifecycle, those changes are made first in the requirements document and then in the use case model. Changes to use cases are then traced down to the other models (Hoffer et al. 2002; Rational 2000).

When discovering use cases, analysts must ensure that they adhere to the essential features of the use case concept. A use case represents (Hoffer et al. 1999; Kruchten 2003; Rumbaugh et al. 2005; Quatrani 2000):

- a *complete* piece of functionality, including the *main flow* of logic, any variations on it (*subflows*) and any exceptional conditions (*alternative flows*)
- a piece of *externally visible* functionality (not an internal function)
- an *orthogonal* piece of functionality (use cases can share objects during execution, but the execution of each use case is independent of the others)
- a piece of functionality *initiated by an actor* (but, once initiated, the use case can interact with other actors) – however, it is possible for an actor to be only on the receiving end of a use case initiated (perhaps indirectly) by another actor
- a piece of functionality that delivers an identifiable *value to an actor* (and that value is achieved in a single use case).

Use cases are discovered from the analysis of:

- requirements identified in the requirements document;
- actors and their purpose in the system.

Requirements management issues were discussed in Section 2.4. We recall that requirements are typed. For the discovery of use cases, we are interested only in *functional requirements*.

Use cases can be determined from the analysis of tasks performed by actors. Jacobson (1992) suggests asking a range of questions about actors. Answers to these questions can result in the identification of use cases.

- What are the main tasks performed by each actor?
- Will an actor access or modify information in the system?
- Will an actor inform the system about any changes in other systems?
- Should an actor be informed about unexpected changes in the system?

In analysis, use cases address identifiable needs of actors. In some way, these are **actor use cases**. Since use cases determine major functional building blocks for a system, there is also a need to identify **system use cases**. System use cases extract commonality from actor use cases and allow generic solutions that are applicable (via inheritance) to a range of actor use cases to be developed. The "actor" of the system use case is the designer/programmer, not the user. System use cases are identified in the design phase.

4.3.1.1 Specifying use cases

Use case specification includes the graphical presentation of actors, use cases and four kinds of relationship:

- association
- include
- extend
- generalization.

The *association* relationship establishes the communication path between an actor and a use case. The *include* and *extend* relationships are stereotyped by the words «include» and «extend». The *generalization* relationship allows a specialized use case to change any aspect of the base use case.

The «include» relationship allows the common behavior in the included use case to be factored out. The «extend» relationship provides a controlled form of extending the behavior of a use case by activating another use case at specific extension points. The «include» relationship differs from the «extend» relationship in that the "included" use case is necessary for the completion of the "activating" use case.

In practice, projects can easily get into trouble by putting too much effort into discovering relationships between use cases and determining which relationships apply for specific pairs of use cases. In addition, high-level use cases tend to be so intertwined that relationship links can dominate and obscure the diagram, shifting the emphasis away from the proper identification of use cases to a focus relationships between use cases.

Examples of use case specifications   4.3.1.2

Example 4.13: university enrolment

Refer to Problem statement 1, for a university enrolment system (Section 1.6.1) and the requirements defined in Examples 4.1 and 4.4 (Section 4.2.1). Our task is to determine use cases from the analysis of functional requirements.

Figure 4.13 shows a high-level use case diagram for a university enrolment system for Example 4.13. The model contains four actors and four use cases. Each use case is initiated by an actor and is a complete, externally visible and orthogonal piece of functionality. All actors, except `Student`, are *initiating* actors. `Student` obtains examination results and enrolment instructions and only then can the program of study for the next semester (term) be entered and validated.

The use case `Provide examination results` *may* «extend» the use case `Provide enrolment instructions`. The former does not always extend the latter use case. For example, for new students, the examination results are not known. This is why we modeled the relationship with the «extend» stereotype, not «include».

The «include» relationship has been established from the use case `Enter program of study` to the use case `Validate program of study`. The «include» relation-

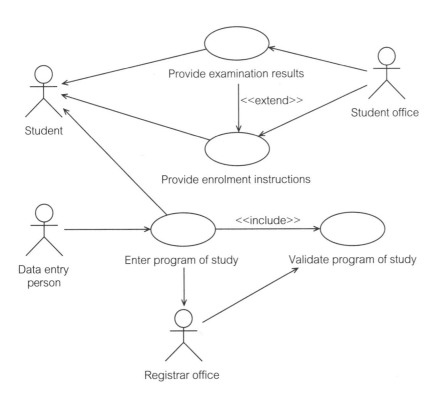

Figure 4.13
A use case diagram for a university enrolment system

ship signifies that the former use case always includes the latter. Whenever the program of study is entered, it is validated for timetable clashes, special approvals, etc.

Example 4.14: contact management

Refer to Problem statement 3, for a contact management system (Section 1.6.3) and the requirements defined in Examples 4.3 and 4.6 (Section 4.2.1). Our task is to determine use cases from the analysis of functional requirements.

There are three actors and five use cases in the use case diagram for a contact management system for Example 4.14, shown in Figure 4.14. An interesting aspect of the model is that the actors are related by generalization relationships. Customer services manager "is a kind of" Customer services employee who in turn "is a kind of" Employee. The generalization hierarchy improves the expressiveness of the diagram. Any event performed by Employee can also be performed by Customer services employee or Customer services manager. Consequently, Customer services manager is implicitly associated with (and can initiate) every use case in the model.

The use case Create task includes Schedule event because of the requirement that the task cannot be created without scheduling the first event. The «extend» relationships signify the fact that the completion of an event can trigger changes to the organization or contact details.

Figure 4.14
A use case diagram for a contact management system

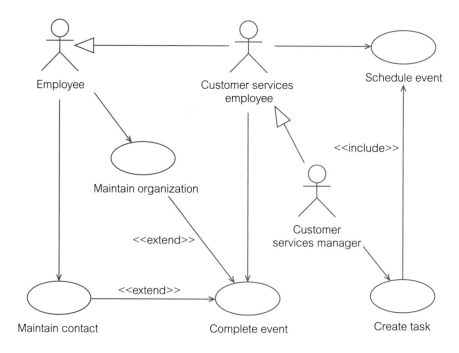

Example 4.15: video store

Refer to Problem statement 2, for a video store system (Section 1.6.2) and the requirements defined in Examples 4.2 and 4.5 (Section 4.2.1). Our task is to determine use cases from the analysis of functional requirements. For one of the use cases, write narrative specifications with the headings summary, actors, preconditions, description, exceptions and postconditions.

There are six use cases and only two actors in the use case diagram for a video store system for Example 4.15, shown in Figure 4.15. Secondary actors, such as `Customer` or `Supplier`, are not shown. These actors do not initiate any use cases. The actor `Employee` initiates *all* use cases. The relationship between actors `Scanning device` and `Employee` is a *dependency*, stereotyped by the analyst with the phrase «`depends on`».

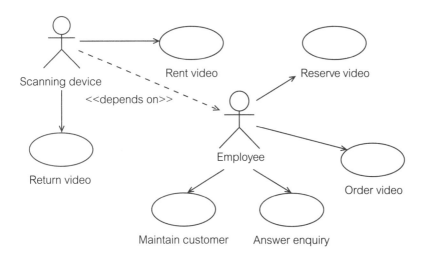

Figure 4.15
A use case diagram for a video store system

Table 4.4 illustrates that the graphical representation of use cases is but one aspect of the complete use case model. Each use case in the diagram has to be documented further in the CASE tool repository. In particular, a narrative description is necessary. Table 4.4 uses one popular structure for the narrative specification of use cases (Section 3.1.4). Section 6.5.3 contains an example of a more realistic use case document that follows similar structure.

Example 4.16: telemarketing

Refer to Problem statement 4, for a telemarketing system in Section 1.6.4 and to the requirements defined in Examples 2.1–2.4 (Sections 2.1.1.2–2.5.2) and Example 4.7 (Section 4.2.1.2.3). Our task is to determine use cases from the analysis of functional requirements.

Table 4.4 Narrative specification for the use case "Rent video" for a video store system

Use case	Rent video
Brief description	A customer wishes to rent a videotape or disk that is picked from the store's shelves or has been previously reserved by the customer. Provided that the customer has a non-delinquent account, the video is rented out once payment has been received. If the video is not returned in a timely fashion, an overdue notice is mailed to the customer.
Actors	Employee and Scanning device.
Preconditions	Videotape or disk is available to be hired. Customer has a membership card. Scanner device works correctly. Employee at the front desk knows how to use the system.
Main flow	A customer may ask an employee about video availability (including a reserved video) or may pick a videotape or disk from the shelves. The videotape and the membership card are scanned and any delinquent or overdue details are brought up for the employee to query the customer about. If the customer does not have a delinquent rating, then he or she can hire up to a maximum of eight videotapes. However, if the rating of the customer is "unreliable", then a deposit of one rental period for each videotape or disk is requested. Once the amount payable has been received, the stock is updated and the videotapes and disks are handed to the customer together with the rental receipt. The customer pays by cash, credit card or electronic transfer. Each rental record stores (under the customer's account) the check-out and due-in dates, together with the identification of the employee. A separate rental record is created for each videotape or disk hired. The use case will generate an overdue notice to the customer if the videotape or disk has not been returned within two days of the due date, and a second notice after another two days (and at that time the customer is noted as "delinquent").
Alternative flows	• A customer does not have a membership card. In this case, the "Maintain customer" use case may be activated to issue a new card. • An attempt to rent too many videotapes or disks. • No videotapes or disks can be rented because of the customer's delinquent rating. • The videotape or disks medium or membership card cannot be scanned because of damage to it. • The electronic transfer or credit card payment is refused.
Postconditions	Videotapes or disks are rented out and the database is updated accordingly.

The solution for Example 4.16, shown in Figure 4.16, consists of a number of use cases. The actors communicate directly with three use cases: `Schedule and make next call`, `Record call outcome` and `Display call details`. The latter can, in turn, be extended to `Display campaign details`, `Display supporter history` and `Display prize details`. The use case `Update supporter` extends `Display supporter history`. `Record ticket sale`, and `Schedule callback` can extend

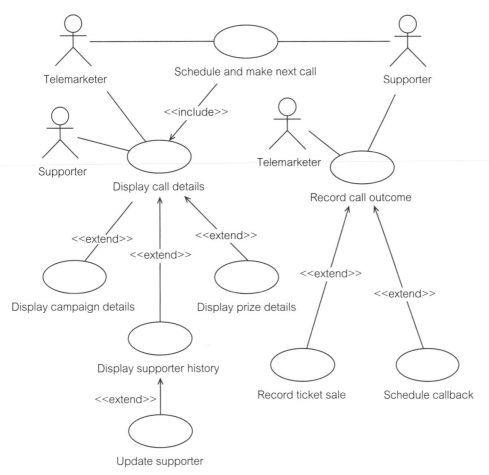

Figure 4.16
A use case
diagram for a
telemarketing
system

`Record call outcome`. It is assumed that the actors can communicate indirectly with the extension use cases, but no explicit communication links are drawn to those use cases.

Modeling activities   4.3.2

Like traditional *flowcharts* and *structure charts* popularized in the structured methods for procedural program design, *activity diagrams* represent the flow of logic in object-oriented programs (albeit at a high level of abstraction). They make it possible to represent a *concurrent control* in addition to any *sequential controls*.

Activity models are used extensively in the *design*. However, they also provide a great technique for expressing computations or workflows at the level of abstraction applied in the *analysis*. *Activity graphs* can be used to show varying levels of detail of a computation.

Activity models can be particularly useful for defining the flow of *actions* in the execution of a use case. Actions are performed by objects (as operations), but activity diagrams do not explicitly visualize the classes of objects that perform the actions.

Consequently, an activity graph can be constructed even if the class model has not been developed or is underdeveloped. Eventually, each activity will be defined by one or more operations in one or more collaborating classes. The detailed design for such collaboration is likely to be modeled in an interaction diagram (Section 3.2).

4.3.2.1 Discovering actions

Each use case can be modeled by one or more activity graphs. An event from an actor that initiates a use case is the same event that triggers the execution of the activity graph. The execution proceeds from one *action* to the next. An action execution completes when its computation has been completed. External event-based interruptions, which would cause the action to complete, are allowed only in exceptional situations. If they are expected to be frequent, then a state machine diagram should be used instead (Section 3.5.2).

Actions are best discovered from the analysis of sentences in the *narrative specifications* of use cases (see Table 4.4). Any phrases with verbs are candidate actions. The description of alternative flows introduces decisions (branches) or forks for concurrent threads.

4.3.2.2 Specifying actions

Activities consist of *actions*. An activity *execution* includes the execution of actions within it. Once the activities have been discovered, their execution specification is the process of connecting action executions by *control flows* and *object flows*. Object flows are used whenever there is a need to model what data are accessed by actions and how actions transform data. Concurrent threads are initiated (*forked*) and *rejoined* with *synchronization bars*. Alternative threads are created (*branched*) and *merged* with *decision diamonds*.

4.3.2.3 Example of activity specifications

Example 4.17: video store

Refer to Example 4.15 (Section 4.3.1.2) and, in particular, to the narrative specification for the use case "Rent video" (Table 4.4). Our task is to design an activity diagram for "Rent video". The diagram should show the sequence of action executions connected by control flows (no need to show object flows).

Figure 4.17 is the activity diagram for the "Rent video" use case for Example 4.17. Not surprisingly, the diagram reflects the narrative specification for the use case (Table 4.4). The processing begins when either a customer card or video medium is scanned. These two actions are considered independent of each other (shown by the use of a fork).

The action `Verify customer` checks the customer's history and the computation proceeds after evaluating the decision (branch) conditions. If a customer is delinquent, then "Rent video" terminates. If a customer is unreliable, then a deposit will be requested before concluding the transaction. If a customer has a good record, then the action `Initiate rent transaction` fires.

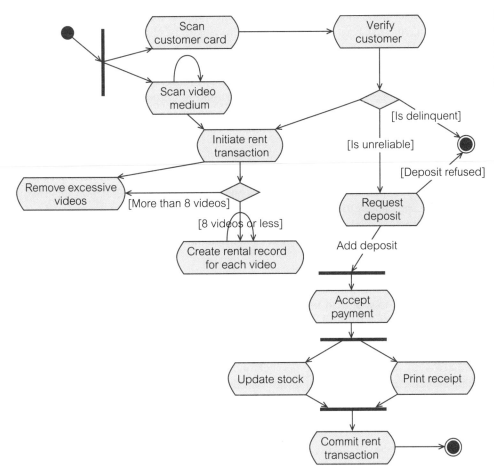

Figure 4.17
An activity
diagram for the
use case "Rent
video" for a video
store system

The second branch condition ensures that no more than eight videotapes are rented out to a single customer. After payment has been accepted, another fork allows for concurrent execution of the actions `Update stock` and `Print receipt`. These concurrent threads are joined before the action `Commit rent transaction` fires and after that the entire processing terminates.

Modeling interactions   4.3.3

Sequence diagrams and *communication diagrams* are two kinds of *interaction diagram*. They show the patterns of **interactions** between objects necessary to accomplish a use case, activity, operation or other behavioral component.

Sequence diagrams show an exchange of messages between objects arranged in a time sequence. Communication diagrams emphasize the relationships between objects along which the messages are exchanged. We find the sequence diagrams more useful in analysis and the communication diagrams in design.

Because interaction models refer to objects, they require that at least the first iteration of state modeling has been completed and major classes of objects have been identified. Although interactions affect the states of objects, interaction diagrams do not explicitly model state changes in objects. This is the domain of state machine diagrams and state change specifications (Sections 3. 5 and 4.4).

Interaction diagrams can be used to determine *operations* (methods) in classes (Sections 3.4.3 and 4.3.4). Any message to an object in an interaction diagram must be serviced by some method in that object's class.

4.3.3.1 Discovering message sequences

The discovery of message sequences follows on from activity models. *Actions* in an *activity diagram* are mapped to *messages* in a *sequence diagram*. If the abstraction levels used in the construction of the activity model and the sequence model are similar, then the mapping between actions and messages is quite straightforward.

4.3.3.2 Specifying message sequences

When specifying messages, it is advantageous to distinguish between a message that is a *signal* and a message that is a *call*: "A message is the transmission of a signal from one object (the sender) to one or more other objects (the receivers), or it is a call of an operation on one object (the receiver) by another object (the sender or caller)" (Rumbaugh et al. 2005: 470). A *signal* denotes an asynchronous interobject communication. The sender can continue executing immediately after sending the signal message. A *call* signifies a synchronous invocation of an operation with provision for the return of control to the sender. From the object-oriented implementation viewpoint, signals imply *event processing* and calls imply *message passing* (Maciaszek and Liong 2005).

Methods activated by messages may or may not return data values to the caller. If no value is to be returned, then the *return type* is void. Otherwise, the return type is some primitive type (such as char) or non-primitive type (a class). Return types are not normally shown on sequence diagrams. If necessary, a special return line (dotted and arrowed) can be used to explicitly show the return type. Note that the return type is not the same as the return (*callback*) message.

4.3.3.3 Examples of sequence specifications

Example 4.18: university enrolment

Refer to Examples 4.9 (Section 4.2.3.3) and 4.12 (Section 4.2.6.2) and to the use case "Enter program of study" in Figure 4.13. Our task is to construct a sequence diagram for this activity of the use case, which is concerned with adding a student to a course offering.

We are not concerned here with the verification of the entered program of study. Another use case ("Validate Program of Study") handles the verification of prerequisites, timetable clashes, special approvals, etc. Our task is only to check whether the course on which the student wants to register is offered in the next semester and if it is still open (if there are places available).

Figures 4.18 and 4.19 illustrate two quite contrasting solutions to the problem in Example 4.18 – one centralized, the other distributed (Fowler 2004). The sequence diagram in Figure 4.18 is a *centralized* solution, reminiscent of a procedural programming style. In this approach, one class (CEnroll) takes charge, doing most of the work. The sequence diagram in Figure 4.19 is a *distributed* solution, in which many objects are involved in fulfilling the service. There is no central point of control. The processing intelligence is distributed among multiple objects. Normally, the distributed approach is preferred for a good (reusable and supportable) object-oriented solution.

In both solutions, an actor (Data entry person) is introduced to initiate processing. In UML, the initiator of processing does not need to be known. The first message – called the *found message* (Fowler 2004) – can come from an undetermined source. However, many CASE tools do not support undetermined sources.

Processing begins when the *control* object CEnroll receives a request to add() a student (identified by argument std) to a course (argument crs) in a semester (argument sem). In both solutions, CEnroll engages EStudent to continue processing. However, in the centralized solution (Figure 4.18), EStudent is only asked to return its eligibility for enrolment (for example, if the student paid the fees). In the distributed solution (Figure 4.19), on the other hand, EStudent is entrusted with checking his or her own eligibility and proceeding to enroll him- or herself, if eligible.

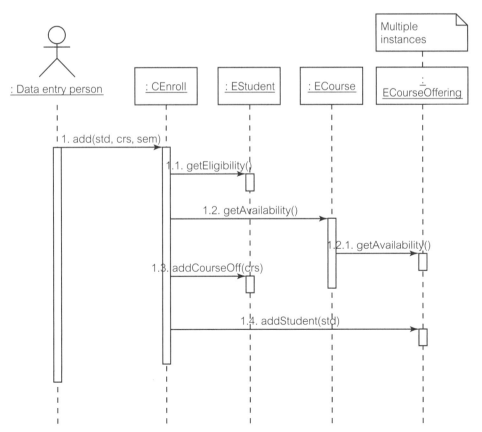

Figure 4.18
A centralized sequence diagram for a university enrolment system

Figure 4.19
A distributed
sequence
diagram for a
university
enrolment system

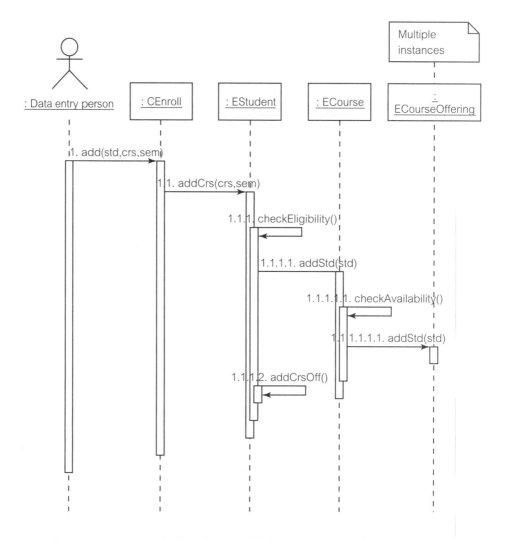

Assuming that EStudent *is* eligible to enroll, in the centralized approach CEnroll is again in charge (pretending to be what is sometimes called a *God class*). In the distributed approach, EStudent takes the responsibility for requesting ECourse to get enrolled. To be able to request services of ECourse, EStudent has been passed crs and sem in the arguments of addCrs().

In reality, EStudent does *not* enroll in ECourse, but in ECourseOffering. This necessitates communication between ECourse and, potentially, multiple instances of ECourseOffering. Enrolling a student in a course offering requires establishing a bi-directional association between relevant EStudent and ECourseOffering objects. Once more, in the case of a centralized solution, CEnroll establishes such an *association*. In the case of a distributed solution, ECourseOffering establishes a *link* to EStudent and returns itself to EStudent so that EStudent can set the link to ECourseOffering.

Modeling operations 4.3.4

A *public interface* of a class is determined by the set of *operations* that the class offers as a service to other classes in the system. Such operations are declared with public visibility. It is only via the public interfaces that objects can collaborate to execute use cases and activities.

Public interfaces are first determined towards the end of the analysis phase, when the state and behavior specifications are largely defined. In analysis, we define only the *signature* of each public operation (operation name, list of formal arguments, return type). In design, we will provide a definition (such as some pseudo-codes) for the algorithms of *methods* that implement operations.

Discovering class operations 4.3.4.1

Class operations are best discovered from sequence diagrams. Every *message* in a sequence model must be serviced by an *operation* in the destination object (Section 3.4.3). If the sequence models are fully developed, the determination of public operations is an automatic task.

In practice, however, the sequence diagrams – even if developed for all use cases and activities – might not provide sufficient detail to permit the discovery of all public operations. In addition, sequence diagrams might not be available for operations that cross use case boundaries (for instance, where a business transaction spans more than one use case).

For these reasons, supplementary methods for operation discovery can be helpful. One such method comes from the observation that objects are responsible for their own destiny and, therefore, must support four primitive operations:

■ create
■ read
■ update
■ delete.

These are known as *CRUD operations* (Section 2.5.2). CRUD operations allow other objects to send messages to an object to request:

■ a new object instance
■ access to the state of an object
■ modification of the state of an object
■ that an object destroys itself.

Specifying class operations 4.3.4.2

At this stage of the lifecycle, a class diagram needs to be modified to include *operation signatures*. The scope of operations may also be determined. By default, *instance scope* is assumed (an operation applies to *instance objects*). *Class (static) scope* must be declared explicitly (the "$" sign in front of an operation name). Class scope states that an operation applies to the *class object* (Appendix, Section A.3.3).

Other properties of operations, such as concurrency, polymorphic behavior and algorithm specification, will be specified later during design.

4.3.4.3 Examples of operation specifications

Example 4.19: university enrolment

Refer to Example 4.18 (Section 4.3.3.3) and to the sequence diagrams in Figures 4.18 and 4.19 there. Our task is to derive operations from the sequence diagrams and add them to the entity classes EStudent, ECourse and ECourseOffering.

The operations specified in the class model in Figure 4.20 for Example 4.19 are obtained directly from the sequence diagram in Figure 4.18. The icons in front of attributes signify that the attributes have *private* scope. The icons in front of the operations inform us that they are *public*.

The class model in Figure 4.20 not only corresponds to the sequence diagram in Figure 4.18 but also supplements it by showing return types for the operations. Establishing the association between EStudent and ECourseOffering is initiated by CEnroll. However, CEnroll must obtain ECourseOffering from ECourse's getAvailability() before it can establish the association.

Figure 4.20
Class operation specifications for centralized interaction for a university enrolment system

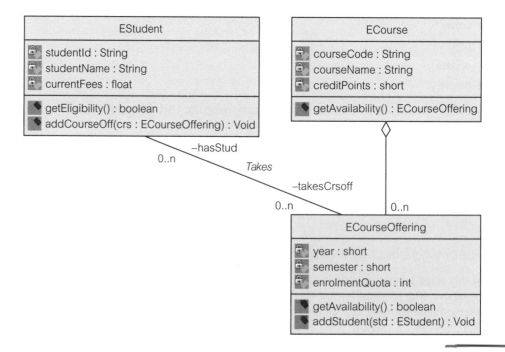

In the distributed solution, `CEnroll` only *initiates* the enrolment process and the rest is done by means of communication between entity objects. Figure 4.21 shows the class operations resulting from the sequence diagram in Figure 4.19. The distributed approach reinforces the spirit of object orientation, which is supposed "to use a lot of little objects with a lot of little methods that give us a lot of plug points for overriding and variations" (Fowler, 2004: 56).

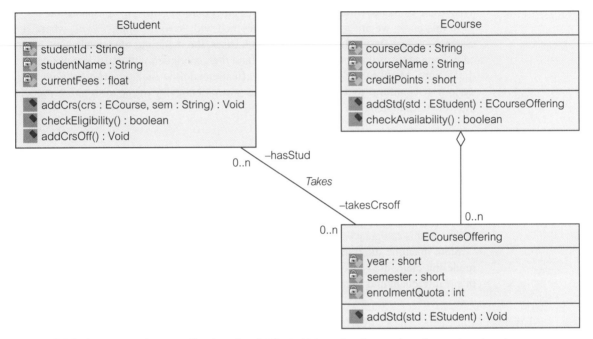

Figure 4.21 Class operation specifications for distributed interaction for a university enrolment system

Review quiz 4.3

RQ1 Do use cases hold the possibility of representing the concurrent flow of control?

RQ2 Can activity diagrams be constructed before a class model is developed?

RQ3 A message can denote an asynchronous interobject communication. How is such a message called?

RQ4 What UML modeling technique is most useful for discovering class operations?

State change specifications

4.4

The state of an object at a point in time is determined by the values of its attributes, including its relationship attributes. State specifications define the class attributes (among other issues). Behavior specifications define the class operations, some of which have *side-effects* – that is, they alter the state of an object. However, to understand how an object can change its state over time, we need a more targeted view of the system. Such a view is provided by the state machine models.

The importance of state change specifications varies between application domains. The modeling of state changes in business applications is much less critical than it is in engineering and real-time applications. Many *engineering and real-time applications* are all about state changes. In modeling such systems, we have to concentrate on state changes from day one. What happens if the temperature is too high? What if the valve is not closed? What if the container is full? These and lots of other questions have to be considered.

In this book, we are predominantly concerned with *business applications*, where state changes are less frequent. Therefore, in such cases, the modeling of state changes is typically done towards the end of the analysis (and then continued with much greater depth in the design). Many of the state change specifications define *exceptional conditions* in the system. It is natural that exceptions to the normal behavior of the system are modeled after the normal behavior has been specified.

4.4.1 Modeling object states

The modeling of object states is done using state machine diagrams (Section 3.5.2). A state graph (state machine) is a graph of states and transitions. State models are built for each class that exhibits interesting *dynamic behavior*. Not all classes in the class diagram will be in this category.

State machine diagrams can also be used to describe the dynamic behavior of other modeling elements – use cases, communications or operations, for example. However, this is infrequent and some CASE tools may not support such functionality.

4.4.1.1 Discovering object states

The process of discovery of object states is based on the analysis of the attribute content in a class and deciding which of these attributes are of special interest to use cases. Not all attributes determine state changes. For example, the modification of a phone number by a customer does not change the state of the `Customer` object. The customer still has the phone; the number of the phone is not relevant. However, the deletion of the phone number may be a state change of interest to some use cases as the customer will not be reachable by phone any more.

Similarly, a change of phone number that includes a change of area code may be an interesting state change, indicating that a customer has moved to another geographical location. This change might need to be noted and modeled in a state machine diagram.

4.4.1.2 Specifying object states

The basic UML notation for state machine specifications has been explained in Section 3.5.2. To use this notation successfully, an analyst must understand how different concepts interrelate, which combinations of concepts are unnatural or not allowed and what notational shortcuts are possible. It is also likely that a CASE tool will introduce some restrictions, but perhaps also some interesting extensions.

A state transition fires when a certain event occurs *or* a certain condition is satisfied. This means, for example, that a transition line does not have to be labeled with an *event name*. A *condition* itself (written in square brackets) can fire the transition whenever an *activity* in the state is completed and the condition evaluates to true.

Some states (such as `Door is closed`) are idle, doing nothing. Other states (`Door is closing`, for example) are more animated and supported by an explicit *activity*. Such an activity within a state is known as a *do activity*. A do activity can be named within a state icon with the `do/` keyword (`do/close the door`, for instance).

In a typical situation, a transition is triggered by a *signal event* or a *call event*. A *signal event* establishes an explicit, asynchronous one-way communication between two objects. A *call event* establishes a synchronous communication in which the caller waits for a response.

Two other kinds of event are *change event* and *time event*. A *change event* signifies that the event of a guard condition (Boolean expression) has been satisfied because of a change to the guard values. A *time event* signifies that an object in a particular state has met a time expression, such as reaching a particular absolute time/date or the passage of a given amount of time. In general, time events that fire transitions based on the absolute or relative notion of time are very useful in some models.

Another consideration in state machine modeling relates to the possibility of specifying *entry actions* inside a state icon (with the `entry/` keyword) or on an incoming transition. Similarly, *exit actions* can be placed inside state icons (with the `exit/` keyword) or on outgoing transitions. Although the semantics are not affected, the choice of which technique to use can influence the readability of the model (Rumbaugh et al. 1991).

Example of state machine specifications 4.4.1.3

Example 4.20: video store

Refer to the class `EMovie` in Example 4.10 (Figure 4.10) (Section 4.2.4.3). Our task is to specify a state machine diagram for `EMovie`.

The state machine for `EMovie` in Example 4.20 is given in Figure 4.22. The diagram demonstrates different ways in which transitions can be specified. The transitions between the states `Available` and `Not in stock` specify parameterized event names, together with action names and guarded conditions. On the other hand, the transition from the state `Reserved` to `Not reserved` lacks an explicit trigger event. It is triggered by the completion of activity in the state `Reserved`, provided that the condition `[no more reserved]` is true.

Review quiz 4.4

RQ1 Do state machine diagrams represent the sequence of state changes?

RQ2 Will the state change always occur when the relevant transition to that state has been fired?

Figure 4.22
A state machine diagram for the class `EMovie` for a video store system

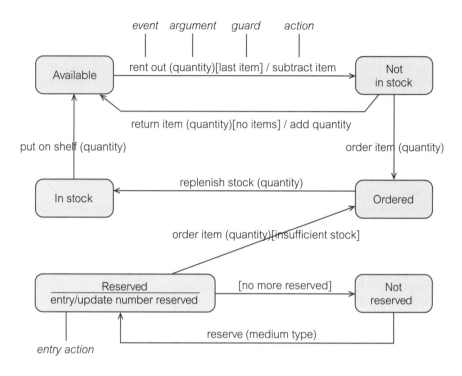

Summary

This has been the nuts and bolts chapter in the book. It has explained the critical importance of architecture in system development and presented UML in full action. The PCBMER architecture introduced in this chapter has been adhered to in UML modeling and will be taken more advantage of in successive chapters.

The case studies introduced in Chapter 1, and used in Chapters 2 and 3, provided the illustrative material for this chapter. All frequently used UML models have been put to the task. The motto of the chapter was "there are no black or white, zero–one, true–false solutions in IS analysis models." For every problem there are many potential solutions. The trick is to arrive at a solution that will both satisfy customers' requirements and work.

■ State specifications describe the IS systems from the *static* perspective of *classes*, their *attribute* content and their *relationships*. There are many methods of *class discovery*, but none of them offers a single "cookbook recipe." A mix of methods that suits the analyst's knowledge and experience is a practical answer to class discovery. Classes are specified in UML *class diagrams*. The diagrams visualize classes and three kinds of relationship between them – *associations*, *aggregations* and *generalizations*.

■ Behavioral specifications describe the IS systems from the *operational* perspective (in order not to use the overloaded term – the *functional* perspective). The driving force for behavioral specifications and, indeed, for requirements analysis and system design in general are *use cases*. *Use case diagrams* provide only simple visualization – the real power of use cases is in their *narrative specifications*. Other behavioral diagrams are derived from use case models. They include *activity diagrams*, *interaction diagrams* and the addition of *operations* to classes.

■ State change specifications describe the IS systems from a *dynamic* perspective. Objects are bombarded by events and some of these cause changes to objects' *states*. *State machine diagrams* allow the modeling of state changes.

Key terms

Abstract class a class that cannot be directly instantiated – it can only have indirect instances via its concrete descendant classes.

Abstract operation "an operation that lacks an implementation – that is, one that has a specification but no method. An implementation must be supplied by any concrete descendant class" (Rumbaugh et al. 2005: 153).

Actor use case a use case that addresses identifiable needs of actors (see also *use case*, Key terms, Chapter 3).

APP Acquaintance Package Principle in PCBMER.

Architectural framework see *architectural meta-model*.

Architectural meta-model a high-level model that defines a framework for a software architecture that concrete system designs can choose to conform to.

Bean a reusable software *component* representing a data object and operations (methods) to access that data. It is also the name of a layer in the PCBMER architecture.

CEP Cycle Elimination Principle in PCBMER.

CNP Class Naming Principle in PCBMER.

Cohesion "a measure of how well the lines of source code within a module work together to provide a specific piece of functionality. Cohesion is an ordinal type of measurement and is usually expressed as "high cohesion" or "low cohesion" when being discussed" (www.en.wikipedia.org/wiki/Cohesion).

Component see *component*, Key terms, Chapters 1 and 3.

Coupling see *dependency*. Coupling is usually contrasted with *cohesion* and the goal is to achieve *low* coupling and *high* cohesion, but low coupling frequently results in lower (that is, worse) cohesion and vice versa.

CRC Class–Responsibility–Collaborators approach.

DDP Downward Dependency Principle in PCBMER.

Dependency "a relationship that signifies that a single or a set of model elements requires other model elements for their specification or implementation. This means that the complete semantics of the depending elements is either semantically or structurally dependent on the definition of the supplier element(s)" (UML 2005: 74).

EAP Explicit Association Principle in PCBMER.

Interaction see *interaction*, Key terms, Chapter 3.

JDBC Java Database Connectivity.

JMS Java Messaging Service.

MVC Model-View-Controller architectural framework.

NCP Neighbor Communication Principle in PCBMER.

PCBMER Presentation-Controller-Bean-Mediator-Entity-Resource architectural framework.

Polymorphism "the ability of objects belonging to different types to respond to method calls of methods of the same name, each one according to the right type-specific behavior. The programmer (and the program) does not have to know the exact type of the object in advance, so this behavior can be implemented at run-time (this is called late binding or dynamic binding)" ([www.en.wikipedia.org/wiki/Polymorphism in-object-oriented programming](www.en.wikipedia.org/wiki/Polymorphism_in-object-oriented_programming)).

Port "a property of a classifier that specifies a distinct interaction point between that classifier and its environment or between the [behavior of the] classifier and its internal parts... A port may specify the services a classifier provides [offers] to its environment as well as the services that a classifier expects [requires] of its environment" (UML 2005: 19). See also *classifier*, Key terms, Chapter 3.

Provided interfaces "the set of interfaces realized by a classifier ... which represent the obligations that instances of that classifier have to their clients" (UML 2005: 99).

Required interfaces "specify services that a classifier needs in order to perform its function and fulfill its own obligations to its clients" (UML 2005: 99).

Requirements specification a detailed, customer-oriented specification of functional and non-functional criteria that an information system under development must meet; requirements specifications are written in a requirements document and they are, therefore, frequently referred to as a requirements document.

Signature "the name and parameter of a behavioral feature, such as an operation or signal. A signature may include optional return types (for operations, not for signals)" (Rumbaugh et al. 2005: 613).

Software architecture see *architecture*, Key terms, Chapter 1.

Substitutability "states that, if S is a subtype of T, then objects of type T in a computer program may be replaced with objects of type S (i.e., objects of type S may be substituted for objects of type T), without altering any of the desirable properties of that program (correctness, task performed, etc.)" (www.en.wikipedia.org/wiki/Substitutability).

Subsystem a unit of hierarchical decomposition for large systems; a kind of component.

System use case a use case that addresses generic needs of the system as the whole. Its functionality can be reused by actor use cases via inheritance.

UNP Upward Notification Principle in PCBMER.

Multiple-choice test

MC1 MVC is a:

   a framework

   b meta-model

   c programming environment

   d all of the above.

MC2 Which of the following is the name of the Core J2EE tier?

   a Business.

   b Integration.

   c Presentation.

   d All of the above.

MC3 Which of the following is the PCBMER layer representing the data classes and value objects that are destined for rendering on user interfaces?

    a Entity.

    b Bean.

    c Presentation.

    d None of the above.

MC4 The process of sending notifications to subscriber objects is called:

    a event processing

    b forwarding

    c delegation

    d none of the above.

MC5 Which of the following class discovery approaches works with the concept of a fuzzy class?

    a CRC.

    b Common class patterns approach.

    c Use case-driven approach.

    d None of the above.

MC6 The properties of transitivity and asymmetry are observed in which of the following categories of aggregation?

    a Owns aggregation.

    b Has aggregation.

    c ExclusiveOwns aggregation.

    d All of the above.

MC7 In a use case model, which one of the following is a relationship that always relates two use cases?

    a Association.

    b Aggregation.

    c Extend.

    d All of the above.

MC8 An event that signifies a guard condition has been satisfied is called a:

    a change event

    b time event

    c signal event

    d call event.

Questions

Q1 Consider the seven PCBMER architectural principles defined in Section 4.1.3.2. Two of these principles are most responsible for delivering hierarchical, rather than network, architectures. What are they? Explain your answer.

Q2 Consider Figure 4.23, which shows classes grouped into three packages and communication dependencies between the classes. Show how these dependencies can be reduced by introducing an interface in each of the three packages. Each interface would define public services available in the respective package. Communication between packages will then be channeled via the interfaces.

Q3 Discuss how functional and data requirements identified in the requirements determination phase relate to state, behavior and state change models of the requirements specification phase.

Q4 Explain the pros and cons of using CASE tools for requirements specification.

Q5 Explain the main differences in the four approaches to class discovery (other than the mixed approach).

Q6 Discuss and contrast the processes associated with the discovery and specification of class attributes and class operations. Would you model attributes and operations in parallel or separately? Why?

Q7 Auto-generation of code for Figure 4.8 (Example 4.8, Section 4.2.2.2.1) will fail. Why?

Figure 4.23
A network of intercommunicating objects
Source: Maciaszek and Liong (2005). Reprinted by permission of Pearson Education Ltd

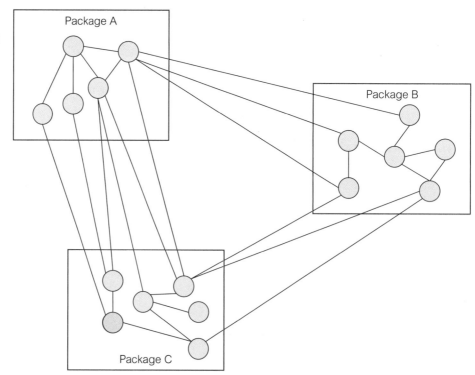

Q8 Refer to the class model in Figure 4.10 (Example 4.10, Section 4.2.4.3). Explain why `EMovie.isInStock` is modeled as a *derived* attribute and `EVideoMedium.percent ExcellentCondition` as a *static* attribute.

Q9 Ternary and derived associations are not desirable in analysis models. Why? Give examples.

Q10 Refer to the class model in Figure 4.8 (Example 4.8, Section 4.2.2.2.1). Consider the top part of the model defining classes and associations between `EPostalAddress`, `ECourierAddress`, `EOrganization` and `EContact`. Think about the different ways of modeling the same requirements. Can the model be made more flexible to accommodate potential changes to the requirements? What are the pros and cons of different solutions?

Q11 Refer to the class model in Figure 4.9 (Example 4.9, Section 4.2.3.3). How would the semantics of the model change if the class `EAcademicRecord` were modeled as an "association as a class" linked to the association *Takes*? How would the model with "association as a class" be influenced if the aggregation between `ECourse` and `ECourseOffering` were reversed – that is, if `ECourseOffering` contained `ECourse`?

Q12 Inheritance without polymorphism is possible but not terribly useful. Why? Give an example.

Q13 Which UML models specifically target behavior specification? Explain their individual strengths and how they interrelate to define the behavior of the system.

Q14 Explain how use cases differ from business functions or business transactions.

Q15 What is the difference between a decision (branch) and a fork in an activity diagrams? Give an example.

Q16 Give an example of an `<<include>>` relationship and an `<<extend>>` relationship between use cases. What is the main difference?

Q17 Give an example of a class with few attributes. Discuss which attributes can trigger a state transition and which attributes are indifferent to state changes.

Exercises: video store

Additional requirements: video store

Consider the following additional requirements for a system for a video store.

- Entertainment media returned late induce a payment equal to an extra rental period. Each entertainment medium has a unique identification number.

- Entertainment items are ordered from suppliers who are generally able to supply entertainment media within one week. Typically, several entertainment items are ordered in a single order to a supplier.

- Reservations are accepted for an entertainment item that is on order and/or because all copies of a particular item are rented out. Reservations are also accepted for items that are neither in store nor on order, but a customer is then asked for a deposit of one rental period.

- Customers can make many reservations, but a separate reservation request is prepared for each entertainment item reserved. A reservation may be canceled due to lack of response from a customer, more precisely one week from the date the customer was contacted to say that the item was available for rental. If a deposit has been paid, it is then credited to the customer's account.

- The database stores the usual information about suppliers and customers – that is, addresses, phone numbers and so on. Each order to a supplier identifies the ordered items, media formats and quantities, as well as an expected delivery date, purchase price and applicable discounts.

- When an entertainment medium is returned by a customer or delivered from a supplier, reservations are satisfied first. This involves contacting the customers who made the reservations. In order to ensure that reservations are properly handled, both the "reserved item has arrived" contact with the customer and the subsequent rental to the customer are related back to the reservation. These steps ensure that reservations are properly carried through.

- A customer can borrow many media, but each borrowed medium constitutes a separate rental record. For each rental, the check-out, due-in, and return dates and times are recorded. The rental record is later updated to indicate that the medium has been returned and the final payment (or reimbursement) has been made. The clerk who has authorized the rental is also recorded. Details about customers and their rentals are kept for a year to enable customer ratings to be determined based on historical information. Old rental details are kept for auditing purposes for the year.

- All transactions are made using cash, electronic money transfer or credit cards. Customers are required to pay the rental charges when the entertainment media are checked out.

- When an entertainment medium item is returned late (or it cannot be returned for whatever reason), a payment is taken either from the customer's account or directly from the customer.

- If an entertainment medium item is overdue by more than two days, an overdue notice is sent to the customer. Once two overdue notices on a single videotape or disk have been sent, the customer is noted as delinquent and the next rental is subject to the manager's decision to remove the delinquent rating.

E1   Refer to the additional requirements above and to Example 4.2 (Section 4.2.1.1.7). What new classes can be derived from the extended requirements?

E2   Refer to the additional requirements above, to Exercise E1 and Example 4.10 (Section 4.2.4.3). Extend the class model in Figure 4.10 (Example 4.10) to include the extended requirements. Show the classes and relationships.

E3   Refer to the additional requirements above and Example 4.15 (Section 4.3.1.2). Study the narrative specification for the use case `Rent video` in Table 4.4 (Example 4.15, same Section). Ignore the last paragraph in the main flow section of the table, as it relates to the use case `Maintain customer`. Develop a separate use case diagram to depict *child* use cases for `Rent entertainment item`.

Exercises: contact management

F1   Refer to Example 4.8 (Section 4.2.2.2.1). Develop a state machine diagram for the class `EEvent`.

F2   Refer to Example 4.8 (Section 4.2.2.2.1). Consider the classes `EOrganization`, `EContact`, `EPostalAddress` and `ECourierAddress`. As an extension to the model in Figure 4.8, allow for a hierarchical structure to organizations – that is, an organization can consist of smaller organizations. Improve the class model by using generalization and, at the same time, extend it to capture the hierarchy of organizations.

Exercises: university enrolment

Additional requirements: university enrolment

Consider the following additional requirements for a university enrolment system.

- The university is organized into divisions. The divisions divide into departments. Academics work for a single department.

- Most degrees are managed by one division, but some are managed jointly by two or more divisions.

- New students receive their acceptance form and enrolment instructions by mail and/or e-mail.

- Continuing students, who are eligible to re-enroll, receive enrolment instructions together with notification of their examination results. All instructions and notifications are also available to students via Web-based access to the university system. A student may also elect to receive instructions and notifications by mail or e-mail.

- Enrolment instructions include the class timetable for the course offerings.

- During enrolment, students may consult an academic adviser in their division on the formulation of a program of study.

- Students are not restricted to studying only courses offered by their division and may at any time change to another by completing a change of program form, available from the student office.

- To take certain courses, a student must first pass the prerequisite courses and achieve the required grade – that is, a straight pass may not be sufficient. A student who has not passed a course satisfactorily may attempt to do the same course again. Special approvals by the delegate of the head of the relevant division are needed to enroll in a course for the third time or when requesting waivers of prerequisites.

- Students are classified as part-time if they are enrolled for the year in course offerings carrying a combined total of fewer than 18 credit points (most courses are worth 3 credit points).

- Special permission needs to be obtained to enroll in a program of course offerings carrying a combined total of more than 14 credit points in a given semester.

- Each course offering has one academic in charge of it, but additional academics may be involved as well.

G1   Refer to the additional requirements above and Example 4.1 (Section 4.2.1.1.7). What new classes can be derived from the extended requirements?

G2   Refer to the additional requirements above, Exercise G1 and Example 4.9 (Section 4.2.3.3). Extend the class model of Figure 4.9 (Example 4.9 Section 4.2.3.3) to include the extended requirements. Show classes and relationships.

G3   Refer to the additional requirements above and Example 4.13 (Section 4.3.1.2). Extend the use case model in Figure 4.13 (Example 4.13) to include the extended requirements.

G4   Refer to the additional requirements above and Example 4.18 (Section 4.3.3.3). Develop a communication diagram (Section 3.4.2) that extends the sequence diagram of Figure 4.18 (Example 4.18) to include the checking of prerequisites – a student will only be added to the course if he or she has passed the prerequisite courses.

G5   Refer to Example 4.19 (Section 4.3.4.3) and to the solution for Exercise G4 above. Use the communication diagram to add operations to classes in the class diagram in Figure 4.20.

Review quiz answers

Review quiz 4.1
RQ1 The prior architectural design, conforming to some recognized architectural framework, is such a condition.
RQ2 Controller objects.
RQ3 The integration tier.
RQ4 The resource layer.

Review quiz 4.2
RQ1 The CRC (class–responsibility–collaborators) approach is a technique for class discovery.
RQ2 Role names can be used to explain more complicated associations – in particular, *self-associations* (recursive associations that relate objects of the same class).
RQ3 Transitivity means that if a subset object C is a part of a subset object B and B is part of another subset object A, then C is necessarily a part of A.
RQ4 The principle of substitutability.

Review quiz 4.3
RQ1 No, they don't. Activity diagrams can represent concurrent flow of control.
RQ2 Yes, they can. This is possible because activity diagrams do not explicitly visualize the classes of objects that perform the actions.
RQ3 A signal.
RQ4 Sequence diagrams.

Review quiz 4.4
RQ1 No, they don't. State machine diagrams are not specific about sequences of state changes, even if such sequences may be expected.
RQ2 Not necessarily. An entry action may be specified and it will then need to be satisfactorily completed before the state change can take place.

Multiple-choice test answers

MC1 d
MC2 d
MC3 b
MC4 a
MC5 d (noun phrase approach works with that concept)
MC6 d
MC7 c
MC8 a

Answers to odd-numbered questions

Q1

The two principles are the NCP and APP.

The NCP principle forbids direct object communication between non-neighboring layers. This enforces hierarchical communication sequences. For example, if A and C are two non-neighboring layers, but B is a neighbor of both A and C, then A needs to communicate with B to get services from C. In a network, A could talk to C.

The APP principle offsets the rigidity of the NCP principle. It is sometimes awkward to force and follow long chains of messages to allow communication between non-neighboring layers, particularly when the layers are far apart. Introducing a separate layer of interfaces that allows objects in non-neighboring layers to be acquainted without undesirable dependencies is a solution to the dilemma created by the APP principle.

Admittedly, the UNP principle also assists hierarchies and counteracts networks. However, the main benefit of the UNP principle is that it reduces object dependencies by eliminating upward dependencies rather than it neutralizes networks. For this reason, the UNP principle is not included in the answer to this question.

Q3

Functional and data requirements captured in the *requirements determination* phase are the *service statements* – they define the desired services of the system in terms of their functions and data. In the *requirements specification* phase, the requirements are formally modeled in state, behavior and state change *diagrams*.

The specification models provide different views of the same set of requirements. A particular requirement may be modeled in all three diagrams, each diagram having a specific viewpoint on the requirement design.

This said, it is also fair to say that *state models* express most of the *data* requirements and *behavior models* capture most of the *function* requirements. *State change models* apply uniformly to both data and functional requirements, as well as to the system constraints (non-functional requirements).

Eventually, the classes in the state model are extended with the detailed design of operations. The final state model embodies all of a system's internal workings and represents both data and functional requirements.

Q5

The four approaches to class discovery are:

- noun phrase approach
- common class patterns approach
- use case-driven approach
- CRC (class–responsibility–collaborators) approach.

The *noun phrase approach* seems to be the easiest and quickest to apply. Lexical tools can support the search for nouns in the requirements document. However, overreliance on the vocabulary to pick up classes may be deceptive and inaccurate.

The *common class patterns approach* is an attractive option when combined with some other approach, but it is unlikely to produce complete results when used alone. The approach seems to be missing a system reference point, be it the list of requirements (noun phrase approach), the set of use cases (use case-driven approach) or workshops with users (CRC approach).

The *use case-driven approach* demands a prior investment in the development of use cases. The classes are discovered by analyzing use case models. The sets of classes from all use cases need to be integrated to arrive at the final class list. Only classes directly demanded by the use cases can be contemplated. This may be a hindrance to the future evolution of the system, because the class models will be strictly matching the system functionality represented in the current use cases.

The *CRC approach* is the most "object-oriented" of the four approaches. It identifies classes to implement discussed business scenarios. It emphasizes the class behavior (operations) and can lead to the discovery of predominantly "behavioral" classes (as opposed to static "informational" classes). However, it also determines the attribute content of each class. In this sense, the CRC approach is at a lower level of abstraction and can be used in addition to one of the previous three approaches.

Q7

The auto-generation will fail because no unique role names are provided for associations between `EEvent` and `EEmployee` and the CASE tool may not be able to generate differently named instance variables for associations to the same class. For example, it is not possible to have three variables named `theEEmployee` in the class `EEvent`. There is a need for variables such as `theCreatedEmp`, `theDueEmp` and `theCompletedEmp`.

Q9

Semantic modeling must be unambiguous. Each model must have only one interpretation. *Ternary associations* lend themselves to multiple interpretations and are therefore undesirable. Consider a ternary association called `FamilyUnit` between `Man`, `Woman` and `Residence` (Maciaszek 1990). Suppose that the association has the multiplicity one at all its ends except that the membership of `Residence` in the association is optional – that is `FamilyUnit` can exist without the `Residence` object.

Such a ternary association poses many uneasy questions. Can the same person participate in more than one `FamilyUnit` if that person has been married twice? Can the same residence house more than one couple? What if the couple splits up and one of the partners takes ownership of the residence? What if that person remarries and his or her husband or wife moves into that residence?

Abandoning the ternary association and replacing it with three binary associations – `Man-Woman`, `Man-Residence` and `Woman-Residence` – provides a solution to difficult questions like those above. In the presence of *generalization*, the association `Person-Residence` could replace the last two associations, further simplifying the model.

A good analysis model should be non-redundant. It should be minimal yet complete. A *derived association* can be removed from the model without any loss of information. A derived association is really a special kind of constraint within the model and it does not need to be explicit in the class diagram.

Consider the following *cycle of associations*. The `Department-Employee` is one to many, as are `Department-ResearchProject` and `ResearchProject-Employee` (Maciaszek 1990). Studying the cycle can reveal that the association `Department-ResearchProject` is redundant. We can always establish research projects run by a department by finding employees of that department and then following the links to the research projects in which these employees participate.

Although the association `Department-ResearchProject` is not necessary in the model, the analyst may still decide to retain it. The clarity of the design justifies showing such an association. This justification extends further to performance gains related to the existence of the direct traversal path between `Department` and `ResearchProject`. Finally, the association is indispensable if a department can negotiate a research project prior to naming any employees who will participate in it.

Q11

This question is a bit devious. The semantics of the model must not change if the model is to reflect the same set of user requirements. If a new model cannot represent certain semantics, then the missing semantics should be expressed by other means – for example, in a narrative attachment. By the same token, if the new model is more expressive, the added semantics must be derived from some narrative document attached to the original model.

Consider the modified model in Figure 4.24. Each instance of the association class `EAcademicRecord` has object references to `EStudent` and `ECourseOffering`, as well as the two attribute values `grade` and `courseCode`. The identity of each instance of `EAcademicRecord` is provided from the object references in it (corresponding to the two roles of the association – -`hasStud` and -`takesCrsoff`). The attribute `grade` informs about the grade of the student in a particular course offering.

The presence of the attribute `courseCode` in `EAcademicRecord` is more controversial. We can argue that this attribute is not needed there because each instance of `ECourseOffering` (pointed to by the object reference -`takesCrsoff` in the `EAcademicRecord` object) is a component of a single instance of `ECourse`. We can therefore follow the "pointer" from `ECourseOffering` to `ECourse` and derive the value of the attribute `courseCode`.

An alternative design is shown in Figure 4.25. `ECourseOffering` contains `ECourse`. The aggregation is "by reference" because `ECourse` is a standalone class that is likely to be linked in other relationships in the complete model. The fact that the attribute `courseCode` is now part of `ECourseOffering` is also evident in `EAcademicRecord` (`courseCode` is removed from it).

The main difference between the models in Figures 4.24 and 4.25 and the model in Figure 4.9 is that the models below support the same semantics with less redundancy (duplication of attribute values). `EAcademicRecord` does not include the attributes `year` and `semester`, and the attribute `courseCode` can also be dispensed with as per the discussion above. However, the information content of `EAcademicRecord` has to be derived from the associated objects rather than stored as part of the `EStudent` object (recall that in the model in Figure 4.9 `EAcademicRecord` is contained "by value" in `EStudent`).

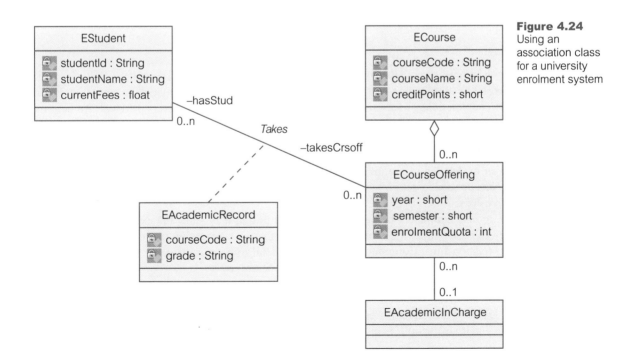

Figure 4.24
Using an association class for a university enrolment system

Figure 4.25
Using an association class after the reversing of aggregation for a university enrolment system

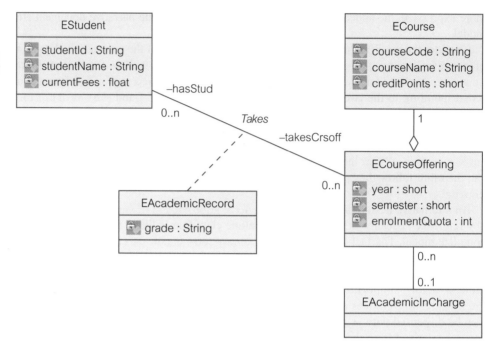

Q13

The UML models that are most applicable for *behavior specification* are:

- activity diagrams
- sequence diagrams
- communication diagrams.

Activity diagrams are best used to model computations – the sequential and concurrent steps in a computational procedure or work flow. Depending on the "granularity" of the actions in the model, an activity diagram can be used to model computations at various levels of abstraction with various levels of detail. An activity diagram can model the computations in a use case or in an operation of the class.

Sequence diagrams demonstrate the exchange of messages between objects in a time sequence. Like activity diagrams, they can be used at different levels of granularity to describe the exchange of generic messages for the whole system or of detailed messages for a single operation. Sequence diagrams are used extensively during analysis. They can be used to determine operations in classes. Unlike communication diagrams, they do not show object relationships.

Communication diagrams compete with sequence diagrams in that they show the exchange of messages between objects. They can use numbering of messages to show the time dimension if necessary. Additionally, they can show object relationships. Communication diagrams tend to be more suitable in the design phase, where they can be used to model the realization of use cases or operations.

All three models have their role and place in behavior specifications. They can be used to show different viewpoints of the same behavior, but, more often, they are used to capture different behavior or the same behavior at different levels of abstraction. Activity diagrams are particularly flexible when used to represent models at different levels of abstraction. Sequence diagrams tend to be used in *analysis*, communication diagrams in *design*.

Q15

A *decision* (*branch*) splits the control flow from an action into two or more flows, each with a separate *guard condition*. To guarantee that an occurrence of an event will trigger one of the split flows, the guard conditions must cover every possibility.

A *fork* is a control flow from an action that results in two or more concurrent actions. If the source action is active and the control flow occurs, all the target actions become active (there is no guard condition to control the activation of target actions).

Figure 4.26 shows an example of a decision and a fork in a banking application that manages customers' accounts.

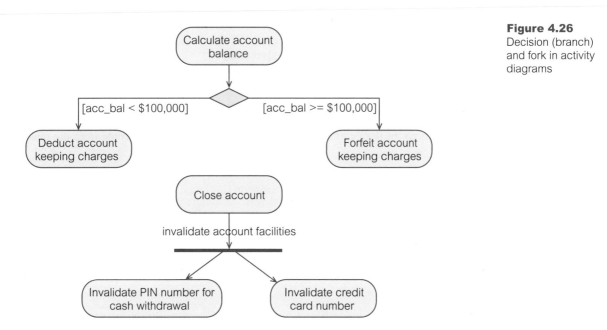

Figure 4.26
Decision (branch)
and fork in activity
diagrams

Q17

Consider the class `ECampaign` in the telemarketing case study (see Figure 4.7). The attributes of that class are listed in Figure 4.27.

Figure 4.27
The `ECampaign`
class for a
telemarketing
system

A class can be analyzed for *state changes* from a number of different perspectives. A separate state model can be built for each perspective. Depending on the perspective, some attributes are considered and other attributes are ignored. For example, from the perspective of using telemarketing to promote the sale of lottery tickets to a charity's supporters, an object of class ECampaign can be in the state of Tickets available or Tickets sold out. To define these states, we are concerned only with the attributes numTickets and numTicketsSold. Other attributes are not relevant.

Similarly, from the perspective of knowing if an ECampaign is Current or Closed, we need to look at the values of attributes dateStart and dateClose. If, additionally, we are interested in modeling the state Closed no more tickets, the values of attributes numTickets and numTicketsSold will have to be considered as well.

Solutions to exercises: university enrolment

G1

Table 4.5 contains the list of proposed classes. The classes established previously in Example 4.1 (Table 4.1, Section 4.2.1.1.7) are underlined. The fuzzy class FullTimeStudent is in square brackets to signify that, although it is not mentioned directly in the extended requirements, it is included to complement the class PartTimeStudent.

Table 4.5 Additional candidate classes for a university enrolment system

Relevant classes	Fuzzy classes
Course	CompulsoryCourse
Degree	ElectiveCourse
Student	StudyProgram
CourseOffering	NewStudent
Division	ContinuingStudent
Department	AcceptanceForm
Academic	EnrolmentInstructions
	ExaminationResults
	ClassTimetable
	AcademicAdviser
	RegistrationDivision
	PrerequisiteCourse
	SpecialApproval
	(SpecialPermission)
	HeadDelegate
	PartTimeStudent
	[FullTimeStudent]
	AcademicInCharge

G2

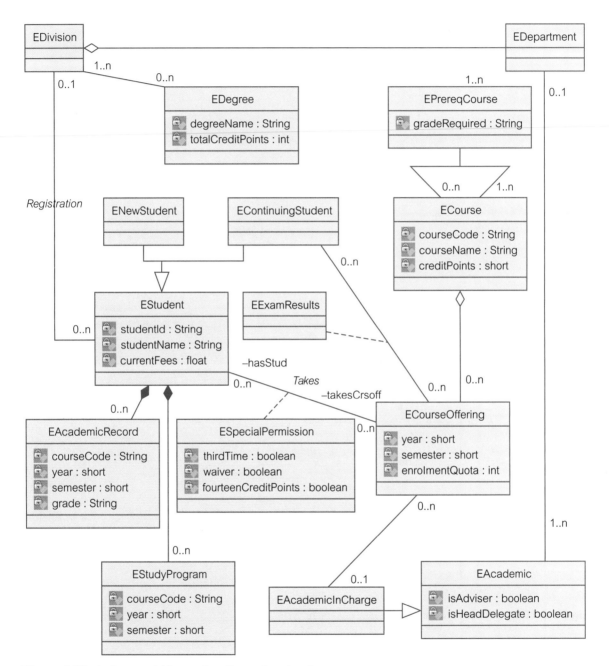

Figure 4.28 A class model for a university enrolment system

G3

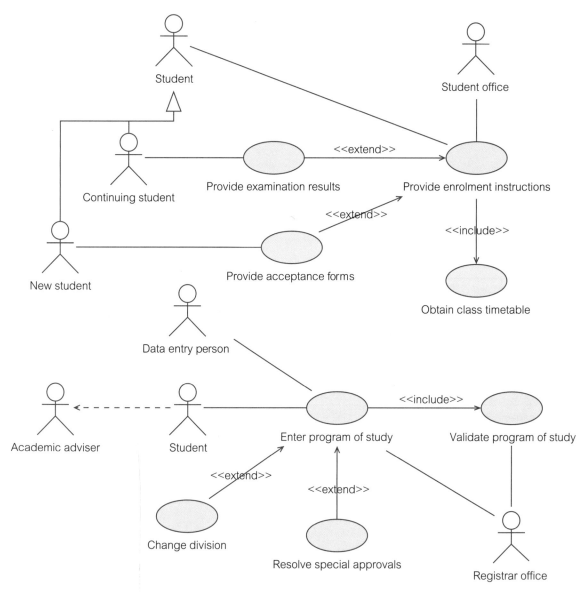

Figure 4.29 A use case model for a university enrolment system

G4

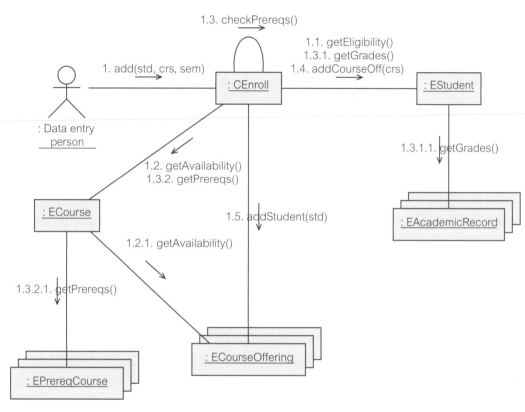

Figure 4.30 A communication diagram for a university enrolment system

G5

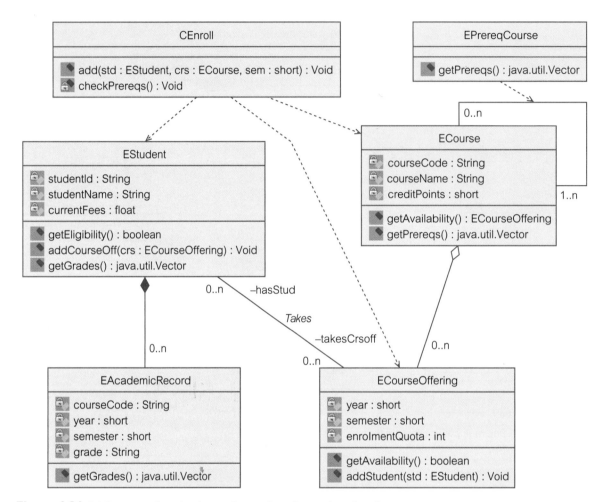

Figure 4.31 Adding operations to classes for a university enrolment system

Chapter

5

Moving from Analysis to Design

Objectives

The previous two chapters have painted a relatively rosy picture of visual object-oriented modeling. The examples were not very demanding, the diagrams produced in UML were attractive and useful and the dependencies between models were apparent. The modeling techniques used were commensurate with the difficulty of the problems posed. They were sufficiently powerful to define the data structures and behavior for the problems.

The realities of software development are more complex. There are no simple solutions to complex problems, as we observed at the very beginning of this book. Objects provide the current technology to construct complex contemporary systems. As such, objects need to provide the technical depth corresponding to the level of complexity they address.

This chapter can be seen as a critical appraisal of object technology and its suitability for solving complex problems. We introduce advanced concepts in class modeling, generalization/inheritance, aggregation/delegation and interaction modeling. Throughout, we compare, pass judgements, give opinions on and suggest alternative solutions for them. Because of their technical character, many topics discussed in this chapter extend directly into system design. This is consistent with the ubiquitous nature of UML and the iterative and incremental process of object-oriented software development.

By reading this chapter you will:

- learn how to customize UML to suit specific needs and the technology of the projects
- gain knowledge of UML features for modeling at lower abstraction levels
- realize that some powerful object technology concepts must not be taken at their face value and applied indiscriminately
- recognize various modeling tradeoffs, particularly with regard to generalization and aggregation
- gain practical knowledge about how to build design-level interaction models.

5.1 Advanced class modeling

The analysis modeling concepts discussed so far are sufficient to produce complete analysis models, but at a level of abstraction that does not exhaust all possible details permissible in analysis modeling – that is, details that do not yet reveal the hardware/software solution but enrich the semantics of the model. UML includes notations for a number of additional concepts that we only alluded to in passing before or have not addressed at all.

The additional modeling concepts include **stereotypes**, **constraints**, **derived information**, **visibility**, *qualified associations*, *association class*, *parameterized class* and so on. These concepts are optional. Many models may be sufficient without them. When used, they have to be applied with care and precision so that any future reader of the model can understand the intention of the writer without misgivings.

5.1.1 Extension mechanisms

The UML standard provides a set of modeling concepts and notations that are universally applicable in software development projects. However, this universality means that some more specific and unorthodox modeling needs may not be catered for by UML. The UML standard, like any standard, is the "lowest common denominator". It would not make sense to complicate UML by trying to provide exotic built-in modeling features that would satisfy specific application domains, software infrastructures or programming languages.

However, there is still a need to use UML beyond its built-in capabilities. To this aim, the UML standard offers extension mechanisms, such as stereotypes, constraints, **tag definitions** and **tagged values**. A coherent set of extensions can materialize in the UML concept of a **profile**. A *profile* extends a reference **metamodel** (that is, UML) for different purposes, such as for different application domains or technology platforms. For example, UML profiles can be built for database modeling, data warehouse design or the development of Web-based systems.

Stereotypes   5.1.1.1

A *stereotype* extends an existing UML modeling element. It varies the semantics of an existing element. It is not a new model element per se. It does not change the structure of UML – it enriches only the meaning of an existing notation. It allows extending and customizing of the model. The possible uses of stereotypes are diverse.

Typically, stereotypes are *labeled* in the models with a name within matched guillemets (quotation symbols in French), such as <<global>>, <<PK>>, <<include>>. An *iconic* presentation of stereotypes is also possible.

Some popular stereotypes are built in – they are predefined in UML. The built-in stereotypes are likely to have icons readily available in a CASE tool. Most CASE tools provide for the possibility of creating new icons at the analyst's will. Figure 5.1 gives an example of a class stereotyped with an icon, label and no stereotype.

The restriction that a stereotype extends the semantics but not the structure of UML is quite insignificant. The bottom line in any object-oriented system is that *everything* in it *is an object* – a class is an object, an attribute is an object, a method is an object. Hence, by stereotyping a class, we can, in effect, create a new modeling element that introduces a new category of objects.

Customer (actor as icon stereotype)

| <<Actor>> |
| Customer (actor as label stereotype) |
| |
| |

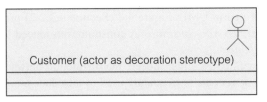

Customer (actor as decoration stereotype)

| Customer (a class with no stereotype defined) |
| |
| |

Figure 5.1 Graphical visualizations of stereotypes

5.1.1.2 Comments and constraints

A **comment** is a textual annotation that can be attached to a set of elements… A comment gives the ability to attach various remarks to elements. A comment carries no semantic force, but may contain information that is useful to a modeler… A comment is shown as a rectangle, with the upper right-hand corner bent (this is also known as a "note symbol"). The rectangle contains the body of the comment. The connection to each annotated element is shown by a separate dashed line.

(UML 2005: 69)

A *constraint* is a condition or restriction expressed in natural language text or in a machine readable language for the purpose of declaring some of the semantics of an element… A constraint represents additional semantic information attached to the constrained elements. A constraint is an assertion that indicates a restriction that must be satisfied by a correct design of the system… A constraint is shown as a text string in braces ({})… For an element whose notation is a text string (such as an attribute, etc.), the constraint string may follow the element text string in braces… For a constraint that applies to a single element (such as a class or an association path), the constraint string may be placed near the symbol for the element, preferably near the name, if any… For a constraint that applies to two elements (such as two classes or two associations), the constraint may be shown as a dashed line between the elements labeled by the constraint string (in braces).

(UML 2005: 70–1)

As constraints can also be expressed as text strings, the difference between a comment and a constraint is not that much in the presentation but in the semantic consequences. A comment does not have semantic force on the model. It is, rather, an additional explanation for modeling decisions. A *constraint* has semantic meaning to the model and (ideally) should be written in a formal constraint language. In fact, UML offers a predefined language for this purpose. The language is called *Object Constraint Language (OCL)*.

Only simpler comments and constraints are shown in a model diagram. More elaborate comments and constraints (with descriptions too long to be shown on a graphical model) are stored in a CASE repository as text documents.

Certain kinds of constraint are predefined in UML. Figure 4.8 (Section 4.2.2.2) provided an example of the use of the predefined *Xor-constraint*. A constraint introduced by the modeler constitutes an *extension mechanism*.

Stereotypes are frequently confused with constraints. Indeed, the distinction between these two concepts is blurred at times. A *stereotype* is frequently used to introduce a new *constraint* into the model – something meaningful to the modeler but not directly supported as a constraint in UML.

Example 5.1: telemarketing

Refer to Example 4.7 (Section 4.2.1.2.3). Consider the classes `ECampaign` and `ECampaignTicket` (Figure 4.7). Establish a relationship between these classes. Add operations to `ECampaign` for the computation of the number of tickets sold and still left, as well as for the computation of overall campaign duration and the number of days left before the campaign is closed.

Annotate the diagram with information that `ECampaign` is different from a bonus campaign. Also, write a reminder on the diagram that operations need to be added to `ECampaignTicket`.

Recall a part of the second requirement listed in Example 4.7 stating that: "All tickets are numbered. The numbers are unique across all tickets in a campaign." Make this statement into a constraint. (In the solution to Example 4.7 (Figure 4.7), we could not capture the above constraint, short of including `campaignCode` (with `ticketNumber`) as a part of a composite primary key for `CampaignTicket`.)

Figure 5.2 represents a simple extension to the class model to satisfy the demands of Example 5.1. The figure defines two comments and a constraint.

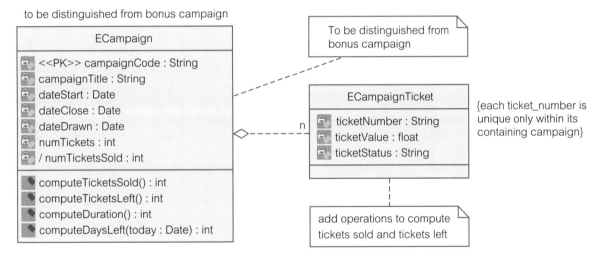

Figure 5.2 Two comments and a constraint for a telemarketing system

Example 5.2: contact management

Refer to Example 4.8 (Section 4.2.2.2.1). Assume that a new requirement has been discovered that the system does not handle the scheduling of events by employees to themselves. This means that an employee who created an event must not be the same as the employee who is due to perform that event.

Extend a relevant part of the class model (Figure 4.8), to include the new requirement.

The solution to Example 5.2 (in Figure 5.3) results in a constraint on association lines. This is shown as a dashed dependency arrow from the association `Created` to the association `Due`. The constraint is *bound* to the arrow.

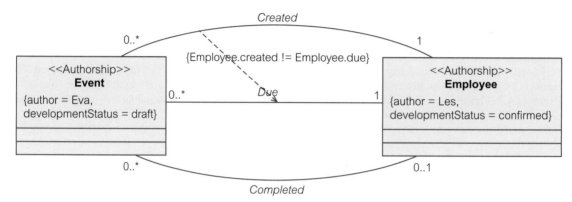

Figure 5.3 Constraints on association for a contact management system

5.1.1.3 Tags

Understanding the concept of tags requires distinguishing between *tag definition* and *tagged values*. A *tag definition* is a property of a stereotype and is shown as an attribute of a class rectangle that contains the stereotype declaration. "A *tagged value* is a name–value pair that may be attached to a model element that uses a stereotype containing a tag definition" (Rumbaugh et al., 2005: 657).

Like constraints, tags represent arbitrary textual information in the model and are presented inside curly brackets. The form is:

```
tag = value - for example:
{analyst = Les, developmentStatus = confirmed}
```

Because a tag can only be represented as an attribute defined on a stereotype, a stereotype with tag definitions must be defined on a model element (such as on a package) before tagged values can be applied to a particular instance of that model element.

Like stereotypes and constraints, few tags are predefined in UML. A typical use of tags is in providing project management information.

Figure 5.4 shows the extended model for Example 5.3 (see overleaf). The stereotype `Authorship` with tag definitions is shown in the upper left-hand corner. A note is used to express the constraint attached to `Task`. (Ideally the note constraint should be visually attached to all three classes, but this is difficult to represent using CASE tools. The reason is that a constraint cannot be defined for a note itself, but must be defined for a model element, such as a class or an association.)

Example 5.3: contact management

Refer to Example 4.8 (Section 4.2.2.2.1) and to Example 5.2 above. Define a stereotype called `Authorship` and make that stereotype applicable to any model element. Declare the tags called `author` and `developmentStatus`. Apply the defined stereotype to classes `Event` and `Employee`. Specify some tagged values.

   Assume that a new requirement has been discovered: that an employee who created a task must also create – in the same transaction – the first event for that task. Extend the relevant part of the class model (Figures 4.8 and 5.3), to include the new requirement. Use for it a note constraint defined for the class `Task`.

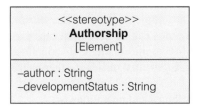

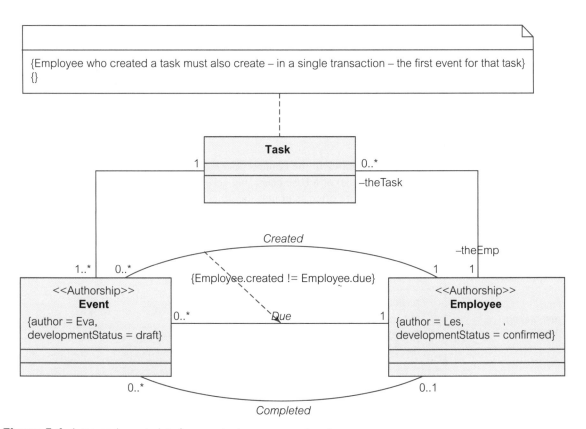

Figure 5.4 A tag and constraints for a contact management system

5.1.2 Visibility and encapsulation

Concepts of *visibility*, and the related notion of *encapsulation*, are explained in the Appendix in relation to visibility in a class – that is *attribute visibility* (Appendix, Section A.3.1.2) and *operation visibility* (Appendix, Section A.3.2.2). In a class, visibility signifies if other classes can access the elements of the class. In the Appendix, we have concentrated on the *public* and *private* visibility of *attributes* and *operations*. The UML standard predefines two more visibility markers – *protected* and *package* visibility.

Also, the visibility can be defined for a *class, interface, association* or *package* (as opposed to the visibility of the class *elements* – that is, *attributes* and *operations*). In an *association*, visibility applies to *role names* (Appendix, Section A.3.1.1). Because role names (called *association end names* in UML 2.0) are implemented as *class attributes*, visibility of role names signifies if the resulting attributes can be used in access expressions to traverse the association. In a *package*, visibility applies to elements contained by the package, such as *classes, associations, nested packages*. It signifies if other packages can access the elements of the package.

The complete set of visibility markers for class attributes and operations is:

+   for public visibility
-      for private visibility
for protected visibility
~   for package visibility.

CASE tools frequently replace this rather dull UML notation with graphically more attractive visibility markers. Figure 5.5 is an example of an alternative notation, complete with corresponding Java code.

5.1.2.1 Protected visibility

Protected visibility applies in the context of *inheritance*. Having the *private properties* (attributes and operations) of a base class only accessible to objects of the base class is not always convenient. More often than not, the objects of a *derived class* (a subclass of the base class) should be allowed to access the otherwise private properties of the base class.

Figure 5.5
Visibility notation in a CASE tool and the corresponding Java code

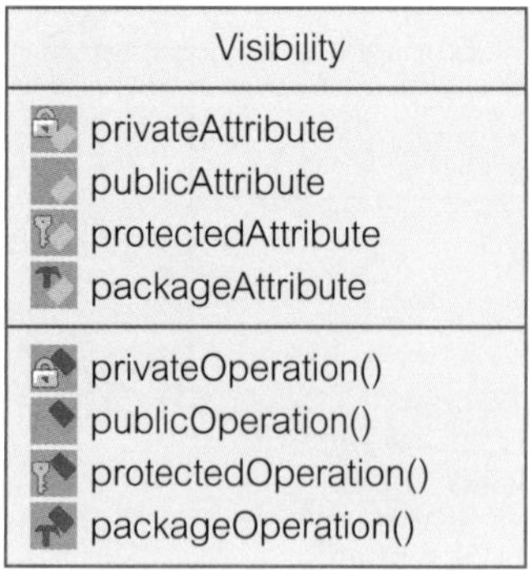

```
public class Visibility
{
    private int privateAttribute;
    public int publicAttribute;
    protected int protectedAttribute;
    int packageAttribute;

    private void privateOperation()
    public void publicOperation()
    protected void protectedOperation()
    void packageOperation()
}
```

Consider a class hierarchy where `Person` is the (non-abstract) base class and `Employee` is a derived class. If `Joe` is an object of `Employee`, then – by definition of generalization – `Joe` must have access to (at least some) properties of `Person` (such as the operation `getBirthDate()`).

In order to allow a derived class to have free access to properties of its base class, these (otherwise private) properties need to be defined in the base class as *protected*. (Recall that visibility applies between classes. If `Betty` is another object of `Employee`, she can access any property of `Joe`, whether public, package, protected or private.)

Example 5.4: telemarketing

Refer to Problem statement 4, for a telemarketing system (Section 1.6.4) and to Example 4.7 (Section 4.2.1.2.3). The problem statement contains the following requirement: "These schemes include special *bonus campaigns* to reward supporters for bulk buying, attracting new contributors and so on." This requirement has not yet been modeled.

Suppose that one of the bonus campaigns involves "ticket books". If a supporter buys the whole book of tickets, an extra ticket from the parent campaign is given free of charge.

Our task is to:

- update the class model to include the class `EBonusCampaign`
- change the visibility of attributes in `ECampaign` (Figure 5.2) so that they can be accessible to `EBonusCampaign`, with the exception of `dateStart`, and make `campaignCode` and `campaignTitle` visible to other classes in the model
- add the following operations to the class `ECampaign` – `computeTicketsSold()`, `computeTicketsLeft()`, `computeDuration()`, `computeDaysLeft()`
- observe that the classes outside the inheritance hierarchy need not be interested in `computeTicketsSold()` – they need only to know `computeTicketsLeft()` – and `computeDuration()` is used only by the operation `ECampaign.computeDaysLeft()`
- the class `EBonusCampaign` stores the attribute `ticketBookSize` and provides an access operation to it called `getBookSize()`.

Figure 5.6 shows a class model and generated Java code corresponding to the points listed in Example 5.4. The operation `computeDuration()` is private in `ECampaign`. The operation `computeTicketsSold()` is protected in `ECampaign`. The remaining two operations in `ECampaign` are public. The operation `getBookSize()` is specific to `EBonusCampaign` and is public.

Accessibility of inherited class properties 5.1.2.2

As remarked in the previous section, *visibility* applies to objects at various levels of granularity. It is usually understood that visibility applies to *primitive objects* – attributes and operations. However, visibility can also be specified with regard to other "containers". This creates a whole tangle of overriding rules.

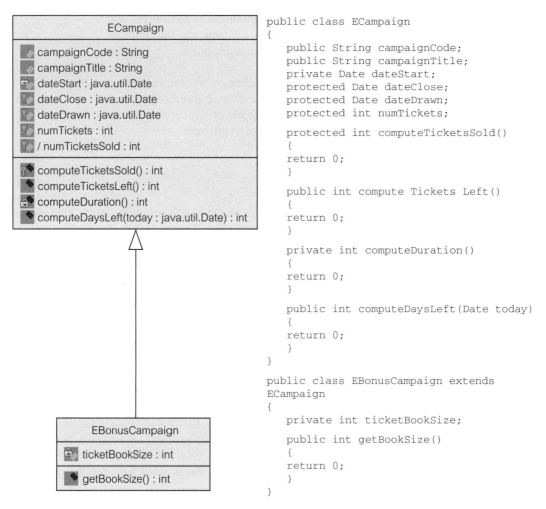

Figure 5.6 Using protected visibility for a telemarketing system

Consider, for example, a situation where visibility is defined in the *inheritance hierarchy* at the level of the base class *and* at the level of *properties* of the base class. Let us say, a class B is a subclass of class A. Class A contains a mixture of attributes and operations – some public, others private, yet others protected. The question is, "What is the visibility of inherited properties in class B?"

The answer to such a question depends on the visibility level given to the base class A when declaring it in the derived class B. In C++, the base class could be defined as public (class B: public A), protected (class B: protected A) or private (class B: private A). In Java, however, classes (other than *inner classes*) can be defined with only public or package visibility (Eckel 2003).

A typical resolution to the C++ scenario is as follows (Horton 1997):

■ the private properties (attributes and operations) of base class A are not visible to class B objects, no matter how base class A is defined in B

- if base class A is defined as `public`, the visibility of inherited properties does not change in derived class B (`public` are still public and `protected` are still protected)
- if base class A is defined as `protected`, the visibility of inherited `public` properties changes in derived class B to `protected`
- if base class A is defined as `private`, the visibility of inherited `public` and `protected` properties changes in derived class B to `private`

Note that, in the context of the above discussion, the notion of *implementation inheritance* means that if a property x exists in a base class A, then it also exists in any class that inherits from A. However, *inheriting* a property does not necessarily mean that the property is *accessible* to the objects of a derived class. In particular, private properties of the base class remain private to the base and are inaccessible to objects of the derived class. This is demonstrated in Figure 5.7, which shows (accessible) properties inherited by EBonusCampaign from Figure 5.6. The private properties of ECampaign – namely dateStart and computeDuration() – are not accessible to EBonusCampaign.

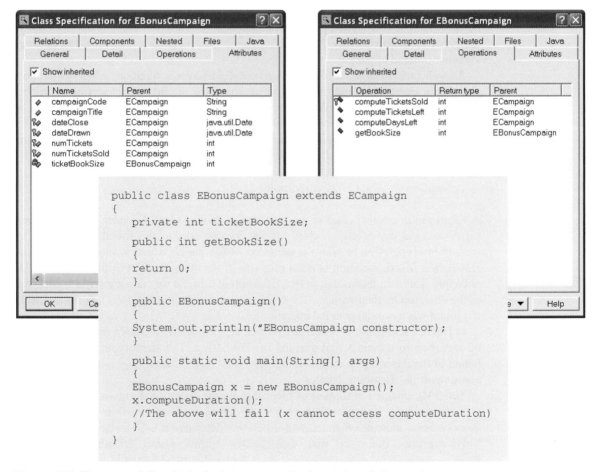

Figure 5.7 The accessibility of inherited class properties for a telemarketing system

5.1.2.3 Package and friendly visibility

There may be circumstances in which selected classes should be given direct access to some properties of another class, whereas for the rest of the classes in the system those properties remain private. Java supports such circumstances with *package* visibility. C++ provides a similar outcome with the definitions of *friends* – friendly operations and friendly classes.

Package visibility is the Java default. If no `private`, `protected` or `public` keyword is specified for a Java attribute or operation (or `public` for the entire class), then the obtained visibility is package, by default. Package visibility means that all other classes in the package concerned have access to such an attribute or operation. However, to all classes in *other* packages, the attribute, operation or class appears to be private.

Protected (and public) also gives package access, but not vice versa. This means that other classes in the same package can access protected properties, but *derived* classes cannot access properties with package visibility if the derived and the base class are in different packages.

Figure 5.8 is a variation on the model in Figure 5.6. In it, the private method (`computeDuration()`) and private data members (`dateStart` and `ticketBookSize`) are given package visibility. Moreover, `EBonusCampaign` as a class now has package visibility (instead of public).

As with Java package visibility, C++ *friendship* addresses situations when two or more classes are intertwined and one class needs to access the private properties of another class. A typical example would be that of the two classes `Book` and `BookShelf` and an operation in `Book` called `putOnBookShelf()`.

One way to solve situations like the one above is to declare the operation `putOnBookShelf()` a *friend* within the class `BookShelf` – something like:

```
friend void Book::putOnBookShelf()
```

A friend can be another *class* or an *operation* of another class. Friendship is not reciprocal. A class that makes another class a friend does not need to be a friend of that class.

A friend (operation or class) is declared *within* the class that grants the friendship. However, a friend operation is not a property of the class, so the visibility attributes do not apply. This also means that in the definition of a friend we cannot reference attributes of the class just by their names – they each have to be qualified by the class name (just as if a friend was a normal external operation).

In UML, a friendship is shown as a dashed *dependency relationship* from a friend class or operation to the class that granted the friendship. The stereotype `<<friend>>` is bound to the dependency arrow. Admittedly, the UML notation does not fully recognize and support the friend's semantics.

The UML notation in support of friendship for the operation discussed in Example 5.5 (see overleaf) is shown in Figure 5.9. A *dependency* relationship, stereotyped as `<<friend>>`, indicates that `ECallScheduled` depends on `ECampaign` for friendship. This captures the fact that `ECampaign` grants some friendship status to `ECallScheduled` (`getTicketsLeft()` is declared a friend within `ECampaign` because `ECampaign` decides who is its friend).

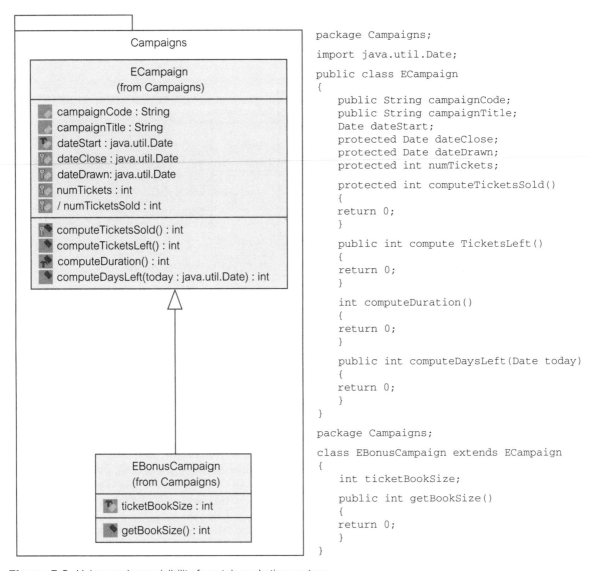

Figure 5.8 Using package visibility for a telemarketing system

Example 5.5: telemarketing

Refer to Example 4.7 (Section 4.2.1.2.3). Consider the relationship between the classes ECampaign and ECallScheduled (Figure 4.7).

Objects of the class ECallScheduled are very active and need special privileges when executing their operations. In particular, they contain an operation called getTicketsLeft() (Figure 5.9), which establishes whether or not any tickets are left so that a supporter's order can be satisfied. It is important that this operation has direct access to the properties of ECampaign (such as numTickets and numTicketsSold).

Our task is to declare the operation getTicketsLeft() and make it a friend of ECampaign.

Figure 5.9
Friend for a
telemarketing
system

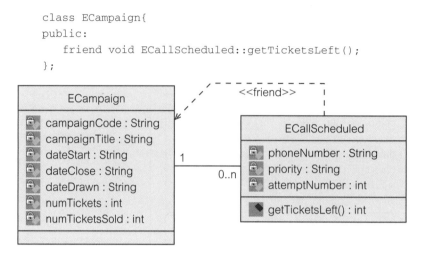

```
class ECampaign{
public:
    friend void ECallScheduled::getTicketsLeft();
};
```

5.1.3 Derived information

Derived information is a kind of *constraint* that applies (most frequently) to an *attribute* or an *association*. The derived information is computed from other model elements. Strictly speaking, the derived information is redundant in the model – it can be computed as needed.

Although derived information does not enrich the semantics of an *analysis model*, it can make the model more readable (because the fact that something can be computed is explicit in the model). The decision to show or not show the information as derived in an analysis model is quite arbitrary, as long as it is applied consistently across the entire model.

The knowledge as to what information is derived is more important in a *design model* where optimization of access to information needs to be considered. In design models, a decision may also be made as to whether some derived information is to be stored (after the derivation) or dynamically computed every time it is needed. This is not a new feature – it was known in old-style network databases under the terms of *actual* (stored) and *virtual* data.

The UML notation for derived information is a slash (/) in front of the name of the derived attribute or association.

5.1.3.1 Derived attribute

Although without explanation, we used derived attributes in passing in a couple of example diagrams. For instance, /numTicketsSold in Figure 5.2 is a derived attribute within the class ECampaign. The value of the attribute /numTicketsSold in Figure 5.2 is computed by the operation computeTicketsSold(). The operation follows the aggregation links from the ECampaign object to the ECampaignTicket objects and checks each ticketStatus. If ticketStatus is "sold", then it is added to the count of sold tickets. When all tickets have been processed, the current value of numTicketsSold has been derived.

Derived association 5.1.3.2

The derived association is a more controversial topic. In a typical scenario, a derived associ-ation happens between three classes already connected by two associations and with no third association that would close the loop. The third association is frequently needed for the model to be semantically correct (this is known as the *loop commutativity*). When not explicitly modeled, the third association can be derived from the other two associations.

> ### Example 5.6: orders database
>
> Consider a simple orders database with classes Customer, Order and Invoice. Consider further that an order is always produced by a single customer and each invoice is generated for a single order.
>   Draw relationships between the three classes. Is it possible to have a derived association in the model?

Yes is the answer to the question in Example 5.6 – yes, it is possible to model a derived association between the classes Customer and Invoice. It is called /CustInv in Figure 5.10. The association is derived due to a slightly unusual business rule that the association multiplicity between Order and Invoice is one to one.
    The derived association has not introduced any new information. We could always assign a customer to an invoice by finding out a single order for each invoice, then a single customer for each order.

Qualified association 5.1.4

The concept of a *qualified association* is a tough and controversial proposition. Some modelers like it; others hate it. Arguably, one can construct complete and sufficiently expressive class models *without* qualified associations. However, if qualified associations are used, they should be used consistently, across the board.

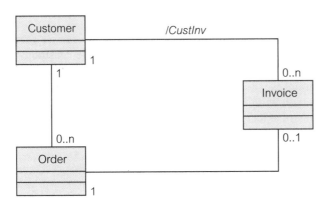

Figure 5.10
Derived
association

A qualified association has an attribute compartment (a *qualifier*) on one end of a binary association (an association can be qualified on both ends, but this is rare). The compartment contains one or more attributes that can serve as an index key for traversing the association from the qualified *source class* via the qualifier to the *target class* on the opposite end of the association.

For example, an association between `Flight` and `Passenger` is many to many. However, when the class `Flight` is qualified by attributes `seatNumber` and `departure`, the multiplicity is reduced to one to one (Figure 5.11). The composite index key introduced by the qualifier (`flightNumber` + `seatNumber` + `departure`) can be linked to only zero or one `Passenger` objects.

Figure 5.11
Qualified
association

In the forward traversal, the association multiplicity represents a number of target objects related by the composite key (qualified object + qualifier value). In the reverse traversal, the multiplicity describes a number of objects identified by the composite key (qualified object + qualifier value) and related to each target object (Rumbaugh et al. 2005).

The uniqueness introduced by a qualifier frequently provides important semantic information that cannot be captured efficiently by other means (such as constraints or an inclusion of additional attributes in the target class). In general, it is not proper nor correct to duplicate a qualifier attribute in the target class.

5.1.5 Association class versus reified class

In the Appendix (Section A.5.4) we explain and exemplify an *association class* – an association that is also a class. An association class is typically used if there is a many-to-many association between two classes and each association instance (a *link*) has its own attribute values. To be able to store these attribute values, we need a class – an *association class*.

Simple as it seems, the concept of an association class carries a tricky constraint. Consider an association class C between classes A and B. The constraint is that there can be only one instance of C for each pair of linked instances of A and B.

If such a constraint is not acceptable, then the modeler has to *reify* the association by replacing class C with an ordinary class D (Rumbaugh et al. 2005). The *reified class* D would have two binary associations to A and B. Class D is independent of classes A and B. Each instance of D has its own identity, so that multiple instances of it can be created to link to the same instances of A and B, if required.

The distinction between an *association class* and *reified class* arises most frequently in the context of modeling temporal (historical) information. An example could be an employee database that maintains information about current and previous salaries of employees.

Model with association class 5.1.5.1

Objects of an *association class*, like objects of any ordinary class, are assigned their OIDs when instantiated (Appendix, Section A.2.3). Apart from the system-generated OIDs, objects can also be identified by their attribute values. In the case of an association class, an object takes its identity from the attributes that designate the associated classes (Appendix, Section A.3.1.1). Other attribute values do not contribute to the object's identification.

Example 5.7: employee database

Each employee in an organization is assigned a unique `empId`. The name of the employee is maintained and consists of the last name, first name and middle initial.

Each employee is employed at a certain salary level. There is a salary range for each level – that is, a minimum and maximum salary. The salary ranges for a level never change. If there is a need to change the minimum or maximum salary, a new salary level is created. The start and end dates for each salary level are also kept.

Previous salaries of each employee are kept, including the start date and finish date at each level. Any changes in the employee's salary within the same level are also recorded.

Draw a class model for the employee database. Use an association class.

The statement in Example 5.7 creates a number of challenges. We know that we need to have a class to store employee details (`Employee`) and a class to store information about salary levels (`SalaryLevel`). The challenge is that of modeling historical and current assignments of salaries to employees. At first it may seem natural to use an association class – `SalaryHistoryAssociation`.

Figure 5.12 presents a class model with the association class `SalaryHistory Association`. This solution is deficient. Objects of `SalaryHistoryAssociation` derive their identity from the composite key created from the references to the primary keys of classes `Employee` and `SalaryLevel` (that is, `empId` and `levelId`).

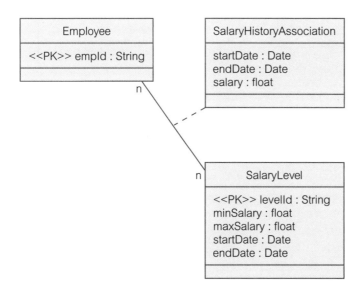

Figure 5.12
Inadequate use of an association class

No two `SalaryHistoryAssociation` objects can have the same composite key (the same links to `Employee` and `SalaryLevel`). This also means that the design in Figure 5.12 will not accommodate the requirement that "any changes in the employee's salary within the same level are also recorded." The solution in Figure 5.12 cannot be sustained – a better model is needed.

5.1.5.2 Model with reified class

An *association class* cannot have duplicates among its object references to the associated classes. A *reified class* is independent of the associated classes and so does not place such a restriction. The primary key of a reified class does not use attributes that designate related classes.

Example 5.8: employee database

Refer to Example 5.7 (Section 5.1.5.1). Draw a class model for the employee database. Use a reified class.

Figure 5.13 demonstrates a class model for Example 5.8 that uses the reified class `SalaryHistoryReified`. The class does not have an explicitly marked primary key. However, we can guess that the key will consist of `empId` and `seqNum`. The attribute `seqNum` stores the sequential number of salary changes for an employee. Every object of `SalaryHistoryReified` belongs to a single `Employee` object and is linked to a single `SalaryLevel` object. The model can now capture an employee's salary changes within the same salary level.

Figure 5.13
A better solution
with a reified class

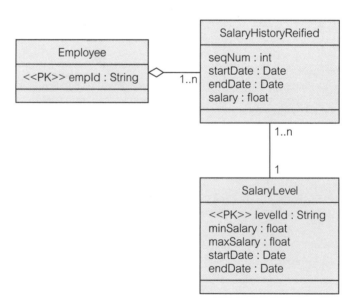

Note that the model in Figure 5.13 would need to be improved further. In particular, it is most likely that the assumption "the salary ranges for a level never change" would need to be relaxed.

Review quiz 5.1

RQ1 What is the most important extension mechanism of UML?

RQ2 How are role names called in UML 2.0?

RQ3 What is the default visibility in Java – that is, if the visibility is not specified?

RQ4 Can a reified class replace an association class without any loss of semantics?

Advanced generalization and inheritance modeling

5.2

There are three main kinds of relationship between classes – association, aggregation and generalization. The topic of generalization and inheritance is discussed in the Appendix (Section A.7), but the careful reader will have noticed that we have devalued the usefulness of generalization in analysis models. *Generalization* is a useful and powerful concept, but it can also create many problems, due to the intricate mechanisms of *inheritance*, particularly in large software projects.

The terms "generalization" and "inheritance" are related but not the same. It is important to know the difference. The price for imprecision is a resulting lack of understanding – frequently evident in the literature. Indeed, unless the difference is acknowledged, it is easy to engage in irrational and groundless discussions about the pros and cons of generalization and inheritance.

Generalization is a semantic relationship between classes. It states that the *interface* of the subclass must include all (public, package and protected) properties of the superclass. *Inheritance* is "the mechanism by which more specific elements incorporate structure and behavior defined by more general elements" (Rumbaugh et al. 2005: 411).

Generalization and substitutablity

5.2.1

From a semantic modeling perspective, *generalization* introduces additional classes, categorizes them into generic and more specific classes and establishes superclass–subclass relationships in the model. Although generalization introduces new classes, it can reduce the overall number of *association* and *aggregation* relationships in the model (because associations and aggregations can be made to more generic classes and still imply the existence of links to objects of more specific classes).

Based on the desired semantics, an association or aggregation from a class can link to the most generic class in the generalization hierarchy (see the class diagrams in Figures 3.11 and 4.10). As a subclass can be *substituted* for its generic class, the objects of the subclass have all the association and aggregation relationships of the superclass. This allows the same model semantics to be captured with a smaller number of association/aggregation relationships. In a good model, the trade-off between the depth of generalization and the consequent reduction in association/aggregation relationships is properly balanced.

When used considerately, generalization improves the expressiveness, understandability and abstraction of system models. The benefits of generalization arise from the *substitutability* principle (Section 4.2.4) – a subclass object can be used in place of a superclass object in any part of the code where the superclass object is accessed. However, and unfortunately, the inheritance mechanism may be used in a way that defeats the benefits of the substitutability principle.

5.2.2 Inheritance versus encapsulation

Encapsulation demands that an object's state (attribute values) be accessible only through the operations in the object's interface. If enforced, the encapsulation leads to a high level of data independence, so that future changes to encapsulated data structures do not necessitate the modification of existing programs. However, is this notion of encapsulation enforceable in applications?

The reality is that encapsulation is *orthogonal* to inheritance and query capabilities and has to be traded off against these two features. In practice, it is impossible to declare all data with *private* visibility.

Inheritance compromises encapsulation by allowing subclasses to access *protected* attributes directly. Computations spanning objects belonging to different classes may require that these different classes be *friends* of each other or have elements with *package* visibility, thus further infringing encapsulation. One also has to realize that encapsulation refers to the notion of the *class*, not the *object*, and, in most object programming environments (with the exception of Smalltalk), an object cannot hide anything from another object of the same class.

Finally, users accessing databases by means of SQL will be justified in expecting to refer directly to attributes in queries, rather than being forced to work with some data access methods that make query formulations more difficult and more error-prone. This requirement is particularly strong in data warehouse applications with OnLine Analytical Processing (OLAP) queries.

Thus, applications should be designed so that they achieve the desired level of encapsulation, but balance this with inheritance, database querying and computational requirements.

5.2.3 Interface inheritance

When *generalization* is used with the aim of *substitutability*, then it may be synonymous with the notion of *interface inheritance* (*subtyping*, *type inheritance*). This is not only a "harmless" form of inheritance but, in practice, a very desirable form (Appendix, Section A.9). Apart from other advantages, interface inheritance provides a means of achieving multiple implementation inheritance in languages that do not support such inheritance (such as Java).

A subclass inherits attribute types and operation signatures (operation names plus formal arguments). A subclass is said to *support* a superclass interface. The implementation of inherited operations may be deferred until later.

There is a difference between the notions of *interface* and *abstract class* (Appendix, Section A.9.1). The difference is that an abstract class can provide partial implementations for some operations, whereas a pure interface defers the definition of all operations.

Figure 5.14 corresponds to Figure A.26 (Appendix, Section A.9.2). The figure demonstrates an alternative visualization of the interface as a "lollipop" and includes the generated Java code.

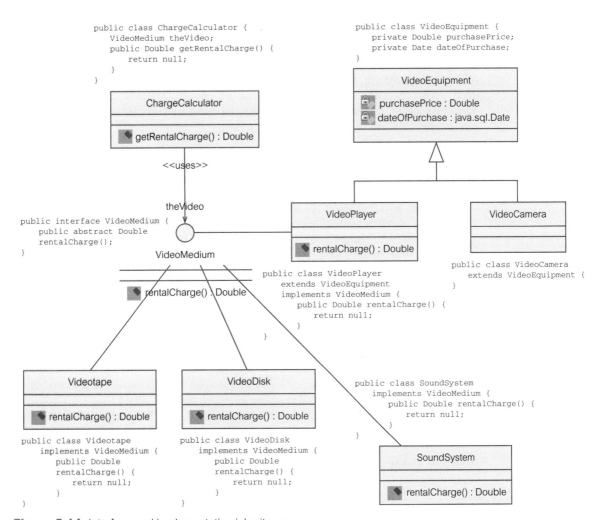

Figure 5.14 Interface and implementation inheritance

5.2.4 Implementation inheritance

As observed in the previous section, *generalization* can be used to imply *substitutability* and it can then be realized by an *interface inheritance*. However, generalization can also be used (deliberately or not) to imply *code reuse* and it is then realized by an *implementation inheritance*. This is a very powerful, sometimes dangerously powerful, representation of generalization. It is also the "default" representation of generalization.

Implementation inheritance – also called *subclassing, code inheritance*, or *class inheritance* – combines the superclass properties in the subclasses and allows them to be *overridden* by new implementations when necessary. Overriding can mean the inclusion (call) of a superclass method in the subclass method and extending it with new functionality. It can also mean a complete replacement of the superclass method by the subclass method. Implementation inheritance allows *property descriptions, code reuse* and *polymorphism* to be shared.

When modeling with generalization, we have to be clear which kind of inheritance is implied. *Interface inheritance* is safe to use as it involves only the inheritance of *contract fragments – operation signatures*. Implementation inheritance involves the inheritance of code – the inheritance of *implementation fragments* (Harmon and Watson 1998; Szyperski 1998). If not carefully controlled and restrained, implementation inheritance can bring more harm than good. The pros and cons of implementation inheritance are discussed next.

5.2.4.1 Proper use of implementation inheritance – extension inheritance

UML is quite specific about the alignment of inheritance with generalization and the proper use of implementation inheritance (Rumbaugh et al. 2005). The only proper use of inheritance is as an incremental definition of a class. A subclass has more properties (attributes and/or methods) than its superclass. A subclass *is a kind of* superclass. This is also known as an *extension inheritance*.

The example in the Appendix in Figure A.21 (repeated here for convenience as Figure 5.15, but with no constructors) represents an extension inheritance. Any `Employee` object *is a kind of* `Person` object and a `Manager` object *is a kind of* `Employee` and `Person` object. This does not mean, though, that a `Manager` object is simultaneously the instance of three classes (see the discussion about multiple classification in the Appendix, Section A.7.4). A `Manager` object is an instance of the class `Manager`.

The method `remainingLeave()` can be invoked on a `Manager` or an `Employee` object. It will perform differently depending on which object is called.

Note that `Person` in Figure 5.15 is not an abstract class. There will be some `Person` objects that are just that – that is, they are not `Employee`).

In extension inheritance, the *overriding* of properties should be used with care. It should be allowed only to make properties more specific (constrain values or make implementations of operations more efficient, for example), not change the meaning of the property. If overriding changed the meaning of a property, then a subclass object could no longer be substituted for the superclass object.

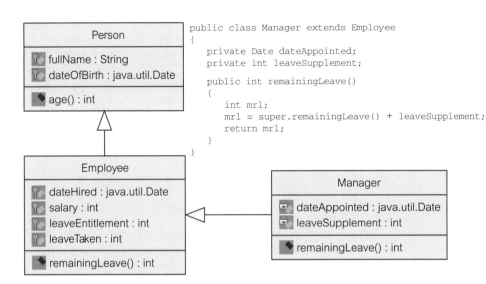

Figure 5.15
Extension
inheritance

Problematic use of implementation inheritance – restriction inheritance

In extension inheritance, the definition of a subclass is extended with new properties. However, it is also possible to use inheritance as a *restriction mechanism*, whereby some of the inherited properties are suppressed (overridden) in the subclass. Such inheritance is called *restriction inheritance* (Rumbaugh et al. 1991).

Figure 5.16 demonstrates two examples of restriction inheritance. Because inheritance cannot be selectively stopped, the class `Circle` would inherit `minor_axis` and `major_axis` from `Ellipse` and would have to replace them with the attribute `diameter`. Similarly, `Penguin` would inherit the flying capability (the operation `fly`) from `Bird` and would have to replace it with the operation `swim` (perhaps flying under a negative altitude could make up for swimming).

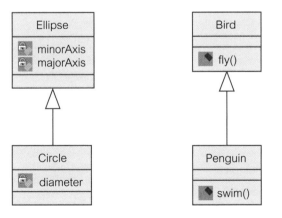

Figure 5.16
Restriction
inheritance

Restriction inheritance is problematic. From a generalization point of view, a subclass does not include all the properties of the superclass. A superclass object can still be replaced by a subclass object, provided that whoever is using that object is aware of the overridden (suppressed) properties.

In restriction inheritance, the properties of one class are used (by inheritance) to implement another class. If overriding is not extensive, restriction inheritance can be of benefit. In general, however, restriction inheritance gives rise to maintenance problems. It is even possible that restriction inheritance would completely suppress the inherited methods by implementing them as empty – that is, doing nothing.

5.2.4.3 Improper use of implementation inheritance - convenience inheritance

Inheritance that is not an extension or restriction inheritance is bad news in system modeling. Such an inheritance can occur when two or more classes have similar implementations, but there is no taxonomic relationship between the concepts represented by the classes. One class is selected arbitrarily as an ancestor of the others. This is called *convenience inheritance* (Maciaszek et al. 1996a; Rumbaugh et al. 1991).

Figure 5.17 provides two examples of convenience inheritance. The class `LineSegment` is defined as a subclass of the class `Point`. Clearly, a *line segment* is not a *point* and therefore the generalization as defined earlier does not apply. However, inheritance can still be used. Indeed, for the class `Point` we can define attributes such as `xCoordinate` and `yCoordinate` and an operation `move()`. The class `LineSegment` would inherit these properties and would define an additional operation `resize()`. The operation `move()` needs to be overridden. Similarly, in the second example, `Car` inherits properties of `Motorbike` and adds some new ones.

Convenience inheritance is improper. It is semantically incorrect. It leads to extensive overriding. The substitution principle is normally invalid because the objects are not of a similar type (`LineSegment` is not a `Point`; `Car` is not a `Motorbike`).

Figure 5.17
Convenience inheritance

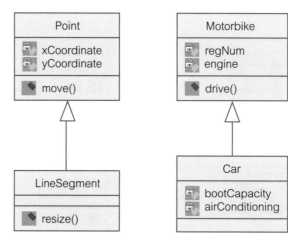

In practice, and regrettably, developers use convenience inheritance because many object programming environments encourage indiscriminate use of implementation inheritance. Programming languages are equipped with a myriad of tools for "power programming" with inheritance, while support for other object features (most notably aggregation) is missing.

The evils of implementation inheritance   5.2.4.4

The previous discussion does not mean that if we forbid *convenience inheritance*, we are fine. *Implementation inheritance* is a risky business by many standards. If not properly controlled and managed, inheritance can be overused and abused and create the kinds of problems that it is supposed to be solving in the first place. This is particularly true in the development of large systems with hundreds of classes and thousands of objects, dynamically changing states of objects and evolving class structures (such as enterprise information systems).

The main risk factors are related to the following troublesome concepts (Szyperski 1998):

- fragile base class
- overriding and callbacks
- multiple implementation inheritance.

Fragile base class   5.2.4.4.1

The *fragile base class* (*superclass*) problem is about making the subclasses valid and operational while allowing the evolution of the *implementation* of their superclass (or superclasses, if multiple inheritance applies) to take place. This is a serious problem in any case, but particularly when we consider that the superclasses may be obtained from external sources, outside of the control of the system development team.

Consider a situation where some superclasses from which your application inherits form part of an operating system, a database system or a GUI. If you buy an object database system for your application development, you really buy a class library with which to implement typical database functions, such as object persistence, transaction management, concurrency and recovery. If your classes inherit from that class library, the impact of new versions of the object database system on your application is unpredictable (and certainly so if no precautions are taken when designing the inheritance model for the application).

The problem of the fragile base class is difficult to harness short of declaring the public interfaces immutable or, at least, of avoiding the implementation inheritance from the superclasses outside our control. Changes to the implementation of a superclass (for which we might not even have the source code) will have a largely unpredictable effect on the subclasses in the application system. This is true even if the superclass' public interface remains unchanged. The situation can be further aggravated if the changes also affect public interfaces. Some examples are (Szyperski 1998):

- changing the signature of a method
- splitting the method into two or more new methods
- joining existing methods into a larger method.

The bottom line is that, to harness the fragile base class problem, developers designing a superclass should know beforehand how people are going to be reusing that superclass now and in the future. However, this is impossible without a crystal ball. As a bumper sticker joke says, "madness is inherited, you get it from your children" (Gray 1994). In Section 5.3, we discuss some alternative object development methods that are not based on inheritance yet deliver the expected object functionality.

5.2.4.4.2   *Overriding, down-calls and up-calls*

Implementation inheritance allows for selective overriding of inherited code. There are five techniques whereby a subclass method can reuse code from its superclass:

- the subclass can inherit the method implementation and introduce no changes to the implementation
- the subclass can inherit the code and include it (call it) in its own method with the same signature
- the subclass can inherit the code and then completely override it with a new implementation with the same signature
- the subclass can inherit code that is empty (that is, the method declaration is empty) and then provide the implementation for the method
- the subclass can inherit the method interface only (that is, the interface inheritance) and then provide the implementation for the method.

Of these five reuse techniques, the first two are the most troublesome when the base class evolves. The third shows contempt for inheritance. The last two techniques are special cases, the fourth is trivial and the fifth does not involve implementation inheritance.

Example 5.9: telemarketing

Refer to Problem statement 4, for a telemarketing system (Section 1.6.4) and to Example 5.4 (Section 5.1.2.1) in particular. Our task is to modify the class model and the generalization relationship between ECampaign and eBonusCampaign (Figure 5.6) to include operations that exemplify the first two reuse techniques listed above and show down-calls and up-calls along the generalization relationship.

To exemplify the first reuse technique and the down-call, consider the operation computeTicketsSold() in ECampaign, which is inherited without modification by EBonusCampaign. The implementation of computeTickets() includes a call to computeTicketsLeft(). The operation computeTicketsLeft() exists in ECampaign and its overridden version in EBonusCampaign.

To exemplify the second reuse technique and the up-call, consider the operation getDateClose() in ECampaign and its overridden version in EBonusCampaign. When invoked on ECampaign, getDateClose() returns the closing date of ECampaign. However, when invoked in EBonusCampaign, it returns the larger (later) date from the comparison of the closing date of ECampaign and EBonusCampaign.

Figure 5.18 shows the model and the code constituting a possible answer to Example 5.9. The class CActioner invokes operations on ECampaign and/or EBonusCampaign. CActioner has a reference (theECampaign) to the subclass EBonusCampaign, but it keeps that reference as the superclass ECampaign type. In reality, the assignment of an EBonusCampaign instance to an ECampaign reference is likely to be done at run-time (Maciaszek and Liong 2005) and not as a static assignment as in Figure 5.18.

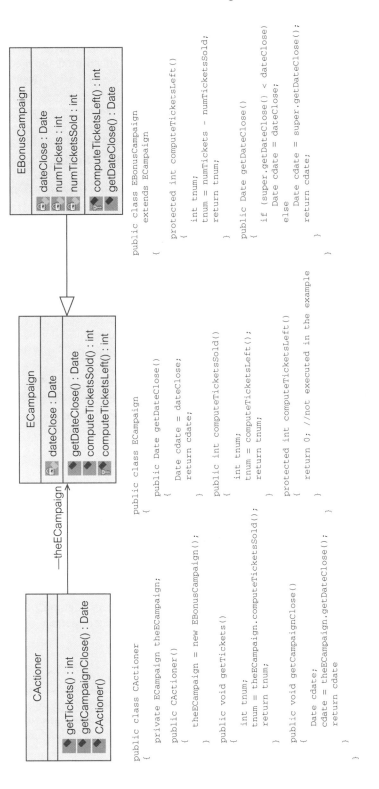

Figure 5.18 Overriding, down-calls and up-calls for a telemarketing system

When `getTickets()` is called on `CActioner`, it executes `computeTicketsSold()` on `ECampaign`. This uses the substitutability principle – the `EBonusCampaign` object held in - `theECampaign` reference is substituted for the `ECampaign` object (because `EBonusCampaign` does not have its own, overridden, version of `computeTicketsSold()`).

Next, `computeTicketsSold()` calls `computeTicketsLeft()`. However, `computeTicketsLeft()` has been overridden in `EBonusCampaign` and therefore this overridden method is called instead. This is an example of a *down-call* from a superclass to its subclass. The result is that the number of tickets left in `EBonusCampaign` will be returned to `CActioner`.

Note that the initialization of the `theECampaign` reference and the successive down-calls have introduced a run-time inheritance dependency from `CActioner` to `EBonusCampaign`. This dependency is not statically legitimized in the compile-time program structure. `CActioner` has an association to `ECampaign`, but not to `EBonusCampaign`. Such run-time dependencies are difficult to manage. They go against the EAP of the PCBMER framework (Section 4.1.3.2).

When `getCampaignClose()` is called in `CActioner`, it executes `getDateClose()` on the object referred to by the - `theECampaign` variable. This is the `EBonusCampaign` object. Accordingly, `getDateClose()` in `EBonusCampaign` is called. Interestingly, `getDateClose()` provides an extension of the method defined in `ECampaign` – it contains a call to `super`. This is an example of an *up-call* (*callback*) from a subclass to its superclass.

Although such a call to `super` is understood, the combination of down-calls and up-calls introduces nasty circular dependencies on the classes involved. Additionally, these dependencies are created at run-time and are, therefore, difficult to manage in view of any changes to classes.

Example 5.9, above, demonstrates how overriding contributes to the fragile base class problem. It also demonstrates that implementation inheritance introduces network-like communication paths, which we argued were unsustainable in large systems (Section 4.1). Message passing with implementation inheritance is all over the place. Apart from simple *down-calls* that follow the inheritance direction, *callbacks* (*up-calls*) are made.

As observed by Szyperski (1998: 104), "In conjunction with observable state, this leads to re-entrance semantics close to that of concurrent systems. Arbitrary call graphs formed by interacting webs of objects abolish the classical layering and make re-entrance the norm."

To do justice to inheritance, callbacks are possible whenever there is a reference between objects. To quote Szyperski (1998: 57) again, "With object reference ... every method invocation is potentially an up-call, every method potentially a callback." Inheritance only adds to the trouble, but it does add considerably.

5.2.4.4.3   *Multiple implementation inheritance*

Multiple inheritance is discussed in the Appendix, Section A.7.3. In Section A.9 the distinction is made between *multiple interface inheritance* (multiple supertyping) and *multiple implementation inheritance* (multiple superclassing). Multiple interface inheritance allows for the merging of interface contracts. Multiple implementation inheritance permits the merging of *implementation fragments*.

Multiple implementation inheritance does not really introduce a new "evil" of implementation inheritance. Rather, it exaggerates the problems caused by the fragile base class, overriding and callbacks. Apart from the need to stop inheritance of any duplicate implementation fragments (if two or more superclasses define the same operation), it may also force the renaming of operations whenever duplicate names are coincidental (and should really mean separate operations).

In this context, it is worthwhile remembering the inherent growth of complexity due to multiple inheritance – the growth that results from the lack of support in object systems for *multiple classification* (Appendix, Section A.7.4). Any orthogonal inheritance branches rooted at a single superclass (Figure A.22, Appendix, Section A.7.3) have to be joined lower in the inheritance tree by specially created "join" classes.

The problems with multiple implementation inheritance have resulted in it being disallowed in some languages – most notably in Java. Java recommends using *multiple interface inheritance* (Appendix, Section A.9) to provide solutions that otherwise would require multiple implementation inheritance.

Review quiz 5.2

RQ1   What related principle makes generalization useful?

RQ2   How does inheritance compromise encapsulation?

RQ3   What concept can be used in lieu of multiple implementation inheritance?

Advanced aggregation and delegation modeling

5.3

Aggregation is the third technique of linking classes in analysis models (Appendix, Section A.6). Compared with the other two techniques (*conventional association* and *generalization*), aggregation has been given the least attention, yet it is the most powerful technique we know for managing the complexity of large systems by allocating classes to hierarchical layers of abstraction.

Aggregation (and its stronger variation – *composition*) is a containment relationship. A *composite class* contains one or more *component classes*. The component classes are elements of their composite class (albeit elements that have their own existence). Although aggregation has been considered a fundamental modeling concept for at least as long as generalization, it has been given only marginal attention in object application development (with the exception of "perfect match" application domains, such as multimedia systems).

In programming environments (including most object databases), aggregation is implemented in the same way as conventional associations – by acquiring references between composite and component objects. Although the compile-time structure of aggregation is the same as for association, the run-time behavior is different. The semantics of aggregation are stronger and it is (unfortunately) the programmer's responsibility to ensure that the run-time structures obey these semantics.

5.3.1 Putting more semantics into aggregation

While current programming environments ignore aggregation, object application development methods incorporate aggregation as a modeling option but give it the least emphasis. Also (or as a consequence of the lack of support in programming environments), the object application development methods do not strive to enforce a rigorous semantic interpretation of the aggregation construct, frequently treating it as just a special form of association.

As discussed in Section 4.2.3, four possible semantics for aggregation can be distinguished (Maciaszek et al. 1996b):

- "ExclusiveOwns" aggregation
- "Owns" aggregation
- "Has" aggregation
- "Member" aggregation.

UML recognizes only two semantics of aggregation – namely *aggregation* (*reference semantics*) and *composition* (*value semantics*) (Appendix, Section A.6). We will now show how stereotypes and constraints can be used to extend the existing UML notation to represent the four different kinds of aggregation identified above.

5.3.1.1 The *ExclusiveOwns* aggregation

The *ExclusiveOwns* aggregation in UML can be represented by a *composition* stereotyped with the keyword <<ExclusiveOwns>> and constrained additionally with the keyword *frozen* (Fowler 2003). The *frozen* constraint applies to a *component class*. It states that an object of the *component class* cannot be *reconnected* (over its lifetime) to another *composite object*. A *component object* can possibly be deleted altogether, but it cannot be switched to another owner.

Figure 5.19 shows two examples of the *ExclusiveOwns* aggregation. The left-hand example is modeled with the UML value semantics (a filled diamond), the right-hand with the UML reference semantics (a hollow diamond).

A `Chapter` object is a part of at most one `CopyrightedBook`. Once incorporated (by value) in a composite object, it cannot be reconnected to another `CopyrightedBook` object. The connection is frozen.

A `BridgeCardPack` contains exactly 52 cards. The UML reference semantics are used to model the ownership. Any `BridgeCard` object belongs to precisely one `BridgeCardPack` and cannot be reconnected to another pack of cards.

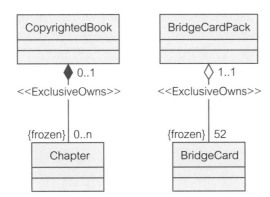

Figure 5.19
The
ExclusiveOwns
aggregation

The *Owns* aggregation

Like the *ExclusiveOwns* aggregation, the *Owns* aggregation can be expressed in UML with a composition's value semantics (a filled diamond) or an aggregation's reference semantics (a hollow diamond). At any point in time, a component object belongs to at most one composite object, but it can be *reconnected* to another composite object. When a composite object is deleted, its component objects are also deleted.

Figure 5.20 demonstrates two examples of the *Owns* aggregation. A `Water` object can be reconnected from one `Jug` to another. Similarly, a `Tire` object can be switched from one `Bicycle` to another. Because of the existence dependency, destruction of a `Jug` or a `Bicycle` propagates down to their component objects.

The *Has* aggregation

The *Has* aggregation would normally be modeled in UML using the aggregation's reference semantics (a hollow diamond). There is no existence dependency in a *Has* aggregation – the deletion of a composite object does not automatically propagate down to the component objects. The *Has* aggregation is characterized by only transitivity and asymmetry.

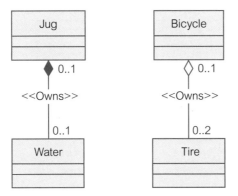

Figure 5.20
The *Owns*
aggregation

An example of a *Has* aggregation is shown in Figure 5.21. If a `Trolley` object has a number of `BeerCrate` objects and a `BeerCrate` object contains a number of `BeerBottle` objects, then the `Trolley` object has these `BeerBottle` objects (*transitivity*). If a `Trolley` has a `BeerCrate`, then a `BeerCrate` cannot have a `Trolley` (*asymmetry*).

Figure 5.21
The *Has* aggregation

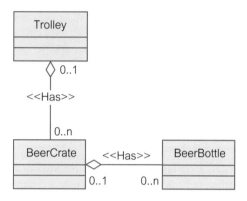

5.3.1.4 The *Member* aggregation

The *Member* aggregation allows for *many-to-many multiplicity* of the relationship. No special assumptions are made about the existence dependency, transitivity, asymmetry or frozen property. If needed, any of these four properties can be expressed as a UML constraint. Because of the many-to-many multiplicity, the *Member* aggregation can only be modeled in UML using the aggregation's reference semantics (a hollow diamond).

Figure 5.22 demonstrates four *Member* aggregation relationships. A `JADSession` (Section 2.2.3.3) object consists of one moderator and one or many scribes, users and developers. Each of the component objects can participate in more than one `JADSession` object.

Figure 5.22
The *Member* aggregation

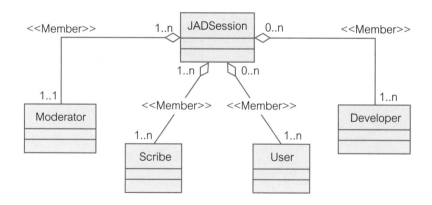

Aggregation as an alternative to generalization   5.3.2

Generalization is a superclass–subclass relationship. *Aggregation* is more like a superset–subset relationship. Notwithstanding this difference, a generalization can be represented as an aggregation.

Consider Figure 5.23. Customers' orders that are not filled can be pending some further action. The pending order can be a back order that is to be filled once sufficient stock is available. The pending order is a future order if it is to be filled at a later date, as specified by the customer.

The left-hand model is a generalization for customers' orders. The class GOrder can be a GPendingOrder. The GPendingOrder can be a GBackOrder or GFutureOrder. Inheritance ensures sharing of attributes and operations down the generalization tree.

Similar semantics can be modeled with the aggregation shown on the right-hand side in Figure 5.23. The classes ABackOrder and AFutureOrder include the attributes and operations of the class APendingOrder, which in turn incorporates the class AOrder.

Although the two models in Figure 5.23 capture similar semantics, there are differences. The main one derives from the observation that the generalization model is based on the notion of class, whereas the aggregation model is really centered on the notion of object.

A particular GBackOrder object is also an object of GPendingOrder and GOrder. There is one *object identifier* (OID) for the GBackOrder. On the other hand, a particular ABackOrder object is built up of three separate objects, each with its own object identifier – the ABackOrder itself, the contained APendingOrder object and the contained AOrder object.

Generalization uses *inheritance* to implement its semantics. Aggregation uses *delegation* to reuse the implementation of component objects. This is discussed next.

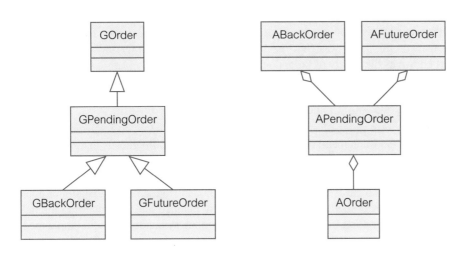

Figure 5.23
Generalization versus aggregation

5.3.2.1 Delegation and prototypical systems

The *computational model* of inheritance is based on the notion of a *class*. However, it is possible to base the computational model on the notion of an *object*. An object-centered computational model structures objects into *aggregation hierarchies*. Whenever a *composite object* (*outer object*) cannot complete a task by itself, it can call on the methods in one of its *component objects* (*inner objects*) – this is called *delegation* (Appendix, Section A.6.3).

In delegation-based approaches, the functionality of the system is implemented by including (*cloning*) the functionality of existing objects in the newly required functionality. The existing objects are treated as *prototypes* for the creation of *new* objects. The idea is to search for the functionality in existing objects (*inner objects*) and then to implement the desired functionality in an *outer object*. The outer object asks for the services of inner objects as required. Systems constructed in this way, from existing prototypical objects, are called *prototypical systems*.

An object may have a *delegation relationship* to any other identifiable and visible object in the system (Lee and Tepfenhart 1997). When an outer object receives a message and cannot complete the service by itself, it will delegate the execution of that service to an inner object. The inner object, if necessary, may forward the message to any of its own inner objects.

The inner object's interfaces may or may not be visible to objects other than the outer object. The four kinds of aggregation identified in Section 5.3.1 can be used to control the level of visibility of inner objects. For example, an outer object may expose the inner objects' interfaces as its own in weaker forms of aggregation (such as in a typical *Has* or *Member* aggregation). In stronger forms of aggregation, an outer object may hide its inner objects' interfaces from the outside world (thus using a stronger form of *encapsulation*).

5.3.2.2 Delegation versus inheritance

It can be shown that a *delegation* can model the *inheritance* and vice versa. This means that the same system functionality can be delivered with *inheritance* or *delegation*. The consensus on this issue was first reached at the conference in Orlando, Florida, in 1987 and is known as the Treaty of Orlando (Stein et al. 1989).

In passing, we discussed the evils of *implementation inheritance*. A pressing question arises if the delegation avoids the disadvantages of implementation inheritance. The answer to this question is not straightforward (Szyperski 1998).

From the *reuse* point of view, delegation comes very close to inheritance. An outer object reuses the implementation of the inner object. The difference is that – in the inheritance case – control is always returned to the object that receives the original message (request for service) after the service has been accomplished.

In the delegation case, once control has been passed from an outer to an inner object, it stays there. Any *self-recursion* has to be explicitly planned and designed into the delegation. In implementation inheritance, self-recursion always happens – it is unplanned and patched in (Szyperski 1998). The *fragile base class* problem is but one undesired consequence of the unplanned/patched reuse.

The other potential advantage of delegation is that the sharing and reuse can be determined dynamically at run-time. In inheritance-based systems, the sharing and reuse is normally determined statically when the object is created. The trade-off is between the safety and execution speed of *anticipatory sharing* of inheritance and the flexibility of *unanticipatory sharing* of delegation.

An argument in favor of delegation is that unanticipatory sharing is more natural and closer to the way people learn (Lee and Tepfenhart 1997). Objects are naturally combined to form larger solutions and can evolve in unanticipated ways. The next section provides another viewpoint on the same issue.

Aggregation and holons – some cerebral ammunition

5.3.3

In Maciaszek et al. (1996a; 1996b), to restrain the complexity of object models, we proposed a new approach for describing software architecture based on Arthur Koestler's interpretation of the structure of natural systems (Koestler 1967; 1978). The central concept is the idea of *holons*, which are interpreted as objects that are both parts and wholes. More precisely, they are considered as self-regulating entities that exhibit both the interdependent properties of parts and the independent properties of wholes.

Living systems are organized hierarchically. Structurally, they are *aggregations* of semi-autonomous units that display both the independent properties of wholes and the interdependent properties of parts. As Arthur Koestler would put it, they are aggregations of holons, from the Greek word *holos*, meaning *whole*, with the suffix changed to *on* to suggest a particle or part (as in proton or neutron) (Koestler 1967).

Parts and wholes in the absolute sense do not exist in living organisms or even in social systems. Holons are hierarchically layered according to complexity. For example, in a biological organism, we can discern a hierarchy of atoms, molecules, organelles, cells, tissues, organs and organ systems. Such hierarchies of holons are called *holarchies*.

Each holarchy layer hides its complexity from the layer above. *Looking downwards*, a holon is something complete and unique, a whole. *Looking upwards*, a holon is an elementary component, a part. Each holarchy layer contains many holons, such as atoms (hydrogen, carbon, oxygen and so on), cells (nerves, muscles, blood cells).

Looking inwards, a holon provides services to other holons. *Looking outwards*, a holon *requests* services of other holons. Holarchies are open-ended. There is no absolute "leaf" holon or "apex" holon, except those identified as such for our interpretative convenience. Because of this characteristic, complex systems can evolve from simple ones.

Individual holons are therefore represented by four characteristics:

- internal charter (interactions between them can form unique patterns)
- self-assertive aggregation of subordinate holons
- integrative tendency with regard to superior holons
- relationships with peer holons.

Successful systems are arranged in holarchies that hide complexity in successively lower layers, while providing greater levels of abstraction within the higher layers of their structures. This concept matches the semantics of aggregation.

Aggregation provides for the separation of concerns – it allows each class to remain encapsulated and focus on a specific behavior (collaborations and services) of the class in a way that is unbound by the implementation of its parent classes (as it is in generalization). At the same time, aggregation allows for free movements between the stratified layers at run-time.

The balance between integration and self-assertion of objects (holons) is achieved by the requirement that aggregation objects must "respect each other's interfaces" (Gamma et al. 1995). Encapsulation is not broken because the objects communicate only through their interfaces. The evolution of the system is facilitated because the object communication is not hard-coded in the implementation by mechanisms similar to inheritance.

Structurally, aggregation can model large quantities of objects by grouping them into various sets and establishing whole–part relationships between them. Functionally, aggregation allows for objects (holons) to look "upwards" and "downwards". However, aggregation is not able to model the necessary interoperability between peer holons so that they can look "inwards" and "outwards". This structural and functional gap can be filled successfully by the generalization and association relationships.

In our recommended approach, aggregation provides a "vertical" solution and generalization a "horizontal" solution to object application development. The aggregation becomes a dominant modeling concept that determines the overall framework of the system. This framework could be further formalized by providing a set of design patterns (Gamma et al. 1995) specifically supporting the holon approach and utilizing the four kinds of aggregation. We hope that the above discussion provides some cerebral ammunition for the reader's own pursuits (refer Maciaszek 2006).

Review quiz 5.3

RQ1 How is aggregation implemented in typical programming environments?
RQ2 Which kind of aggregation needs to be specified with the "frozen" constraint?
RQ3 What does aggregation use to reuse the implementation of component objects?

5.4 Advanced interaction modeling

We have discussed the basics of interaction modeling in Chapter 3 (Section 3.4) and Chapter 4 (Section 4.3.3). Here, we will explain some more advanced features of interaction diagrams and demonstrate how their flexibility and precision allows for a smooth transition to the abstraction level demanded by detailed design.

Of the two types of interaction diagrams, *sequence diagrams* are more popular than *communication diagrams*. They express similar information, but sequence diagrams concentrate on the sequence of messages, while communication diagrams emphasize object relationships. CASE tools tend to be better equipped to visualize sequence diagrams and better support the intricacies of interaction modeling in sequence diagrams. The same is not necessarily true for communication diagrams. A notable advantage of communication diagrams, though, is that they can be used as hand-drawn sketches in meetings and discussions. Communication diagrams are much more space-efficient and correction-friendly than sequence diagrams in such face-to-face situations.

Lifelines and messages   5.4.1

Two of the most visible concepts in interaction diagrams are *lifelines* and *messages*. A *lifeline* represents a participant in the interaction; it signifies the existence of an object at a particular time during an interaction. A *message* represents a communication between lifelines of an interaction. A lifeline/object receiving a message activates the relevant operation/method. The time when the flow of control is focused in an object is called in UML 2.0 an *execution specification* (previously called an *activation*).

Figure 5.24 demonstrates the UML notation for lifelines and messages. *Lifelines* are shown as named boxes extended by vertical lines (which are typically dashed). A lifeline box can be named to represent:

- an unnamed instance of a class – :Class1
- a named instance of a class – c2:Class2
- a class – that is, an instance of a **metaclass** – :Class 3 – to show static method calls to a class itself
- an interface – :Interface1.

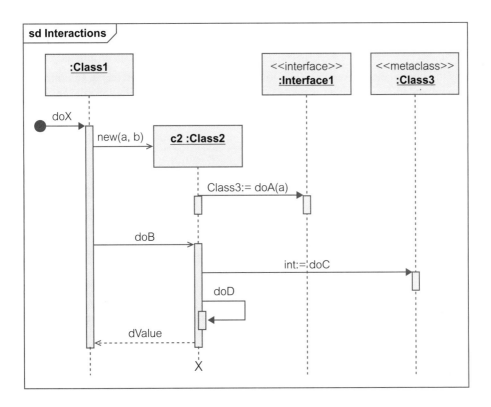

Figure 5.24
Lifelines and messages

Figure 5.24 shows a variety of message types allowed in interaction modeling:

■ *synchronous messages* in which the caller blocks – that is, it waits for a response – represented by a filled arrowhead – doX, doA, doC, doD

■ *asynchronous messages* in which the caller does not block, thus allowing multi-threaded executions – represented by an open arrow, such as doB

■ *object creation messages* – frequently (but not necessarily) named using keywords such as new or create and represented by a line with an open arrow – new(a,b), where a and b are the parameters supplied to a constructor in Class2

■ *reply messages* that transmit output values of an interaction to the caller that initiated the action – represented by a dashed line with an open arrow and frequently labeled with a description of the returning value – dValue.

Note that a *reply message* is just one of two ways of showing the return result from a message. The other is to indicate the return variable in the message syntax, such as Class3 = doA(a) or int = doC (Larman 2005). Depending on the abstraction level on which the diagram is formed, returns and replies from messages may or may not be shown.

Figure 5.24 also shows a so-called *found message* – doX – which represents a message, the sender of which is not specified. In other words, the origin of the found message is outside the scope of the model as presented.

Object destruction is indicated on the diagram by the large X. It is normally assumed that objects created in the interaction model will also be destroyed within the context of the same interaction model (such as c2:Class2). For languages that do not have automatic garbage collection (such as C++), another object in the model should initiate the destruction in a separate <<destroy>> message.

In the case of a lifeline represented by an interface (:Interface1) or an abstract class, the obvious implication is that the called method executes from a class that implements the interface or a concrete class that inherits from the abstract class. In both cases, a recommended practice is to provide separate interaction diagrams for relevant implementations of the interface or for each polymorphic concrete case (Larman 2005).

5.4.1.1 Accounting for basic technology

Even when carrying out interaction modeling at a relatively high level of abstraction, consideration may need to be given to the *software technology* chosen for the development project. Contemporary programming languages are, rather, *programming environments* with ready-to-use components, class libraries, XML configuration files, custom tags, database connections and so on. Consequently, much of the work performed by the application is not really custom-programmed but reused or otherwise executed by the environment.

It turns out that providing details of interactions between the custom code and the environment is difficult using UML interaction modeling, yet some such details are necessary to "bridge the gaps" in the models. As a minimum, and a starting point, it is important to appropriately stereotype the lifelines of the sequence diagram to refer to the technology used. For readers familiar with the technology, such stereotyped lifelines can provide sufficient bridges. (This book assumes that the reader is familiar with basic software technologies. Nevertheless, for completeness and assuredness sake, we undertake to briefly explain the technologies used in examples, case studies, exercises, and so on)

In the Java world, the basic technology used for Web applications will invariably use Java Server Pages (JSPs), servlets and JavaBeans. A *servlet* is a Java program deployed and run inside a Web server. Typically, a servlet does not have a graphical user interface (GUI) and, therefore, can cleanly belong to the Controller layer. The GUI is supplied by the servlet's clients, such as a server page or an applet.

Java Server Pages (JSP) are HTML pages with Java code pieces embedded in them. To run the application, an actor requests a JSP page by typing in a URL something like www.myserver.com/myJsp.jsp. JSPs belong to the Presentation layer.

JavaBeans are Java classes that can store data and follow predefined rules allowing users to `get()` and `set()` the data. Java provides a mechanism on beans that allows JSP form values to be automatically loaded/unloaded from/into beans. JavaBeans reside in the Bean layer.

Example 5.10: currency converter

Refer to Problem statement 7, for a currency converter (Section 1.6.7). Assume that the application will consist of two web pages – one for entering the calculation request data and the other for displaying the results of the calculation. The application needs to obtain currency conversion rates from a database.

Draw a sequence diagram for the currency converter application. Design the model for the Java technology consisting of Java Server Pages (JSPs), servlets and JavaBeans. Conform to the PCBMER architecture, but there is no need to use the entity layer (Section 4.1.3.1). There is no need to show parameters or return types.

Figure 5.25 is a sequence diagram corresponding to the implementation scenario described in Example 5.10. The design uses the PCBMER Class Naming Principle (CNP), according to which each class name is prefixed with the first letter of the package/subsystem name. So, for example, `PRequest` indicates that the class belongs to the Presentation package/subsystem.

The narrative for the sequence diagram in Figure 5.25 is as follows. `PRequest.jsp` sends a post (or get) request to the servlet – the `CCalculator` class in our case. `CCalculator` asks `MMediator` to `getRate()` and `MMediator` delegates this request to `RQuery`. `RQuery` gets the exchange rate from the database and the rate value is returned all the way back to `CCalculator`. `CCalculator` can now instantiate and populate a `BBean` object. `CCalculator` also knows (declares) a JSP page (`PResult` in our case) to which the response information should go. `PResult` can then access the `BBean` data to render it in the Web browser. Finally, `CCalculator` gets any `startOver()` messages from `PResult` and directs them to `PRequest`.

Setting response information and other details, such as accessing and using the user's session and fetching request details in the first place, are the responsibility of the Web container. So, in effect, `CurrencyConverter` merely communicates to the Web container that `PResult` will need to obtain response details and that the control needs to go back to `PRequest` when the user wants to start over.

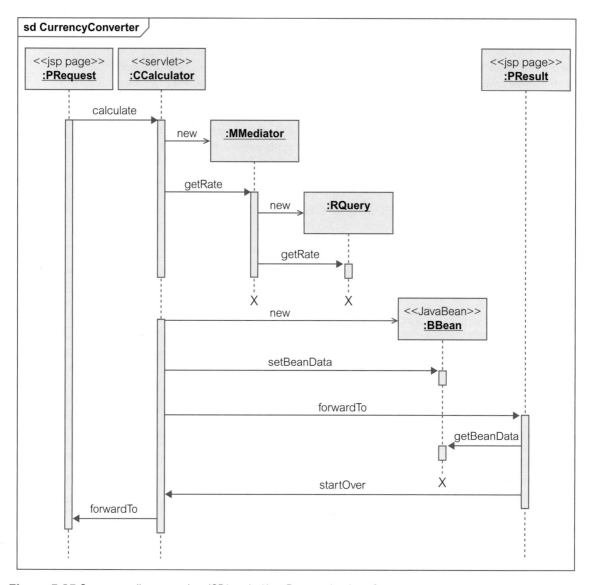

Figure 5.25 Sequence diagram using JSP/servlet/JavaBean technology for a currency converter system

5.4.1.2 Visualizing technology contributions in interaction models

Stereotyping lifelines with references to the software technology is helpful but it does not show exactly how the custom code and technology code collaborate to make the application execute. As mentioned before, building interaction models just for the custom code and not accounting for the technology contributions leaves significant gaps in the models and can make them quite useless. On the other hand, visualizing technology contributions in interaction models can be a real challenge because UML is meant to be technology independent.

Even if a technology-related UML profile (Section 5.1.1) exists (or is developed within the project), the richness and constant changes of the technology can make it really hard to show in visual models what is (or will be) happening during the code execution.

With the above proviso, let us consider a simple case of an application consisting just of a JSP page providing a HTML form and a servlet responsible for the application logic and rendering computation output in a Web browser. Using JSP/servlet technology takes advantage of the class library called `javax.servlet.*`. It also uses a *deployment descriptor* file, called `web.xml`, in which deployment instructions specific to a particular Web application need to be provided by the developer. Among other things, `web.xml` contains the name of the servlet to invoke when encountering a specific uniform resource locator (URL) pattern. That URL address is what users invoke or type in the Web browser in order to display the initial JSP page. Consequently, when users submit that page, the Web server (the *container*) knows which servlet to activate.

The servlet is then concerned with picking up the JSP input and generating an output. In doing so, the servlet relies on the implementations of `javax.servlet.*` interfaces called `HttpServletRequest` (for inputs) and `HttpServletResponse` (for outputs). In many cases, the servlet class consists of just one method – `doGet()` or `doPost()` – able to take inputs, conduct computations and generate outputs. `doGet()` is used for GET requests in which the request information is sent as part of the URL, while `doPost()` is used for POST requests in which the data is sent as part of the message body and not as part of the URL. POST requests are normally used when the values of fields in a HTML form need to be submitted to a servlet.

Example 5.11: currency converter

Refer to Problem statement 7, for a currency converter (Section 1.6.7) and to Example 5.10 in the previous section. Consider a simplistic implementation of the currency converter, converting money from only one currency (such as from Australian dollars) to another currency (such as to US dollars). The user needs to type in both the money value to be converted and the current exchange rate between the two currencies. On submitting this information, the application computes the money value in the target currency and displays the results in three fields – the money value to be converted, exchange rate and money value obtained from the conversion.

Draw a sequence diagram to show the above scenario for the currency converter application. Design the model for Java technology, consisting of only a JSP and a servlet. To show the user's interactions, create an actor called `The User`. Use another actor, called `web.xml`, to model the mapping between the JSP and the servlet. Show also the lifelines for `HttpServletRequest` and for `HttpServletResponse`. Show the message parameters and return types, if not void.

Figure 5.26 is a sequence diagram for the implementation scenario described in Example 5.11. Although the diagram is quite explicit and hopefully self-explanatory, some modeling elements have to be taken with a grain of salt. For example, the interactions with `The User` have been modeled using asynchronous messages, although, except for `submitForm`, other "messages" signify only the supply of data. Similarly, the visualization of the mapping encoded in `web.xml` from the JSP to the servlet is quite arbitrary, if not controversial. The calls to `HttpServletRequest` and `HttpServletResponse` demonstrate how the Java/J2EE API (or rather its implementation provided by the Web or application server) facilitates programming of Web applications.

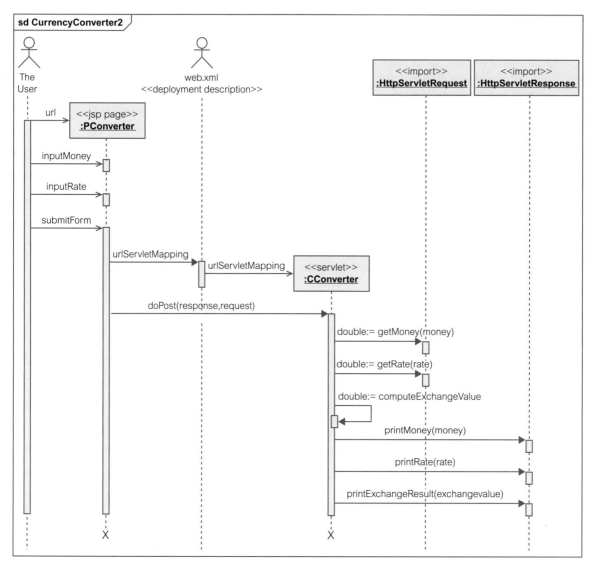

Figure 5.26 Detailed sequence diagram using JSP/servlet technology for a currency converter system

5.4.2 Fragments

A piece of interaction is called an **interaction fragment**. Interactions can contain smaller interaction fragments called *combined fragments*. The semantics for a combined fragment are determined by the *interaction operator*. UML 2.0 predefines a number of operators, of which most important are (Larman 2005; UML 2005):

- `alt` – alternative fragment for if-then-else conditional logic expressed in guard conditions
- `opt` – option fragment that executes if a guard condition is true
- `loop` – loop fragment that is repeated many times subject to the loop condition
- `break` – break fragment that executes instead of the rest of the enclosing fragment if the break condition is true
- `parallel` – a parallel fragment that allows for interleaved execution of contained behaviors.

Figure 5.27 presents how fragments are represented in sequence diagrams. The model shows an *alternative fragment* – `alt` – that, in turn, contains an *option fragment* – `opt`. The *option fragment* executes only within the `else` condition of the alternative fragment and only if its own guard condition `y<=0` is true.

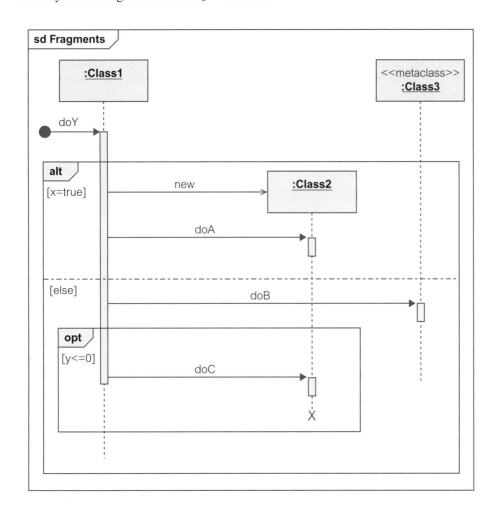

Figure 5.27
Fragments

Example 5.12: currency converter

Refer to Problem statement 7, for a currency converter system (Section 1.6.7). Consider a desktop GUI implementation of the currency converter for converting money both ways between two currencies (such as between Australian dollars and US dollars). The application consists of one Java class called `CurrencyConverter`.

The frame holds three fields – for accepting the values of Australian dollars, US dollars and the exchange rate. It also holds three buttons (`btn`) called `USD to AUD`, `AUD to USD` and `Close` (for exiting the application). The class contains an `actionPerformed()` method. When any of the three buttons is clicked, this method is called with an `ActionEvent` object. The `getSource()` method called on the `ActionEvent` object allows the system to determine which button was clicked and what computation should follow.

Draw a sequence diagram for the above scenario of the currency converter application. Use an alternative fragment for the if-then-else conditional logic required to determine which button was clicked.

Figure 5.28 is a sequence diagram corresponding to the implementation scenario described in Example 5.12. A three-way alternative fragment is used to model mutually exclusive conditional processing activated by three buttons (the `[else]` condition reacts to the `Close` event by executing the `exit` method). The whole application consists of one class – `CurrencyConverter`. `ActionEvent` is an object provided by the Swing library.

Figure 5.28
Sequence
diagram using
Swing technology
for a currency
converter system

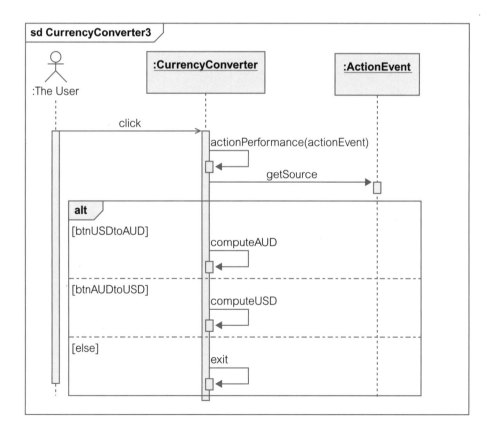

Interaction uses

Apart from containing combined fragments, interactions can contain other interactions. Such a reference to an interaction from an enclosing interaction is called an **interaction use**. The enclosing interaction is labeled with the tag sd (sequence diagram), as can be seen in Figures 5.24–5.28. Interaction use is labeled with the tag ref (reference) and it refers to another sd interaction created separately.

The notion of interaction use allows for the extraction and sharing of common behavior. It is a reuse facility. It is also useful to simplify a complex interaction model by dividing it into a number of separately defined interaction uses. Figure 5.29 is a simple example of how interaction uses are modeled.

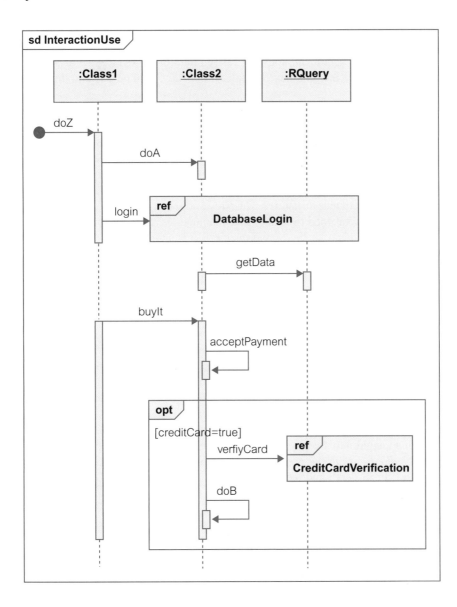

Figure 5.29
Interaction uses

Review quiz 5.4

RQ1 What interaction modeling concept needs to be used to specify multithreaded execution?

RQ2 What interaction modeling concept needs to be used to specify an interaction from an unknown sender?

RQ3 What architectural layer does a servlet belong to?

RQ4 What tag is used to label interaction use?

Summary

In this chapter, we have completed our discussion of requirements analysis and bridged analysis and systems design. The object technology support for large-scale systems development was scrutinized. The chapter has been technically difficult in places, but has offered insights into object technology not easily found in books on systems analysis and design. Many of these insights have revealed important weaknesses and downsides of object technology.

Stereotypes are the main extensibility technique of UML. In the extensibility task, they are assisted by *constraints* and *tags*. Extensibility mechanisms allow modeling beyond the predefined UML features. Because of the resourceful nature of this chapter, the UML extensibility mechanisms – in particular stereotypes – were used frequently.

Public and *private* visibilities, discussed in previous chapters, give only basic support to the important notion of *encapsulation*. *Protected* visibility permits control of encapsulation within the inheritance structures. The *friend* notion and *package* visibility allow the encapsulation to be weakened to handle special situations. *Class visibility* (as opposed to the visibility of individual attributes and operations) is another important concept related to inheritance.

UML offers a number of additional modeling concepts to improve the expressiveness of class models. They include *derived attributes*, *derived associations* and *qualified associations*. One of the most intriguing aspects of class modeling is the choice between an *association class* and a *reified class*.

The concept of *generalization and inheritance* is a double-edged sword in system modeling. On the one hand, it facilitates software reuse and improves the expressiveness, understandability and abstraction of system models. On the other hand, it has the potential for self-destruction, ruining all these benefits if not used properly.

The concept of *aggregation and delegation* is an important modeling alternative to generalization and inheritance. *Delegation and prototypical systems* have an additional benefit of backing the hierarchical architectural structures. The *holon* abstraction provides an interesting insight into the way in which complex systems should be constructed.

Sequence diagrams are the preferred visual tool for interaction modeling and provide good support for in-depth and technology-relevant modeling tasks. *Combined fragments* have been added to interaction models in UML 2.0 to account for detailed programming logic, such as loops and conditional statements. Complex models can be structured with the assistance of *interaction uses*.

Key terms

Comment an annotation attached to a model element or a set of elements. It does not directly define or change the semantics of the model.

Constraint "a condition or restriction expressed in natural language text or in a machine readable language for the purpose of declaring some of the semantics of an element" (UML 2005: 70).

Derived information "an element that can be computed from other elements and is included for clarity or for design purposes even though it adds no semantic information" (Rumbaugh et al. 2005: 315).

Interaction fragment "a structural piece of an interaction" (Rumbaugh et al. 2005: 409).

Interaction use "a reference to an interaction within the definition of another interaction" (Rumbaugh et al. 2005: 412).

Metaclass "a class whose instances are classes… typically used to construct metamodels" (Rumbaugh et al. 2005: 458).

Metamodel "a model that defines the language for expressing other models" (Rumbaugh et al. 2005: 459).

Profile "defines limited extensions to a reference metamodel with the purpose of adapting the metamodel to a specific platform or domain" (UML 2005: 642).

Stereotype "defines how an existing metaclass may be extended, and enables the use of platform or domain specific terminology or notation in place of, or in addition to, the ones used for the extended metaclass" (UML 2005: 649).

Tag definition a property of a stereotype, shown as an attribute of a class rectangle that contains the stereotype declaration.

Tagged value "a name–value pair that may be attached to a model element that uses a stereotype containing a tag definition" (Rumbaugh et al. 2005: 657).

Visibility "an enumeration whose value (public, protected, private, or package) denotes whether the model element to which it refers may be seen outside of its enclosing namespace" (Rumbaugh et al. 2005: 678).

Multiple-choice test

MC1 Which is not a UML extension mechanism?

    a Constraint.

    b Stereotype.

    c Derived attribute.

    d Tag value.

MC2 Which of the following is another name for interface inheritance?

    a Subtyping.

    b Substitutability.

    c Polymorphism.

    d None of the above.

MC3 The inheritance in which some inherited properties are overridden in the subclass is called:

    a extension inheritance

    b convenience inheritance

    c restriction inheritance

    d none of the above.

MC4 Self-recursion always happens in:

    a delegation

    b interface inheritance

    c forwarding

    d implementation inheritance.

MC5 The time when the flow of control is focused in an object is called in UML 2.0:

    a interaction use

    b execution specification

    c lifeline

    d none of the above.

MC6 Which of the following operators defines a parallel fragment that allows for interleaved execution of contained behaviors?

    a Opt.

    b Loop.

    c Alt.

    d None of the above.

Questions

Q1 What is a profile in UML? Search on the Internet using the words "UML profile" and list some published profiles available to software developers.

Q2 At times, a class is allowed to instantiate only immutable objects – that is, objects that cannot change after instantiation. How can such a requirement be modeled in UML?

Q3 Explain the difference between a constraint and a note.

Q4 Is encapsulation the same as visibility? Explain.

Q5 The visibility of inherited properties in a derived class depends on the visibility level given to the base class in the declaration of that derived class. What is this visibility if the base class is declared as private? What are the consequences for the rest of the model? Give an example.

Q6 The concept of a friend applies to a class or an operation. Explain the difference. Give an example (other than those in this book) where the use of a friend could be desirable.

Q7 What are the modeling benefits of derived information?

Q8 When should a reified class replace an association class? Give an example (choose a different one from that used in this book).

Q9 What is the substitutability principle? Explain your answer.

Q10 Explain the difference between interface inheritance and implementation inheritance. Refer in your answer to the issues related to inheritance from an interface, abstract class and concrete class.

Q11 What is the fragile base class problem? What are the main reasons for fragile base classes?

Q12 Explain the difference between the *ExclusiveOwns* and *Owns* aggregations. What is the modeling advantage gained by distinguishing between these two kinds of aggregation?

Q13 Compare inheritance and delegation. What are the similarities? What are the differences?

Q14 A common processing logic is to iterate over all objects of a collection (such as an array or list) and send the same message to each. How can this be modeled in a sequence diagram? Give an example.

Q15 Would it be advantageous to combine activity and sequence diagrams to create a useful modeling notation? Explain your answer.

Exercises

E1 Refer to Figure A.14 (Appendix, Section A.5.2). Suppose that a teacher who *manages* a course offering must also *teach* that course offering. Modify the diagram in Figure A.14 to capture this fact.

E2 Refer to Figures A.20 (Appendix, Section A.7) and A.21 (Appendix, Section A.7.1). Combine the two figures into a single class model. Design the visibility into the class model. Explain your answer.

E3 Refer to Figure A.16 (Appendix, Section A.5.4). Suppose that the system has to monitor students' assessments in multiple course offerings of the same course. This is because of the constraint that a student can fail the same course only three times (a fourth enrolment is not permitted). Extend the diagram from Figure A.16 to model the above constraint. Use a reified class. Model and/or explain any assumptions.

E4 Refer to Example 4.10 (Section 4.2.4.3). Redraw the diagram in Figure 4.10 using aggregation in place of generalization. Explain the pros and cons of the new model.

E5 Refer to Example 4.18 (Section 4.3.3.3). Improve the sequence diagram in Figure 4.18 by taking advantage of combined fragments and other advanced interaction modeling notions.

E6 Refer to Example 4.18 (Section 4.3.3.3). Improve the sequence diagram in Figure 4.19 by taking advantage of combined fragments and other advanced interaction modeling notions.

Exercises: time logging

Additional information

Refer to Problem statement 6, for a time logging tool (Section 1.6.6). Consider the function in which an employee uses the stopwatch facility of the Time Logger tool to create a new time record. This function is the responsibility of a use case subflow called "*Create Time Record – Stopwatch Entry.*" The GUI window supporting this subflow is shown in Figure 5.30.

The stopwatch entry window is a modeless dialog box. This allows the user to access the time records in the primary window's row browser, the menus and other features of Time Logger while the stopwatch is running. The display in Figure 5.30 shows the stopwatch in the "Running" state after it has been started from the `Stopwatch` menu.

The window has buttons for starting/stopping the stopwatch. When the stopwatch is running, the person can use the picklist fields and the `Description` field to fill in information about what he or she is doing. When the `Stop` button is pushed, Time Logger adds a new time record in the row browser.

The `Duration` is calculated based on the contents of the `Start`, `Now` and `Pause Duration` fields. The `Now` fields are not editable. The buttons `Pause` and `End Pause` control pause duration.

The `Reset` button cancels the stopwatch without storing a time record in the database. The `Hide` button hides the stopwatch and makes it run in the background. The hidden stopwatch can be displayed again from the `Stopwatch` menu.

The iconic buttons – plus, pencil and minus – provide create, update, and delete functions on corresponding picklists.

Figure 5.30
Stopwatch
window for a time
logging system

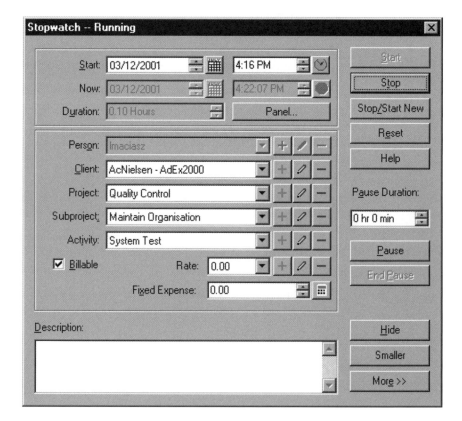

F1 Design a high-level communication diagram for the *"Create Time Record – Stopwatch Entry"* subflow. The diagram should show only the main program classes and the flow of messages between them. The messages do not need to be numbered. There is no need to specify signatures of messages. The design should adhere to the PCBMER framework, except that there is no need for Mediator and Bean classes. Explain assumptions and potentially unclear or ambiguous messages.

F2 Based on your solution to Exercise F1, design a class diagram for the *"Create Time Record – Stopwatch Entry"* subflow. The diagram should show operations, but there is no need to show attributes. The classes need to be connected with necessary static relationships. Dependency relationships should be used between classes without static relationships, but which communicate at run time. Explain assumptions and potentially unclear or ambiguous parts of the model.

Exercises: advertising expenditure

Additional information

Refer to Problem statement 5, for an advertising expenditure measurement system (Section 1.6.5). Refer also to Solutions to exercises: AE near the end of Chapter 2. Consider the function in which an employee maintains the lists of categories and corresponding advertised products. This function is the responsibility of a use case subflow called *"Maintain Category–Product Links."* A part of the GUI window supporting this subflow is shown in Figure 5.31.

The "Maintain Category–Product Links" window consists of two panes, called `Categories` and `Products for [Active Category]` – in this case, Products for consolidated loans. The `Categories` pane is a tree browser. The category view can be expanded or collapsed by clicking the plus or minus sign, respectively. Categories containing subcategories are identified with a folder icon. Categories at the bottom of the tree (with no subcategories) are shown using a note icon.

On selecting (highlighting) a category that does not have any subcategories, the list of products in that category is shown in the right-hand row browser's pane. Selecting a category that contains subcategories has no effect on the products' pane.

Although not part of the exercise, double clicking on any category opens an "Update Category" window. The pop-up menu contains a `Reassign From` item, which is used to reassign a product to a different category.

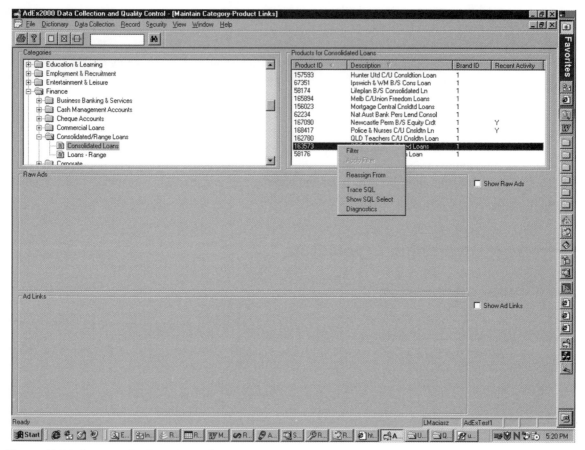

Figure 5.31 Category–Product window for an advertising expenditure system
Source: Courtesy of Nielsen Media Research, Sydney, Australia

G1 Design a high-level communication diagram for the "*Maintain Category–Product Links*" subflow. The diagram should show only the main program classes and the flow of messages between them. The messages do not need to be numbered. There is no need to specify signatures of messages. The design should adhere to the PCBMER framework, except that there is no need for Mediator and Bean classes. Explain your assumptions and any potentially unclear or ambiguous messages.

G2 Based on your solution to Exercise G1, design a class diagram for the "*Maintain Category–Product Links*" subflow. The diagram should show operations, but there is no need to show attributes. The classes need to be connected with the necessary static relationships. Dependency relationships should be used between classes without static relationships, but which communicate at run-time. Explain your assumptions and any potentially unclear or ambiguous parts of the model.

Review quiz answers

Review quiz 5.1
RQ1 Stereotype.
RQ2 Association end names.
RQ3 The package visibility.
RQ4 Yes, a reified class can always replace an association class without any loss of semantics (but the converse is not true).

Review quiz 5.2
RQ1 The substitutability principle.
RQ2 By allowing subclasses to access protected attributes directly.
RQ3 Interface inheritance.

Review quiz 5.3
RQ1 It is implemented as conventional associations, by acquiring references between composite and component objects.
RQ2 The *ExclusiveOwns* aggregation.
RQ3 Delegation.

Review quiz 5.4
RQ1 Asynchronous messages.
RQ2 Found message.
RQ3 The Controller layer.
RQ4 The `ref` (reference) tag.

Multiple-choice test answers

MC1 c
MC2 a
MC3 c
MC4 d
MC5 b
MC6 d (the operator is called parallel)

Answers to odd-numbered questions

Q1
"A *profile* takes a part of the UML and extends it with a coherent group of stereotypes for a particular purpose, such as business modeling" (Fowler 2003: 63). The profile stereotypes would normally introduce new graphical icons to visually reflect domain-specific concepts. The profiles are frequently needed in *design modeling*; less so in *analysis modeling*. A good example is the profile for building Web applications published by Conallen (2000).

Concerted efforts are made to introduce profiles for software development. Links to various UML profile specification documents are provided at: www.jeckle.de/uml_spec.htm#profiles

A quick Internet search conducted at the time of this book's writing produced links to the UML profiles for (in no particular order):

- data modeling
  www.agiledata.org/essays/umlDataModelingProfile.html
- CORBA (Common Object Request Broker Architecture)
  www.omg.org/technology/documents/formal/profile_corba.htm
- Web modeling, XSD schema, business process modeling
  www.sparxsystems.com.au/uml_profiles.htm
- MOF (Meta-Object Facility) – Object Management Group (OMG) standard for model driven engineering
  mdr.netbeans.org/uml2mof/profile.html
- profiles for business modeling and software services
  www-128.ibm.com/developerworks/rational/library/5167.html
  www-128.ibm.com/developerworks/rational/library/05/419_soa/
- model-based risk assessment
  coras.sourceforge.net/uml_profile.html
- real-time embedded systems
  www-omega.imag.fr/profile.php

Q3

A *constraint* is a semantic condition or limitation placed on a UML modeling element. A constraint can be rendered graphically as a text string enclosed in curly brackets or in a note symbol (a rectangle with its upper right-hand corner bent over).

Typically, more complex constraints are represented as notes. Because the note is a distinct graphical element, it can be linked visually – by relationships – to other UML modeling elements.

The note is only a graphical medium that can be used to express a constraint. The note symbol does not have semantic clout by itself. As such, the note can be used to contain information that does not make a semantic statement. For example, the note symbol can contain a *comment*.

Q5

The implementation of *visibility* can differ significantly among object-oriented languages (Fowler 2004; Page-Jones 2000). With regard to the question, the private properties of that class remain private to that class and are not accessible to objects of the derived class (independently of which kind of class inheritance is used – private, protected or public).

If base class A is declared private in subclass B (`class B: private A`), then the visibility of properties inherited from A changes in B to private. That is, the properties that are public or protected in A become private properties in B. The consequence is that further specialization of B (such as `class C: public B`) will make it impossible for C to access any properties of A. That is, despite the fact that class C inherited properties of A, the objects of class C cannot access the private properties of A (and the private properties of B). Properties of class A have become invisible to objects of class C, although the definitions of some properties in C could have been derived from their parent properties in A.

The example in Figure 5.32 is loosely based on the C++ example in Meyers (1998). The protected attribute `tax_file_number` in `Person` becomes a private attribute of `Student`. If `std` is an object of `Student`, then an assignment like `x = std.tax_file_number` is not permitted. Similarly, the call `std.sing()` will result in error.

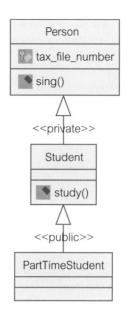

Figure 5.32
Private class
visibility

C++ code corresponding to the above model would look like this:

```
class Person
{
protected:
    int tax_file_number;
public:
    void sing(){};
};
class Student : private Person
{
};
void main()
{
    Student std;
    int x = std.tax_file_number;        //compiler error
    std.sing();                          //compiler error
}
```

To quote Meyers (1998), "in contrast to public inheritance, compilers will generally *not* convert a derived class (such as `Student`) into a base class object (such as `Person`) if the inheritance relationship between the classes is private."

An unhappy conclusion is that *private inheritance* is the antithesis of the "is a kind of" inheritance that we advocate in this book (such as in Section 4.2.4.1). A `Student` is not a `Person` any more. "Private inheritance means is implemented in terms of. If you make a class D privately inherit from a class B, you do so because you are interested in taking advantage of some of the code that has already been written for class B, not because there is any conceptual relationship between objects of type B and objects of type D" (Meyers 1998).

Private class inheritance is, in many ways, synonymous with *convenience inheritance*, discussed in Section 5.2.4.3 of the textbook as an improper variation of implementation inheritance.

Q7

Derived information does not really provide new information to a UML model, but it can enrich its semantics. It clarifies the model by bringing to light information that would otherwise be hidden from direct observation.

In an *analysis* model, derived information may be used to provide a name or definition for a noteworthy concept or user requirement. In a *design* model, derived information may be used to signify that the value of that information needs to be recomputed once the values it depends on change.

In most practical situations, derived information specifies a *constraint* on existing properties, such as some value that can be computed based on existing values. Used judiciously, derived information has the potential to simplify the model even though the information per se is "redundant."

Q9

The substitutability principle states that "given a declaration of a variable or parameter whose type is declared as X, any instance of an element that is a descendant of X may be used as the actual values without violating the semantics of the declaration and its use. In other words, an instance of a descendant element may be substituted for an instance of an ancestor element" (Rumbaugh et al. 2005: 632).

The "*is a kind of*" generalization relationship (Section 4.2.4.1) supports *substitutability*. Since, furthermore, the "is a kind of" relationship is implemented with *public class inheritance* (see Q5), the substitutability principle demands public inheritance. Public inheritance asserts that everything applicable to superclass objects is also applicable to subclass objects (a subclass cannot renounce or modify properties of its superclass).

Q11

The *fragile base class* problem refers to the undesirable impact that the evolution of superclasses (base classes) has on all application programs that contain subclasses that inherited from these superclasses. The impact of such changes is largely unpredictable as the designers of superclasses cannot know how subclasses are going to be reusing the superclasses' properties.

Short of demanding that a designer of a base class be a prophet, the fragile base class problem is unavoidable in object-oriented implementations. Any changes to public interfaces in the base class will necessitate adjustments in subclasses. Changes to implementation of operations inherited by subclasses may have even more dramatic consequences, albeit frequently more subtle and more difficult to recognize (this is particularly the case for default implementations that have been arbitrarily redefined in subclasses).

A special kind of the fragile base class problem arises in *multiple inheritance* (Section 5.2.4.4.3). In essence, any multiple inheritance conflict is a variation of the fragile base class problem encountered by a subclass even before a superclass has been modified.

Q13

Inheritance is a *reuse* technique in generalization relationships. *Delegation* is a *reuse* technique in aggregation relationships. In most cases, the decision as to whether to use inheritance (generalization) or delegation (aggregation) is straightforward – the "is a kind of" semantics demand generalization; the "has a" semantics demand aggregation.

However, as evidenced in this book with a contrived example (Figure 5.23 Section 5.3.2), generalization can be implemented with aggregation. Barring such forceful modeling practices, inheritance should be used with "is a kind of" semantics and delegation with "has a" semantics.

The similarities between these two techniques amount to the fact that both are *reuse techniques*. The differences stem from the fact that inheritance is a reuse technique between *classes*, while delegation is a reuse technique between *objects*. This makes delegation more powerful than inheritance.

First, delegation can simulate inheritance, but not vice versa. Second, delegation is a run-time notion that supports the dynamic evolution of systems, whereas inheritance is a compile-time static notion. Third, a delegating (outer) object can reuse both behavior (operation implementations) and state (attribute values) of delegated (inner) objects, whereas inheritance does not inherit the state.

Q15

A combination of activity and sequence diagrams could be beneficial to express the control logic of more complex programs. In fact, the need for such combined modeling has been recognized in UML 2.0 with the introduction of interaction overview diagrams.

An *interaction overview diagram* divides the problem space into interaction uses and combined fragments (from sequence diagrams) and into flow control constructs (decision and fork notation from activity diagrams). The control constructs provide an overview of the control flow, while the specific computational nodes are modeled as interaction uses and combined fragments. It is possible to "drill into" the uses and fragments to find out the interaction details.

Solutions to odd-numbered exercises

E1

An easy solution to this question can be achieved by placing a *constraint* on the two associations (Figure 5.33). The constraint named {subset} informs that a teacher in charge must be one of the teachers teaching the course offering.

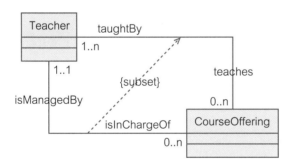

Figure 5.33
Constraint on associations

E3

The solution in Figure 5.34 (p. 300) has been obtained by converting the association class in Figure A.16 (Appendix, Section A.5.4) into an independent, fully fledged class Assessment. The constraint note (to capture the "up to three assessments" rule) has been added and linked to Assessment and its associations to two other classes.

E5

Figure 5.35 (p. 301) demonstrates an improved sequence diagram for a "centralized" solution to the university enrolment system example. The model uses three combined fragments – an alternative, loop and option.

Figure 5.34
Modeling a
constraint

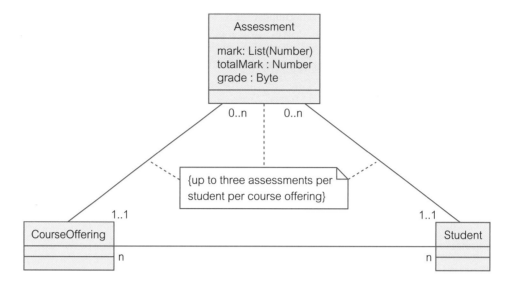

Solutions to exercises: time logging

F1

Figure 5.36 (p. 302) contains a communication model for the stopwatch entry subflow. The subflow starts when the user activates the stopwatch from a :CMenuItem. The dialog box :PStopwatch opens up and needs to be populated with data. To this aim, it instantiates a :CStopwatchInitializer, which takes over the responsibility to refreshView().

An entity object – :ETimeRecord – is instructed to getTimeRecord(), to be displayed in the dialog box. This action triggers a number of messages to other entity objects – to getDate(), getTime(), getPerson(), getClients(), getProjects(), getSubprojects() and getActivities().

The objects that are the targets of these messages will involve :RReader to access the information in the database. That is not precisely what is shown in our model. Our model is simplified and shows that only :ETimeRecord uses the services of :RReader.

Once the dialog is populated with data, the user can edit many fields. To edit picklist fields, the user involves the :CMouseEvent objects. An item selected by the mouse results in a pickCurrent() message on a corresponding container object (:EClientList, :EProjectList or :EActivityList). As before, :RReader encapsulates access to the database.

Finally, the stop() request from :CButton to :CStopwatchInitializer results in a saveTimeRecord() message to :ETimeRecord. The task of generating the SQL update statements to modify the database is given to :RUpdater.

F2

Figure 5.37 (p. 303) contains a class model for the stopwatch entry subflow. The model has been obtained from the solution to F1 above. The diagram exemplifies the PCBMER approach. The control class CStopwatchInitializer is in the center of the design, but the main tasks of getting and saving time records are coordinated by the entity class ETimeRecord. ETimeRecord performs many of its services with the assistance of its component classes. For communication with the database, ETimeRecord depends on RReader and RUpdater.

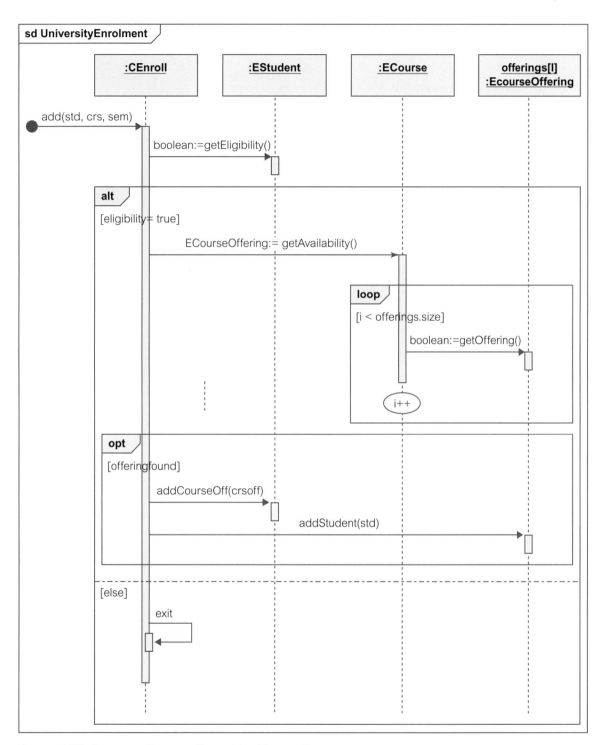

Figure 5.35 Sequence diagram with combined fragments

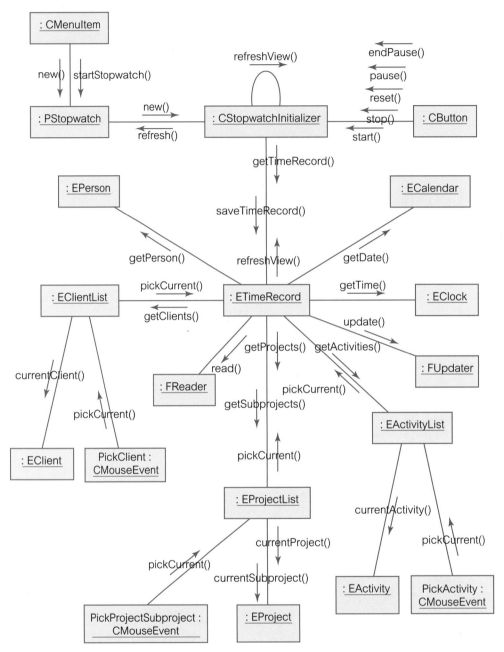

Figure 5.36 Communication model for stopwatch for a time logging system

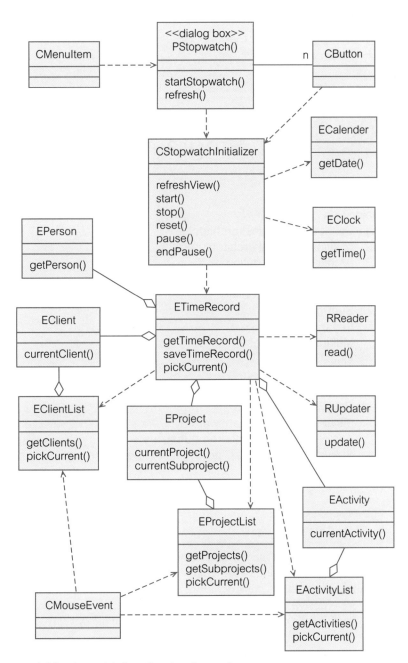

Figure 5.37 Class model for stopwatch for a time logging system

Chapter

6

System Architecture and Program Design

Objectives

In an iterative and incremental software development, the analysis models are continually "elaborated" with technical details. Once the technical details include software/hardware considerations, an analysis model becomes a design model. *System design* encompasses two major issues – the architectural design of the system and the detailed design of the programs in the system.

Architectural design is the description of a system in terms of its modules. It includes decisions about the solution strategies for the client and server components of the system. The architecture defines the layered organization of classes and packages, assignment of processes to computing facilities, reuse and component management. Architectural design resolves the issues with regard to a *multi-tier* physical architecture as well as with regard to a *multilayer* logical architecture.

The description of the internal workings of each module (use case) is called the *detailed design*. The detailed design develops complete algorithms and data structures for each module. These algorithms and data structures are tailored to all (reinforcing and obtrusive) constraints of the underlying implementation platform. The *detailed design* addresses the collaboration models required for the realization of the program's demanded functionality captured in use cases.

By reading this chapter you will:

- understand the differences between typical distributed physical architectures
- appreciate the overriding importance of a multilayer logical architecture for building quality systems
- learn how to compute the complexity of logical architectures
- gain practical knowledge of applying patterns in general and architectural design in particular.
- understand the differences between artifacts used for architectural modeling
- become aware of key principles of good program design
- become acquainted with different reuse strategies
- gain practical knowledge of collaboration modeling and how it is related to use case modeling and interaction modeling.

Distributed physical architecture

6.1

Architectural design has *physical* and *logical* aspects. *Physical architectural design* is concerned with the selection of a deployment solution and with the workload of the system being distributed across multiple processors. The physical **architecture** resolves the **client** and **server** issues as well as any middleware needed to "glue" the client and the server. It allocates processing **components** to computer **nodes**. From the UML modeling perspective, the physical architectural design uses nodes and *deployment diagrams* (Section 3.6.3).

Although the physical architecture resolves the client and server issues, the client and server are logical concepts (Bochenski 1994). The *client* is a computing process that makes requests of the server process. The *server* is a computing process that services the client requests. Normally, the client and the server processes run on different computers, but it is perfectly possible to implement a client/server system on a single machine.

In a typical scenario, the *client process* is responsible for controlling the display of information on the user's screen and handling the user's events. The *server process* is any computer node with a database of which data or processing capability may be requested by a client process.

The *client/server* (*C/S*) architecture can be extended to represent an arbitrary distributed system. The need for distribution can arise from many factors, such as:

- a requirement for specialized processing on a dedicated machine
- the need to access the system from various geographical locations
- economic considerations – using multiple small machines may be cheaper than a large, pricey computer
- an adaptiveness requirement to ensure that future extensions to the system can scale up nicely.

In a *distributed processing system*, the client can access any number of servers. However, the client may be allowed to access only one server at a time. This means that in a single request it may not be possible to combine data from two or more database servers. If this is possible, then the architecture supports a *distributed database* system.

6.1.1 Peer-to-peer architecture

Any computer node with a database can be a client in some business transactions and a server in other transactions. Connecting such nodes by means of a communication network can give rise to an architectural style known as *peer-to-peer*, often referred to as **P2P** (Figure 6.1).

In the peer-to-peer architectural style, any process or node in the system may be both client and server. Accordingly, "this architectural style defines a single type of system element (the **peer**) and a single type of connector that is a network connection (an inter-peer connection)… The central organizational principle of the system is that any peer is free to communicate directly with any other peer, without needing to use a central server. Peers typically locate each other by automatically exchanging lists of known peers (although central peer lists are also used in some cases)" (Rozanski and Woods 2005:147).

Clearly, offloading work to peer machines has to be assessed against the workload demanded by interpeer network communication. Minimization of network traffic while maximizing overall system throughput is a special consideration in peer-to-peer architectures. Attention has to be given to potential *deadlocks* between processes (when two or

Figure 6.1
Peer-to-peer
architecture

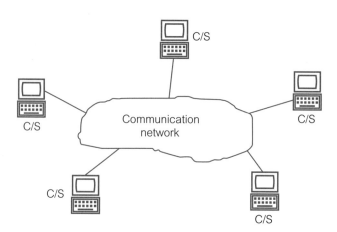

more processes are in a "deadly" embrace and cannot proceed because they hold resources on which other processes are waiting). Also, guaranteeing a consistent response time from a peer-to-peer system is a challenge.

On the positive side, peer-to-peer systems tend to be quite resilient to network and single peer failures (as it should be possible to dynamically redirect the processing). Moreover, because of the uniform distribution of processing among peers, this architectural style is likely to be quite scalable and adaptive.

Tiered architecture

Most enterprise information systems use a multi-tier architectural style. As opposed to the peer-to-peer architectural style, a *tiered architecture* defines a hierarchy of tiers of computation. Like in the case of peers, each **tier** in the middle of the hierarchy acts as both the client and the server. However, a tier can only be a client to the next tier in the hierarchy and can only act as a server for a caller higher up in the hierarchy.

One of the most important recognized practices in the development of large database-centered enterprise systems is the necessary separation of at least three implementation concerns – GUI presentation issues, enterprise-wide business rules and data services. This separation of concerns aligns with the *three-tier architecture* in which a separate business logic middle tier is introduced between the GUI client and the database server.

In practice, the separation of concerns may go beyond just three issues and include other services, such as Web processing, network communication or printing. A resulting *tiered architecture* differs from a peer-to-peer architecture in that it imposes hierarchical dependencies between the tiers of hardware and software. These dependencies align well with hierarchical layers of software modules recommended by what are in essence logical architectural frameworks, such as the J2EE architecture (Section 4.1.2) or PCBMER architecture (Section 4.1.3).

Figure 6.2 illustrates a possible alignment between PCBMER layers and potential deployment tiers. In it, the presentation, control and bean layers are shown as being implemented in a Web server. The remaining PCBMER layers are implemented in the application server, while engaging the database server from the resource subsystem.

One of the most talked-about tiers is the **application server**. This is also perhaps the least understood concept of multi-tier architecture. The confusion relates to misunderstandings about the notions of application and business services. For the database community, these two notions are clearly different. An *application service* is what each single program executing on a database does. A *business service* is what a database enforces as business rules on all executing programs. This business rules enforcement is frequently done programmatically (by means of database triggers and stored procedures).

As a result, a three-tier architecture can be presented as consisting of application services, business services and data services. Alas, the above distinction between an application and a business service is not always followed. It is frequent, for example, to use the term *application server* to mean a tier that handles business components and also takes care of business rules (while still providing a separate thread of the application service to each program). At the same time, a **Web server** is given the task of handling the application's control events and GUI presentation. This is how application and Web servers are presented in Figure 6.2.

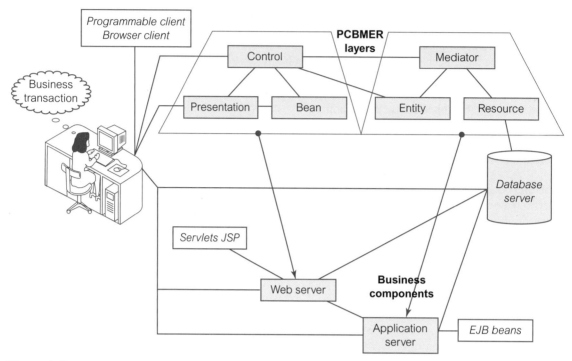

Figure 6.2 Alignment between PCBMER layers and deployment tiers

This said, the *application process* is a logical concept that may or may not be supported by dedicated hardware. The application logic can run equally well on a client or a server node – that is, it can be compiled into the client or the server process and implemented as a dynamic link library (DLL), application programming interface (API), remote procedure calls (RPC) and so on.

When the application logic is compiled into the client, then we talk about a *thick client architecture* ("a client on steroids"). The thick client assumes workstations for user–program interaction. Normally, a thick client architecture uses only two tiers (thick client and database server).

When the application logic is compiled into the server, then we talk about a *thin client architecture* ("a skinny client"). The thin client assumes network computers for user–program interaction. It also assumes that the client is a Web browser accessing HTML pages, Java applets, beans, servlets and so on.

Intermediate architectures – in which application logic is partly compiled into the client and partly into the server – are also possible.

6.1.3 Database-centered architecture

This book is predominantly concerned with the development of business applications and enterprise information systems. Database software plays a crucial role in such systems (Chapter 8). Accordingly, databases influence physical software architectures.

Independently of where the application logic resides, the program (client) interacts with the database (server) to obtain information for display and the user's manipulation. However, modern databases can be programmed as well. We say that those modern databases are *active*.

A database program is called a *stored procedure*. A stored procedure is stored in the database itself (it is a **persistent object**). It can be invoked from a client program (or from another stored procedure) by a normal procedure/function call statement.

A special kind of stored procedure – called a **trigger** – cannot be explicitly called. A trigger fires automatically on an attempt to change the content of the database. Triggers are used to implement enterprisewide business rules, which have to be enforced in a way that is independent of the client programs (or stored procedures). Triggers enforce integrity and consistency of the database. They do not allow individual applications to break the database-imposed business rules.

We need to decide which parts of the system should be programmed into the client and which into the database. The "programmable" parts to consider include:

- user interface
- presentation logic
- application (control) function
- integrity logic
- data access.

The *user interface* part of a program knows how to display information on a particular GUI, such as a Web browser, Windows or Macintosh. The *presentation logic* is responsible for handling the GUI objects (forms, menus, action buttons and so on) as required by the application function.

The *application function* contains the main logic of the program. It captures what the application does. It is the glue that puts the client and the database together. From the perspective of the PCBMER approach (Section 4.1.3), the application function is implemented in the classes of the *control* subsystem.

The *integrity logic* is responsible for the enterprisewide business rules. These are the rules that apply across all the application programs – that is, all programs have to conform to them. The *data access* knows how to access persistent data on the disk.

Figure 6.3 shows a typical scenario. The user interface and presentation logic belong to the *client*. The data access and integrity logic (triggers) are the responsibility of the *database*. The application function is frequently programmed (as SQL queries) into the client during the early development phase, but it is moved to the database (as stored procedures) for the final deployment of the software product.

Review quiz 6.1

RQ1 Which architectural style defines only a single type of system element?

RQ2 What is the middle tier in the three-tier architecture?

RQ3 By what programming means are enterprisewide business rules implemented in a database?

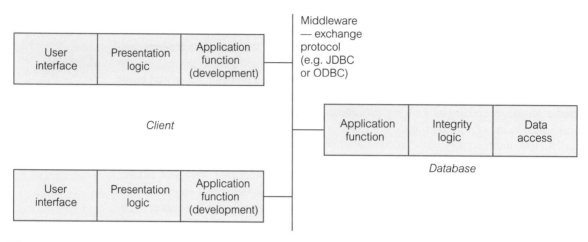

Figure 6.3 Application–database interaction

6.2 Multilayer logical architecture

Software developers know that the difficulty of producing a small system cannot be compared with the difficulty of delivering a large-scale solution. A small system is often easy to understand, implement and deploy. A large enterprise system consists of very many objects responding to random events that invoke a mesh of interrelated operations (methods). Without a clear architectural design and rigorous processes, large software projects are likely to fail.

A well-known cognitive psychology principle – *the 7 ± 2 rule* – states that the short-term memory of a human brain can *simultaneously* handle up to nine (7 + 2) things (graphical elements, ideas, concepts and so on). The lower bound of five (7 – 2) indicates that fewer than five things constitutes a trivial problem.

The rules of cognitive psychology do not change the fact that we have to produce large systems, and large systems are complex. Much of this complexity is human-generated or *accidental* rather than essential (Section 1.1). Accidental difficulties are unnecessary complications. They have the potential to turn an inherently complex system into a needlessly *complicated system*. A complicated system, that is also sufficiently complex, is not adaptive.

The main culprit is system modeling that allows for unrestricted communication between objects. Objects in such systems form *networks* – webs of cross-referenced objects. Message passing is allowed from anywhere to anywhere in the system. Down-calls and up-calls are possible. In networks, the number of communication paths between objects grows exponentially with the addition of new objects. As noted by Szyperski (1998: 57), "object references introduce linkage across arbitrary abstraction domains. Proper layering of system architectures thus lies somewhere between the challenging and impossible."

Successful systems are organized in hierarchies – any network substructures within such hierarchies are restricted and carefully controlled. *Hierarchies* reduce the complexity from exponential to polynomial. They introduce layers of objects and constrain intercommunication between **layers**. As already discussed in Section 4.1, virtually all logical architectural frameworks for enterprise systems are multilayer hierarchies. As shown vividly for example by the PCBMER framework (Section 4.1.3), the hierarchies are not strict, but *relaxed,* in the sense that higher layers can depend on several layers below in the hierarchy (Buschmann et al. 1996).

In the following subsections, we define complexity as a concept and show why hierarchies are superior to networks. We also discuss the most important architectural patterns aimed at reducing complexity.

Architectural complexity   6.2.1

To talk about the **complexity** of object systems, we need to agree on a measurement. How do we measure complexity? Complexity has different kinds and shapes. A simple, but very illustrative, measurement is the number of communication paths between classes. We define a *communication path* as the existence of a persistent or transient link between classes (Appendix, Section A.2.3). We say in the jargon that the *complexity* of modern enterprise and e-business systems is *"in the wires".*

This definition of complexity is consistent with the reality of contemporary computing, which has experienced all kinds of changes, from the Turing machine model based on *algorithms* (with its inability to compute more than the computable function can do) to an open *interaction* model. As noticed by Wegner (1997: 80);

> The paradigm shift from algorithms to interaction captures the technology shift from mainframes to workstations and networks, from number-crunching to embedded systems and graphical user interfaces, and from procedure-oriented to object-based and distributed programming. The radical notion that interactive systems are more powerful problem-solving engines than algorithms is the basis for a new paradigm for computing technology built around the unifying concept of interaction... Algorithms yield outputs completely determined by their inputs, while interactive systems, like PCS, airline reservation systems, and robots, provide history-dependent services over time that can learn from and adapt to experience.

Short of stating that complexity is in the eye of the beholder, there are certainly various meanings to the concept. Fenton and Pfleeger (1997) identify four interpretations of complexity:

- *Problem complexity* the complexity of the problem domain itself. This is also known as a computational complexity. Problem complexity is an offshoot of Brooks' essential characteristics of software, discussed in Section 1.1.1.

- *Algorithmic complexity* aiming at measuring the efficiency of software algorithms. This is a kind of complexity with diminishing relevance (at least from the viewpoint of software adaptiveness) due to the shift from algorithms to interactions in the computing paradigm, as explained above.

- *Structural complexity* aiming at establishing the relationship between the structure of the software and the ease of its maintenance and evolution. The measurements are applied to **dependencies** between software objects.

- *Cognitive complexity* measuring the effort required to understand the software – that is, capture the program's *flow of logic* and measure the flow's various properties.

From the adaptivity viewpoint, the cognitive complexity metrics contribute to the quality of understandability and the structural complexity metrics contribute to the qualities of maintainability and scalability. The two categories are related. A relatively small (good) value of cognitive complexity is a necessary, although not sufficient, condition for a low structural complexity. This is consistent with the requirement that to modify the code, you have to understand it first.

6.2.1.1 Spatial cognitive complexity

Arguably, the most suitable metrics for computing the cognitive complexity of modern programs are *spatial complexity metrics* (Gold et al., 2005). Their aim is to measure the *distance* that a software engineer must move within the code to build a mental model of it. Spatial complexity metrics come in different flavors.

As an illustration, Douce et al. (1999) present two types of spatial complexity metrics – *functional* (*procedural*) and *object-oriented*. Both have weaknesses and the object-oriented formulas are badly grounded and quite misguided. Therefore, the formulas for *functional* programming are presented here.

The complexity value is derived in two steps. First, the complexity values for each function in the program are calculated. Second, these values are summed to give a complexity value for the whole program.

$$FC = \sum_{i=1}^{totalcalls} dist_i \qquad \text{Equation 6.1}$$

where *totalcalls* is the number of calls to the function, *dist* is the distance in lines of code from a call to the function's definition and *FC* is the function spatial complexity.

$$PC = \sum_{i=1}^{totalfunctions} FC_i \qquad \text{Equation 6.2}$$

where *totalfunctions* is the number of functions in the program and *PC* is the program spatial complexity.

The main weakness of the above formulas is that the distance is calculated in lines of code. The lines of code measure lacks relevancy for more modern programming practices and ways of visualizing program code when doing analysis. Also, in this case, the lines of code have the distorted meaning of "spatial" – they mean, skip these lines of code to get to the function definition (the question to ask would be is "skipping" a factor in the program's comprehension?) Nevertheless, the presented metrics do give us an idea as to the the purpose of spatial complexity measurements.

Structural complexity   6.2.1.2

If *cognitive* complexity concentrates on the program's flow of logic, the *structural* complexity metrics address the dependencies between a program's objects. We are reminded, from Chapter 4, that *dependency* between two system objects exists if a change to the object that supplies a service may necessitate a change in client objects that demand that service (Maciaszek and Liong 2005). This definition is consistent with the UML standard (UML 2005: 74), which states that "A dependency signifies a supplier/client relationship between model elements where the modification of the supplier may impact the client model elements. A dependency implies the semantics of the client is not complete without the supplier."

If all dependencies in a system are identified and understood, the system is said to be *adaptive* – that is, it is understandable, maintainable and scalable. A necessary condition for adaptiveness is that dependencies are tractable. Consequently, the task of the software engineer is to minimize dependencies.

In software systems, dependencies can be identified for objects of varying granularity – components, **packages**, classes, methods. The dependencies between more specific objects at lower levels of granularity propagate up to create dependencies at higher level of granularity. Accordingly, dependency management necessitates a detailed study of the program code to identify all relationships between data structures and code invocation between software objects. The following explains structural complexity regarding dependencies between classes. More detailed discussion of these issues can be found in Maciaszek (2006) and related publications.

Structural complexity of networks   6.2.1.2.1

Each communication path would typically allow for a bidirectional interaction between classes – from *A* to *B* and from *B* to *A*. Figure 6.4 illustrates the complexity of a network of seven classes. The complexity is given by the formula:

$$_{net}CCD = n(n-1)$$ Equation 6.3

where *n* is the number of objects (nodes in the graph) and $_{net}CCD$ is a cumulative class dependency in a fully connected network (assuming that objects refer to classes).

This formula, applied to seven classes, gives us the CCD value of 42. Clearly, the growth of complexity in network systems is exponential. It is exponential not in the sense of the *actual dependencies* between objects, but because the flat network structure, as in Figure 6.4 (with no restrictions on communication paths between objects), creates *potential* dependencies between any (all) objects in the system. A change in an object can potentially impact (can have a *ripple effect* on) any other object in the system.

Note that we measure complexity in relation to the number of classes, not the number of objects. In programs, the objects – not the classes – send messages to other objects of the same or different class. This introduces additional difficulty to the programmer responsible for delivering the application logic and managing the program's variables and other data structures. However, that additional difficulty is negligible in the context.

Figure 6.4
The complexity of
networks

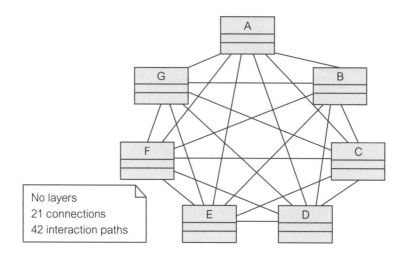

No layers
21 connections
42 interaction paths

An object can send a message to another object *only* if there is a persistent or transient link between them. The transient (run-time) links are resolved within a single program invocation and may or may not be directly visible in the program structures. The persistent (compile-time) links, on the other hand, exist only if there is a connection (such as an association) defined in the class model.

6.2.1.2.2 *Structural complexity of hierarchies*

The solution to complexity control lies in reducing the network structures by grouping classes into *class hierarchies* (or rather *holarchies* (Section 5.3.3) to be precise). In this way, classes can form naturally into layers that emphasize a hierarchical decomposition *between* layers while allowing for network-like interactions *within* the layers.

The hierarchical layering offers reductions in complexity by restricting the number of potential interaction paths between classes. The reduction is achieved by stratifying classes into layers and allowing for direct class interactions only within a layer and with "adjacent" layers below if in the hierarchy.

In practice, the complexity of hierarchical structures is further improved by the enforcement of various architectural principles, such as those described in Section 4.1.3.2. One such principle is the *DDP (downward dependency) principle*, stating that dependencies between layers are only downwards. In other words, communication paths between layers are single-directional, meaning that the number of interaction paths between layers is the same as the number of connections. Any upward communication between layers is realized by "dependency-less" loose **coupling** facilitated by interfaces placed in lower layers but implemented in higher layers and/or by event processing instead of message passing and/or by the use of meta-level technologies (such as the Struts framework for Java programming).

The DDP constraint applies to interlayer communication, too. For intralayer communication, a similar effect is achieved by the application of the *CEP (cycle elimination) principle*. Cycles within layers can be eliminated by using interfaces, but also refactoring techniques that extract circularly-dependent functionality into separate objects/components (Section 4.1.3.2; for further details, see Maciaszek and Liong 2005).

Assuming that the dependencies between layers are only downwards and the dependencies within layers have no cycles, Figure 6.5 shows the complexity of a seven-class hierarchy that has its classes grouped into four layers. In comparison to the network structure in Figure 6.4, the complexity has been reduced from 42 to just 13 interaction paths.

Let the layers be $l_1, l_2 \dots l_n$. For any layer l_i, let:

- $size(l_i)$ be the number of objects in l_i
- l_1 be the number of parents of l_i
- $P_j(l_j)$ be the jth parent of l_i

Then, the cumulative class dependency *CCD* for a holarchy (i.e. a hierarchy that permits more than parent layer as in the PCBMER framework) is calculated according to Equation 6.4:

$$_{holarchy}CCD = \sum_{i=1}^{n} \frac{size(l_i) * (size(l_i) - 1)}{2} + \sum_{i=1}^{n} \sum_{j=1}^{l_i} (size(l_i) * size(p_j(l_i))) \qquad \text{Equation 6.4}$$

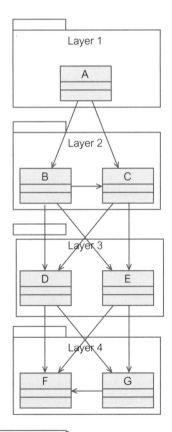

Figure 6.5
The complexity of hierarchies

where n is the number of classes in each layer i (that is, layers 1, 2, 3, and so on) and $_{hier}CCD$ is a cumulative class dependency in the hierarchy.

The first part of the formula in Equation 6.4 computes the number of potential (all possible) single-directional paths between all classes in each layer. The second part computes the number of potential (all possible) single-directional paths between the classes in each pair of adjacent layers.

Even in the case of only seven classes, the complexity reduction between a *network* (Figure 6.4) and a *hierarchy* (Figure 6.5) is significant. The complexity of the former grows exponentially, while the complexity of the latter grows polynomially. The formulas calculate the worst possible values of CCD. Hence, the CCD for Figure 6.5 is 13, not 12 as would be the case in a particular situation shown on the diagram (because there is no dependency between D and E). Incidentally, the value 13 is calculated as follows:

- 0 connections within layer 1
- plus 1 connection within layers 2, 3, and 4 (that is, 3 altogether)
- plus 2 connections between layers 1 and 2
- plus 4 connections between layers 2 and 3
- plus 4 connections between layers 3 and 4.

The complexity formulas for hierarchies can differ depending on the specific constraints additionally placed on the hierarchy. One such constraint, not used in Figure 6.5, results from the **Façade** pattern, explained next in Section 6.2.2.1. The Façade pattern defines a single entry point (a dedicated interface or class) to each layer/subsystem/package in the hierarchy, thus further reducing the possible dependencies between layers.

Maciaszek (2006) provides the structural complexity formulas for some of the variants on hierarchies. As already observed, all formulas for hierarchies lead to only polynomial growth of complexity with the addition of more classes in the system.

6.2.2 Architectural patterns

When presenting the PCBMER architectural framework (or meta-architecture) in Chapter 4, we listed a number of principles that the framework must conform to (Section 4.1.3.2). Every framework must have such principles defined. However, the realization of these principles in any concrete system design will need to follow more specific *design* **patterns**.

"A design pattern provides a scheme for refining the elements of a software system or the relationships between them. It describes a commonly recurring structure of interconnected design elements that solves a general design problem with a particular context" (Rozanski and Woods 2005: 138). When used in the context of architectural design, a design pattern can be called an *architectural pattern*.

In the following subsections, we describe design patterns of particular value to architectural design. These are known as the *Gang of Four* (**GoF**) patterns (named after the four authors of a book (Gamma et al. 1995), who popularized the patterns' discipline and defined some of the most widely used patterns today). The explanation of the architectural patterns below borrows from the more detailed discussion and application of architectural patterns in Maciaszek and Liong (2005).

Façade

Gamma et al. (1995: 185) define the *Façade* pattern as "a higher-level interface that makes the subsystem easier to use". The goal is to "minimize the communication and dependencies between subsystems".

A "higher-level interface" is not necessarily fully descriptive of the concept of interface (Appendix, Section A.9). It can be a *concrete class* (called then a *dominant class*) or an *abstract class* (Appendix, Section A.8). The point is that a higher-level interface encapsulates the main functionality of the layer (subsystem, package) and provides the main or even the only entry point for the clients of the layer. In general, a layer may define more than one façade to target different clients in higher layers.

As sketched in Figure 6.6, client objects communicate with the layer via the façade object – the object `EFacadeImpl`, which implements the interface `EFacade`. `EFacadeImpl` keeps references (associations) to appropriate layer classes (`EClass1` and `EClass5`) and delegates client requests to them. The layer classes handle work assigned by the façade, but they keep no reference to the façade. There is no need for the façade to keep references to all classes in the layer because some classes perform subservient work for other classes in that layer. In the case of specialization from an abstract class (such as `EClass1`), the model shows the reference to the abstract class, but, in the implemented system, the `EFacadeImpl` will have references to the concrete subclasses `EClass2` and `EClass3`.

Although the façade object is allowed to do some work itself, it normally delegates the work to other objects in the layer. The consequence is the reduction of communication paths between layers and the number of objects that clients of the layer deal with. The other consequence may be that the layer classes get hidden behind the façade object, but this is a side-effect rather than the objective of the Façade pattern. The objective is to provide a simpler interface to a layer and reduce dependencies to it, but clients who need more elaborate options can still directly communicate with the layer's classes (Stelting and Maassen 2001).

Example 6.1: university enrolment

Consider Problem statement 1, for a university enrolment system (Section 1.6.1) and consult the examples for that case study in Chapter 4. Refer in particular to the "centralized" interactions from Example 4.18 (Figure 4.18) and Example 4.19 (Figure 4.20). Apply the Façade pattern to the entity layer and draw a class diagram for it. Show the operations that the facade needs to define. Explain the model. Discuss possible variations on the diagram for a "distributed" model (Figures 4.19 and 4.21).

Figure 6.7, for Example 6.1, shows how the `EFacade` object creates a single point of entry to the `Entity` package. It defines the four operations that `CEnroll` needs to directly invoke (as per the sequence diagram in Figure 4.18). `EFacade` would delegate execution of these operations to appropriate entity classes.

Figure 6.6
The Façade
pattern

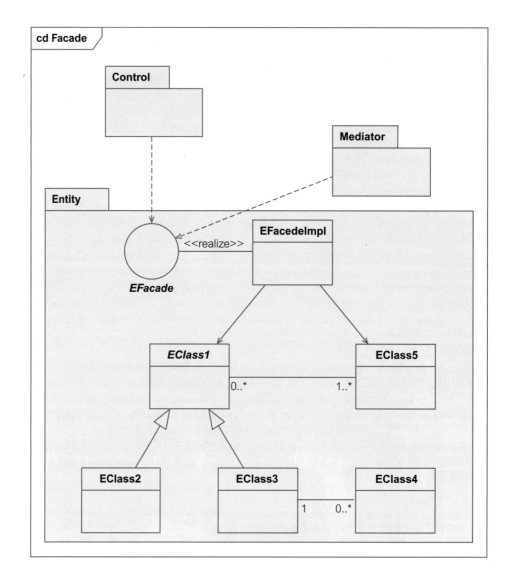

In the case of the "distributed" model, EFacade would be further simplified and contain only one operation, namely addCrs(crs,sem) (Figures 4.19 and 4.21). The execution of this operation would be delegated to EStudent – the object that takes responsibility for talking to ECourse and ECourseOffering and completing the enrolment processing.

6.2.2.2 Abstract Factory

The **Abstract Factory** pattern provides "an interface for creating families of related or dependent objects without specifying their concrete classes" (Gamma et al. 1995: 87). As opposed to the Façade pattern, where a "higher-level interface" could mean a concrete class, an interface in Abstract Factory is either a *true interface* (preferably) (Appendix, Section A.9) or an *abstract class* (Appendix, Section A.8).

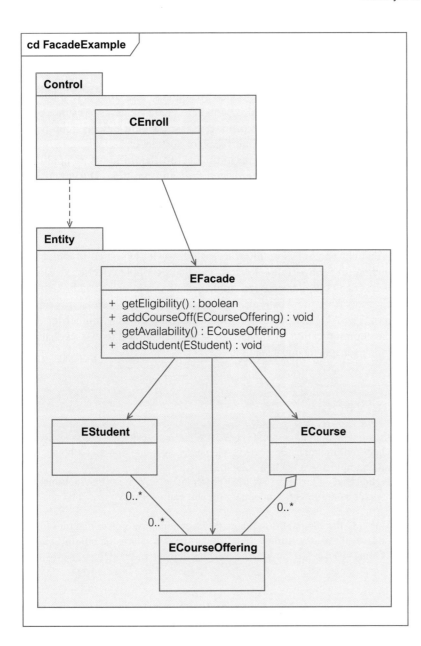

Figure 6.7
The Façade
pattern for a
university
enrolment system

Abstract Factory enables the application to behave differently by accessing one of several families of objects hidden behind the Abstract Factory interface. A configuration parameter value can control which family should be accessed. A typical function of Abstract Factory is when an application needs to use different *resources* depending on run-time circumstances – to use a different file, launch a different GUI window or display information in different languages, for example.

Figure 6.8 (overleaf) is a visualization of the Abstract Factory pattern. `EAbstractFactory` is an interface (but it could have been an abstract class) that defines create methods for several product objects (different resources). `EAbstractProductA` and `EAbstractProductB` are abstract classes (but they could have been interfaces) defining the general behavior of the products (resources) that will be used by the application. Abstract Factory is implemented by concrete factory classes. Abstract products are extended (implemented) by concrete product classes. Client objects keep references to abstract factory and abstract product interfaces (or abstract classes).

"An Abstract Factory helps to increase the overall flexibility of an application. This flexibility manifests itself both during design time and run-time. During design, you do not have to predict all future uses for an application. Instead, you create the generic framework and then develop implementations independently from the rest of the application. At run-time, the application can easily integrate new features and resources" (Stelting and Maassen 2001: 14).

Because Abstract Factory is an interface, which is implemented in entire families of classes, extending it to support new families may have a ripple effect on existing concrete classes. Gamma et al. (1995) discuss few implementation solutions to address this problem.

On closer inspection, the Abstract Factory pattern can be seen as a variation on the Façade pattern. The Abstract Factory interface can be used as a "higher-level interface" via which the communication to a package is channeled and the classes that do the real work inside the package are encapsulated.

Example 6.2: telemarketing

Consider Problem statement 4, for a telemarketing system (Section 1.6.4) and consult the examples for that case study explaining the difference between a regular (dedicated) telemarketing campaign and a bonus campaign (Example 2.5 in Section 2.5.3 and Example 5.9 in Section 5.2.4.4.2).

It is characteristic of telemarketing that campaigns may be of different sorts, may or may not include bonus campaigns, new categories of campaigns are likely to be emerging and campaigns are launched and closed as time passes.

Apply the Abstract Factory pattern to the campaigns in the entity layer and draw a class diagram for it. Show the factory operations (no need to show operations in products). Show also a mediator class called `MCampaignLauncher` that needs to have access to the Abstract Factory objects. Explain the model.

The design in Figure 6.9 (p. 322) for Example 6.2 refers to two categories of campaign products – dedicated campaigns and bonus campaigns. Two concrete products for each abstract category are shown. `MCampaignLauncher` is immune to changes to concrete classes as it communicates with these classes only via operations defined in the abstract factory and abstract products.

The generic Abstract Factory framework makes adding new campaigns a painless exercise, involving only the creation of a new concrete product class. Extending the system to support additional categories of campaigns is also relatively easy. With each additional campaign, we would only need to define an additional concrete factory class, a matching abstract product interface and any concrete product classes.

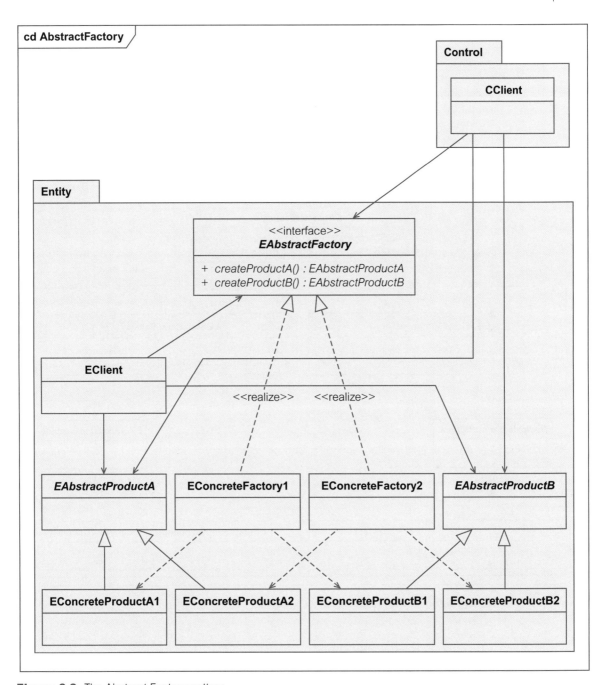

Figure 6.8 The Abstract Factory pattern

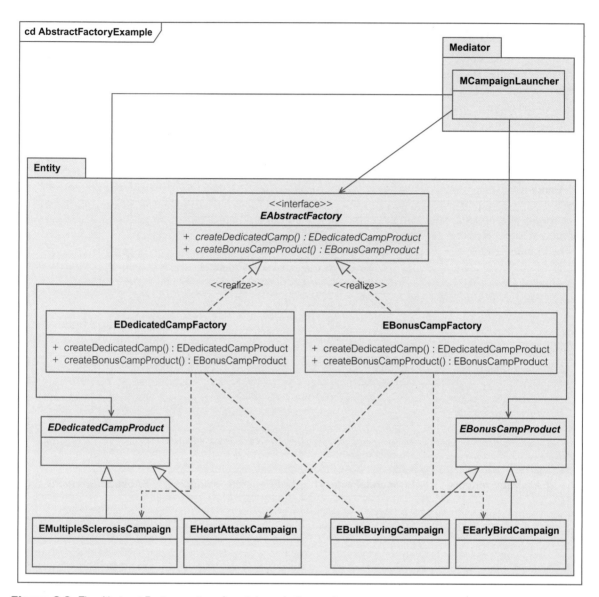

Figure 6.9 The Abstract Factory pattern for a telemarketing system

6.2.2.3 Chain of Responsibility

The intent of the **Chain of Responsibility** pattern is to "avoid coupling the sender of a request to its receiver by giving more than one object a chance to handle the request" (Gamma et al. 1995: 223). The Chain of Responsibility can be seen as a variant of the concept of *delegation,* understood as a referral chain of messages (Appendix, Section A.6.3; also Section 5.3.2.1).

The chain of messages starts with an object that produces the message. If the object itself (a "this" or "self" object) cannot respond to the message, it will delegate the message to some other object, which, in turn, can delegate it further. The process ends when some object replies to the message or the termination condition is reached (in which case, either a default object is returned or some other default result, indicating the success or failure of the chain).

In its most frequent form, "the Chain of Responsibility is implemented with a parent–child or container–contained model. With this approach, messages not handled by a child object are sent to the parent, and potentially the parent's parent, until a suitable handler object is reached. The Chain of Responsibility is well-suited for a variety of object-oriented GUI activities. GUI help functions, component layout, formatting, and positioning all might use this pattern. In business models, the pattern is sometimes used with whole–part models. For example, a line item on an order might send a message to the order it's on – the order composite – for action" (Stelting and Maassen 2001: 36).

The Chain of Responsibility pattern is also beneficial in situations where a set of classes, possibly in different architectural layers, can potentially respond to a particular initial message. In the PCBMER framework, the Chain of Responsibility makes it possible to enforce the *NCP (neighbor communication) principle* whenever the client class in a higher architectural layer needs to be serviced by a method in a class residing in a non-neighboring lower layer. If the Chain of Responsibility is involved, a client object that sends a message does not have a direct reference to an object that ultimately supplies the service.

Figure 6.10 is a possible way of thinking about the Chain of Responsibility pattern. It shows a presentation client PClient sending a handleClientRequest() message to one of the classes implementing the interface – CHandler. If the concrete handler can service the request, it will do so. If it cannot, it will delegate it to another object. This other object could be another concrete class implementing CHandler or it could be a class in the next architectural layer. In the case of delegating to lower layers, the existence of the CHandler interface may not be needed.

Example 6.3: contact management

Consider Problem statement 3, for a contact management system (Section 1.6.3) and consult the examples for that case study in Chapter 4. Refer to Figure 4.11 (Example 4.11 in Section 4.2.5.3) to understand the information content of the class EContact.

Consider a scenario that requires a presentation object (PWindow) to display information about a particular contact. To obtain data, PWindow needs to communicate with a control object (let's call it CActioner). CActioner (being a control class) does not contain the necessary data and will need to delegate the request further. This Chain of Responsibility can go as far as to the resource layer if the contact information has to be retrieved from the database.

Apply the Chain of Responsibility pattern to the above scenario. Consider all layers of the PCBMER framework. There is no need to use the CHandler interface as presented in Figure 6.10. Explain the model.

Figure 6.11 represents the Chain of Responsibility scenario for displaying contact information for Example 6.3. PWindow sends the original request to CActioner. Assuming that CActioner does not know of the existence of the EContact object with the current

Figure 6.10
The Chain of
Responsibility
pattern

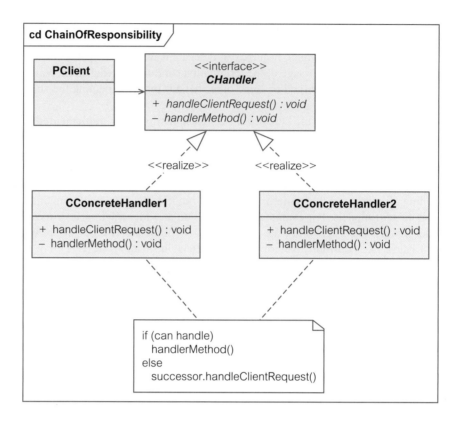

contact data, it will delegate `retrieveContact()` to `MBroker`. `MBroker` delegates it further to `RReader` so that the data can be retrieved from the database. Once retrieved and returned to `MBroker`, an instance of `EContact` can be created and returned to `CActioner`. `CActioner` can now ask `EContact` for its data so that it can instantiate `BContact` and return `BContact`'s reference to `PWindow`. `PWindow` is now able to get the `BContact` data for rendering on the screen.

6.2.2.4 Observer

The intent of the **Observer pattern** (also known as the Publish-Subscribe pattern) is to "define a one-to-many dependency between objects so that when one object changes state, all its dependents are notified and updated automatically" (Gamma et al. 1995: 293).

The pattern relates two types of objects:

■ the object that is observed called *subject* or *publisher*

■ the objects that are observing called *observers* or *subscribers* or *listeners*.

A subject may have many observers that subscribe to it. All observers are notified of subject state changes and can then perform the necessary processing to synchronize their states with the subject state. Observers are not related to each other and can do different processing in response to notifications of state changes in subjects.

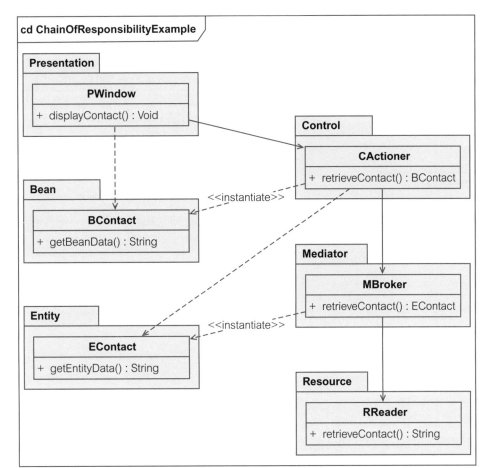

Figure 6.11
The Chain of
Responsibility
pattern for a
contact
management
system

Figure 6.12 sketches the modus operandi of the Observer pattern (modified from a wizard implemented for this pattern in Sparx Systems' CASE tool called Enterprise Architect). The abstract class `Subject` keeps references to its observers and defines operations for attaching, detaching and notifying observer objects. These operations are implemented in `ConcreteSubject`, which inherits from `Subject`. `ConcreteSubject` manages its state and notifies observers when its state changes. The abstract class (or interface) `Observer` defines an `onUpdate()` operation implemented in `ConcreteObserver`. `ConcreteObserver` may keep a reference to a `ConcreteSubject` object and, when notified of the state change in the subject, updates its own state to maintain consistency with the subject.

Although the GoF definition of the Observer pattern mentions dependencies, the pattern promotes low coupling between subjects and observers. Subjects know about observers indirectly via the `Observer` interface. Registration and deregistration of observers with the subject is done dynamically and can be achieved by a separate "handshaking" `Registrator` object. The notifications of state changes in the subject are broadcast automatically to observers. Subjects and observers execute in separate threats, thus further enhancing the low coupling.

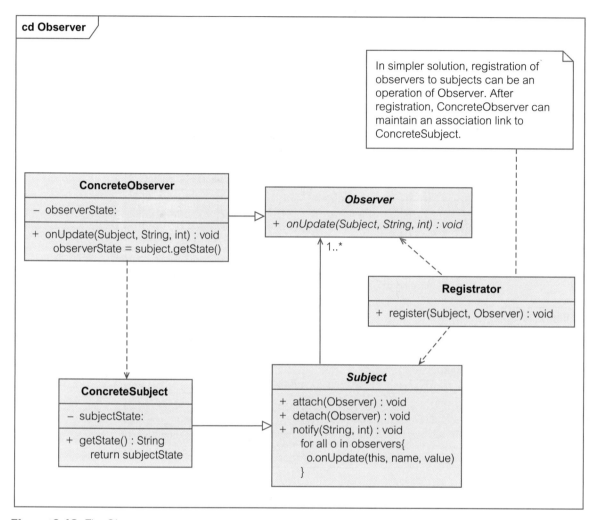

Figure 6.12 The Observer pattern

The Observer pattern has been popularized by its extensive use in GUI event handling libraries, such as Java Swing. For example, a Swing JMenuItem is a subject that publishes an "action event" when it gets selected. Any observer needing to know that a menu item was selected would subscribe to JMenuItem events. In Java and in C#.NET implementations of Observer, the event's data is stored as an object of the event class (PMenuItemEvent, for example). The event object is then passed as a parameter in the event message to observers (Larman 2005; Maciaszek and Liong 2005).

The low coupling of the Observer pattern can (and should) be taken advantage of in layered architectural frameworks to support both the downward and upward communication between layers – in particular when the subject and observers are not in adjacent layers. The PCBMER framework recommends using the Observer pattern in the *UNP (upward notification) principle* (Section 4.1.3.2). This, in turn, gives rise to the *APP (acquaintance package) principle*, defined in Section 4.1.3.2, but not directly used so far in this book (Maciaszek and Liong 2005).

The APP principle adds the *acquaintance* package/subsystem to the six PCBMER layers. The acquaintance package is quite orthogonal to the six layers – that is, it does not extend the layer hierarchy. The package consists only of interfaces that are allowed to be *implemented* in any PCBMER layer. Other layers can access these implementations by *using* the interfaces. Depending on whether the "using" layer is above or below the "implementation" layer, the acquaintance package permits downward or upward communication, including direct communication with non-neighboring layers.

Example 6.4: contact management

Refer to Problem statement 3, for a contact management system (Section 1.6.3) and Example 6.3 (Section 6.2.2.3).

Consider a scenario in which EContact is a subject that needs to notify its observers of the changes to its state. For the purpose of the example, take only into account one observer – PContact (a presentation window that displays the current information about the contact). EContact publishes its change event by sending onContactChange() message to PContact. PContact implements an observer interface located in the Acquaintance package.

Apply the Observer pattern to the above scenario. Draw a class model for it. Explain the model.

Figure 6.13 shows the class diagram built according to the Observer pattern described in Example 6.4. CRegistrator is used to subscribe the observer (PContact) to the subject (EContact). AObserver is an interface in the Acquaintance package, implemented by PContact and used by EContact to notify of its state change. When notified of the change, PContact can communicate directly with EContact to getState(). The state data is needed by displayContact() to perform its function.

Mediator   6.2.2.5

The **Mediator** pattern defines classes that encapsulate intercommunication between other classes, likely from different layers. The pattern "promotes loose coupling by keeping objects from referring to each other explicitly, and it lets you vary their interaction independently" (Gamma et al. 1995: 273).

The Mediator pattern allows us to group complex processing rules, including complex business rules, in dedicated Mediator class(-es). This relieves other implicated objects (called *colleagues* in the pattern) from doing the processing by exchanging possibly very many messages to do the job. As a result, colleague objects become more cohesive and much simpler. They become more independent from the business rules and, therefore, more reusable.

As with most other patterns, the architect/designer has to strike a proper balance regarding the depth to which the Mediator pattern is used. As noted in Gamma et al. (1995), the Mediator pattern may seem to contradict the commitment of object-oriented design to uniform distribution of behavior among objects. However, too much distribution also means an object model with excessive connections and dependencies between objects.

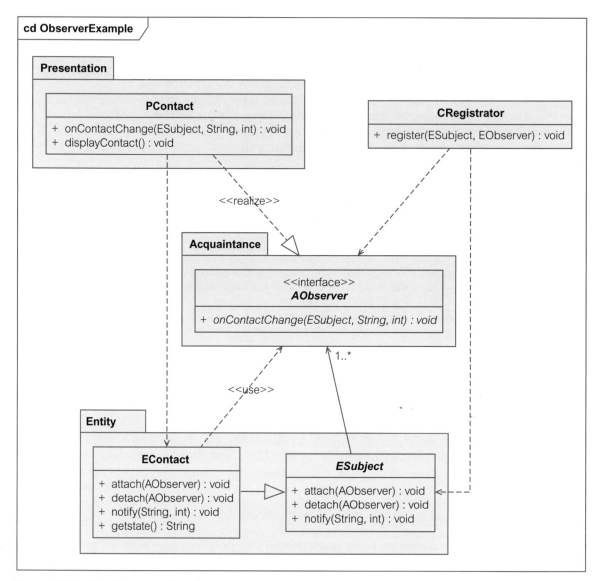

Figure 6.13 The Observer pattern for a contact management system

Figure 6.14 presents a conceptual model of the Mediator pattern. The `Mediator` interface defines some `coordinate()` operation to do the work that involves `Colleague` objects. When a `Client` object invokes some `coordinate()` method, the `ConcreteMediator` object uses its references to `ConcreteColleague` objects to do the coordination work without forcing them to communicate with other colleagues (that is, the work is master-minded by `ConcreteMediator`). However, if necessary, the `ConcreteMediator` can route requests between the `ConcreteColleague` objects in order to implement the mediation behavior.

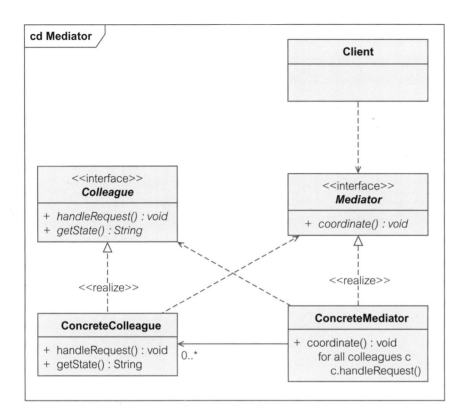

Figure 6.14
The Mediator
pattern

Note, that each `ConcreteColleague` object knows its mediator, but that knowledge is indirect via the `Mediator` interface. This said, there is no obligation to define the `Mediator` interface in simpler systems that require only one mediator. In such cases, the Observer pattern can be used for communication from colleagues to the mediator (that is, colleagues would act as subjects notifying the mediator whenever they change state and the mediator would respond by transmitting the effects of the change to other colleagues). In the Observer pattern, the mediator object that encapsulates complex update semantics between subjects and observers is known as a *change manager* (Gamma et al. 1995).

Example 6.5: telemarketing

Consider Problem statement 4, for a telemarketing system (Section 1.6.4) and consult its class model (Example 4.7 in Section 4.2.1.2.3, Figure 4.7).

The main responsibility of telemarketing is to be able to dynamically schedule the next call for each telemarketer who has just finished a conversation. This involves finding out about the state of each current phone conversation and creating a new call instance.

Apply the Mediator pattern to the above scenario. Draw a class diagram conforming to the PCBMER framework. Use the CNP (class naming) principle (ref. Section 4.1.3.2). Explain the model.

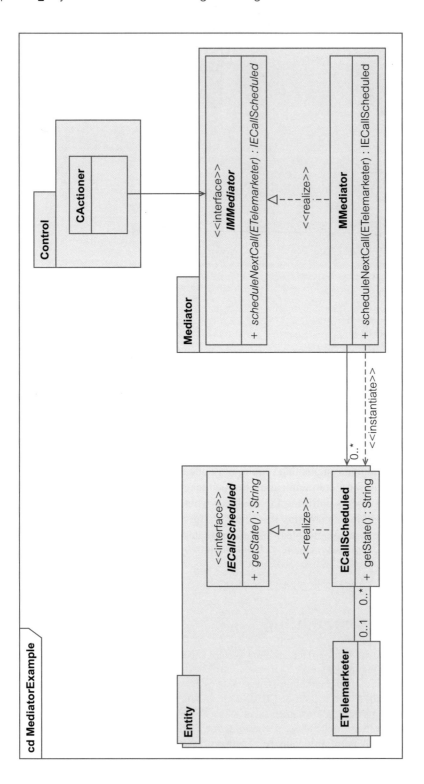

Figure 6.15 The Mediator pattern for a telemarketing system

In PCBMER, a separate layer is named after the mediator pattern. The mediator layer decouples the control, entity and resource layers. The Mediator interface or class can also act as a façade (Section 6.2.2.1) to the Mediator layer. Moreover, the control layer is an application of the Mediator pattern in that it has the capability to mediate between the presentation, bean, entity and mediator layers.

The design in Figure 6.15 for Example 6.5 assumes that control object `CActioner` is a client that initiates the scheduling of phone calls to telemarketers. It communicates this task to the concrete mediator `MMediator` via the interface `IMMediator`. `MMediator` contains the implementation of the business logic that governs the scheduling activity (in `scheduleNextCall()` (and possibly in other methods not shown in the model). `MMediator` maintains a collection of references to all currently active `ECallScheduled` objects so that it can get their state, decide the supporter and the campaign for which the next call should be scheduled and create a new instance of `ECallScheduled` associated with the concerned `ETelemarketer`.

Review quiz 6.2

RQ1 What are the two main, and contrasting, computational models?

RQ2 Is structural complexity computed with regard to a program's classes or its objects?

RQ3 What is the name of the pattern that defines a higher-level interface that makes the subsystem easier to use?

RQ4 Which pattern makes it possible to enforce the NCP (neighbor communication) principle?

Architectural modeling

6.3

In UML, *architectural modeling* is supported by facilities for *implementation modeling* (Section 3.6). Implementation models are centered on such concepts as a node, component, package and subsystem. Beyond implementation models, UML supports architectural modeling via *constraints* designed into class diagrams. The main form this facility takes is the visualization of dependency relationships in class and other models. Dependencies are the cornerstone of architectural frameworks (Section 4.1). They also determine the architectural complexity (Section 6.2.1).

Packages

6.3.1

UML provides the notion of the *package* (Section 3.6.1) as a way of representing a group of classes (or other modeling elements, such as use cases). Packages serve to partition the logical model of an application program. They are clusters of highly related classes that are themselves cohesive but are loosely coupled relative to other such clusters (Lakos 1996).

Packages can be *nested*. An outer package has access to any classes directly contained in its nested packages. A class can be owned by only one package. This does not inhibit the class from appearing in other packages or communicating with classes in other packages. By declaring the visibility of a class within a package, we can control the communication and dependencies between classes in different packages (Section 5.1.2.2).

A package is shown by means of a folder icon (Figure 6.16). A nested package is drawn inside its outer package. Each package has its own class diagram, which definines all classes owned by the package. Figure 6.16 illustrates different ways to show the assignment of classes to packages (Fowler 2004) and reflects the fact that a Java programmer has the option of importing a `Date` class from either the `java.sql` or `java.util` library packages.

Packages can be related in two kinds of relationship: *generalization* and *dependency*. Dependency from package A to package B states that changes to B may require changes in A. Dependencies between packages are, by and large, due to message passing – that is, a class in one package is sending a message to a class in another package.

UML specifies a number of different categories of the dependency relationship (a *usage* dependency, *access* dependency or *visibility* dependency, for example). However, determining the category of dependency is not particularly helpful. Instead, the true nature of each dependency can be specified as a descriptive constraint of the system model.

Note that a *generalization* between packages also implies a dependency. The dependency is from a subtype package to the supertype package. Changes in the supertype package affect the subtype package.

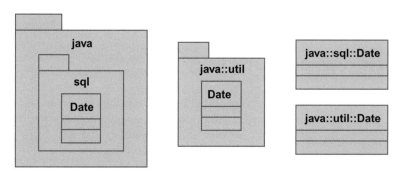

Figure 6.16
Packages and classes

Figure 6.17 shows the packages and relationships between them for Example 6.6. Enrolment depends on `Grades` and `Timetable`. `Timetable` depends on `Calendar`. There can be four different calendars, shown by a generalization relationship. `Gregorian Calendar` depends on `java::sql::Date`.

Components

A *component* (Section 3.6.2) is a physical part of the system, a piece of implementation, or a software program (Booch et al. 1999; Lakos 1996; Rumbaugh et al. 2005; Szyperski 1998). Components are typically perceived as binary executable (EXE) parts of the system. However, a component can also be a part of the system that is not directly executable (such as a source code file, data file, DLL (dynamic link library) or a stored procedure in a database).

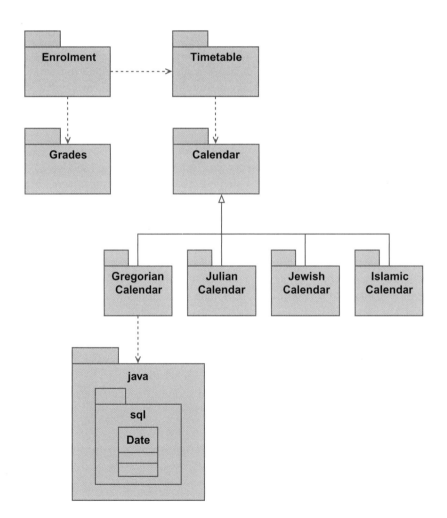

Figure 6.17
Packages for a
university
enrolment system

The component notation is shown in Figure 6.18 (refer also to Figure 3.19 in Section 3.6.2). UML allows the modeling of component interfaces using the "lollipop" notation. If a dependency between components is negotiated via interfaces, then a component that realizes the same set of interfaces can replace another component.

The characteristics of a component are that it (Rumbaugh et al. 2005; Szyperski, 1998):

■ is a unit of independent deployment – it is never deployed partially

■ is a unit of third-party composition – that is, it is sufficiently documented and self-contained to be "plugged into" other components by a third party

■ has no persistent state – it cannot be distinguished from copies of it and, in any given application, there will be at most one copy of a particular component

■ is a replaceable part of a system – it can be replaced by another component that conforms to the same interface

■ fulfills a clear function and is logically and physically cohesive

■ may be nested in other components.

A component diagram shows components and how they relate to each other. Components can be related by *dependency relationships*. A dependent component requires the services of the component pointed to by the dependency relationship (the use of dependency relationships for components has been discussed in Section 3.6.2)

6.3.2.1 Component versus package

A *package* is a grouping of modeling elements under an assigned name (Section 3.6.1). At the logical level, every class belongs to a single package. At the physical level, every class is implemented by at least one component and it is possible that a component implements only one class. Abstract classes and interfaces are frequently implemented by more than one component.

Packages are typically larger architectural units than components. They tend to group classes in a *horizontal* way – by static proximity of classes in the application domain. *Components* are *vertical* groups of classes with behavioral proximity – they may come from different domains, but they contribute to a single piece of business activity, perhaps a use case.

The above orthogonality of packages and components makes it difficult to establish dependencies between them. A frequent situation is that a logical package depends on a few physical components.

Figure 6.18
Component
notation

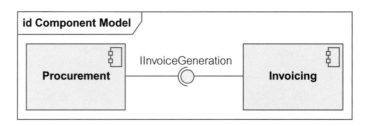

Example 6.7: university enrolment

Refer to the packages identified in Example 6.6 (Section 6.3.1). Consider the Timetable package. Assume that the package will be implemented as a C# program that embodies the logic of the allocation of university rooms to classes. The program accesses a database for room and class information. Two stored procedures will be implemented to provide that service to the program.

Draw a component diagram that demonstrates the dependencies between the package and the necessary components.

Figure 6.19 shows the component model for Example 6.7. Three components are identified – `RoomAllocEXE`, `RoomUSP` and `ClassUSP`. The package `Timetable` depends on these components.

Component versus class and interface 6.3.2.2

Like classes, components realize interfaces. The difference is twofold. First, a *component* is a physical abstraction deployed on some computer node. A *class* represents a logical thing that has to be implemented by a component to act as a physical abstraction.

Second, a component reveals only some interfaces of the classes that it contains. Many other interfaces are encapsulated by the component – they are used internally, only by collaborating classes and are not visible to other components.

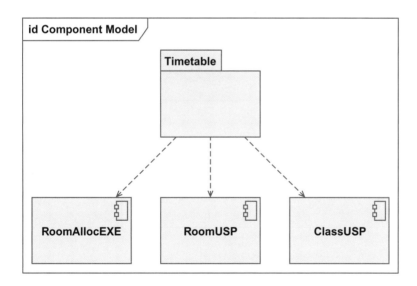

Figure 6.19
Package versus component for a university enrolment system

Example 6.8: university enrolment

Refer to the three components identified in Example 6.7 (Section 6.3.2.1). Assume that the component `RoomAllocEXE` initiates the allocation of rooms to courses by providing the component `RoomUSP` with the class identification. To this end, `RoomUSP` realizes the interface called `Allocate`.

The component `ClassUSP` does the rest of the job by obtaining the room details from the component `ClassUSP`. To provide that service, `ClassUSP` implements the interface called `Reserve`.

Figure 6.20 shows the component diagram corresponding to the requirements given in Example 6.8. It features two ways to present the provided and required interfaces.

6.3.3 Nodes

In UML, a distributed physical architecture (Section 6.1) or any other architecture for the system is rendered as a *deployment diagram* (Section 3.6.3). A computational resource (a run-time physical object) in a deployment diagram is called a *node*. As a minimum, the node has a memory and some computing capability. The node can also be a database server. This signi-fies the fact that contemporary databases are active servers (they are programmable).

Figure 6.20
The interfaces in a component diagram for a university enrolment system

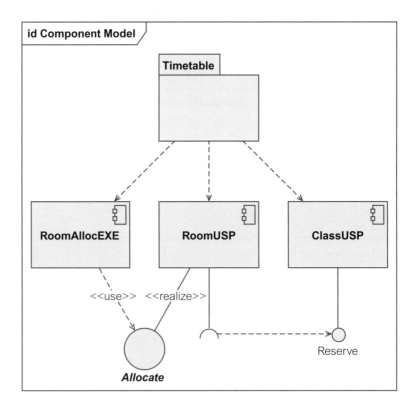

In UML, a *node* is rendered graphically as a cube. The cube can be stereotyped and contain constraints. The stereotyped cube can be an icon. Every node is given a unique name (a textual string).

A **deployment** diagram shows the nodes and how they relate to each other. Nodes can be related by *associations*, and these can be named to indicate the network protocol used (if applicable) or to characterize the connection in some other way. Also, as with any association, the association between nodes can be modeled showing typical association properties, such as the degree, multiplicity and roles.

Figure 6.21 shows four nodes in a deployment diagram. The connection relationships indicate the form the communication between the nodes takes.

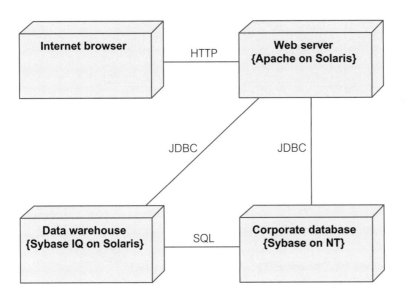

Figure 6.21
Nodes

Nodes are the locations of the hardware on which the components run. Nodes execute components. Components are deployed on a node. A node together with its components is sometimes called a *distribution unit* (Booch et al. 1999).

Figure 6.22 shows two graphical notations for a node with components deployed on it (or contained in it). The node called `Corporate Database` runs two stored procedures, which are represented as the components `CustomerUSP` and `InvoiceUSP`. The "containment" notation can be extended so that the entire component diagram can be placed on a deployment diagram.

Review quiz 6.3

RQ1 What kinds of relationships are used to relate packages?

RQ2 Does a component have a persistent state?

RQ3 Can a class be implemented by more than one component?

Figure 6.22
A node with
deployed/contained
components

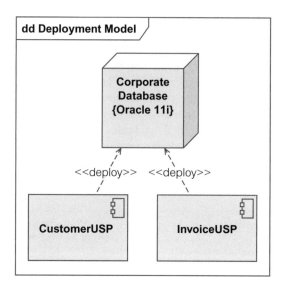

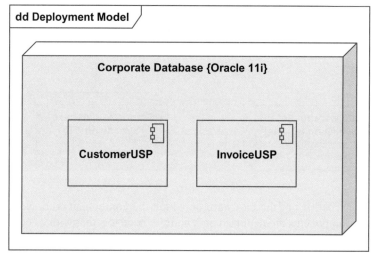

6.4 Principles of program design and reuse

Program design is an intrinsic part of overall system design. The *architectural design* (Sections 4.1 and 6.1–6.3) establishes the generic execution framework. The *detailed design* of the GUI and database specifies the front end and the back end of that framework. The program design fills in the gaps in this generic framework and leads to a design document that can be handed over to a programmer for implementation.

Program design concentrates on one application program at a time. In this sense, it is a direct extension of *user interface design*, discussed in Chapter 7. Program design is also an extension of *database design*, discussed in Chapter 8. In particular, the procedural aspects of database design, which include stored procedures and triggers, are inherently related to program design.

The program's execution logic is split between the client and the server processes. The *client process* embodies most of the dynamic object collaboration in the program. A proper balance between object cohesion and coupling can harness the complexity of that collaboration. The *server process* takes care, among other things, of executing business transactions initiated by the *client process*.

Class cohesion and coupling   6.4.1

In passing, we have identified the main principles of good program design, albeit more in the context of overall system design and in the context of architectural design. *Class layering* is the cornerstone of writing understandable, maintainable and scalable programs. The proper use of *inheritance* and *delegation* is necessary to avoid delivering object-oriented programs that become legacy systems the day after deployment to the stakeholders.

A good program design ensures well-balanced **cohesion** and *coupling* of classes. The terms "cohesion" and "coupling" were coined by the structured design methods. However, the terms have a similar connotation and importance in object-oriented design (Larman 2005; Page-Jones 2000; Schach 2005).

Class cohesion is the degree of the inner self-determination of a class. It measures the strength of the class's independence. A highly cohesive class performs one action or achieves a single goal. The stronger the cohesion the better.

Class coupling is the degree of the connections between classes. It measures the class's interdependence. The weaker the coupling the better (however, the classes have to be "coupled" to cooperate!)

Cohesion and coupling are at odds with each other. Better cohesion induces worse coupling, and vice versa. The task of the designer is to achieve the best balance of the two. Riel (1996) proposed a number of heuristics to address this issue:

- two classes should either not depend on one another or one class should depend only on the public interface of another class

- attributes and the related methods should be kept in one class (this heuristic is frequently violated by classes that have many *accessor* (get, set) methods defined in their public interface)

- a class should capture one and only one abstraction – unrelated information, when a subset of methods operates on a proper subset of attributes, should be moved to another class

- the system intelligence should be distributed as uniformly as possible (so that classes share the work uniformly).

A good example of trade-offs between cohesion and coupling was provided by the university enrolment system in Section 4.3.3.3. The example presented two contrasting sequence diagrams – one for a "centralized" solution (Figure 4.18) and the other for a "distributed" solution (Figure 4.19).

From the viewpoint of a proper cohesion/coupling balance, the distributed solution is clearly the winner. It results in better (lower) coupling from CEnroll to the entity classes (while not affecting the degree of coupling within the entity layer, as can be seen in the class diagrams for both solutions in Section 4.3.4.3 – Figures 4.20 and 4.21). It also results in better (higher) cohesion because it avoids turning CEnroll into a so-called *bloated controller* (Larman 2005), which does unrelated tasks and does too much work.

6.4.1.1 Kinds of class coupling

In order for two classes to communicate, they need to be "coupled". *Coupling* between class X and class Y exists if class X can refer *directly* to class Y. Larman (2005: 30) lists six common forms of coupling:

- X contains Y or it has an attribute (data member or instance variable) that refers to an instance of Y
- X has a method that references an instance of Y by any means, such as it uses a parameter or local variable of type Y or the object of type Y was returned to it from a message
- X calls on services of (sends messages to) Y
- X is a direct or indirect subclass of Y
- X has a method with an input argument of class Y
- Y is an interface and X implements that interface.

6.4.1.2 The Law of Demeter

Class coupling is necessary for object communication, but it should be confined, as much as possible, to *within* the class layers – that is, to *intralayer coupling*. *Interlayer coupling* should be minimized and carefully channeled. A point of additional guidance for restricting the arbitrary communication between classes is offered in the *Law of Demeter* – known in the popular formulations as "don't talk to strangers" and "talk only to your friends" (Lieberherr and Holland 1989).

The **Law of Demeter** specifies what targets are allowed for the messages within the class methods. It states that the target of a message can only be one of the following objects (Larman 2005; Page-Jones 2000):

- the method's object itself – that is, this in C# and Java, self and super in Smalltalk
- an object that is an argument in the method's signature
- an object referred to by the object's attribute (including an object referred to within a collection of attributes)
- an object created by the method
- an object referred to by a global variable.

To restrict the coupling induced by inheritance, the third rule can be limited to the attributes defined in the class itself. An attribute inherited by the class cannot then be used to identify a target object for the message. This constraint is known as the *Strong Law of Demeter* (Page-Jones 2000).

In practical terms, the Law of Demeter enforces only the recommendations of good architectural design (Section 6.2) and the principles of architectural frameworks (Section 4.1.3.2). In particular, the NCP (neighbor communication) principle is realized by applying the Law of Demeter to classes in neighboring layers – "friends". "Strangers" are non-neighboring layers. Remember, though, that in many architectures (including PCBMER), a layer can have more than one neighboring layer.

Accessor methods and mindless classes 6.4.1.3

As mentioned in Section 6.4.1, attributes and the related methods should be kept in one class (Riel 1996). A class should decide its own destiny. A class can restrict other classes from accessing its own state by limiting the accessor methods in its interface. **Accessor methods** define the **observer** (get) or **mutator** (set) operations.

Accessor methods "open up" a class to internal manipulation by other classes. While coupling implies access to other classes, an excessive availability of accessor methods may lead to a non-uniform distribution of intelligence among classes. A class with many accessor methods risks becoming *mindless* – other classes decide what is good for it.

This said, there are situations when a class has to open up to other classes. This happens whenever there is a need to implement a policy between two or more classes (Riel 1996). Examples abound.

Suppose that we have two classes, `Integer` and `Real`, and we need to implement a "policy" for the conversion of integer and real numbers. In which of the two classes is the policy to be implemented? Do we need a `Converter` class to implement the policy? Either way, at least one of these two classes must allow accessor methods, and it will then become "mindless" with regard to that policy.

A famous quote from Page-Jones (at OOPSLA'87) is appropriate:

On an object-oriented farm there is an object-oriented milk. Should the object-oriented cow send the object-oriented milk the uncow_yourself message, or should the object-oriented milk send the object-oriented cow the unmilk_yourself message?"

Example 6.9: university enrolment

Assume that we need to add a student to a course offering. To do so, we need to do two checks. First, we have to find out the prerequisite courses for that course offering. Second, we have to check the student's academic record to establish whether or not the student satisfies the prerequisites. With this knowledge, we can decide whether the student can be added to the course offering or not.

Consider that a message `enrol()` is to be sent by a control object `CEnroll`. Consider that three classes – `ECourseOffering`, `ECourse` and `EStudent` – *collaborate* to accomplish the task. `EStudent` knows how to get the academic record and `ECourse` knows how to find its prerequisites.

Our task is to design a range of possible interaction diagrams to solve the problem. Discuss the pros and cons of different solutions.

Figure 6.23 illustrates the first solution to the task detailed in Example 6.9 by means of both a sequence diagram and a communication diagram. The control object CEnroll initiates the transaction by sending the enrol() message to ECourse. ECourse asks EStudent for the academic record and checks it against its prerequisites. ECourse decides if EStudent can or can't be enrolled and requests that ECourseOffering adds EStudent to its list of students if he or she can be.

The scenario in Figure 6.23 gives too much power to the class ECourse. ECourse is the policy maker and EStudent is mindless. The solution is unbalanced, but there is no clear way out.

We could switch the emphasis from ECourse to EStudent, obtaining the solution presented in Figure 6.24. Now CEnroll asks EStudent to do the main job. EStudent invokes the observer method getPrereq() on ECourse. EStudent decides whether or not the enrolment is possible and instructs ECourseOffering to enroll the student if it is.

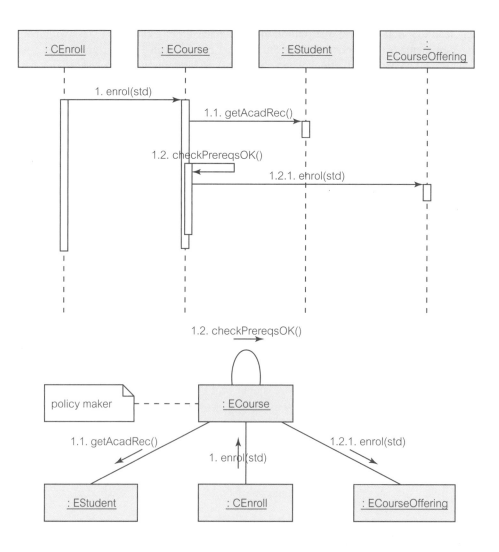

Figure 6.23
ECourse as policy maker for a university enrolment system

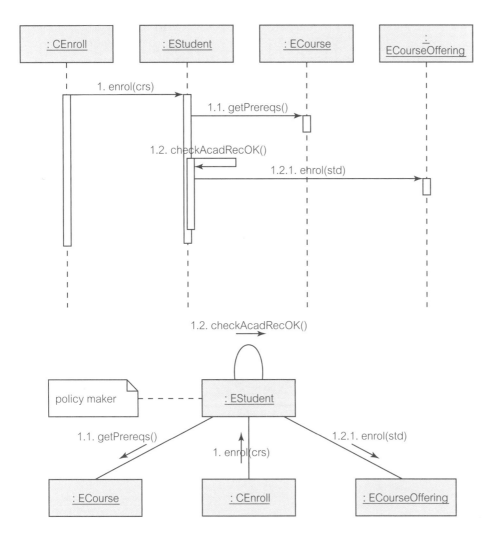

Figure 6.24
EStudent as
policy maker for a
university
enrolment system

Figure 6.25 illustrates a more balanced solution in which ECourseOffering is the policy maker. The solution is impartial with regard to ECourse *and* EStudent, but it does make these two objects quite idle and mindless. ECourseOffering acts like the "main program" (a *"God" class* in Riel's parlance (1996)).

All the solutions so far have been *distributed* in nature, very much as advocated in Section 4.3.3.3. A *centralized* solution is also possible. Such a solution could rely on CEnroll as the policy maker. However, a better approach would be to have a separate class for the task. Such a class could be placed in the PCBMER's *mediator* layer and called MEnrolmentPolicy.

The mediator class MEnrolmentPolicy in Figure 6.26 decouples the three entity classes from the enrolment policy. This is beneficial because any changes to the enrolment policy are encapsulated in a single mediator class. However, there is a risk that the class MEnrolmentPolicy can grow into a "God" class.

Figure 6.25
ECourseOffering
as policy maker for
a university
enrolment system

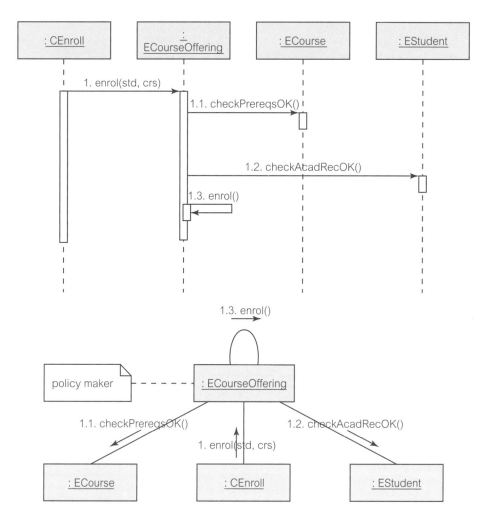

6.4.1.4 Dynamic classification and mixed-instance cohesion

In Appendix, Section A.7.5, we raise the issue of *dynamic classification* and observe that the popular object-oriented programming environments do not support it. The price for this lack of support is frequently reflected in designing classes with *mixed-instance cohesion*.

Page-Jones (2000) states that "a class with *mixed-instance cohesion* has some features that are undefined for some objects of the class." Some methods of the class apply only to a subset of objects in that class and some attributes make sense only for a subset of objects. For example, the class Employee may define objects that are "ordinary" employees and managers. A manager is paid an allowance. Sending a message payAllowance() to an Employee object does not make sense if that Employee object is not a manager.

To eliminate mixed-instance cohesion, we need to extend the generalization hierarchy to identify Employee subclasses, such as OrdinaryEmployee and Manager. However,

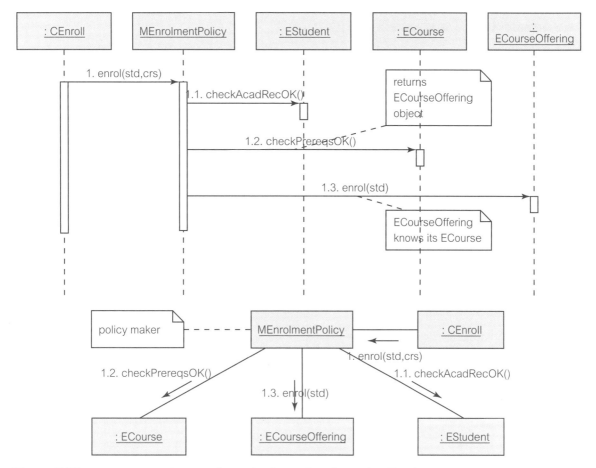

Figure 6.26 MEnrolmentPolicy as policy maker for a university enrolment system

an Employee object may be an OrdinaryEmployee at some point in time and a Manager at another time or vice versa. To eliminate the mixed-instance cohesion, we need to allow objects to change classes dynamically at run-time – the proverbial Catch-22 situation, if the dynamic classification is not supported.

To eliminate the mixed-instance cohesion mentioned in Example 6.10 (overleaf), we need to specialize Student into two subclasses, PartTimeStudent and FullTimeStudent (Figure 6.27). If every student must be either part-time *or* full-time, then the class Student is *abstract*. The message payExtraFee(crsoff) will never be sent to an object of class FullTimeStudent, because FullTimeStudent does not have a method for it.

Granted, we still have a problem. A part-time student may have a preference for day-time course offerings – that is, eveningPreference = 'False' – and no extra fees are then paid. In other words, we still have *mixed-instance cohesion* in PartTimeStudent. Sending a message payExtraFee(crsoff) to a PartTimeStudent will not make sense if the student takes a daytime course offering.

Example 6.10: university enrolment

Consider the following variations for Example 6.9 above:

- evening course offerings are available only to part-time students
- full-time students may enroll only in daytime course offerings
- there is a small extra fee if a part-time student wants to enroll in an evening course offering
- a part-time student is automatically considered full-time when enrolled in courses providing more than six credit points (more than two course offerings, for example, if each course is worth three credit points) in a given semester and vice versa.

Our task is to propose a highly cohesive class model but with no mixed-instance cohesion. The model should then be critically appraised and an alternative solution that avoids the problem of dynamic classification should be suggested and discussed.

Figure 6.27
A class model
eliminating mixed-
instance cohesion
for a university
enrolment system

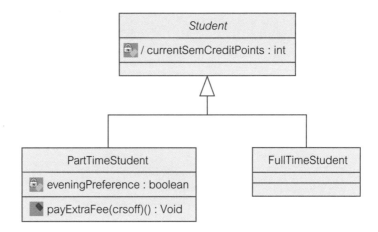

Figure 6.28 extends the design to eliminate this second example of mixed-instance cohesion. The class `DayPrefPartTimeStudent` does not have the method `payExtraFee(crsoff)`. However, what if a `DayPrefPartTimeStudent` is *forced* to take an evening course offering because there are no more places available in daytime course offerings? Perhaps some other fee would then apply. Should we specialize further to derive a class `UnluckyDayPrefPartTimeStudent`?

Short of getting into ridiculous situations, we may opt to abandon the idea of pushing the elimination of mixed-instance cohesion any further. We have not even mentioned the dynamic classification yet. In reality, the current value of the attribute `currentSemCreditPoints` determines if a student is part-time or full-time.

Similarly, a student can change his or her preference for the evening or daytime course offerings at any time. In the absence of the programming environment's support for *dynamic classification*, it would be a programmer's responsibility to allow an object to change the class at run-time. That's tough – very tough in the case of persistent objects with OID values containing class identifiers.

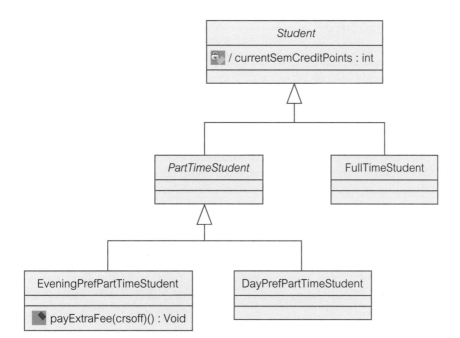

Figure 6.28
A class model
eliminating
another aspect of
mixed-instance
cohesion for a
university
enrolment system

The alternative is to restrict the depth of the inheritance hierarchy, eliminate the need for dynamic classification and reintroduce a certain amount of mixed-instance cohesion. For example, we can hang on to the class model in Figure 6.27 and resolve the problem of the evening preference by allowing an object to respond differently to the message payExtraFee(crsoff) depending on the value of the attribute eveningPreference. This can be programmed with an if statement, as shown in the following pseudo-code:

```
method payExtraFee(crsoff) for the class PartTimeStudent
if eveningPreference = 'False'
     return
else
     do it
end method
```

Although the use of if statements in object-oriented code signifies an abandoning of inheritance and polymorphism, it may be unavoidable for purely pragmatic reasons. Rather than struggle with *dynamic classification*, the programmer introduces the *dynamic semantics* to a class. An object responds differently to the same message depending on its current local state. A state machine diagram would be used to design the dynamic semantics for the class. Admittedly, the *cohesion* of the class suffers in the process.

6.4.2 Reuse strategy

UML defines **reuse** as "the use of a pre-existing artifact" (Rumbaugh et al. 2005: 575). In passing, we discussed the object-oriented *techniques* for software reuse, such as inheritance and delegation (Sections 5.2 and 5.3). We also indicated that painting the implementation inheritance as an indispensable feature of object orientation and the main reuse technique is a dangerous practice. To quote again Rumbaugh et al. (2005: 575), "Bear in mind that reuse can occur through other means than inheritance, including copying of code. One of the great errors in modeling is to force inappropriate generalization in an attempt to achieve reuse, which instead often causes confusion."

In this section, we address the *strategies* of software reuse. It turns out that the strategies also imply the granularity at which the reuse is done. The *granularity* can be the:

- class
- component
- solution idea

Associated with granularity, there are three corresponding strategies for reuse (Coad et al. 1995; Gamma et al. 1995):

- toolkits (class libraries)
- frameworks
- analysis and design patterns.

6.4.2.1 Toolkit reuse

A *toolkit* emphasizes *code reuse* at a *class* level. In this kind of reuse, the programmer "fills the gaps" in the program by making calls to *concrete classes* in some library of classes. The main body of the program is not reused – it is written by the programmer.

There are two kinds (levels) of toolkit (Page-Jones 2000):

- foundation toolkits
- architecture toolkits.

The *foundation classes* are widely provided by object programming environments. They include classes to implement primitive data types (such as `String`), structured data types (such as `Date`) and collections (such as `Set`, `List` or `Index`).

The *architecture classes* are normally available as part of system software, such as an operating system, database software or GUI software. For example, when we buy an object database system, what we really get is an architecture toolkit that implements the expected functionalities of the system, such as persistency, transactions and concurrency.

6.4.2.2 Framework reuse

A *framework* emphasizes design reuse at a component level (Sections 3.6.2 and 6.3.2). As opposed to toolkit reuse, a framework provides the skeleton of the program. The programmer then "fills the gaps" in this skeleton (customizes it) by writing the code that the framework needs to call. Apart from concrete classes (for the framework itself), a framework provides a large volume of abstract classes to be implemented (customized) by the programmer.

A framework is a customizable application software. The best examples of frameworks are ERP (enterprise resource planning systems) such as SAP, PeopleSoft, Baan or J.D. Edwards. However, the reuse in those systems is not based on pure object-oriented techniques.

Object-oriented frameworks for IS development are proposed within distributed component technologies, such as J2EE/EJB and .NET. They are known as *business objects* – "shippable" products to meet specific business or application needs. For example, a business object could be an accounting framework with customizable classes, such as `Invoice` or `Customer`.

While frameworks are an attractive reuse proposition, they also have a number of drawbacks. Perhaps the most significant one is that the generic, lowest common denominator solutions that they deliver are suboptimal or even obsolete. As a result, they do not give a competitive advantage to their adopters and can create a maintenance burden when chasing state-of-the-art solutions.

Pattern reuse 6.4.2.3

Patterns emphasize reuse in the course of the development approach (Section 6.2.2). They provide ideas and examples of object interactions that are known to represent good development practices, leading to understandable and scalable solutions. Patterns can apply to the analysis phase of the development lifecycle, the architectural design or detailed design. Hence, *analysis patterns*, *architectural patterns* and *design patterns* (in a more general sense, design patterns include architectural patterns).

A *pattern* is a documented solution that has been shown to work well in a number of situations. These situations have been identified and can be used as an index entry for the developer seeking a solution to a problem. Any known disadvantages or side-effects of a pattern are listed to allow the developer to make informed decisions.

Pattern reuse is largely conceptual, though many design patterns contain sample code for the programmer's reuse. The *scope* of a *design pattern* (Gamma et al. 1995, for example) is that of an interaction sequence – typically larger than a class but smaller than a component. The *scope* of an *analysis pattern* (Fowler 1997, for instance) depends on the level of modeling abstraction at which the pattern applies.

Review quiz 6.4

RQ1 What term is used to define the degree of inner self-determination of a class?

RQ2 Mixed-instance cohesion results from a particular weakness of object-oriented programming environments. What is that weakness?

RQ3 What can design reuse at the component level be called?

6.5 Collaboration modeling

The *architectural design* makes an impact on the *detailed design* in that it determines the target hardware/software platform that the detailed design must conform to. Apart from that, the detailed design is a direct continuation of the analysis. The objective is to turn the analysis models into detailed design documents from which the programmers can implement the system.

In *analysis*, we simplify the models by abstracting away the details that interfere with the presentation of a particular viewpoint on the system. In *design*, we tend to do exactly the opposite. We take one architectural part of the system at a time and add technical details to the models or create brand new design models at a low level of abstraction.

In passing, we have used the term **collaboration** freely, sometimes interchangeably with the term *interaction*, to refer to sets of objects collaborating to perform a task. Historically in UML, the meaning of the term "collaboration" has been underspecified and changed between versions. Starting from UML 2.0, the notion of collaboration has become more precise and been placed within the context of so-called **composite structures**. The term *composite structure* refers to "a composition of interconnected elements, representing run-time instances collaborating over communications links to achieve some common objectives" (UML 2005: 157). Composite structures can be modeled in separate *composite structure diagrams*.

6.5.1 Collaboration

A *collaboration* describes a structure of collaborating elements (roles), each performing a specialized function, which collectively accomplish some desired functionality. Its primary purpose is to explain how a system works and, therefore, it typically only incorporates those aspects of reality that are deemed relevant to the explanation... A collaboration is represented as a kind of classifier and defines a set of cooperating entities to be played by instances (its roles), as well as a set of connectors that define communication paths between the participating instances.

(UML 2005: 164)

As shown in Figure 6.29, a collaboration is visualized as a dashed ellipse with a collaboration *name* and rectangular icons representing the cooperating entities (*roles*). The roles are connected by *connectors*. Although a collaboration is itself a classifier, it typically describes the structure and behavior of some other classifier, such as a use case, class, interaction fragment, activity. The name of that classifier can then be noted, following the name of the collaboration, as demonstrated in Figure 6.29.

A *role* may have a *type* to which the instances of the role are bound. The type is a classifier, typically a class. Showing the type of the role is optional. Roles are meaningful only within a collaboration and the same object/instance can play different roles in different collaborations.

Similarly, a *connector* – being a relationship between two roles – is meaningful only within a collaboration. The connector "may be an instance of an association, or it may

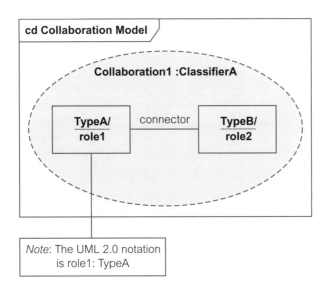

Figure 6.29
Collaboration
notation

represent the possibility of the instances being able to communicate because their identities are known by virtue of being passed in as parameters, held in variables or slots, or because the communicating instances are the same instance. The link may be realized by something as simple as a pointer or by something as complex as a network connection. In contrast to associations, which specify links between any instance of the associated classifiers, connectors specify links between instances playing the connected parts only" (UML 2005: 170).

Example 6.11: university enrolment

Consider Example 6.9 in Section 6.4.1.3, referring to the activity of enrolling a student on a course by adding that student to an offering (a class) of that course. Consider the business (entity) objects identified in the solutions to Example 6.9. Draw a collaboration model for the enrolment activity by specifying the roles that the business objects play and the connectors between these roles.

Figure 6.30 shows the collaboration named `Enrolment`, drawn in answer to the task set in Example 6.11. The collaboration consists of three roles – `/student`, `/course to enroll` and `/class to attend`. The last two roles have their types (classes) specified. Each role is connected to the two other roles.

Composite structure   6.5.2

UML 2.0 offers an alternative notation to model collaborations for situations in which the types (classifiers) of the roles are explicit. This notation is shown in Figure 6.31. Although labeled in UML 2.0 as merely an alternative notation, the explicit representa-

Figure 6.30
Collaboration
model for a
university
enrolment system

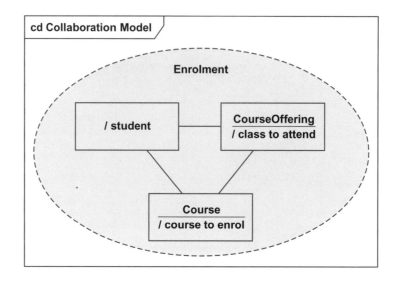

tion of classes leads to the creation of a kind of a class diagram, called in UML 2.0 a *composite structure diagram*.

Example 6.12: university enrolment

Consider Example 6.11 in Section 6.5.1, which shows a collaboration for the enrolment activity. Draw a corresponding composite structure diagram.

Converting a collaboration into a composite structure for Example 6.12 is as simple as extracting all the roles from the collaboration ellipse into the classes (thus defining any missing types for the roles), connecting the collaboration to the classes and defining the role names for all connectors. Because composite structures are frequently modeled in parallel with interaction diagrams, the properties (in particular the methods) can be named within classes/interfaces. Figure 6.32 is the result of this conversion applied to Figure 6.30.

Figure 6.31
Composite
structure notation

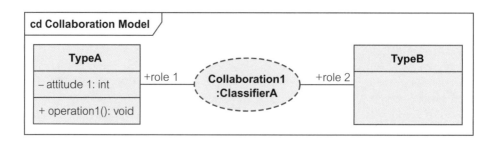

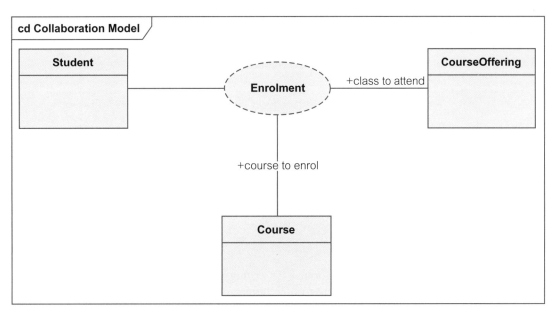

Figure 6.32 Composite structure for a university enrolment system

A composite structure is particularly useful for representing a collaboration as a reusable *pattern* (Sections 6.2.2 and 6.4.2.3). To put it another way, patterns can be documented using composite structures. The collaboration is then the name of the pattern. The classes/interfaces, together with their properties, define the pattern structure. Any additional rules describing the pattern behavior can be shown as constraints (possibly within the notes).

From use case to composite collaboration   6.5.3

Collaborations can be specified for classifiers at various levels of abstraction and can, therefore, represent both analysis *and* design models. Corresponding to successive layers of collaborations is the possibility of modeling collaborations as compositions of other collaborations. A *composite collaboration* consists of (is implemented in terms of) *subordinate collaborations*. Each subordinate collaboration can in turn be a composite collaboration for other subordinate collaborations. Visually, a composite collaboration can be shown as in Figure 6.33.

In one of its most useful incarnations, a composite collaboration can represent a use case and subordinate collaborations can represent requirements of the use case. As explained in Sections 3.1 and 4.3.1, use cases draw their strength from text descriptions of flows of events, not from the graphical visualization of use cases in diagrams. Without undermining this fact, composite collaboration models can show a nested structure of subflows and requirements of a use case. Each subordinate collaboration can be later specified in its own collaboration and/or composite structure model.

Figure 6.33
Composite
collaboration
notation

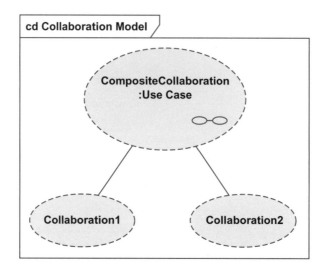

There are many possible formats for writing a use case document. Section 3.1.4 presented one such format. Irrespective of the format, a use case document must be detailed enough to answer most, if not all, a programmer's questions. To assist in this task, use case documents are sometimes supplemented with the sketches of GUI designs.

Example 6.13: advertising expenditure

Refer to the exercises for advertising expenditure measurement at the ends of Chapters 2 and 5. In particular, the category–product GUI window in Figure 5.31 (Exercises: advertising expenditure, end of Chapter 5) can help in understanding the context of this example.

The AE system measures the expenditure (costs) for advertising various products via different media. To do it properly, the AE system must maintain a coherent list of products, classify the products into categories and recognize various brand names of products.

Table 6.1 is a use case document for maintaining product information in the AE system. Because typical maintenance activities consist of four operations – create, read, update and delete product data – the use case is named *CRUD Product*. As is the case with many use case documents, the document in Table 6.1 is supplemented with a design for a GUI window.

Our task in this example is to draw a composite collaboration for the use case CRUD Product. Only one level of collaboration nesting needs to be shown.

Table 6.1 Use case document for CRUD Product for an advertising expenditure system

Use case	CRUD Product
Brief description	This use case enables the user of the AE system to maintain information about products. It includes facilities to view (read) a list of products, create a new product, delete a product and update the information about a product
Actors	`Data Collection Employee`, `Data Verification Employee`, `Valorization Employee`, `Reporting Employee`
Preconditions	The actor possesses system privileges to maintain products. Any `Employee` can view a list of products. Only a `Data Collection Employee` and a `Data Verification Employee` can create, update or delete products
Main flow	***1 Basic flow*** This use case starts when an `Employee` chooses to work with `Products` by selecting the `Maintain Products` option of the AE system The system retrieves and displays the following information for all products in a browse window. The `Read Products` subflow is performed The `Data Collection Employee` or `Data Verification Employee` can choose to create, update or delete a product. A corresponding dialog box window is displayed consisting of a group of fields. Non-editable fields are grayed and the cursor cannot be placed on them Most fields have names (prompts). The fields display the following information: `product_id, product_name, category_name, brand_name, product_status, created_by, last_modified_by, created_on, last_modified_on, notes` The dialog box window does not have an associated menu – events are activated by the command buttons: "ok" and "cancel". The "ok" button applies the values in the window to the database and closes the window. The "cancel" button ignores all changes, cancels the operation the user chose and closes the window There are three operation modes of dialog box window: `Insert Product`, `Update Product` and `Delete Product` The `Record` menu in the main menu bar is a principal way of opening a dialog box window in a particular mode. The corresponding toolbar buttons provide for accelerated opening of a dialog box window The dialog box window is modal – the user has to complete interaction within this window and close it before continuing with any further interaction outside the window Navigation between fields can be done from the keyboard by pressing "tab" (next field) and "shift+tab" (previous field). Pressing "enter" navigates to the default command button – the "ok" button If the `Data Collection and Verification Supervisor` chooses to create a new product, the `Create Product` subflow is performed If the `Data Collection and Verification Supervisor` chooses to modify information about a product, the `Update Product` subflow is performed If the `Data Collection and Verification Supervisor` chooses to delete a product, the `Delete Product` subflow is performed If the `Quality Control Person` chooses to exit, the use case ends

Table 6.1 (cont'd)

Use case	CRUD Product

2 Subflows

2.1 Read products
The following information is displayed in the AE row browser window: `product_name`, `category_name`, `notes`, `created_by`, `last_modified_by`, `created_on`, `last_modified_on`

The information is displayed in a tabular (columns and rows) view, with vertical and horizontal scroll bars, if necessary

The display is named `Products` and all columns are named

The order of columns on screen can be changed (using a drag and drop action)

The user can add more columns to the browser (using a right-click pop-up menu from the column bar). Optional columns that can be added are `product_id`, `category_id`, `brand_id`, `brand_name`, `product_status`

The user can remove any column from the browser except `product_name` (using a right-click pop-up menu from the column bar)

The values displayed in the rows are not editable. Double-clicking on the row opens up an `Update Product` window

Rows can be sorted on two designated columns – `product_name` and `product_id`. Sort columns are distinguished visually from other columns. The current sort column is also visually distinct

2.2 Create product
The system displays the `CreateProduct` dialog box window

The non-editable fields are `product_id`, `created_by`, `last_modified_by`, `created_on`, `last_modified_on`. These fields have prompts but no values

The value of the `product_id` field is automatically assigned by the database's identifier creation capability when a product is inserted into the database

The editable fields are `product_name`, `category_name`, `brand_name`, `product_status`, `notes`

The fields that allow values to be typed in are `product_name and notes`

The fields that allow a value to be selected from a database picklist (which opens by clicking at the down-arrow button) are `category_name`, `brand_name`, `product_status`

Alternative flows are `AF1`, `AF2`

2.3 Update product
The system displays the `Update Product` dialog box window and displays the product name in the title bar

The non-editable fields are `product_id`, `created_by`, `last_modified_by`, `created_on`, `last_modified_on`. These fields have prompts and values

The editable fields are `product_name`, `category_name`, `brand_name`, `product_status`, `notes`

Table 6.1 (cont'd)

Use case	CRUD Product
	The fields that allow new values to be typed in are `product_name, notes` The fields that allow a new value to be selected from a database picklist (which opens by clicking at the down-arrow button) are `category_name, brand_name, product_status` Alternative flows are *AF1, AF2, AF4* *2.4 Delete product* The system displays the `Delete Product` dialog box window and displays the product name in the title bar All fields are non-editable and the system displays values in all fields Alternative flows are *AF3, AF4*
Alternative flows	*AF1* The system will not allow a product to be created/updated with a `product_name` that already exists in the database
	AF2 The system will not allow a product to be created/updated without assigning the product to a `category_name` and `brand_name`
	AF3 The system will not allow a product linked to adlinks to be deleted
	AF4 The system will not allow any two update/delete dialog box windows to be opened for the same product by more than one user
Postconditions	After a product has been successfully created/updated, the browser window highlights the row with that product information After a product has been successfully deleted, the browser window is refreshed and highlights the first visible row After the user exits from the use case, the `Products` window is closed

Constructing a composite collaboration model for the detailed use case description as given above is a simple exercise in treating the use case as a composite collaboration and extracting subflows into subordinate collaborations. This is shown in Figure 6.34.

From collaboration to interaction   6.5.4

A collaboration defines connectors over which the roles exchange messages, but it does not identify messages per se. The specification of message flows within the collaboration is the domain of interaction models. Consequently, collaborations can be used as a stepping stone for the production of sequence and communication diagrams. To do so, collaboration roles become *lifelines* on the sequence diagrams and the connectors are replaced by *messages* in an interaction.

Figure 6.34
Composite
collaboration
model for an
advertising
expenditure
system

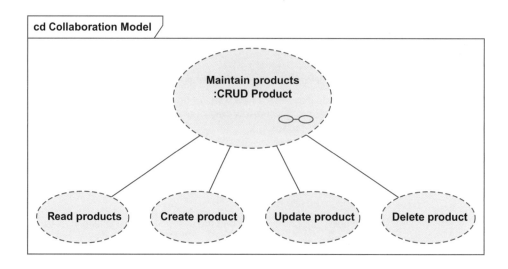

Example 6.14: advertising expenditure

Refer to Example 6.13 (Section 6.5.3) and the Update Product window in Figure 6.35. Consider also the *Update Product* subflow in the use case document in Table 6.1. Assume a scenario for the `Update Product` subflow restricted to the following actions: 1 a new update product window is launched from the product browser window (a primary window that lists the products); 2 initialize editable fields in the window (ignore non-editable fields), 3 assume that only the `categoryName` field is updated and 4 the user clicks the "ok" button to save changes.

Create a collaboration model for the update product scenario as described. Use stereotypes for roles to identify the PCBMER architectural layers to which the roles belong. Assume that the collaboration requires only roles in three layers – presentation, control and entity. Use dependency arrows on connectors to demonstrate the downward communication principle (DCP) of the PCBMER architecture.

Figure 6.36 presents a collaboration model for Example 6.14. The model identifies seven roles – two in the presentation layer, two in the control layer and three in the entity layer. The collaboration shows that the `product browser` role (product browser window) instantiates the `single product` role (update product window). The connector from `/single product` to the `/data getter` role is used to populate the update product window with the information from the business objects of type `Product`, `Brand`, and `Category`.

The connector from `/single product` to the `/data setter` role is used to update the business objects `Product` and `Category` after the `categoryName` for the product has been changed in the update product window. Because the `categoryName` identifies a new `Category` object that the `Product` object links to, the change of the `categoryName` means really a relinking of `Product` and `Category` – that is, the `Product` needs to be linked to another `Category` and vice versa, the `Category` concerned must now have a link to that `Product`.

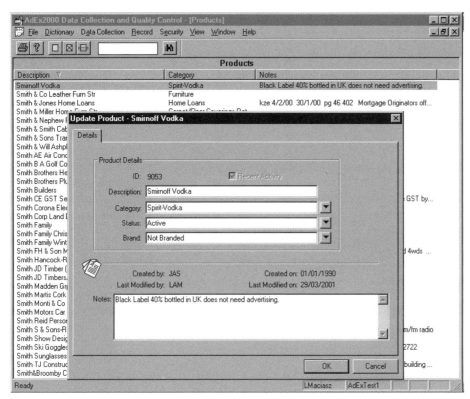

Figure 6.35
Update Product
window for an
advertising
expenditure
system
Source: Courtesy of
Nielsen Media
Research, Sydney,
Australia

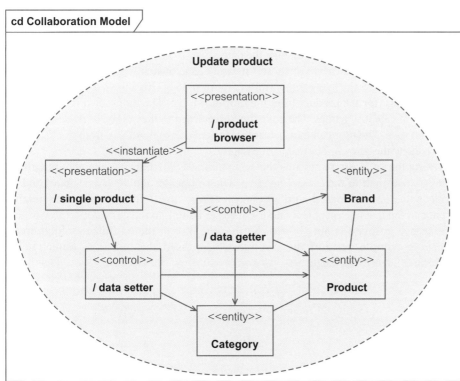

Figure 6.36
Collaboration
model for an
advertising
expenditure
system

Example 6.15: advertising expenditure

Refer to Example 6.14 above and to the update product window in Figure 6.35 (there is no need to be concerned about the `Status` and `Notes` fields). Consider the collaboration model for the update product scenario shown in Figure 6.36 and described in the answer to Example 6.14.

Use the collaboration model to develop a sequence diagram for the same scenario. Explain your interaction model and comment on how the model would change (improve) if a bean object(s) were allowed.

The sequence diagram for the update product scenario requested in Example 6.15 is shown in Figure 6.37. The roles of the collaboration model serve now as lifelines of the sequence diagram. The diagram uses the popular icons to represent presentation, control and entity objects.

The /`product browser` lifeline instantiates a /`single product` lifeline – that is, an update product window with no data content. However, the constructor is passed the `Product` object in the `new()` message. The /`single product` has to get the data to display in its window. It asks the /`data getter` in three separate messages to return `ProductName` (for the `Description` field), `categoryName` (for the `Category` field) and `BrandName` (for the `Brand` field). The /`data getter` responds by accessing the three entity objects to get the data. Prior to getting `categoryName` and `BrandName`, the /`data getter` obtains from the `Product` object references to the `Category` and `Brand` objects.

Sending three separate messages from /`single product` to /`data getter` is clearly a substandard solution. To improve it, a bean object would need to be introduced to hold all the data needed by the update product window for rendering on the screen. Such a bean object could be instantiated as empty by the /`single product`, passed to the /`data getter` and then populated with data by the /`data getter`. The /`single product` would get the bean to display the data.

The `populateCategoryList()` self-message is activated when the user presses the down-arrow next to the `Category` field (Figure 6.35). This allows the user to select another category for the product from the drop-down list. The drop-down list is a collection (a list) of category names. The collection is returned to the /`single product` by the /`data getter`. The user can then select the desired `CategoryName` from the list, which is displayed by the `showSelected()` message.

Clicking the `OK` button activates the `saveChanges()` message, which contains the `updateLink()` call to the /`data setter`. The call passes the `Product` object and the `categoryName` value. Based on the `CategoryName`, the `Product` object can obtain a reference to the `Category` object and use it to set its link to the `Category` (how exactly the reference is found is not shown). Setting the link in the `Category` object to the `Product` is simple because the `Category` is passed the `Product` object in the `setProductLink()` message.

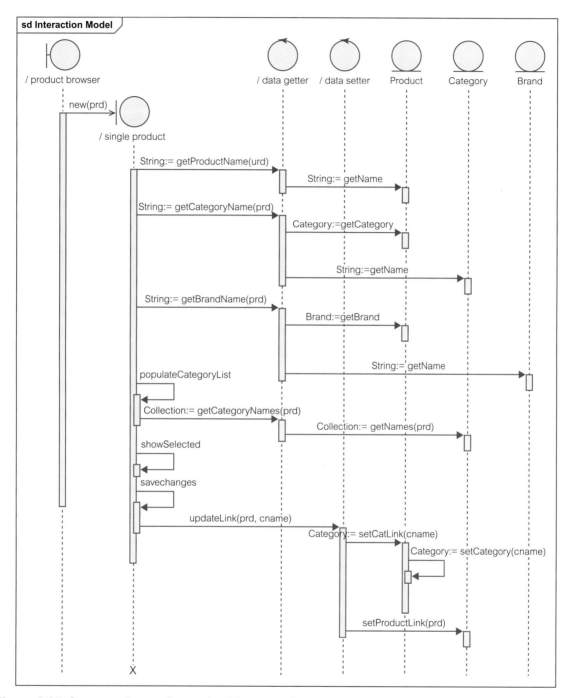

Figure 6.37 Sequence diagram for an advertising expenditure system

6.5.5 From interaction to composite structure

Collaboration has a behavioral and a structural part. The structural part represents the static aspect of collaboration. It can be shown in a *composite structure diagram* – a kind of a class diagram corresponding to the scope of collaboration. In a typical manifestation, relationships between classes are not depicted in composite structure diagrams. However, these diagrams are normally "elaborated" with other implementation details. In particular, the signatures of class/interface operations can be stated. The operations can be naturally obtained from an interaction model designed for the collaboration.

Example 6.16: advertising expenditure

Refer to Example 6.15 and to the sequence diagram in Figure 6.37. Use that sequence diagram to construct the corresponding composite structure diagram.

Figure 6.38 is a composite structure diagram obtained by giving proper names to classes and showing the operation signatures in those classes. The operations have been identified from the sequence diagram in Figure 6.37. Otherwise, this composite structure is an enhanced version of the collaboration in Figure 6.36, but with no relationships shown.

Review quiz 6.5

RQ1 In what collaboration model are the roles always typed (have a type explicitly defined)?
RQ2 Do collaboration models identify messages?

Summary

If the previous chapter moved us from analysis to design, this chapter has made it clear that design is about system implementation. The chapter has addressed the two main (and distinct) aspects of design – the architectural design of the system and the detailed design of the programs in the system.

Typical IS applications are based on the *client/server* architectural principle. As much as the C/S principle is sometimes pictured as old hat, it is, in reality, a primary concept in virtually all distributed physical architectures, including *peer-to-peer architecture*. *Multi-tier systems* extend the basic C/S architecture by placing an application/business logic and the Web services on separate tiers. *Database* technologies make an important contribution to modern system architectures.

Modern software systems are very complex. It is important that the modeling solutions simplify and reduce this inherent complexity as much as possible. The most important mechanism for handling software *complexity* is the *hierarchical layering* of system archi-

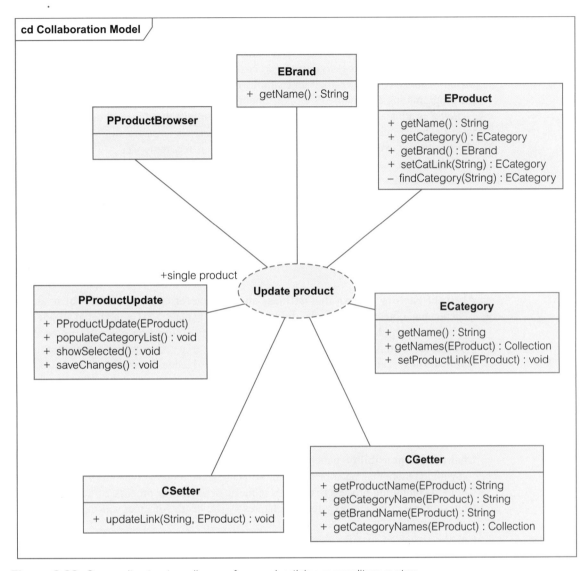

Figure 6.38 Composite structure diagram for an advertising expenditure system

tectures. Proper structuring of classes in *layers* (packages, subsystems), organized according to the PCBMER or similar framework, is an important architectural objective. Layered architectures allow us to reduce the growth of *structural complexity* of software from exponential to polynomial. *Architectural patterns* are essential for enforcing desirable architectural principles in software.

Architectural modeling encompasses the allocation of software elements (classes, interfaces, and so on) to packages, components and nodes. There are intricate dependencies and interactions between these concepts – mostly because they intersect with logical and physical program and data structures.

A well-designed program maximizes *class cohesion* while minimizing *class coupling*. The coupling and cohesion principles can be achieved if the design obeys the *Law of Demeter*, which specifies which object targets for the messages are allowed within the class methods. The excessive use of *accessor methods* can lead to *mindless classes*. *Mixed-instance cohesion*, albeit undesirable, may need to be allowed sporadically because the programming environments do not support *dynamic classification*.

Reuse is a major design consideration affecting architectural as well as detailed design issues. The choices are between *toolkit reuse*, *framework reuse* and *pattern reuse*. The choices are not exclusive – a mix of reuse strategies is recommended.

The detailed design concentrates on *collaborations*. A *collaboration model* specifies collaborating elements (*roles*) and the communication paths (*connectors*) between the roles needed to accomplish a desired functionality. *Composite structure diagrams* can be used to visualize collaborations. There are well-defined mappings between the use cases and collaborations, collaborations and interactions, and interactions and composite structure.

Key terms

Abstract Factory pattern that defines "an interface for creating families of related or dependent objects without specifying their concrete classes" (Gamma et al. 1995: 87).

Accessor method a class method that enables the state of an object to be accessed (*observer* method) or modified from other objects of a program (*mutator* method).

Application server an architectural *tier* that handles business components and also takes care of business rules.

Architecture see *architecture*, Key terms, Chapter 1. "The organizational structure of the system, including its decomposition into parts, their connectivity, interaction mechanisms, and the guiding principles that inform the design of a system" (Rumbaugh et al. 2005: 170).

Chain of Responsibility pattern to "avoid coupling the sender of a request to its receiver by giving more than one object a chance to handle the request" (Gamma et al. 1995: 223)

Client a computing process that makes requests of the *server* process.

Cohesion see *cohesion*, Key terms, Chapter 4. The degree of inner self-determination of the class.

Collaboration "a specification of a contextual relationship among instances that interact within a context to implement a desired functionality" (Rumbaugh et al. 2005: 227)

Complexity a property of software that refers to the difficulty of understanding and managing the software solution because of having a lot of different but related parts.

Component see *component*, Key terms, Chapters 1 and 3. "A modular part of a system design that hides the implementation behind a set of external interfaces" (Rumbaugh et al. 2005: 253).

Composite structure a structure that "describes an interconnection of objects within a context to form an entity with an overall purpose" (Rumbaugh et al., 2005: 264)

Coupling see *coupling*, Key terms, Chapter 4. The degree of connections between classes.

Dependency see *dependency*, Key terms, Chapter 4. A relationship between system parts such as one part needs another part to continue operating.

Deployment "the assignment of software artifacts to physical nodes during execution" (Rumbaugh et al. 2005: 312).

GoF Gang of Four patterns.

Façade pattern that defines "a higher-level interface that makes the subsystem easier to use" and the goal of which is to "minimize the communication and dependencies between subsystems" (Gamma et al. 1995: 185).

Law of Demeter a design guideline that specifies what targets are allowed for the messages within class methods. Its purpose is to restrict allowed communication between objects.

Layer one of several levels in an architectural hierarchy. Similar to tier, but typically implying a logical architectural level.

Mediator pattern that "promotes loose coupling by keeping objects from referring to each other explicitly, and it lets you vary their interaction independently" (Gamma et al. 1995: 273).

Mutator a class method that changes the state of an objecton which it is invoked. Also called a setter.

Node see *node*, Key terms, Chapter 3. "A run-time physical object that represents a computational resource, which generally has at least a memory and often processing capability" (Rumbaugh et al. 2005: 479).

Observer a class method that enables the state of an object to be accessed but does not change its state. Also called a getter.

Observer pattern pattern to "define a one-to-many dependency between objects so that when one object changes state, all its dependents are notified and updated automatically" (Gamma et al. 1995: 293).

Package see *package*, Key terms, Chapter 3. "A general-purpose mechanism for organizing elements into groups, establishing ownership of elements, and providing unique names for referencing elements" (Rumbaugh et al. 2005: 504).

Pattern "a parameterized collaboration that represents a set of roles for parameterized classifiers, relationships, and behavior that can be applied to multiple situations by binding elements from the model (usually classes) to the roles of the pattern" (Rumbaugh et al. 2005: 517).

P2P Peer-to-peer.

Peer a computing process that is free to communicate directly with any other peer, without needing to use a central *server*.

Persistent object an object that lasts beyond the program's execution time because it will be peristently stored in the database before the program exits. Also used for any object already in the database.

Reuse see *reusability*, Key terms, Chapter 2. "The use of a pre-existing artifact" (Rumbaugh et al. 2005: 575).

Server a computing process that services the *client* requests.

Tier one of several levels in an architectural hierarchy. Similar to *layer*, but typically implying a physical architectural level.

Trigger a procedural code that is automatically invoked and executed in response to modifications performed in a database table.

Web server an architectural *tier* responsible for handling the application's control events and GUI presentation.

Multiple-choice test

MC1 Which of the following architectural styles admit the notions of client and server processes?

    a Peer-to-peer architecture.

    b Tiered architecture.

    c Database-centered architecture.

    d All of the above.

MC2 Measuring the effort required to understand the software is called:

    a structural complexity

    b cognitive complexity

    c algorithmic complexity

    d problem complexity.

MC3 Pattern that "promotes loose coupling by keeping objects from referring to each other explicitly, and it lets you vary their interaction independently" is called:

    a observer

    b façade

    c Abstract Factory

    d none of the above.

MC4 Which of the following is another name for an observer object in the Observer pattern?

    a Listener.

    b Spectator.

    c Watcher.

    d Viewer.

MC5 Which of the following cannot be the target of a message within the class method according to the Law of Demeter?

    a An object referred to by a global variable.

    b An object that is an argument in the method's signature.

    c An object referred to by the attribute of an object of an associated class.

    d An object created by the class method.

MC6 Which of the following is not a legitimate artifact of reuse?

    a An object.

    b A class.

    c A solution idea.

    d A component.

MC7 Roles in a collaboration communicate along:

  a associations

  b connectors

  c links

  d relationships.

Questions

Q1 Explain the difference between a distributed processing system and a distributed database system.

Q2 What is a three-tier architecture? What are its advantages and disadvantages?

Q3 What do we mean by an active database?

Q4 What is the structural complexity of a network of nine classes? Draw a hierarchy with four layers for these nine classes. Assume that the dependencies between layers are only downwards. What reduction in complexity is achieved in your four-layer hierarchy?

Q5 Suppose that a class model for a banking application contains a class called `InterestCalculation`. What PCBMER layer does that class belong to? Explain.

Q6 What are the benefits of the Façade pattern? In what circumstances would you use this pattern?

Q7 What are the benefits and drawbacks of the Mediator pattern?

Q8 Explain how the Chain of Responsibility pattern can be used to implement a help system for typical pull-down cascading menus (so that a help information can be provided for menu items).

Q9 How are components and packages related to each other?

Q10 How is the design affected by the principles of class cohesion and coupling?

Q11 What is a "mindless class"?

Q12 Explain the correlations between dynamic classification and mixed-instance cohesion.

Q13 How could we classify message/method types (apart from constructors and destructors)?

Q14 A sender of a message may or may not send itself (its OID) to the target object. Does this statement apply to asynchronous messages? Explain your answer.

Q15 What is the difference between overriding and overloading?

Q16 Compare toolkit and framework reuse.

Q17 Which UML diagrams can be used for designing the behavioral aspect of collaboration?

Q18 Object systems implement the multiplicity of an association link by means of some collection (set, list) of references. In Java, the implementation would normally use the `Collection` interface from a Java library `java.util.Collection`. In C++, the implementation would normally use the notion of a parameterized type known as a class template. Discuss how the associations in class models in Figures 5.12 and 5.13 (Section 5.1.5.1) would be implemented in Java and in C++.

Exercises: video store

Additional requirements

Consider the following additional requirements for a system for a video store (from the end of Chapter 4, repeated here for your convenience).

■ Entertainment media returned late induce a payment equal to an extra rental period. Each entertainment medium has a unique identification number.

■ Entertainment items are ordered from suppliers who are generally able to supply entertainment media within one week. Typically, several entertainment items are ordered in a single order to a supplier.

■ Reservations are accepted for an entertainment item that is on order and/or because all copies of a particular item are rented out. Reservations are also accepted for items that are neither in store nor on order, but a customer is then asked for a deposit of one rental period.

■ Customers can make many reservations, but a separate reservation request is prepared for each entertainment item reserved. A reservation may be canceled due to lack of response from a customer, more precisely one week from the date the customer was contacted to say that the item was available for rental. If a deposit has been paid, it is then credited to the customer's account.

■ The database stores the usual information about suppliers and customers – that is, addresses, phone numbers, and so on. Each order to a supplier identifies the ordered items, media formats and quantities, as well as an expected delivery date, purchase price and applicable discounts.

■ When an entertainment medium is returned by a customer or delivered from a supplier, reservations are satisfied first. This involves contacting the customers who made the reservations. In order to ensure that reservations are properly handled, both the "reserved item has arrived" contact with the customer and the subsequent rental to the customer are related back to the reservation. These steps ensure that reservations are properly carried through.

■ A customer can borrow many media, but each borrowed medium constitutes a separate rental record. For each rental, the check-out, due-in, and return dates and times are recorded. The rental record is later updated to indicate that the medium has been returned and the final payment (or reimbursement) has been made. The clerk who has authorized the rental is also recorded. Details about customers and their rentals are kept for a year to enable customer ratings to be determined based on historical information. Old rental details are kept for auditing purposes for the year.

■ All transactions are made using cash, electronic money transfer or credit cards. Customers are required to pay the rental charges when that entertainment media are checked out.

■ When an entertainment medium item is returned late (or it cannot be returned for whatever reason), a payment is taken either from the customer's account or directly from the customer.

■ If an entertainment medium item is overdue by more than two days, an overdue notice is sent to the customer. Once two overdue notices on a single video-tape or disk have been sent, the customer is noted as delinquent and the next rental is subject to the manager's decision to remove the delinquent rating.

F1 Refer to the additional requirements above, the various examples for a video store system in Chapters 3 and 4 – in particular the use case model in Figure 4.15 (Section 4.3.1.2).

F1a Design a composite collaboration diagram for the "Reserve video" use case.

F1b Design a collaboration diagram for the "Reserve video" use case. Consider only the business objects (entity classes).

F1c Design an interaction diagram for the "Reserve video" use case. Assume that the business objects have been preloaded onto the entity subsystem and the interaction involves only the presentation, control and entity layers. Use architectural patterns as required.

F2 Refer to the requirements above, the various examples for a video store system in Chapters 3 and 4 – in particular to the use case model in Figure 4.15 (Section 4.3.1.2).

F2a Design a composite collaboration diagram for the "Return video" use case.

F2b Design a collaboration diagram for the "Return video" use case. Consider only the business objects (entity classes).

F2c Design an interaction diagram for the "Return video" use case. Assume that the business objects have been preloaded onto the entity subsystem and the interaction involves only the presentation, control and entity layers. Use architectural patterns as required.

F3 Refer to the additional requirements above, the various examples for a video store in Chapters 3 and 4 – in particular the use case model in Figure 4.15 (Section 4.3.1.2).

F3a Design a composite collaboration diagram for the "Order video" use case.

F3b Design a collaboration diagram for the "Order video" use case. Consider only the business objects (entity classes).

F3c Design an interaction diagram for the "Order video" use case. Assume that the business objects have been preloaded onto the entity subsystem and the interaction involves only the presentation, control and entity layers. Use architectural patterns as required.

F4 Refer to the additional requirements above, the various examples for a video store system in Chapters 3 and 4 – in particular to the use case model in Figure 4.15 (Section 4.3.1.2).

F4a Design a composite collaboration diagram for the "Maintain customer" use case.

F4b Design a collaboration diagram for the "Maintain customer" use case. Consider only the business objects (entity classes).

F4c Design an interaction diagram for the "Maintain customer" use case. Assume that the business objects have been preloaded onto the entity subsystem and the interaction involves only the presentation, control and entity layers. Use architectural patterns as required.

Exercises: advertising expenditure

Additional information

Consider the following requirements for the AE system. For the purposes of further analysis, refer to the screenshot in Figure 6.39, which delineates the requirements and provides a visual context for them.

■ The AE system maintains associations between an ad, the product it advertises, the advertiser who pays for the exposure of the ad and the agency responsible for booking that exposure. These associations are called *ad links*. Outlets that have exposed (advertised) the ad can be derived from the descriptions of instances of that ad.

■ The AE system allows the business relationships of an *ad link* to be changed – that is, to change the advertiser, agency or product associated with an ad. This may be done as a simple update when a correction is required (when a human error occurred before, for example). This may also be done as a business change (when a different agency starts booking the ad, for instance). In the latter case, the historical business relationships (historical *ad links*) are retained.

■ The use case "*Relink ad link as correction*" enables the user to modify an ad link by changing its advertiser, agency or product ("relinking an ad" and "modifying an ad link" are conceptually the same function). The use case starts when the user selects an ad link in the Ad link row browser window, uses a mouse right-click to open a pop-up menu and activates the "Modify ad link" menu item.

■ The resulting dialog box window, called "Modify ad links", serves a double purpose of relinking ads as corrections and relinking ads as business changes. Only one of these two options can be activated at a time (by means of the user selecting one of two option buttons provided in the dialog box).

■ The "Modify ad links" window shows the ad link information (copied from the selected ad link in the browser window) and allows the user to change the ad link's agency and/or advertiser and/or product. Only agencies, advertisers and products currently stored on the database can be used for the ad link modification. Any change of agency, advertiser or product is immediately visible in the "Modify ad links" window, but the changes to the database are made only after the user presses the "save" button. The changes can be canceled at any time prior to the user initiating the "save" action.

■ In most circumstances, the modification of an ad link as a correction will be defining a new association of the ad to advertiser, agency and product where the advertiser–agency link has been defined before (in an existing ad link). In cases where a new relationship between the advertiser and agency is being created, only users with the system privileges to perform this task may create the new advertiser–agency link unless the association with the agency is the first for the advertiser (that is, it is a new advertiser that has not been linked to an agency yet).

■ The "Modify ad links" window in Figure 6.39 is shown with the ad link row browser window in the background. The analysis of *both* windows reveals that an ad can be linked several times to the same advertiser/agency/product. There are a few reasons for this being the case, but this exercise does not explain these reasons (apart from the requirement that historical ad links are to be retained on the database). Consequently, there is no expectation that a solution to the exercise will allow the possibility of an ad being linked several times to the same advertiser/agency/product.

■ When the "Modify ad links" screen is opened, all command buttons (except "cancel") and entry fields are disabled until the user selects the "Change mode" "Correction or Business Change" option button. The pane with ad links contains a row with the details of the ad link to be modified. Once the mode has been selected, the user can press a command button "Select Agency", "Select Advertiser", or "Select Product". Each of these command buttons pops up a picklist from which an agency, advertiser or product can be selected into the corresponding fields.

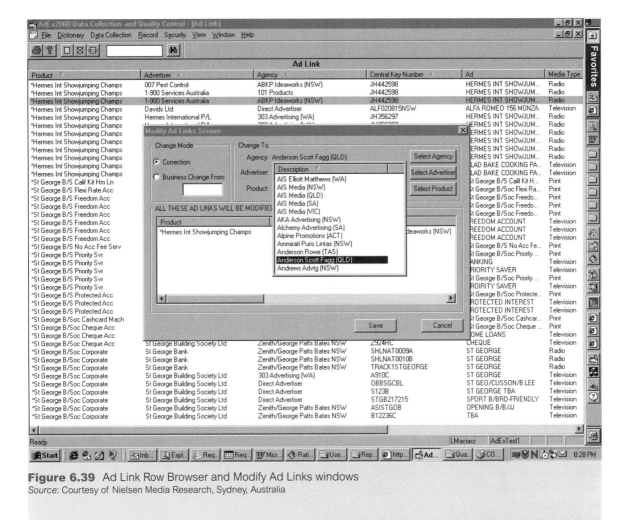

Figure 6.39 Ad Link Row Browser and Modify Ad Links windows
Source: Courtesy of Nielsen Media Research, Sydney, Australia

■ Pressing "Save" modifies the ad's ad link, linking it with a new agency and/or advertiser and/or product. The dialog box is then dismissed and the primary window highlights the modified ad link and shows the corrected information. The "Cancel" button dismisses the dialog box without modifying the ad link.

G1 Draw a composite collaboration model for the part of the AE system described by the above requirements. Explain your model.

G2 Identify business (entity) objects involved in the "*Relink ad link as correction*" use case. Draw a collaboration model for this use case by specifying the roles that the business objects play and the connectors between these roles. Explain your model.

G3 Identify PCBE (presentation, control, bean and entity) objects involved in the "*Relink ad link as correction*" use case – that is, assume that the business objects in the entity layer are an exact image of the persistent database state and there is no need to involve mediator and resource layers). Draw a collaboration model for this use case by specifying the roles that the PCBE play and the connectors between these roles. Use stereotypes for roles to identify the PCBE layers to which the roles belong. Use dependency arrows on connectors to demonstrate the downward communication principle (DCP) of the PCBMER architecture and show object instantiations. Explain your collaboration model.

G4   Use the collaboration model from Exercise G3 (Figure 6.42, p. 378) to develop a sequence diagram for the same scenario. For simplicity, consider that only a different advertiser was selected for the ad link (no changes to the agency nor the product were made). Explain your interaction model.

Review quiz answers

Review quiz 6.1
RQ1   The peer-to-peer architectural style. A peer is the only system element.
RQ2   Business logic and enterprisewide business rules.
RQ3   By triggers.

Review quiz 6.2
RQ1   The Turing machine model, based on algorithms and an open interaction model.
RQ2   Classes.
RQ3   The Façade pattern.
RQ4   Chain of Responsibility.

Review quiz 6.3
RQ1   Generalization and dependency relationships.
RQ2   No, it does not (the component cannot be distinguished from copies of its own and, in any given application, there will be at most one copy of a particular component).
RQ3   Yes, it can.

Review quiz 6.4
RQ1   Class cohesion.
RQ2   The lack of support for dynamic classification.
RQ3   Framework reuse.

Review quiz 6.5
RQ1   Composite structure diagram.
RQ2   No, they do not. Interaction models serve that purpose.

Multiple-choice test answers

MC1   d
MC2   b
MC3   d (it is called the Mediator pattern)
MC4   a

MC5   c
MC6   a
MC7   b

Answers to odd-numbered questions

Q1

A distributed database system is a superset of a distributed processing system. In a *distributed processing system*, a client program can connect to multiple databases, but each database access/update statement in such a program can be addressed to only one of these databases.

A *distributed database system* relaxes the above restriction. This means that a client program can contain access statements that combine data from multiple databases and update statements that modify data in multiple databases (Date 2000). Ideally, the access/update statements should operate "transparently" on data – that is, the user must not be aware where the data resides. The databases may be "heterogeneous" – that is, they may be managed by different database management systems.

Distributed database systems are difficult to implement. The difficulties derive mostly from stiff requirements for transaction management and query processing.

Q3

An *active database* is capable of storing not only data but also programs. Such stored programs can be invoked by their names or can be triggered by events that attempt to update the database.

Contemporary commercial database management systems are active. They provide programmatic extensions to SQL – such as PL/SQL in Oracle or Transact SQL in Sybase or Microsoft SQL server – that allow programs to be written and stored in a database dictionary. These programs can be invoked from application programs or triggered as a result of modification events on the database.

Programs in active databases are "computationally complete" but they are not "resource complete". They are able to execute any computation, but they may not be able to access external resources, such as talking to a GUI window or an Internet browser, sending an e-mail or SMS or monitoring an engineering device.

Q5

Such a class would naturally belong to the *control* layer. This class embodies the logic activated by a user event (which is the main purpose of the control layer). The class `InterestCalculation` provides a level of indirection between user events (presentation layer) and the database content (represented at run-time by classes of the entity layer). Changes to the way in which the interest calculation is computed (program logic) will be localized to the class `InterestCalculation` and will not affect the presentation or entity classes.

Q7

Persistent entity objects tend to have complex associations and convoluted business logic. Business transactions operating on such sets of entity objects are inherently difficult to program. The Mediator pattern provides a simplified solution to these dilemmas. Its main advantage is that it takes responsibility for handling the application logic that deals with the communication between entity objects to perform business transactions. A related advantage is that any changes to business transactions and the communication strategy between entity objects are localized in the mediator. Centralizing application-specific behavior in the mediator improves system adaptiveness because business transactions are separated from business (entity) objects.

An obvious drawback of the Mediator pattern is that its own complexity grows significantly as the number of entity objects grow and the business transactions become more complex. This can fly in the face of an object-oriented principle to ensure a uniform distribution of intelligence between all classes in the system. An answer to that drawback is the creation of multiple mediators focused on groups of business transactions and/or groups of entity classes.

Q9

In a typical situation, components and packages represent sets of classes. However, these representations are at different levels of abstraction and frequently orthogonal.

Package is a logical concept that does not have immediate implementation connotations and is not a unit of software reuse (although individual classes within a package can be designed for reuse).

Component is a physical concept, normally distributed for *reuse* as a run-time executable. A component "publishes" its external interface (its services) in a contractual manner. The internal implementation of the operations in a component's interface is not published. Components can be interconnected via their interfaces even if they are implemented in different programming languages.

Component is a compilation unit. Component can contain many classes, but only one of these classes can be *public* (that is, can have public visibility). The name of the component's compilation unit (such as `Invoice.java`) must correspond to the name of its public class (`Invoice`). Some visual modeling tools (such as Rational Rose) create components automatically when the Java code is generated for public classes (one component per public class).

A *package* is an architectural grouping of classes. The grouping is obtained by static proximity of classes in the application domain. A *component* offers a set of operations to the environment in which it functions. This set of operations captures the behavioral proximity of classes and may be of use in more than one application domain.

Q11

A *well-designed class* provides services to other classes, it does not just reveal its attribute values. A well-designed class also takes responsibility for controlling its state space and does not allow other classes to set its attribute values. A class that is not well designed (as per these two observations) is *mindless*.

A class is mindless if its public interface consists mostly of accessor methods – that is, observer (`get`) methods and mutator (`set`) methods. In practice, most classes provide some accessor methods to allow sufficient coupling between otherwise cohesive classes.

Q13

Messages can be classified in a number of ways. The principal classification can be to divide messages into (Page-Jones 2000):

- *read messages* interrogative, present-oriented messages
- *update messages* informative, past-oriented messages
- *collaborative messages* imperative, future-oriented messages.

A sender of a *read message* requests information from the receiver (target object) of the message. A method that executes as a result of a read message is sometimes called an *observer* (`get`) method.

A sender of an *update message* provides information to the receiver so that the receiver can update its state with the information provided. A method invoked by an update message is sometimes called a *mutator* (`set`) method.

Read and update messages are also known as *accessor* messages. The related observer and mutator methods are termed accessor methods.

A *collaborative message* is sent to an object responsible for a larger task that demands the collaboration of multiple objects. A collaborative message is a message in a chain of messages. Each collaborative message can be a read or update message.

As an aside, we note that UML classifies messages into signals and calls (Rumbaugh et al. 2005). A *signal* is a one-way asynchrononous communication from sender to receiver, so that the arrival of a signal is an event for the receiver. A *call* is a two-way synchronous communication in which the sender invokes an operation on the receiver. The classification into read, update and collaborative messages relates to calls.

Q15

Both overriding and overloading imply that there are several methods with the same name. The difference is as follows.

- *Overriding* relates to inheritance and polymorphism. A method in a superclass can be overridden by a method in a subclass. Not only has the overridden method the same name as the superclass method but also the signatures of both methods must be the same. (An abstract operation must be polymorphic and its implementation must be provided in subclasses. This is not considered overriding because the abstract operation does not have a method in the superclass.)
- *Overloading* relates to the existence of multiple methods with the same name in the same class. Clearly, the signatures of the overloaded set of methods are different.

Q17

The design of the behavioral aspect of collaboration is concerned with capturing the dynamics of method invocations or events that lead to the implementation of a behavior (typically the implementation of a use case). The collaboration itself is modeled using a *collaboration diagram*, including its special form known as a *composite structure diagram*. Although connectors between roles in a collaboration diagram represent the communication paths along which the behavior is achieved, collaboration diagrams are in principle similar to *class diagrams* (and class diagrams capture first of all the structure of the system while still representing the behavior in class operations).

Accordingly, the behavioral design requires additional models to represent these details of the collaboration that are not captured by collaboration diagrams. These additional models are predominantly *interaction diagrams* – that is, sequence diagrams and communication diagrams.

When choosing between sequence and communication diagrams, we need to consider that *sequence diagrams* do not visualize the static relationship links (mostly associations) used for message passing. However, collaboration diagrams express the relationship semantics by means of connectors. Accordingly, sequence diagrams can build nicely on prior collaboration diagrams. *Communication diagrams*, on the other hand, visualize the relationship links. As such, they can be potentially used as a replacement for collaboration diagrams.

Another important tool in behavioral design is a *state machine diagram*. State machines can supplement other behavioral models to show the states in which an object or an interaction can be as a result of the behavior (events) performed on that object or interaction.

Solutions to exercises: advertising expenditure

G1

Figure 6.40 shows a composite collaboration model. The model distinguishes two collaborations as corresponding to two use cases, which in turn are represented by the primary and secondary windows in Figure 6.39. The `Modify ad link` composite collaboration consists of two alternative but similar collaborations – `Modify ad link` as `correction` and `Modify ad link` as `business change`. These two collaborations are alternatives in the sense that the user has to select which one of these collaborations to perform. They are similar in the sense that they perform similar functions except that the business change relinking does not delete the old ad link and records the change date.

Figure 6.40
Composite
collaboration
model for an
advertising
expenditure
system

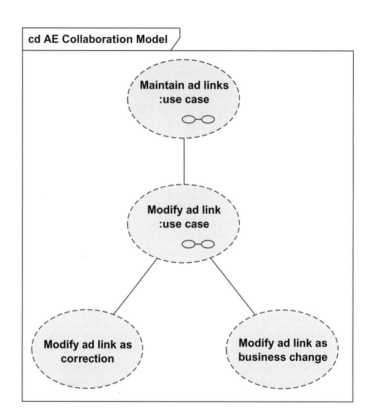

G2

The collaboration model for business objects only is shown in Figure 6.41. This is a generic and static model in which the roles map directly to the persistent data structures (tables or classes) in the database. No multiplicities are shown but the role names inform that an ad has many ad links. Each ad link links an agency, advertiser and product. Agencies, advertisers and products are mutually connected.

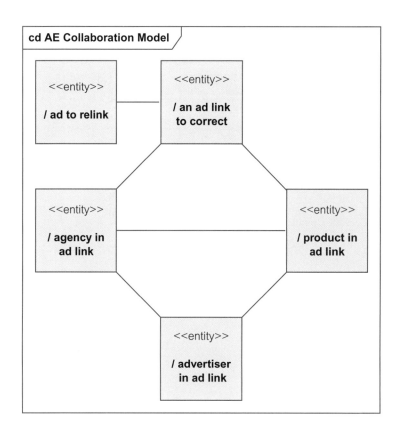

Figure 6.41
Collaboration model for business objects for an advertising expenditure system

G3
The collaboration model for PCBE objects is shown in Figure 6.42. The thrust of the model is as follows:

- `PAdLinkBrowser` instantiates the `Modify ad links screen` (Figure 6.39) using the data that it already has (that is, we are not validating if the data are still correct and we are not reretrieving the data if not correct).
- When the user selects any of the three drop-down list arrows, `/a picklist` opens up. To populate the list, `/a picklist` involves `/data getter`, which accesses `/ agencies`, `/advertisers` and `/products` as needed. This enables the getter to instantiate `/picklist suppliers` and supply to it the names of `/agencies`, `/advertisers` and `/products` so that appropriate beans can be created. The beans are used by `/picklist` to display drop-down lists to the user as requested.
- After the user selects the desired entries in the drop-down lists, an `/ad link after correction` becomes ready for saving. This involves a `/data setter` so that a `/new ad link for the ad` can be created with appropriate links to an agency, advertiser and product.

G4
The sequence diagram corresponding to the collaboration model in Figure 6.42 is shown in Figure 6.43. The diagram is self-explanatory when analyzed together with its collaboration model. In principle, it only defines messages that flow over connectors between the roles.

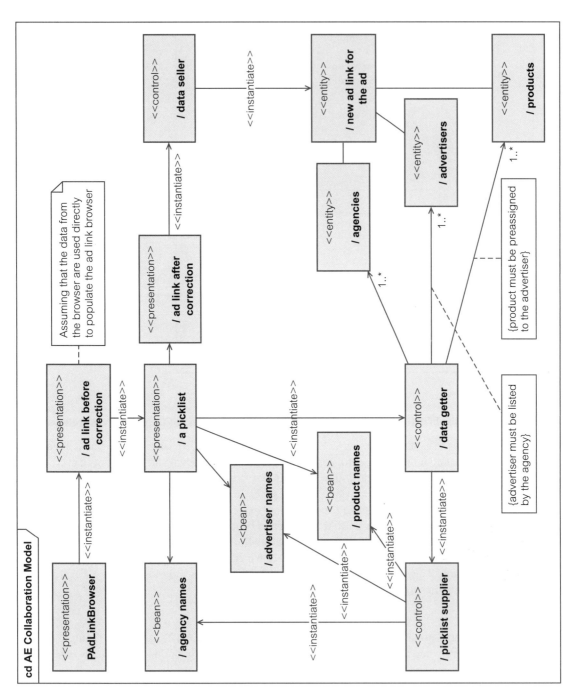

Figure 6.42 Collaboration model involving PCBE layers for an advertising expenditure system

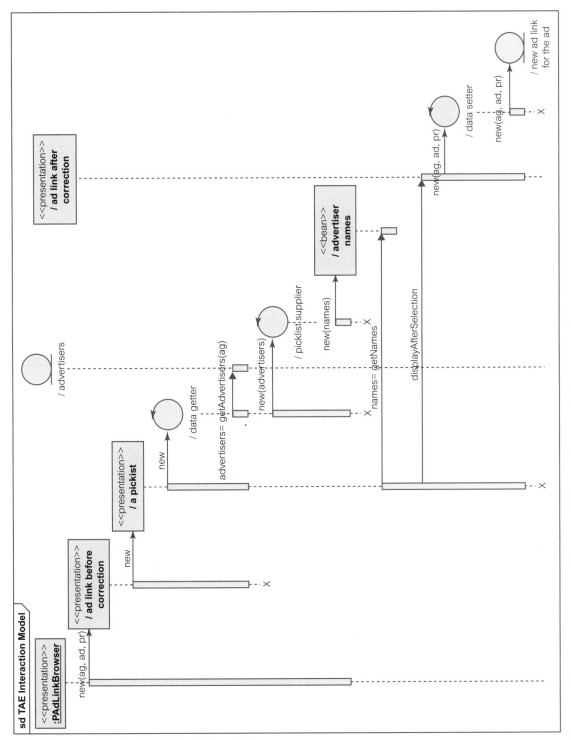

Figure 6.43 Sequence diagram involving PCBE layers for an advertising expenditure system

Chapter

7

Graphical User Interface Design

Objectives

The days when user interface (GUI) screens were dumb and green and a keyboard was the only input device are gone. Contemporary graphical user interface (GUI) screens are not just vibrant but also interactive. The user is equipped with a mouse (not to mention voice and touch) to control the program's execution. The program can still be designed to disallow illegal or unauthorized events, but the shift of control from the program *algorithm* to user *interaction* has changed the way that GUI systems are designed and implemented.

GUI design is a very comprehensive task, requiring a diverse mix of skills ranging from visual art to software programming. Many books have been written to emphasize different aspects of GUI design (Constantine and Lockwood 1999; Fowler 1998; Fowler and Stanwick 2004; Galitz 1996; Olsen 1998; Ruble 1997; Sklar 2006; Windows 2000, for example). In this chapter, we concentrate on what the system designer must know to collaboratively design a successful desktop or Web GUI and specify navigation between GUI windows or web pages.

By reading this chapter you will:

- become aware of the principles of good GUI design
- understand the similarities and differences between desktop and Web GUI design
- become acquainted with enabling technology for GUI design
- learn about GUI visual elements – containers, menus, controls and so on
- realize various ways in which to navigate design
- gain practical knowledge of how to model GUI navigation.

Principles of GUI design

7.1

The development of user interfaces begins with early sketches of GUI windows in the requirements analysis phase. These sketches are used for requirements gathering, in story-boarding sessions with the customers, for prototyping and inclusion in the use case documents. During the design process the GUI windows for an application are developed to conform to the underlying GUI presentation software and the peculiarities and constraints of the chosen programming environment.

In Chapter 6 and elsewhere, we emphasized that enterprise information systems are invariably client/server (C/S) solutions. It is true to say that if server solutions *make* the software, client solutions *sell* the software.

GUI clients can be divided into programmable clients on *desktop platforms* and browser clients on *Web platforms* (Maciaszek and Liong 2005; Singh et al. 2002). A **programmable client** is, typically, a *thick client* (Section 6.1.2) with a program residing and executing on it and access to the client's machine storage resources. A **browser client**, on the other hand, is a Web-based GUI and needs a server to obtain its data and programs. This is a *thin client*. It is also called a Web client.

Whatever the client, the GUI design must follow some universal principles of good GUI design while taking advantage of the latest technologies in human–computer interaction. GUI design is a *multidisciplinary activity*. It requires the skills of a *team* – a single person is unlikely to have all the knowledge demanded by the multifaceted considerations of GUI design. Good GUI design requires the combined skills of a graphic artist, requirements analyst, system designer, programmer, technology expert, social and behavioral scientist and perhaps a few other professions, depending on the nature of the system.

From GUI prototype to implementation

7.1.1

A typical process involving the GUI design for IS applications begins with *use cases*. The *analyst* describing the flow of events for a use case has some visual image of the GUI to support the human–computer interaction. In some cases, the analyst may choose to insert graphical depictions for user interfaces in the use case document. Complex human–computer interactions cannot be adequately described in prose alone. Occasionally, the process of gathering and negotiating customers' requirements necessitates the production of GUI sketches.

The *designer* involved in specifying collaborations for the realization of use cases must have a clear visual image of GUI screens. If the analyst has not done this before, the designer will be the first person to produce depictions of user interfaces. The designer's depictions must conform to the underlying GUI technology – windowing and widget toolkits, Internet browsers and so on. A *technology expert* may need to be consulted to exploit technological features successfully.

Before collaboration designs (Section 6.5) are passed on to programmers for implementation, a user-friendly prototype of GUI screens needs to be constructed. This task should engage *graphic artists* and *social and behavioral scientists*. Together, they can offer a GUI that is attractive and usable.

The *programmer's* task is not just to blindly implement the screens but also suggest changes motivated by the programming environment. In some cases, the changes may be improvements. In other cases, they may worsen the design, due to programming or performance restrictions.

The central issue in GUI design is that the *user is in control* (with the proviso that the system, not the user, controls system integrity, safety and security). A modern object-oriented program is *event-driven*. Objects respond to events and messages. Internal communication between objects is initiated by external user-activated events.

The GUI's look and feel sells the software product to the customer. A GUI prototype can serve the double purpose of enabling an evaluation of the feel of the GUI screen and conveying its functions. However, the real look of the screen is delivered in the implementation phase.

Example 7.1: contact management

Refer to Problem statement 3, for a contact management system (Section 1.6.3) and the successive examples in Chapter 4. In particular, consider the design of the class `Organization` in Examples 4.6 (Section 4.2.1.2.3) and 4.8 (Section 4.2.2.2.1).

The purpose of this example is to demonstrate the change that a GUI screen for updating information about `Organization` can undergo during the design process as it progresses from an initial prototype to final implementation. We assume that the underlying GUI technology is Microsoft Windows.

A GUI prototype for `Organization` for Example 7.1, developed during early requirements analysis, is presented in Figure 7.1. Its main purpose is to enable us to visualize data and control objects in the window. The feedback obtained from users and the ideas given by the GUI development team will change not only the window's look and feel but perhaps also its content.

Figure 7.2 shows how the `Maintain organizations` window can potentially be presented during the system design phase. As can be seen, the designer opted for a dialog box with tabbed pages and a number of other look and feel changes. The changes have been made to conform to Microsoft Windows' GUI design principles and accommodate functional requirements overlooked in the initial prototype.

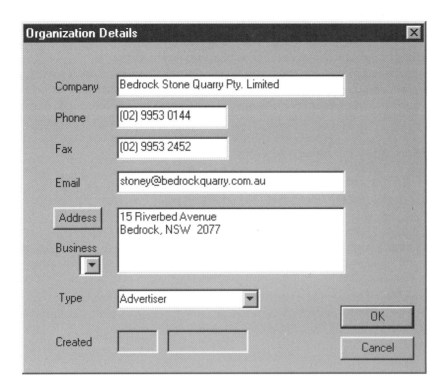

Figure 7.1
Analysis-phase
window prototype
for a contact
management
system
Source: Courtesy of
Nielsen Media
Research, Sydney,
Australia

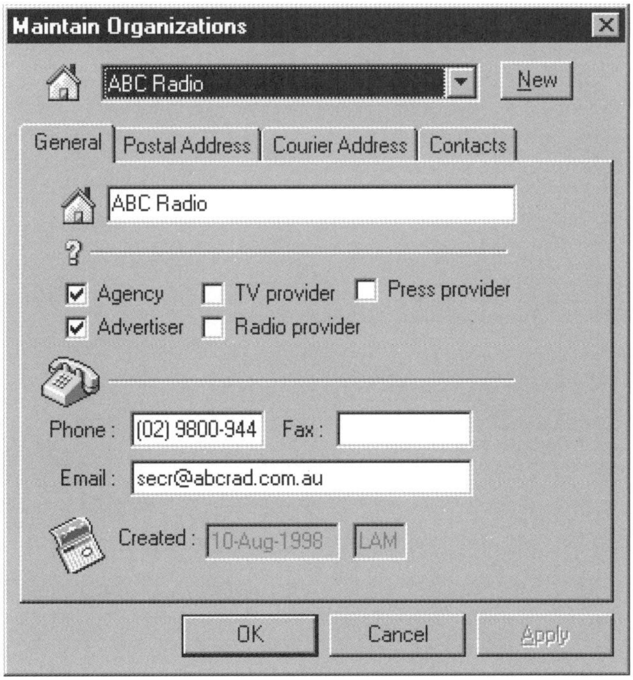

Figure 7.2
Design-phase
window prototype
for a contact
management
system
Source: Courtesy of
Nielsen Media
Research, Sydney,
Australia

The design in Figure 7.2 still has problems with regard to the look and feel, implementation constraints and satisfying functional requirements. As a result, the final implemented window is different again, as demonstrated in Figure 7.3.

The implemented window in Figure 7.3 disallows a drop-down list for selecting the organization's name (a dialog box is a secondary window opened to allow a particular organization to be updated). The `Classification` possibilities of `Organization` are now disabled for editing (because an organization cannot have its classification changed by the user of this application). Other changes include larger sizes of fields, the introduction of a group of fields called `History` and so on.

7.1.2 Guidelines for good GUI design

The GUI design centers on the users. Associated with this observation is a range of guidelines for software developers. The guidelines are published by the manufacturers of GUIs (such as Windows 2000). They are also discussed in many books (Galitz 1996; Ruble 1997, for example).

The *GUI guidelines* constitute the foundations on which a developer builds. They should be at the back of the developer's mind in all GUI design decision making. Some of the guidelines sound like ancient pieces of ubiquitous wisdom; others have been motivated by modern GUI technology.

Figure 7.3
Implemented window for a contact management system
Source: Courtesy of Nielsen Media Research, Sydney, Australia

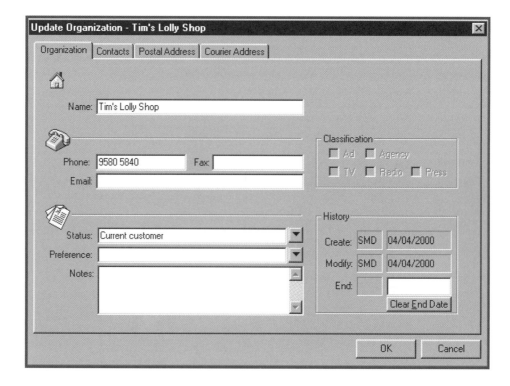

User in control

The *user in control* is the principal GUI guideline. This could be better called the *user's perception of control*. Some call it the *no mothering* principle – the program should not act like your mother and do things for you (Treisman 1994). The underlying meaning is that users initiate actions and if, as a result, the program takes control, then users obtain the necessary *feedback* (an hourglass, wait indicator or similar).

Figure 7.4 demonstrates a typical flow of control in a human–computer interaction. A user event (a menu action, mouse-click, screen cursor movement) can open a GUI window or invoke a program – typically, a program accessing the database and taking advantage of its SQL procedures. The program temporarily takes control from the user.

Program execution can return control back to the same or another window. Alternatively, it can call another SQL module or invoke an external routine. In some cases, the program can in fact do things for the user. This may happen, for example, when the program needs to do a computation that is normally associated with an explicit user event or if the program moves the cursor to another field on the screen and the event of leaving the original field has exit processing associated with it.

Consistency

Consistency is arguably the second most important guideline of good interface design. Consistency really means adherence to standards and the usual way of doing things. There are at least two dimensions to consistency:

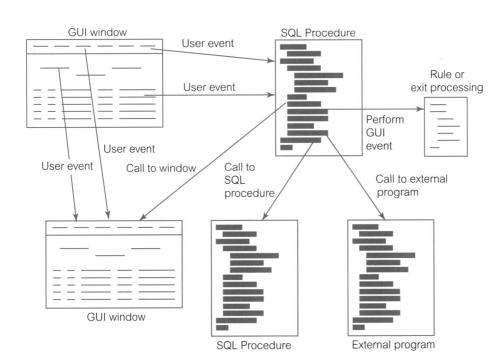

Figure 7.4
GUI program flow
of control

- conformance to the GUI vendor's standards
- conformance to the naming, coding and other GUI-related standards developed internally by the organization.

Both of these dimensions are important and the second (over which the developers have influence) must not contradict the first. If an application is developed for Windows, then the Windows look and feel must be delivered. On a Macintosh, replacing the celebrated apple menu with a kangaroo menu, as your author once attempted to do, is not a good idea!

A GUI developer must not be too creative or innovative in the interface design. This will erode the confidence and ability of users – they should be presented with a familiar and predictable environment. As Treisman (1994) observed, imagine what a car designer would do to the driving community if new cars were released with the accelerator and brake pedals swapped around!

Conformance to naming, coding, abbreviations and other internal standards cannot be underestimated either. This includes the naming and coding of the menus, action buttons and screen fields. It also includes any standards for the placement of objects on the screen and consistent use of other GUI elements across all internally developed applications.

7.1.2.3 Personalization and customization

Personalization and *customization* (known jointly as *adaptability*) are two related guidelines. GUI personalization is simply customization for personal use, whereas customization – as we understand it here – is an administrative task of tailoring the software to different groups of users.

An example of personalization is when a user reorders and resizes columns in a row browser (grid) display and saves these changes as his or her personal preference. The next time the program is activated, the personal preferences are taken into account.

An example of customization is when the program can operate differently for novice and advanced users. For instance, novice users may be offered explicit help and extra warning messages for user events perceived to be dangerous.

In many cases, the distinction between personalization and customization is blurred or negligible. Changing menu items and creating new menus are cases in point. If done for personal use, it is personalization. If done by a system administrator for the user community at large, it is customization.

An Internet-age feature related to personalization and customization is the user's *locale* information (Lethbridge and Laganière 2001). An application can adapt to the user's locale (such as the user's spoken language, character set, currency and date formats) by simply querying the operating system on which the program executes.

Another important adaptability issue is that the application can adjust to people with disabilities. For example, blind people would require that the application delivers Braille or speech. Deaf people would require that visual output be substituted for sound. Other disabilities may require their own special measures.

Forgiveness 7.1.2.4

A good interface should allow users to experiment and make mistakes in a forgiving way. *Forgiveness* encourages exploration because the user is allowed to take erroneous routes and yet can be "rolled back" to the starting point if necessary. Forgiveness implies a multilevel *undo* operation.

This is easily said, difficult to implement. The implementation of forgiveness in the interface is a particular challenge in multi-user database applications. The user who withdrew (and spent) money from a bank account could not possibly undo that operation! He or she could only rectify the problem by depositing the money back into the account in another transaction. Whether or not a forgiving interface should warn users of the consequences of cash withdrawal is a debatable issue (and one that relates to the personalization guideline).

Feedback 7.1.2.5

The *feedback* guideline is a spin-off of the first guideline – user in control. To be in control implies knowledge of what is going on when the control is temporarily with the program. The developer should build into the system visual and/or audio cues for every user event.

In most cases, an hourglass or wait indicator is sufficient feedback to show that the program is doing something. For those parts of the application that may experience occasional performance problems, a more vivid form of feedback may be necessary (such as the display of an explanatory message). Either way, the developer must never assume that the application performs so quickly that the feedback is unnecessary. Any surge in application workload will prove the developer painfully wrong.

Aesthetics and usability 7.1.2.6

Aesthetics are about the system's visual appeal. *Usability* is about the ease, simplicity, efficiency, reliability and productivity associated with using the interface. Ultimately, both are about *user satisfaction*. This is where the GUI developer needs the assistance of a graphic artist and a social and behavioral expert.

There are many golden rules for an aesthetic and usable design (Constantine and Lockwood 1999; Galitz 1996). Issues to consider include the fixation and movement patterns of the human eye, use of colors, sense of balance and symmetry, alignment and spacing of elements, sense of proportion and groupings of related elements.

The guideline to attend to aesthetics and usability turns the GUI developer into an artist. It is good to remember in this context that simple is beautiful. In fact, *simplicity* is frequently considered to be yet another GUI guideline, but strongly related to aesthetics and usability. Simplicity in complex applications is best achieved by the "divide and conquer" approach – the progressive disclosure of information so that it is shown only as and when needed, possibly in separate windows.

7.2 Desktop GUI design

There are two main aspects of GUI design for *desktop programmable applications* – the design of windows and the design of windows' input and editing controls. Both depend on the underlying GUI environment. In the following discussion, we concentrate on the Microsoft Windows environment (Maciaszek and Liong 2005; Windows 2000).

A typical Windows application consists of a single main application window, the **primary window**. The *primary window* is supported by a set of *pop-up windows* – the **secondary windows**. A *secondary window* supports the user's activities in the primary window or other secondary window. Many activities supported by secondary windows are *CRUD* (create, read, update and delete) operations on the database.

From the programming perspective, windows are GUI **containers**. These are rectangular areas of a GUI screen that contain other containers, menus and controls (such as action buttons). Containers can be primary windows, but also dialogs (secondary windows), **panes** and **panels**.

Together, containers, menus and controls constitute GUI *components*. Java provides a GUI component kit for building applications and applets called **Swing**, which is a library of classes and interfaces. Swing's *concrete classes* are named starting with the letter J – JDialog, JButton and so on.

7.2.1 Primary windows

A *primary window* has a border (**frame**). The *frame* contains a title bar (caption bar) for the window, a menu bar, toolbars, status bar and the window's viewable and modifiable content. Horizontal and vertical scroll bars are used to scroll through the content, if required.

The window's viewable and modifiable content can be organized into *panes*. Panes permit different but related information content to be seen and manipulated. Figure 7.5 demonstrates a primary window that would display after a successful login to an application. The pane on the left contains an application map in the Windows Explorer style. The window (and therefore the application) can be (presumably) closed from the File menu or by means of the Close button in the upper right-hand corner of the window's pane. The annotation explains the visual vocabulary of Windows' features.

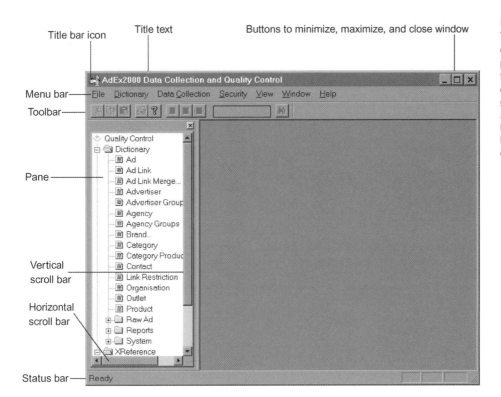

Figure 7.5
The main
components of a
primary window
for an advertising
expenditure
system
Source: Courtesy of
Nielsen Media
Research, Sydney,
Australia

A typical feature that distinguishes a primary from a secondary window is that the former has a menu bar and toolbar whereas a secondary window does not. The toolbar contains action icons for the most frequently used menu items. The toolbar icons duplicate these menu items. They provide a quick way of executing frequently repeated actions.

Example 7.2: advertising expenditure

Refer to Problem statement 5, for an advertising expenditure system (Section 1.6.5) and to Examples 6.13–6.15 (Section 6.5). In particular, consider Figure 6.35 (Section 6.5.4) and show the design of the primary window from which the update product dialog box is launched. Include in the design a pane similar to the one shown on the left-hand side of Figure 7.5.

Figure 7.6 demonstrates the primary window for Example 7.2. The left-hand pane contains a *tree browser* (Section 7.2.1.2). The tree browser allows the selection of a particular "data container" to be displayed in the right-hand pane. The right-hand pane is a *row browser* (Section 7.2.1.1).

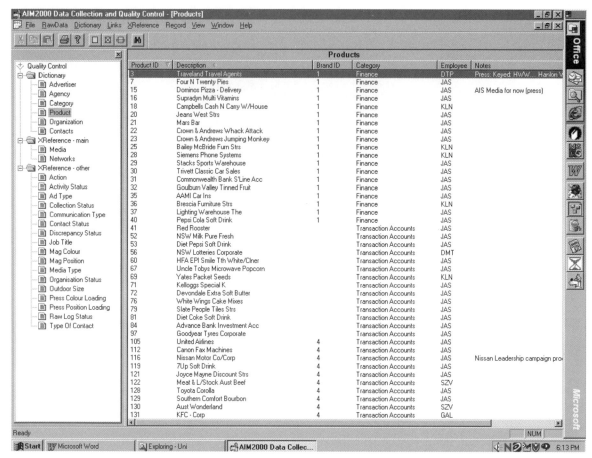

Figure 7.6 A primary window showing a list of products for an advertising expenditure system

Source: Courtesy of Nielsen Media Research, Sydney, Australia

7.2.1.1 Row browsers

A frequent use of the primary window in IS applications is to provide a row browser display of database records, such as employee records. Such a window is sometimes called a *row browser*. The user can browse up and down through the records using the vertical scroll bar or keys on the keyboard (Page Up, Page Down, Home, End and up and down arrows).

Figure 7.7 is an example of a row browser. The document – labeled `Ad Link` – inside the primary window is a *child window*. The child window has its own set of *window buttons* – minimize, restore, close – placed in the right-hand corner of the menu bar. The columns of the browser's grid are *resizable* and their positions can be *rearranged*. The circular dents next to column names indicate that the column is *sortable* – clicking at the column will sort the records into ascending or descending order of that column's values.

At any particular time, only one row (record) is active in the browser. Double-clicking on that record would normally display an *edit window* with details of that record. The *edit window* allows the content of the record to be modified.

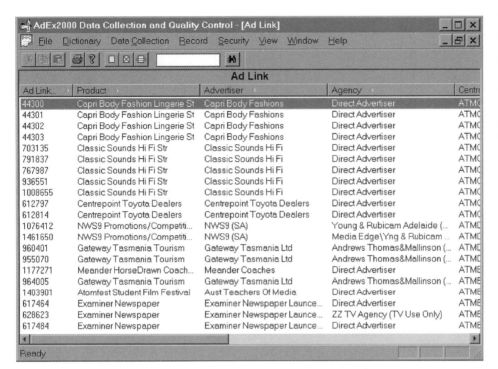

Figure 7.7
A row browser
window for an
advertising
expenditure
system
Source: Courtesy of
Nielsen Media
Research, Sydney,
Australia

Panes can be used to split the window vertically or horizontally, or even both ways. Figure 7.8 demonstrates a horizontal split. As the window's title informs us, the three panes are used to display the products by advertiser and by agency. The middle pane shows the advertisers belonging to the advertising agency currently selected – highlighted in the top pane. The bottom pane then shows the products advertised by the selected advertiser.

Tree browsers

7.2.1.2

The other popular way to use a primary window is as a *tree browser*. A tree browser displays related records as an indented list. The list has controls that allow the tree to be expanded or collapsed. A well-known example of a tree browser is the display of computer folders in Windows Explorer.

Unlike a row browser, a tree browser would allow in-place modifications to be made – that is, it would allow the content of the window to be modified without activating an edit window. Modifications in a tree browser are done by means of drag and drop operations.

Figure 7.9 demonstrates a tree browser in the left pane of the window. The right pane is a row browser. Selecting an agency group record in the tree browser displays the agencies of that agency group in the row browser.

Figure 7.8
A multipane row
browser window
for an advertising
expenditure
system
Source: Courtesy of
Nielsen Media
Research, Sydney,
Australia

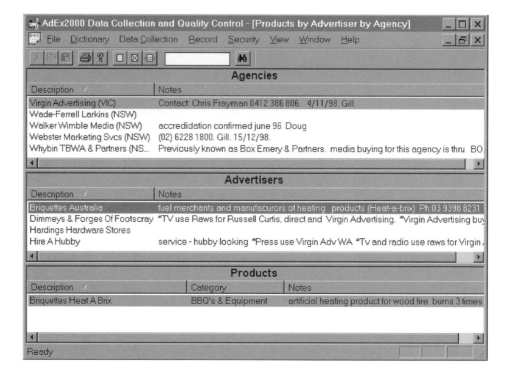

Figure 7.9
A window with
tree browser and
row browser
panes for an
advertising
expenditure
system
Source: Courtesy of
Nielsen Media
Research, Sydney,
Australia

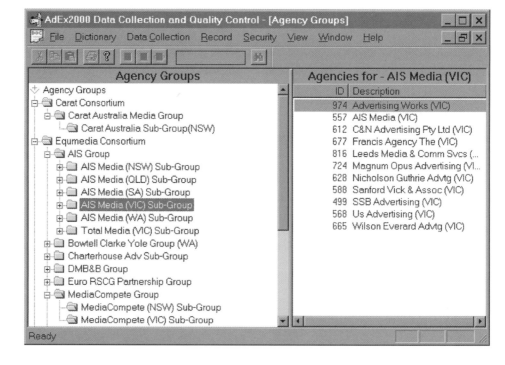

Secondary windows

Disregarding some trivial IS applications, a *secondary window* supplements its primary window. It extends the functionality of the primary window, in particular for operations that modify the database (the insert, delete and update operations).

A secondary window is typically *modal* with respect to the primary window. The user must respond and close the secondary window before interacting with any other window of the application. *Modeless* secondary windows are possible but not recommended.

Technically, the *logon window* is an example of a secondary window, but conceptually it is a standalone window that is not launched in the context of the primary window. In fact, it can lead to the display of the application's primary window on successful login. In general, simple applications can consist of only one or more secondary windows.

The logon example in Figure 7.10 demonstrates the main visual differences between the primary and secondary windows. A secondary window does not have any bars – a menu bar, toolbar, scroll bars or status bar. User events are achieved with *command buttons* (*action buttons*), such as "OK", "Cancel" and "Help".

Secondary windows come in various forms and shapes. A secondary window can be a:

- dialog box
- tab folder
- drop-down list
- message box.

Dialog boxes

A *dialog box* is almost synonymous with the concept of the secondary window. It captures the most frequently needed properties of that window. It supports the dialog between the user and the application. The word "dialog" is used as the user enters some information to be considered by the application.

Figure 7.11 contains an example of a dialog box. It is an insert window, used for inserting new TV ad instances for the database. The user can insert/modify any *editable field* value in the white field boxes. Some fields are placed within named frames (such as `Ad Instance Attributes` in the upper right-hand corner). The window provides the option of inserting new values and closing the window ("Save and Close" button) or inserting new values and clearing the fields for the next insertion ("Save and Next" button).

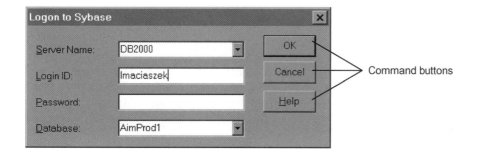

Figure 7.10
A simple secondary window – a logon window for an advertising expenditure system
Source: Courtesy of Nielsen Media Research, Sydney, Australia

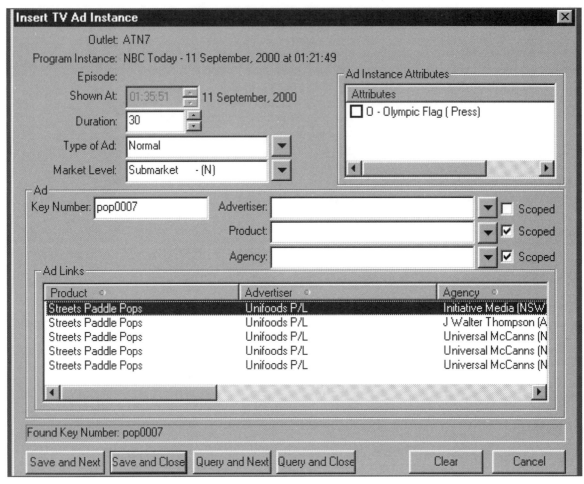

Figure 7.11 A dialog box for an advertising expenditure system
Source: Courtesy of Nielsen Media Research, Sydney, Australia

Example 7.3: currency converter

Refer to Problem statement 7, for a currency converter system (Section 1.6.7) and to examples for it in Chapter 5. In particular, consider the specification for Example 5.12 (section 5.4.2), of which the following parts of the specification are especially relevant:

> Consider a desktop GUI implementation of the currency converter for converting money both ways between two currencies (such as between Australian dollars and US dollars)… The frame holds three fields – for accepting the values of Australian dollars, US dollars and the exchange rate. It also holds three buttons called USD to AUD, AUD to USD and Close (for exiting the application).

Design a dialog box for the desktop currency converter as specified above.

Figure 7.12 illustrates the dialog box for a currency converter system for Example 7.3 consisting of three fields and three action buttons. The window shows the outcome of a money conversion action.

Tab folders

A *tab folder* is useful when the amount of information to be displayed in a secondary window exceeds the window's "real estate" and the subject matter can be broken apart, into logical information groups. At any point in time, information from one tab is visible on the top of the stack of tab sheets. (The Microsoft Windows name for a tab folder is a *tabbed property sheet* and each tab is called a *property page*.)

Figure 7.13 demonstrates a tab folder for inserting information about a new contact person. The three tabs divide the large volume of information to be entered by the user into three groups. The command buttons at the bottom of the screen apply to the whole window, not just to the currently visible tab page.

Drop-down lists

In some cases, a *drop-down list* (or a set of drop-down lists) is a convenient substitute for a tab page. A drop-down list provides a *picklist* of choices from which the user can select one that applies. For insert operations, the user can type in a new value to be added to the drop-down list the next time it is opened.

In general, a drop-down list does not need to be restricted to a simple list of values, as in Figure 7.14. It can be a tree browser of values.

Message boxes

A *message box* is a secondary window that displays a message to the user. The message can signify a warning, explanation, exceptional condition and so on. Command buttons in the message box offer one or more reply choices to the user.

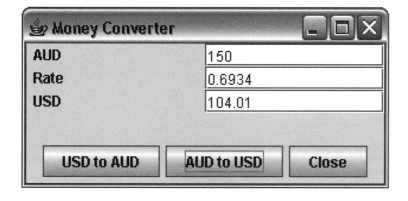

Figure 7.12
A dialog box for a currency converter system

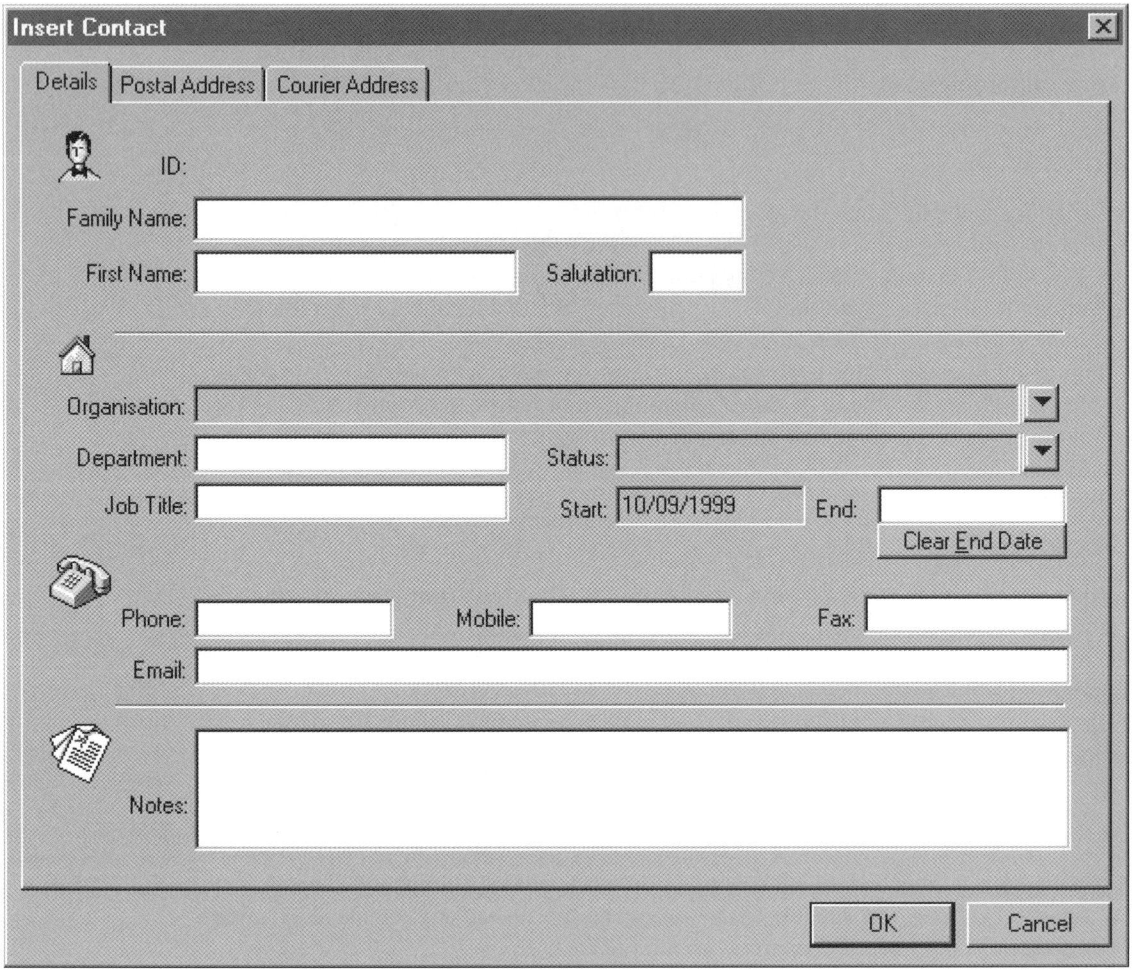

Figure 7.13 A tab folder for an contact management system
Source: Courtesy of Nielsen Media Research, Sydney, Australia

Figure 7.15 shows a message that requires acknowledgment (the "OK" button) from the user.

7.2.3 Menus and toolbars

The GUI components include menus and toolbars. In the Java Swing library, the names of the classes imply the provided functionality of the menus – JMenuBar, JMenu, JMenuItem, JCheckBoxMenuItem, JRadioButtonMenuItem, for example.

Menu items are grouped into lists, which can be opened by means of actions called *pull-down*, *cascading* or *pop-up* (the latter is activated by pressing the right-hand mouse button).

Figure 7.18 is a visualization of Swing controls such that the names for controls are the names of the classes used to implement them (Maciaszek and Liong 2005).

The differences between various buttons are sometimes subtle, so some explanation may be in place. JButton fires an event as soon as it is pressed and pops up again (unless the event results in a new window and hides the button). By contrast, JToggleButton remains pushed down (after a mouse-click on it) until it is pressed again.

JRadioButton and JCheckBox are two categories of JToggleButton. JRadioButton is used to implement a group of buttons, such that only one of these buttons is selected at any one time. JCheckBox is an independent control that can be set to either true (with a checkmark) or false (without a checkmark).

JList, JTree and JComboBox are controls with direct applicability to the implementation of some containers discussed earlier. JList is used in the implementation of a row browser (Section 7.2.1.1), JTree in the implementation of a tree browser (Section 7.2.1.2) and JComboBox in the implementation of a drop-down list (Section 7.2.2.3).

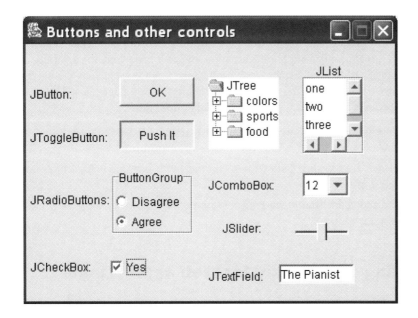

Figure 7.18
Buttons and other controls
Source: Maciaszek and Liong (2005). Reprinted by permission of Pearson Education Ltd

Review quiz 7.2

E1   What is the main characteristic that distinguishes primary from secondary windows?

E2   What GUI component is a property page part of?

E3   What GUI component is an accelerator key related to?

7.3 Web GUI design

"A Web application is a Web system that allows its users to execute business logic with a Web browser" (Conallen 2000: 10). The *business logic* can reside on the server and/or the client. A **Web application** is therefore a kind of distributed C/S system (Section 6.1) rendered in an Internet browser.

An Internet client *browser* renders **web pages** on a computer screen. A *Web server* delivers the web pages to the browser. Web page documents can be *static* (unmodifiable) or *dynamic*. A web page document can be a *form* that a user fills in. *Frames* can be used by the application to divide the screen's real estate so that the user can view multiple web pages at the same time.

A *web page* – when used as an entry point of a Web application – can be seen as a special kind of primary window. Unlike in desktop IS applications though, the menu bar and toolbar of a web page are not used for specific application tasks. They are used for generic Web-surfing activities, but can also be used for generic tasks related to the application's web page content (such as printing or copying). The user events in Web applications are programmed via *menu items*, action *buttons* and active *links* (hyperlinks).

Figure 7.19 is an example of a web page within a website, rather than as part of a Web application. Even in this simple reincarnation, the web page contains a variety of ways to call other pages of the website and to execute some functions (such as the `Search` button in the upper right-hand corner, enabling searching for web pages based on entered keywords). The links to other web pages are available from the:

- *menu bar* underneath the web page header (`About the Book`, `Readers Area`, and `Instructors Area`)
- *breadcrumb* area located below the menu bar (with just one breadcrumb item on this page called *Main*)
- left-hand and right-hand *menu panels* (with possible downward and side navigation to additional menu lists).

7.3.1 Enabling technology for Web applications

Central enabling technology for most Web applications is a *Web server* that serves the web pages for rendering in the browser. However, the heavy-duty processing is normally performed by an *application server* (Section 6.1.2). The application server manages the application logic (business transactions and business rules). The importance of the application server is such that it frequently performs also, almost as a side-effect, the functionality of a Web server (the Web server becomes a function of an application server).

The application server maintains the *application state* to keep track of the actions of online users. A simple technique for monitoring the state is to store a *cookie* in the browser – a short string of characters that represents the state of an online user. Because the number of online users to be monitored by the Web or application server is arbitrarily large, a *session timeout* may be imposed on the online user's activity. If the user is not

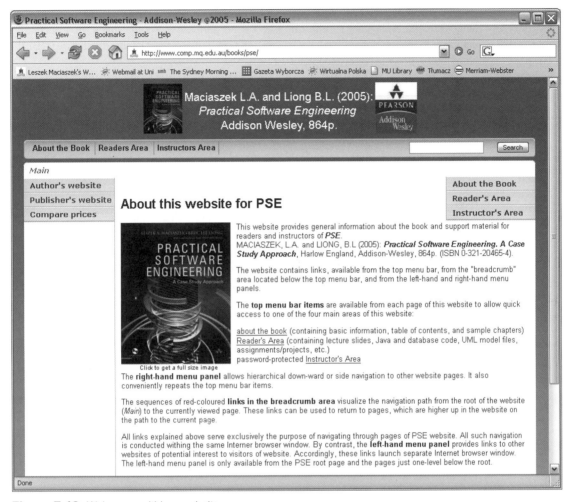

Figure 7.19 Web page within a website

active for 15 minutes (the typical timeout), the server disconnects from the client. The cookie itself may or may not be removed from the client's machine.

Scripts and applets are used to make the **client page** dynamic. A *script* (written in JavaScript, for example) is a program interpreted by the browser. An **applet** is a compiled component that executes in the browser's context but has only limited access to other resources of the client's computer (for security reasons). We say that an applet executes in a *sandbox*.

A web page can also have scripts executed by the server. Such a page is called a **server page**. A server page has access to all the resources of the database server. Server pages manage client sessions, place cookies on the browser and build client pages (build page documents from the server's business objects and send them to the client).

Standard *data access libraries* are used to allow the scripts in the server pages to access the database. Typical enabling technologies include Open Database Connectivity

(ODBC), Java Database Connectivity (JDBC), Remote Data Objects (RDO) and ActiveX Data Objects (ADO). In a situation where an organization standardizes on a particular database management system, low-level function calls to the Database Library (DBLib) allow more direct access to the database.

The enabling technology for the *Web server* is likely to be scripted HyperText Markup Language (HTML) pages, Active Server Pages (ASP) or Java Server Pages (JSP). The enabling technology for *web pages* can be client scripts (JavaScript or VBScript), eXtensible Markup Language (XML) documents, Java applets, JavaBeans or ActiveX controls.

Clients use HyperText Transfer Protocol (HTTP) to obtain web pages from the Web server. The page may be scripted or it may contain compiled and directly executable Dynamic Link Library (DLL) modules, such as Internet Server Application Programming Interface (ISAPI), Netscape Server Application Programming Interface (NSAPI), Common Gateway Interface (CGI) or Java **servlets** (Conallen 2000).

The *cookie* serves as a primitive mechanism for maintaining a connection between the client and the server in what is otherwise a *connectionless Internet* system. More sophisticated mechanisms for connecting clients and servers turn the Internet into a *distributed object system*. In such a system, objects are uniquely identified with OIDs (Appendix, Section A.2.3) and communicate by obtaining each other's OIDs. The principal mechanisms are CORBA, DCOM and EJB. With these technologies, objects can communicate without using HTTP or going through a Web server (Conallen 2000).

The deployment architecture capable of supporting more sophisticated Web applications includes four tiers of computing nodes (Section 6.1.1):

1 client with browser

2 Web server

3 application server

4 database server.

The browser of the *client node* can be used to display static or dynamic pages. Scripted pages and applets can be downloaded and run within the browser. Additional functionality can be supplied to the client's browser with objects such as ActiveX controls or JavaBeans. Running application code on the client, but outside the browser, may satisfy other GUI requirements.

The *Web server* handles page requests from the browser and dynamically generates pages and code for execution and display on the client. The Web server also deals with customization and parameterization of the session with the user.

The *application server* is indispensable when distributed objects are involved in the implementation. It manages the business logic. The business components publish their interfaces to other nodes via component interfaces such as CORBA, DCOM or EJB.

The business components encapsulate persistent data stored in a database, probably a relational database. They communicate with the *database server* via database connectivity protocols such as JDBC or ODBC. The database node provides for scalable storage of data and multi-user access to it.

Content design   7.3.2

Web content design is a topic in its own right that has led to a new and "hot" profession – Web content designer. *Content design* has to do with how a website's or Web application's visual content is presented to a user in a Web browser. Like in desktop GUI design, Web content design requires the combined skills of a visual artist at one end of the spectrum and a software developer at the other end. The principles of good GUI design apply equally well to Web content design (Section 7.1.2).

The distinguishing factor between desktop and Web content design seems to be that the audience of a website or application is not necessarily known to the designer. Accordingly, the design has to be even more accommodating and take into consideration varying users' needs, interests, skills and preferences. This makes all the guidelines discussed in Section 7.1.2 even more important.

The content has to match the nature and the purpose of a website or application. Sklar (2006) distinguishes the following content goals on the scale from websites to Web applications:

- *billboard* – it establishes a Web presence for an organization
- *publishing* – it publishes newspapers and periodicals
- *portal* – it publishes its own informational content while acting as a gateway to Web services and resources, such as shopping, searching, e-mail (advertising content is the main source of revenue)
- *special interest, public interest and non-profit organizations* – it contains news, contact information, links, downloadable files and so on, according to the purpose
- *blog* – short for weblog, it contains private or limited scope pages that reflect the unique interests or endeavor of the blog's creator and invite contributions from other "bloggers"
- *virtual gallery* – it contains samples of the textual, visual and audiovisual work of writers, artists, photographers, musicians and so on (typically the material is copyrighted using digital watermarking technology)
- *e-commerce, catalog and online shopping* – it (undoubtedly an application, not just a site) makes it possible to conduct business over the Internet
- *product support* – it disseminates information, instructions, upgrades, advice, documentation, tutorials and other support to the products' users and consumers
- *Intranet and extranet* – it allows employees to access an organization's software applications as well as documentation, policies, e-mail and so on via its private local area networks (all this is also accessible via the Internet in the case of an extranet).

Website to Web application continuum   7.3.2.1

This book is about modeling software applications, but, in the case of Web applications (as observed in passing), the demarcation line between a site and an application is blurred. Instead of distinguishing between the two, we should instead be talking about a *continuum* of Web-based developments in which a site can somewhat transparently turn into an application. As an example, consider a book's website in Figure 7.19, discussed at the beginning of Section 7.3. Does the `Search` capability (in the upper right-hand corner of the page) transform this site into an application? What if the site provided online tests for students?

Associated with the site-to-application continuum is *another continuum* – a desktop application to Web application continuum. After all, many applications are first developed for the desktop platform and are only later made available for the Internet medium. A Web-based transactional business application demands at least the same kind of robust modeling and engineering as a corresponding desktop application. If anything, the ease of accessibility and the unknown user base of Web applications means that they require even more engineering rigor (in areas such as security, for example).

Unfortunately, from the software development perspective, the two continuums are in a bit of conflict. The transformation of a website into a Web application brings with it a risk that the sound engineering may be nowhere to see in the resulting application. The most important danger is the emergence of an application that is not based on a sound architectural backbone and, therefore, not adaptive (see Sections 4.1, 6.2 and elsewhere in the book).

Despite the discussed continuums, the definition of a Web application can be quite clearcut. One such definition was given at the very beginning of Section 7.3 – "A Web application is a Web system that allows its users to execute business logic with a web browser" (Conallen 2000: 10). One of the best-known Web development tools – Macromedia Dreamweaver – defines a Web application as "a collection of web pages that interact with visitors, with each other, and with various resources on a web server, including databases."

The above two definitions of a Web application make it clear that the nature of the interaction capabilities that are provided for the user and Web browser determine when a website becomes an application. From the software perspective, the difference is between working with *static* as opposed to *dynamic* web pages. Macromedia Dreamweaver clarifies this point as follows:

> A Web application is a website that contains pages with partly or entirely undetermined content. The final content of a page is determined only when the visitor requests a page from the Web server. Because the final content of the page varies from request to request based on the visitor's actions, this kind of page is called a dynamic page.

Incidentally, the distinction between static and dynamic web pages is also reflected in the distinction between a Web server and application server. A *Web server* manages static pages. It finds them on the request from the browser and sends them to the browser. An *application server* manages dynamic pages. It receives an incomplete page from the Web server, scans the page for instructions, communicates with the database for requested information, inserts new information into the page and passes the page to the Web server.

7.3.2.2 Forms

A Web application executes within the browser's overall *frame*, which includes the frame's title bar, menu bar, button bar and URL address bar (Figure 7.20). The application's content area consists of its own frames, including the navigation frames, action buttons and **forms**.

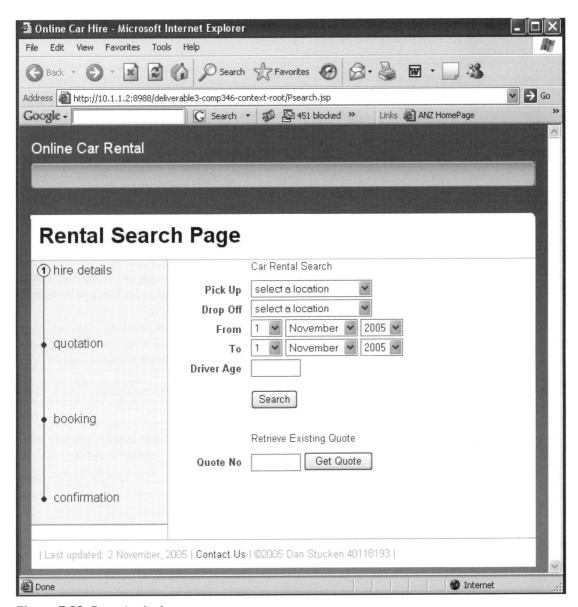

Figure 7.20 Example of a form

A *form* displays information to the user, allows data entry and sends collected information to the server to process and display the results in the page. As seen in Figure 7.20, the form consists of *fields* in which information can be entered. The data input can be facilitated by having various controls that are familiar from desktop applications, such as drop-down or open list boxes, checkboxes or radio buttons. Forms can also be constructed as tab folders, contain tables, display message boxes and so on.

The design guidelines for fields on a Web form are also similar to those for desktop applications. Fowler and Stanwick (2004) list and discuss the following guidelines:

- decide the field type (Should it take an arbitrary text? Should it be restricted to predefined values? Is it required – that is, the value *must* be provided?)
- make the fields the right size – typically, make the size of the field frame or box the same as the field length, but remember that the fields can scroll horizontally and the size can be smaller than a length for big fields
- make the application format the field values, if possible – text justified to the left, numbers justified to the right and so on
- provide both keyboard and mouse navigation within fields (but remember that data entry people prefer entering data via the keyboard and hate being forced to switch to the mouse, so don't make them)
- if the application logic allows it, retain the browser's cut, copy and paste facility on field values
- label the fields and align them either to the left or to the right (left-alignment may be preferred when the fields are different lengths and/or the users are likely to be entering data by tabbing from field to field – see Figure 7.21)
- break long forms into a number of separate forms or (in the case of a single-transaction form) ensure that there are no "false bottoms" – that is, any visual indications between the fields that may suggest that the bottom of the form has been reached
- group fields in a visually appealing manner (not necessarily in boxes or frames)
- make sure that there are clear visual indications of any value-restrictive and required fields, including text for visually impaired people
- use drop-down lists when possible, but replace them with open pop-up lists with scroll bars when the number of items on the list is too long for a drop-down display
- if possible, use checkboxes and radio buttons (these also help to prevent data entry errors).

Example 7.4: currency converter

Refer to Problem statement 7, for a currency converter system (Section 1.6.7), to examples for it in Chapter 5 and Example 7.3 (Section 7.2.2.1). Assume that the currency converter should be able to convert money from only Australian dollars, but to any other major currency. Allow also for conversion of different currency types, including cash and money transfers. Assume that the result of the conversion will be displayed in a separate form on a separate web page.

Design a Web form for the Web-based currency converter as specified above.

Figure 7.22 illustrates the web form for a currency converter provided as a service to customers by the National Australia Bank (NAB), as per Example 7.4. The form consists of three fields and two action buttons. Two of the fields supply drop-down lists to selected relevant entries.

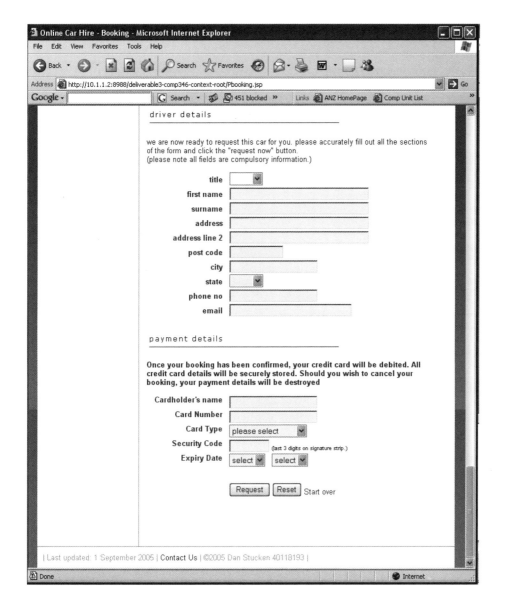

Figure 7.21
Form fields

Example 7.5: currency converter

Refer to Example 7.4 above. Design a Web form for the result of the currency conversion. The form should display the exchange rate applied, the amount of money after conversion and the date of exchange. It should also allow the user to return to the data entry form to conduct the next conversion.

Figure 7.22
Form design for
entering data for a
currency
converter system

Print Page | Increase Font Size | Close

Foreign Exchange calculator

Pocket currency converter

Use this Pocket Currency Converter to make up a handy wallet size currency converter which you can use as an approximate refrence while travelling.

1. Select your required currency
2. Press 'Calculate'
3. Print 'Results' screen
4. Cut and fold

Select a currency to convert

Choose currency [United States Dollar ▼]

◄ cancel │ calculate ►

© National Australia Bank Limited. Use of the information contained on this page is governed by Australian law and is subject to the disclaimers which can be read on the disclaimer page. View the NAB Privacy Policy.

Figure 7.23 illustrates the result form for the NAB's currency converter for Example 7.5.

A Web form works within a browser and some standard browser's menu and toolbar functions can act on the form, unless explicitly restricted by the Web application. Functions that may need to be restricted include (Fowler and Stanwick 2004):

■ back and forward buttons to navigate between web pages in a way not controlled by the application (such navigation can cause the loss of the user's input or interrupt a business transaction)

Figure 7.23
Form design for
displaying the
currency
converter's results

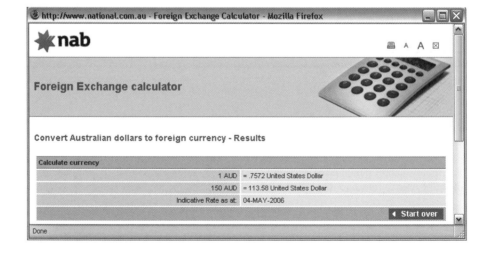

- buttons and menu items that can close the browser and, therefore, exit the application in an uncontrolled manner
- editing, downloading and printing capabilities for applications in which access to information must be restricted to legitimate users.

Navigation design   7.3.3

Navigation between GUI screens (windows, web pages) happens as a result of either an action by the user or the application code. In desktop applications, users' navigation between windows is enabled by menu items, toolbar buttons, command buttons and keyboard strokes. Similar capabilities exist in Web applications although visual representations may vary, in particular for menu items and toolbar buttons. In fact, menu bars and toolbars in the desktop sense do not normally exist in Web applications. On the other hand, active links (hyperlinks) for users' navigation in Web applications do not exist in desktop applications.

If anything, navigation in Web applications tends to be more user-friendly than in desktop applications. There is no distinction between primary and secondary windows – each web page can present any mix of navigation capabilities; *menus* of various kinds can coexist with *buttons*, *links* and *breadcrumbs* (navigation panels). Figure 7.19 shows a web page featuring a number of menus (explained in the content panel of the page) and some active links (the text underlined in the content panel). Figure 7.20 demonstrates a web page with action buttons and a menu on the left-hand side showing the current step in the workflow process leading to renting a car.

Navigation between an application's web pages has to be carefully planned. There must be some clear underlying logic in navigation that the user can understand, either intuitively or with the assistance of navigation panels visible in pages. The user should never feel lost in the "hyperspace" of web pages.

Navigation styles vary depending on the nature and complexity of a Web application. Transaction-based business applications, as in Figure 7.20, tend to enforce a workflow of activities on sequences of pages. They allow exploration in the initial stages when the user is searching for a product or service, but later they guide the user towards the payment. Data entry applications tend to consist of a small number of longer pages with little navigation to facilitate fast typing without the need to switch between pages. Applications that target retrieval operations, such as library systems, provide search facilities by different criteria, linear browsing through the retrieved items, scanning the content of selected items and so on. Some applications may also provide site maps to connect to and from all pages.

Menus and links   7.3.3.1

Menus and links are two of the main facilities for navigating between web pages. Figure 7.24 is a fragment of the page shown in Figure 7.19, with menus and links indicated. Menus and links have similar *affordance*. Affordance is a term used for the behavior that users expect from a GUI item (Fowler and Stanwick 2004). The *affordance of a link* is that it leads to another web page. The *affordance of a menu* is also to move to another page, but occasionally a menu item can additionally do something in the process of presenting another page. Moreover, menus can be hierarchical, so some menu items may in fact not move to a new page but just present a drop-down list of *submenu* items (see Figure 7.25).

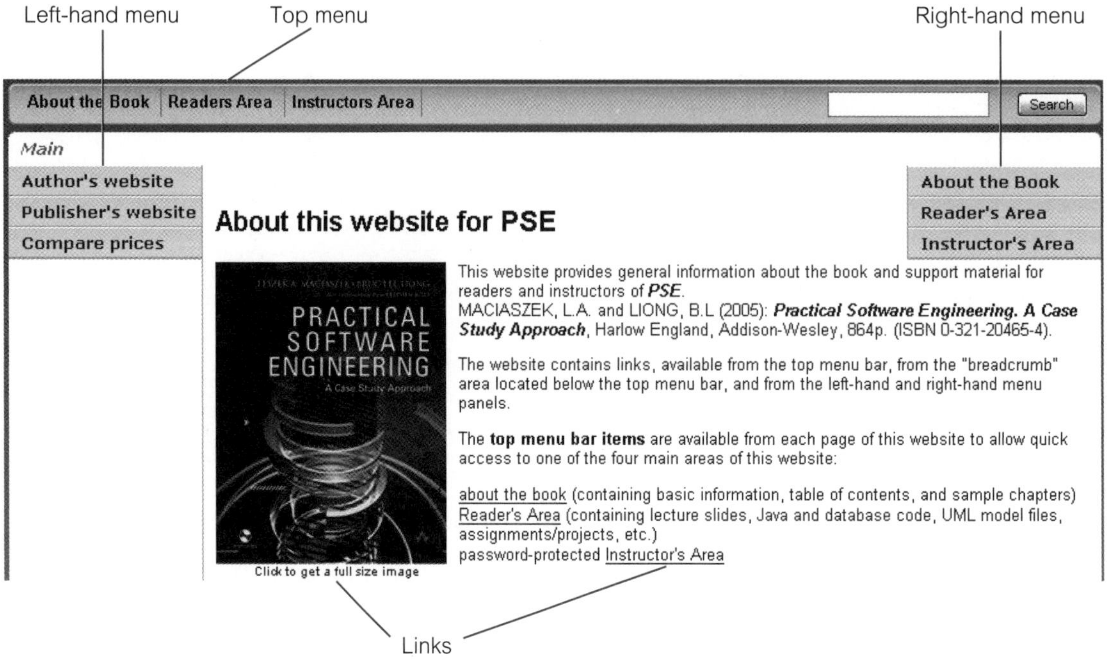

Figure 7.24 Menus and links

We can distinguish between:

- ∎ top menus
- ∎ left-hand menus
- ∎ right-hand menus.

A *top menu* is typically used for sitewide navigation. The design rules for left-hand and right-hand menus are more flexible. In Figure 7.24, the *left-hand menu* is used for navigations that reach pages beyond the control of the website, whereas the *right-hand menu* displays pages within the scope of the website. An argument could be made for reversing these two menus. Such an argument could be made on at least two grounds. Many applications (as opposed to sites) would have a single exit facility and not allow for back and forth movements to outside sites or applications. Moreover, research into how people scan pages informs us that typical users scan pages from the left, then look at the top and, finally, to the centre and to the right (Fowler and Stanwick 2004). Consequently, it may be more sensible for the menu that concentrates on the essence of the site or application to be placed on the left-hand side where users will look first.

Breadcrumbs and navigation panels

There are special kinds of menus, the main function of which is informational rather than to facilitate movement between pages. These are breadcrumbs and other navigation panels – they offer a visualization of the location of the current page within the sequence of pages and are used to navigate to that page.

A *breadcrumb* area is customarily placed at the top of the page just below the top menu, if any (Figure 7.25). The area consists of a set of linked labels that tell users where they are (which page they are currently working with). So, the breadcrumb items change as the user navigates between pages. Typically, they also allow the user to move back to the pages they visited before.

Navigation panels (Figure 7.26) are similar to breadcrumbs, but they are likely to be used in transactional applications, show all steps in a transactional workflow and may not permit movement to the previous steps without canceling the transaction's progress. Frequently, forward movement to the pages in the workflow is achieved by actions on buttons on the previous page rather than by clicking in the navigation panel. Also, the location of a navigation panel on the page is up to the discretion of the designer and is perhaps not at the top of the page.

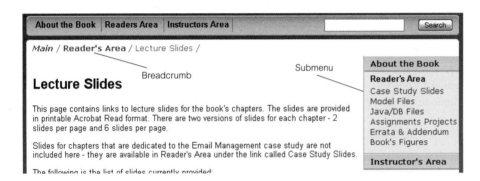

Figure 7.25
Breadcrumb and submenu

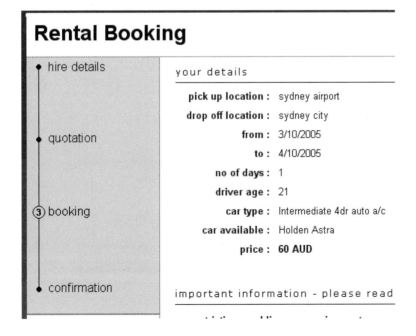

Figure 7.26
Navigation panel

7.3.3.3 Buttons

In desktop applications, computational actions are called, sometimes interchangeably, by menu items and buttons. In Web applications, *buttons* (Figure 7.27) are the main facility for invoking actions, while menu items serve just a navigational purpose. The *affordance of a button* is to do something when it is pressed (Fowler and Stanwick 2004).

The design principles for buttons in desktop applications apply also to buttons in web pages. The buttons should be (Fowler and Stanwick 2004):

- the same size as each other if they are placed in a related group of buttons and if the amount of text on them does not differ dramatically
- kept together in their own area on the page and separately from data entry fields
- repeated at the top and bottom of the page if the page is longer than the window size
- carefully placed in tab frames to distinguish between the actions that apply to individual tabs and those that apply to a whole tab frame
- programmed to ignore multiple presses by impatient users
- named to precisely indicate the action they will take (in particular, to indicate when the action results in saving to the database as opposed to a temporary saving that could be "undone" by the user).

Figure 7.27
Buttons

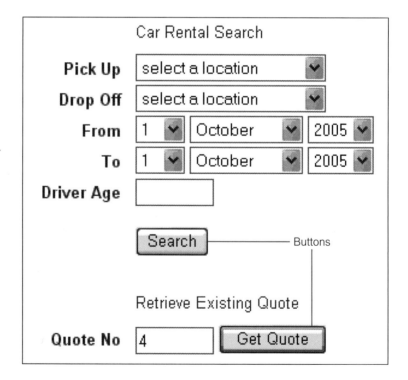

Using GUI frameworks to leverage Web design   7.3.4

Developers use system software to build application software. As a classic and long-standing example, developers invariably rely on database management systems for persistent storage of data. Except in exotic cases, building application-specific persistency mechanisms is not even contemplated. Similarly, Enterprise Resource Planning (ERP) systems provide standard solutions for accounting, human resources and manufacturing systems.

Likewise, on the GUI-end of application development, various software frameworks exist to leverage GUI design. Integrated Development Environments (IDEs) that programmers use are just that – *environments*, not programming languages. Modern programming is more an activity that involves composing software from pre-existing reusable components than developing new lines of source code. This places special expectations and demands on programmers, but also on system designers, architects and even analysts.

By a *GUI framework*, we understand here any technology, software library or other GUI-directed system software that developers can use to leverage GUI design. Typical frameworks in this category include the Swing library, Java Server Faces, Struts, Spring and so on. The frameworks take some implementation responsibilities from the application code, thus reducing the complexity of the application software. A particular development objective should be to use technologies that not only ease programming but also allow systems to be constructed in compliance with the chosen architectural design. It turns out, as discussed next, that certain technologies can be indispensable for ensuring that some of the most important architectural objectives and design principles are achieved.

The MVC dilemma   7.3.4.1

One of the architectural issues that is tricky is the separation and elimination of cycles between `Presentation` and `Control` in both programmable client and Web-based applications. The issue is tricky because an interactive style of communication between the user and the system creates natural cycles of processing – `Presentation` submits requests for `Control` services and `Control` decides the `Presentation` object that should receive the response.

Perhaps not surprisingly, related technologies divide into centralized (known as *Model 1*) and decentralized (*Model 2*). In *Model 1*, each `Presentation` object is paired with a `Control` object (as in Java Swing or Microsoft Foundation Classes (MFC)). In *Model 2*, advocated by the Core PCBMER framework, a physical separation exists between `Presentation` and `Control`. Hence, for Web-based applications, JSPs are placed in the `Presentation` layer and servlets in the `Control` layer. However, decoupling alone is not a big gain unless circular dependencies are eliminated by making servlets independent from JSPs. As JSPs, being HTML pages, cannot implement interfaces or subscribe to events, we face a dilemma when deciding how to solve the problem under the Model-View-Controller (MVC) umbrella (Section 4.1.1).

As shown in Figure 7.28, in answer to the task set in Example 7.6 (overleaf), the processing starts when a `Request` web page accepts a user's input, instantiates a `Calculator` object and asks it to `calculate()` the exchange amount. To be able to do the calculation, `Calculator` needs to `getRate()` from the database. This task is performed by a `Query` object. After obtaining the exchange rate, `Calculator` instantiates a `Bean` object and sets its content with data ready for display in a `Result` web page. `Calculator` instantiates a `Result` object and passes to it the reference to `Bean`. This enables `Result` to get `Bean`'s data and render it to the screen. A user's request to `startOver()` results in passing the control back to the `Request` web page.

Figure 7.28
Sequence
diagram for an
initial design for a
currency
converter

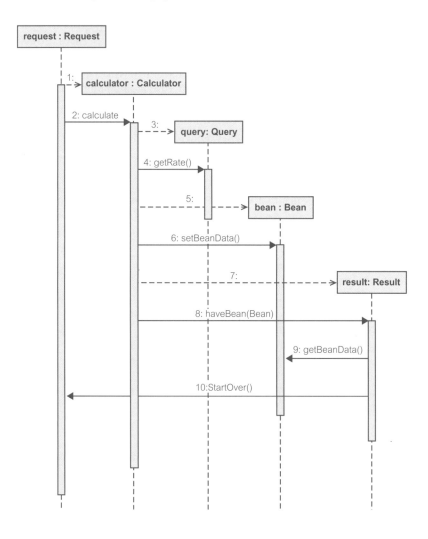

Example 7.7: currency converter

Refer to Example 7.6 above. Design a class dependency diagram for the sequence diagram in Figure 7.28. What can you observe? What is the structural complexity of the design?

Figure 7.29 is a class dependency diagram for the sequence diagram in Figure 7.28 for Example 7.7. The diagram shows a worrying cyclic dependency between `Request`, `Calculator` and `Result`. For the particular case in Figure 7.28, the actual number of origin/destination communication links is 6. However, the actual measure cannot be used as an indicator of structural complexity (Section 6.2.1.2). The design is a network structure for which the *cumulative class dependency* (*CCD*) is given by Equation 7.1 (based on Equation 6.3 in Section 6.2.1.2.1).

$$_{net}CCD = n(n-1) = 5 \times 4 = 20 \qquad \text{Equation 7.1}$$

Using Struts technology

7.3.4.2

The designs for the currency converter above are clearly unsatisfactory. Assistance can come in the form of GUI frameworks, such as Jakarta Struts (Sam-Bodden and Judd 2004).

Figure 7.30 shows how **Struts** can be used for a simple Web application. The application starts from a JSP page (`PX`). In a configuration file `web.xml`, Struts defines an `ActionServlet` class that is loaded on startup and is configured to receive submit requests. The servlet implementation acts as a hub for the `Controller` package and delegates application-specific functionality to `Action` classes. Struts encapsulates the request information in an `ActionForm` object implemented as a JavaBean. The mapping between JSPs, actions and forms is maintained in the Struts main configuration file `struts-config.xml`.

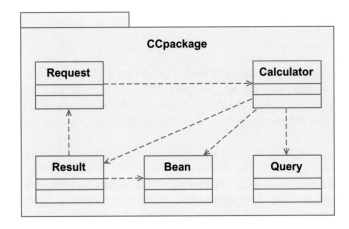

Figure 7.29
Class dependency diagram for an initial design for a currency converter

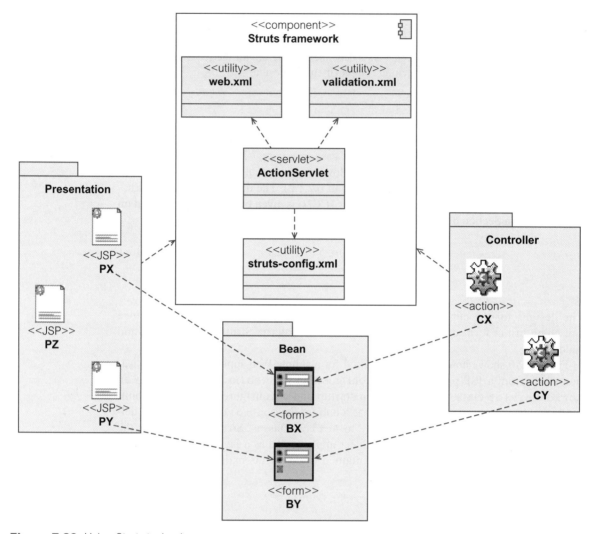

Figure 7.30 Using Struts technology

Struts also provides support for validation of a user's input. The validation code can be placed in the `validate()` method, which is called before the `Action`'s `execute()` method. A configuration file `validation.xml` informs Struts where to pass the control to display an error message (such as to PZ) when the `validate()` method discovers inputting errors.

On successful validation of a user's input, `ActionServlet` passes control to an action class. The `struts-config.xml` mapping ties `Action` classes to `ActionForm` classes. For example, BY would contain data set by CY and prepared for display in a JSP page. When CY finishes, it returns forward and this is used to determine a JSP page to gain control on success (such as PY) or determine a JSP that would report a failure (such as PX) (the forward is returned to `ActionServlet`, which consults `struts_config.xml` to determine the presentation component to forward the request to).

Apart from the elements shown Figure 7.30, Struts includes many other features that make Web development easier and the end result conform even better to the MVC framework. So, tag libraries are provided as a replacement for Java code in JSPs and as a replacement for functionality that would otherwise be implemented in servlets. The Struts Tiles framework provides a separate layout JSP to simplify common visual elements and page layouts.

All in all, Struts presents a powerful framework technology for addressing dependency concerns with MVC and architectural designs that build up on the MVC ideas, such as PCBMER. Figure 7.31 generalizes Figure 7.30 to show that "technology-managed" dependencies from the application components to Struts virtually eliminate dependencies between `Presentation` and `Controller`. To be precise, dependencies exist, but they are managed by a meta-layer of Struts software that provides declarative means of defining dependencies and takes responsibility for managing the flow of application logic. Accordingly, as shown in Figure 7.31, `Presentation` and `Controller` depend on Struts, but do not depend on each other.

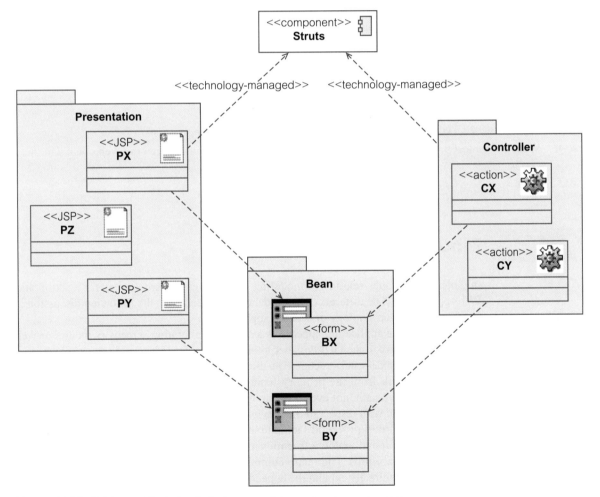

Figure 7.31 Relying on Struts to eliminate upward dependencies and cycles

Example 7.8: currency converter

Refer to Examples 7.6 and 7.7. Use Struts technology to make the design for a currency converter compliant with PCBMER architecture and design a relevant class dependency diagram. Refer to the Struts component in a generic sense, as in Figure 7.31. Assign classes to appropriate PCBMER layers (but there is no need to use the `Entity` layer). What is the structural complexity of the design?

Figure 7.32 represents a PCBMER-compliant Struts design for a currency converter application in answer to Example 7.8. Struts provides a brokerage service between `Presentation` and `Controller`, which effectively replaces *architecture-managed* dependencies with *technology managed* dependencies.

The resulting CCD for the design using Struts technology is given by Equation 7.2 below (based on Equation 6.4 in Section 6.2.1.2.2):

$$_{holarchy}CCD = \sum_{i=1}^{n} \frac{size(l_i) * (size(l_i) - 1)}{2} + \sum_{i=1}^{n} \sum_{j=1}^{l_i} (size(l_i) * size(p_j(l_i))) = 2 + 8 = 10$$

Equation 7.2

Review quiz 7.3

RQ1 What are the GUI components for programming user events in Web applications?

RQ2 What is the most primitive mechanism for maintaining a connection between the Web client and the server?

RQ3 What is the affordance of a link?

7.4 Modeling GUI navigation

In general, the issues relating to modeling GUI navigation are similar for desktop and Web applications. The differences are in details. Consequently, the following discussion is conducted in the terminology of desktop applications.

To the user, the application appears as a set of collaborating screens (windows or web pages). It is the task of the GUI designer to organize the dependencies between screens in a coherent, easy to understand structure. The user should never feel lost among opened screens.

Ideally, the link from the primary window to the top secondary window currently opened should be a path, not even a hierarchy. This can be achieved by making a secondary window *modal* with respect to the previous window.

While the GUI design should facilitate the user's exploration of the interface, a good design of the *menu* and *toolbar* structures remains the principal technique to explain the application's capabilities. The menu commands available to the user in pull-down and slide-off menus indirectly explain the dependencies between windows.

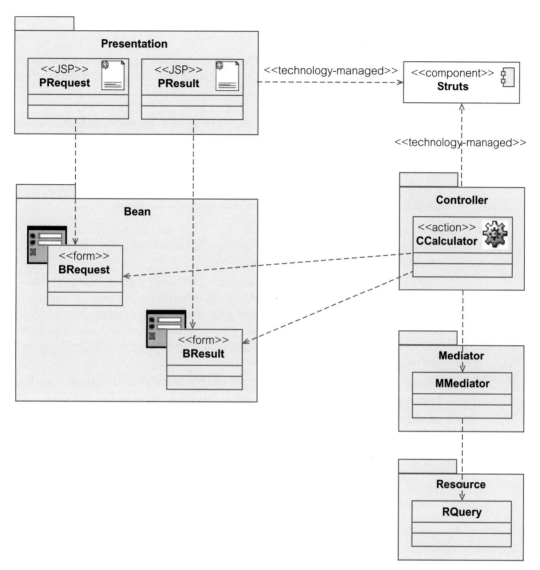

Figure 7.32 Class dependency diagram for a Struts design for a currency converter system

The graphical depiction of GUI windows – using prototyping or other GUI layout tools – does not inform how the windows can actually be *navigated* by the user. We still need to design the *window navigation*. A window navigation model should consist of diagrams visualizing screen containers and components and showing how the user can traverse from one window to another.

7.4.1 User experience storyboards

Sketching the structure and logic behind the application's presentation and navigation choices is sometimes called *storyboarding* (Sklar 2006). UML lacks a direct storyboard modeling capability but UML profiles have been offered to address that shortcoming. One such profile is the *user experience* (**UX**) *storyboards* (Heumann 2003).

In the absence of UX storyboards or similar window navigation models, the designer might have no choice but to enrich the use case specifications by including window prototypes as part of the use case documents. This has been the approach used in this book so far whenever we have felt that the understanding of use case descriptions lacked precision without presenting screen prototypes.

Modeling with UX storyboards consists of five steps (Heumann 2003).

1 *Add actor characteristics to the use case* This includes a definition of the actor's (user's) (Section 3.1.1) computer literacy, domain knowledge and frequency with which he or she will be accessing the system.

2 *Add usability characteristics to the use case* Usability (Section 7.1.2.6) is a non-functional requirement, normally defined as system constraints in supplementary specifications (Section 2.6.4). The usability characteristics include helpful hints (such as how to make the GUI easier to use or easier to implement) and any rigorous requirements that must be conformed to (system response time, acceptable error rates, learning times and so on, for example).

3 *Identify UX elements* This involves the identification of GUI containers and components. A specially stereotyped class model is used to represent UX elements.

4 *Model the use case flows with the UX elements* This is UX-driven behavioral collaboration modeling (Section 7.4.3). UML sequence and class diagrams are used to depict the interaction between the user and the GUI presentation screens or between the GUI screens themselves.

5 *Model screen navigation for the use case* This is UX-driven structural collaboration modeling (Section 7.4.4). Stereotyped UML class diagrams are used to depict associations along which the navigation between UX elements takes place.

All in all, UX storyboards aim to give justice to the GUI design as an inherent part of system design. They represent the modeling aspects of GUI design and are concerned with issues such as (Kozaczynski and Thario 2003):

■ user's presentation screens

■ user-instigated screen events that the system must react to

■ data that the system displays on the screen

■ data that the user enters on the screen for further processing

■ the screen's decomposition to smaller areas that should be managed separately by other areas

■ transitions (navigation) between screens.

The UX storyboarding profile introduces several stereotypes for classes. The main stereotypes are <<screen>>, <<input form>> and <<compartment>>. These stereotypes are at a relatively high level of abstraction. A more complete list of stereotypes could consider other UX elements, perhaps classified by structural and behavioral collaboration. A possible list is as follows.

1 Structural UX elements:
   - primary window
     - pane in primary window
   - row browser
   - tree browser.

2 Secondary window:
   - dialog box
   - message box
   - tab folder.

3 Window data:
   - text box
   - combo box
   - spin box
   - column
   - row
   - group of fields.

4 Behavioral UX elements:
   - drop-down menu item
   - pop-up menu item
   - toolbar button
   - command button
   - double-click
   - list selection
   - keyboard key
   - keyboard function key
   - keyboard accelerator key
   - scrolling button
   - window close button.

Modeling UX elements   7.4.2

The UX profile offers only a few stereotypes to serve as the primary UX modeling elements. The most encompassing is a stereotype for a *package* called <<storyboard>>. This stereotype defines a package that contains a UX storyboard.

The UML *classes* can be stereotyped as:

- <<screen>> – the screen abstraction defines a window rendered on the screen

- `<<input form>>` – this stereotype represents a window's container form through which the user can interact with the system by entering data or by activating some actions. The input form is a part of a screen. This can be a class derived from Java Swing library, such as `JInternalFrame`, `JTabbedPane`, `JDialog`, or `JApplet`

- `<<compartment>>` – this stereotype represents any region of a screen that can be reused by multiple screens. This can be, for example, a toolbar.

The UX class elements contain the GUI dynamic content (fields on the screen) and any actions associated with screens, input forms and compartments. The UX profile predefines some tags (Section 5.1.1.3) associated with the *fields* (Kozaczynski and Thario 2003). Other tags can be added by the UX designers. Three most interesting tags specify if a field is:

- *editable* indicates if the field can be modified by the user or not
- *visible* indicates if the field is displayed on the screen or hidden from the user's view (but still accessible to the program)
- *selectable* indicates if the field can be selected (highlighted or otherwise shown as active).

For example, a field can have tag values such as `{editable = true, visibility = visible}` or `{editable = false, visibility = hidden}`. Alternatively, the fact that a field is visible can be indicated by marking it with a public visibility icon (a plus (+) symbol in front of the name). For hidden visibility, a private visibility marker (a minus (–) sign) can be used.

There are two categories of *action* to be listed in the UX classes – user actions and environmental actions (Heumann 2003). *User actions* are any GUI events coming from the user. *Environmental actions* are any GUI events coming from the system. Navigation to a new screen is one of the most noticeable environmental actions. The UX profile recommends that environmental actions be distinguished with a dollar sign prefixing the action's name.

Example 7.9: advertising expenditure

Refer to Figure 7.5 (Section 7.2.1). Our task is to identify the main UX modeling elements (class-level stereotypes) that are being used to represent the content of the screen in this figure.

Figure 7.33 presents a UX class model that represents the content of the screen in Figure 7.5 for Example 7.9. The screen consists of four compartments and one input form.

7.4.3 Behavioral UX collaboration

Once the class-level UX elements are known, it is possible to start modeling the UX flows of events between these elements. The UX flows of events capture the behavioral aspect of a UX communication. Accordingly, the UML interaction diagrams (sequence and/or collaboration diagrams) are used to represent UX flows of events.

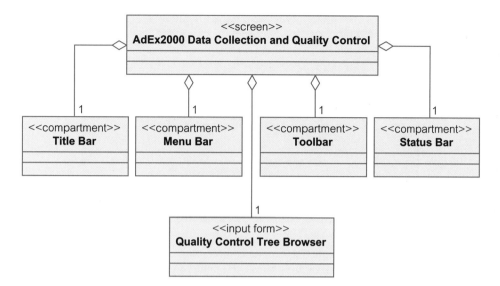

Figure 7.33
UX elements for
the primary
window for an
advertising
expenditure
system

Example 7.10: contact management

Refer to Figures 7.3 (Section 7.1.1) and 7.6 (Section 7.2.1). Figure 7.3 is the "Update Organization" window. The window features a field (drop-down list) named "Status". This field defines the status of the organization from the contact management perspective (that the organization is a potential, past or current client, say).

The list of organization statuses is short and relatively fixed (Figure 7.34), but there is an occasional need to modify the list (insert, update or delete a list item). The user can display the current list (possibly for updating or deleting) by double-clicking on the "Organization Status" option in the tree browser seen on the left-hand side in Figure 7.6. However, to insert a new organization status, the user has to select (highlight) the "Organization Status" option in the tree browser and then use an "Insert" action from the menu bar (this is the "Record" item in Figure 7.6) or from a toolbar (a small square icon in Figure 7.6).

Our task in this example is to identify the UX elements and design a behavioral UX collaboration for the process of inserting a new organization status. Normally, modeling with UX storyboards replaces the need for window prototypes, but, to assist us in this example, Figure 7.35 shows a possible "Insert Organization Status" window.

Organization Status		
Code ▽	Org Status ○	
1	Prospective customer in long term	
2	Prospective customer soon	
3	Current customer	
4	Past customer	
5	Current customer with contract soon t...	
6	Uncertain if a good prospect	

Figure 7.34 Organization status in a contact management system

Source: Courtesy of Nielsen Media Research, Sydney, Australia

Figure 7.35
A window to insert
new organization
status for a
contact
management
system
Source: Courtesy of
Nielsen Media
Research, Sydney,
Australia

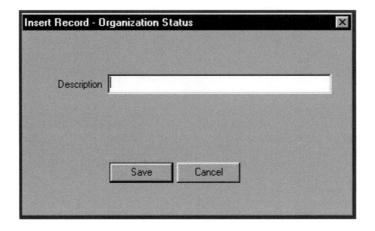

The UX elements for Example 7.10 include three classes from Figure 7.33, namely `Quality Control Tree Browser`, `Menu Bar` and `Toolbar`. The UX class model in Figure 7.36 presents the remaining classes needed for Example 7.10. These are the classes associated with the window to insert the new organization status data (Figure 7.35).

Figure 7.37 is a sequence diagram for the *behavioral UX collaboration* necessary to fulfill the requirements of Example 7.10. The model shows branching due to the conditionality of some of the users' actions. For example, they have the option to obtain the `Insert Organization Status` screen by using either a `Menu Bar` (event 2) or a `Toolbar` (event 3). The branched event flows can be rejoined at some point (such as at events 4 and 5). Note that after pressing the `Save` or `Cancel` button, users are presented with the main screen containing the `Quality Control Tree Browser`.

UX collaboration models are restricted to human–computer interaction. This means, from the PCBMER perspective, that the only classes involved are from the `Presentation` layer. Hence, for example, the model in Figure 7.37 does not show any processing involved in saving a new organization status in the database and showing this new status in the "Organization Status" row browser (Figure 7.34).

Similarly, the model does not make any reference to the fact that when a status description is saved, the database generates a `Code` for it (Figure 7.34). The fact that the code needs to be displayed in the "Organization Status" row browser is a matter for another UX collaboration model (but such a model is beyond Example 7.10).

Figure 7.36
UX elements for a
dialog box for a
contact
management
system

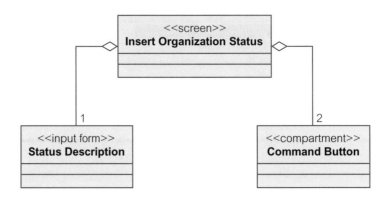

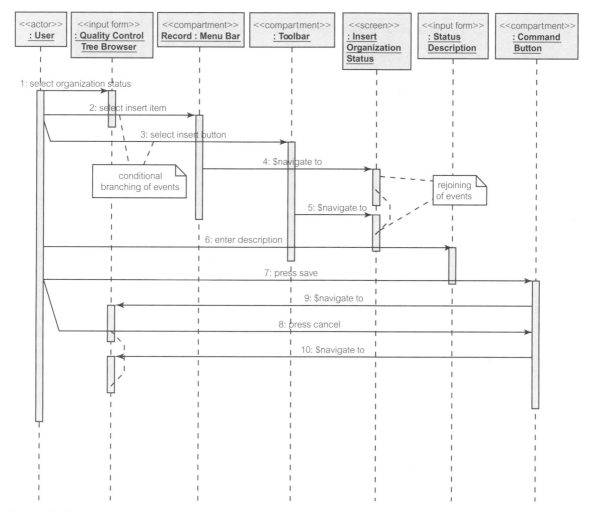

Figure 7.37 A sequence diagram for behavioral UX collaboration model for a contact management system

Strucural UX collaboration

The structural aspect of UX collaboration is largely derivable from the behavioral UX collaboration. *Structural UX collaboration* produces a UX-stereotyped class diagram. The attribute box of each class presents the dynamic content for a screen, input form or compartment. The operation box of each class presents user and environmental events.

The structural UX collaboration model serves as a *navigation diagram* for the use case that is the basis of the UX storyboard. To this end, the structural UX model shows arrowed relationships between classes to indicate possible navigations between screens, input forms and compartments.

Example 7.11: contact management

Refer to Example 7.10 (Section 7.4.3). Our task is to produce a structural UX collaboration model corresponding to the behavioral UX collaboration model in Figure 7.37.

The model requested for Example 7.11 is demonstrated in Figure 7.38. The classes and the events within classes have been derived directly from the sequence diagram in Figure 7.37. The dynamic content for the classes has been specified according to the windows shown in Figures 7.6 and 7.35 (however, we emphasize again that, in most situations, UX storyboards alleviate the need for developing window layouts or prototypes).

The dynamic content of the UX classes in Figure 7.38 is annotated with tag values. The tags specify the editability and selectability of fields. The visibility of fields is marked with a plus sign in front of their names (meaning that the fields are visible).

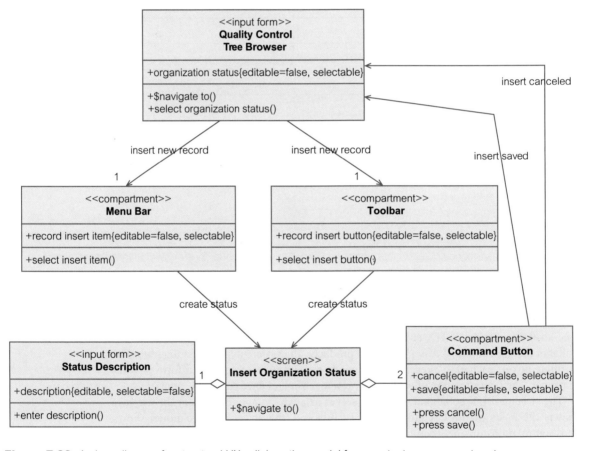

Figure 7.38 A class diagram for structural UX collaboration model for a contact management system

Navigation diagrams like that in Figure 7.38 should be defined for all use cases in the system. It is also possible to build navigation diagrams for the actions of activity diagrams. Higher-level navigation diagrams, showing the main navigation paths between all screens in the system, may be desirable as well.

Review quiz 7.4

RQ1 What is the name of a UX stereotype representing screen regions?

RQ2 How is a hidden field modeled in a UX storyboard?

RQ3 What UML diagram is used for modeling a behavioral UX collaboration?

Summary

The development of the GUI spans the software production lifecycle – starting in the analysis phase and extending to implementation. In this chapter, we have addressed GUI design for both *desktop* and *Web* clients. With regard to desktop clients, the Microsoft Windows environment has been emphasized. We have discussed both GUI visual elements and the navigation between GUI windows or web pages. We have also introduced a UML profile called a UX storyboard that offers a graphical notation to depict the window design and navigation.

GUI design is a *multidisciplinary activity*, requiring the combined expertise of different professions. The guidelines for good GUI design address such issues as the "user in control" principle, consistency, personalization, customization, forgiveness, feedback, aesthetics and usability.

The design of a GUI requires familiarity with the various containers and components available for a particular client platform. The *containers* define various windows and web pages used in the application. Containers are considered to be one category of GUI *component*. Menus, toolbars, links, buttons and so on are other kinds of component. A Java Swing library for desktop design and Jakarta Struts framework for Web design are examples of technologies that offer customizable solutions for GUI design.

The visual design of individual windows is only one aspect of GUI development. The second relates to *window navigation*, which captures the possible navigation paths between application GUI containers. In this chapter, we introduced a UML profile – *UX storyboard* – to address this issue.

Key terms

Applet a program executing on the client machine and running in the context of another program (Web browser) with its processing capabilities being controlled (restricted) by the browser.

Browser client a thin client that represents a Web-based GUI and needs a server to obtain its data and programs.

Client page a web page rendered by a Web browser and that may have programming logic interpreted by the browser.

Container a desktop GUI component that can be a window, *panel* or *pane*.

Form a part of a web page consisting of a collection of input fields.

Frame a rectangular viewing area that contains a web page or another frame.

Pane a *container* that is a part of a window, such as a scroll pane or a tab pane.

Panel a *container* into which other GUI components can be inserted.

Primary window main application window in desktop applications.

Programmable client a thick client with a program residing and executing on it and with access to the client's machine storage resources.

Secondary window a pop-up window that supports the user's activities in the *primary window* or other secondary window.

Server page a web page that has programming logic executed by a server.

Servlet a program executing on the server machine that is capable of receiving requests from the client's Web browser and generating responses to the requests.

Struts a technology framework supporting GUI implementation of Web applications.

Swing a class library supporting GUI implementation of desktop applications.

UX User eXperience.

Web application a website that contains dynamic pages, the content of which can change between a user's requests.

Web page an application's "window" in a Web application.

Multiple-choice test

MC1 Which GUI guideline is the concept of locale related to?

   a Personalization.

   b Adaptability.

   c Customization.

   d All of the above.

MC2 A GUI desktop window can be divided into:

   a frames

   b forms

   c panes

   d panels.

MC3 A GUI Web screen's real estate can be divided into:

   a web pages

   b forms

   c frames

   d panes.

MC4 The concept sandbox is related to:

    a Web applications

    b desktop applications

    c applets

    d server pages.

MC5 Which PCBMER layer do JSPs belong to?

    a Bean.

    b Presentation.

    c Control.

    d Entity.

MC6 Which PCBMER layer do Struts' action forms belong to?

    a Bean.

    b Presentation.

    c Control.

    d Entity.

MC7 Which is not a UX stereotype?

    a Window.

    b Input form.

    c Screen.

    d Compartment.

Questions

Q1 Refer to Figures 7.4 (Section 7.1.2.1) and 7.15 (Section 7.2.2.4). Figure 7.15 presents a message box informing us that a business rule has been violated by an attempt to delete information about a `Program` ("program" refers to a TV or radio program). Figure 7.4 shows that business rule processing is invoked from an SQL procedure, not from a GUI window. Why? Could a business rule, such as that in Figure 7.15, be activated directly as a GUI window event?

Q2 Which of the GUI design guidelines has been, according to you, most fundamental in the shift from procedural to object-oriented programming? Justify your standpoint.

Q3 A programmable client or a browser client may represent an application GUI. What are these clients? What deployment options do they offer?

Q4 How is a primary window different from a secondary window?

Q5 The notion of an interface is used in software engineering in multiple contexts and with different meanings. What are the popular uses of the word "interface" in software development?

Q6 What is a pane? How is it useful in Windows GUI design?

Q7 The Java Swing library consists mostly of so-called lightweight components, but some Swing components are heavyweight. Search the literature and/or Internet to find out about these two kinds of Swing components and describe the difference between them.

Q8 JavaServer Faces (JSF) is a new technology that aims at defining something like a Swing library for Web-based user interfaces. Search the Internet to establish the current status of JSF. Describe your findings.

Q9 Java Web applications feature a combined use of servlet and JSP technologies. What is the relationship between these two technologies?

Q10 Explain why the UX profile recommends tags to describe the properties of the dynamic content of UX classes. Could tags be replaced by constraints?

Exercises: contact management

F1 Refer to Problem statement 3, for a contact management system (Section 1.6.3) and to the successive examples in Chapter 4. Users require that the contact management application be modeled on the functionality of the Calendar window in Microsoft Outlook (Figure 7.39).

The primary window should display the activities scheduled for the day for the employee who is using the system. The `Calendar` control can display past and future activities. The events scheduled for a particular time of the day (timed events) are to be displayed as in the Microsoft Outlook left pane. However, there is also a requirement to show and handle untimed, outstanding (due in the past) and completed events.

Design a primary window for contact management that conforms to the above requirements.

Figure 7.39
Microsoft Outlook
– Calendar
window
Source: Screenshot
reprinted by
permission from
Microsoft Corporation

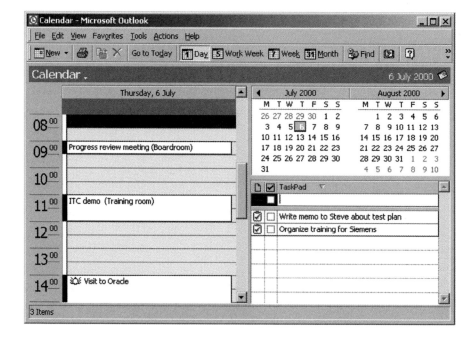

F2   Refer to Problem statement 3, for a contact management system (Section 1.6.3) and to the successive examples in Chapter 4. Refer also to Exercise F1 above and to the solution provided.

Assume that the primary window for contact management does not permit certain manipulations of events. For example, entering a new event or updating an existing event must be done via a secondary window – a dialog box.

By double-clicking on an event in the primary window, a dialog box should appear showing full details for that event. The dialog box displays not just the event information but also the data about its encompassing task, as well as the organization and contact to which the event relates.

The event details that can be displayed and possibly modified include the event type (called action), a longer description (called notes), the date, time and user (employee) for an event's creation, and the scheduled, due and completion time for the event.

Design a dialog box for event manipulation that conforms to the above requirements.

F3   Refer to Problem statement 3, for a contact management system (Section 1.6.3) and to the successive examples in Chapter 4. Refer also to Exercises F1 and F2 above and to the solutions provided.

Consider the tab folder for "Update Organization" in Figure 7.3 (Section 7.1.1). One of the tabs is called "Contacts". The purpose of it is to allow access to and modification of contact data (EContact class) from this tab folder. Otherwise, the user would always have to return to the primary window and activate a separate secondary window for "Contacts".

Design the content of the "Contacts" tab.

F4   Refer to Examples 7.10 (Section 7.4.3) and 7.11 (Section 7.4.4). As stated in Example 7.10 with reference to Figure 7.6 (Section 7.2.1), the user can display the current list of organization statuses by double-clicking on the "Organization Status" option in the tree browser. This action will display the list of statuses (as a row browser) in the right-hand pane of the window. The list will be displayed as in Figure 7.34 (Section 7.4.3).

If the user wants to update any status, she or he has to select (highlight) the status record on the list. There are three possibilities for obtaining the "Update Status" dialog box: (1) by double-clicking on the selected record; (2) by selecting an Update action from the menu bar (the "Record" item in Figure 7.6); or (3) by clicking on a toolbar button (a square with an overlapping rectangle in Figure 7.6).

Design a behavioral UX collaboration for the process of updating organization status. Make sure that a successful update gets reflected in the list of statuses (Figure 7.34). Show only the third option (a toolbar button) for navigation to the "Update Status" window.

F5   Refer to Exercise F4 and to its provided solution (Figure 7.43). Produce a structural UX collaboration model corresponding to the behavioral UX collaboration model in Figure 7.43.

Exercises: telemarketing

Additional requirements

Consider the following additional requirements for a telemarketing system.

■ The `Telemarketing Control` window is the primary control interface for the telemarketing application. The window displays to the telemarketer a list of the calls in the current queue. When the telemarketer requests a call from the queue, the system establishes the connection and the telemarketer is able to process a connected call. The `Call Summary` information displays on the screen – it shows the start time, finish time and duration of the current call.

■ Once connected, the `Telemarketing Control` window displays information about the current call – who has been called, about what campaign and what kind of call is being made. If there is more than one call scheduled for the current phone number, then the telemarketer is given the option of cycling through these calls.

■ At any stage during the conversation, the telemarketer can view the supporter's history (the `Supporter History` window) with regard to previous campaigns. Similarly, details about the campaign to which the current call is pertaining can be viewed (the `Campaign` window).

■ The GUI provides for quick recording of call outcomes. The possible outcomes are placement (that is, tickets have been ordered), callback, unsuccessful, no answer, engaged, machine (answering machine), fax, wrong (wrong number) and disconnected.

■ The `Campaign` window displays campaign details, ticket details and prize details for the campaign. The campaign details include the identifying number, title, start, close and prize draw dates. The ticket details include the number of tickets in the campaign, how many have been sold and how many are still available. The prize details include the prize description, prize value and place of the prize (the first, second or third).

■ The `Supporter History` window shows the past call history and the past campaign history for the supporter. The call history lists the recent calls, types of these calls, outcomes and identification of the campaigns and telemarketers. The campaign history informs about ticket placements and prize winnings by the supporter.

■ On selecting the `Placement` action, the `Placement` window is activated. The `Placement` window allows the user to allocate tickets to the supporter and record payment.

■ On selecting the `No Answer` or `Engaged` action, the "no answer" or "engaged" outcome is recorded in the system for each of the current calls. The calls are then rescheduled by the system for another time tomorrow, provided that each call is below the limit for attempts determined by the type of call.

■ On selecting the `Machine` action, the "machine" outcome is recorded in the system. The duration of the call is set for the first of the current calls only. The calls are then rescheduled by the system for another time tomorrow, provided that each call is below the limit for attempts determined by the type of call.

■ On selecting the `Fax` or `Wrong` action, the "fax" or "wrong" outcome is recorded in the system. The duration of the call is set for the first of the current calls only. The supporter data is then updated to "bad phone" for each supporter with the current phone number.

■ On selecting the `Disconnected` action, the "disconnected" outcome is recorded in the system. The supporter data is then updated to "bad phone" for each supporter with the current phone number.

■ On selecting the `Callback` action, the "callback" outcome is recorded in the system. The duration of the call is set for the first of the current calls only. The `Call Scheduling` window is invoked to obtain the date and time for the callback to be arranged. The calls are then rescheduled by the system (with the new priority) for the date and time obtained by the `Call Scheduling` window. The types of new calls are set to "callback".

■ On exiting the `Placement` window, if all of the remaining tickets in the campaign have just been allocated, then all further calls to supporters for that campaign are pointless. Any such calls must be removed from the call queue.

G1 Refer to Problem statement 4, for a telemarketing system (Section 1.6.4) and the examples in Chapters 4 and 5. Consider the class diagram for Example 4.7 (Section 4.2.1.2.3).

Modify and extend the class diagram in Figure 4.7 to support the additional requirements specified above.

G2 Refer to the telemarketing requirements, including the additional requirements above. Also consider your solution to Exercise G1.

Design and sketch the primary window for the telemarketing system. The window should contain a row browser with the list of calls currently scheduled to telemarketers. Some calls would be explicitly scheduled to a specific telemarketer – perhaps as a result of a specific request from the supporter. The window should provide the facilities to refresh the display of the queue (by polling the database server), request the next call from the queue and switch to the next campaign.

G3 Refer to the telemarketing requirements, including the additional requirements above. Also consider your solutions to Exercises G1 and G2.

Design and sketch the main secondary window for the telemarketing system. The window, called "Current Call", shows the primary set of information and actions available to the telemarketer when the phone connection to the supporter is being attempted and established by the automatic dialing capability of the system. The command buttons in the window should be grouped into three categories: call details, call outcome and two generic buttons (`Next Call` and `Cancel`).

G4 Refer to the telemarketing requirements, including the additional requirements above. Also consider your solutions to Exercises G1, G2 and G3.

Design and sketch the `Supporter History` window. The window should present five groups of fields: calls in this campaign, address/phone, history/winnings, preferred hours and payment status.

G5 Identify the main UX modeling elements (class-level stereotypes) representing the content of the primary window from your solution to Exercise G2.

G6 Identify the main UX modeling elements (class-level stereotypes) representing the content of the main secondary window from your solution to Exercise G3.

G7 Identify the main UX modeling elements (class-level stereotypes) representing the content of the secondary window from your solution to Exercise G4.

G8 Design a behavioral UX collaboration for the process defined in the third requirement in the list of additional requirements above. The requirement states:

At any stage during the conversation, the telemarketer can view the supporter's history (the `Supporter History` window) with regard to previous campaigns. Similarly, details about the campaign to which the current call is pertaining can be viewed (the `Campaign` window).

G9 Design a structural UX collaboration corresponding to the behavioral UX collaboration that you have developed as your solution to exercise G8.

Review quiz answers

Review quiz 7.1
RQ1   GUI clients are classified into programmable clients on desktop platforms and browser clients on Web platforms.
RQ2   User in control.
RQ3   Feedback.

Review quiz 7.2
RQ1   The existence of the menu bar and toolbar in primary windows.
RQ2   Property page is Windows' name for a tab of a tab folder.
RQ3   Menu item.

Review quiz 7.3
RQ1   Menu items, buttons and links.
RQ2   Cookie.
RQ3   The affordance of a link is that it moves to another web page.

Review quiz 7.4
RQ1   <<compartment>>.
RQ2   By a tag value called visible.
RQ3   Sequence diagram.

Multiple-choice test answers

MC1   d
MC2   c
MC3   c
MC4   c
MC5   b
MC6   a
MC7   a

Answers to odd-numbered questions

Q1
Business rules are defined for the system as a whole, not for each individual window or even an individual application program. An attempt to delete a `Program` may be initiated by a user from a GUI window, but it should invariably result in an invocation of a SQL procedure executing within the database environment (not within the client code). The database procedure will then attempt to delete the `Program` information from the database. At this point, the database will check the deletion against the business rules, normally implemented as *trigger* programs within the database. The message in Figure 7.15 comes from such a trigger. Triggers cannot be explicitly called. They are "triggered" by events, such as the delete event.

Technically, a delete event could come directly from a client program. This would happen if the delete event from the user were serviced by a SQL `Delete` command (from the client straight to the database), rather than by calling a SQL procedure (a stored procedure). However, this would not be a recommended practice. Apart from other drawbacks, issuing SQL commands from the client would force the client code to service any error messages returned by the server (instead of using the stored procedure to interpret such errors for the client).

Q3

Client and *server* are logical concepts. They do not refer to physical machines, but, rather, to logical processes/computations that execute on machines. Hence, a client/server application can reside on a single machine – the only requirement is that client and server are separate processes.

Client and server take on a slightly different meaning when addressed from a *user perspective* and when addressed from a *developer perspective*. "From a user's point of view, the client *is* the application. It must be useful, usable, and responsive. Because the user places high expectations on the client, you must choose your client strategy carefully, making sure to consider both technical forces (such as the network) and non-technical forces (such as the nature of the application)" (Singh et al. 2002: 51).

"From a developer's point of view, a J2EE application can support many types of clients. J2EE clients can run on laptops, desktops, palmtops, and cell phones. They can connect from within an enterprise's intranet or across the World Wide Web, through a wired network or a wireless network or a combination of both. They can range from something thin, browser-based and largely server-dependent to something rich, programmable, and largely self-sufficient" (Singh et al. 2002: 51).

A *programmable client* is an application that resides and executes on the user's machine and has access to that machine's resources (files and programs). Such a client can download data from a server data source, perform necessary computations and render some outputs and reports into its GUI. A programmable client is also called a *thick* or *rich* client ("client on steroids").

A *browser client* is an application that renders the views to a user's GUI, but the logic for the views is likely to be downloaded from the server as needed (although some logic can be programmed into the client). A browser client can validate a user's input, communicate with the server to request its functionality and manage application's conversational state. The latter tracks information as a user goes through the steps of a business transaction (although the conversational state may – and frequently should – be managed on a server). A browser client is also called a *Web* or *thin* client ("hopefully not anorexic").

The distinction between a programmable and a browser client is not necessarily clear-cut. There are different levels of thickness or thinness. However, under the most typical understanding, a *browser client* is very thin – it displays data to the user and relies on the server-side application for what it does. That is, the application for a browser client is deployed on a server, typically a Web server.

On the other hand, a *programmable client* is very thick and installed (deployed) explicitly on a client's machine. However, it is possible to deploy a programmable *client on demand* using, for example, Java Web Start technology. Once downloaded on demand and cached, the programmable client can be relaunched without having to download the information again.

Q5

There are at least four meanings of the concept *interface*. First, the notion of *interface* brings to mind the *GUI* (Graphical User Interface) – the display, the computer screen on which information is rendered.

Second, interface brings to mind the *API* (Application Programming Interface). The API is a set of software routines and development tools that provide function-calling conventions to application programs so that the programs can access services provided by some lower-level modules (such as the operating system, device drivers, JVM – that is, Java Virtual Machine).

Third, interface brings to mind *public interface* – that is a *protocol* or a set of publicly visible operations (methods) that other software components can use to access the support functions defined in the classes offering that interface. The scope of a public interface can be a single class, a set of classes (such as a package or subsystem) or the entire application.

Fourth, "interface" brings to mind *UML or Java interface* – that is, a definition of a semantic type with attributes (perhaps restricted to constants only) and operations, but without declarations of operations (that is, without implementations). UML/Java interface is a modeling/programming way of defining the public interface. In this context, we can distinguish between a *provided interface* and a *required interface*.

Q7

Maciaszek and Liong (2005) provide a direct answer to this question in the following excerpts:

> The *Swing component kit* enables delivery of applications with *pluggable look and feel*. "Pluggable" has several meanings. It can mean the conformance to the GUI platform on which the program executes (Windows, Unix, etc.). It can mean a uniform cross-platform look and feel that has identical manifestation on any execution platform. Swing calls this the Java look and feel. Finally, it can mean a programmer-customizable look and feel unique to an application.
>
> To achieve *pluggability*, most Swing components are themselves platform-independent or *lightweight*, sometimes called peerless. A lightweight component is programmed without any use of platform-specific (peer) code. Unfortunately, not all Swing components are lightweight – some are *heavyweight*. In most cases where heavyweight components are used, Swing provides workarounds to hide the peer code so that pluggable look and feel is still achievable.
>
> (Maciaszek and Liong 2005: 514)
>
> Swing has a variety of classes able to produce container objects. Four of these classes are *heavyweight*: JWindow, JFrame, JDialog, and JApplet. In most situations, a top-level container of a program is an instance of a heavyweight container. Lightweight container classes need heavyweight components for screen painting and event handling. *Lightweight* classes include: JInternalFrame, JDesktopPane, JOptionPane, JPanel, JTabbedPane, JScrollPane, JSplitPane, JTextPane, and JTable.
>
> (Maciaszek and Liong 2005: 515)

Q9

A *servlet* is (Java) code that dynamically creates HTML pages. It is Java code with embedded HTML elements. A *server page* (a Java Server Page – JSP) is the opposite – an HTML page with embedded Java code (tags and scriplets) to manage the dynamic content of the page and supply data to it (Maciaszek and Liong 2005).

If we consider that the servlet code may be supported by Java Server Pages and that JSP is compiled to a servlet prior to running, the difference is quite insignificant. What is more important is that once a servlet is loaded in a Web server, it can connect to a database and maintain the connection for more than one client. This is called *servlet chaining*. It allows one servlet to pass a client request to another servlet.

It is a common practice to use JSP to query a servlet for data to be displayed on the screen. The reason for this is the simplicity of JSP programming, which allows Java code to be embedded with a set of HTML tags and, therefore, allows reusing of the programmer's existing knowledge of HTML.

JSP can also invoke another JSP or even include the output of another JSP as part of its own output. This allows JSP to combine the output (HTML) to provide a richer display. A servlet, on the other hand, when it invokes another servlet, is usually for the purpose of data retrieval rather than data display.

Solutions to exercises: contact management

F1

Figure 7.40 shows the primary window for contact management. The `Calendar` control is designed as a detachable "floating" window to conserve space. It can be closed if so desired. For each event in the left-hand pane, the event's short description and either an organization or contact name is shown. For some events, additional information may be shown as well, such as the organization's or contact's phone number, a fax number, or address. Although not clearly visible in the black and white reproduction here, color is used in the left pane to signify the priority assigned to the event (high in red, normal in black and low in blue).

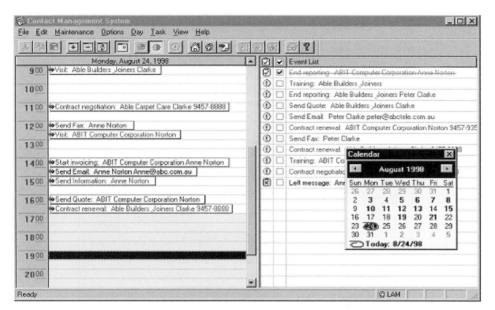

Figure 7.40
A primary window
for a contact
management
system
Source: Courtesy of
Nielsen Media
Research, Sydney,
Australia

The right-hand pane serves three purposes. It displays three kinds of event. *Completed* events are removed from the left-hand pane and placed at the top of the right-hand pane. The text is in blue type and crossed out. The main reason for not removing a completed event altogether from the display is that it may need to be "uncompleted" (perhaps we thought prematurely that the event was done but found out later that it was not quite done).

The *outstanding* events are listed in the right pane. They are in red. Finally, the *untimed* events are shown in black and listed at the bottom of the right pane. The left-hand side column in the pane is designed with color-blind users in mind. The icons there signify the three kinds of event possible in the right pane.

F2

Figure 7.41 is the proposed solution to the example. Note that the `Organization` and `Contact` fields are not editable, because the "target" of the event cannot be changed. Similarly, the field values next to the prompt `Created` are not editable.

The field values adjacent to the prompt `Completed` are not editable in the sense that the user cannot type in them. However, pressing the `Complete` button will automatically insert the date, time and user values in these fields. After completing the event, the user still has the possibility of "uncompleting" it because the `Complete` button is then renamed `Uncomplete`.

It is possible for the user to save changes to the database and return to the primary window by clicking the `OK` button. Alternatively, the user can `Cancel` the changes and stay in the dialog box. Finally, the user can press the `New Event` button, which will save the changes (after the user's confirmation), clear all the fields in the dialog box and allow the user to create a new event (without returning to the primary window).

F3

As shown in Figure 7.42, the `Contacts` tab displays only the names of the contacts in an organization. However, the tab has its own set of command buttons to `Add`, `Edit` or `Delete` the currently highlighted contact. An action to `Add` or `Edit` a contact will result in a `Maintain Contacts` secondary window opening up on top of the `Maintain Organizations` window. The `Maintain Contacts` window will be modal with regard to the `Maintain Organizations` window.

Figure 7.41
A dialog box for a contact management system
Source: Courtesy of Nielsen Media Research, Sydney, Australia

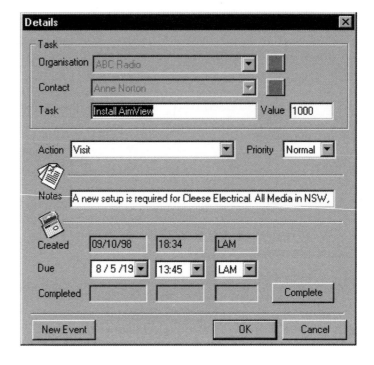

Figure 7.42
A tab folder for a contact management system
Source: Courtesy of Nielsen Media Research, Sydney, Australia

F4

Figure 7.43 presents a solution to Exercise F4. The solution should be self-explanatory.

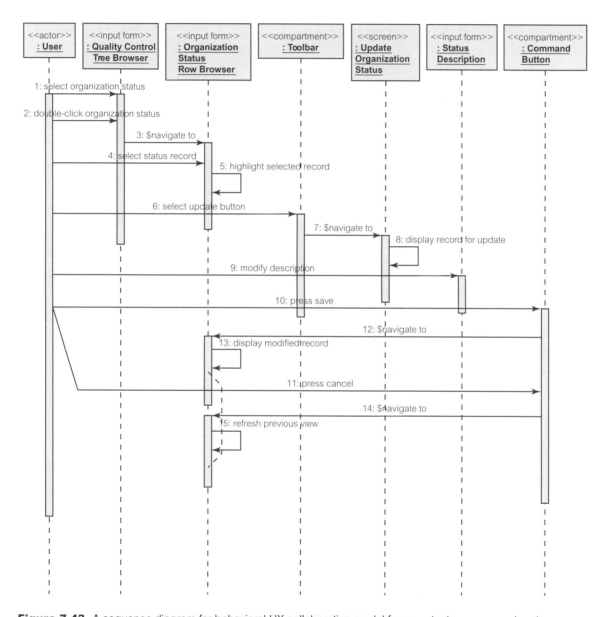

Figure 7.43 A sequence diagram for behavioral UX collaboration model for a contact management system

F5

Figure 7.44 presents a solution to Exercise F5. The solution should be self-explanatory, but the comparison with a structural UX collaboration for inserting a new status in Figure 7.36 may have educational value. Note, for example, that the status code is now a dynamic content of `Update Organization Status`, while description is a dynamic content of `Status Description`. However, because `Status Description` is contained in `Update Organization Status`, description is also included in the dynamic content of `Update Organization Status`.

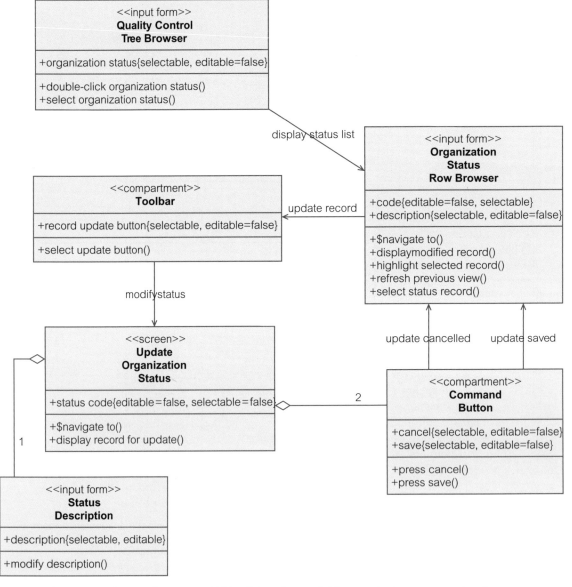

Figure 7.44 A class diagram for structural UX collaboration model for a contact management system

Chapter

8

Persistence and Database Design

Objectives

Information systems are, by definition, multi-user systems. *Database management systems* (DBMSs) provide the technology to support concurrent access by large numbers of users and application programs to the same data store. Application programs depend on databases not just for data but also for database-provided functions that resolve any concurrency conflicts, ensure secure access to data, guarantee data consistency, take care of recovering from transaction failures, and so on. Some of these functions are an inherent part of the DBMS software. Other functions on which application programs depend must be coded by the database programmers. The conclusion is obvious – a good database design that can accommodate and support *all* application programs is the necessary condition for an information system to deliver the intended functionality.

In UML, class diagrams define the data structures required by an application. The data structures that have persistent presence in the database are modeled as the entity classes ("business objects") and relationships between entity classes. The entity classes need to be mapped to the data structures recognized by the database. These data structures vary depending on the underlying database model, which is likely to be relational, but can also be object-oriented or object-relational.

By reading this chapter you will:

∎ comprehensively understand the connection between business objects and persistence

∎ learn about the relational database model

∎ gain practical knowledge about the mapping of objects to databases and vice versa

∎ find out about the principal patterns for managing persistent objects

∎ learn about design and implementation issues related to database access and transaction processing.

8.1 Business objects and persistence

Throughout the book, we have been carefully distinguishing between the development of a client application and the design of a server database. We have emphasized that the class models and PCBMER subsystems contain the application classes, not the storage database structures.

The *entity classes* represent persistent database objects in the application. They are *not* persistent classes in the database. They are *called* persistent with the understanding that, prior to the application program's termination, the latest images of entity objects will be stored persistently in the database. This allows future activation of the same or other application programs to obtain entity objects again by loading them from the database to the program's memory. Consequently, the interaction between business objects and a persistent database has to be carefully designed.

8.1.1 Database management systems

A database can be *relational* (such as Sybase, DB2, Oracle), *object-relational* (UniSQL, Oracle) or *object-oriented* (ObjectStore, Versant). It is unlikely that the storage model for a new contemporary system can be any of the older models, such as hierarchical (IMS), network (IDMS) or inverted or similar model (Total, Adabas). In some cases, but not really in modern IS applications, the persistence can be implemented in simple flat files.

The *Relational Database (RDB)* model dominates the database software scene. It has replaced the earlier hierarchical and network database models. In the second half of the 1990s, vendors of *Relational Database Management Systems (RDBMS)* were, however, put on notice by the *Object Database (ODB)* model, the *Object Database Management Group (ODMG)* standards and various *Object Database Management System (ODBMS)* products.

As a consequence, hybrid *Object-Relational Database Management Systems (ORDBMS)* emerged and may still be destined to play a dominant role in the future. Traditional RDBMS vendors, such as Oracle and IBM, offer the most influential of these products today, while Microsoft's push into this market has grown significantly. In the meantime, pure ODBMS products have not increased their market share – they have shifted to become *object storage APIs* to support interoperability between client applications and any server data sources, in particular relational databases.

Although the long-term future may no longer belong to the RDB model, business inertia is such that a decade or more will pass before large systems migrate to ORDB or ODB technology. There will also be many new applications developed using RDB technology, simply because businesses will not need the sophisticated and difficult-to-master object solutions.

This said, the latest database standard, known as SQL:1999, calls itself an object-relational database standard (Melton 2002), while also being the standard for traditional relational databases (Melton and Simon 2001). SQL:1999 adds object-oriented features to the relational model, while keeping the relational model conceptually intact. The object-oriented features fall short of the expectations of object-oriented software developers, but they constitute a step in the right direction.

Because the relational model dominates in business systems, it is the only model discussed in detail in this chapter. Curiously enough, the first edition of this book contained discussions on object and object-relational databases. We can only hope that these two models gain more of a presence in enterprise information systems to warrant presenting them again in future editions of this book.

Levels of data models 8.1.2

The database community has developed its own view on the world of modeling. Databases *store data*. Historically, the database community has concentrated on *data models* (static models in the UML parlance). The current capability of databases to *store and execute programs* has extended this perspective to include *behavior models* (centered on **triggers** and **stored procedures**), but data modeling remains the "bread and butter" of database development.

A **data model** (also called a *database schema*) is an abstraction that presents the database structures in more understandable terms than as raw bits and bytes. A popular classification of the data model's layers recognizes three abstractions:

- external (conceptual) data model
- logical data model
- physical data model.

The *external schema* represents a high-level *conceptual data model* required by a single application. Because a database normally supports many applications, multiple external schemas are constructed. They are then integrated into one conceptual data model.

The most popular conceptual data modeling technique uses *entity-relationship* (**ER**) *diagrams* (Maciaszek 1990, for example). Although ER modeling remains popular among database designers, it gives way to UML class modeling as the technique of choice for all conceptual modeling – that is, the conceptual modeling of applications and databases.

The *logical schema* (also sometimes called the *global conceptual schema*) provides a model that reflects the logical storage structures (tables and so on) of the database model to be used for system implementation (typically, a relational model). The logical schema is a global integrated model to support any current and expected applications that need to access information stored in the database.

The *physical schema* is specific to a particular DBMS (such as Oracle or SQL Server). It defines how data are actually stored on persistent storage devices, typically disks. The physical schema defines such issues as the use of indexes and clustering of data for efficient processing.

The *lower-engineering CASE tools* (the CASE tools targeting system design and implementation) normally provide a data-modeling technique that targets a vast variety of specific DBMSs. In effect, they provide a capability for constructing a combined logical/physical model and immediately generating the relevant SQL code.

8.1.3 Integrating application and database modeling

Modeling of an *application* program and modeling of a *database* are disjoint activities. The former is done by application developers, the latter by database administrators or designers. The reason for this split is that a database must be developed independently of applications (but not "in spite of" the applications!) A single database must serve multiple and different application programs. It must be a compromise solution that resolves any conflicts and overlaps in data access demands by applications.

An application developer is usually given a model for a database that the application needs to access. Having this, the application developer needs to design the necessary mappings between the program model and the database model.

Figure 8.1 demonstrates how UML models for an application relate to persistent database models. The arrows show the dependencies between modeling elements. The downward dependency principle (DDP) of the PCBMER architectural framework (Section 4.1.3.2) extends on the communication between the application and the persistent database.

The *resource* subsystem is solely responsible for communication with the database. All SQL queries and calls to stored procedures from the application are generated by the resource classes and passed to the database server. Any data and other results returned by the database server are first delivered to the resource classes before they can make their way up to the entity subsystem.

Classes of the *entity* subsystem represent the *business objects* placed in the memory of an application program. The mapping rules between business objects and their corresponding records in database tables must be carefully defined.

The mapping rules are used by the *mediator* subsystem, which is responsible for managing the application's memory cache and any movement of objects between the memory and the database. This means that the mediator subsystem is the first port of call when a control class needs to access a business object and it does not have a prior handle (reference) on that object. This also means that the mediator subsystem must manage **business transactions** within which any sequences of database access and modification are conducted.

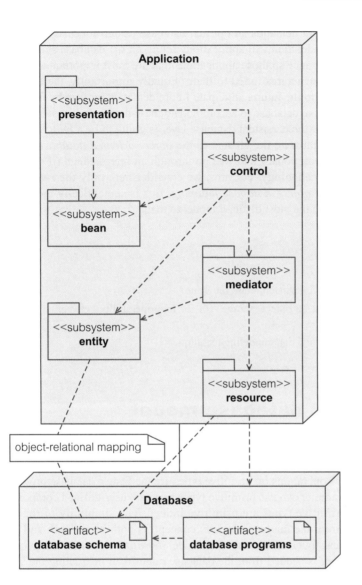

Figure 8.1
Integrating
application and
database
modeling

Underpinnings of object–database mapping 8.1.4

The *mapping* between the application and the database may be a convoluted issue. There are two fundamental reasons for the mapping difficulty. First, the storage structures of the database may have little to do with the object-oriented paradigm. Second, the database is almost never designed for a single application.

The first reason amounts to the conversion of *non-object-oriented structures* – typically, relational tables – into classes in the entity subsystem. Even if the target database is an object database, the peculiarities of the database will necessitate careful conversion.

The second reason demands an optimal database design for *all* applications, not just the one under consideration. All applications acting on the database should be prioritized for business significance so those applications that are most important to the organization have the database structures tuned to them. Equally importantly, the database designer should always look to the future, anticipate future demands for data by forthcoming applications and design the database to accommodate these demands.

The odds are that the persistent database layer is going to be a *relational database*. For large enterprise databases, the change to the *object-oriented database* technology, if it happens, will be evolutionary and will go through an intermediate (if not final) stage of *object-relational* technology. For now, we consider here only the *relational database* model. In terms of *object–database mapping*, this is semantically the most restrictive model and therefore the most difficult model to map.

Review quiz 8.1

RQ1   Are the notions of entity class and persistent class the same?

RQ2   Which database model is used as an object storage API for interoperability between client applications and any server data sources?

RQ3   What is the most popular conceptual data modeling technique?

8.2   Relational database model

Databases, like programming languages, provide built-in data types as basic building blocks for modeling and programming. Such built-in data types are called **primitive types**. Databases operations on primitive types are the fastest database programming constructs. A programmer can use primitive types to create user-defined compositive types.

The RDB primitive types are primitive indeed. The simplicity of the RDB model, which derives from the mathematical *set* concept, is both its strength and its weakness. The mathematical foundations make the model *declarative* (rather than *procedural*). The user declares *what* is needed from the database rather than instructing the system *how* to find the information (an RDBMS knows how to find data in its own database).

However, what is simple at first becomes quite complex when the problem to solve is complicated. There are no simple solutions for complex problems. To solve them, we need sophisticated machinery. To start with, we need sophisticated primitive types.

Perhaps the best way to characterize the RDB model is to state what it does *not* support. From the major primitive types available in the ODB and/or ORDB models, the RDB does not support:

- object types and associated concepts (such as inheritance or methods)
- structured types
- collections
- references.

The main primitive type in the RDB model is a **relational table** that consists of columns. Table *columns* can take only *atomic values* – structured values or collections of values are not permitted.

The RDB model is adamant about any user-visible *navigational links* between tables – they are explicitly *precluded*. The relationships between tables are maintained by comparing values in columns. There are no persistent links. The ORDB utility to maintain predefined relationships between tables is called the **referential integrity**.

Figure 8.2 shows RDB primitive types and the dependencies between them. All concepts are named with singular nouns, but some dependencies apply to more than one instance of the concept. For example, a referential integrity is defined on one or more tables. The concepts shown in Figure 8.2 are discussed next in this chapter.

Columns, domains and rules

8.2.1

Relational databases define data in tables of **columns** and **rows**. A data value stored on the intersection of any column and row must be a simple (indivisible) and a single (not repeating) value. We say that the *columns* have *atomic domains* (data types).

A **domain** defines the legal set of values that a column can take. The domain can be anonymous (such as `gender char(1)`) or named (such as `gender Gender`). In the latter case, the domain `Gender` has been defined earlier and used in the definition of the column. A possible syntax for the domain definition could be:

```
create domain Gender char(1);
```

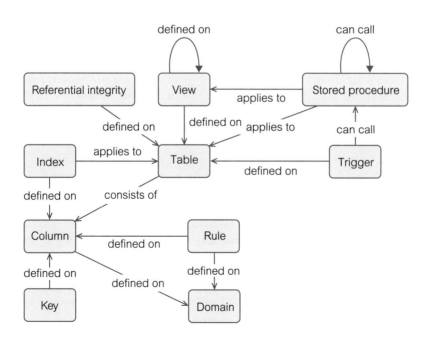

Figure 8.2
Dependencies between database primitive types

A *named domain* can be used in the definition of many columns in different tables. This enforces consistency between these definitions. Changes to the domain definition are automatically reflected in column definitions. Although an attractive option at first glance, the domain's use is impeded once the database has been *populated* – that is, loaded with data.

Columns and domains can have *business rules* that constrain them. Such rules can define:

- *default value* – if no value is provided for city, assume "Sydney" for example
- *range of values* – the allowed age is in the range 18 to 80, for example
- *list of values* – the allowed color is "green", "yellow" or "red", for example
- *case of value* – the value must be in upper or lower case, for example
- *format of value* – the value must start with the letter "K", for example.

Only very simple business rules concerning single columns or domains can be defined using the *rule* facility. More complex rules spanning tables can be defined as *referential integrity* constraints. The ultimate mechanism for defining business rules is a *trigger*.

8.2.2 Tables

A *relational table* is defined by its fixed set of columns. Columns have built-in or user-defined types (domains). Tables can have any number of *rows* (records). As the table is a mathematical *set*, there are no duplicate rows in a table.

A column value in a particular row may be allowed to be null. The null value means one of two things: "the value is at present unknown" (such as, I don't know your birth date) or "the value does not apply" (you cannot have a maiden name if you are a man, for example). The null value is not zero or a space (empty) character value but a special stream of bits that denotes the null value.

A consequence of the RDB model's requirement of "no duplicate rows" is that every table has a **primary key**. A **key** is a *minimal* set of columns (possibly one) and the values in these columns *uniquely* identify a single row in the table. A table can have many such keys. One of these keys is arbitrarily chosen as the most important for the user – this is the *primary key*. Other keys are called *candidate* or *alternate keys*.

In practice, an RDBMS table does not have to have a key. This means that a table (without a unique key) may have duplicate rows – a pretty useless feature in a relational database as two rows with the same values for all their columns are not distinguishable. This is different for ODB and ORDB systems, where the OID provides such a distinction (two objects may be equal but not identical, as with two copies of this book, for example).

Although UML can be stereotyped for modeling relational databases, it is more convenient to use a specifically targeted diagramming technique for the logical modeling of relational databases. Figure 8.3 demonstrates one such notation. The target database is DB2.

The table Employee has nine columns. The column dept_id and the last three columns accept null values. The column emp_id is the primary key. The column dept_id is a **foreign key** (explained in the next section). The columns {family_name,

Employee			
emp_id	CHAR(7)	<pk>	not null
dept_id	SMALLINT	<fk>	not null
family_name	VARCHAR(30)	<ak>	not null
first_name	VARCHAR(20)		not null
date_of_birth	DATE	<ak>	not null
gender	Gender		not null
phone_num1	VARCHAR(12)		null
phone_num2	VARCHAR(12)		null
salary	DEC(8,2)		null

Figure 8.3 Table definition in an RDB

date_of_birth} define a candidate (alternate) key. The column gender is defined on the domain Gender.

Because of the RDB restriction that a column can take only atomic single values, we have encountered difficulty with modeling employee names and phone numbers. In the former case, we used the two columns family_name and first_name. The columns are not grouped or otherwise related in the model. In the latter case, we also opted for a solution with two columns – phone_num1 and phone_num2 – allowing a maximum of two phone numbers per employee.

Once the table has been defined in a CASE tool, the code to create the table can be generated automatically, as shown in Figure 8.4. The generated code includes the definition of the domain Gender and the definition of the business rule defined on that domain.

```
--==================================================================
-- Domain: "Gender"
--==================================================================
create distinct type "Gender" as CHAR(1) with comparisons;
--==================================================================
-- Table: "Employee"
--==================================================================
create table "Employee" (
   "emp_id"                CHAR(7)                          not null,
   "dept_id"               SMALLINT,
   "family_name"           VARCHAR(30)                      not null,
   "first_name"            VARCHAR(20)                      not null,
   "date_of_birth"         DATE                             not null,
   "gender"                "Gender"                         not null
       constraint "C_gender" check ("gender" in ('F','M','f','m')),
   "phone_num1"            VARCHAR(12),
   "phone_num2"            VARCHAR(12),
   "salary"                DEC(8,2),
primary key ("emp_id"),
unique ("date_of_birth", "family_name")
);
```

Figure 8.4 SQL generated for table definition

8.2.3 Referential integrity

The RDB model maintains relationships between tables by means of *referential integrity* constraints. The relationships are not fixed row-to-row connections (using pointers, references or similar navigational links). Instead, an RDB "discovers" row-to-row connections each time the user requests the system to find a relationship. This "discovering" is done by comparing the *primary key* values in one table with the *foreign key* values in the same or another table.

A *foreign key* is defined as a set of columns in one table, the values of which are either NULL or required to match the values of the primary key in the same or another table. That primary-to-foreign key correspondence is called the *referential integrity*. The primary and foreign keys in a referential integrity must be defined on the same domain, but they do not have to have the same names.

Figure 8.5 shows a graphical representation of referential integrity. As the result of drawing a relationship between the tables Employee and Department, the foreign key dept_id is introduced to the table Employee. For each Employee row, the foreign key value must either be null or match one of the dept_id values in Department (otherwise an employee would work for a department that does not exist).

The additional description on the relationship line defines *declaratively* the behavior associated with the referential integrity. There are four possible *declarative referential integrity constraints* associated with *delete* and *update* operations. The question is what to do with Employee rows if a Department row is deleted or updated (that is, when dept_id is updated). There are four possible answers to this question.

- Upd(R); Del(R) – *restrict* the update or delete operation (that is, do not allow the operation to go ahead if there are still Employee rows linked to that Department).
- Upd(C); Del(C) – *cascade* the operation (that is, delete all linked Employee rows).
- Upd(N); Del(N) – *set null* (that is, update or delete the Department row and set dept_id of the linked Employee rows to null).
- Upd(D); Del(D) – *set default* (that is, update or delete the Department row and set dept_id of the linked Employee rows to the default value).

Department			
dept_id	SMALLINT	<pk>	not null
dept_name	VARCHAR(50)		not null
address	VARCHAR(120)		null

dept_id = dept_id
Upd(R); Del(N)

0..n

Employee			
emp_id	CHAR(7)	<pk>	not null
dept_id	SMALLINT	<fk>	null
family_name	VARCHAR(30)	<ak>	not null
first_name	VARCHAR(20)		not null
date_of_birth	DATE	<ak>	not null
gender	Gender		not null
phone_num1	VARCHAR(12)		null
phone_num2	VARCHAR(12)		null
salary	DEC(8,2)		null

Figure 8.5 Graphical representation of referential integrity

Although not shown in Figure 8.5, the *change parent allowed* (*cpa*) *constraint* could also be defined for a referential integrity. The *cpa constraint* states that records in a *child (foreign)* table can be reassigned to a different record in a *parent* table. For example, the cpa constraint could, in fact, be defined on the relationship in Figure 8.5, as it is normally expected that an `Employee` can be reallocated to another `Department`. The cpa constraint is the opposite of the *frozen constraint* that is enforced by the *ExclusiveOwns* aggregation (Section 5.3.1.1).

Figure 8.6 shows the SQL statements generated automatically based on the graphical model in Figure 8.5. The foreign key in the table `Employee` is dropped in the first `alter` statement and then recreated in the second `alter` statement. Note that the referential integrity is specified for the delete operations, but not for the update. The reason is that `restrict` is the only declarative constraint allowed for the update operations, so `restrict` is implicitly assumed.

The modeling of referential integrity becomes complicated when the relationship between tables is many to many, as between `Student` and `CourseOffering` (Figure 4.9 in Section 4.2.3.3). To be able to manage the problem under the RDB restriction that a column cannot take multiple values, we need to introduce an *intersection table*, such as `StdToCrsOff` in Figure 8.7. The only purpose of the table is to model the many-to-many relationship and specify the declarative referential integrity constraints.

Note from Figure 8.7 that, because the primary key in `CourseOffering` is a composite key consisting of two columns (`crs_name` and `semester`), the corresponding foreign key in `StdToCrsOff` is also composite. Although not indicated in the model, the primary key for `StdToCrsOff` is a composite key consisting of all three columns in the table.

```
alter table "Employee"
    drop foreign key "RefToDepartment";

alter table "Employee"
    add foreign key "RefToDepartment" ("dept_id")
        references "Department" ("dept_id")
        on delete set null;
```

Figure 8.6
SQL generated for referential integrity

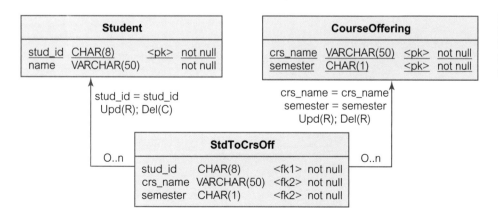

Figure 8.7
Referential integrity for a many-to-many relationship

8.2.4 Triggers

The *rules* and *declarative referential integrity* constraints allow simple *business rules* to be defined on the database. They are not sufficient to define more complex rules or any exceptions to the rules. An RDB solution to this problem (standardized in SQL:1999) is a *trigger*.

A *trigger* is a small program, written in an extended SQL, that is executed automatically (triggered) as a result of a modification operation on a table on which the trigger has been defined. A modification operation can be any of the SQL modification statements – insert, update or delete.

A trigger can be used to implement business rules that go beyond the capability of the SQL rule statement (Section 8.2.1). For example, the business rule that forbids changes to the Employee table during weekends can be programmed into a trigger. Any attempt to issue an SQL insert, update or delete on the table during a weekend will result in the trigger firing and the database refusing to execute the operation.

A trigger can also be used to enforce more complex referential integrity constraints. For example, our business rule may state that, on deleting a Department row, the Employee who is the manager of that department should also be deleted, but all other employees should have dept_id values set to null. Such a business rule cannot be enforced declaratively. We need a procedural trigger to enforce it.

Once triggers are used to enforce referential integrity in the database, the declarative referential integrity constraints are normally abandoned. Mixing procedural and declarative constraints is a bad idea because of occasionally intricate interdependencies between them. Consequently, the dominant practice today in enterprise databases is to program the referential integrity in triggers alone. The issue is not as daunting as it may look because a good CASE tool can generate much of the code automatically. For example, the trigger code generated by a CASE tool for the Sybase RDBMS is shown in Figure 8.8. The trigger implements the Del(R) declarative constraint – that is, it does not allow the Department row to be deleted if there are still Employee rows associated with it.

Figure 8.8
SQL trigger generated from a data model definition

```
create trigger keepdpt
   on Department
   for delete
   as
   if @@rowcount = 0
      return /* avoid firing trigger if no rows affected */
   if exists
      (select * from Employee, deleted
      where Employee.dept_id =
         deleted.dept_id)
      begin
         print 'Test for RESTRICT DELETE failed. No deletion'
         rollback transaction
         return
      end
      return
go
```

The `if` statement checks whether or not the SQL `delete` operation (which fired the trigger) is going to delete any rows at all. If not, the trigger does not proceed – no harm can be done. If `Department` rows can be deleted, then Sybase stores these (about to be deleted) rows in an internal table called `deleted`. The trigger then does an *equality join* operation on `dept_id` on the tables `Employee` and `deleted` to find out if there are any employees working for the department(s) to be deleted. If so, the trigger refuses the `delete` action, displays a message and rolls back the transaction. Otherwise, the `Department` rows are allowed to be deleted.

Triggers are a special kind of *stored procedure* (Section 8.2.5, next) that cannot be called – they trigger themselves on insert, update or delete events on a table. This implies that each table can have up to three triggers. Indeed, in some systems this is the case (Sybase, SQL Server, for example). In other systems (Oracle, DB2), additional variants of events are identified, leading to the possibility of having more than three triggers on each table. (The availability of more kinds of trigger does not provide more expressive power in trigger programs, though.)

Triggers can be programmed to enforce *any business rules* that apply to the database and cannot be violated by any client program or an interactive SQL Data Manipulation Language (DML) statement. A user of a client program may not even be aware that the triggers "watch" what is being modified in the database. If the modifications do not violate business rules, the triggers are not visible to the programs. A trigger makes itself known to the user when a DML command cannot be allowed. The trigger will notify the user of the problem by displaying an informational message on the application's screen and refusing to perform the DML operation.

Stored procedures   8.2.5

The Sybase RDBMS first introduced *stored procedures*, but they are now part of every major commercial DBMS. Stored procedures turn a database into an active programmable system.

A *stored procedure* is written in an extended SQL that allows for such programming constructs as variables, loops, branches and assignment statements. A stored procedure is given a name, can take input and output parameters and is compiled and stored in the database. A client program can call a stored procedure as if it was any internal subroutine.

Figure 8.9 illustrates the advantages of a client program calling a stored procedure rather than sending a complete query to the server. A query constructed in a client program is sent to the server database over the network. The query may contain syntax and other errors, but the client is not able to eliminate them – the database system is the only place where such verification can be done. Once verified, the DBMS checks whether or not the caller is authorized to run the query. If so, the query is optimized to determine the best access route to the data. Only then can it be compiled, executed and the results returned to the client.

On the other hand, if a query (or the whole set of queries) is written as a stored procedure, then it is optimized and compiled into the server database. A client program does not need to send a (possibly large) query over the network. Instead, it sends a short call with the procedure name and a list of actual parameters. If lucky, the procedure may reside in the DBMS memory cache. If not, it will be brought to memory from the database.

Figure 8.9
A comparison of
client SQL and
stored procedure
invocation

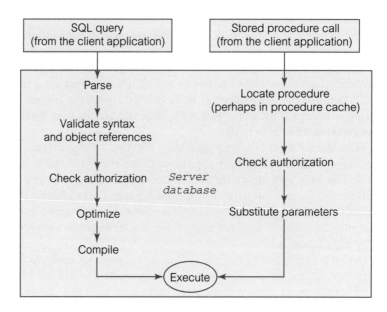

The user's authorization is scrutinized as it is in the case of an SQL query. Any actual parameters replace formal parameters and the stored procedure executes. The results are returned to the caller.

As can be seen in the above scenario, stored procedures provide a much more efficient way of accessing the database from a client program. The performance advantages are due to the savings in *network traffic* and the fact that there's no need for *parsing and compilation* each time a client request is received. Even more importantly, a stored procedure is *maintained in a single place* and can be called from many client programs.

8.2.6 Views

A *relational view* is a stored and named SQL query. Because a result of any SQL query is a transient table, a view can be used in place of a table in other SQL operations. A view can be derived from one or more tables and/or one or more other views (see Figure 8.2).

Figure 8.10 shows a graphical representation together with the generated code for the view `EmpNoSalary` – the view displays all information from the table `Employee` except the salary column. The `create view` statement below the figure demonstrates that a view is really a named query that executes each time an SQL query or update operation is issued on the view.

Theoretically, a view is a very powerful mechanism with many uses. It can be used in support of *database security* by restricting users from seeing table data. It can present data to users in *different perspectives*. It can *isolate the application from changes* to table definitions, if the changed definition is not part of the view. It allows for the easier expression of *complex queries* – the query can be built in a "divide and conquer" fashion by using multiple levels of views.

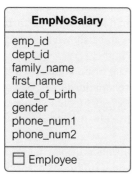

Figure 8.10
A relational view
and the code
generated

```
::::::::::::::::::::::::::::::::::::::::::::::::::::::::::::::::::::::::::::::
- - View: "EmpNoSalary"                                          — —
::::::::::::::::::::::::::::::::::::::::::::::::::::::::::::::::::::::::::::::
create view "EmpNoSalary" as
      select Employee.emp_id, Employee.dept_id,
             Employee.family_name, Employee.first_name,
             Employee.date_of_birth,Employee.gender,
             Employee.phone_num1, Employee.phone_num2
    from Employee;
```

In practice, the use of the view concept in the RDB model is severely restricted by its inability to allow view updates. A *view update* is the possibility of sending a modification operation (an SQL insert, update or delete) to the view and changing the underlying base table(s) as a result. SQL support for view updating is very limited and takes advantage of special triggers, so-called *instead of triggers*.

Normal forms

8.2.7

Arguably, one of the most important but at the same time least understood concepts in the RDB design is **normalization**. A relational table must be in a *normal form* (*NF*). There are six normal forms:

■ 1st NF
■ 2nd NF
■ 3rd NF
■ BCNF (Boyce–Codd NF)
■ 4th NF
■ 5th NF.

A table that is in a higher NF is also in all lower NFs. A table must be at least in the 1st NF. A table with no structured or multivalued columns is in the 1st NF (and that is the fundamental requirement of the RDB model).

A table in a low NF can exhibit so-called **update anomalies**. An *update anomaly* is an undesirable side-effect as a result of a modification operation (insert, update, delete) on a table. For example, if the same information is repeated many times in the same column in the table, then an update of that information must be performed in all places or the database will be left in an incorrect state. It can be shown that update anomalies are incrementally eliminated with the table reaching higher NFs.

So how do we normalize a table to a higher NF? We can bring a table to a higher NF by splitting it vertically along columns into two or more smaller tables. These smaller tables are likely to be in higher NFs and they replace the original table in the RDB design model. However, the original table can always be reconstructed by joining the smaller tables in an SQL join operation.

The scope of this book does not allow us to treat normalization theory in any detail. The reader is referred to such textbooks as those by Date (2000), Maciaszek (1990), Ramakrishnan and Gehrke (2000) and Silberschatz et al. (2002). The main point that we would like to make is that a good RDB design naturally arrives at a good normalization level.

What do we mean by a "good design" in the normalization context? A *good design* is one where we understand how the RDB is going to be used by a mix of update and retrieval operations. If the database is very dynamic – it is subjected to frequent update operations – then we will naturally create smaller tables to better localize and facilitate these updates. The tables will be in higher NFs and the update anomalies will be reduced or eliminated.

On the other hand, if the database is relatively static – we frequently search for information but we update the database content sporadically – then a *denormalized design* will pay off. This is because a search in a single large table is going to be much more efficient than the same search in multiple tables, that need to be joined together before the search starts.

Review quiz 8.2

RQ1 What mathematical concept is a relational database model based on?

RQ2 What are the two main features of a key?

RQ3 Can a foreign key have null values?

RQ4 What term is used for an undesirable side-effect that can result from a modification operation on a table?

8.3　Object-relational mapping

Object-relational mapping – mapping from a UML class model to the RDB schema design – has to consider the limitations of the RDB model. The issue is that of trading some *declarative semantics* of class diagrams for the *procedural solutions* in logical schema designs. In other words, it might not be possible to express some built-in declarative semantics of classes in the relational schema. Such semantics will have to be resolved procedurally in database programs – that is, in stored procedures (Section 8.2.5).

Mapping to the RDB models has been extensively studied in the context of the ER and extended ER modeling – Elmasri and Navathe (2000) and Maciaszek (1990), for example. The principles are the same, and all major issues have been identified in those studies. The mapping must not simply conform to an RDB standard (SQL92 or SQL:1999) but also relate to the target RDBMS implementation.

Mapping entity classes 8.3.1

The mapping of entity classes to relational tables must obey the 1st NF of tables. The columns must be atomic. This restriction of the relational model turns out not to be an issue because UML has a similar restriction. Attributes of UML classes are defined on *atomic data types* and, depending on the target programming language, on a few *built-in structured data types* (`Date`, `Currency`). Similar structured data types are likely to be supported by an RDBMS.

Still, doubts remain. What about simple questions such as, "What if an employee has many phone numbers? How should I model this during analysis? Do I really need to have a separate class of phone numbers?" A similarly troublesome question seems to be, "Can I model an employee name as a single attribute but with the internal structure recognizing that the name consists of the family name, first name and middle initial? Do I really need to have a separate class of employee names?"

Example 8.1: contact management

Refer to the class specifications for contact management in Example 4.6 and Figure 4.6 (Section 4.2.1.2.3). Consider the classes `EContact` and `EEmployee`.

`EContact` has the attributes `familyName` and `firstName` but does not have the concept of a contact name. Similarly, `EEmployee` contains `familyName`, `firstName` and `middleName`, but we could not ask the database about an employee name because such a concept does not exist.

`EContact` has the attributes `phone`, `fax` and `e-mail`. The current model does not allow for a contact to have more than one `phone`, `fax` or `e-mail` – quite an unrealistic assumption in practice.

Map the classes `EContact` and `EEmployee` to an RDB design in such a way that a number of alternative mapping strategies are demonstrated.

A solution to Example 8.1 is shown in Figure 8.11. The target RDBMS is DB2. The solution assumes the Oracle RDBMS. We modeled `contact_name` as an atomic data type in the table `Contact`. Each `Contact` is allowed only one `fax` and one `email`. However, we do allow any number of `phones`. The table `ContactPhone` serves this purpose.

In the table `Employee`, we maintain three separate attributes for `family_name`, `first_name` and `middle_initial`. However, the database does not have any knowledge of `employee_name` as a combined concept for these three attributes.

Mapping associations 8.3.2

The mapping of associations to a RDB involves the use of *referential integrity* constraints between tables. Any association that is one-to-one or one-to-many can be directly expressed by inserting a *foreign key* in one table to match the primary key of the other table.

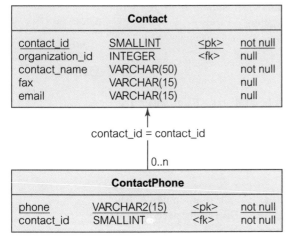

Figure 8.11 Mapping entity classes to RDB design for a contact management system

In the case of a *one-to-one association*, the foreign key can be added to either table (to be decided on the basis of the association usage patterns). Also, in the case of a one-to-one association, it may be desirable to combine the two entity classes in one table (depending on the desired normalization level).

For *recursive* one-to-one and one-to-many associations, the foreign key and primary key are in the same table. Each *many-to-many association* (whether recursive or not) requires an intersection table, as demonstrated in Figure 8.19 later in this chapter.

Example 8.2: contact management

Refer to the association specifications for a contact management system in Example 4.8 and Figure 4.8 (Section 4.2.2.2.1).

   Map the diagram in Figure 4.8 to an RDB model.

Example 8.2 proves to be quite straightforward, due to the lack of many-to-many associations in the UML association specifications. The RDB diagram (for the DB2 RDBMS) is shown in Figure 8.12. Consistently with RDB principles, we created a number of new columns as primary keys. We decided to retain the model in Figure 8.11 as a partial solution to this example. To conserve space, we suppressed the display of the columns' null definitions and key indicators.

   The referential integrity constraints between `PostalAddress` and `CourierAddress` on the one hand and `Organization` and `Contact` on the other are modeled with foreign keys in the address tables. This is slightly arbitrary, and the constraints could have been modeled in the opposite direction (that is, with foreign keys in `Organization` and `Contact`).

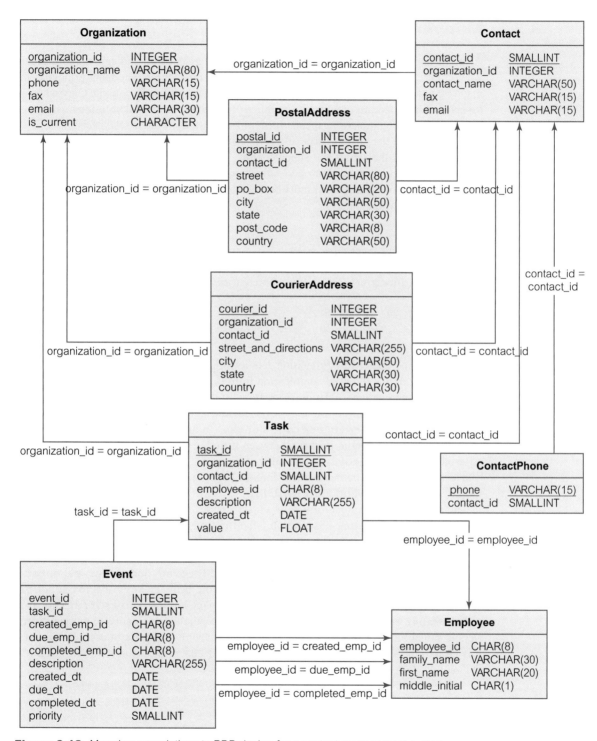

Figure 8.12 Mapping associations to RDB design for a contact management system

8.3.3 Mapping aggregations

An RDB does not understand the difference between association and aggregation, except when implemented procedurally in triggers or stored procedures. The main principles for mapping associations (Section 8.3.2) apply to the mapping of aggregations. Only when an association can be converted into a number of resultant relational solutions would the semantics of aggregation (as a special form of association) influence the decision.

In the case of the strong form of aggregation (*composition*), an attempt should be made to combine the subset and superset entity classes in a single table. This is possible for *one-to-one aggregations*. For *one-to-many aggregations*, the subset class (in the strong and weak forms of aggregation) must be modeled as a separate table (with a foreign key linking it to its owning table).

Example 8.3: university enrolment

Refer to the aggregation specifications for a university enrolment system in Example 4.9 and Figure 4.9 (Section 4.2.3.3).
Map the diagram in Figure 4.9 to an RDB model.

Example 8.3 includes two aggregation relationships – a composition from `Student` to `AcademicRecord` and a weak aggregation from `Course` to `CourseOffering`. Both are one-to-many aggregations and require separate "subset" tables.

In the UML model in Figure 4.9, we assumed (naturally enough) an indirect navigational link from `AcademicRecord` to `Course`. In an RDB design, we may want to establish a direct referential integrity between the tables `AcademicRecord` and `Course`. After all, `AcademicRecord` has the attribute `course_code` as part of its primary key. The same attribute can be made into a foreign key to the table `Course`. This is shown in Figure 8.13 (for the IBM Informix RDBMS).

The *many-to-many association* between the classes `Student` and `CourseOffering` leads to another interesting observation, albeit not related to the aggregation mapping. The association results in an intersection table `StdToCrsOff` with the primary key to be composed from the primary keys of the two main tables.

The primary key for `CourseOffering` could be {`course_code`, `year`, `semester`}. However, such a key would result in a cumbersome primary key for `StdToCrsOff`. We opted, therefore, for a system-generated primary key in `CourseOffering`. It is called `crsoff` and its type is `SERIAL` (in Informix, the type to generate unique identifiers is called `SERIAL`; the same type may be called something else in other RDBMSs – it is called `IDENTITY` in Sybase, `UNIQUEIDENTIFIER` in SQL Server and `SEQUENCE` in Oracle).

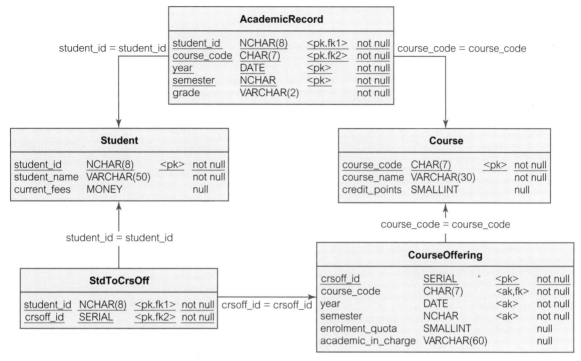

Figure 8.13 Mapping aggregations to RDB design for a university enrolment system

Mapping generalizations 8.3.4

The mapping of generalization relationships to an RDB can be done in a variety of ways, but the principles are less convoluted than might be expected. However, it must be remembered that expressing a generalization in an RDB data structure ignores issues that make the generalization tick – inheritance, polymorphism, code reuse, and so on.

To illustrate the generalization mapping strategies, consider the example in Figure 8.14. There are four strategies for converting a generalization hierarchy to an RDB design model (although some further variations of these strategies are possible):

- map each class to a table
- map the entire class hierarchy to a single "superclass" table
- map each concrete class to a table
- map each disjoint concrete class to a table.

The first mapping strategy is illustrated in Figure 8.15. Each table has its own primary key. The solution presented does not tell us if a "subclass" table "inherits" some of its columns from the "superclass" table. For example, is `person_name` stored in `Person` and "inherited" by `Employee`, `Student` and `StudentEmployee`? "Inheriting" really means a join operation and the performance penalty of the join may force us to have `person_name` duplicated in all tables of the hierarchy.

Figure 8.14
Generalization
hierarchy to
exemplify
mapping to an
RDB

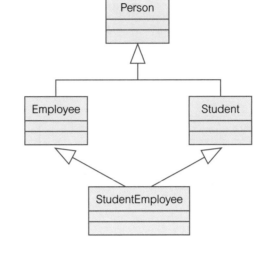

Figure 8.15
Mapping each
class to a table

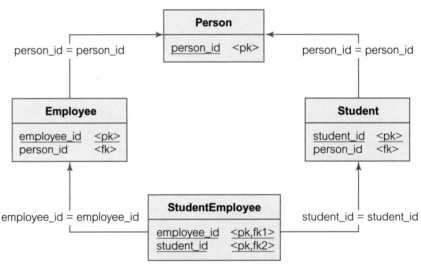

The second mapping strategy is illustrated in Figure 8.16 (in SQL Server RDBMS). The
table `Person` would contain the combined set of attributes in all classes of the generalization hierarchy. It also contains two columns (`is_employee` and `is_student`) to record
whether a person is an employee, a student or both.

Figure 8.16
Mapping the class
hierarchy to a
table

Person			
person_id	uniqueidentifier	<pk>	not null
is_employee	char(1)		null
is_student	char(1)		null

To illustrate the third mapping strategy, we assume that the class `Person` is abstract. Any attributes of the class `Person` are "inherited" by the tables corresponding to the concrete classes. The result will be similar to that shown in Figure 8.17.

Still assuming that the class `Person` is abstract, the last strategy is illustrated in Figure 8.18 (in Informix RDBMS). As opposed to the model in Figure 8.15, we assume that whether or not an employee is also a student, and vice versa, is always known. Hence, `not null` is entered for the two `BOOLEAN` columns.

Example 8.4: video store

Refer to the generalization specifications for a video store system in Example 4.10 and Figure 4.10 (Section 4.2.4.3).

Our task is to map three classes from the diagram in Figure 4.10 to an RDB model. We will use the third strategy of mapping each concrete class to a table. The classes to be mapped are `EMovie`, `EVideotape` and `EDVD`.

We need to consider how to handle the derived attribute `/isInStock` and the static attribute `percentExcellentCondition`.

The RDB design (for Sybase RDBMS) in Figure 8.19 for Example 8.4 contains a table for each of the three concrete classes (`Movie`, `Videotape` and `DVD`). The tables include inherited columns.

The columns `different_languages`, `different_endings` and `is_in_stock` are typed as `bit`. By definition, the `bit` type does not allow `null` values (`bit` is either zero or one).

The column `is_in_stock` is set to true (one) if there is at least one tape or disk with a particular movie in stock. This is not terribly useful information if a customer is interested in only one of the two media. A better solution would be to have two `bit` columns

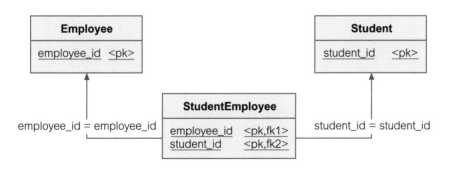

Figure 8.17
Mapping each concrete class to a table

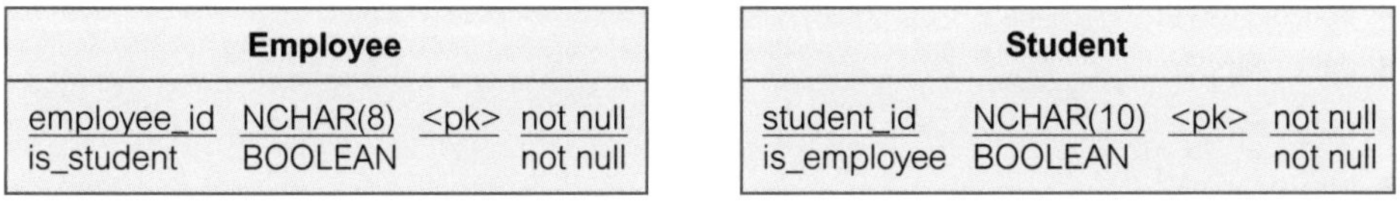

Figure 8.18
Mapping each disjoint concrete class to a table

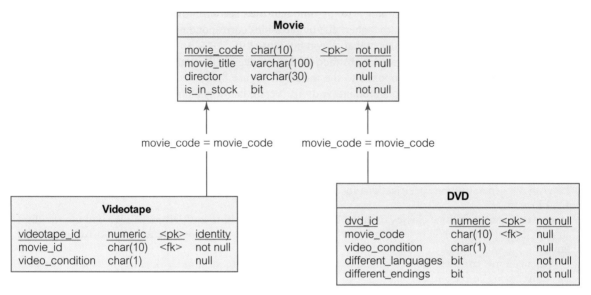

Figure 8.19 Mapping generalizations to RDB design for a video store system

or to assume that this information is never stored – that is, it is derived (calculated) whenever a customer requests a tape or disk.

The static attribute `percentExcellentCondition` is not stored in any table in our design. The only table where it could be sensibly stored is `Movie`. If stored, the same considerations as for the attribute `/is_in_stock` would apply.

Review quiz 8.3

RQ1 In what kind of mapping is an intersection table required?

RQ2 How is polymorphism addressed in mapping of generalization relationships to a relational model?

8.4   Patterns for managing persistent objects

The management of **persistent objects** is undoubtedly the main challenge in application programming. This is the area that particularly requires a good set of *design patterns*. Such a set is provided by the *Patterns of Enterprise Application Architecture* (**PEAA**) patterns (Fowler 2003). Maciaszek and Liong (2005) describe a few of these patterns, including:

- identity map
- data mapper
- lazy load
- unit of work.

The **identity map** pattern offers a solution to the problem of assigning object identifiers (OIDs) to persistent objects held in memory, mapping these OIDs to memory addresses of these objects, mapping other identifying attributes of objects to their OIDs and providing a single registry of object identifiers that other objects in the program can use to access objects by their OIDs.

The **data mapper** pattern offers a solution in which the program knows at all times if a required object is in a memory cache or has to be retrieved from the database. If the object is in memory, then a data mapper can find out if it is *clean* – that is, if its state (data content) in memory is in sync with the corresponding record in a database table. If the object is *dirty* (not clean), then a data mapper initiates a new retrieval from the database. The knowledge of whether an object is clean or dirty can be kept by the data mapper, but a better solution is to keep this information in the identity map or even in the entity object itself.

The **lazy load** pattern is defined by Fowler (2003: 200) as "an object that doesn't contain all of the data you need but knows how to get it." The need for this pattern arises from the fact that the data in the database are very interrelated, but an application can load only a limited number of objects to the memory cache. However, it is important for the program to be able, at any time, to load more data related to the objects already in memory.

The **unit of work** pattern offers a solution in which the program knows which objects in memory are embraced by a business transaction and, therefore, should be handled in unison with regard to committing any changes in these objects to the database. This pattern makes the application program aware of business transactions. It "maintains a list of objects affected by a business transaction and coordinates the writing out of changes and the resolution of concurrency problems" (Fowler 2003: 184).

Searching for persistent objects   8.4.1

As discussed in Section 8.1.3 and elsewhere, the PCBMER architecture addresses enterprise applications and can accommodate the PEAA and similar patterns. Figure 8.20 is an activity diagram presenting transition flows that are typical of when the application program searches for a persistent object (Maciaszek and Liong 2005).

In a typical scenario, a user would request an entity object (such as invoice information) by interacting with some presentation object (say, a UI window). In the PCBMER framework, such a request would be forwarded to a *control object* (an object in the control subsystem). The control object would ask a *data mapper object* to get the entity object. The data mapper class is normally placed within the mediator subsystem.

A data mapper object would have a number of overloaded methods providing different search strategies depending on what information is passed to the mapper by the control object. Typical possibilities are that a control object knows (Maciaszek and Liong 2005):

- the OID of an object and passes it to a data mapper object
- some attribute values of an object and passes them to a data mapper object
- of another object X that holds a reference to the entity object that is the search target and passes X to a data mapper object.

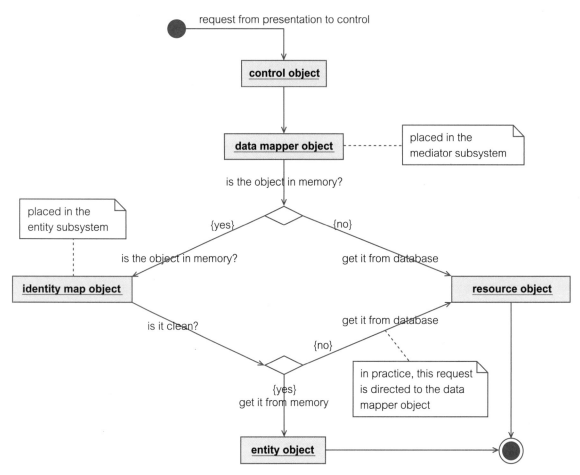

Figure 8.20 Searching for a persistent object

Note that, in the first case, the control object may elect to enquire an identity map object directly and so circumvent the data mapper object. This is possible because the control subsystem can communicate directly with the entity subsystem (Figure 8.1).

In the second case, the data mapper uses the attribute values obtained from the control object to construct a proper message to the identity map object. The identity map object will then initiate a further search based on the attribute values.

In the third case, the data mapper object cannot be of immediate help, so the request must be delegated to the identity map object. Once the object holding the reference is retrieved, the identity map can ascertain whether the reference links to an entity object held in memory. If the object is in memory, it can be returned to the control object (and further up to the presentation object). If not, a database retrieval is necessary.

As shown in Figure 8.20, it is not enough to find an entity object in memory. The object should be clean – that is, it should contain the current data values as in the database. The information about whether or not an object is clean is normally held in the object itself (by some kind of marker, so that each entity object is marked as clean or dirty).

In cases when an entity object is found but is dirty or when it is not found in the memory cache, a data mapper object initiates the search in the database. The note in Figure 8.20 makes it clear that the data mapper object mediates all searches to the database and, therefore, the entity subsystem does not communicate directly with the resource subsystem (as per the PCBMER framework – Figure 8.1).

Because a data mapper object has such an important mediating role, sending messages from the control subsystem directly to the entity subsystem should be restricted to those situations where a control object is certain that a clean entity object exists in memory. As, most of the time, a control object cannot have such a certainty, the communication should go through a data mapper object in the mediator subsystem.

Loading persistent objects   8.4.2

The diagram in Figure 8.20 does not explain what it takes to *load* a persistent object from a database to memory if that object does not exist in the program's memory or is there but is marked as dirty. The load operation is also known as a *check-out* operation – meaning that an object is "checked out" from the database to memory.

Figure 8.21 is a sequence diagram for loading an `EContact` object from the `Contact` table (Example 8.1, Section 8.3.1). The model assumes that `MDataMapper` knows that the `EContact` object is not in memory and immediately proceeds to the database to get the object. To make the search possible, `CAdmin` passes `contactName` as a search condition value in the argument `getContact()`.

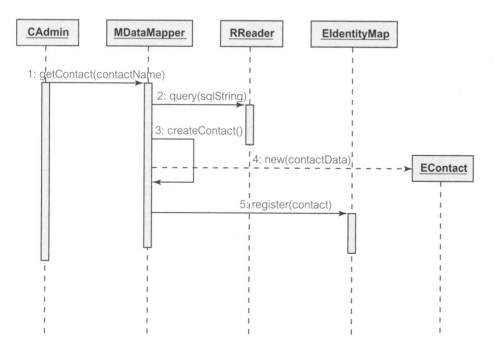

Figure 8.21
Loading a persistent object for a contact management system

In the model in Figure 8.21, `MDataMapper` builds an SQL search string and passes it to `RReader` in the `query()` message. `RReader` then handles any communication with the database and obtains the data from the `Contact` table. These data are then returned to `MDataMapper`. In general, the SQL query could be fully constructed in `RReader`, rather than in `MDataMapper`.

`MDataMapper` now has data to build an `EContact` object. This process is initiated in the `createContact()` method. This method is responsible for the construction of a new `EContact` object. The message `new()` does this.

To conclude the loading process, `MDataMapper` requests that `EIdentityMap` register the newly created `EContact` object (and mark it as clean). The registration involves adding `EContact`'s OID to various maps managed by `EIdentityMap`. The most obvious map is the map between `EContact`'s OID and the `EContact` object itself. Another map may exist to link `EContact`'s OID with its `contactName` (assuming the `contactName` is a unique identifier).

8.4.3 Unloading persistent objects

Unloading (also known as *check-in*) is the opposite operation to loading. There are three main circumstances when an entity object needs to be unloaded (Maciaszek and Liong 2005). These are when the application has:

■ created a new entity object and it needs to be persistently stored in the database

■ updated an entity object and the changes need to be persistently recorded in the database

■ deleted an entity object and the corresponding record must be deleted from a database table.

Figure 8.22 demonstrates the interaction sequence for the third situation, where an object is deleted by the application. Assuming that `CAdmin` knows that an `EContact` object needs to be deleted, it invokes the `deleteContact()` service on `MDataMapper`. `MDataMapper` constructs an SQL string for the `delete()` operation and asks `RWriter` to get the database to delete the pertinent record from the `Contact` table.

Once `RWriter` returns (to `MDataMapper`) the information that the database record has been deleted, `MDataMapper` sends an `unregister()` message to `EIdentityMap`. Following successful removal of any `EContact` information from the maps maintained by `EIdentityMap`, `MDataMapper` requests `EContact` to `destroy()` itself.

Review quiz 8.4

RQ1 What does PEAA stand for?

RQ2 Which pattern has knowledge of objects currently in the memory cache?

RQ3 Which pattern is responsible for handling business transactions?

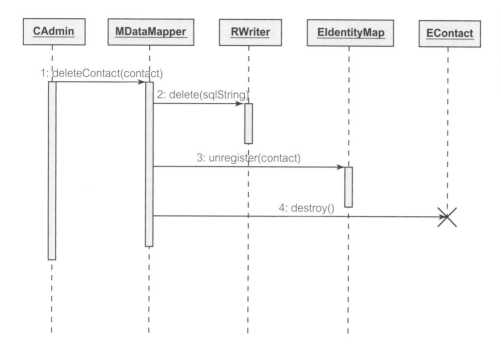

Figure 8.22
Unloading a
persistent object
for a contact
management
system

Designing database access and transactions

8.5

Applications programs interact with databases for data. A client program must use a database language – typically SQL – to access and modify the database. As shown in Section 8.4, the resource subsystem (and classes such as RReader, RWriter) is responsible for communication with the database. However, the models in Section 8.4 did not show *how* this communication is implemented. Moreover, the models did not explain how the *consistency* of business transactions can be ensured.

Levels of SQL programming

8.5.1

To understand how a client program communicates with a database server, we need to recognize that SQL comes in different dialects and can be used at different levels of programming abstraction. Figure 8.23 distinguishes five levels of SQL interface.

- *Level 1* SQL is used as a data-definition language (DDL). DDL is a specification language for defining the database structures (database schema). Database designers and database administrators (DBAs) are the main users of Level 1 SQL.

- *Level 2* SQL is used as a data-manipulation language (DML) or as a query language. However, the term *query language* is a misnomer, because SQL at level 2 serves the purpose of not only retrieving data but also modifying it (with insert, update and delete operations).

Figure 8.23
SQL interfaces

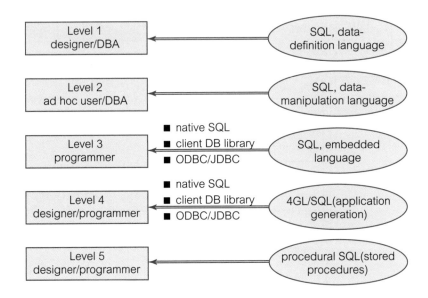

A wide range of users use level 2 SQL, from "naive" ad hoc users to experienced DBAs. SQL at this level is *interactive*, which means that a user can formulate a query outside any application programming environment and immediately run it on a database. Level 2 SQL is an entry point to learning the more elaborated SQL at the next levels.

Application programmers use SQL at levels above level 2. At these higher levels, SQL permits *record-at-a-time processing* in addition to the *set-at-a-time processing* facility available (as the only option) at level 2. The set-at-a-time processing takes one or more tables (sets of records) as the input to a query and returns a table as the output. Although a powerful facility, it is difficult and dangerous to use with complicated queries.

To be certain that a query returns correct results, it must be possible for the programmer to browse through the records returned by a query one by one and decide what to do with these records on a one-at-a-time basis. Such a record-at-a-time processing capability is called a *cursor* and is available in SQL at levels above level 2.

■ *Level 3* SQL is *embedded* in a conventional programming language, such as C or COBOL. Because a programming language compiler does not understand SQL, a precompiler (preprocessor) is needed to translate SQL statements into function calls in the DB library provided by the DBMS vendor. A programmer may elect to program using the DB library functions directly, in which case the precompiler is not needed.

A popular way of interfacing a client program with databases is via *Open DataBase Connectivity* (**ODBC**) or *Java Database Connectivity* (**JDBC**) standards. To program in this way, an ODBC or JDBC software driver for a particular DBMS is required. ODBC and JDBC provide a standard database language, above SQL, which is translated by the driver into the native DBMS SQL.

ODBC/JDBC have the advantage of decoupling the program from the native DBMS SQL. If the program needs to be migrated in the future to a different target DBMS, then the straightforward process replacing of the driver should do the trick. More importantly, working with ODBC/JDBC allows a single application to issue queries to more than one DBMS.

The disadvantage of ODBC/JDBC is that it is the "lowest common denominator" for SQL. A client application cannot take advantage of any special SQL features or extensions supported by a particular DBMS vendor.

- *Level 4* SQL at this level uses the same strategies for embedding SQL in client programs as level 3. However, at level 4, SQL provides a more powerful programming environment of an application generator or a fourth-generation language (4GL). A 4GL comes equipped with "screen painting" and UI-building capabilities. As IS applications require sophisticated GUIs, a 4GL/SQL is a frequent choice for building such applications.

- *Level 5* SQL at this level complements levels 3 and 4 by providing the possibility of moving some SQL statements from the client program to an active (programmable) server database. SQL is used as a programming language (PL/SQL in Oracle or Transact SQL in Sybase and SQL Server, for example). The server programs can be called from within the client programs, as discussed in Section 8.2.5.

Designing business transactions 8.5.2

A **transaction** is a logical unit of work that comprises one or more SQL statements executed by a user. A transaction is a unit of *database consistency* – the state of the database is consistent after the transaction completes. To ensure that consistency, the transaction manager of a DBMS serves two purposes – *database recovery* and *concurrency control*.

According to SQL standards, a transaction begins with the first executable SQL statement (in some systems, an explicit *begin* transaction statement may be required). A transaction ends with a *commit* or *rollback* statement. The commit statement writes the changes persistently to the database. The rollback statement erases any changes made by the transaction.

The transaction is *atomic* – the results of all SQL statements in the transaction are either committed or rolled back. The user determines the duration (size) of a transaction. Depending on the business needs, application domain and user–computer interaction style, a transaction can be as short as one SQL statement or involve a series of SQL statements.

Short transactions 8.5.2.1

Most conventional IS applications require *short transactions*. A short transaction contains one or more SQL statements that must be completed as quickly as possible so that other transactions are not held up.

Consider an airline reservation system in which many travel agents make flight bookings for travelers around the world. It is essential that each booking transaction is performed quickly by the DBMS so that the availability of flight seats is updated and the database gets ready to process the next transaction waiting in the queue.

Pessimistic concurrency control 8.5.2.1.1

Conventional DBMSs, with the notable exception of ODBMSs, have been designed with short transactions in mind. These systems work according to *pessimistic concurrency control*. **Locks** are acquired on every persistent object that a transaction processes. There are four possible kinds of lock that are put on an object:

- *exclusive (write) lock* other transactions must wait until the transaction holding such a lock completes and releases the lock

- *update (write intent) lock* other transactions can read the object, but the transaction holding the lock is guaranteed to be able to upgrade it to the exclusive mode as soon as it has such a need

- *read (shared) lock* other transactions can read, and possibly obtain, an update lock on the object

- *no lock* other transactions can update an object at any time, so this is only suitable for applications that allow *dirty reads* – that is, a transaction reads data that can be modified or even deleted (by another transaction) before the transaction completes.

8.5.2.1.2   *Levels of isolation*

Associated with the four kinds of lock described above are the four *levels of isolation* between concurrently executing transactions. It is the responsibility of the system designer to decide which level of isolation is appropriate for the mix of transactions on the database. The four levels are (Khoshafian et al. 1992):

- *dirty read possible* transaction t1 modified an object, but it has not committed yet; transaction t2 reads the object; if t1 rolls back the transaction, then t2 has obtained an object that, in a sense, never existed in the database

- *non-repeatable read possible* t1 has read an object; t2 updates the object; t1 reads the same object again, but this time obtains a different value for the same object

- *phantom possible* t1 has read a set of objects; t2 inserts a new object into the set; t1 repeats the read operation and then sees a "phantom" object

- *repeatable read* t1 and t2 can still execute concurrently, but the interleaved execution of these two transactions will produce the same results as if the transactions executed one at a time (this is called *serializable execution*).

Typical GUI-based interactive IS applications require short transactions. However, the level of isolation may differ for different transactions in the same application. The SQL statement set transaction can be used for that purpose. The trade-off is obvious – increasing the level of isolation reduces the overall concurrency of the system.

However, one crucial design decision is independent of the above considerations. The beginning of the transaction must always be delayed to the last second. It is unacceptable to start a transaction from a client window and then make the transaction wait until it obtains some additional information from the user before it can actually complete the job.

The user may be very slow in providing that information or may even elect to shut the computer down while the transaction is running. The *transaction timeout* will eventually roll back the transaction, but by then the harm to the overall system throughput will already have been done.

Murphy's law states that if something can go wrong, it will. Programs may contain errors, running processes can hang or be aborted, the power supply can fail, a disk head can crash, and so on. Fortunately, a DBMS provides *automatic recovery* for most situations. Only in the case of the physical loss of disk data is a DBA's intervention necessary to instruct the DBMS to recover from the last database *backup.*

Depending on the state of the transaction at failure point, a DBMS will automatically perform a *rollback* or *roll forward* of the transaction as soon as the cause of the problem has been eliminated. The recovery process is automatic, but a DBA can control the amount of recovery time by setting the frequency of **checkpoints**. A *checkpoint* is an action taken by the DBMS to identify currently active (still executing) transactions. To this end, a checkpoint record is written to the **log** that is used during the recovery process. A log, as its name suggests, is a written record of a "transactional journey" – it contains a sequence of data record processed so far in the transactions. As a minimum, any recovery process needs to scan back to the last checkpoint record before deciding what recovery actions must be taken.

Figure 8.24 illustrates the issues involved in automatic recovery from failure (Kirkwood 1992). Transaction t1 was committed after the checkpoint but before the system failure. As a DBMS does not know if all changes after the checkpoint have been physically written to the database, it will *roll forward* (*redo*) transaction t1 after it recovers from the failure.

Transaction t2 had a rollback applied to it between the checkpoint and the failure. As in the case of transaction t1, the DBMS does not know if the rollback changes reached the disk, so the DBMS will perform the *rollback* again.

Other transactions started after the checkpoint. Transaction t3 will be *rolled forward* to guarantee that its changes are effected in the database. Similarly, transaction t4 will be repeated – that is *rolled back.*

Transaction t5 would not require any remedial action by the DBMS, because it was executing at the time of failure. Any changes done by t5 before the failure have not been written to the database. All intermediate changes have only been written to the log file.

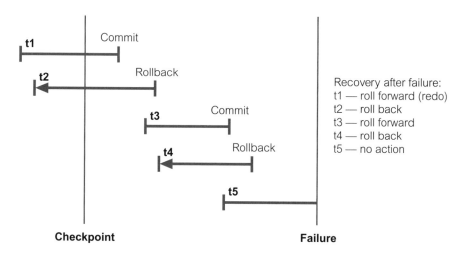

Figure 8.24
Automatic
recovery

Recovery after failure:
t1 — roll forward (redo)
t2 — roll back
t3 — roll forward
t4 — roll back
t5 — no action

The user is aware that the transaction was executing at the time of failure and may resend the transaction when the DBMS is up and running again.

8.5.2.1.4 Programmable recovery

While unexpected system failures are automatically recovered from by a DBMS, designers and programmers should control any anticipated transaction problems. A DBMS provides a range of rollback options to apply in the program so that it can recover gracefully from a problem, possibly without the user realizing that things went wrong at some point.

To start with, UI guidelines such as the user in control and forgiveness (Section 7.1.2) demand that a program allows the user to make mistakes and recover from them. A programmer-controlled rollback applied in the right places in the program can restore the database to its previous state (that is, *undo* the mistake), provided that the transaction has not committed.

If the transaction *has* committed, then the programmer may still have the option of writing a *compensating transaction*. The user can then request the execution of the compensating transaction to undo the changes to the database. Compensating transactions are designed specifically to allow programmable recovery and should be modeled in use cases.

A **savepoint** is a statement in a program that divides a longer transaction into smaller parts. *Named savepoints* are inserted in strategic places in the program. The programmer then has the option of rolling back the work to a named savepoint rather than to the beginning of the transaction. For example, a programmer may insert a savepoint just before an update operation. If the update fails, then the program rolls back to the savepoint and attempts to execute the update again. Alternatively, the program may take any other action to avoid aborting the transaction altogether.

In larger programs, savepoints may be inserted before each subroutine. If a subroutine fails, it may be possible to roll back to the beginning of that subroutine and re-execute it with revised parameters. If necessary, a specially designed and programmed recovery subroutine can do the mopping up so that the transaction can resume execution.

A *trigger rollback* is a special kind of savepoint. As explained in Section 8.2.4, a trigger can be used to program a business rule of any complexity. At times, it may be undesirable to roll back the *whole* transaction when a trigger refuses to modify a table (due to the transaction's attempt to breach a business rule). The transaction may want to take remedial action. For this reason, a DBMS may provide a trigger programming possibility to roll back either the whole transaction or just the trigger. In the latter case, the program (possibly a stored procedure) can analyze the problem and decide on further action. Even if the whole transaction eventually has to be rolled back, it may be possible for the program to better interpret the cause of the error and display a more intelligible message to the user.

8.5.2.1.5 Designing stored procedures and triggers

The *window navigation* approach presented in Section 7.4 could be extended to the application program logic related to the management of transaction states. The resulting *program navigation* models could identify stored procedures and triggers. The purpose, definition and detailed design of each stored procedure and trigger would then need to be provided. In particular, some pseudo-code notation ought to be employed to define the algorithms.

As an example, we present an algorithm for the stored procedure `DeleteEvent` related to a contact management system (Figure 8.25). The procedure checks if the user (employee) attempting to *delete* an event is the same employee who *created* the event. If not, the delete operation is rejected. The procedure also checks if the event is the only one remaining for the task. If so, the task is deleted as well.

The stored procedure `deleteEvent` contains delete statements to delete records from the tables `Event` and `Task`. These delete statements would fire delete triggers on these tables, if present. If the algorithms for these triggers go beyond the normal referential integrity checking, the designer should provide pseudo-code specifications for them as well (including the decision on rollback strategy – whether to have a trigger rollback or transaction rollback).

Long transactions

8.5.2.2

Some new classes of IS application encourage cooperation between users. These applications are known as *workgroup computing* applications or *Computer-Supported Cooperative Work (CSCW)* applications. Examples include many office applications, collaborative authoring, computer-aided design, (CAD) and CASE tools.

In many ways, workgroup computing applications have database requirements that are orthogonal to the traditional database model, with short transactions that isolate users from each other. Workgroup computing applications require long transactions, version management and collaborative concurrency control.

The ODB model provides a framework for workgroup computing and many ODBMS products target this application domain. Users in a workgroup computing application share information and are made aware of the work they do on shared data. They work in

```
BEGIN
INPUT PARAMETERS (@event_id, @user_id)
Select Event (where event_id = @event_id)
IF @user_id = Event.created_emp_id
    THEN
        delete Event (where event_id = @event_id)
        IF no more events for
            Task.task_id = Event.task_id AND
            Event.event_id = @event_id
        THEN
            delete that Task
        ENDIF
    ELSE
        raise error ('Only the creator of the event can
                    delete that event')
    ENDIF
END
```

Figure 8.25
Pseudo-code for a stored procedure for a contact management system

their own *workspaces* using personal databases of data *checked-out* (copied) from the common workgroup database. They work in a *long transaction* that can span computer sessions (users can take breaks then continue working in the same long transaction after returning).

The dominant aspect of a long transaction is that it is not allowed to be rolled back automatically without being traced by the system because of failures. To appreciate this requirement, imagine my despair if the text and figures for this book were now to be rolled back due to a computer failure! The effects of a rollback of a long transaction can be controlled by means of *savepoints* that persistently store objects in users' private databases.

The notion of a *short transaction* is not eradicated from a workgroup computing application. Short transactions are necessary to guarantee atomicity and isolation *during* the check-out and check-in operations between the group database and private databases. *Short locks* are released afterwards and *long persistent locks* are imposed by the group database on all checked-out objects.

Related objectives of the long transaction model include (Hawryszkiewycz et al.1994; Maciaszek 1998):

■ allowing the exchange of information (even if temporarily inconsistent) between cooperating users

■ detecting data inconsistencies and mediating their resolutions

■ taking advantage of object versionability to provide controlled sharing without loss of work in case of system failures.

Review quiz 8.5

RQ1   Record-at-a-time processing is possible from which SQL programming level?

RQ2   What are the two main responsibilities of a DBMS transaction manager?

RQ3   What isolation level ensures serializable execution of transactions?

RQ4   How can a DBA control the amount of recovery time?

RQ5   How can a programmer control the effects of a rollback of a long transaction?

Summary

This chapter has reflected on the paramount importance of databases in software development. All major issues related to application–database interaction have been discussed. The target database model was assumed to be the relational model.

There are three levels of data model: external, logical and physical. In this chapter, we have concentrated on the *logical model*. The *mapping of objects to databases* has been understood as the mapping of a UML class model to a logical data model within a relational database.

Mapping to the *RDB logical model* is occasionally cumbersome because of the underlying semantic simplicity of relational databases. The RDB model does not support object types, inheritance, structured types, collections or references. Data are stored in *tables* related by *referential integrity* constraints. *Triggers* can be used to program the semantics captured in business rules implied in UML class models. *Stored procedures* and *views* can be used to capture some modeling constraints that cannot possibly be expressed in tabular data structures. *Normalization* can further influence the mapping.

An application program needs to communicate with a database. The communication must not break the adopted *architectural framework*. The PCBMER framework integrates very well with database design. There are various design patterns for managing *persistent objects* in the application code. Models for searching, loading and unloading persistent objects have been shown.

When designing the application–database collaboration, consideration needs to be given to the five levels of *SQL interface*. *Level 5* SQL is of particular interest because it allows the user to program the database directly. Stored procedures and triggers heavily influence the server aspect of program design.

A *transaction* is a logical unit of database work that starts in a consistent database state and ensures that the next consistent state is established when it has finished. Transactions ensure *database concurrency* and *database recovery*. Conventional database applications require *short transactions*, while some new database applications work in *long transactions*.

Key terms

Business transaction a logical unit of work, from the business (application) perspective, that can consist of a number of (system) transactions.

Checkpoint A DBMS action that writes a checkpoint record, containing the identities of all the active transactions, to the *log* so that the time required to recover from failures can be reduced.

Column a named vertical dimension in a table that has a specific data type and represents a particular domain of data. See also *row*.

Data mapper pattern that defines "a layer of Mappers that moves data between objects and a database while keeping them independent of each other and the mapper itself" (Fowler 2003: 165).

Data model a model of data structures in the database. It may also define behavioral structures, such as triggers and stored procedures.

Domain the legal set of values that a column can take.

ER Entity-relationship.

Foreign key a key included in the definition of a referential integrity constraint (a key that references a primary key in the referenced table).

Identity map pattern that "ensures that each object gets loaded only once by keeping every loaded object in a map. Looks up objects using the map when referring to them" (Fowler 2003: 195).

JDBC Java DataBase Connectivity.

Key a column or a set of columns defining certain integrity constraint between tables and columns in a relational database.

Lazy load pattern that is defined as "an object that doesn't contain all of the data you need but knows how to get it" (Fowler 2003: 200).

Lock a DBMS action that 'locks' the data records (and other internal data structures) by allocating them to a single SQL statement within a transaction so that the execution of that statement is isolated with respect to other concurrently executing transactions.

Log a special file maintained by the DBMS that contains all records from the database that have been changed by transactions (the images of records both before and after changes have been recorded).

Normalization a process of designing a database table to avoid update anomalies.

Object-relational mapping a facility or software concerned with the transfer of application objects to a relational database and vice versa.

ODBC Open DataBase Connectivity.

PEAA Patterns of Enterprise Application Architecture.

Persistent object see *persistent object,* key terms, Chapter 6.

Primary key a key that uniquely identifies rows in a table. A table can have only one primary key.

Primitive type a built-in data type provided by a programming language or a database in support of its basic operations. Primitive types can be used by a programmer to create user-defined composite types.

Referential integrity a rule defined on a (foreign) key in one table that guarantees the values in that key match the values in a (primary) key in a related table (the referenced value). A way of implementing associations in a relational database.

Relational table see *Table (relational)* below.

Row (record) a collection of column information corresponding to a single row in a table. A relational database counterpart of a programming language object. See also *column.*

Savepoint A statement in a database program that indicates a point within the program that the transaction can be rolled back to without affecting work done in the transaction prior to reaching that savepoint.

Stored procedure a program stored in a database and that can act on the database when invoked.

Table (relational) the basic unit of data definition and data storage in a relational database. All user-accessible data is stored in tables.

Transaction (system transaction) a logical unit of work that comprises one or more SQL statements and all statements of a transaction are committed or rolled back together.

Trigger see *trigger*, Key terms, Chapter 6.

Unit of work pattern that "maintains a list of objects affected by a business transaction and coordinates the writing out of changes and the resolution of concurrency problems" (Fowler 2003: 184).

Update anomaly an undesirable side-effect as a result of a modification operation (insert, update, delete) on a table.

View a stored and named SQL query that presents itself to the user as a virtual table.

Multiple-choice test

MC1 SQL:1999 is the standard for which database?

    a Relational.

    b Object-relational.

    c Object-oriented.

    d All of the above.

MC2 Which of the following is not supported by the RDB model?

    a Structured types.

    b References.

    c Collections.

    d All of the above.

MC3 A view can be used:

    a to program business rules

    b in support of database security

    c to define domains

    d none of the above.

MC4 Which is not the permissible strategy for generalization mapping?

    a Map the entire class hierarchy to a single "superclass" table.

    b Map each disjoint concrete class to a table.

    c Map each abstract class to a table.

    d None of the above – all are permissible.

MC5 Which pattern is defined as "an object that doesn't contain all of the data you need but knows how to get it"?

    a Unit of work.

    b Identity map.

    c Data mapper.

    d Lazy load.

MC6 Which kind of lock permits "dirty reads"?

    a Write intent lock.

    b Read lock.

    c Shared lock.

    d None of the above.

Questions

Q1 Explain the three levels of data model.

Q2 Refer to Figure 8.1 (Section 8.1.3) and explain the meaning of the dependencies involving the resource subsystem, database schema and database programs.

Q3 What is referential integrity? How is it useful for mapping from a UML class model?

Q4 Explain the four declarative referential integrity constraints.

Q5 What is a trigger? How is it related to referential integrity?

Q6 Can a stored procedure call a trigger? Explain your answer.

Q7 What is a good normalization level for a database? Explain your answer.

Q8 Refer to Figure 8.11 (Section 8.3.1). Assume that each `ContactPhone` must be linked to `Contact` and cannot be allocated (switched) to another Contact. How can these constraints be enforced in the database?

Q9 Refer to Figure 8.22 (Section 8.4.3). Consider a situation in which an entity object needs to be unloaded to the database as a result of an update operation, instead of delete. How would the sequence diagram differ in such a case?

Q10 Describe briefly the five levels of SQL programming interfaces.

Q11 What are the advantages of a stored procedure call over an SQL query submitted from the client program to the database? Are there any circumstances that would make us use an SQL query instead of a stored procedure call?

Q12 Describe briefly the locks in pessimistic concurrency control.

Q13 Describe briefly the levels of transaction isolation.

Q14 Can the amount of database recovery time be controlled by the designer/DBA? Explain your answer.

Q15 What is a compensating transaction? How can it be used in program design?

Q16 What is a savepoint? How can it be used in program design?

Exercises: contact management

F1 Refer to Example 7.10 (Section 7.4.3) and to Exercise F4 in the Exercises: contact management section at the end of Chapter 7. Consider Figure 7.43, which is the solution to this exercise in the Solutions to exercises: contact management section, also at the end of Chapter 7. Refer to message number 8 in Figure 7.43 (`display record for update`). Extend the sequence diagram (starting from message 8) to account for the management of persistent objects, as discussed in Section 8.4. Explain the model.

F2 Refer to Example 7.10 (Section 7.4.3) and to Exercise F4 in the Exercises: contact management section at the end of Chapter 7. Consider Figure 7.43, which is the solution to this exercise in the Solutions to exercises: contact management section, also at the end of

Chapter 7. Refer to message number 10 in Figure 7.43 (`press save`). Extend the sequence diagram (starting from message 10) to account for the management of persistent objects, as discussed in Section 8.4. Explain the model.

F3   Refer to Problem statement 3, for a contact management system (Section 1.6.3) and to the successive examples in Chapters 4, 5, 7 and 8. In particular, consider Example 5.3 (Section 5.1.1.3). Identify the database triggers for the Event table.

F4   Refer to Problem statement 3, for a contact management system (Section 1.6.3) and to the successive examples for contact management in Chapters 4, 5, 7 and 8. Identify the database triggers for the `Task` table.

F5   Refer to Problem statement 3 contact management for (Section 1.6.3) and to the successive examples for contact management in Chapters 4, 5, 7 and 8. Identify the stored procedures to act on the `Event` table. Also specify pseudo-code algorithms for the stored procedures identified.

Exercises: telemarketing

G1   Refer to exercise G1 in the Exercises: telemarketing section at the end of Chapter 7. Consider the class diagram that you obtained as your solution to this exercise. Map the class diagram to a relational database model. Explain the mapping.

G2   Refer to exercise G8 in the Exercises: telemarketing section at the end of Chapter 7. Consider the sequence diagram that you obtained as your solution to this exercise. Identify any events (messages) in the diagram that will result in actions related to the management of persistent objects, as discussed in Section 8.4. Extend the diagram to include the management of persistent objects. Explain the model.

Review quiz answers

Review quiz 8.1
RQ1   No, it is not the same. An entity class is "destined" to be persistent and it has a persistent representation in the database, but it is not persistent per se. This distinction is even more blurred in object-oriented databases that store objects of entity classes as objects (relational databases store them in tables as records).
RQ2   Object-oriented database model.
RQ3   Entity relationship (ER) diagrams.

Review quiz 8.2
RQ1   The set theory (and predicate logic).
RQ2   A key must be unique and minimal.
RQ3   Yes, it can.
RQ4   Update anomaly.

Review quiz 8.3

RQ1 In mapping many-to-many associations.

RQ2 It is not addressed; it is ignored.

Review quiz 8.4

RQ1 Patterns of Enterprise Application Architecture.

RQ2 The data mapper pattern.

RQ3 The unit of work pattern.

Review quiz 8.5

RQ1 From level 3.

RQ2 Database recovery and concurrency control.

RQ3 Repeatable read.

RQ4 By setting the frequency of checkpoints.

RQ5 By means of savepoints that persistently store objects in the users' private databases.

Multiple-choice test answers

MC1 b

MC2 d

MC3 b

MC4 c

MC5 d

MC6 d (the "no lock" lock permits dirty reads)

Answers to odd-numbered questions

Q1

Data modelers – people specializing in modeling database structures – distinguish three levels of data model, which are the external, logical and physical.

The external and logical models are *conceptual models* that do not consider the intricacies of a particular DBMS, but normally conform to the model that is dominant today – the relational database model. This adherence to the relational model is frequently reflected in a trimmed-down expressiveness of the entity–relationship (ER) diagramming technique typically used for external and logical modeling ("trimming down" is due to the underlying semantic simplicity of the relational model).

The *external data model* is constructed for the scope of a single application system. The application is normally defined as one executable program that connects to a database. The external data model defines the database structures needed for that application.

Usually, a database supports many applications. The database requirements of these applications may overlap and conflict. It is, therefore, necessary to integrate the external models in a single *logical data model*. A well-designed logical data model is almost dissociated from individual applications and provides a database structure on which any existing and future applications can be built.

The *physical data model* is obtained by transforming the logical model into a design that corresponds to a particular DBMS and a particular release of that DBMS. The resulting physical model enables the designer to generate code to create database schemas (including triggers and indexes) and, possibly, load test data into the database tables.

Q3

Referential integrity is the principal RDB technique for ensuring that the data in the database is accurate and correct. Referential integrity states that a database must not contain foreign key values that do not match some primary key values.

Referential integrity is an RDB way of implementing associations between data structures. Consequently, associations (and aggregations) in UML class diagrams are mapped to primary-to-foreign-key relationships in RDB models.

Q5

A *trigger* is a procedural (programmatic) way of implementing the business rules on data. Some business rules on relationships between data in the database cannot be implemented declaratively and triggers then provide the only way of programming such referential integrity rules.

In effect, triggers subsume *declarative referential integrity*. The trigger code can be generated automatically to account for any declarative referential constraint. This code can then be manually extended or reprogrammed to enforce more exotic business rules.

Q7

A good *normalization level* delivers a database schema that is optimal – in terms of performance and maintenance – for the ways in which the database is used. As database usage patterns consist of a mixture of retrieval and update operations, a good normalization level implies a trade-off between retrieval and update, such that the most important retrieval and update operations get preferential treatment as far as the normalization of tables is concerned.

Database tables that are *dynamic* (their content is frequently updated) should be normalized to a high NF. On the other hand, tables that are relatively *static* (possibly updated by some batch processes outside peak hours) should be denormalized to a low NF. As a result, some tables in the database may be in a high NF and other tables in a low NF.

Q9

The question is slightly hypothetical as the extent of the update is not specified and the exact design of the entity classes (`EIdentityMap` and `EContact`) is not known. For example, it is possible to have only one instance of `EIdentityMap` in the program or a separate instance of it for each entity class. In the latter case, the status of an entity object (clean or dirty) may be maintained in `EIdentityMap` instead of in the entity object itself.

The main difference between the delete and update scenarios is that unloading due to an update does not (normally) lead to the destruction of the entity object. The object is "unloaded" to the database by executing an SQL update operation on the `Contact` table. However, the `EContact` object will be retained in the memory cache. Moreover, the `EContact` object is clean and should be marked as such. The marking will involve a `setClean()` or similar message from `MDataMapper` to either `EIdentityMap` or directly to `EContact`.

Q11

Stored procedures have important performance advantages over SQL queries submitted from the client. The advantages are the much reduced network traffic and the fact that stored procedures are optimized, compiled and ready to "fire".

In large systems, stored procedures allow highly modularized code to be written that can be reused and nested in larger stored procedures as well as invoked from many different application programs.

An SQL query may still need to be used from a client program in circumstances in which the user is given an opportunity to construct (indirectly through the UI) *dynamic queries* to the database – in other words, when the client program cannot know ahead of time what processing (query criteria) will be demanded by the user.

Q13

SQL supports four levels of *transaction isolation*. These four levels have been given different names in this chapter to facilitate readers' understanding and follow the book's flow of logic. The four levels are (the chapter's descriptions are in parentheses):

1 read uncommitted (dirty read possible)
2 read committed (non-repeatable read possible)
3 repeatable read (phantom possible)
4 serializable (repeatable read).

Read uncommitted means that the database does not issue read (shared) locks while reading data. Consequently, another transaction can read an uncommitted transaction that might be rolled back later (hence "dirty read"). This isolation level only ensures that physically corrupt data will not be read.

Read committed means that the database will require read locks to read data. Only committed data can be read, but the data can be changed before the end of the transaction.

Repeatable read means that locks are placed on all data used in a transaction and other transactions cannot update the data. However, other transactions might insert new items into the data set and, if the transaction reads from that data set again, then "phantom reads" may occur.

Serializable means that locks are placed on all data that are used in a transaction and other transactions cannot update or insert items into that data set.

Note that if a database supports only *page-level locking* (there is no support for row-level locking), then the repeatable read and serializable levels are synonymous. This is because other transactions cannot insert individual rows of data before the first transaction is finished as the entire page of data is locked.

Q15

A *compensating transaction* reverses the effect of a transaction that has already committed. Compensation is an important recovery mechanism in situations where the user must undo changes made to the database and expects that the program will provide such an undo operation (such as a menu item). In some cases, it may be possible and desirable to design into the program a compensating transaction that can undo to a number of levels (one undo after another more than once).

In some *advanced transaction models* that employ savepoints, subtransactions are allowed to commit changes to the database. A recovery from the successive failure of a transaction will then require a compensating transaction so that a committed subtransaction can be undone without causing a cascading abort of (perhaps many) other transactions.

Solutions to exercises: contact management

F1

The screen `Update Organization Status` in Figure 7.43 is similar to the window presented in Figure 7.34 (Section 7.4.3), except that the `statusCode` is also shown as a non-editable field. When the program navigates into this screen, there is a need to find the latest value for `statusDescription`. Accordingly, a message is sent to `CAdmin` to `getOrgStatus()` (Figure 8.26). `CAdmin` delegates this request to `MDataMapper`.

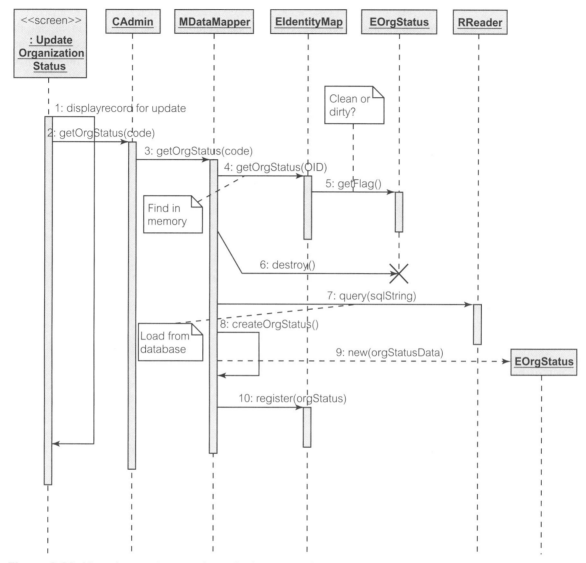

Figure 8.26 Managing persistency after a display request for a contact management system

As discussed in Section 8.4.1 (Figure 8.20), MDataMapper attempts to obtain the EOrgStatus object from the memory cache. If the EOrgStatus object exists in memory and is clean, processing will terminate (after the EOrgStatus object is returned and displayed in the Update Organization Status screen).

Otherwise, the program has to search for the EOrgStatus object in the database (after destroying any dirty EOrgStatus object, if such a dirty object is in the cache). The remaining messages follow the pattern described in Section 8.4.2 (Figure 8.21).

F2

Making a change to an organization status record necessitates updating the database as well as modifying the entity object held in the memory cache. As seen in Figure 8.27, the `save()` request is forwarded by CAdmin to `MDataMapper`. The request passes the `OID` of `EOrgStatus` as well as modified `orgStatusData`. With this information, `MDataMapper` can engage `RWriter` to update the database.

Provided that the database update is successful, `MDataMapper` engages `EIdentityMap`, so that the memory-held `EOrgStatus` object is modified with a new `statusDescription`. The model in Figure 8.27 assumes that `EOrgStatus` holds a flag indicating whether or not it is clean. The flag value is modified with the `setClean()` message.

F3

There is a need for two *triggers* on the `Event` table, namely:

1 on `insert` (ti_event)

2 on `update` (tu_event)

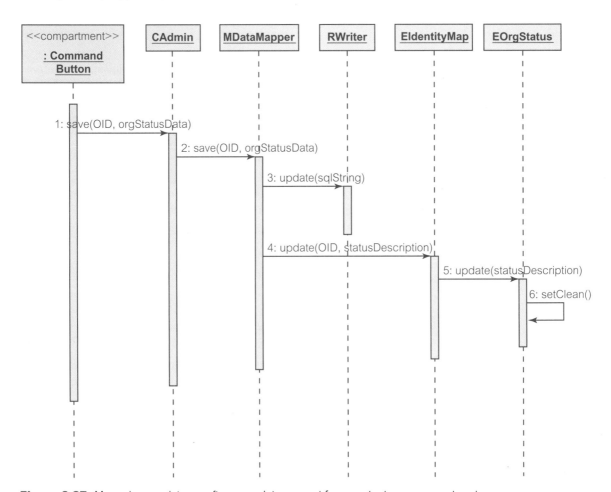

Figure 8.27 Managing persistency after an update request for a contact management system

The *insert trigger* will ensure that:

- foreign key `Event.task_id` must correspond to an existing `Task.task_id`
- foreign key `Event.created_emp_id` corresponds to an existing `Employee.emp_id`
- foreign key `Event.due_emp_id` corresponds to an existing `Employee.emp_id`
- foreign key `Event.completed_emp_id` corresponds to an existing `Employee.emp_id` or be `null`

The *update trigger* will ensure that the same business rules apply as for the insert trigger in case an attempt is made to update the foreign key columns:

- `Event.task_id`
- `Event.created_emp_id`
- `Event.due_emp_id`
- `Event.completed_emp_id.`

F4

There is a need for three *triggers* on the `Task` table, namely:

1 on insert (ti_task)
2 on update (tu_task)
3 on delete (td_task)

The *insert* trigger will ensure that:

- foreign key `Task.contact_id` corresponds to an existing `Contact.contact_id`
- foreign key `Task.created_emp_id` corresponds to an existing `Employee.emp_id`

The *update trigger* will ensure that:

- foreign key `Task.contact_id` cannot be modified to a non-existent `Contact.contact_id`
- foreign key `Task.created_emp_id` cannot be modified to a non-existent `Employee.emp_id`
- primary key `Task.task_id` cannot be modified if associated events still exist in the `Event` table

The *delete trigger* will ensure that on the deletion of a task:

- all associated events in the `Event` table are also deleted (the "cascade" of deletion stops at the `Event` table).

F5

Stored procedures to further support transactional integrity of the `Event` table (that is, modify `Event` and cooperate with the triggers) include those to:

- save an event (`SaveTaskEvent_SP`)
- delete the last event for the task (`DeleteEvent_SP`).

Stored procedures that modify the `Event` table without the risk of violating foreign key references to other tables include (note that a stored procedure that modifies a table without the risk of violating foreign key references is either not modifying any of the foreign key columns or the application program ensures that foreign key values are correct, by, for example, using database-driven picklists for value selections) ones that:

- store the fact that an event has been completed (`CompleteEvent_SP`)

Stored procedures that only retrieve information from the database and "touch" on the Event table include ones that:

■ find the daily activities of employees in the contact management subsystem (DailyActivity_SP).

The following algorithm is obeyed by the procedure SaveTaskEvent_SP:

```
BEGIN
INPUT PARAMETERS (all known (not null) fields corresponding to columns in tables Task and Event)
IN/OUT PARAMETERS (@task_id, @event_id)
IF @task_id is null
  AND other Task fields are not nulls
   (except @value that can be null)
  THEN
        insert into Task
  ELSE
        IF @task_id is not null
            AND at least one other Task field is not null
            THEN
                    update Task
        ENDIF
ENDIF
IF @task_id is not null
  IF @event_id is null
        AND other required Event fields are not nulls
        THEN
                insert into Event
        ELSE
                IF @event_id is not null
                    THEN
                    update Event
                ENDIF
  ENDIF
ENDIF
```

Any other case not allowed by the application, but if allowed the triggers will roll back the transaction with appropriate error message

```
END
```

The *algorithm* for the procedure DeleteEvent_SP is:

```
BEGIN
INPUT PARAMETERS (@event_id, @user_id)
Select Event (where event_id = @event_id)
IF @user_id = Event.created_emp_id
  THEN
        delete Event (where event_id = @event_id)
        IF no more events for
```

```
                Task.task_id = Event.task_id AND
                Event.event_id = @event_id
          THEN
              delete that Task
          ENDIF
    ELSE
      raise error ("Only creator of the event can delete that event")
  ENDIF
END
```

The *algorithm* for the procedure `CompleteEvent_SP` is:

```
BEGIN
INPUT PARAMETERS (@event_id, @completed_dt, @completed_emp_id)
IF all parameters are not null
  THEN
      update Event (where event_id = @event_id)
  ELSE
      raise error
ENDIF
END
```

The *algorithm* for the procedure `DailyActivity_SP` is:

```
BEGIN
INPUT PARAMETERS (@date, @user_id)
OUTPUT PARAMETERS (all columns from tables Task, Event, and selected columns from tables
Contact and PostalAddress)
LOOP (until no more Events found)
  Select Event (where (due_dt <= @date OR
                completed_dt = @date) AND
                due_emp_id = @user_id)
  Select Task for that Event.task_id
  Select ActionXref for that Event.action_id
  Select Contact for that Task.contact_id
  Select PostalAddress for that Contact.contact_id
ENDLOOP
END
```

Chapter

9

Quality and Change Management

Objectives

9.1 Quality management

9.2 Change management

    Summary

    Key terms

    Multiple-choice test

    Questions

    Review quiz answers

    Multiple-choice test answers

    Answers to odd-numbered questions

Objectives

In this chapter we refer back to the most fundamental issues in systems development as defined in Chapter 1 and, in a sense, close the development lifecycle loop. Issues that we are concerned with here – quality and change management – determine whether or not an IT organization is capable of attaining the two highest levels of CMM process maturity (Section 1.1.2.2.2).

Quality management divides into *quality assurance* and *quality control*. *Quality assurance* is about proactive ways to build quality into a software system. *Quality control* is about (mostly reactive) ways to test the quality of a software system.

Change management is the underlying aspect of overall project management – change requests must be documented and the impact of each change on development artifacts tracked and retested after the change has been realized.

By reading this chapter you will:

- understand the interplay between quality and change management
- recognize the difference between quality assurance and quality control
- learn about conventional quality assurance techniques – checklists, reviews and audits
- become aware of test-driven development as a quality assurance approach

- learn about testing as the principal quality control mechanism
- become conscious of the difference between testing system services and system constraints
- appreciate the need for prescribed change management processes originating with a formal change request
- recognize that traceability is a necessary condition for change management.

Quality management

9.1

Quality management is part of an overall *software process management*, along with such other activities as people, risk and change management. Some aspects of quality management interweave with other management undertakings.

An exception is *project management* (scheduling, budget estimation, tracking project progress). It is desirable that quality management is performed in parallel with and in addition to project management. Quality management should have its own budget and schedule and one of its tasks should be to ensure quality in project management. This said, the actions and outcomes of quality and change management may involve changes to the project schedule and budget baselines, also known as the *performance measurement baselines* (Heldman 2002).

Quality management targets software *products* as well as *processes* that are used during the development of the products. There are many desired *software qualities* that vary in importance for different software projects. These qualities are in addition to the most important objective of the system – namely, that the functional requirements are satisfied by the software product. Maciaszek and Liong (2005) list the following qualities as being necessary to achieve this aim:

- correctness
- reliability
- robustness
- performance
- usability
- understandability
- maintainability (repairability)
- scalability (evolvability)
- reusability
- portability
- interoperability
- productivity
- timeliness
- visibility.

Three of these qualities have been emphasized in this book and are the most important for long-term viability and competitiveness of enterprises. They are understandability, maintainability and scalability – together known as *adaptiveness*.

9.1.1 Quality assurance

Quality assurance is concerned with defining quality processes and standards that will assure quality in the resulting products. In this sense, the process standards and frameworks discussed in Section 1.1.2.2 belong to the realm of quality assurance.

Because of its independence from project management, quality assurance should be governed by a separate body – a *software quality assurance (SQA) team*. The SQA team should consist of some of the best people in the organization. The team must not be associated with the project, except in the capacity of quality assurance. The SQA group (not the original developers!) is made responsible for the final quality of the product. The SQA team should report to functional management at the level commensurate with the significance and scope of the development project. So, this could be the level of operational, tactical or even strategic management.

9.1.1.1 Checklists, reviews and audits

Checklists, reviews and audits are the three most widely used techniques of quality assurance. A *checklist* is what the name suggests – a predefined list of "to do" points that need to be scrupulously checked off during the development process. Any IT enterprise with an established software development process has its own checklist of activities that developers have to adhere to. Standards organizations also define checklist items, and enterprises can verify their conformance to standards by checking their activities against these lists.

Because no two projects are the same, the processes must differ from project to project. Consequently, checklists cannot be fixed forever – they need to be "generated" separately for each project. Also, the "baseline" checklists need to be modified to account for new IT technologies and changes in IT development paradigms.

A *review* is a kind of hands off form of testing. It is a formal, document-driven meeting of developers, and possibly managers, to review a work product or process. There are two popular kinds of review: **walkthroughs** and **inspections**.

A *walkthrough* is a type of formal brainstorming review that can be conducted in any development phase. It is a friendly meeting of developers, carefully planned and with clear objectives, an agenda, set duration and membership. Many IS development teams conduct walkthroughs on a weekly basis.

A few days prior to a walkthrough meeting, the participants are handed the materials (models, documents, program code and so on) that are to be reviewed at the meeting. The materials are collected and distributed to the participants by the walkthrough moderator. The participants study the materials and supply the moderator with their comments, also prior to the meeting.

The meeting itself is relatively short (two to three hours at most). During the meeting, the moderator presents the comments that were made and opens a discussion on each of the items. The purpose of the meeting is to pinpoint any problems, not harass the developer! The developer behind the problem is not important and may even be anonymous (although normally this would not be the case). The whole idea is to confirm the existence of a problem. A solution to the problem must not even be attempted.

Acknowledged problems are entered on a *walkthrough issues list* (Pressman 2005), which is given to the developer after the meeting. The list is used by the developer to make corrections to the software product or process reviewed. Once the corrections have been made, the developer informs the moderator, who makes a decision as to whether or not a follow-up walkthrough is necessary.

There is lots of evidence that walkthroughs work very well. They introduce rigor and professionalism to the development process, contribute to productivity and the meeting of deadlines, have very important informational outcomes and improve software quality.

Like a walkthrough, an *inspection* is a friendly meeting, but carried out under close supervision by the project's management. Its purpose is also to identify any **defects**, validate that they are in fact defects, record them and schedule when and by whom they have to be fixed.

Unlike the walkthroughs, inspections are conducted less frequently, may target only selected and critical issues and are more formal and more rigorous. An inspection is organized in a number of stages. It starts with the *planning stage*, which identifies the inspection membership and the inspection target area.

Prior to the inspection session, a short informational meeting may be arranged. During the informational meeting, the developer whose product is to be inspected introduces the subject. The inspection materials are handed over to the participants during or before the informational meeting.

The informational meeting usually takes place one week before the inspection meeting. This gives the inspection team time to study the materials and prepare for the meeting. During the meeting, any defects are identified, recorded and numbered. Immediately after the meeting, the moderator prepares the *defect log* – ideally, recorded in a *change management tool* associated with the project.

The developer is normally asked to resolve the defects quickly and record the resolution in the change management tool. The moderator would verify that this had solved the problem and decide if *reinspection* was needed. Once satisfied with the resolution, the moderator – in consultation with the project manager – submits the development module to the SQA group in the organization (if such a group exists).

An **audit** in a system development project is a quality assurance process that is modeled on and similar, in terms of the resources required, to traditional accounting audits. It is a very formal process and has an undertone of the management overseeing things and exerting its power. An audit is prepared well in advance and involves studies of the product to be audited and/or process, interviews and inspections.

An audit is always positioned within the overall management of the software process. It places risk management in its view. It relates to the strategic importance of IT to the enterprise and addresses IT governance. It looks at the alignment of the audited project with IT investments in the context of the enterprise's mission and business objectives.

Unhelkar (2003) lists the following differences between an audit and other quality assurance techniques:

- the producer of the audited product or process is usually a team, not a single person
- an audit can be performed without the presence of the producer
- audits make extensive use of checklists and interviews and less so of reviews
- audits can be external – that is, conducted by auditors external to the organization
- an audit can last from a day to a week or more, but always tightly adheres to a strictly defined scope and objectives.

9.1.1.2 Test-driven development

Test-driven development, popularized by agile software development methods, is a very practical way of conducting quality assurance. It builds quality into a software system by means of its outright demand that test code has to be written before the application code and that the application must pass the test to be quality assured.

Agile software development methods (Section 1.5.4) popularized test-driven development. The idea is to write **test cases** and **test scripts** as well as test programs before the application code (the unit under test) is developed (designed and programmed). This reversing of the "normal" sequence of activities causes the application code to be written as a response to a test code, and the test code can be used to test the application code as soon as it is available.

Test-driven development has numerous advantages, notwithstanding the fact that it allows users' requirements (and the use case specifications) to be clarified before the programmer writes the first line of the application code. The test code includes *verification points* to check whether or not all the users' requirements are met by the application. In a way, the test code is written to challenge and fail the application code.

Because the test code exists beforehand, the programmer can write the application code to specifically address all the test's verification points in order to assert the functionality it demands. Consequently, test-driven development takes a very proactive role and, in fact, drives the software development, not just the software verification.

The popularity of test-driven development has resulted in the availability of relevant patterns and frameworks. These provide ideas as well as libraries of classes and interfaces in support of test-driven development. One of the most popular *testing frameworks* for Java development is an open source tool called JUnit (JUnit 2004).

JUnit is a framework developed according to one of the best-known design patterns, called the *composite pattern* (Gamma et al. 1995). JUnit offers a Java interface named Test. The interface is implemented by the two classes `TestCase` and `TestSuite`. A `TestResult` class, associated with `TestCase`, collects the test's outcomes. Figure 9.1 shows the class model for JUnit. The model uses the GoF composite pattern.

As per its adherence to the composite pattern, `TestSuite` is a composite class that implements the `Test` interface, but it can also contain one or more `Test` interfaces. Because `Test` is implemented by both `TestCase` and `TestSuite`, a `TestSuite` object can contain one or more `TestCase` objects and/or one or more other `TestSuite` objects.

A *test unit*, such as `XXXTest`, is implemented as a subclass of `TestCase`, which can manipulate the concrete objects in the composition via the `Test` interface. In effect, `XXXTest` implements test cases to execute on a test unit indicated in the model by the

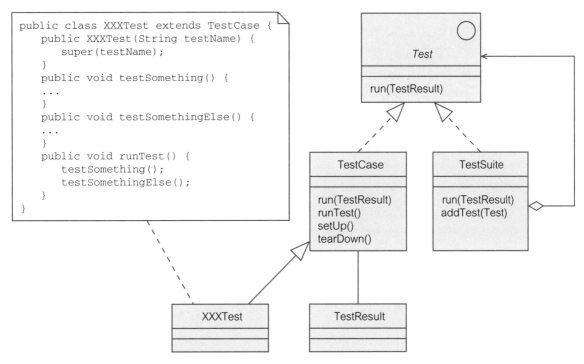

```
public class XXXTest extends TestCase {
    public XXXTest(String testName) {
        super(testName);
    }
    public void testSomething() {
    ...
    }
    public void testSomethingElse() {
    ...
    }
    public void runTest() {
        testSomething();
        testSomethingElse();
    }
}
```

Figure 9.1 JUnit as the composite pattern
Source: Maciaszek and Liong (2005). Reprinted by permission of Pearson Education Ltd

xxx prefix (xxx may be a name of a class to be tested, for example). As shown in the code fragment in Figure 9.1, xxxTest would use its runTest() method to run a test unit by calling the desired test cases. JUnit offers a visual interface to run tests, indicate test progress and report test results (Maciaszek and Liong 2005).

Quality control   9.1.2

While quality assurance is about building quality into a software product or process, **quality control** is about testing the quality of a product or process. Quality assurance is proactive, while quality control is reactive. Quality assurance has a strategic dimension, while quality control is tactical or even operational in its nature.

Being a predominantly *software testing* activity, quality control spans the lifecycle of system development. Prior to the existence of any testable software product, "testing" takes the form of quality assurance and is applied to software modeling artifacts and project documents. Conformance to checklists and reviews are the early "testing" activities.

Once a software product (application code) becomes available, testing starts with unit testing. As noticed by Pfleeger (1998) and observed in Figure 9.2, the sequence of testing tends to address software artifacts in the reverse order of to the steps involved in producing

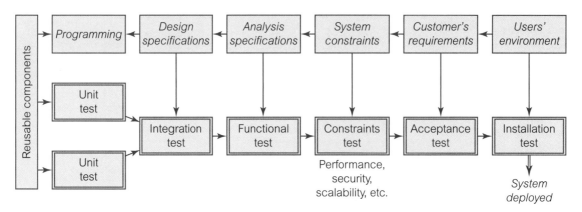

Figure 9.2 Testing activities versus development phases
Source: Maciaszek and Liong (2005). Reprinted by permission of Pearson Education Ltd

them. Accordingly, integration testing relates to design specifications, functional testing derives from analysis specifications, constraints testing refers to non-functional requirements (constraints) and so on.

9.1.2.1 Test concepts and techniques

Testing is an important part of the overall quality management plan. A **test plan** should address such issues as test schedules, budget, tasks (test cases) and resources. A test plan would also normally encroach on change management issues, such as the handling of defects and **enhancements**.

The test and change management *documentation* is an integral part of the other system documents, including the use case documents (Figure 9.3). The system's *features*, identified in the business use case model (Section 2.5.2), can be used to write the initial test plan. The use case model is then used to write test case documents and determine **test requirements**. *Defects* found during testing are documented in the defects document. Any unimplemented use case requirements are listed in the enhancements document.

When a CASE tool is used, the developers can use one or the other of the following options:

- produce narrative documents and then use them to create the requirements (test requirements, use case requirements and so on) in the CASE repository
- use the CASE tool to enter the requirements into the repository and then generate documentation.

Figure 9.4 shows an excerpt from a test case document used to enter test requirements into the repository. Rather like use case requirements, test requirements are numbered and organized hierarchically. Many test requirements correspond directly to use case requirements. Hence, the main section in the document shown in Figure 9.4 is called "Conformance to use case specs".

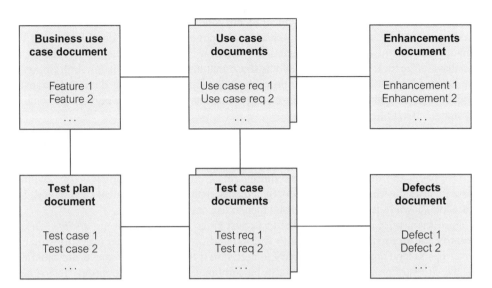

Figure 9.3
Main documents
in quality control

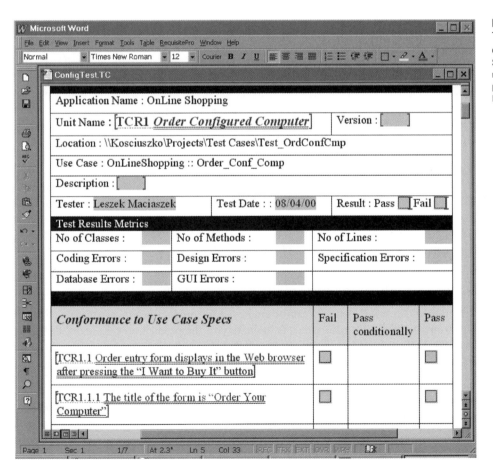

Figure 9.4
Test case
document
Source: Screenshot
reprinted by
permission from
Microsoft Corporation

Other sections of a test case document identify the requirements for GUI testing, database testing and testing of generic reusable components. These kinds of tests must be included as part of the testing of functional units for two reasons. First, to test the GUI, database or generic components (such as those that end up in the dynamic link library), we need the functional context within which the input and output data make sense. Second, the GUI, database and generic components may show defects only in the context of some, but not all, functional tests.

The test case documents are used to record test outcomes, hence the three columns next to each test requirement in Figure 9.4. A test requirement can fail the test, pass it conditionally (in which case an explanation is required) or pass it unconditionally.

Use cases and the resulting test requirements are used to develop *test cases*, which were identified earlier in the *test plan*. Statements in a test case document can (should) be traceable, down to test requirements and then to use case requirements.

For the purpose of conducting the tests, test cases are realized in *test scripts*. These identify the *steps* (that a tester has to follow) and *verification points* (questions that a tester has to find answers to) necessary to ascertain if the test's requirements are satisfied by the software product. Test scripts can be combined into larger **test suites**. Test suites can create a hierarchy in which larger test suites contain smaller test suites.

The interplay of the test concepts discussed above is shown in Figure 9.5 as a class model (Maciaszek and Liong 2005). The class model also shows that some test scripts can be automated and others can only be tested manually.

A *manual test* is conducted by a human tester, who simply executes the unit (application program) under test and observes the outcome. An *automated test* is performed by a virtual tester, which is a dedicated test workstation set up to launch the unit under test and automatically perform the steps and verification points of a test script.

A virtual tester is a *capture/playback tool*. First, the tool creates a test script by capturing the GUI and other events occurring during the execution of the unit under test. Then, the tool can play back the recorded script and check over and over again whether or not the unit under test performs as expected (as prerecorded). Accordingly, automated testing is used extensively for regression testing. "**Regression testing** is the re-execution of relevant acceptance tests on successive code iterations. The aim of regression testing is to ensure that iterative extensions (increments) to the code have not resulted in unintended side-effects and errors in the old parts of the code that were not supposed to change during the iteration" (Maciaszek and Liong 2005: 396).

9.1.2.2 Testing system services

Selecting which *test techniques* can be employed for product or process testing depends on various factors. The main factor is the nature of the product/process under test. It is clear that different test techniques are demanded by a software program, software model and document. Another factor is the required coverage and scrutiny of the test. Also, different techniques need to be used for the testing of *system services* and *system constraints* (Section 9.1.2.3).

Schach (2005) distinguishes between *informal* and *methodical* testing of system services. Every developer performs an *informal test* while modeling or implementing a system service. By its nature, informal testing is imperfect. A person who developed a service is the least likely person to find faults in that service.

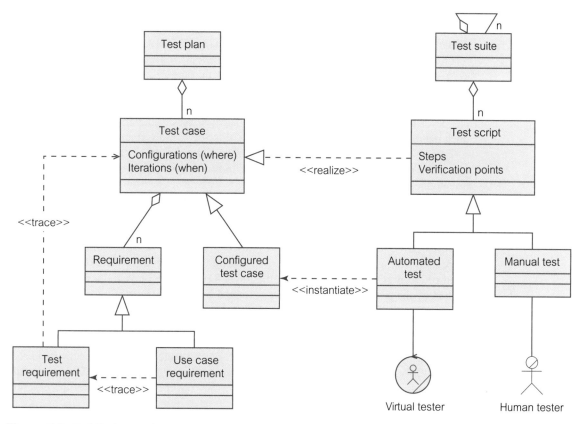

Figure 9.5 Test Environment
Source: Modified from Maciaszek and Liong (2005). Reprinted with permission of Pearson Education Ltd.

The informal testing is only of marginal significance and it must be supplemented by methodical testing. There are two main kinds of *methodical testing* (Schach 2005):

- non-execution-based – formal reviews (Section 9.1.1.1):
  - walkthroughs
  - inspections
- execution-based:
  - **testing to specs**
  - **testing to code**.

Testing to specs is an execution-based test type. It applies to executable software products, not documents or models. It is also known under a variety of different names, such as *black box testing*, functional testing and input-/output-driven testing.

The principle of testing to specs is that the developer treats the test module as a black box that takes some input and produces some output. No attempt is made to understand the program's logic or its computational algorithms.

Testing to specs requires that the *test requirements* are derived from the *use case requirements* and then identified and documented in a separate test plan and test case documents. These documents provide a test scenario for the tester. The scenarios can be recorded in a *capture–playback tool* and used repeatedly for *regression testing*.

Testing to specs is likely to discover defects that are normally difficult to catch by other means. In particular, it discovers *missing functionality* – something that (hopefully) has been documented as a use case requirement (and, therefore, a test requirement), but has never been programmed in. It can also discover missing functionality that was never documented in the use cases but is manifestly missing in the system implementation.

Testing to code is the second form of execution-based testing. It is also known under the names of *white box testing*, *glass box testing*, *logic-driven testing* and path-oriented testing.

Testing to code starts with the careful analysis of the program's algorithms. Test cases are derived to *exercise the code* – that is, guarantee that all possible execution paths in the program are verified. The test data are specially contrived to exercise the code.

Testing to code can be supported by the capture–playback tools and then used for regression testing. However, the nature of testing to code requires the extensive involvement of the programmer in utilizing the tools. Many of the playback scripts need to be written by the programmer rather than generated by the tool. Even if generated, they may need to be extensively modified by the programmer.

Like all other forms of execution-based testing, testing to code cannot be exhaustive because of the combinatorial explosion in the number of possible test cases with even a modest growth in the program's complexity. Even if it were possible to test every execution path, we could not guarantee that we have detected every defect. The old testing adage holds: testing can eliminate only some errors, but it cannot prove that the program is correct!

9.1.2.3 Testing system constraints

The *testing of system constraints* is predominantly *execution-based*. Its purpose is to determine that the system constraints have been implemented as listed in the requirements and test documents and includes such issues as:

- user interface testing
- database testing
- authorization testing
- performance testing
- stress testing
- failover testing
- configuration testing
- installation testing.

The first two types of system constraint test – the *user interface* and *database testing* – are very closely associated with the testing of the system's services. They are normally conducted in parallel with tests of these services. As such, they are included in test documents produced for testing the system's services.

Graphical user interface testing

GUI testing is intertwined with the overall software development process. It starts as early as in the requirements phase, with activities such as storyboarding, the inclusion of window drawings in use case documents and GUI prototyping. These early GUI tests concentrate on the fulfillment of functional requirements and usability.

Later, when the system has been implemented, methodical *post-implementation GUI testing* is required. Tests are conducted first by the developers, then by the testers and – prior to the software's release – customers (*pilot tests*). The following is a sample of the kinds of questions that would appear in a test document designed for post-implementation GUI tests (Bourne 1997).

- Does the window name correspond to its function?
- Is the window modal or modeless? Which should it be?
- Is a visual distinction made between the required and optional fields?
- Can the window be resized, moved, closed and restored? Should it be?
- Are any fields missing?
- Are there any spelling mistakes in titles, labels, prompt names and so on?
- Are command buttons (`OK`, `Cancel`, `Save`, `Clear` and so on) used consistently in all dialog boxes?
- Is it always possible to abort the current operation (including the delete operation)?
- Are all static fields protected from editing by users? If the application can change the static text, is this being done correctly?
- Are consistent font types and sizes applied to static text fields? Are they spelled correctly?
- Do the sizes of edit boxes correspond to the ranges of values that they take?
- Are all edit boxes initialized with their correct values when the window opens?
- Are the values entered into edit boxes validated by the client program?
- Are the values in drop-down lists populated correctly from the database?
- Are edit masks used in entry fields as specified?
- Are error messages legible and easy to act on?

Database testing

As with GUI testing, database testing is inherent in many other kinds of test. Much of the black box testing (testing to specs) is based on database input and output. However, separate methodical database testing is still necessary.

Post-implementation database testing includes extensive white box (to code) testing. The most significant part of database testing is the testing of concurrent execution of transactions and the results that they produce. Some other aspects of the database's operation can be extracted into separate tests – performance and security/authorization, for example.

As with the GUI tests, the same database tests need to be conducted repeatedly for all different application functions. The issues to be addressed in the database tests should be extracted into a generic document. This document should then be attached to all function (system services) tests. The following is an exemplary set of issues that the database tests should address (Bourne 1997).

■ Verify that the transaction executes as expected with the correct input. Is the system's feedback to the UI correct? Is the database content correct after the transaction?

■ Verify that the transaction executes as expected with the incorrect input. Is the system's feedback to the UI correct? Is the database content correct after the transaction?

■ Abort the transaction before it finishes. Is the system's feedback to the UI correct? Is the database content correct after the transaction?

■ Run the same transaction concurrently in many processes. Deliberately make one transaction hold a lock on a data resource needed by other transactions. Are users getting understandable explanations from the system? Is the database content correct after the transactions have terminated?

■ Extract every client SQL statement from the client program and execute it interactively on the database. Are the results as expected and the same as when the SQL is executed from the program?

■ Perform interactive white box testing of all the more complex SQL queries (from a client program or from a stored procedure) involving outer joins, union, subqueries, null values, aggregate functions and so on.

9.1.2.3.3 *Authorization testing*

Authorization testing may be treated as an inherent extension of the first two types of system constraints test. Both the client (user interface) and server (database) objects should be protected from unauthorized use. Authorization testing should verify that the security mechanisms built into the client and the server will, in fact, protect the system from unauthorized penetration.

Although ultimately the database bears the consequences of security breaches, protection starts at the client. The *user interface* of the program should be able to configure itself dynamically to correspond to the *authorization* level of the current user (*authenticated* by the user ID and password). Menu items, command buttons or even entire windows should be made inaccessible to users if they do not have the proper authorization.

Not all security loopholes can be addressed at the client. The support for authorization is a significant component of any DBMS. *Server permissions* (*privileges*) fall into two categories. A user may be given selective permission to:

■ access individual *server objects* – tables, views, columns, stored procedures and so on

■ execute SQL statements – select, update, insert, delete and so on.

Permissions for a user may be assigned directly at a *user level* or at a *group level*. Groups allow the security administrator to assign permissions to a group of users in a single entry. A user may belong to none or many groups.

To allow greater flexibility with managing authorization, most DBMSs introduce one more authorization level – the *role level*. The role allows the security administrator to grant permissions to all users who play a particular role in an organization. Roles can be nested – that is, the permissions granted to different role names can overlap.

In larger IS applications, *authorization design* is an elaborate activity. Frequently, an *authorization database* is set up alongside the application database to store and manipulate the client and server permissions. The application program consults the database after the user's logon in order to identify his or her authorization level and configure itself to that user.

Any changes to database permissions are driven from the authorization database – that is, nobody, even the security administrator, is allowed to change the application database permissions directly without first updating the authorization database.

Testing of other constraints   9.1.2.3.4

The testing of system constraints also includes:

- performance testing
- stress testing
- failover testing
- configuration testing
- installation testing.

Performance testing measures the performance constraints demanded by the customer. The constraints relate to *transaction speed and throughput*. The tests are conducted for different system workloads, including any anticipated *peak loads*. Performance testing is an important part of *system tuning*.

Stress testing is designed to break the system when abnormal demands are placed on it – low resources, an unusual contention for resources, abnormal frequency, quantity or volume. Stress testing is frequently coupled with performance testing and may require similar hardware and software *instrumentation*.

Failover testing addresses the system's response to a variety of hardware, network or software malfunctions. This kind of testing is closely related to the *recovery* procedures supported by the DBMS.

Configuration testing verifies how the system operates on various software and hardware configurations. In most production environments, the system is expected to run successfully on various client workstations that connect to the database using a variety of network protocols. The client workstations may have different software installed (such as drivers) that can conflict with the expected setups.

Installation testing extends configuration testing. It verifies that the system operates properly on every platform installed. This means that the tests of the system's services are rerun.

Review quiz 9.1

RQ1   Which technique of quality assurance is also known as non-execution-based testing?

RQ2   Which quality assurance technique produces a defect log to act on?

RQ3   What is a popular testing framework for Java applications?

RQ4   How are test cases realized (specified)?

RQ5   Which kind of testing can discover missing functionality?

9.2   Change management

The meaning of *change management* is as diverse as the concept of change itself. Change is omnipresent and affects all aspects of enterprise. It has a business dimension and a system dimension.

Change management can be (and frequently is) discussed from the perspective of the *business value of systems* (Laudon and Laudon 2006). It applies then to financial analysis and capital budgeting models. It is conducted in the context of scheduling, budgeting and planning of capital projects, including software projects. The business perspective of change management emphasizes behavioral and organizational impacts of change associated with new information systems. It addresses people management issues – motivational theories, employees' concerns about change, forms and lines of communication between individuals and groups.

A narrower understanding of **change** management (as discussed next) concentrates on a *system's fitness for purpose* in the face of changes in the users' requirements and quality objectives missed in the implementation. In this sense, change management is the process of managing software products and processes and managing the teamwork activities involved in an evolving software system. As shown in Figure 9.6 (Maciaszek and Liong 2005), change management is intrinsically related to quality management.

Quality control reveals *defects*, which need to be fixed. To be fixed, the defects must be submitted as *change requests* and allocated to developers. Some change requests may relate to *enhancements* rather than defects. Both defects and enhancements undergo status changes, may be prioritized, have owners and need to be traced to their origins in test and use case documents.

Figure 9.6
The relationship between change and quality management
Source: Modified from Maciaszek and Liong (2005). Reprinted by permission of Pearson Education Ltd.

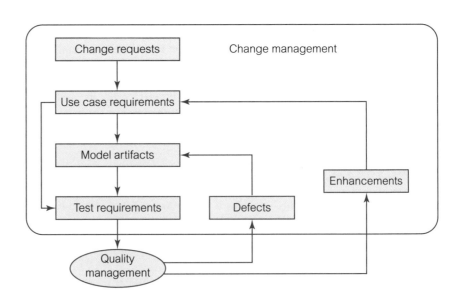

Instrumenting and managing change requests   9.2.1

Managing change is a big task in any multideveloper software project. Consider the scenario where two different defects are allocated to two different developers to fix, but it turns out that correcting these seemingly unrelated defects requires changes to be made to the same code component. Unless the developers are made aware of the possible conflict, both could simultaneously work on the corrections and, eventually, the more recent fix would undo the earlier one.

To manage change properly, a *change request management tool* is necessary (Figure 9.7). The tool allows changes to be managed online and ensures that all developers work with the latest documents. Changes to documents introduced by one project member are immediately available to fellow developers. Potential conflicts are resolved by *locking* or *version control* mechanisms. In the former case, a locked document is temporarily unavailable to other developers. In the latter case, multiple versions of the same document can be created and any conflicts between versions are resolved by means of negotiations at some later time.

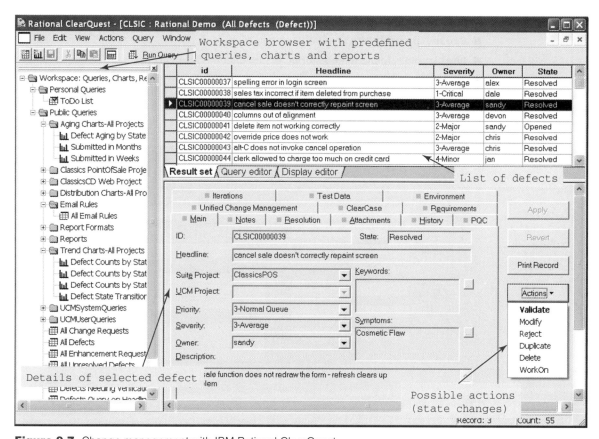

Figure 9.7 Change management with IBM Rational ClearQuest
Source: Rational Suite tutorial (Rational, 2002); Maciaszek and Liong (2005). Reprinted by permission of Pearson Education Ltd.

9.2.1.1 Submitting a change request

Typically, a *change request* is either to fix a defect or create an enhancement. A change request is entered into the project's repository. Once it has been entered into the repository, the developers can monitor the progress made on the change request, observe its *status* and act on it. *Actions* that can be performed on a change request depend on its current status.

Figure 9.8 shows the main tab in the dialog box for entering defects (Rational 2000). A defect is numbered and described in detail. The priority, severity, project and owner information can be entered from the drop-down lists of applicable choices (the attribute values in the drop-down lists and elsewhere on the form can be customized to suit the project's needs). Other fields allow descriptive information to be entered, including the possibility of attaching related documentation, such as code fragments.

The action of *submitting* a change request can result in automatic *e-mail notifications* to team members. The status of the change request is then `Submitted`. The project management can customize the tool to allow predefined actions for each status. For example, when in the `Submitted` status, the possible actions can be (Figure 9.9):

- `Assign` – to a team member
- `Modify` – some details of the request
- `Close` – probably as a result of fixing it
- `Duplicate` – found to be reported before under a different ID
- `Postpone` – don't worry about it for now
- `Delete` – without fixing
- `WorkOn` – we'll keep working on it.

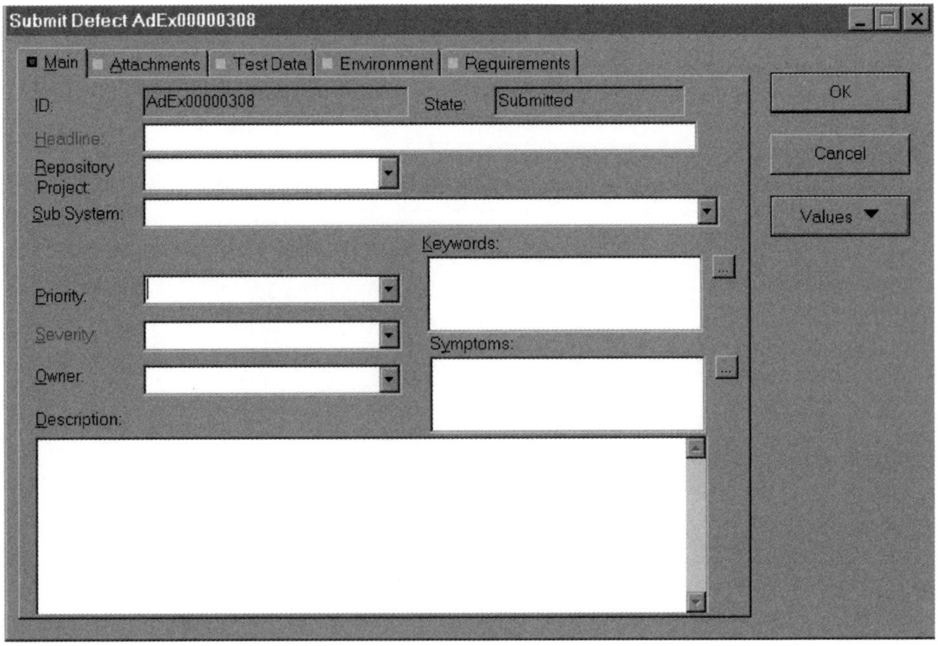

Figure 9.8
ClearQuest interface to submit a defect

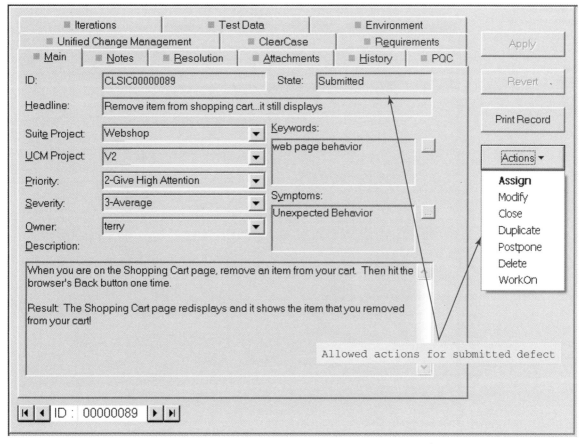

Figure 9.9 Defect management with IBM Rational ClearQuest
Source: Rational Suite tutorial (Rational, 2002); Maciaszek and Liong (2005). Reprinted by permission of Pearson Education Ltd

Keeping track of change requests

9.2.1.2

Each change request is assigned to a team member. The team member can `Open` the change request. When in the `Open` state, no other team member can modify the state of that request.

When the change request has been resolved, the developer can execute the `Resolve` action on it. The details of the resolution can be entered and e-mail notification can be sent to the project managers and testers. The testers may need to perform the `Verify` action on the resolved change request.

At any stage, the change request management tool can track the requests and produce easy-to-understand charts and reports (*project metrics*). These can be used to assess the number of unassigned defects, reveal the workloads of each team member and show how many defects are still unresolved.

Figure 9.10 shows a chart of active defects by priority for a project. We can see that 6 defects are to be resolved immediately, 55 should be given a high level of attention, 67 are in the normal queue and 68 are of low priority.

Figure 9.10
Metric chart of
defects by priority

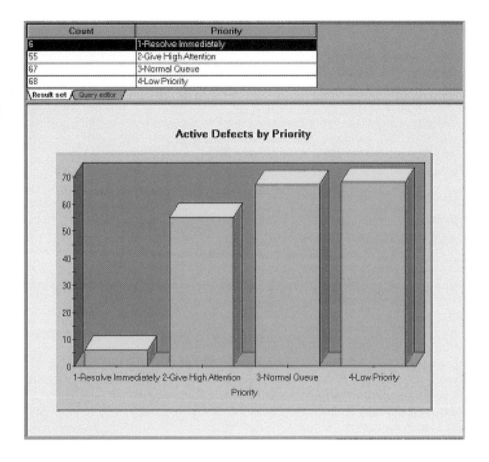

Count	Priority
6	1-Resolve Immediately
55	2-Give High Attention
67	3-Normal Queue
68	4-Low Priority

9.2.2 Traceability

Traceability underlies testing and change management. The aim is to capture, link and track all the important development artifacts, including requirements. The ultimate aim is to enable the generation of complete system documentation that is guaranteed to be correct and consistent across various documents and models – from the requirements to technical and user documentation.

The traceability items can be textual statements or graphical models. Traceability establishes explicit links between these items. The links can be direct or indirect. The links allow an impact analysis to be undertaken if any item on the traceability path is changed.

Earlier in the book, we distinguished between system services and system constraints. Traceability, quality, and change management are frequently associated with system services that manifest themselves in the use case requirements. However, one must not forget that enforcement of system constraints must also be tested and managed.

Traceability, testing and change management are not aims in themselves and must not be overdone. The developers should concentrate on developing, not tracing, testing or managing change. There is a significant cost to the project associated with these issues.

However, there is also a significant long-term cost to the project associated with *not* managing these issues.

As traceability underpins quality and change management, a *cost–benefit analysis* should be used to determine the scope and depth of project traceability. As a minimum, traceability should be maintained between the use case requirements and defects. In a more elaborated model, the test requirements could be added between the use case requirements and defects on the traceability path. In an even more sophisticated model, the traceability agenda can include system features, test cases, enhancements, test verification points and other software development artifacts.

In the rest of this chapter, we will consider the traceability model in line with the links between system documents shown in Figure 9.3. The business use case document lists *system features*. The test plan document identifies *test cases*. Features are linked to test cases and to *use case requirements* in the use case documents. *Test requirements* in the test case documents can be traced back to test cases and use case requirements. Test requirements are linked to *defects* and *enhancements* are traced to use case requirements. The trace from defects to *enhancements* is not needed.

System features to use cases and use case requirements 9.2.2.1

A *system feature* is a generic piece of functionality to be implemented in the system. It is a business process shown as an important benefit of the system. Normally, a system feature corresponds to a *business use case* in a business use case model (Section 2.5.2). If a business use case model is not formally developed, then system features are identified in a *vision document* (or similarly named strategic project document).

Each system feature is realized by a set of *use case requirements* in one or more *use cases*. Tracing use cases back to stakeholder needs (expressed in system features) helps to validate the correctness of the use case model. This strategy "scopes" requirements capture and facilitates completion of the requirements phase. It can also assist in the incremental development and delivery of the product.

A problem may arise with this strategy if the use case requirements within each use case are only indirectly linked to features. This can lead to situations where there is a trace between a feature and a use case, yet most use case requirements have nothing to do with the feature. Deciding whether or not the trace between the feature and the use case is still valid may prove to be a daunting and unsustainable task.

To avoid the scalability and long-term problems associated with this strategy, the traceability matrix should trace the features not only to the use cases but also directly to the use case requirements. This is possible if each use case is itself treated as the highest-level use case requirement with a hierarchy of specific use case requirements under it.

This is shown in Figure 9.11. The columns contain use cases and use case requirements within use cases. The hierarchical display of use case requirements can be expanded or collapsed. The arrows in the matrix signify the traces from features listed on the left-hand side to use cases and use case requirements above. Some arrows are crossed through. These are *suspect traces*. A trace becomes suspect when a *from* or *to* requirement changes. The developer needs to examine the suspect links before clearing them.

Figure 9.11
Traceability from features to use cases and use case requirements
Source: Courtesy of Nielsen Media Research, Sydney, Australia

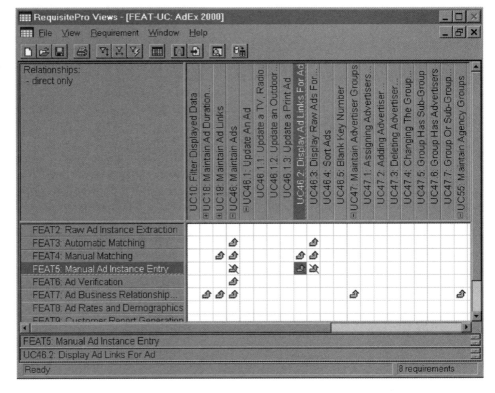

9.2.2.2 Test plans to test cases and test requirements

A *test plan* document is for test cases what a business use case document is for use cases. The test plan identifies the high-level project information and the software components (*test cases*) that should be tested. The test plan also describes the testing strategy for the project, required test resources, effort and cost.

Each test case identified in the test plan is to be written as a test case document. Mapping test requirements to test cases and test plans brings similar benefits to those for the traceability between features, use cases and use case requirements – the scoping of test capture, scalability and so on.

Figure 9.12 shows the traceability matrix from the test plan to test cases and test requirements within test cases. The hierarchical display of test requirements can be collapsed and expanded.

9.2.2.3 UML diagrams to documents and requirements

Traceability and change management do not apply just to narrative documents and textual requirements stored in the CASE repository. The repository also stores UML models. The graphical objects in UML diagrams can be hyperlinked to documents and requirements.

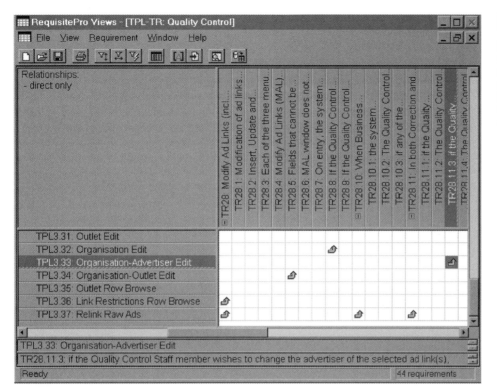

Figure 9.12
Traceability from
test plan to test
case and test
requirements
Source: Courtesy of
Nielsen Media
Research, Sydney,
Australia

The traceability between UML visual artifacts and any other repository records (in particular documents and requirements) can be established for various UML *graphical icons*. Perhaps the most important of these icons are the use cases in use case diagrams.

Figure 9.13 shows a dialog box for hyperlinking a use case graphical icon (`Maintain Ads`) to a document. The hyperlinking is done from within a UML use case diagram. The linked document can be any of the documents in the repository, including those shown in Figure 9.3.

Figure 9.14 shows a dialog box for hyperlinking a use case graphical icon (`Maintain Ads` again) to a use case requirement. In general, it is possible to link the icon to a requirement of any type.

Use case requirements to test requirements 9.2.2.4

Traceability between use case requirements and test requirements is critical in assessing whether or not the application meets the business requirements established for it. The links between these two requirement types allow the user to track defects via the test requirements back to the use case requirements and system features (Figure 9.3).

Figure 9.15 shows the traceability matrix with traces between the use case requirements and test requirements. Note that both the use case requirements and test requirements are structured hierarchically. The hierarchical levels at which the traces are defined can be predetermined.

Figure 9.13
Hyperlinking
document to use
case graphical
icon
Source: Courtesy of
Nielsen Media
Research, Sydney,
Australia

Figure 9.14
Hyperlinking
requirement to
use case
graphical icon
Source: Courtesy of
Nielsen Media
Research, Sydney,
Australia

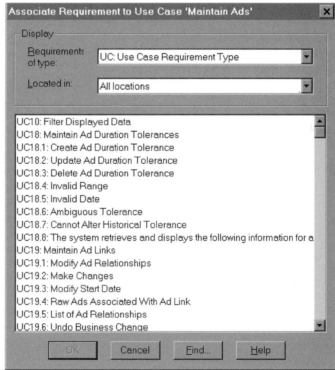

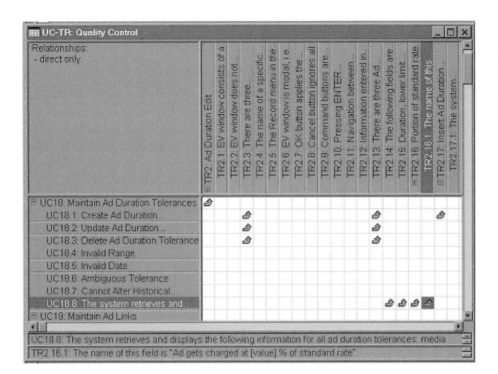

Figure 9.15
Traceability from
use case
requirement and
test requirement
Source: Courtesy of
Nielsen Media
Research, Sydney,
Australia

Test requirements to defects

9.2.2.5

Test case documents are written in the form of scripts containing the test requirements to be verified when testing. The scripts are used in *manual* tests, but many of these scripts can be *automated* (coded) within *capture-and-playback* testing tools. Test requirements in test case documents can then be used to establish verification points in these automated tests.

A *verification point* is a requirement in the script that is used (in *regression testing*) to confirm the state of a test object across different versions (builds) of the application under test (AUT). There are various types of verification point (Rational 2000). A verification point can be set to check that a text has not changed, numeric values are accurate, two files are the same, a file exists, menu items have not changed, computation results are as expected and other such items.

Automated testing requires working with two data files – a baseline data file and an actual data file. During *capture*, the verification point records object information in the *baseline data file*. The information is the baseline against which to compare in subsequent tests (*playbacks*). The results of these comparisons are stored in the *actual data file*. Each *failed verification point* needs to be investigated further and, if necessary, entered into the change management tool as a *defect*.

Ultimately all defects – whether discovered using automated or manual tests – must be linked to the test requirements. Figure 9.16 shows a tool that displays all defects in the row browser in the upper part of the window. A currently selected defect can be associated with one or more test requirements. In the example, two test requirements are traced to the highlighted defect.

Figure 9.16
Traceability from
test requirement
to defect
Source: Courtesy of
Nielsen Media
Research, Sydney,
Australia

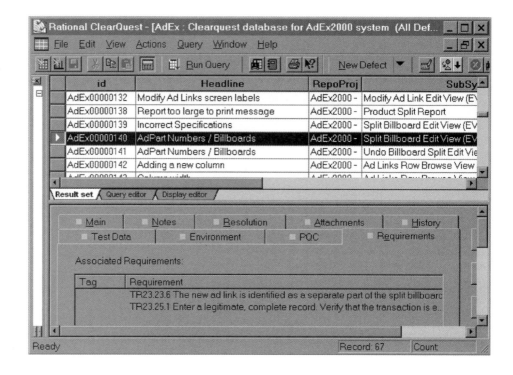

9.2.2.6 Use case requirements to enhancements

Defects need to be traced directly to the test requirements. Enhancements (to be implemented in a future release of the product) must be explained in the use case requirements. In rare situations when a defect has been converted into an enhancement, the traceability links between use case requirements and test requirements would allow the user to trace the defect to the enhancement.

Figure 9.17 demonstrates that a single tool (see Figure 9.16) can be used to manage enhancements *and* defects or, indeed, any other change requests.

Figure 9.17
Enhancements
Source: Courtesy of
Nielsen Media
Research, Sydney,
Australia

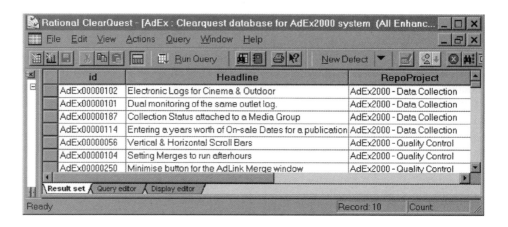

Review quiz 9.2

RQ1 What needs to be done to originate a change?

RQ2 What technique is used to determine the scope and depth of project traceability?

RQ3 What tools can automate test scripts?

Summary

In this chapter, we have addressed quality and change management issues. These two activities span the development lifecycle. They require specialized *documentation*, such as test plans, test case documents and defect and enhancement documents. *Test requirements* are identified in the *test case documents* and linked to the use case requirements in the use case documents.

A *quality management* agenda has two, quite orthogonal, dimensions. It is a reactive (*post factum*) activity when used as a *quality control* mechanism. However, it can be a very proactive *quality assurance* activity when used within the framework of *test-driven development*.

Quality control relates to the testing of a system's services and constraints. *Testing of system services* can be non-execution-based or execution-based. *Non-execution-based testing* includes walkthroughs and inspections – formal review meetings that flow on from quality assurance practices. *Execution-based testing* can take the form of *testing to specs* or *testing to code*.

The *testing of system constraints* includes a large range of relatively disparate tests that relate to such issues as the user interface, database, authorization, performance, stress, failover, configuration and installation. Some system constraints tests are conducted in parallel with the system's services tests; others are done independently.

A *change request* is normally originated to deal with either a *defect* or an *enhancement*. A change management tool allows a change request to be submitted and kept track of as the developers address it. A vital part of the change management tool relates to the establishment of *traceability* paths between change requests and other system artifacts – in particular, test requirements and use case requirements.

Key terms

Audit a formal quality assurance process, possibly performed by competent external auditors.

Change any expected or unexpected occurrence that results in a variation being made to a system's requirements and/or requires attention in terms of the implementation code and design models.

Checklist a quality assurance technique based on a predefined list of "to do" points that need to be scrupulously checked off in the development process.

Defect a change that requires corrective action.

Enhancement a change that it is envisaged will be acted on in the future.

Inspection a more formal review meeting closely supervised by the project's management.

Quality assurance a process of proactively building quality into software products and processes.

Quality control a process of verifying quality in developed software artifacts, products and applied processes.

Regression testing re-execution of previosuly run acceptance tests to check that previously fixed or new defects have not emerged in successive code iterations.

Review a quality assurance technique conducted as a formal, document-driven meeting of developers, and possibly managers, to review a work product or process.

Test case document that defines the test requirements.

Test-driven development an agile software development technique to write test cases and test programs before the application code is written.

Test plan a quality control document that identifies the test cases and defines the schedule, budget and resources required for the testing process.

Test requirement a functional requirement or non-functional constraint that is documented for testing.

Test script a manual or (partly) automated script that defines the sequence of test steps and verification points.

Test suite a set of test scripts.

Testing to code an execution-based form of testing that is based on a careful analysis of the control logic of the program under test.

Testing to specs an execution-based form of testing that treats the program being tested like a black box that merely takes some input and is expected to produce some output.

Traceability a lifecycle process to capture, link and track all the important development artifacts for a system, including its requirements.

Walkthrough a less formal review meeting, likely not to be attended by project managers.

Multiple-choice test

MC1 Which is not a technique of quality assurance?

    a Walkthrough.

    b Checklist.

    c Retrospection.

    d Inspection.

MC2 Questions that a tester has to find answers for are called:

    a verification points

    b script queries

    c test inquiries

    d none of the above.

MC3 Re-execution of relevant acceptance tests on successive code iterations is called:

    a white box testing

    b regression testing

    c black box testing

    d coverage testing.

MC4 Black box testing is also called:

    a testing to specs

    b functional testing

    c input/output driven testing

    d all of the above.

MC5 White box testing is also called:

    a functional testing

    b testing to specs

    c path-oriented testing

    d coverage testing.

Questions

Q1 Quality and change management span the development lifecycle. What other activities span the lifecycle? Explain the aims of these activities.

Q2 Refer to Figure 9.3 (Section 9.1.2.1). Explain the interplay between enhancements and defects. Why is the enhancements document linked to the use case documents and the defects document linked to the test case documents? Should there not be a link between the enhancements document and the defects document?

Q3 Refer to Figure 9.5 (Section 9.1.2.1). Why does a virtual tester have to be a dedicated test workstation?

Q4 How is a walkthrough different from an inspection?

Q5 What is the role of the SQA group in an organization?

Q6 What is an authorization database? What is its role in system development and testing?

Q7 What other system constraints testing is stress testing closely related to? Explain your answer.

Q8 What other system constraints testing is installation testing closely related to? Explain your answer.

Q9 What actions would you allow on an enhancement in an opened state? Explain the meaning of these actions.

Q10 Visit the web page for JUnit (www.junit.org). Report briefly on the latest improvements to the JUnit framework.

Q11 What is a verification point?

Q12 What is a suspect trace? Give an example.

Q13 Explain the difference between a baseline data file and an actual data file.

Q14 What is the role and place of traceability in project management? What questions does it answer?

Review quiz answers

Review quiz 9.1
RQ1 Review (walkthrough and inspection).
RQ2 Inspection.
RQ3 JUnit.
RQ4 By means of test scripts.
RQ5 Testing to specs.

Review quiz 9.2
RQ1 It originates with a formal change request.
RQ2 Cost–benefit analysis.
RQ3 Capture-and-playback tools.

Multiple-choice test answers

RQ1 c
RQ2 a
RQ3 b
RQ4 d
RQ5 c

Answers to odd-numbered questions

Q1
Important lifecycle-spanning activities, apart from testing and change management, are (Maciaszek and Liong 2005):

- project planning (Section 1.4.3.1)
- metrics (Section 1.4.3.2)
- configuration management
- people management
- risk management.

Project planning (and tracking) is a lifecycle activity aiming at the estimation (and verification) of how much time, money, effort and resources are consumed by the project. In its broader meaning, project planning also encompasses quality assurance, people management, risk analysis and configuration management.

To be able to plan for the future, we need to measure the past. *Metrics* collection is the activity of measuring the software product and process. Metrics is a complex and tricky domain, as not everything of value in software development can be assigned quantitative numbers. Nevertheless, an approximate number is better than no number and there is lots of evidence that the collection of metrics is a necessary condition for success in system development.

Configuration management goes hand in hand with change management. Configuration management adds the "teamwork" dimension to change management. The aim of configuration management is to store versions of software artifacts produced by the development team, make these versions available on demand to various members of the team and combine the versions into configured software models and products.

An information system is a social system. It is not possible to produce a successful software product without proper attention to the people component. *People management* embraces such activities as acquiring staff, creating and motivating teams, establishing effective communications between people, resolving conflicts and other team development issues (such as team organization, training, appraisals, performance reports and external feedback).

Risks are "potentially adverse circumstances that may impair the development process and the quality of products" (Ghezzi et al. 2003: 416). "Risk management is a decision-making activity that assesses the impact of risks (uncertainties) on decisions. It weighs distributions of possible project outcomes versus the probabilities of arriving at these outcomes" (Maciaszek and Liong 2005: 72–3). Clearly, risk management spans the life-cycle and monitors the project from inception to conclusion. It may, in fact, demand that the project be terminated at any point when risks become too high and indefensible.

Q3

A *virtual tester* is a capture/playback computing environment for regression testing. It replays the test scripts previously recorded and monitors whether or not the application code behaves as before – that is, whether or not it produces the same events and outputs as written in the test script. It is, therefore, essential that the entire test environment be fixed and stable.

Only a workstation dedicated solely to testing and not used for any other purpose can ensure a fixed and stable testing environment. It is essential that the workstation uses the same version of the operating system for all tests on that machine and has a minimal (and the same) amount of additional system software installed.

In particular, the workstation must not be connected to the Internet, e-mail facilities and so on. This is because any Internet event can be intercepted by the test program running and interpreted as an (unexpected) event generated by the application under test.

Q5

The *SQA (software quality assurance)* group is responsible for a planned and systematic evaluation of the quality of software products and processes. The group checks that software standards and procedures exist and are followed throughout the software development lifecycle. To ensure that the role of the SQA group is fulfilled, the group – not the developers – is made responsible for the quality of the delivered product.

Software quality is evaluated by means of process monitoring, product evaluation, formal reviews, audits and testing. The evaluation is undertaken at quality assurance *approval points*, determined in software development and control processes. The product of SQA is an *audit report* to management containing the findings of reviews, tests and so on and recommendations to bring the development into conformance with standards and procedures.

Q7

Stress testing executes a system for abnormal conditions – low resources, peak loads, frequencies, quantities or volumes. Stress testing is closely related to *performance testing* because performance degradations frequently occur when the system executes in stress conditions.

In practice, stress testing and performance testing can be performed concurrently, use similar test scripts, similar hardware and software instrumentation.

Q9

Actions allowed on an opened enhancement request depend on the development practice adopted. The list of permitted actions is normally customizable in CASE tools to suit the software process. A possible list of actions is:

- `Close` – as a result of its resolution or by managerial decision
- `Modify` – some details of the enhancement
- `Delete` – without addressing it; perhaps recorded in error
- `WorkOn` – we keep working on it
- `Postpone` – we can address it at some future time.

Q11

A *verification point* is a point in a regression test script that shows whether or not a test requirement has been met. It is used to verify the state of a test object across different program versions. Verification points can be set to:

- test for a numeric or other value, a number within a range, a blank field and so on
- compare the contents of two files or other data sets
- check for the existence of a file, database table and so on
- capture and compare the state of the GUI menu items, common controls, data windows and so on
- check for the existence of a GUI window or a specified software module in the memory
- capture and compare websites.

During program *capture* (recording), the verification point intercepts the test object information and stores it as the baseline of expected behavior. During *playback*, the verification point obtains the test object information and compares it with the baseline. A *regression test* is passed if the playback script confirms that the program performs as intended and verification points return correct data.

Q13

Most verification points create a *baseline data file*. If, during playback, the captured data is different from that in the stored baseline data file, the verification point fails and an *actual* (failed) *data file* is created.

If the script is played many times and fails many times, a separate actual data file is created each time (typically with the same name but with consecutively numbered file extensions). The name of the actual file is normally the same as that of the verification point.

Chapter

10

Tutorial-style Review and Reinforcement

Objectives

This is a review and reinforcement chapter. It exemplifies all the important models and processes in the software development lifecycle. The explanations are pivoted on a single application domain – online shopping – and adopt the style of a comprehensive and complete tutorial. The sequence of points in the discussion and the presentation of answers and solutions follow the sequence adopted in the book. Indeed, it is possible (and even recommended) to refer to this chapter, to reinforce the knowledge gained, when going through previous chapters in the book.

Apart from its RR (review and reinforcement) purpose, this chapter has a value-added aspect. It demonstrates all the important software development artifacts (models, diagrams, documents and so on) as an integrated set and shows how they all fit together. Moreover, the tutorial refers to a Web-based application and, as such, it challenges the developer with cutting-edge technology.

By reading this chapter you will:

- acknowledge to yourself that modeling results in interrelated and partially overlapping sets of models
- better understand the changes in abstraction levels when moving from analysis to design and implementation
- learn about the typical analysis and design tasks required when modeling for the popular Web application domain of online shopping
- review and reinforce your knowledge of UML diagrams and how they interact.

Use case modeling

Tutorial statement: online shopping (customer order processing)

A computer manufacturer offers the possibility of purchasing computers via the Internet. Customers can select computers on the manufacturer's web page. The computers are classified into servers, desktops and portables. Customers can select a standard configuration or build a desired configuration online. The configurable components (such as memory) are presented as drop-down lists (picklists) of available options. For each new configuration, the system can calculate the price.

To place their orders, customers must fill out the shipment and payment information. Acceptable payment methods are credit cards and checks. Once the order has been entered, the system sends confirmation e-mail messages to customers with details of their orders. While waiting for the arrival of the computers, customers can check the status of their orders online at any time.

The back-end order processing consists of the steps needed to verify customers' credentials and payment methods, request the ordered configurations from the warehouse, print invoices and request the warehouse to ship the computers to the customers.

10.1.1 Actors

Step 1: online shopping

Refer to the tutorial statement above and consider the following extended requirements to find actors in the online shopping application.

■ Each customer uses the manufacturer's online shopping web page to view the standard configuration of the chosen server, desktop or portable computer. The price is also shown.

■ The customer chooses to view the details of the configuration, perhaps with the intention of buying it as is or to build a more suitable configuration. The price for each configuration can be computed at the customer's request.

■ The customer may choose to order a computer online or request that a salesperson contact him or her to explain the details of the order, negotiate the price and so on before the order is actually placed.

■ To place an order, the customer must fill out an online form with shipment and invoice address and payment details (credit card or check).

■ After the customers' order has been entered into the system, the salesperson sends an electronic request to the warehouse with details of the configuration ordered.

■ The details of the transaction, including an order number and a customer account number, are e-mailed to the customer so that he or she can check the status of the order online.

■ The warehouse obtains the invoice from the salesperson and ships the computer to the customer.

Figure 10.1 shows the three actors that are manifestly present in the specifications. These are the `Customer`, `Salesperson` and `Warehouse`.

Customer Salesperson Warehouse

Figure 10.1
Actors for an
online shopping
system

Use cases 10.1.2

Step 2: online shopping

Refer to Step 1 of the tutorial (Section 10.1.1) and find the *use cases* for the online shopping application.

Table 10.1 Assignment of requirements to actors and use cases for the online shopping application

Requirement no.	Requirement	Actor	Use case
1	The customer uses the manufacturer's online shopping web page to view the standard configuration of the chosen server, desktop or portable computer. The price is also shown.	Customer	Display standard computer configuration
2	The customer chooses to view the details of the configuration, perhaps with the intention of buying it as is or to build a more suitable configuration. The price for each configuration can be computed on the customer's request.	Customer	Build computer configuration
3	The customer may choose to order a computer online or may request that the salesperson contact him or her to explain details of the order, negotiate the price and so on before the order is actually placed.	Customer Salesperson	Order configured computer Request salesperson contact
4	To place an order, the customer must fill out an online form with shipment and invoice address and payment details (credit card or check).	Customer	Order configured computer Verify and accept customer payment
5	After the customer's order has been entered into the system, the salesperson sends an electronic request to the warehouse with details of the configuration ordered.	Salesperson Warehouse	Inform warehouse about order
6	The details of the transaction, including an order number and a customer account number, are e-mailed to the customer so that he or she can check the status of the order online.	Salesperson Customer	Order configured computer Display order status
7	The warehouse obtains the invoice from the salesperson and ships the computer to the customer.	Salesperson Warehouse	Print invoice

To address this tutorial problem, we can construct a table that assigns the functional requirements to the actors and use cases. Note that some potential business functions may not be within the scope of the application – they are not to be transformed into use cases.

Table 10.1 assigns the function requirements listed in Step 1 of the tutorial to the actors and the use cases. The warehouse's tasks of configuring the computer and shipping it to the customer are considered to be *out-of-scope* functions.

Figure 10.2 demonstrates the use cases for online shopping in the UML graphical notation.

Figure 10.2
Use cases for an online shopping system

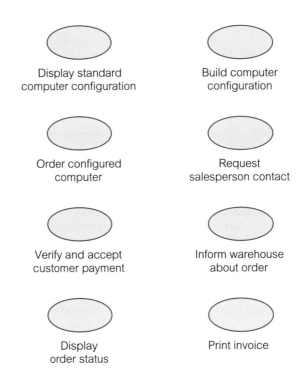

Display standard computer configuration

Build computer configuration

Order configured computer

Request salesperson contact

Verify and accept customer payment

Inform warehouse about order

Display order status

Print invoice

10.1.3 Use case diagram

Step 3: online shopping

Refer to the previous steps of the tutorial and draw a use case diagram for the online shopping application.

A solution to this tutorial step can be obtained directly from the information contained in the previous steps. The only additional consideration may be the relationships between the use cases. The diagram is presented in Figure 10.3. The meaning of the <<extend>>

relationship is that the use case `Order configured computer` can be extended by `Customer` with the use case `Request salesperson contact`.

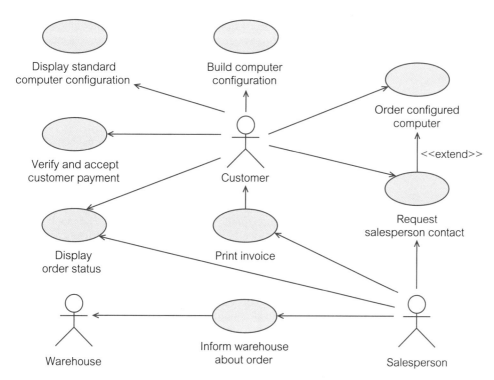

Figure 10.3
Use case diagram for an online shopping system

Documenting use cases

10.1.4

Step 4: online shopping

Refer to the previous tutorial steps and write a use case document for the use case "Order configured computer". Use your general knowledge of typical order processing tasks to derive details not stated in the requirements.

The solution to this tutorial step is presented in Table 10.2.

Table 10.2 Narrative specification for the use case "Order configured computer" for the online shopping example

Use case	Order configured computer
Brief description	This use case allows a `Customer` to enter a purchase order. This includes providing a shipment and invoice address as well as payment details.
Actors	`Customer`
Preconditions	The `Customer` points an Internet browser to the computer manufacturer's order entry web page. The page displays the details of a configured computer together with its price.
Main flow	The use case begins when the `Customer` decides to order the configured computer by choosing the `Continue` (or similarly named) function when the order details are displayed on the screen.
	The system requests that the `Customer` enter the purchase details, including name of the salesperson (if known), shipment details (customer's name and address), invoice details (if different from shipment details), a payment method (credit card or check) and any comments.
	The `Customer` chooses the `Purchase` (or similarly named) function to send the order to the manufacturer.
	The system assigns a unique order number and a customer account number to the purchase order and stores the order information in the database.
	The system e-mails the order number and customer number to the `Customer`, together with all the order details, as confirmation of acceptance of the order.
Alternative flows	The `Customer` activates the `Purchase` function before providing all mandatory information. The system displays an error message and requests that the missing information be supplied.
	The `Customer` chooses the `Reset` (or similarly named) function to revert to an empty purchase form. The system allows the `Customer` to enter the information again.
Postconditions	If the use case was successful, the purchase order is recorded in the system's database. Otherwise, the system's state is unchanged.

10.2 Activity modeling

10.2.1 Actions

Step 5: online shopping

Refer to Step 4 of the tutorial. Analyze the main and alternative flows in the use case document. Find the actions for the use case "Order configured computer" in the online shopping application.

Table 10.3 lists the statements in the main and alternative flows of the use case document and identifies the actions. Note the system's (not actor's) viewpoint is given when naming actions.

Table 10.3 Finding the actions in the main and alternative flows

No.	Use case statement	Action
1	The use case begins when the `Customer` decides to order the configured computer by choosing the `Continue` (or similarly named) function when the order details are displayed on the screen.	`Display current configuration` `Get order request`
2	The system requests that the `Customer` enter the purchase details, including the name of the salesperson (if known), shipment details (customer's name and address), invoice details (if different from shipment details), a payment method (credit card or check) and any comments.	`Display purchase form`
3	The `Customer` chooses the `Purchase` (or similarly named) function to send the order to the manufacturer.	`Get purchase details`
4	The system assigns a unique order number and a customer account number to the purchase order and stores the order information in the database.	`Store order`
5	The system e-mails the order number and customer number to the `Customer`, together with all order details, as confirmation of the order's acceptance.	`E-mail order details`
6	The `Customer` activates the `Purchase` function before providing all mandatory information. The system displays an error message and requests that the missing information be supplied.	`Get purchase details` `Display purchase form`
7	The `Customer` chooses the `Reset` (or similarly named) function to revert to an empty purchase form. The system allows the `Customer` to enter the information again.	`Display purchase form`

The actions identified in Table 10.3 are drawn in Figure 10.4.

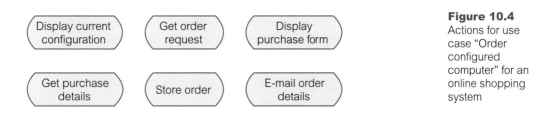

Figure 10.4
Actions for use case "Order configured computer" for an online shopping system

10.2.2 Activity diagram

Step 6: online shopping

Refer to Steps 4 (Section 10.1.4) and 5 (Section 10.2.1) of the tutorial and draw an activity diagram for the use case "Order configured computer" in the online shopping application.

Figure 10.5 shows an activity diagram for Step 6 of the tutorial. `Display current configuration` is the initial action. When performing the action `Display purchase form`, the timeout condition can terminate the execution of the activity model. Alternatively, the action `Get purchase details` is activated. If the purchase details are incomplete, the system again reaches the action `Display purchase form`. Otherwise, the system performs `Store order`, followed by `E-mail order details` (which is a final action).

Note that only those branch conditions that (always) appear on exits from an action are shown. The branch conditions that are internal to an action are not explicit in the diagram. They can be inferred from the presence of multiple exit transitions, possibly with a guarded condition name in square brackets on the transition (such as `[timeout]` on exit from `Display purchase form`).

Figure 10.5
Activity diagram
for use case
"Order configured
computer" for an
online shopping
system

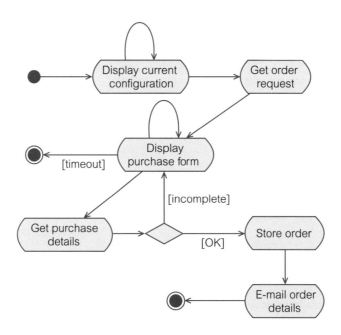

Class modeling

Classes

Step 7: online shopping

Refer to the requirements defined in the Tutorial statement at the beginning of this chapter and in Step 1 of the tutorial (Section 10.1.1). Find candidate entity classes in the online shopping application.

Table 10.4 (overleaf) assigns the functional requirements in the tutorial to the entity classes. The list of classes poses many questions, such as the following.

■ What is the difference between ConfiguredComputer and Order? After all, we are not going to store ConfiguredComputer unless an order for it has been placed, or are we?

■ Is the meaning of Shipment in requirements 4 and 7 the same? Probably not. Do we need the Shipment class if we know that the shipment is the warehouse's responsibility and is therefore out of scope?

■ Could not ConfigurationItem be just a set of attributes in ConfiguredComputer?

■ Is OrderStatus a class or an attribute of Order?

■ Is Salesperson a class or an attribute of Order and Invoice?

Answering these and similar questions is not easy and requires an in-depth knowledge of application requirements. For the purpose of this tutorial, we have chosen the list of classes as shown in Figure 10.6.

Attributes

Step 8: online shopping

Refer to Steps 5, 6 and 7 of the tutorial. Think about the attributes for the classes in Figure 10.6. Consider only attributes with primitive types (Appendix, Section A.3.1).

Figure 10.7 shows the classes with primitive attributes. Only the most interesting attributes have been shown. The attributes of ConfigurationItem warrant brief explanation. The attribute itemType will have values such as processor, memory, screen and hard drive. The attribute itemDescr will further describe the item type. For example, the processor in the configuration may be an Intel 4000 MHz with 2,048 k cache.

Table 10.4 Assignment of requirements to entity classes for the online shopping example

Requirement no.	Requirement	Entity class
1	The customer uses the manufacturer's online shopping web page to view the standard configuration of the chosen server, desktop or portable computer. The price is also shown.	`Customer, Computer,` `(StandardConfiguration,` `Product)`
2	The customer chooses to view the details of a configuration, perhaps with the intention of buying it as is or to build a more suitable configuration. The price for each configuration can be computed at the user's request.	`Customer,` `ConfiguredComputer,` `(ConfiguredProduct),` `ConfigurationItem`
3	The customer may choose to order a computer online or request that a salesperson contact him or her to explain the details of the order, negotiate the price and so on before the order is actually placed.	`Customer,` `ConfigureComputer,` `Order, Salesperson`
4	To place an order, the customer must fill out an online form with shipment and invoice address and payment details (credit card or check).	`Customer, Order,` `Shipment, Invoice,` `Payment`
5	After the customer's order has been entered into the system, the salesperson sends an electronic request to the warehouse with details of the configuration ordered.	`Customer, Order,` `Salesperson,` `ConfiguredComputer,` `ConfigurationItem`
6	The details of the transaction, including an order number and a customer account number, are e-mailed to the customer so that he or she can check the status of the order online.	`Order, Customer,` `(OrderStatus)`
7	The warehouse obtains the invoice from the salesperson and ships the computer to the customer.	`Invoice, (Shipment),` `(Salesperson),` `Computer, Customer`

Figure 10.6
Classes for an online shopping system

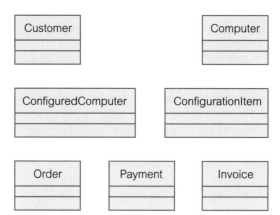

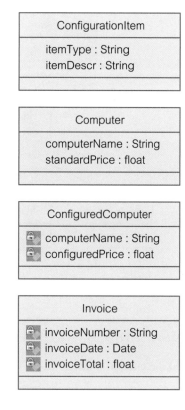

Figure 10.7
Primitive attributes
in classes for an
online shopping
system

Associations

Step 9: online shopping

Refer to the previous steps of the tutorial. Consider the classes shown in Figure 10.7. Think what access paths between these classes are required by the use cases. Add associations to the class model.

Figure 10.8 shows the most apparent associations between the classes. We made a few assumptions when determining association *multiplicities* (Appendix, Section A.5.2). Order is from a single Customer, but Customer may place many Orders. Order is not accepted unless the Payment has been specified (hence, one-to-one association). Order does not have to have an associated Invoice, but Invoice is always related to a single Order. An Order is for one or many ConfiguredComputers. A ConfiguredComputer may be ordered many times or not at all.

Figure 10.8
Associations for
an online
shopping system

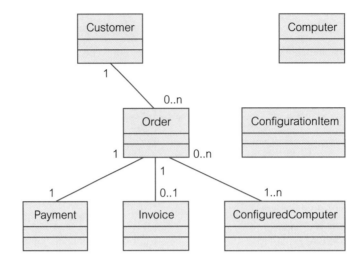

10.3.4 Aggregations

Step 10: online shopping

Refer to the previous steps of the tutorial. Consider the models in Figures 10.7 and 10.8. Add aggregations to the class model.

Figure 10.9 adds two aggregation relationships to the model. `Computer` has one or more `ConfigurationItems`. Likewise, `ConfiguredComputer` consists of one or many `ConfigurationItems`.

Figure 10.9
Aggregations for
an online
shopping system

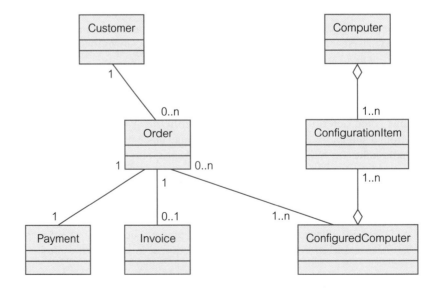

Generalizations 10.3.5

Step 11: online shopping

Refer to the previous steps of the tutorial. Consider the models in Figures 10.7 and 10.9. Think how you can extract any common attributes in the existing classes into a higher-level class. Add generalizations to the class model.

Figure 10.10 shows a modified model with the class `Computer` changed to a generic *abstract* class for two *concrete* subclasses: `StandardComputer` and `ConfiguredComputer`. `Order` and `ConfigurationItem` are now linked to `Computer`, and `Computer` can be either `StandardComputer` or `ConfiguredComputer`.

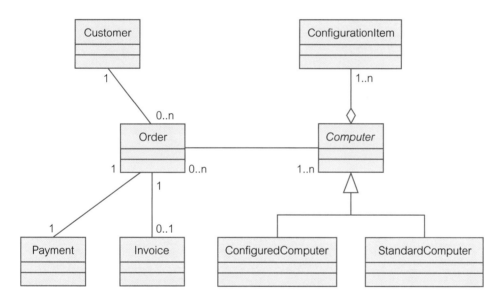

Figure 10.10
Generalization for an online shopping system

Class diagram 10.3.6

Step 12: online shopping

Refer to the previous steps of the tutorial. Combine the models in Figures 10.7 and 10.10 to show a complete class diagram. Modify the attribute content of classes as necessary due to the introduction of the generalization hierarchy.

Figure 10.11 is a class diagram for the online shopping application. It is not a complete solution as, for example, more attributes would be required in a pragmatic solution.

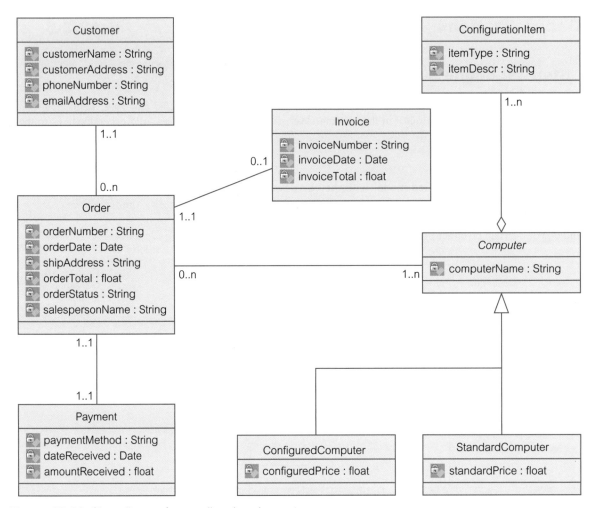

Figure 10.11 Class diagram for an online shopping system

10.4 Interaction modeling

10.4.1 Sequence diagram

Step 13: online shopping

Refer to the activity diagram in Figure 10.5 (Section 10.2.2). Consider the first action in the diagram, `Display current computer`. Construct a sequence diagram for this action. As per the PCBMER framework, prefix the names of the classes involved with a letter indicating the PCMR subsystem to which the class belongs. However, show only the presentation and entity classes and assume that the presentation layer can communicate directly with the entity layer.

For a better understanding of the task, refer to Figures 10.12 and 10.13. Figure 10.12 (Sony 2004) shows a possible "custom configuration" web page, via which a customer can set up the required (current) configuration. Figure 10.13 (Sony 2004) is a web page that displays summary information about the current configuration after the customer has pressed a submit button on the web page in Figure 10.12.

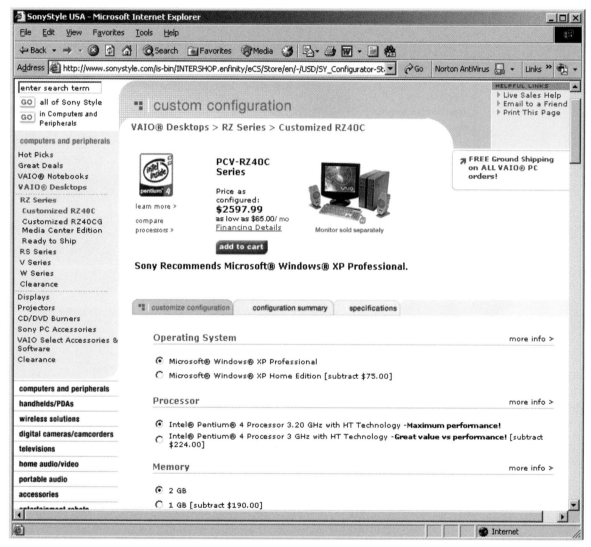

Figure 10.12 Example of a custom configuration web page for an online shopping system
Source: Sony Electronics Inc. (2004)

Figure 10.13
Example of a
configuration
summary web
page for an online
shopping system
Source: Sony
Electronics Inc. (2004)

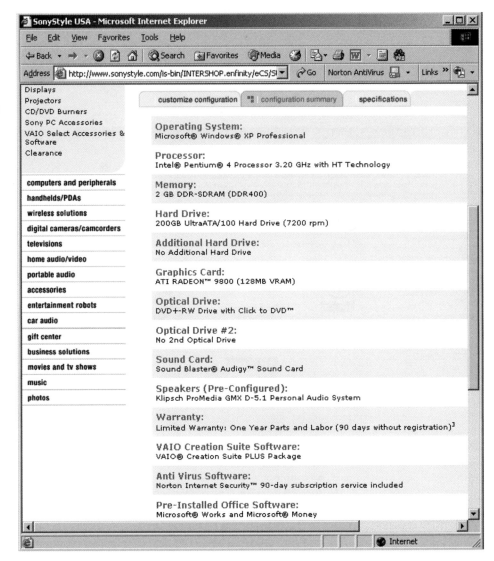

A sequence diagram for "display current configuration" is shown in Figure 10.14. When the outside actor (Customer) chooses to display the configuration of a computer, he or she presses the Submit button on the PCustomConfiguration web page. This event is serviced by a self-method submit().

The submit() method sends a getCurrentConf() to EComputer. EComputer is an abstract class, so in reality the message will be sent to either EStandardComputer or EConfiguredComputer (Figure 10.11). The model assumes that PCustomConfiguration knows whether or not the actor modified the standard configuration and can, therefore, resolve to which concrete class the getCurrentConf() message should go.

Because PCustomConfiguration *has* an EComputer object, it could request all details directly. However, the model in Figure 10.14 makes EComputer combine all the

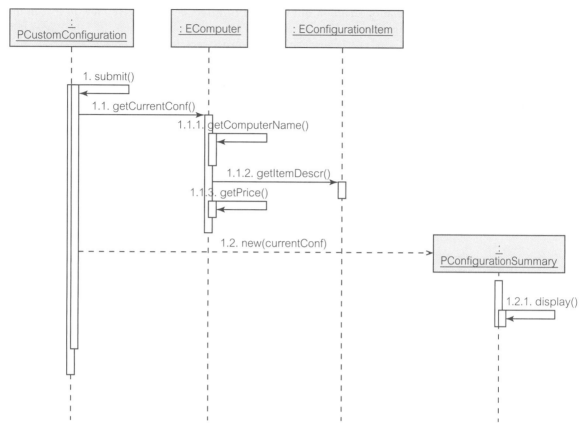

Figure 10.14 Sequence diagram for action "Display current configuration" for an online shopping system

information (computerName, itemDescr and price) and then return all of it (in a Java collection), to PCustomConfiguration. In fact, EConfigurationItem is itself a collection of objects, and getItemDescr() works on this collection. The model does not explain how exactly the getPrice() method works.

When equipped with all the requested information, PCustomConfiguration constructs a new PConfigurationSummary web page. The constructor receives all information in the argument of the new() message. As a result, the constructor of PConfigurationSummary contains a self-method display(), so that the current configuration can be displayed on the screen.

Communication diagram   10.4.2

Step 14: online shopping

Convert the sequence diagram in Figure 10.14 into a communication diagram.

The communication diagram in Figure 10.15 offers an alternative view to that in the sequence diagram in Figure 10.14. The view is enriched by the fact that `EConfigurationItem` is now explicitly shown as a collection of objects.

Figure 10.15
Sequence diagram for action "Display current configuration" for an online shopping system

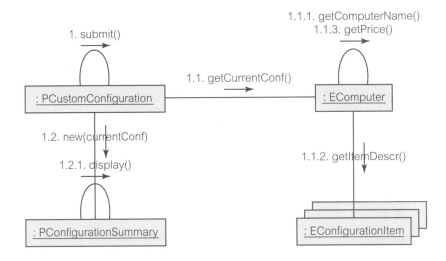

Step 15: online shopping

Refer to the class diagram in Figure 10.11 and the communication diagram in Figure 10.15. For each message in the sequence diagram, add an operation to a relevant class in the class diagram. Do not redraw the whole class diagram – only show the classes extended with operations. Show the dependency relationships for classes not already related by other relationships.

The solution to this simple tutorial step is shown in Figure 10.16. Operations are added as expected. Note that the `new()` message results in invoking a constructor on `PConfigurationSummary`. `PCustomConfiguration` depends on *EComputer* and on `PConfigurationSummary`.

The class *EComputer* is an *abstract class*. The operations *getCurrentConf()* and *getPrice()* are abstract, inherited and implemented by the subclasses `EConfiguredComputer` and `EStandardComputer`.

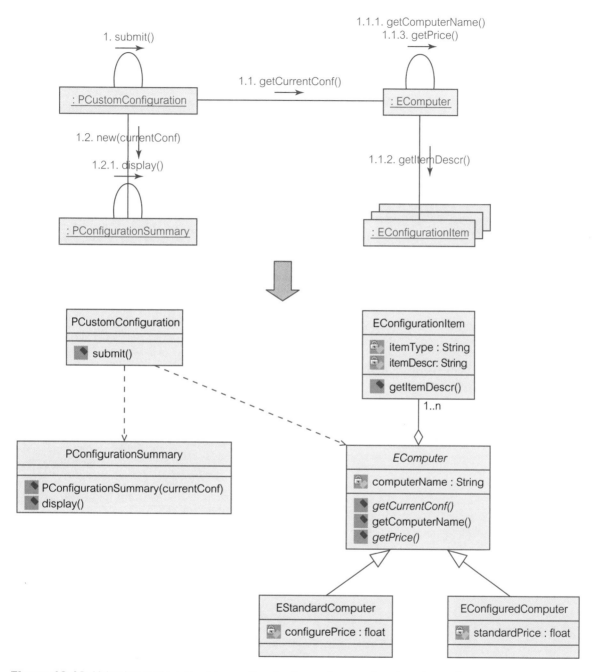

Figure 10.16 Using interactions to add operations to classes for an online shopping system

State machine modeling

10.5.1 States and transitions

Step 16: online shopping

Consider the class `Invoice` in the online shopping application. We know from the use case model that a customer specifies the payment method (credit card or check) for the computer when the purchase form is filled out and submitted to the vendor. This results in the generation of an order and, subsequently, in the preparation of an invoice. However, the use case diagram has not clarified when the payment is actually received in relation to the invoice. We can assume, for example, that payment can be made before or after the invoice has been issued and partial payments are allowed.

From the class model, we know that the invoice for the order is prepared by a salesperson but is eventually handed over to the warehouse. The warehouse sends the invoice to the customer, together with the computer shipment. It is important that the payment status of the invoice be maintained in the system so that invoices are properly annotated.

Draw a state machine diagram that captures possible invoice states as far as payments are concerned.

Figure 10.17 is a state machine model for the class `Invoice`. The initial state of `Invoice` is `Unpaid`. There are two possible transitions out of the `Unpaid` state. On the partial payment event, the `Invoice` object goes into the `Partly Paid` state. Only one partial payment is allowed. The final payment event, when in an `Unpaid` or `Partly Paid` state, fires a transition to the `Fully Paid` state. This is the final state.

Figure 10.17
States and events for the class `Invoice` for an online shopping system

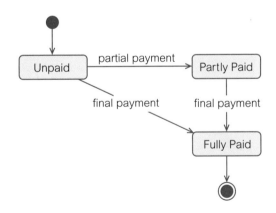

State machine diagram

Step 17: online shopping

Refer to the previous steps of the tutorial. Consider the class `Order` in the online shopping application. Think about the states in which `Order` can be – starting from its submission to the system and culminating in its fulfilment.

Consider that an ordered computer can be in stock or may need to be individually configured to satisfy your requirements. You may also specify that you want to receive the computer on some day in the future, even if the computer is in stock.

You are allowed to cancel your order any time prior to the computer's shipment. You don't need to model any penalty that may be involved in late cancelling.

Draw a state machine diagram for the class `Order`.

A state machine diagram for `Order` is shown in Figure 10.18. The initial state is `New Order`. This is one of the `Pending` states, the others being `Back Order` and `Future Order`. There are two possible transitions out of any of the three states nested in the `Pending` state.

The transition into the `Canceled` state is guarded by the condition `[canceled]`. It would be possible – without violating the state machine modeling rules – to replace the guard by the event `cancel`. The transition to the state `Ready to Ship` is labeled with a complete description containing the event, guard, and action.

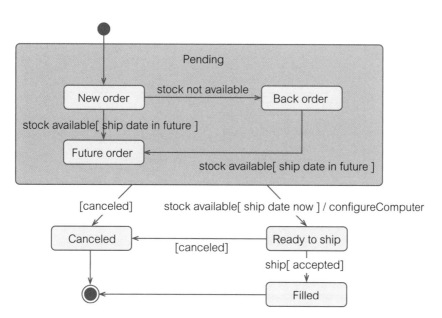

Figure 10.18
State diagram for the class `Order` for an online shopping system

10.6 Implementation models

10.6.1 Subsystems

Step 18: online shopping

The layers of the PCBMER architectural framework have been modelled as subsystems. This has been consistent with an expectation (and a requirement) that the services of a subsystem are encapsulated by interfaces (Section 3.6.1).

Extend an architectural diagram for PCBMER, presented in Figure 4.3 (Section 4.1.3.1), such that provided and required interfaces for subsystems are explicitly indicated. Use the lollipop notation (see, for example, Figure 3.19 in Section 3.6.2)

Figure 10.19 is (hopefully) a self-explanatory answer to Step 18. For example, the Bean subsystem provides interfaces that are required by Presentation and Control.

Figure 10.19
PCBMER subsystems with their interfaces for an online shopping system

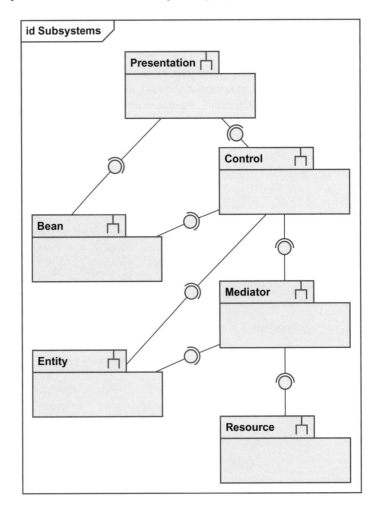

Packages

Step 19: online shopping

Refer to the previous steps of the online shopping tutorial. Naturally enough, most classes that we have defined so far represent persistent business objects. A more complete model for the system would require that other application classes be identified. This will be done successively as the design progresses. Even though we do not have the application classes yet, we can still speculate about packages that would group classes into coherent units according to the PCBMER approach.

Out task in this step is to think about possible packages in the online shopping example and the main dependencies between them. Extend the model in Figure 10.19 to include packages.

The best way to approach the online shopping example is to "impersonate the system" and imagine what needs to be done to accept a customer's order for a configured computer. The most obvious observation is that the system handles two separate functions – the computer configuration and order entry. These two functions require separate GUI windows, so we can create two *Presentation* packages: `configuration view` and `order view` (Figure 10.20). The data for rendering in these views will be supplied by the *Bean* packages `configuration bean` and `order view` (created by the *Control* subsystem).

On the "business side" of the class spectrum, we identified a range of classes in the class diagram (Figure 10.11). These *Entity* classes can be grouped naturally into three *Entity* packages – `customers`, `computers` and `orders` (the latter would also include the classes `Invoice` and `Payment`). Moreover, we will require a package to assign `OID`s to entity objects and maintain `OID` maps (Section 8.4). Let us call it the `identity map` package.

Next, we need to identify packages that glue the presentation and entity classes together – *Control* packages. We need a package to configure computers and calculate configuration prices sensibly. Let us call such a package `configuration provider`. We also need a package responsible for entering and recording orders – an `order monitor` package.

Not a great deal is known about the *Mediator* subsystem, but we know from the discussion about patterns for managing persistent objects (Section 8.4) that at least three *Mediator* packages may be needed. The packages can be named after the patterns – that is, `data mapper`, `lazy load` and `unit of work`.

Finally, there is a need for one or more *Resource* packages. The main resource package can be called `crud` – create, read, update, delete (Section 4.3.4.1). The `crud` communicates with the database tables whenever the application needs to access or modify database content.

The `crud` package depends on two other resource packages, called `connection` and `schema`. Classes in the `connection` package are responsible for handling database connections. The `schema` package contains the current information about the database schema objects – tables, columns, stored procedures and so on. The application can instantiate the schema objects when it starts so that it can validate that the database objects exist in the database before actually attempting to access the database (for example, before a stored procedure is called, the application can verify, using an in-memory schema object, that the stored procedure still exists).

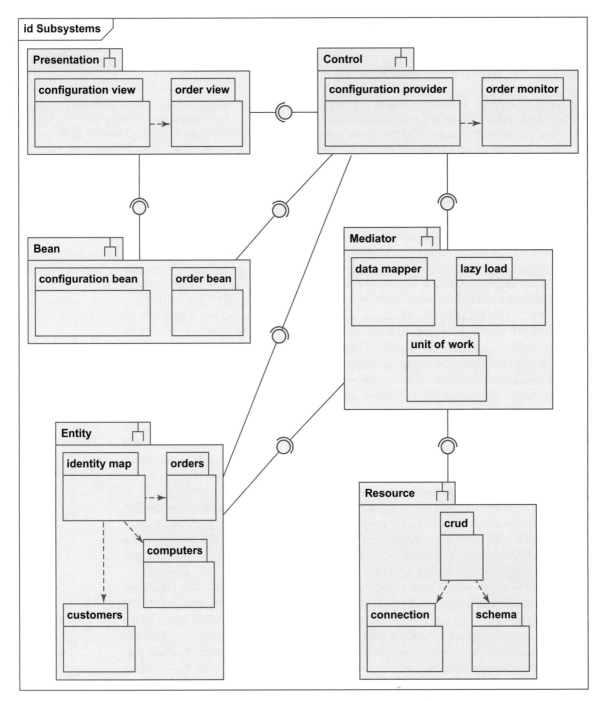

Figure 10.20 Packages for an online shopping system

Components

Step 20: online shopping

Propose a component diagram for business objects in the online shopping example. You will recall that a component is a cohesive functional unit with clear interfaces so that it becomes a replaceable part of the system. As the implementation platform for the online shopping example has not been specified, the identification of smaller components (such as libraries and stored procedures) is not possible at this stage.

One way to address this tutorial step is to consider the typical sequence involved when a customer accesses web pages and wishes to purchase a computer online. The guidelines can be obtained from the analysis of use cases in Section 10.1.

The first web page that an online customer would visit is the vendor's page, listing product categories (such as servers, PCs, laptops), highlighting the latest offers and discounts and providing links to web pages that list the products and give short descriptions of each one. The short descriptions would include prices for standard product configurations. This part of the system would be concerned with advertising the products to an online shopper. It needs to be a cohesive unit of functionality that could constitute the component called `ProductList`.

The customer's next step would be to ask for technical specifications for a chosen product. This would include a visual display of the product from different angles. It would be a standalone web page and a good candidate for the next component called `ProductDisplay`.

Assuming that the previous web pages would have attracted the customer to a product, different configurations for the product could then be requested to satisfy the customer's special needs and budget. This would be done via dynamic web pages where configurations could be built interactively and displayed, complete with a configured price. This is another good candidate for a component. Let us call it `Configuration`.

If the customer then decided to buy a product, he or she would be presented with a purchase order form. The details that would need to be entered would include the name and address for shipment and the invoice. The payment method would also be chosen and the relevant details submitted via some secure transfer protocol. This is the fourth component – `Purchase`.

The last component that we need to identify in this tutorial has to do with order fulfillment and tracking. From the customer's perspective, this would make it possible to view the status of the order on a web page (after the customer number and the order number have been entered). This component can be called `OrderTracking`.

The five components identified in the above discussion are shown in Figure 10.21. The main dependencies between components are shown by specifying the required and provided interfaces. Components are physical, tangible units of self-governing deployment – they have to be carefully designed and implemented, even for small systems.

Figure 10.21
Component
diagram for an
online shopping
system

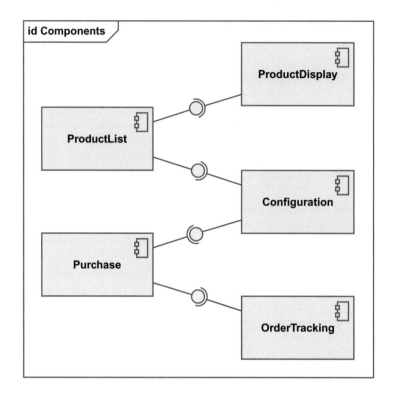

10.6.4 Notes

Step 21: online shopping

Refer to the implementation models in Steps 18–20 and propose a deployment diagram for the online shopping example. In particular, consider if there is a need in this example for an application server.

The connectionless nature of the Internet makes the *deployment* of a Web application significantly more difficult than that of a client/server database application. To start with, the Web server has to be set up as the routing middleware between all client browsers and the database.

If session management cannot be solved satisfactorily with *cookie* technology, then *distributed objects* need to be engaged. Deploying distributed objects would require a separate architectural element – an application server – to be placed between the Web server and the database server.

The deployment design must also address security issues. Secure transfer and encryption protocols make additional deployment demands. Careful planning is also needed with regard to network loads, Internet connections, backups and so on.

The deployment architecture capable of supporting more sophisticated Web applications includes four tiers of computing nodes:

1 client with browser

2 Web server

3 application server

4 database server.

The browser of the *client node* can be used to display static or dynamic pages. Scripted pages and applets can be downloaded and run within the browser. Additional functionality can be supplied to the client's browser with objects such as ActiveX controls or JavaBeans. Running application code on the client, but outside the browser, may satisfy other UI requirements.

The *Web server* handles page requests from the browser and dynamically generates pages and code for execution and display on the client. It also deals with the customization and parameterization of the session with the user.

The *application server* is indispensable when distributed objects are involved in the implementation as it manages the business logic. The business components publish their interfaces to other nodes via component interfaces such as CORBA, DCOM or EJB.

The business components encapsulate persistent data stored in a database, probably a relational database. They communicate with the *database server* via database connectivity protocols, such as JDBC, SQLJ or ODBC. The database node provides for scalable storage of data and multi-user access to it.

As shown in Figure 10.22, the online shopping application can be deployed without a separate application server. The Web server would execute the code in the server pages. The potential advantage of an application server is that the application components they

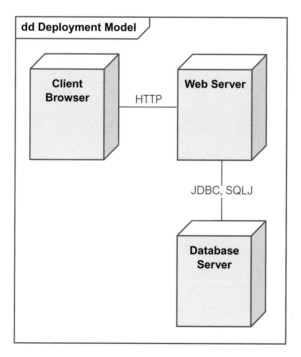

Figure 10.22
Deployment diagram for an online shopping system

house can be reused by other Web applications to invoke the same business logic. However, online shopping is a standalone system and no other Web applications to take advantage of its business logic could be identified.

10.7 Object collaboration design

Collaborations define the realization of use cases and more intricate operations (simple operations do not have to be modeled as collaborations). The design of collaborations invariably leads to the *elaboration* (modifications and extensions) of existing class diagrams and the production of new interaction diagrams (sequence and/or communication diagrams). Other kinds of diagram – in particular, state machine diagrams – may also need to be developed or elaborated.

An important spin-off (or even a prerequisite) of collaboration design is the need to *elaborate use cases*. The use cases documented during requirements analysis are unlikely to contain a sufficient level of detail to use as they are to design collaborations. The use case specifications therefore have to be elaborated into design documents. New design-level use case specifications must include the system-level demands yet at the same time maintain the actors' perspective.

Figure 10.23
Excerpt from a use case document managed by a CASE tool
Source: Screenshot reprinted by permission from Microsoft Corporation

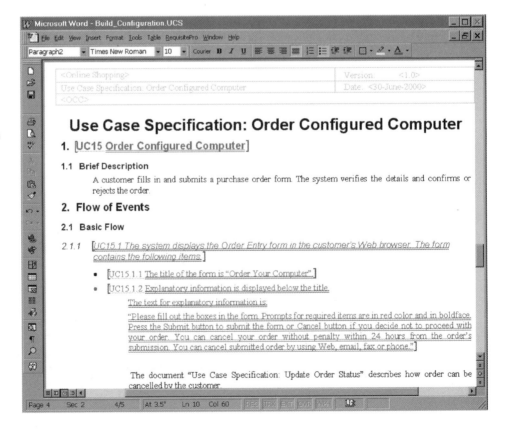

If the requirements management (Section 2.4) was fairly laid back during the analysis phase, there is now a last opportunity to become more formal and disciplined.

The requirements need to be numbered (Section 2.4.1) and structured (Section 2.4.2). Both activities can best be accomplished with the assistance of a CASE tool. If the requirements are then stored in a CASE tool repository, this ensures proper change and traceability management. Attempts to track changes to requirements manually are destined to fail. With a CASE tool, the renumbering and restructuring of requirements is easy.

Figure 10.23 shows a fragment of a use case specification document. Note the numbered requirements and hierarchial structure. The requirements are numbered using the Dewey decimal system, with the prefix UC (use case). The prefix is helpful when a use case document contains more than one type of requirement. Note that the requirements are enclosed in square brackets, underlined and displayed in green (though you will have to take our word for it on that last point).

Once entered into a CASE repository, the requirements can be viewed and modified by other tools supported by the CASE toolkit. Figure 10.24 demonstrates one such display in which the hierarchy of requirements is emphasized. The designer can use this display to modify any requirement or to attach various attributes to it.

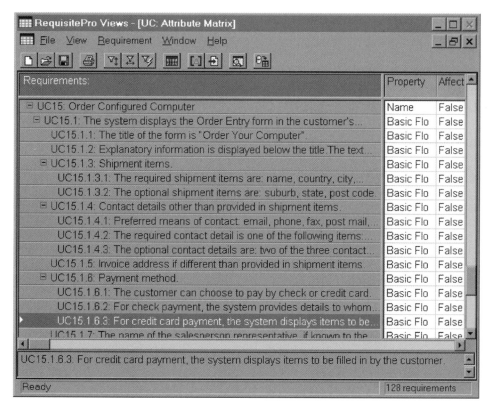

Figure 10.24
Requirements management in a CASE tool

10.7.1   Use case design specifications

Step 22: online shopping

Refer to the use case analysis document for online shopping in Section 10.2.2 (Table 10.2). The document is for the use case "Order configured computer". It is not sufficient on its own to design a collaboration model from.

The purpose of this tutorial step, therefore, is to show how to elaborate the use case document so you have a design-level use case specification. The elaborated document is to be organized as shown in Figure 10.23. In fact, Figures 10.23 and 10.24 reveal parts of the solution to this tutorial step.

The text proper for the use case design document is shown below. Note that the document can be printed differently from the format presented here. For example, the display and printing of the use case numbers can be suppressed.

Use case specification: Order configured computer

1   [UC15 Order configured computer]

1.1   Brief description

A customer fills out and submits a purchase order form. The system verifies the details and confirms or rejects the order.

2   Flow of events

2.1   Basic flow

[UC15.11 The system displays the order entry form in the customer's Web browser. The form contains the following items.]

[UC15.11.1 The title of the form is "Order your computer."]
[UC15.11.2 The order summary information and the explanatory information are displayed below the title. The text for explanatory information is:

"Please fill out the boxes in the form. Prompts for required items are in red color and in bold face. Press the Submit button to submit the form or Cancel button if you decide not to proceed with your order. You can cancel your order without penalty within 24 hours from the order's submission. You can cancel the submitted order by using Web, e-mail, fax or phone."]

The document "Use case specification: update order status" describes how an order can be canceled by the customer.
[UC15.11.3 Shipment items.]
[UC15.11.3.1 The required shipment items are: name, country, city, street, courier directions.]
[UC15.11.3.2 The optional shipment items are: suburb, state, postcode.]
[UC15.11.4 Contact details other than provided in shipment items.]

[UC15.11.4.1 Preferred means of contact: e-mail, phone, fax, post mail, courier mail.]

[UC15.11.4.2 The required contact detail is one of the following items: e-mail, phone, fax.]

[UC15.11.4.3 The optional contact details are: two of the three contact items listed as required, postal address (if different to that provided in shipment items).]

[UC15.11.5 Invoice address if different to that provided in shipment items.]

[UC15.11.6 Payment method.]

[UC15.11.6.1 The customer can choose to pay by check or credit card.]

[UC15.11.6.2 For check payment, the system provides details to whom the check should be made out and to what address it should be mailed. It also informs the customer that it takes three days to clear the check once received.]

[UC15.11.6.3 For credit card payment, the system displays items to be filled out by the customer. The items are: the picklist of acceptable credit cards, credit card number, credit card expiry date.]

[UC15.11.7 The name of the salesperson representative, if known to the customer from previous dealings.]

[UC15.11.8 Two action buttons: Submit and Cancel.]

[UC15.12 The system prompts the customer to enter order details by placing the cursor on the first editable field (the Name item).]

[UC15.13 The system allows information to be entered in any order.]

[UC15.14 If the customer does not submit or cancel the form within 15 minutes, the alternative flow "Customer Inactive" executes.]

[UC15.15 If the customer presses the Submit button and all required information has been provided, the order form is submitted to the Web server. The Web server communicates with the database server to store the order in the database.]

[UC15.16 The database server assigns a unique order number and a customer account number to the purchase order. The system confirms receipt of the order by displaying the assigned order number and account number.]

[UC15.17 If the database server is unable to create and store the order, the alternative flow "Database exception" executes.]

[UC15.18 If the customer submits the order form with incomplete information, the alternative flow "Incomplete information" executes.]

[UC15.19 If the customer provided an e-mail address as the preferred means of communication, the system e-mails the order and customer numbers to the customer, together with all order details, as the confirmation of the order's receipt. The use case terminates.]

[UC15.20 Otherwise, the order details will be mailed to the customer and the use case terminates as well.]

[UC15.21 If the customer presses the Cancel button, the alternative flow "Cancel" executes.]

2.2 Alternative flows

Customer inactive

[UC15.14.1 If the customer is inactive for more than 15 minutes, the system terminates the connection with the browser. The order entry form closes. The use case terminates.]

Database exception

[UC15.17.1 If the database raises an exception, the system interprets it and informs the customer about the nature of the error. If the customer has disconnected, the system e-mails the error message to the customer and to a salesperson. The use case terminates.]
If the customer is not reachable by Internet or e-mail, the salesperson needs to contact the customer by other means.

Incomplete information

[UC15.18.1 If the customer has not filled out all required items, the system invites the customer to provide the missing information. The list of missing items is displayed. The use case continues.]

Cancel

[UC15.11.1 If the customer presses the Cancel button, the form fields are cleared. The use case continues.]

3   Preconditions

3.1 The customer points the Internet browser to the system's web page. The page displays details of the configured computer together with its price. The customer presses the Purchase button.

3.2 The customer presses the Purchase button within 15 minutes from requesting the last computer configuration to be built and displayed in the browser's page.

4   Postconditions

4.1 If the customer's order submission is successful, the purchase order is recorded in the system's database. Otherwise, the system's state is unchanged.

10.7.2   User interface prototyping

Step 23: online shopping

In practice, the use case design specifications at the level of detail presented in Section 10.7.1 are still insufficient as the basis for producing an object collaboration design that is sufficient for programming tasks. There are two main techniques used to provide more information for programmers. Both are *storyboarding* techniques. The first is reminiscent of the technique used in the film industry – UX storyboards (Section 7.4.1 and 10.8)

The purpose of this tutorial step is to produce a prototype for a web page that displays the current status of an order to the customer.

Figure 10.25 presents a plain design for an order status page. A more complete design would also include a *client logon* page. The logon page would request that the user enters his or her account number and order number (sent when the order was originally placed). The system would then validate the user before showing the order's status.

The design in Figure 10.25 reveals (in the URL) that the order status is implemented as an *active server page (ASP)*. The layout consists of five informational fields. The gray background of the fields indicates that the user cannot modify the fields' values (the fields are read-only). The hyperlink at the bottom of the screen enables the user to logout from the order status page.

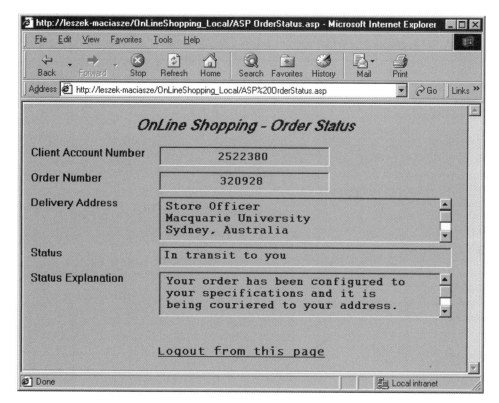

Figure 10.25
Prototype for a "Display order status" web page for an online shopping system

Sequence diagram   10.7.3

Step 24: online shopping

Refer to Step 23 of the tutorial. Design a sequence diagram for "Display order status."

Consider in the design the patterns for managing persistent objects (Section 8.4 and Solutions to exercises: contact management at the end of Chapter 8). Make the design consistent with the class diagram in Figure 10.11 and the package diagram in Figure 10.20. For simplicity, ignore the bean objects.

Assume that the data mapper knows the memory cache does not contain "clean" order status information and that a trip to the database is necessary. Once the status information has been obtained from the database, the memory cache needs to be refreshed. Assume that the refreshing means updating EOrder and creating a new EOrderStatus object.

Figure 10.26 offers a solution to Step 24. Note that `MDataMapper` proceeds immediately to the database and returns the order status data to the `Order Status` screen via `CStatusMonitor` (the "screens" could have been modeled as presentation objects – say, `POrderStatus` – but we opted for the notation of the UX storyboards profile). The `Order Status` screen uses the `display()` message to render the data to the screen. At the same time, `MDataMapper` takes care of refreshing the entity objects in the memory cache. First, it updates `EOrder`. Next, it creates a new `EOrderStatus`. The model does not explain what should be done to link `EOrderStatus` to its `EOrder` object.

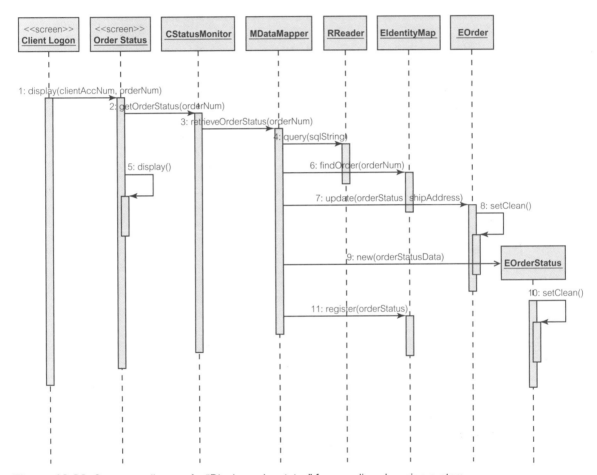

Figure 10.26 Sequence diagram for "Display order status" for an online shopping system

Design-level class diagram

10.7.4

> ## Step 25: online shopping
>
> Refer to Step 24 of the tutorial. Design a class diagram for "Display order status". There is no need to include data members, just methods, in all but the entity classes. Show return types of methods. Relationships, including dependency relationships, should also be defined.

The design-level class model in Figure 10.27 is derived directly from the model in Figure 10.26. The main additions are the return data types for the methods and data types for attributes. The Java data types are used. The `orderStatus` attribute in `Order` (Figure 10.11) is replaced by an association to the `EOrderStatus` class in `EOrder`.

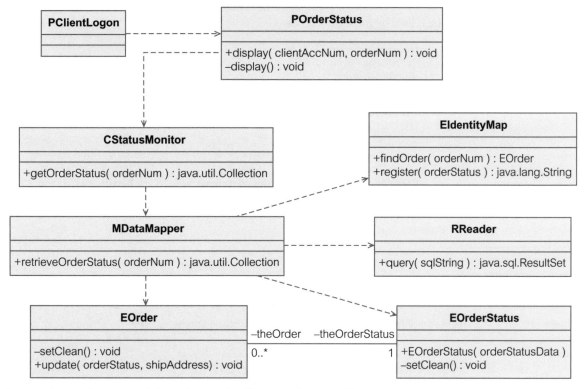

Figure 10.27 Design-level class diagram for "Display order status" for an online shopping system

10.8 Window navigation design

10.8.1 User experience (UX) elements

Step 26: online shopping

Refer to Step 22 of the tutorial. Study the use case design specifications to identify the UX elements. Draw properly stereotyped UX classes for the use case "Order configured computer".

Figure 10.28 is a class diagram featuring the user experience (UX) elements and relationships between them. The `Computer Order` screen contains one `Order Entry` form, two `Command Button` compartments (for `Submit` and `Cancel`) and possibly one `Order Confirmation` screen. The `Incomplete Order Entry` form is a kind of `Order Entry`. `Database Exception` is modeled as a compartment to emphasize that it can be reused by multiple screens.

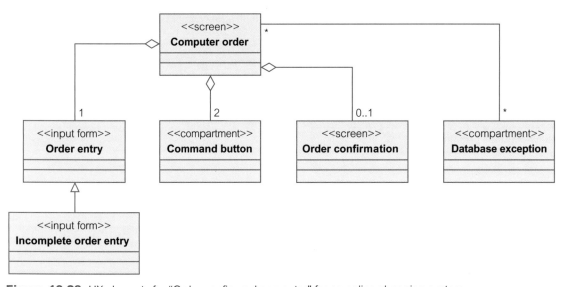

Figure 10.28 UX elements for "Order configured computer" for an online shopping system

10.8.2 Behavioral UX collaboration

Step 27: online shopping

Refer to Steps 22 and 26 of the tutorial. Draw a sequence diagram for behavioural UX collaboration for the use case "Order configured computer". Do not be unduly concerned with individual fields in the order entry form. Treat them as group entries as classified in the use case specifications – that is, shipment items, contact details, invoice address, payment method and salesperson name.

The sequence diagram in Figure 10.29 is a solution to Step 27. Only a couple of points may need explanation. Apart from the usual environmental actions of $navigate to, there are two $display actions that are also environmental. The branching of actions is quite extensive to address the alternative flows in the use case.

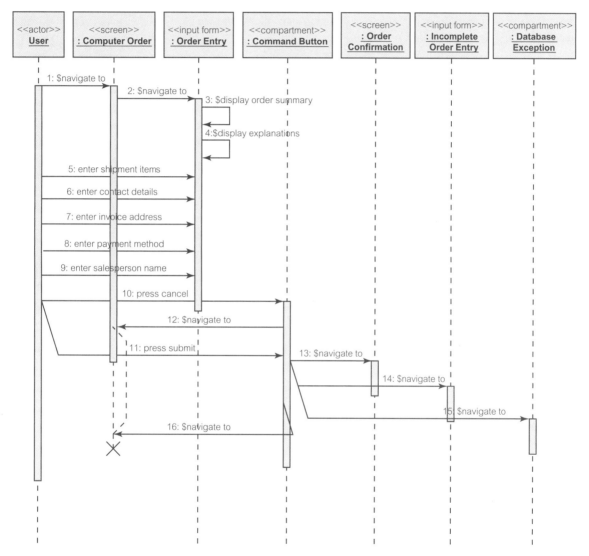

Figure 10.29 Sequence diagram for behavioral UX collaboration for "Order Configured Computer" for an online shopping system

10.8.3 Structural UX collaboration

Step 28: online shopping

Refer to Steps 22, 26 and 27 of the tutorial. Develop a class diagram for structural UX collaboration for the use case "Order configured computer". There is no need to apply the UX tags to the dynamic content of the UX elements (the fields in the UX classes).

Figure 10.30 presents a solution to Step 28. The solution is derived from the previous models – in particular, from the sequence diagram in Figure 10.29.

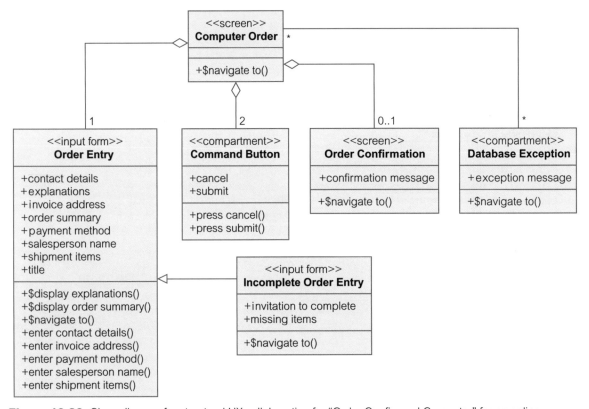

Figure 10.30 Class diagram for structural UX collaboration for "Order Configured Computer" for an online shopping system

Database design

Object-relational mapping

Step 29: online shopping

Refer to Step 12 of the tutorial. Map the class diagram in Figure 10.11 to a database schema model. Also consider the need, identified in Step 25, for the order status table. Show the tables, relationships between them, column types and null indicators. Also show multiplicities on relationships.

The mapping resulted in the 12 tables shown in Figure 10.31. Most mapping decisions were routine and followed the recommendations defined in Section 8.3. The generalization in Figure 10.11 was mapped using the third strategy listed in Section 8.3.4 – namely, to map each concrete class to a table.

In Figure 10.11, the association between Order and Computer is many to many and such that an Order must be associated with at least one computer. The mapping in Figure 10.31 has introduced two "relationship tables" to convert a many-to-many association to two one-to-many relationships (separately for linking to StandardComputer and to ConfiguredComputer). In this mapping, the constraint that an Order must be associated with at least one computer is not maintained in the database model. The note on the diagram indicates that the constraint must be enforced procedurally (say, by a trigger).

Surprisingly, a very similar model was obtained for the aggregation from Computer to ConfigurationItem (Figure 10.11). The class model did not indicate that a ConfigurationItem object can be a component of more than one Computer object (it is so because a ConfigurationItem defines a type of an item, not a concrete instance of an item). Accordingly, the aggregation is really a many-to-many relationship and has to be mapped with "relationship tables" as shown in Figure 10.31.

The only other not obvious decision relates to the relationship between Order and Invoice. This relationship could be modeled by placing a foreign key in either of these two tables. The decision was taken to place the foreign key in the Order table. However, note that the foreign key (invoice_number) accepts nulls. This is caused by the 0..1 multiplicity from Order to Invoice in the class diagram (Figure 10.11).

Referential integrity design

Step 30: online shopping

Refer to Step 29 of the tutorial and the database schema model in Figure 10.31. Consider various declarative referential integrity constraints for the delete operations (Section 8.2.3). Show which relationships in Figure 10.31 should have Del(C) or Del(N) constraints, rather than Del(R). Also show on the diagram which of the relationships allow "Changing parents" (that is, permit the cpa (change parent allowed) constraint).

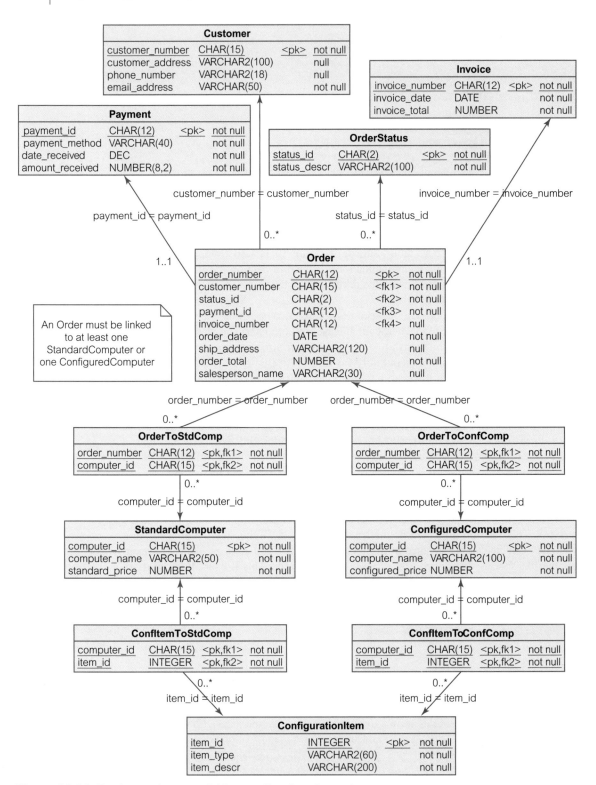

Figure 10.31 Database schema model for an online shopping system

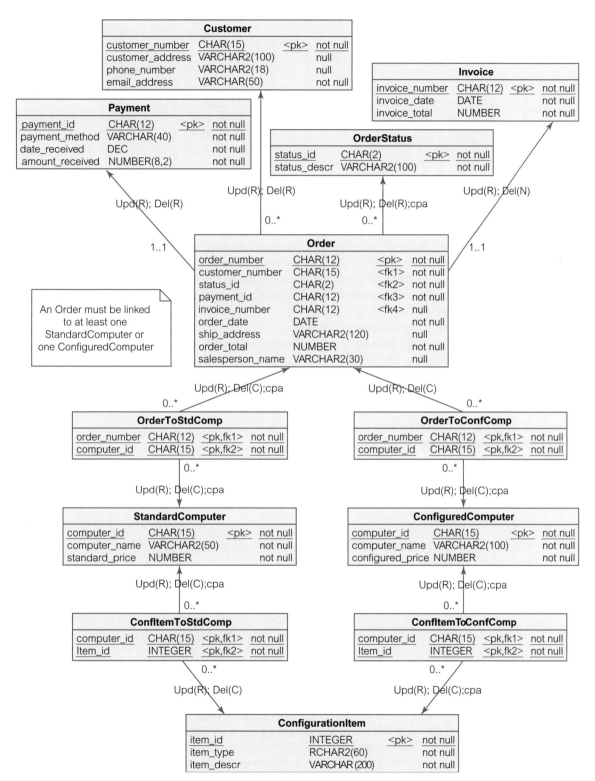

Figure 10.32 Database schema model with referential integrity constraints for an online shopping system

Figure 10.32 is a modified database schema model that shows the allowed delete actions and whether the `cpa` constraint is permitted. The `cpa` constraint is permitted on the relationship between `Order` and `OrderStatus` (an order can change `status_id`). The `cpa` constraint is also allowed on most relationships involving the "relationship tables" in the lower part of the diagram. There are two exceptions, which are that a configured computer cannot change an order and a standard computer cannot change a configuration item.

The deletion of an invoice will set the foreign key in `Order` to null. Records in the "relationship tables" can be freely deleted if their parent record has been deleted. This is signified by the `Del(C)` constraints on the relationships involving these tables. All other delete constraints are `Del(R)`.

Summary

This last chapter of the book has been motivated by an important (if not the most important) educational principle – to review and reinforce the studied material. This RR principle is embraced by most university courses – the last week of study frequently being dedicated to material review and reinforcement. For such courses, this chapter would have come in very handy.

The chapter applied the RR principle in a tutorial style. A single application domain – an online shopping example – was used to present all the important steps of requirements analysis and system design. Altogether, the material was presented in 30 interrelated software development steps. The steps were grouped into nine consecutive topics:

1. use case modeling
2. activity modeling
3. class modeling
4. interaction modeling
5. state machine modeling
6. implementation models
7. collaboration design
8. window navigation design
9. database design.

This chapter is in no way a substitute for the rest of the book. It does not explain (with few exceptions) the theory behind the modeling decisions and solutions. Also, a tutorial contained in a single chapter cannot address all modeling and design intricacies. The exercises address but a few of the other important analysis and design issues.

Exercises: online shopping

G1   Refer to Step 2 (Section 10.1.2).

Point 6 in Table 10.1 says that the customer is to be e-mailed so that he or she can check the status of the order online. There is no use case that shows this happening. Should there be? Explain your answer.

G2 Step 3 (Section 10.1.3) identifies `Display order status` as one of the use cases. The use case is to allow a customer to check the status of the computer order.

Write a use case document for the use case `Display order status`. Use the document format as in Step 4 (Section 10.1.4).

G3 Refer to Step 9 (Section 10.3.3).

In Figure 10.8, the class Customer is not associated directly with the classes `Payment`, `Invoice` and `ConfiguredComputer`. Should it be associated? If so, modify the diagram. Explain your answer.

G4 Refer to Step 11 (Section 10.3.5).

Figure 10.10 is a relatively simple example of generalization. What complications might arise if differences are required between the information on invoices for `StandardComputer` sales and `ConfiguredComputer` sales? For example, there might be additional charges depending on the modifications required for `ConfiguredComputer` systems and a discount for bulk purchases of `StandardComputer` systems.

Modify the diagram to reflect such complications. Explain your answer briefly.

G5 Refer to Step 6 (Section 10.2.2).

Draw an analysis-level sequence diagram for the action `Display purchase form` (Figure 10.5). As reference, consider Figure 10.14 (step 13, Section 10.4.1) to be an analysis-level sequence diagram.

G6 Refer to your solution to Exercise G5 above.

Add operations to the classes denoted by the objects in the sequence diagram. Show the relationships, including dependency relationships, between the classes.

G7 Refer to Step 16 (Section 10.5.1).

The state machine diagram in Figure 10.17 conforms to the restriction that only one partial payment is allowed. Suppose that this is not the case and that more partial payments are allowed. Modify the diagram accordingly.

Provide two solutions. The first solution should be for the situation in which partial payments are a priori designated as partial. The second solution should be for the situation in which the system has to calculate whether a payment is partial or in full.

G8 Refer to Step 12 (Section 10.3.6).

Consider a part of the model with classes `Customer`, `Order`, and `Invoice`. Is it possible to introduce a derived association to the model? If so, add it to the diagram.

G9 Refer to Step 12 (Section 10.3.6).

Consider a part of the model with classes `Order` and `Computer`. Change the association between `Order` and `Computer` to a qualified association to explicitly capture the constraint "a single order item per computer on order."

G10 Refer to Step 5 (Section 10.2.1).

Design a sequence diagram for the action "E-mail Order Details". Take an approach similar to that in Step 24 (Section 10.7.3).

G11 Refer to Step 5 (Section 10.2.1).

Produce a design-level class diagram for the action "E-mail order details". Take an approach similar to that in Step 25 (Section 10.7.4).

G12 Refer to Step 3 (Section 10.1.3).

Produce a design-level use case specification for the use case "Verify and accept customer payment". Take an approach similar to that in Step 22 (Section 10.7.1).

G13 Refer to your solution to Exercise G12.

Study the use case design specifications to identify the UX elements. Draw properly stereotyped UX classes for the use case "Verify and accept customer payment." Take an approach similar to that in Step 26 (Section 10.8.1).

G14 Refer to your solutions to Exercises G12 and G13.

Draw a sequence diagram for behavioral UX collaboration for the use case "Verify and accept customer payment". Take an approach similar to that in Step 27 (Section 10.8.2).

G15 Refer to your solutions to Exercises G12, G13 and G14.

Draw a class diagram for structural UX collaboration for the use case "Verify and accept customer payment". Take an approach similar to that in Step 28 (Section 10.8.3).

G16 Refer to Step 29 (Section 10.9.1).

Develop an alternative database schema model to that in Figure 10.31. Attempt to produce a model that is as different as possible from it while ensuring the same (or very close) declarative semantics and efficiency.

G17 Refer to Step 30 (Section 10.9.2).

Consider the relationship between `Invoice` and `Order`. Write database triggers (can be in pseudo-code) for these two tables that enforce the referential integrity between them, as specified in Figure 10.32.

Appendix A

Fundamentals of Object Technology

Virtually all modern software systems are object-oriented and developed using object-oriented modeling. The omnipresence of objects in information systems places knowledge demands on virtually all stakeholders of software projects – not just developers but also customers (users and system owners). To be able to communicate effectively, all stakeholders must have a common understanding of the object technology and object modeling language. For customers, the knowledge of objects must be just sufficient to understand the main concepts and modeling constructs. For developers, the knowledge must be in-depth and at the level where it can be applied to build models and implement the software.

The main difficulty in learning *object technology* relates to the absence of an obvious starting point and the lack of a clear path of investigation. There is not a top-down or bottom-up learning approach that we know of. By necessity, the approach has to be a sort of "middle-out". No matter how much we advance the learning process, we always seem to be in the middle of that learning (as new issues keep emerging). The first major test of a successful learning process is passed when the reader understands the in-depth meaning of the fact that, in an object-oriented system, "everything is an object".

The concepts of object technology are best explained using visual representations of the Unified Modeling Language (UML). Accordingly, this appendix uses UML to represent all the fundamental concepts of object technology.

A.1 Real-life analogy

A good way to explain object orientation in information systems is to provide an analogy with real-life concrete objects. The world around us consists of *objects* in some observable *states* (determined by current values of the objects' attributes) and exhibiting some *behavior* (determined by operations (functions) performed by these objects). Each object is uniquely *identified* among other objects.

For example, a coffee mug on my desk is in a filled *state* because it is shaped to hold liquids and there is still coffee in it. When there is no more coffee in it, the state of the mug can be defined as empty. If it falls on the floor and breaks, it will be in a broken state.

My coffee mug is passive – it does not have *behavior* of its own. However, the same cannot be said of my dog or a eucalyptus tree outside my window. My dog barks, the tree grows and so on. So, some real-life objects do have behavior.

All real-life objects also have *identity* – a fixed property by which we distinguish one object from another. If I had two coffee mugs on my desk from the same mug set, I could say that the two mugs are *equal* but not *identical*. They are equal because they have the same state – the same values for all their attributes (so, they are the same size and shape, are black and are empty). However, in object-oriented parlance, they are not identical because there are two of them and I have a choice of which one to use.

Real-life objects that possess these three properties – state, behavior, identity – build up *natural behavioral systems*. Natural systems are by far the most *complex systems* that we know. No computer system has come close to the inherent complexity of an animal or a plant.

Despite their complexity, natural systems tend to work very well – they exhibit interesting behavior, can adjust to external and internal changes, can evolve over time and so on. The lesson is obvious. Perhaps we should construct *artificial systems* by emulating the structure and behavior of natural systems (Maciaszek et al. 1996b).

Artificial systems are models of reality. A coffee mug on my computer screen is as much a model of the real thing as is a dog or a eucalyptus tree on my screen. A coffee mug can, therefore, be modeled to have behavioral properties. It can, for example, fall on the floor if knocked over. The "fall" action can be modeled as a behavioral *operation* of the mug. Another consequential operation of the mug may be to "break" when hitting the floor. Most, if not all, objects in a computer system "come alive" – they have behavior.

A.2 Instance object

An object is an *instance* of a thing. It may be one of the many instances of the same thing. My mug is an instance in the set of possible mugs.

A generic description of a thing is a *class*. Hence, an object is an instance of a class. However, as discussed later in this chapter, a class itself may also need to be instantiated – it may be an object. For this reason, we need to distinguish between an *instance object* and a *class object*.

For brevity, an instance object is frequently called an *object* or an *instance*. It is confusing to call it an "object instance". Likewise, it is confusing to use the term "object class". Yes, a class is a template for objects with the same attributes and operations, but a class itself can be instantiated as an object (and it would be strange to call such a creation an "object class object").

An object-oriented system consists of collaborating objects. Everything in an object-oriented system is an object, be it an object of an instance (*instance object*) or an object of a class (*class object*).

Object notation

The UML notation for an object is a rectangle with two compartments. The upper compartment contains the name of an object and the name of a class to which the object belongs. The syntax is:

> objectname: classname

The lower compartment contains the list of attribute names and values. The types of attributes can also be shown. The syntax is:

> <u>attributename</u>: [type] = value

Figure A.1 demonstrates four different ways in which an object can be shown graphically. The example shows a `Course` object named `c1`. The object has two attributes. The types of the attributes are not shown – they have been specified in the definition of the class. The compartment for attribute values may be suppressed if attribute values do not need to be shown in a particular modeling viewpoint. Similarly, the object name may be omitted when representing an anonymous object of the given class. Finally, the class of the object may be suppressed. The presence or absence of the colon indicates whether the given label represents a class or an object.

It is important to note that the object notation does not provide a compartment for listing the *operations* that an instance object can execute. This is because the operations are identical for all instance objects, so it would be redundant to store them repeatedly in each instance object. Operations may be stored in a *class object* or associated with instance objects by other means (implemented in the underlying object-oriented system software).

As an aside, there are some less well-known programming languages, such as Self, that allow operations to be attached to objects (not just classes) at run-time. These languages are known as *prototypical* or *delegation-based* languages. For such situations, UML allows a third compartment containing operations as a language-specific extension (UML 2005).

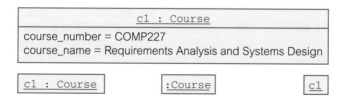

Figure A.1
An instance object

A.2.2 How do objects collaborate?

The number of objects of a particular class can be very large. This is true in particular for *business objects* representing business concepts (known as *entity classes*, such as `Invoice` or `Employee`). It is impractical and infeasible to visualize many objects on a diagram.

Objects are normally drawn only to exemplify a system at a point in time or how they *collaborate* over time to do certain tasks. For example, to order products, a *collaboration* may need to be established between a `Stock` object and a `Purchase` object. To be precise, objects on collaboration diagrams are *roles* that objects play, not objects per se – they describe many possible objects. Graphically, the roles are presented using the notation of an anonymous object.

System tasks are performed by sets of objects that invoke *operations* (behavior) on each other. We say that they exchange *messages*. The messages call operations on objects that can result in the change of objects' states and invoke other operations.

Figure A.2 shows the flow of messages between four objects. The parentheses after the message names indicate that a message can take parameters (like in a traditional programming call to a function). The object `Order` requests the object `Shipment` to "ship itself" (to this end, `Order` passes itself to `Shipment` as an actual parameter to `shipOrder()`). `Shipment` asks `Stock`, in a `getProducts()` message, to provide the appropriate quantity of products. At this point, `Stock` analyzes its inventory levels for products to be shipped by performing `analyze Levels()`. If the stock requires replenishment, `Stock` requests `Purchase` to reorder more products in a `reorder()` message.

Although the object collaboration model in Figure A.2 is shown as a sequence of numbered messages, in general the flow of messages does not impose a strict temporal order on the activation of objects. For example, `analyzeLevels()` can be activated independently of `shipOrder()` and `get Products()`, not in a way related to shipments. For these reasons, the numbering of messages is frequently not used in object collaboration models.

Figure A.2
Object
collaboration

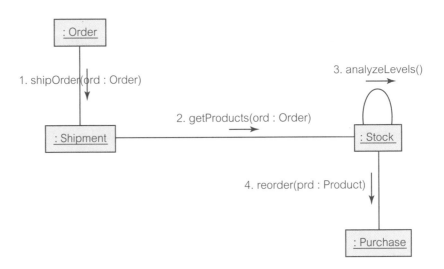

Identity and object communication

The question is how an object knows the *identity* of another object to which it wants to send a message. How does an `Order` object know the `Shipment` object so that the message `shipOrder()` reaches its destination?

The answer is that each object is given an *object identifier* (OID) when it is created. The OID is the *handle* on that object – a unique number that remains with the object for its entire life. If object `X` wants to send a message to object `Y`, then `X` has somehow to know the OID of `Y`. There are two practical solutions to establishing OID *links* between objects. These solutions involve:

- persistent OID links
- transient OID links.

The distinction between these two kinds of link has to do with the longevity of objects. Some objects live only as long as the program executes – they are created by the program and destroyed during the program's execution or when the program finishes its execution. These are *transient objects*. Other objects outlive the execution of the program – they are stored in the persistent disk storage when the program finishes and are available for the next execution of the program. These are *persistent objects*.

Persistent link

A *persistent link* is an object reference (or a set of object references) in one object in persistent storage that links that object to another object in persistent storage (or to the set of other objects). Hence, to persistently link a `Course` object to its `Teacher` object, the object `Course` must contain a link attribute, the value of which is the OID of the object `Teacher`. The link is persistent because the OID is physically stored in the object `Course`, as shown in Figure A.3.

The OID of object `c1` is marked here as `CCC888`. The object contains a link attribute named `teacher`. The type of this attribute is `identity`. Its value is the OID of a `Teacher` object, shown here as `TTT999`. The OID is a logical address of the object. This can be implemented as the computer identification number plus the time in milliseconds when the object was instantiated. The programming language environment is able to convert the logical address to the physical disk address where the object `Teacher` is *persistently* stored.

Once the objects `Course` and `Teacher` are transferred to the program's memory, the value of the `teacher` attribute will be *swizzled* to a memory pointer, thus establishing a

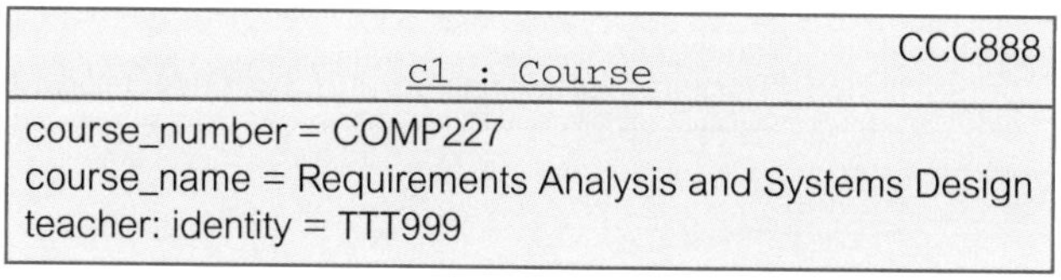

c1 : Course	CCC888
course_number = COMP227 course_name = Requirements Analysis and Systems Design teacher: identity = TTT999	

Figure A.3
The representation of a persistent link

memory-level collaboration between the objects. (Swizzling is not the UML term – it is used in object databases where the transfers of objects between persistent storage and transient memory are frequent.)

Figure A.3 illustrates how persistent links are represented in objects. In UML modeling, the links between objects can be drawn as in Figure A.4. The links are represented as *instances of an association* between the objects Course and Teacher.

Normally, collaboration links on business objects allow for *navigation* in both directions. Each Course object is linked to its Teacher object and a Teacher object can navigate to Course objects. It is possible, though not frequent in the case of business objects, to allow for navigation in only one direction.

A.2.3.2 Transient link

What if no persistent link is defined between Course and Teacher and there is still a need to send a message from object t1 to object c1 to invoke the operation getCourseName()? The application program must have other means to find out the identity of object c1 and create a *transient link* from object t1 to object c1 (Riel 1996).

Fortunately, a programmer has many techniques that can lead to initialization of a reference variable – called, for example, crsRef – with an OID of memory-resident object c1. To start with, it is possible that earlier in the program a link between objects c1 and t1 has been established and crsRef still holds the correct OID. For example, the program has executed a search operation on the teacher t1's availability for teaching and on the timetable for courses and has determined that teacher t1 should teach course c1.

An alternative possibility is that the program has access to a persistently stored table that maps course numbers to teacher names. It can then search on Course objects to find all courses taught by teacher t1 and request the user to determine the course that the message getCourseName() is to be sent to.

It is also possible that the very task of a program is to create courses and teachers before storing them in a database. There is no persistent link between teachers and courses, but the user enters the information so that each course clearly identifies a teacher in charge. The program can then store the transient links in the program's variables (such as crsRef) and these variables can be used later (during the same program execution) to send messages between Teacher and Course objects.

In short, there are quite a few ways to establish transient links between objects that are not persistently linked by associations between relevant classes. *Transient links* are program variables that contain OID values of objects that are currently in the program's memory. The mapping (*swizzling*) between the transient and persistent OIDs should be the responsibility of the underlying programming environment, such as an object database system.

Figure A.4
Persistent links in a UML object model

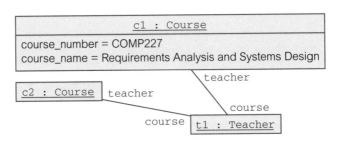

Message passing

Once an object is linked to another object, it can send a message along the link to request a *service* from the other object. That is, an object can invoke an *operation* on another object by sending a *message* to it. In a typical scenario, to point to an object, the sender will use a program's variable containing a link value (OID value) of that object. For example, a *message* sent by an object `Teacher` to find the name of an object `Course` could look like:

```
crsRef.getCourseName(out crs_name)
```

In the example, the specific object of class `Course` that will execute `getCourseName()` is pointed to by the current value of the link variable `crsRef`. The output (`out`) argument `crs_name` is a variable to be initialized with the value returned by the operation `getCourseName()` implemented in the class `Course`.

The example assumes that the programming language distinguishes between input (`in`), output (`out`) and input/output (`inout`) arguments. Popular object-oriented languages, such as Java, do not make such distinctions. In Java, message arguments of primitive data types (such as `crs_name` in the example) are passed to operations by value. *Pass by value* means that these are effectively input arguments – the operation cannot change the value passed. The change is not possible because the operation acts on a copy of the argument.

In the case of message arguments of non-primitive data types (that is, arguments that are references to user-defined objects), pass by value means that the operation receives the reference to the argument, not its value. Because there is only one reference (not two copies of it), the operation can use it to access and possibly modify the attribute values within the passed object. This, in effect, eliminates the need for explicit input/output arguments.

Finally, the need for explicit output arguments is substituted in Java by a return type of an operation invoked by a message call. The return type may be primitive or non-primitive. An operation can return the maximum of one return value or no value at all (a return type of `void`). When multiple values need to be returned, the programmer has an option of defining a non-primitive aggregate object type that can contain all the values to be returned.

Class

A *class* is the descriptor for a set of objects with the same attributes and operations. It serves as a *template* for object creation. Each object created from the template contains the attribute *values* that conform to attribute *types* defined in the class. Each object can invoke operations defined in its class.

Graphically, a class is represented as a rectangle with three compartments separated by horizontal lines, as shown in Figure A.5. The top compartment holds the class name. The middle compartment declares all attributes for the class. The bottom compartment contains definitions of operations.

Figure A.5
A class
compartment

A.3.1 Attribute

An attribute is the *type–value* pair. Classes define *attribute types*. Objects contain *attribute values*. Figure A.6 illustrates two classes with attribute names and attribute types defined. Two different attribute-naming conventions are shown. The attribute names in `Course` use the notation popularized by the database community. However, the programming language community prefers the convention shown in `Order`.

Figure A.6
Attributes

Course
course_number : String
course_name : String

Order
orderNumber : Integer
orderDate : Date
orderValue : Currency
customer : Customer

An attribute type can be a built-in *primitive type* or user-defined *non-primitive type*. A primitive type is the type directly understood and supported by the underlying object-oriented software environment. All attribute types in Figure A.6, except `customer`, designate primitive types. The type of `customer` is a *class* (non-primitive type). However, note that, in UML analysis models, non-primitive attribute types are not visualized within the attributes compartment (this is discussed next).

A.3.1.1 Attribute type that designates a class

An attribute type can also designate a class. In a particular object of the class, such an attribute contains an object identifier (OID) value pointing to an object of another class. In UML analysis models, attributes with class-based types (rather than primitive types) are not listed in the middle class compartment. Instead, the *associations* between classes represent them. Figure A.7 shows such an *association* between two classes.

The two names on the association line (`theShipment` and `theOrder`) represent so-called role names. A *role name* identifies the meaning for the association end and is used to *navigate* to an object of the other class in the association.

Figure A.7
Association
between classes
with role names
(analysis model)

Order
orderNumber : Integer
orderDate : Date
orderValue : Currency

theOrder

theShipment

Shipment
ShipOrder(ord : Order)

In the implemented system, the role name (on the opposite end of the association) becomes a class attribute, its type being the class pointed to by the role name. This means that an attribute represents an association with another class. Figure A.8 shows two classes from Figure A.7 as eventually implemented.

Order
orderNumber : Integer
orderDate: Date
orderValue : Currency
the Shipment : Shipment

Shipment
theOrder: Order
shipOrder(ord : Order)

Figure A.8
Attributes that designate classes (implementation model)

Attribute visibility

A.3.1.2

As explained in Section A.2.2, objects collaborate by sending messages to each other. A message invokes a class operation. The operation services the calling object's request by accessing attribute values in its own object and, if necessary, by sending messages to other objects. For this scenario to be possible, the operations must be *visible* to the outside objects (messages must see the operations). Such operations are said to have *public visibility*.

In a well-designed and implemented object-oriented system, most operations are *public* but most attributes are *private*. Attribute values are hidden from other classes. Objects of one class can only request the services (operations) published in the public interface of another class. They are not allowed to manipulate other objects' attributes directly.

It is said that operations *encapsulate* attributes. However, note that the encapsulation applies to classes. One object cannot hide (encapsulate) anything from another object of the same class. Visibility is normally designated by a plus or minus symbol:

+ for public visibility
− for private visibility

These symbols are replaced in some CASE tools by graphical icons. Figure A.9 demonstrates two graphical representations to signify attribute visibility. The graphical icon of a lock designates private visibility.

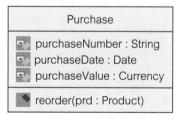

Purchase
− purchaseNumber : String
− purchaseDate : Date
− purchaseValue : Currency
+ reorder(prd : Product)

Figure A.9
Private attributes and public operations

A.3.2 **Operation**

An object contains *data* (*attributes*) and *algorithms* (*operations*) to act on these data. An operation is declared in a class. A procedure that implements the operation is called a *method*. The operation (or the method, to be precise) is invoked by a message sent to it. The name of the message and the name of the operation are the same. The operation can contain a list of formal arguments (parameters) that can be set to specific values by means of actual arguments in the message call. The operation can return a value to the calling object.

The operation name, together with a list of formal argument types, is called the *signature* of an operation. The signature must be unique within a class. This means that a class may have many operations with the same name, provided that the lists of parameter types vary.

A.3.2.1 Operations in object collaboration

An object-oriented program executes by reacting to random events from the user. The events come from the keyboard, mouse-clicks, menu items, action buttons and other input devices. A user-generated *event* converts to a *message* sent to an *object*. To accomplish a task, many objects may need to collaborate. Objects collaborate by invoking *operations* in other objects (Section A.2.2).

Figure A.10 shows operations in classes necessary to support the object collaboration demonstrated in Figure A.2. Each message in Figure A.2 requires an operation in the class designated by the message's destination.

The classes `Order` and `Product` (the latter not shown in Figure A.2) do not have any operations in this simple example. The `Order` is initiated by the `Order` object when it requests that a `Shipment` object ship it. As a result of the shipment, the stock may need to be replenished with new products.

The `getProducts()` operation demonstrates the return type of `Collection`. This refers to a *collection* (set, list or something similar) of products returned by `Stock` to `Shipment`. The `Collection` type is provided by the programming language. The Java `collection` comes from the library `java.util.Collection`.

Figure A.10
Operations in object collaboration

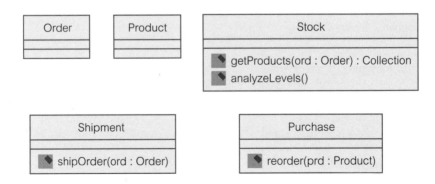

Operation visibility and scope

The visibility of an operation defines whether or not the operation is visible to objects of classes other than a class that defines the operation. If it is visible, then its visibility is *public*. It is *private* otherwise. The icons in front of the operation names in Figure A.10 denote that their visibility is public.

Most operations in an object-oriented system would have public visibility. For an object to provide a service to the outside world, the service's operation must be visible. However, most objects will also have a number of internal housekeeping operations. These will be given private visibility. They are accessible only to objects of a class in which they have been defined.

Operation visibility needs to be distinguished from *operation scope*. The operation may be invoked on an *instance object* (Section A.2) or on a *class object* (Section A.3.3). In the former case, the operation is said to have the *instance scope*, in the latter case the *class scope*. For example, the operation to find an employee's age has instance scope, but the operation to calculate the average age of all employees has class scope.

Class object

In Section A.2, the distinction was made between *instance objects* and *class objects*. A *class object* is an object with class-scope attributes and/or class-scope operations. The class scope implies here a global attribute or operation that can be accessed/called on the class itself, not necessarily on an instance object. However, note that, in practice, most programming languages do not implement the concept of a class object, nor do they allow us to instantiate such an object. Instead, they provide a syntax capability to refer to the class name in order to access a class-scope attribute or call a class-scope operation.

The commonest *class-scope attributes* are those that hold default values or aggregate values (such as sums, counts and averages). The most common *class-scope operations* are those that create and destroy instance objects and operations that calculate aggregate values.

Figure A.11 shows the class `Student` with two class-scope attributes (underlined) and a class-scope operation (identified by the stereotype `<<static>>`). Note that the attribute `numberOfStudents` is private, but the attribute `maxCoursesPerSemester` is public. Every student has the same allowed maximum number of courses per semester. The operation to calculate the average age of students has class scope because it needs to access the individual ages of students (in `Student` instance objects), sum them and divide the sum by the total number of students kept in `numberOfStudents`.

Figure A.11 also shows Java code corresponding to the graphical model. Java uses the keyword `static` to distinguish between instance and class properties. In effect, Java defines two kinds of object (instance and class objects) in one class definition (Lee and Tepfenhart 2002).

The two instance attributes (`studentId` and `studentName`) result in their own copies (storage space) in each instance of the class. Because these two attributes have private visibility, they are accessible only to operations defined in `Student` class.

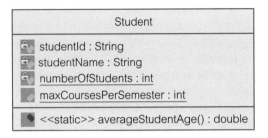

```
public class Student
{
    private String studentId;   //accessible via Student's operations
    private String studentName; //accessible via Student's operations
    private static int numberOfStudents;
    //accessible only to Student's static methods, such as averageStudentAge()
    public static int maxCoursesPerSemester;
    // accessible via Student:: maxCoursesPerSemester

    public static double averageStudentAge()
    { implementation code here }
    //callable by referring to the class name – Student::averageStudentAge()
    //callable also with an object of the class – std.averageStudentAge()
}
```

Figure A.11 Java class with class-scope attributes and operations

Class-scope (static) attributes are stored as single copies (occupy single storage space). In the case of a private static attribute (`numberOfStudents`), this single storage space is shared with all instances of `Student` and is accessible to `Student`'s static operations. In the case of a public static attribute (`maxCoursePerSemester`), the single storage space is shared with all instances of all classes and is accessible with the class name – that is, `Student::numberOfStudents`.

Class-scope (static) operations are callable, if public, from any instance of any class. They can be called by referring to the class name (`Student::averageStudentAge()`) or with an object of the class (such as, `std.averageStudentAge()`).

A.4   Variables, methods and constructors

The discussion so far has used, as far as possible, the generic terminology present in UML analysis models. However, to explain object implementation principles, you need to know the terminology used in UML design models and programming languages, such as Java. Frequently, the analysis and design terminology are the same, but sometimes there are some differences and the mapping between corresponding analysis and design/implementation terms is not exactly one to one.

This section introduces the concepts of variable and method. A variable maps from the notion of an attribute (variable implements an attribute). A method maps from the notion of an operation (method implements an operation).

A *variable* is the name for a storage space that may contain values for a specific data type. A variable can be declared a class or an operation (method body) of the class. In the first case, the variable is a *data member* of the class. In the second case, the variable is not a data member – it is a *local variable*. A local variable is valid only within the scope of the method (that is, as long as the method is executing).

Data members can have instance scope (*instance variables*) or class scope (*class variables*) (Section A.3.3). There are two categories of instance variable – those that implement *attributes* and those that implement *associations*. The former are variables with a primitive data type (they store attribute values). The latter are variables with a non-primitive data type (they store references to objects and, therefore, implement associations).

It is important to understand that variables storing references to objects are not objects, although they make it possible to act on objects (Lethbridge and Laganière 2001). During a single program execution, the same variable can refer to different objects and the same objects can be referred to by different variables. A variable can also contain a null value, which means that it does not refer to any object at all.

Data members (instance and class variables) can be initialized to any *non-constant* or *constant* value/object. A constant variable cannot change its value after the value has been assigned to it. Constants cannot be defined for local variables. In Java, constants are defined with the final keyword.

Instance variables that implement attributes can be initialized at the time they are defined within a class. Instance variables that implement associations are normally initialized programmatically, frequently in the constructor, which initializes objects of the class concerned.

A *method* is the implementation of an operation (a service) that belongs to a class (Lee and Tepfenhart 2002). A method has a name and a *signature* – the list of formal arguments (parameters). Two methods with the same name but different signatures are considered different. Such methods are known as *overloaded* methods.

A method may *return* (to the calling object) a single value of some primitive or non-primitive type. Formally, all methods must have a return type, but the type may be void. The method name, its signature and its return type are together known as the method *prototype*.

A *constructor* is a special method (the purists would argue that it is not a method at all) that serves the purpose of instantiating objects of the class. Each class must have at least one constructor, but it can have more than one (constructors can be overloaded). A constructor name is the same as the name of the class for which it is declared. Constructors do not have return types. In Java, a constructor is called with the new keyword, such as:

```
Student std22 = new Student();
```

The constructor Student() in the example is the so-called default constructor, generated automatically by Java if the programmer has omitted it in the class definition. The default constructor creates an object with default values assigned for all class variables. In Java, the default values are 0 for numbers, '0' for characters, false for Booleans and null for objects.

A.5 Association

An *association* is one kind of relationship between classes. Other kinds of relationship include generalization, aggregation and dependency.

An association relationship provides a linkage between objects of given classes. Objects needing to communicate with each other can use the linkage. If possible, messages between objects should always be sent along association relationships. This has an important documentary advantage – the static compile-time structures (associations) document all possible dynamic message passing that is allowed at run-time.

Figure A.12 shows the association named *OrdShip* between the classes Order and Shipment. The association allows for an Order object to be shipped (to be linked to) more than one Shipment object (indicated by the association multiplicity of n). A Shipment object can also carry (be linked to) more than one Order object.

In the simplest case of one-to-one association between an Order object and a Shipment object, the processing scenario could be as follows. An Order object needs to be shipped. To this end, it instantiates a new Shipment object by invoking one of Shipment's constructors. As a result of instantiation, Order obtains the reference to the new Shipment object.

Knowing this, Order can send the shipOrder() message to Shipment, passing itself to Shipment in the actual argument of ShipOrder(). This way, Shipment obtains the reference to Order. The only remaining action to establish the association is to assign the Shipment reference to the variable theShipment and, conversely, the Order reference to the variable theOrder.

Typically, associations on entity classes (business objects), as in Figure A.12, are bi-directional. However, uni-directional associations may be sufficient in associations on other categories of classes, such as between classes representing a GUI window, programming logic or user events.

Figure A.12
Association

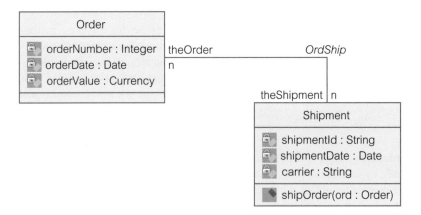

Association degree

Association degree defines the number of classes connected by the association. The most frequent association is of degree 2. This is called a *binary association*. The association in Figure A.12 is binary. Association can also be defined on a single class. This is called a *unary* (or *singular*) *association* (Maciaszek 1990). The unary association establishes links between objects of a single class.

Figure A.13 is a typical example of a unary association. It captures the hierarchical structure of employment. An `Employee` object is `managedBy` one other `Employee` object or by nobody (in the case of an employee who is, say, the chief executive officer (CEO), who is not managed by anybody). An `Employee` object may be the `managerOf` many employees, unless the employee is at the bottom of the employment ladder and so is not managing anybody. Associations of degree 3 (*ternary associations*) are also possible but not recommended (Maciaszek 1990).

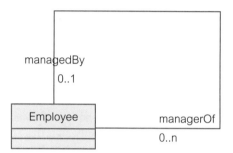

Figure A.13
Unary association

Association multiplicity

Association multiplicity defines how many objects may be represented by a *role name*. The multiplicity states how many objects of a target class (pointed to by the role name) can be associated with a single object of the source class.

Multiplicity is shown as a range of integers – $i1..i2$. The integer $i1$ defines the minimum number of connected objects and $i2$ the maximum number (the maximum number can be shown as n if the precise maximum integer value is not known or is not fixed). The minimum number does not have to be specified if such information is not essential in the model at the level of abstraction applied (as in Figure A.12).

The most frequent multiplicities are:

```
0..1
0..n
1..1
1..n
n
```

Figure A.14 demonstrates two associations on the classes `Teacher` and `CourseOffering`. One association captures the assignment of teachers to current course offerings. The other determines which teacher is in charge of an offering. A teacher can teach many offerings or none (if a teacher is on leave, for example). One or more teachers teach a course offering. One of these teachers is in charge of the offering. In general, a teacher can be in charge of many course offerings or none. One, and only one, teacher manages a course offering.

Figure A.14
Association
multiplicity

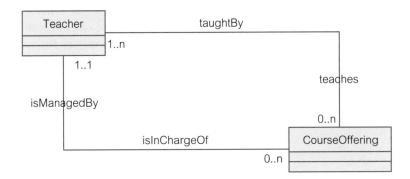

Association multiplicity in UML is an imprecise term. The "zero" and "one" minimum multiplicity can be seen as a distinct semantic notion of *membership* or *participation* (Maciaszek 1990). The "zero" minimum multiplicity signifies an *optional membership* of an object in the association. The "one" multiplicity signifies a *mandatory membership*. For example, a `CourseOffering` object must be managed by a `Teacher` object.

The membership property has some interesting semantics of its own. For example, a particular mandatory membership may additionally imply that the membership is *fixed*, meaning that, once an object is linked to a target object in the association, it cannot be reconnected to another target object in the same association.

A.5.3 Association link and extent

An association *link* is an instance of the association. It is a *tuple* of references to objects. The tuple can be, for example, a *set* of references or a *list* (ordered set) of references. In general, the tuple can contain one reference only. The link also represents the *role name*, as discussed earlier. The *extent* is a set of links.

Figure A.15 is a particular instantiation of the association *OrdShip* in Figure A.12. There are five links in Figure A.15. Hence the extent of the association is five. The understanding of association links and extents is important for an overall comprehension of the association concept, but the links and extents are not meant to be modeled or otherwise apparent.

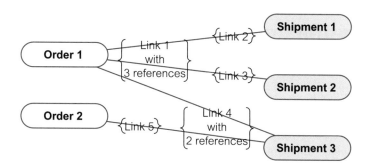

Association class

Sometimes an association has attributes (and/or operations) of its own. Such an association must be modeled as a class (because attributes can only be defined in a class). Each object of an *association class* has attribute values and links to the objects of associated classes. Because an association class is a class, it can be associated with other classes in the model in the normal way.

Figure A.16 shows the association class `Assessment`. An object of the class `Assessment` stores the list of marks, the total mark and the grade obtained by a `Student` in a `CourseOffering`.

The type of the attribute mark is `List(Number)`. This is a so-called *parameterized type*. Number is the parameter of the class `List`, where `List` defines an ordered set of values. The attribute mark contains the list of all marks that a student obtained in a class offering. That is, if the student "Fred" takes the course offering "COMP227", there will eventually be a list (an ordered set) of marks for him for that course offering. That list of marks will be stored in an `Assessment` object that represents the association between "Fred" and "COMP227".

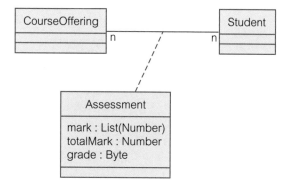

A.6 Aggregation and composition

An *aggregation* is a whole–part relationship between a class representing an assembly of components (*superset class*) and the classes representing the components (*subset classes*). A superset class contains a subset class (or classes). The containment property can be strong (*aggregation by value*) or weak (*aggregation by reference*). In UML, aggregation by value is called *composition* and aggregation by reference is simply called *aggregation*.

From the system modeling perspective, aggregation is a special kind of association with additional semantics. In particular, aggregation is *transitive* and *asymmetric*. *Transitivity* means that if class A contains class B and class B contains class C, then A contains C. *Asymmetry* means that if A contains B, then B cannot contain A.

Composition has an additional property of *existence dependency*. An object of a subset class cannot exist without being linked to an object of the superset class. This implies that if a superset object is deleted (destroyed), then its subset objects must also be deleted.

A *composition* is signified by the *filled diamond* "adornment" on the end of the association line connected to the superset class. *Aggregation* that is *not* composition is marked with a *hollow diamond*. However, note that the hollow diamond can also be used if the modeler does not want to make the decision as to whether the aggregation is a composition or not.

Figure A.17 shows a composition on the left and a normal aggregation on the right. It means that any Book object is a composition of Chapter objects, and any Chapter is a composition of Section objects. A Chapter object does not have an independent life; it exists only within the Book object. The same cannot be said about BeerBottle objects. The BeerBottle objects *can* exist outside of their container – a Crate object.

Aggregation and composition (as well as the associated notion of *delegation* – introduced in Section A.6.3) are very useful concepts in object technology. However, it is

Figure A.17
Composition and aggregation

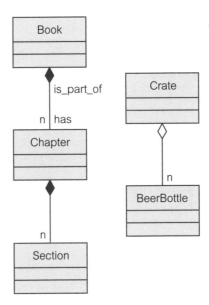

unfortunate that commercial programming languages give relatively little support to them. In many languages, aggregation and composition are implemented no differently than the implementation of association – that is, by means of *buried references* (Lee and Tepfenhart 2002); Section A.6.1). Java provides an alternative implementation by means of *inner classes* (Section A.6.2).

Buried reference   A.6.1

A *buried reference* implements an aggregation by means of a variable with private visibility that references the subset object. This is no different to the implementation of an association by means of a private reference. Such implementation does not support any other semantics of aggregation. Hence, for example, to ensure that the deletion of a super-set object also deletes its subset objects, the programmer has to implement such deletions in the application code.

Figure A.18 is an example of buried references. `Book` is modeled as the composition of many `Chapter` objects and one `TableOfContents` object. Consequently, the `Book` class has two buried references – the private variables `theChapter` and `theTableOfContents`. Making these references `private` hides the identities of the book's chapters and its table of content from other classes. However, this is of little benefit, because the visibility of classes cannot be private with regard to other classes. In the example, `Chapter` and `TableOfContents` have *package* visibility (this is implied by the absence of the keyword `public` in front of these classes' names). The package visibility makes the classes visible to all classes in the same package (in Java, every class must be assigned to one and only one package).

The presence of backward references from `Chapter` and `TableOfContents` to `Book` is also the result of imperfect implementation of aggregation/composition. Subset objects must somehow know their owner.

Figure A.18 illustrates how the superset object can demonstrate to the outside world that it is the owner of subset objects. This is shown in the implementation of the `search()` operation. The service to search for some string in the book is available in the `Book` class. The requester can send the `search()` message to a `Book` object. The `Book` object can then forward this request to its `Chapter` objects by invoking the `search()` method on these objects. In effect, the requester relies exclusively on the `Book` object to get the search results back.

Inner class   A.6.2

In Java, it is possible to define a class as an internal member of another class. The member class can have class scope – that is, be declared as `static`. It is then called a *nested class*. Alternatively, the member class can have instance scope and it is then called an *inner class* (Eckel 2003). It turns out that the inner class could be used as the best Java-supported implementation of aggregation/composition.

An inner class reflects the relationship between the superset instance and its inner subset instances. The superset instance has natural control over its subset objects because

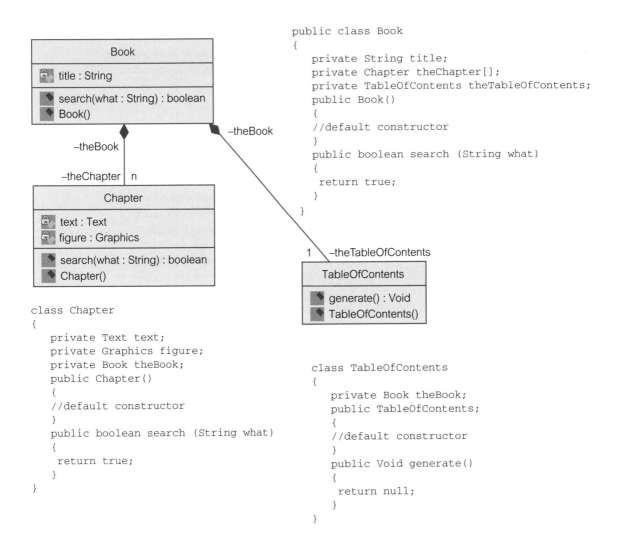

```
public class Book
{
    private String title;
    private Chapter theChapter[];
    private TableOfContents theTableOfContents;
    public Book()
    {
    //default constructor
    }
    public boolean search (String what)
    {
        return true;
    }
}
```

```
class Chapter
{
    private Text text;
    private Graphics figure;
    private Book theBook;
    public Chapter()
    {
    //default constructor
    }
    public boolean search (String what)
    {
        return true;
    }
}
```

```
class TableOfContents
{
    private Book theBook;
    public TableOfContents;
    {
    //default constructor
    }
    public Void generate()
    {
        return null;
    }
}
```

Figure A.18 A buried reference

it owns them. In the opposite direction, the subset instances have direct access to all members of the superset object, including the private members.

Figure A.19 shows how what is essentially the same model as in Figure A.18 can be implemented with inner classes. In typical situations, an outer class obtains a reference to an inner class by either instantiating the inner object within its own constructor or having a method that instantiates the inner object. The example uses the former approach. The `Book()` constructor instantiates `TableOfContents` and `Chapter` objects from its constructor (but it could construct them from other private methods to achieve the same level of encapsulation). `Book` redirects all queries to its content to appropriate `TableOfContents` or `Chapter` objects.

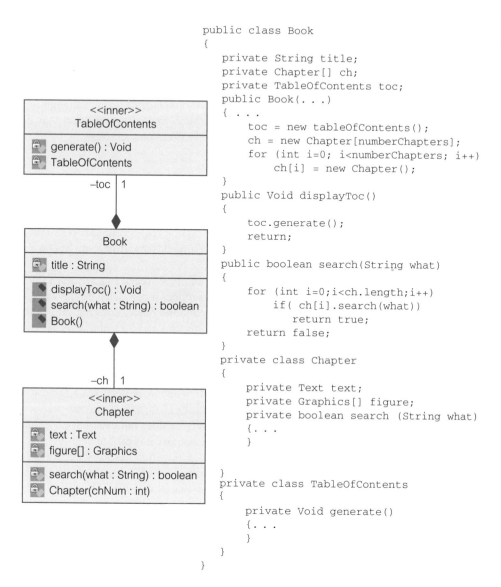

```
public class Book
{
    private String title;
    private Chapter[] ch;
    private TableOfContents toc;
    public Book(. . .)
    { . . .
        toc = new tableOfContents();
        ch = new Chapter[numberChapters];
        for (int i=0; i<numberChapters; i++)
            ch[i] = new Chapter();
    }
    public Void displayToc()
    {
        toc.generate();
        return;
    }
    public boolean search(String what)
    {
        for (int i=0;i<ch.length;i++)
            if( ch[i].search(what))
                return true;
        return false;
    }
    private class Chapter
    {
        private Text text;
        private Graphics[] figure;
        private boolean search (String what)
        {. . .
        }

    }
    private class TableOfContents
    {
        private Void generate()
        {. . .
        }
    }
}
```

The inner classes have an additional advantage in the implementation of aggregation/composition – they can be made *private* (whereas the normal classes can have only public or package visibility). Private inner classes can be accessed only from the outer class. This completely hides the implementation of inner classes from all but the outer class and reduces dependencies due to changes in the implementation. In Figure A.19, `TableOfContents` and `Chapter` are known only to `Book`, not to other classes in the system.

Other important benefits of using inner classes are related to the notions of *interface* and *inheritance*. Both these notions are discussed later in the Appendix (Sections A.7 and

A.9). To those already familiar with these concepts, suffice it to say that an inner class can implement an interface as well as extend (inherit from) a class (Eckel 2003). The first technique can further reduce dependencies of the program's classes on the inner class, even if the inner class is public. Everything that is made available to the program's classes are references to one or more interfaces that the inner class invisibly implements. The second technique, in effect, allows *multiple implementation inheritance*, even though Java is a single-inheritance language. The multiple inheritance comes from the fact that the outer class and its inner classes can inherit independently from other classes.

A.6.3 Delegation

Associated with aggregation/composition is the powerful technique of *delegation*. Delegation is a good replacement for inheritance as the code reuse technique (Gamma et al. 1995). Although delegation can be used between any classes, it is at its best when applied to classes related by aggregation/composition.

The idea of delegation is as its name suggests. If an object receives a request to perform one of its services and is unable to deliver the service, it can delegate the work to one of its component objects. Delegating the work to another object does not relieve the original recipient of the message from responsibility for the service – the *work* is delegated, not the *responsibility*.

Figure A.19 gives an example of delegation involving an inner class. The delegation can happen on the `search()` method. The `Book` class has `search()` in its public interface, thus promising this service to the outside world. When `Book` receives a request to perform a `search()`, it delegates the work to its `Chapter` objects. `Chapter` performs the work, `Book` gets the glory. The requester of the service does not even have a choice regarding directing the message to `Chapter` because `Chapter` has private visibility.

Technically, the scenario in Figure A.19 is known as *forwarding* the message, not *delegating*. Delegation is a more complex form of forwarding, such that an object delegating the service is passing along a reference to itself (Gamma et al. 1995). However, in the case of inner classes, there is no need to pass a reference for the delegating object because inner objects have direct access to all members of the outer class (by means of language-implemented hidden references).

Figure A.19 does not illustrate the *code reuse* aspect of delegation and the related benefit of improved *supportability* of programs relying on this kind of delegation. The benefits of reusability and supportability require delegation to be combined with interfaces and/or abstract classes (both concepts are discussed later, Sections A.8 and A.9).

The idea is that changes to objects that do the work (those to which the work was delegated) do not affect the program as long as the work is done. As an example, assume that `Chapter` and `Section` objects have the same type – they inherit from the same superclass (ideally abstract class) or implement the same interface. It will then be possible to replace the `Chapter` instances with `Section` instances at run-time when doing the `search()` operation. This replacement will not be noticed by the client object that requested the `search()` service.

Generalization and inheritance

A *generalization* relationship is a kind of relationship between a more generic class (*superclass* or *parent*) and a more specialized kind of that class (*subclass* or *child*). The subclass is a kind of superclass. An object of the subclass can be used where the superclass is allowed. Generalization makes it unnecessary to restate already defined properties. The attributes and operations already defined for a superclass may be *reused* in a subclass. A subclass is said to *inherit* the attributes and methods of its parent class. Generalization facilitates incremental specification, exploitation of common properties between classes and better localization of changes.

A generalization is drawn as a hollow triangle on the relationship end connected to the parent class. In Figure A.20, `Person` is the superclass and `Employee` is the subclass. The class `Employee` inherits all attributes and operations of the class `Person` (but the private members of `Person` are not accessible to the `Employee` objects). The inherited properties are not visibly shown in the subclass box – the generalization relationship forces the inheritance into the background.

Note that inheritance applies to classes, not objects. It applies to types, not values. The class `Employee` inherits the definitions of attributes `fullName` and `dateOfBirth`. This is by virtue of the fact that an instance of `Employee` is also an instance of `Person`. Hence, the constructor `Employee()` can set the values for `fullName` and `dateOfBirth` and for the remaining four data members.

There is a twist, though. The two attributes in `Person` have private visibility. This implies that the class `Employee` cannot access the `fullName` and `dateOfBirth` values in a `Person` object. This is logical. Somebody named "Joe Guy" is either an employee and a person or he is just a person. If Joe is an employee (and a person), he has his own values for `fullName` and `dateOfBirth` (as well as for `dateHired` and so on). If Joe is just a person (and not an employee), he again has values for `fullName` and `dateOfBirth` (but not for `dateHired` and so on).

Although an instance of `Employee` has no right to access attribute values in an instance of `Person`, it can call the `Person`'s `age()` method without referring to the `Person` class name. The inherited `age()` method will access the `dateOfBirth` value of an object on which it is called (the `Employee` object). Other classes in the program can also call the `age()` method (because of its public visibility), but any such call must either refer to the `Person` class name (`Person::age()`) or call it with a `Person` instance (`person.age()`).

The two private operations in `Person` (two `getYear()` methods) are used internally by the `age()` method to compute the current `age` of a `Person` object. Java support for manipulating date values is a bit awkward. Java provides several libraries to do the job (as per the `import` statements in Figure A.20). The first method, `getYear()`, returns the current year. The second parameterized method, `getYear(Date date)`, returns the year for some date in the past.

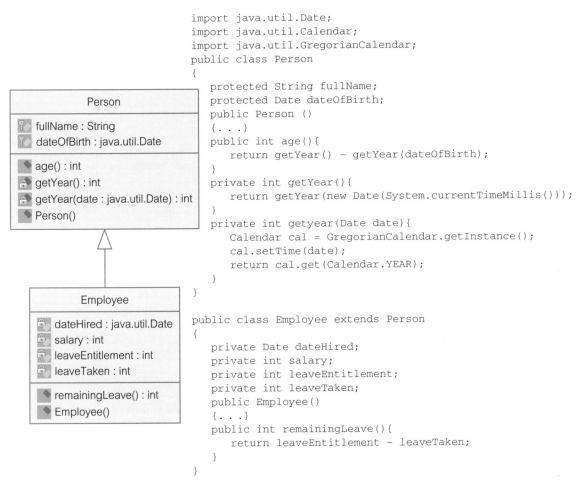

```
import java.util.Date;
import java.util.Calendar;
import java.util.GregorianCalendar;
public class Person
{
    protected String fullName;
    protected Date dateOfBirth;
    public Person ()
    {. . .}
    public int age(){
        return getYear() - getYear(dateOfBirth);
    }
    private int getYear(){
        return getYear(new Date(System.currentTimeMillis()));
    }
    private int getyear(Date date){
        Calendar cal = GregorianCalendar.getInstance();
        cal.setTime(date);
        return cal.get(Calendar.YEAR);
    }
}

public class Employee extends Person
{
    private Date dateHired;
    private int salary;
    private int leaveEntitlement;
    private int leaveTaken;
    public Employee()
    {. . .}
    public int remainingLeave(){
        return leaveEntitlement - leaveTaken;
    }
}
```

Figure A.20 Generalization

A.7.1 Polymorphism

A method inherited by a subclass is frequently used as inherited in that subclass (that is, without modification). The operation age() works identically for the objects of classes Person and Employee. However, there are times when an operation needs to be *overridden* (modified) in a subclass to correspond to semantic variations of the subclass. For example, Employee.remainingLeave() is computed by subtracting leaveTaken from leaveEntitlement (Figure A.20). However, the employee who is a manager gains a yearly leaveSupplement. If we now add the class Manager to the generalization hierarchy (as shown in Figure A.21), the operation Manager.remainingLeave() would override the operation Employee.remainingLeave(). This is indicated in Figure A.21 by duplicating the operation name in the Manager subclass.

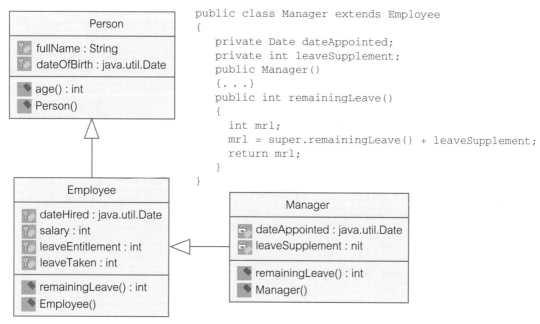

```
public class Manager extends Employee
{
    private Date dateAppointed;
    private int leaveSupplement;
    public Manager()
    {. . .}
    public int remainingLeave()
    {
        int mrl;
        mrl = super.remainingLeave() + leaveSupplement;
        return mrl;
    }
}
```

Figure A.21 Polymorphism

The operation `remainingLeave()` has been *overridden*. There are two implementations (two *methods*) for the operation. We can now send the message `remainingLeave()` to an `Employee` object or to a `Manager` object and we will get different methods executed for each. We may not even know or care which object is targeted as, `Employee` or `Manager`, the proper method will execute.

The operation `remainingLeave()` is *polymorphic*. There are two implementations (*methods*) for this operation. Both methods have the same name and identical *signatures* – the number and types of parameters (in this case, the parameter list is empty).

Polymorphism and inheritance go hand in hand as polymorphism *without* inheritance is of limited use. *Inheritance* permits the incremental description of a subclass by reusing and then extending the superclass descriptions. The operation `Manager.remainingLeave()` is probably implemented by invoking the functionality of `Employee.remainingLeave()` and then adding `leaveSupplement` to the value returned from `Employee.remainingLeave()`.

Overriding versus overloading   A.7.2

Overriding must not be confused with overloading. *Overriding* is the mechanism used to achieve polymorphic operations. Overriden methods have identical names and signatures and are placed in different classes of the same inheritance hierarchy. The decision as to which method is invoked is taken dynamically at run-time. The decision is based on the class of the object to which the variable (from which the method is called) points to and not on the type of the variable (Lee and Tepfenhart 2002).

If the variable points to a subclass object in the inheritance tree and the overridden method exists for that subclass, then this overridden method will be invoked. However, if the method is *not* declared in the subclass, the programming environment will search up the inheritance tree to find the method in a superclass of the subclass. The search will continue up to the base class if the method has not been overridden in any subclasses. If this is the case, the method of the base class will be invoked.

Overloading refers to a situation when multiple methods with the same name are declared in the same class. The methods have the same names, but they have different signatures and possibly also different return types. Unlike overriding, which is a run-time phenomenon, overloading can be resolved at compile-time.

Figure A.20 illustrates overloading in the private methods `getYear()` and `getYear(Date date)`. The former returns the current calendar year. The latter returns the calendar year of some concrete date passed to it as a parameter. The program decides statically which method to call. In fact, both methods are called by the public `age()` method declared within the same class (the `Person` class).

A.7.3 Multiple inheritance

In some languages, such as C++, a subclass can inherit from more than one superclass. This is called *multiple implementation inheritance*. *Multiple inheritance* can lead to inheritance conflicts,and these have to be explicitly resolved by the programmer.

In Figure A.22, the class `Tutor` inherits from the classes `Teacher` and `PostgraduateStudent`. `Teacher` in turn inherits from `Person` and so does `PostgraduateStudent` (via `Student`). As a result, `Tutor` would inherit twice the attributes and operations of `Person` unless the programmer were to instruct the programming environment to inherit only once by using either the left or right inheritance path (unless the programming environment enforces some default behavior, acceptable to the programmer, that eradicates the duplicated inheritance).

Note that Java does not permit multiple implementation inheritance. It provides alternative mechanisms, in particular interfaces (including multiple interface inheritance) and inner classes, to implement the class structures and behavior corresponding to the model in Figure A.22.

A.7.4 Multiple classification

In most current object-oriented programming environments, an object can belong to only one class. This is a troublesome restriction because, in reality, objects can belong to multiple classes.

Multiple classification is different from multiple inheritance. In multiple classification, an object is simultaneously the instance of two or more classes. In multiple inheritance, a class may have many superclasses, but an object is created as an instance of only one of these classes. The "knowledge" of other classes is only available to the object via inheritance.

In the multiple inheritance example in Figure A.22, each `Person` object (such as Mary or Peter) belongs to a single class (the most *specific* class that applies to it). If Mary is a `PostgraduateStudent`, but not a `Tutor`, then Mary's class is `PostgraduateStudent`.

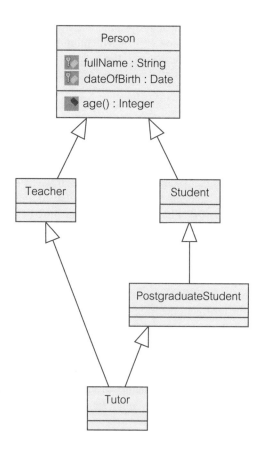

Figure A.22
Multiple
inheritance

The problem arises if `Person` is specialized in a few orthogonal hierarchies. For example, a `Person` can be an `Employee` or `Student`, `Male` or `Female`, `Child` or `Adult`. Without multiple classification, we would need to define classes for each legal combination of the orthogonal hierarchies to have, for example, a class for a `Person` object who is a child female student – a class that could be called `ChildFemaleStudent` (Fowler 2004).

Dynamic classification   A.7.5

In most current object-oriented programming environments, an object cannot change its class after it has been instantiated (created). This is another troublesome restriction because, in reality, objects *do* change classes dynamically.

Dynamic classification is a direct consequence of multiple classification. An object not only belongs to multiple classes but can also gain or lose classes over its lifetime. Under the dynamic classification scheme, a `Person` object can be just an employee one day and a manager (and employee) another day. Without dynamic classification, business changes such as the promotion of employees are hard (or even impossible) to implement. The implementation problem arises because definitions of object identifiers (OIDs) include the identification of the class to which an object belongs. Dynamic classification would necessitate changes of OIDs, which would defeat the very idea of OIDs (Section A.2.3).

The lack of support for multiple and dynamic classification in programming languages translates to a similar lack of support in UML modeling. Consequently, no graphical models are shown here to enhance the explanation.

A.8 Abstract class

The *abstract class* is an important modeling concept that follows on from the notion of inheritance. An abstract class is a parent class that will not have direct instance objects. Only subclasses of the abstract parent class can be instantiated.

In a typical scenario, a class is abstract because at least one of its operations is abstract. An *abstract operation* has its name and signature defined in the abstract parent class, but the implementation of the operation (the method) is deferred to *concrete* child classes.

An abstract class cannot instantiate objects because it has at least one abstract operation. This is because, if an abstract class was allowed to create an object, then a message to that object's abstract operation would cause a run-time error (as there would not be an implementation for the abstract operation in the class of that object).

A class can be abstract only if it is a superclass that is completely partitioned into subclasses. The partitioning is complete if the subclasses contain all possible objects that can be instantiated in the inheritance hierarchy – there are no "stray" objects (Page-Jones 2000). The class `Person` in Figure A.22 is not abstract because we may want to instantiate objects of `Person` that are not teachers or students. It is also possible that we may want to add more subclasses of `Person` in the future (such as `AdminEmployee`).

Figure A.23 shows the abstract class `VideoMedium` (in UML, the names of abstract classes are shown in italics). The class contains the abstract operation *rentalCharge()*. Understandably, rental charges are calculated differently for videotapes and for videodisks. Therefore, there has to be two different implementations of `rentalCharge()` – in classes `Videotape` and `VideoDisk`.

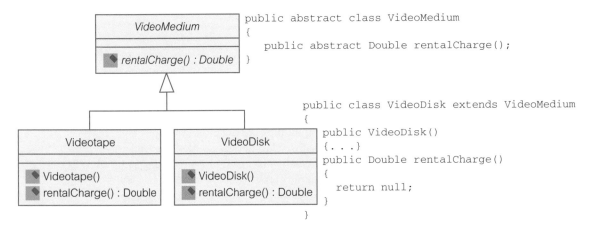

Figure A.23 An abstract class

Abstract classes do not have instances, but they are very useful in modeling. They create a high-level modeling "vocabulary" without which the modeling language would be deficient.

Interface

The idea of abstract classes is brought to complete fruition in Java interfaces. An *interface* is a definition of a semantic type with attributes (constants only) and operations, but without actual declarations of operations (that is, without implementation). The actual declarations are provided by one or more classes that undertake to implement the interface.

A program can use an interface variable in lieu of a class variable, thus separating the client class from the actual supplier of the implemented method. The client object can determine the value of the interface variable and invoke an appropriate method on the supplier object as determined at run-time.

Interface versus abstract class

Abstract classes constitute a powerful mechanism, but they are not helpful in resolving multiple inheritance problems and are not free from other undesired side-effects of implementation inheritance (Section 5.2.4). One such side-effect is the *fragile base class* problem – any change in the implementation of the base class has a largely unpredictable effect on the subclasses that inherit from that base class. As an abstract class can have some methods fully or partially implemented, it can become a fragile base class.

Figure A.24 demonstrates how an abstract class is of no help when resolving a modeling situation that seems to ask for multiple inheritance. Assuming that the video store (Section 1.6.2) rents not just movies but also videotape- and disk-playing equipment, the modeler may be tempted to inherit from `VideoMedium`. However, due to Java's single-

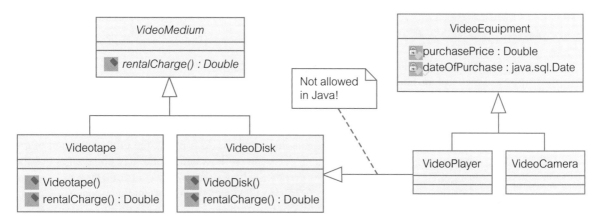

Figure A.24 Multiple implementation inheritance is not allowed in Java for a video store system

inheritance mechanism, such inheritance will not be allowed. This is because `VideoPlayer` already inherits from `VideoEquipment` and *VideoMedium* is a class (albeit abstract).

The notion of an *interface* comes to the rescue and provides other advantages in the process (Lee and Tepfenhart 2002; Maciaszek and Liong 2005). Like an abstract class, an interface defines a set of attributes and operations, but no objects of it can be instantiated. Unlike an abstract class, an interface does not implement (even partially) any of its methods.

The total lack of implementation in an interface seems to be similar to the notion of a *pure abstract class*, available in C#, but even here there is a difference. In the case of a pure abstract class, the only classes that can implement the pure methods must be subclasses of that pure abstract class. In the case of an interface, any class in the system can implement the interface. Moreover, the class can implement any number of interfaces.

A.9.2 Implementing an interface

Figure A.25 shows a video store model in which the abstract class of Figure A.24 has been replaced by the *VideoMedium* interface. Graphically, the interface is marked by putting a circle in the name compartment (this is one of the few possible UML graphic elements). All methods of an interface are implicitly public and abstract, so there is no need to use these keywords in the method's prototype.

Although not shown in Figure A.25, a Java interface can also include constant declarations (attributes that are public, static and final). This is a restriction. A more powerful mechanism should allow declaration in the interface of any attribute typed as another interface or class. In effect, this would allow the declaration of associations between interfaces and between an interface and classes. Such a mechanism is not yet supported by Java, but it has been envisaged for introduction in the forthcoming UML standards.

Also not shown in Figure A.25, an interface can inherit from another interface (it can extend another interface). Figure A.26 illustrates how a class (`VideoPlayer`) can extend a class (`VideoEquiment`) and at the same time implement one or more interfaces (`VideoMedium`).

A.9.3 Using an interface

The power of interfaces does not come only from providing a handy resolution to multiple implementation inheritance. Even more importantly, an interface defines a *reference type* that allows separation of client objects from the implementation changes in the supplier objects.

An interface name can be referred to anywhere in the program where the client needs to refer to the class that implements this interface. As a result, the implementation of the interface can change and the client class can work as before and may not even notice the change. This feature of interfaces greatly facilitates the *adaptiveness* of a system.

As an aside, note that Figure A.26 also illustrates the use of unidirectional association. The «uses» association is unidirectional from `ChargeCalculator` to `VideoMedium` (this is indicated graphically by the arrow). A `ChargeCalculator` object "knows" of the

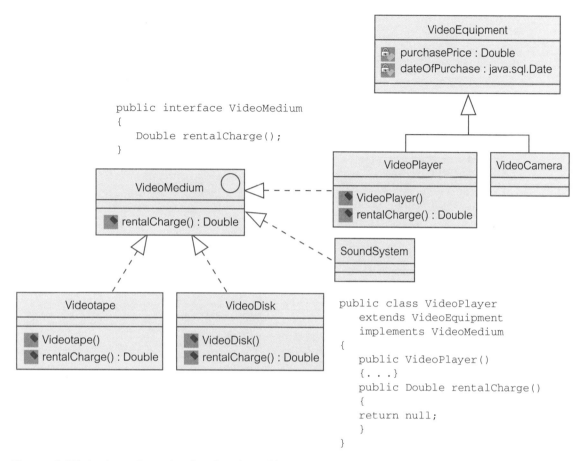

```
public interface VideoMedium
{
    Double rentalCharge();
}
```

```
public class VideoPlayer
    extends VideoEquipment
    implements VideoMedium
{
    public VideoPlayer()
    {...}
    public Double rentalCharge()
    {
    return null;
    }
}
```

Figure A.25 Implementing a Java interface for a video store system

VideoMedium object (in the theVideo variable), but the model does not maintain the reverse link from VideoMedium to ChargeCalculator.

Summary

This appendix has covered quite a lot of ground. It has explained the fundamental terminology and concepts of object technology.

An object system consists of collaborating *instance objects*. Each object has a state, behavior and identity. The concept of *identity* may well be the most critical to a proper understanding of object systems – it is also the most difficult to appreciate for people with some of the baggage of experience with conventional computer applications. Navigation along *links* is the *modus operandi* of object technology – something that a reader educated in relational database technology may have difficulty digesting.

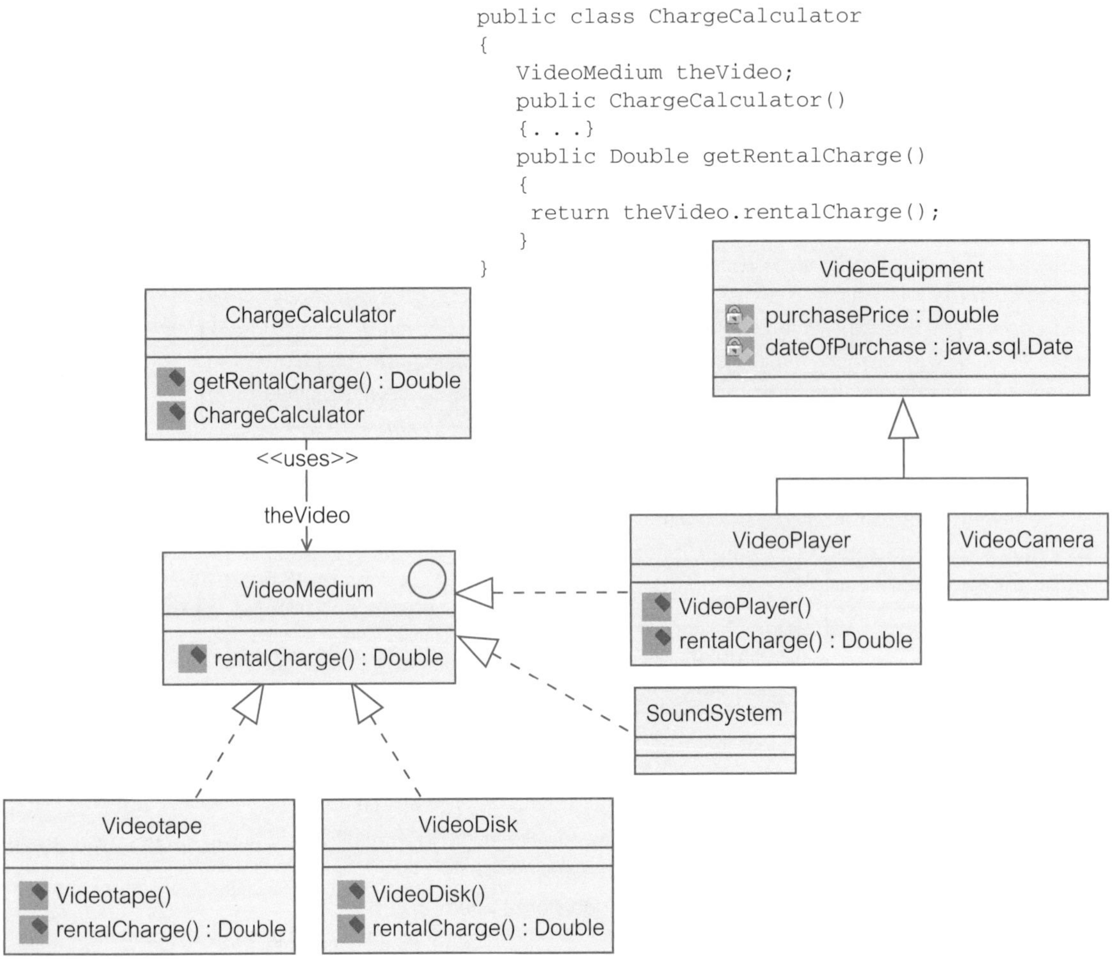
public class ChargeCalculator
{
VideoMedium theVideo;
public ChargeCalculator()
{. . .}
public Double getRentalCharge()
{
return theVideo.rentalCharge();
}
}
ChargeCalculator
getRentalCharge() : Double
ChargeCalculator
<<uses>>
theVideo
VideoMedium
rentalCharge() : Double
Videotape
Videotape()
rentalCharge() : Double
VideoDisk
VideoDisk()
rentalCharge() : Double
VideoEquipment
purchasePrice : Double
dateOfPurchase : java.sql.Date
VideoPlayer
VideoPlayer()
rentalCharge() : Double
VideoCamera
SoundSystem

Figure A.26 Using an interface to eliminate a dependency on the supplier for a video store system

A *class* is the template for object creation. It defines the *attributes* that an object can contain and the *operations* an object can invoke. Attributes can have primitive types or designate other classes. The attributes that designate other classes declare the *associations*. The association is one kind of relationship between classes. Other kinds are *aggregation* and *generalization*.

A class may have attributes or operations that apply to the class itself, not to any one of its instance objects. Such attributes and operations require the notion of a *class object*. Attributes and operations defined in classes during system analysis are referred to during system design/implementation as *variables* and *methods*, respectively.

A complete method prototype includes the method name, its *signature* (the list of formal arguments) and its return type. A *constructor* is a special method that serves the purpose of instantiating objects of the class.

An *association* relationship provides a linkage between objects of given classes. Association *degree* defines the number of classes connected by the association.

Association *multiplicity* defines how many objects may be represented by a *role name*. An association *link* is an instance of the association. An association that has attributes (and/or operations) of its own is modeled as an *association class*.

An *aggregation* is a whole–part relationship between a class representing an assembly of components (*superset class*) and the classes representing the components (*subset classes*). In UML, aggregation by value is called *composition*, while aggregation by reference is simply called *aggregation*. Aggregation/composition is frequently implemented by means of *buried references*. Java provides an alternative implementation by means of *inner classes*. Associated with aggregation/composition is the powerful technique of *delegation*.

A *generalization* relationship is a kind of relationship between a more generic class (*superclass* or *parent*) and a more specialized kind of that class (*subclass* or *child*). Generalization provides the basis for *polymorphism* and *inheritance*. *Overriding* is the mechanism for achieving polymorphic operations. Commercial programming environments can support *multiple inheritance*, but they do not normally support *multiple* or *dynamic classification*.

Related to inheritance are the notions of abstract class and interface. An *abstract class* is a class that may have partial implementations (some operations may be declared), but cannot be instantiated. An *interface* is a definition of a semantic type with attributes (constants only) and operations but without any implementation. A class that inherits the interface must provide the implementation.

Questions

Q1 Why do we need to distinguish between an instance object and a class object?

Q2 What is an object identifier? How can it be implemented?

Q3 What is the distinction between a transient object and a persistent object?

Q4 What are a transient link and a persistent link? How are they used during program execution?

Q5 What do we mean when we say that an attribute type designates a class? Give an example.

Q6 Why are most attributes private and most operations public in a good object model?

Q7 What is the difference between operation visibility and scope?

Q8 What is the difference between "public static" and "private static" members as far as their accessibility is concerned? Give an example.

Q9 In what modeling situations must an association class be used? Give an example.

Q10 "Buried reference" and "inner class" are two mechanisms for implementing aggregation/composition. Do these mechanisms provide sufficient and complete implementation of the semantics assumed in aggregation/composition? Explain your answer.

Q11 Explain the observation that, in a typical object programming environment, inheritance applies to classes, not to objects.

Q12 What is the connection between overriding and polymorphism?

Q13 How is multiple classification different from multiple inheritance?

Q14 What are the modeling benefits of an abstract class versus the modeling benefits of an interface? Explain by means of examples.

Answers to odd-numbered questions

Q1

Most processing in an object system is accomplished by the collaboration of instance objects. *Instance objects* send messages to other instance objects to activate their methods. Hence, a `Student` instance object can send a message to an `Instructor` instance object to request consultation. There may be many `Instructor` objects, but the `Student` instance is interested in talking to a specific `Instructor` instance.

At times, however, a message needs to be sent to a group of instance objects. For example, a `Student` may need to get the list of all `Instructor` instance objects before deciding on the instance from which the consultation will be requested. An `Instructor` *class object* is the only object that knows about its `Instructor` instance objects. The `Student` instance object should therefore send the message to the `Instructor` class object to obtain the list of `Instructor` instance objects.

In general, a class object contains services (methods) that implement efficient access to all instance objects of that class. Such services are essential in order to obtain the current list of instance objects and perform statistical calculations on instance objects (such as sums, counts, averages). Equally importantly, a class object is responsible for the *creation* of new instance objects.

Q3

A *transient object* is created and destroyed within a single execution of the program. A *persistent object* outlives the execution of the program. A persistent object is stored in persistent storage – typically in a database held on a magnetic disk.

A persistent object is read to program memory for processing and may be returned to persistent storage before the program terminates. Of course, the program may choose to destroy a persistent object, thus removing it from the database.

Q5

An attribute of a class can take values of a built-in type or a user-defined type. The set of *built-in types* supported by an object programming environment is known as *a priori*. The built-in types can be *atomic* (such as `int` or `boolean`) or *structured* (such as `Date` or `Time`).

A *user-defined type* designates a new *object type* required by the application. That type can be used to implement a *class* so that *objects* of that class can be instantiated.

An *attribute* can be assigned a user-defined object type. A value of such an attribute is an OID to an object of that user-defined type. An attribute is linked to an object of another (or the same) class. We say that the attribute type designates a (user-defined) class. An example is an attribute called `theCust` in the class called `Invoice`. The type of that attribute may be a class called `Customer`.

Q7

Operation visibility declares the ability of an outside object to reference the operation. Visibility can be public, private package (the default visibility in Java) or protected (related to the notion of inheritance).

The *operation scope* declares whether the owner of the operation is an instance object (*object scope*) or a class object (*class scope*). Constructor operations, which instantiate new objects, necessarily have class scope. Class scope implies centralized global information about instance objects and should be carefully controlled, in particular in a distributed object system.

Q9

An *association class* must be used when the association itself has properties (attributes and/or operations). This frequently occurs with many-to-many associations and sometimes with one-to-one associations. An association class with one-to-many association is unusual.

A many-to-many association between classes `Employee` and `Skill` may demand an association class if we want to store such information as `dateSkillAcquired`. The one-to-one association between `Husband` and `Wife` may result in an association class to store `marriageDate` and `marriagePlace`.

Q11

In a typical object programming environment, *inheritance* is an incremental definition of a class. It is a mechanism by which more specific classes incorporate definitional elements (attributes and operations) defined by more general classes. As such, inheritance applies to *types* (classes), not objects.

Objects are instantiated after inherited elements have been added to the class definition. The values of inherited elements are instantiated in the same way as the values of non-inherited elements.

In general, it is possible to imagine that inheritance can be extended to allow the *inheritance of values* (*inheritance of objects*). Value inheritance may be useful for setting default values of attributes.

For example, a `Sedan` object inheriting from a `Car` object may inherit the default number of wheels (four), the default transmission (automatic) and so on. These values may be modified (overridden), if necessary. Some knowledge base tools support the inheritance of values.

Q13

Multiple classification is a program execution regime in which an object is an instance of (and it, therefore, directly belongs to) more than one class. *Multiple inheritance* is a semantic variation of generalization in which a class can have more than one parent class (and it, therefore, inherits from all parent classes).

Multiple classification is not supported by popular object programming languages. This creates problems whenever an object can play multiple roles, such as a `Person` who is both a `Woman` *and* a `Student`. Without multiple classification, we may have to use multiple inheritance to create a specialized class `FemaleStudent`.

Defining classes for each legal combination of parent classes is not necessarily a desirable option, particularly if the objects are likely to change roles over time. Multiple classification can be combined with *dynamic classification* to allow objects to change classes during run-time.

Bibliography

Agile (2006) www.agilealliance.org (last accessed February 2007).

Alhir, S.S. (2003) *Learning UML*, O'Reilly & Associates.

Allen, P. and Frost, S. (1998) *Component-Based Development for Enterprise Systems: Applying the SELECT Perspective™*, Cambridge University Press.

Alur, D., Crupi, J. and Malks, D. (2003) *Core J2EE Patterns: Best practices and design strategies*, 2nd edition, Prentice Hall.

Arthur, L.J. (1992) *Rapid Evolutionary Development: Requirements, prototyping and software creation*, John Wiley.

Bahrami, A. (1999) *Object Oriented Systems Development*, McGraw-Hill.

Beck, K. (1999) *Extreme Programming Explained: Embrace challenge*, Addison-Wesley.

Bennett, S., McRobb, S. and Farmer, R. (2002) *Object-Oriented Systems Analysis and Design Using UML*, 2nd edition, McGraw-Hill.

Benson, S. and Standing, C. (2002) *Information Systems: A business approach*, John Wiley.

Bloch, J. (2001) *Effective Java: Programming language guide*, Addison-Wesley.

Bochenski, B. (1994) *Implementing Production-quality Client/Server Systems*, John Wiley.

Boehm, B.W. (1988) "A spiral model of software development and enhancement", *Computer*, May, pp. 61–72.

Booch, G., Rumbaugh, J. and Jacobson, I. (1999) *The Unified Modeling Language: User guide*, Addison-Wesley.

Bourne, K.C. (1997) *Testing Client/Server Systems*, McGraw-Hill.

BPMN (2006) http://en.wikipedia.org/wiki/BPMN (last accessed February 2007).

Brainstorming (2003) www.brainstorming.co.uk/contents.html (last accessed February 2007).

Brooks, F.P. (1987) "No silver bullet: essence and accidents of software engineering", *IEEE Software*, 4, pp. 10–19; reprinted in C.F. Kemerer (ed.) *Software Project Management: Readings and cases* (1997), Irwin, pp. 2–14.

Buschmann, F., Meunier, R., Rohnert, H., Sommerland, P. and Stal, M. (1996) *Pattern-oriented Software Architecture: A system of patterns*, John Wiley.

CMM (1995) *The Capability Maturity Model: Guidelines for improving the software process*, Addison-Wesley.

COBIT (2000) *COBIT Framework*, 3rd edition, IT Governance Institute.

COBIT (2005) *Aligning COBIT®, ITIL® and ISO 17799 for Business Benefit*, IT Governance Institute, www.itsmf.com/images/news/ITIL-COBiT.pdf (last accessed February 2007).

Coad, P. with North, D. and Mayfield, M. (1995) *Object Models: Strategies, patterns, and applications*, Yourdon Press.

Conallen, J. (2000) *Building Web Applications with UML*, Addison-Wesley.

Connolly, T.M. and Begg, C.E. (2005) *Database Systems: A practical approach to design, implementation and management*, 4th edition, Addison Wesley.

Constantine, L.L. and Lockwood, L.A.D. (1999) *Software for Use: A practical guide to the models and methods of usage-centered design*, Addison-Wesley.

Date, C.J. (2000) *An Introduction to Database Systems*, 7th edition, Addison-Wesley.

Davenport, T.H. (1993) *Process Innovation: Reengineering work through information technology*, Harvard Business School Press.

Davenport, T.H. and Short, J. (1990) "The new industrial engineering: Information technology and business process redesign", *Sloan Management Review*, Cambridge, summer, pp. 11, 17.

Douce, C.R., Layzell, P.J. and Buckley, J. (1999) "Spatial measures of software complexity", *Proceedings of the 11th Annual Workshop of Psychology of Programming Interest Group*, Leeds, UK, www.ppig.org/papers/11th-douce.pdf (last accessed February 2007).

Eckel, B. (2003) *Thinking in Java*, 3rd edition, Prentice Hall.

Elmasri, R. and Navathe, S.B. (2000) *Fundamentals of Database Systems*, 3rd edition, Addison-Wesley.

Extreme (2006) www.xprogramming.com (last accessed February 2007).

Feature (2006) www.featuredrivendevelopment.com (last accessed February 2007).

Fenton, N.E. and Pfleeger, S.L. (1997) *Software Metrics: A rigorous and practical approach*, 2nd edition, PWS Publishing Company.

Ferm, F. (2003) "The what, how, and why of a subsystem", *The Rational Edge*, June, http://download.boulder.ibm.com/ibmal/pub/software/dw/rationaledge/jun03/TheRationalEdge_June2003.pdf (last accessed February 2007).

Fowler, M. (1997) *Analysis Patterns: Reusable object models*, Addison-Wesley.

Fowler, M. (2003) *Patterns of Enterprise Application Architecture*, Addison-Wesley.

Fowler, M. (2004) *UML Distilled: A brief guide to the standard object modeling language*, 3rd edition, Addison-Wesley.

Fowler, S. (1998) *GUI Design Handbook*, McGraw-Hill.

Fowler, S and Stanwick, V. (2004) *Web Application Design Handbook: Best Practices for Web-based software*, Morgan Kaufmann.

Galitz, W.O. (1996) *The Essential Guide to User Interface Design: An introduction to GUI design principles and techniques*, John Wiley.

Gamma, E., Helm, R., Johnson, R. and Vlissides, J. (1995) *Design Patterns: Elements of reusable object-oriented software*, Addison-Wesley.

Ghezzi, C., Jazayeri, M. and Mandrioli, D. (2003) *Fundamentals of Software Engineering*, Prentice Hall.

Glass, R.L. (2005) "IT failure rates – 70 percent or 10–15 percent?", *IEEE Soft*, May/June, pp. 110–111, 112.

Gold, N.E., Mohan, A.M and Layzell, P.J. (2005) "Spatial complexity metrics: an investigation of utility", *IEEE Transactions on Software Engineering*, 31 (3) pp. 203–12.

Grady, R. (1992) *Practical Software Metrics for Project Management and Process Improvement*, Prentice Hall.

Gray, N.A.B. (1994) *Programming with Class*, John Wiley.

Hammer, M. (1990) "Reengineering work: don't automate, obliterate", *Harvard Business Review*, July/August, p. 104.

Hammer, M. and Champy, J. (1993a) *Reengineering the Corporation: A manifesto for business revolution*, Allen & Unwin.

Hammer, M. and Champy, J. (1993b) "The promise of reengineering", *Fortune*, 9, p. 94.

Hammer, M. and Stanton, S. (1999) "How process enterprises really work", *Harvard Business Review*, November/December, pp.108–18.

Harmon, P. and Watson, M. (1998) *Understanding UML: The Developer's Guide: With a Web-based application in Java*, Morgan Kaufmann.

Hawryszkiewycz, I., Karagiannis, D., Maciaszek, L. and Teufel, B. (1994) "RESPONSE: requirements specific object model for workgroup computing", *International Journal of Intelligent & Cooperative Information Systems*, 3, pp. 293–318.

Heldman, K. (2002) *PMP: Project management professional: study guide*, Sybex Inc.

Henderson-Sellers, B. (1996) *Object-oriented Metrics: Measures of complexity*, Prentice Hall.

Heumann, J. (2003) "User experience storyboards: building better UIs with RUP, UML, and use cases", *The Rational Edge*, November, www.-128.ibm.com/developerworks/rational/library/content/RationalEdge/nov03/f_usuability_jh-pdf (last accessed February 2007).

Hirschfeld, R. and Hanenberg, S. (2005) "Open aspects", *Computer Languages, Systems & Structures*, 32, pp. 87–108.

Hoffer, J.A., George, J.F., and Valacich, J.S. (2002) *Modern Systems Analysis and Design*, 3rd edition, Prentice Hall.

Hohpe, G. and Woolf, B. (2003) *Enterprise Integration Patterns*, Addison-Wesley.

Horton, I. (1997) *Beginning Visual C++ 5*, Wrox Press.

ITIL (2004) *The IT Infrastructure Library: An introductory overview of ITIL*, Version 1.0a, itSMF, www.itsmf.no/bestpractice/itil_overview.pdf (last accessed February 2007).

Jacobson, I. (1992) *Object-Oriented Software Engineering: A use case-driven approach*, Addison-Wesley.

Jordan, E.W. and Machesky, J.J. (1990) *Systems Development: Requirements, evaluation, design, and implementation*, PWS-Kent.

JUnit (2004) www.junit.org (last accessed February 2007).

Khoshafian, S., Chan, A., Wong, A. and Wong, H.K.T. (1992) *A Guide to Developing Client/Server SQL Applications*, Morgan Kaufmann.

Kiczales, G., Lamping, J., Mendhekar, A., Maeda, C., Lopes, C.V., Loigntier, J.-M. and Irwin, J. (1997) "Aspect-oriented Programming", *Proceeding of the European Conference on Object-Oriented Programming (ECOOP 97)*, LNCS 1242, Springer, pp. 220–42.

Kifer, M., Bernstein, A. and Lewis, P. (2006) *Database Systems: An application-oriented approach: Complete version*, 2nd edition, Addison-Wesley.

Kimball, R. (1996) *The Data Warehouse Toolkit: Practical techniques for building dimensional data warehouses*, John Wiley.

Kirkwood, J. (1992) *High Performance Relational Database Design*, Ellis Horwood.

Kleppe, A., Warmer, J. and Bast, W. (2003) *MDA Explained: The model-driven architecture: practice and promise*, Addison-Wesley.

Koestler, A. (1967) *The Ghost in the Machine*, Hutchinson.

Koestler, A. (1978) *Janus: A summing up*, Hutchinson.

Kotonya, G. and Sommerville, I. (1998) *Requirements Engineering: Processes and techniques*, John Wiley.

Kozaczynski, W. and Thario, J. (2003) "Transforming User Experience Models to Presentation Layer Implementations', http://se2c.uni.lu/tiki/se2c-bib.php and download paper from [262] of the LASSY Bibliography listing (last accessed February 2007).

Krasner, G.E. and Pope, S.T. (1988) "A cookbook for using the model view controller user interface paradigm in Smalltalk-80", *Journal of Object-oriented Programming*, August–September, pp. 26–49.

Kruchten, P. (2003) *The Rational Unified Process: An introduction*, 3rd edition, Addison-Wesley.

Kruchten, P., Obbink, H. and Stafford, J. (2006) "The past, present, and future of software architecture", *IEEE Software*, March/April, pp. 22–30.

Lakos, J. (1996) *Large-scale C++ Software Design*, Addison-Wesley.

Larman, C. (2005) "Applying UML and patterns", *An Introduction to Object-oriented Analysis and Design and Iterative Development*, 3rd edition, Prentice Hall.

Laudon, K.C. and Laudon, J.P. (2006) *Management Information Systems: Managing the digital firm*, 9th edition, Prentice Hall.

Lee, R.C. and Tepfenhart, W.M. (1997) *UML and C++: A practical guide to object-oriented development*, Prentice Hall.

Lee, R.C. and Tepfenhart, W.M. (2002) *Practical Object-oriented Development with UML and Java*, Pearson Education.

Lethbridge, T.C. and Laganière, R. (2001) *Object-Oriented Software Engineering: Practical software engineering using UML and Java*, McGraw-Hill.

Lieberherr, K.J. and Holland, I.M. (1989) "Assuring good style for object-oriented programs", *IEEE Software*, 9, pp. 38–48.

Linthicum, D.S. (2004) *Next Generation Application Integration: From simple information to Web services"*, Addison-Wesley.

Maciaszek, L.A. (1990) *Database Design and Implementation*, Prentice Hall.

Maciaszek, L.A. (1998) "Object-oriented development of business information systems – approaches and misconceptions", *Proceedings of the 2nd International Conference on Business Information Systems BIS '98*, Poznan, Poland, pp. 95–111.

Maciaszek, L.A. (2006) "From hubs via holons to an adaptive meta-architecture – the 'AD-HOC' approach", in *Software Engineering Techniques: Design for Quality*, ed. K. Sacha, Springer, pp. 1–13.

Maciaszek, L.A. and Liong, B.L. (2005) *Practical Software Engineering: A case study approach*, Addison-Wesley.

Maciaszek, L.A., De Troyer, O.M.F., Getta J.R. and Bosdriesz, J. (1996a) "Generalization versus aggregation in object application development – the 'ad-hoc' approach", *Proceedings of the 7th Australasian Conference on Information Systems ACIS '96*, 2, Hobart, Australia, pp. 431–42.

Maciaszek, L.A., Getta, J.R. and Bosdriesz, J. (1996b) "Restraining complexity in object system development – the 'ad-hoc' approach", *Proceedings of the 5th International Conference on Information Systems Development ISD '96*, Gdansk, Poland, pp. 425–35.

MDA (2006) www.omg.org/mda (last accessed February 2007).

Melton, J. (2002) *Advanced SQL:1999: Understanding object-relational and other advanced features'*, Morgan Kaufmann.

Melton, J. and Simon, A. (2001) *SQL:1999: Understanding relational language components*, Morgan Kaufmann.

Meyers, S. (1998) *Effective C++: 50 specific ways to improve your programs and design*, 2nd edition, Addison-Wesley.

Michelson, B.M. (2005) *Business Process Execution Language (BPEL) Primer: Understanding an important component of SOA and integration strategies*, Patricia Seybold Group, http://elementallinks.typepad.com/bmichelson/2005/09/view_bpel_proce.html (last accessed February 2007).

Murphy, G. and Schwanninger, C. (2006) "Aspect-oriented programming", *IEEE Software*, January–February, pp. 20–3.

Olsen, D.R. (1998) *Developing User Interfaces*, Morgan Kaufmann.

OMG (2004) www.omg.org/uml (last accessed February 2007).

Oz, E. (2004) *Management Information Systems*, 4th edition, Thomson.

Page-Jones, M. (2000) *Fundamentals of Object-Oriented Design in UML*, Addison-Wesley.

Pfleeger, S.L. (1998) *Software Engineering: Theory and practice*, Prentice Hall.

Polikoff, I., Coyne, R. and Hodgson, R. (2006) *Capability Cases: A solution envisioning approach*, Addison-Wesley.

Poppendieck, M. and Poppendieck, T. (2003) *Lean Software Development: An agile toolkit for software development managers*, Addison-Wesley.

Porter, M. (1985) *Competitive Advantage: Creating and sustaining superior performance*, Free Press.

Porter, M.E. and Millar, V.E. (1985) "How information gives you competitive advantage", *Harvard Business Review*, July/August, pp. 149–61.

Pressman, R.S. (2005) *Software Engineering: A practitioner's approach*, 6th edition, McGraw-Hill.

Quatrani, T. (2000) *Visual Modeling with Rational Rose 2000 and UML*, Addison-Wesley.

Ramakrishnan, R. and Gehrke, J. (2000) *Database Management Systems*, McGraw-Hill.

Rational (2000) *Rational Solutions for Windows*, online documentation, April 2000 edition, Rational Software.

Rational (2002) *Rational Suite Tutorial*, Version 2002.05.00, Rational Software.

Responsive (2003) www.responsivesoftware.com/timelog.htm (last accessed February 2007).

Riel, A.J. (1996) *Object-oriented Design Heuristics*, Addison-Wesley.

Robertson, J. and Robertson, S. (2003) *Volere Requirements Specifications Template*, 9th edition, Atlantic Systems Guild, www.atlsysguild.com (accessed February 2007).

Robson, W. (1994) *Strategic Management and Information Systems: An integrated approach*, Pitman.

Roy-Faderman, A., Koletzke, P. and Dorsey, P. (2004) *Oracle JDeveloper 10g Handbook*, McGraw-Hill/Osborne.

Rozanski, N. and Woods, E. (2005) *Software Systems Architecture: Working with stakeholders using viewpoints and perspectives*, Addison-Wesley.

Ruble, D.A. (1997) *Practical Analysis and Design for Client/Server and GUI Systems*, Yourdon Press.

Rumbaugh, J. (1994) "Getting started: using use cases to capture requirements", *Journal of Object-oriented Programming*, September, pp. 8–10, 12, 23.

Rumbaugh, J., Blaha, M., Premerlani, W., Eddy, F., and Lorensen, W. (1991) *Object-oriented Modeling and Design*, Prentice Hall.

Rumbaugh, J., Jacobson, I. and Booch, G. (2005) *The Unified Modeling Language Reference Manual*, 2nd edition, Addison-Wesley.

RUP (2003) www-306.ibm.com/software/awdtools/rup/ (last accessed February 2007).

Rus, I. and Lindvall, M. (2002) "Knowledge management in software engineering", *IEEE Software*, May/June, pp. 26–38.

Sam-Bodden, B. and Judd, C.M. (2004) *Enterprise Java Development on a Budget: Leveraging Java open source technologies*, Apress (Springer).

Schach, S. (2005) *Classical and Object-Oriented Software Engineering*, 6th edition, McGraw-Hill.

Schmauch, C.H. (1994) *ISO 9000 for Software Developers*, ASQC Quality Press.

Selic, B. (2003) "The subsystem: a curious creature", *The Rational Edge*, July, www-128.ibm.com/developerworks/rational/library/content/RationaleEdge/jul03/k_subsystem_bs.pdf (last accessed February 2007).

Silberschatz, A., Korth, H.F. and Sudershan, S. (2002) *Database System Concepts*, 4th edition, McGraw-Hill.

Singh, I., Stearns, B., Johnson, M. and Enterprise Team (2002) *Designing Enterprise Applications with the J2EE Platform*, 2nd edition, Addison-Wesley.

Sklar, J. (2006) *Principles of Web Design*, Thomson Course Technology.

Smith, J. (2003) "A Comparison of the IBM Rational Unified Process and eXtreme Programming". www3.software.ibm.com/ibmdl/pub/software/rational/web/ whitepapers/2003/TP167.pdf (last accessed February 2007).

Smith, J.M. and Smith, D.C.P. (1977) "Database abstractions: aggregation and generalization", *ACM Transactions on Database Systems*, 2, pp. 105–33.

Sommerville, I. and Sawyer, P. (1997) *Requirements Engineering: A good practice guide*, John Wiley.

Sony (2004) www.sonystyle.com (last accessed February 2007).

Sowa, J.F. and Zachman, J.A. (1992) "Extending and formalizing the framework for information systems architecture", *IBM Systems Journal*, 3, pp. 590–616.

Stein, L.A., Lieberman, H. and Ungar, D. (1989) "A shared view of sharing: the Treaty of Orlando", in W. Kim and F.H. Lochovsky (eds), *Object-oriented Concepts, Databases and Applications,* Addison-Wesley, pp. 31–48.

Stelting, S. and Maassen, O. (2001) *Applied Java Patterns*, Prentice Hall.

Stevens, P. and Pooley, R. (2000) *Using UML Software Engineering with Objects and Components*, Addison-Wesley.

Szyperski, C. (1998) *Component Software: Beyond object-oriented programming*, Addison-Wesley.

Treisman, H. (1994) "How to design a good interface design", *Software Magazine*, Australia, August, pp. 32–6.

UML (2003) *OMG Unified Modeling Language Specification*, Version 1.5, OMG.

UML (2005) "Unified Modeling Language: Superstructure", Version 2.0, formal/05-07-04, www.uml.org/#UML2.0 (last accessed February 2007).

Unhelkar, B. (2003) *Process Quality Assurance for UML-based Projects*, Addison-Wesley.

Wegner, P. (1997) "Why interaction is more powerful than algorithms", *Communications of the ACM*, 40(5) pp. 80–91.

White, S.A. (2004) "Introduction to BPMN", www.bpmn.org/Documents/Introduction%20to%20BPMN.pdf (last accessed February 2007).

White, S.A. (2005) "Using BPMN to model a BPEL process", www.bpmn.org/Documents/Mapping%20BPMN%20to%20BPEL%20Example.pdf (last accessed February 2007).

Whitten, J.L. and Bentley, L.D. (1998) *Systems Analysis and Design Methods*, 4th edition, McGraw-Hill.

Windows (2000) *The Windows Interface Guidelines for Software Design*, MSDN Library, CD-ROM collection, Microsoft.

Wirfs-Brock, R. and Wilkerson, B. (1989) "Object-oriented design: a responsibility-driven approach", in *OOPSLA '89 Proceedings, SIGPLAN Notices*, 10, ACM, pp. 71–5.

Wirfs-Brock, R., Wilkerson, B., and Wiener, L. (1990) *Designing Object-Oriented Software*, Prentice Hall.

Wood, J. and Silver, D. (1995) *Joint Application Development*, 2nd edition, John Wiley.

Yourdon, E. (1994) *Object-Oriented Systems Design: An integrated approach*, Yourdon Press.

Zachman, J.A. (1987) "A framework for information systems architecture", *IBM Systems Journal*, 3, pp. 276–92.

Zachman, J.A. (1999) "A framework for information systems architecture", *IBM Systems Journal*, 2/3, pp. 454–70.

Index